Stepping Out of the Traffick is breathtaking. Ea theory, theology, biblical acumen, and practicali drawing from divergent theological frames of r offers ultimately a reflection on the goodness of G... in the person of Jesus Christ.

Dr. Dan B. Allender
The Seattle School of Theology & Psychology,
Founding President and Professor

Holistic theological probing is evident throughout this book and we find ourselves rethinking freedom and forgiveness and what these mean in the lives of those who suffer. *Stepping Out of the Traffick* offers us the opportunity to pause and seize the chance to create new pathways for Christians that are more ethical, more empowering, more effective. It is an opportunity not to be missed and this outstanding book provides a resource which is second to none.

Dr. Elaine Storkey
Oxford Scholar, *BBC* Broadcaster, and Past President of *Tearfund*

What a much-needed resource this book is! It is a timely reminder to all involved in anti-trafficking of the importance of regularly pausing and reflecting on what we are doing, and the importance of having our response anchored in a solid theological foundation. The Triangle around which this book is structured provides a framework for ministry reflection; a framework that not only enables us to better understand the problems we are up against in anti-trafficking, but how our theology impacts our response, and how we can integrate this knowledge and understanding to ensure more focused and effective ministry. This is a book that will ensure the anti-trafficking movement is fully equipped to continue the fight and bring freedom to all. There is much here to pause and reflect upon.

Sarah Scott Webb
SIM "For Freedom" Co-Director & Founder and *World Evangelical Alliance Mission Commission* Anti-Trafficking Synergist

Whether you are new or have worked in the anti-trafficking movement for many years, this book invites you to go deeper than you have gone before, to consider and re-consider the issues around trafficking and its responses, and to be deeply challenged in your understanding and own response to it. *Stepping Out of the Traffick* is deeply rooted in the challenges that the Bible poses to us as we look at freedom in the lives of victims and ourselves.

Binia Nightingale
former Consultant for the Anti-Trafficking Movement in Asia

Sexual exploitation and trafficking may be out of our sight most of the time, but it affects all – directly or indirectly. As we step out of the traffick and reflect on our responses, may we learn rhythms to participate in God's calling to mercy, justice, peace and hope for all. Around the world, awareness and concern for people caught in trafficking has grown, and through reading this book many will be equipped to hear the nudge of God, pause and become inspired practitioners.

Ruth Robb,
Azalea, CEO & Co-Founder

I am a firm believer in knowledge equals responsibility! Therefore, no Christians working in this sector of human trafficking and modern slavery have any excuse to not having access to thoughtful, professional and deeply researched topics that are able to contribute to our responses, whether those are within non-profits, communities or churches. Packed with theological and practical content, this book presents a wide range of contexts and perspectives, challenging our own paradigms and norms and pushing us to reframe our responses and programs. As Christians in this movement, it is crucial for us to be humbler and more open – to take a critical look at the language we use, the theological frameworks we have never questioned, and the power imbalances that we perpetrate.

Helen Sworn
Chab Dai, Founder and Former Executive Director

Stepping Out of the Traffick is an important and timely book for anyone who does anti-trafficking work or is interested in it. As the editors state, "what we do matters." This book deeply and deftly explores how our understanding of sexual exploitation and our theology (or the "why we do what we do") is vital to forming a better, more holistic, and dignified response to exploitation. I love the deep theological reflections found throughout the book and how the authors apply these reflections to all aspects of our approach to doing anti-trafficking work. It is very easy for us to put our heads down and focus on the hard work we do and forget to pause and reflect on how or why we are doing it. This book calls us to slow down for a moment, look up, and readjust what we do to better align with why we do it. It has given me so much to ponder. I give this book my wholehearted recommendation.

Brian Leak
WorldVenture Global Anti-Trafficking Team, European Liaison

Stepping Out of the Traffick is a powerful resource that presents the interplay of theology, issues of sexual exploitation, and response in a creative way. It highlights that each person's way of engaging in the solution to sexual trafficking is significant. Great care was taken in the composition of the contributors: voices of experts all over the world. While reading the book, I was able to hear the voices of the survivors of exploitation. It was a sacred experience. Understanding trafficking in the perspectives of practitioners, theologians, and academicians provides a cognitive dissonance that urges readers to be keener at reading the Scriptures with new lenses. The book paints unapologetically the horrible conditions that many women, children, and men have suffered in the hands of the unmerciful; however, it also brilliantly portrays that there is freedom in Jesus Christ! The book issues out a clarion call to all people in authority – police, pastors, practitioners in government, non-government and faith-based organizations, theologians, and the universal church – to be Jesus' hands and feet to the exploited, to the abused, to the downtrodden!

Dr. Nativity A. Petallar
Asia-Pacific Nazarene Theological Seminary, Associate Dean of PhD Studies

Any attempt to make a positive and lasting social impact on the complexities of human trafficking and related human rights violations cannot be done without an ongoing reflection and inquiry into the worldviews that inform our humble attempts to support individual survivors. *Stepping Out of the Traffick* makes this ongoing reflection and inquiry possible by challenging the status quo and preconceived ideas, and by keeping the questions open.

Dr. Stephen Morse
Unchained Solutions, CEO

This book should be prescribed reading for students and the entire public, private and civil society sectors that work to end human trafficking, including seminary students and missions organisations. "Selah", to pause and reflect, describes the impact this timely book made on me. Written from the heart of people who count the cost and remain committed to giving their best to the most vulnerable, it charges us to engage with the Dance of The Triangle of theology, practice and sexual exploitation. Let's allow the words of this book to dance in our hearts. Faith challenges us to say, "Yes" to bearing authentic love, compassion, and commitment to the freedom journey of those we serve. Faith mobilises us, despite our own brokenness. God's love compels us to assess the relevance and quality of our service. Human trafficking can only be effectively addressed if we choose to bridge the gaps between our silos, choose to step out of the boots that keep us stuck, choose to think, plan and work like God – creative, compassionate and consistent.

Anita du Plessis
Freedom Ports Alliance, Executive Director

Stepping Out of the Traffick challenges the Christian community to take a fresh look at trafficking of persons, pausing for a time and learning about the theology of the topic in order to 'do good work better.' The variety of authors help readers to see the context of the biblical person described in a new way, revealing the full horror of the abuse the person has suffered, and giving a deeper understanding, not only about the biblical person, but also about our response to people who similarly suffer today. The challenge to us, as we read through the chapters of the book, is: How do we see and reach out to the exploited and the exploiters in our places and ministries with a new, theologically-informed view. The book's theological reflections and case studies, as well as the reflection questions at the end of every chapter, help individuals as well as churches to reconsider their response to trafficking and empower them to get involved in a healthy manner.

Dr. Barbara Rüegger
World Without Orphans Europe

If you've ever been stuck (in a problem, a relationship, a thought, or anything else) and could not get out, you would know what it means to be helpless and even desperate. If you've ever known and truly understood what sexual exploitation is (or worse – have ever experienced it yourself), you would want to seek and find ways of stepping out of the routine and trying to contribute to ending it. This is what this book offers its readers: stepping out of the traffick of sexual exploitation and offering a genuine Christian response in resolving its devastating consequences both for individuals and the society in general. Although it offers a Christian response, it can benefit everyone who has a heart for the vulnerable and exploited. I'm delighted to commend this account which faithfully considers the various theological and practical responses to sexual exploitation and trafficking.

Valentin Kozhuharov
International Association for Mission Studies,
Chair of Academic Committee and Executive Committee Member

The great strength of *Stepping Out of the Traffick* is that it not only faces up to complexities of the field of sexual exploitation and explores the responsive disciplines and services designed to combat it; it also insists on a third component: Christian theology. The book seeks to show the many ways in which faith can fruitfully interact with the other components, not to establish some form of control, but rather through living a life rooted in prayer, which opens up the truth of our limited and frail human situation, and calls us to stand with and for others, so enabling a mutual giving and patiently sensing the right direction towards a horizon of genuine hope. This is a challenge to those, whether Christian or of another persuasion, who would confine the faith to a private ghetto. Whilst the book commits to working with the secular world, it is at the same time a critique of its prevailing assumption that all problems can be solved by calculations of utility, and a vital contribution to a far deeper response to the God who has taken responsibility for the world's mess in the life, death and resurrection of Jesus Christ.

Dr. Alan M. Suggate
Durham University, Department of Theology,
Senior Lecturer (past) and *Pace UK*, Board of Trustees Secretary

Many organizations have opened their doors to help people who have experienced horrific sexual harm in the twenty years since the passage of the Trafficking Victims Protection Act of 2000. The bulk of these organizations are faith based and there has been much good work done. Now is a time to step back and pause to ask good questions: Where is God in this work? How do we see Him moving? How is He guiding us in this work and what steps are needed for us to see as He sees? The contributors to this book include practitioners, theologians, and scholars who have spent years in the anti-trafficking field. Not only have they been 'boots on the ground' but they have also thought deeply about this work. In this book, they have stepped back, thought, reflected and written through their individual lenses, deeply weaving and integrating theology into the issue of trafficking for us to pause, read, and savor. This book brings together both story and biblical text. For those of us that have worked in this field for many years, we know the stories, but to weave those stories into a deeper framework alongside the biblical text makes them come alive with a depth of color and humanity that can sometimes become lost. These chapters will encourage and invite the reader to hunger for more – more of God. It is He who is able to bring about the impossible (Ephesians 3:20).

Corinne Vance
International Christian Alliance on Prostitution (ICAP), North America Leadership Team, Trauma Therapist at *The Wellhouse*, and Assistant Internship Director, *The Seattle School of Theology and Psychology*

REGNUM STUDIES IN MISSION

Stepping Out of the Traffick

Pausing for Theological Reflection on Christian Response to Sexual Exploitation and Trafficking

Series Preface

Regnum Studies in Mission are born from the lived experience of Christians and Christian communities in mission, especially but not solely in the fast growing churches among the poor of the world. These churches have more to tell than stories of growth. They are making significant impacts on their cultures in the cause of Christ. They are producing 'cultural products' which express the reality of Christian faith, hope and love in their societies.

Regnum Studies in Mission are the fruit often of rigorous research to the highest international standards and always of authentic Christian engagement in the transformation of people and societies. And these are for the world. The formation of Christian theology, missiology and practice in the twenty-first century will depend to a great extent on the active participation of growing churches contributing biblical and culturally appropriate expressions of Christian practice to inform World Christianity.

Series Editors

REGNUM STUDIES IN MISSION

Stepping Out of the Traffick

Pausing for Theological Reflection on Christian Response to Sexual Exploitation and Trafficking

Edited by
Glenn Miles and Christa Foster Crawford
with Bill Prevette

First published 2024 by Regnum Books International

Regnum is an imprint of the Oxford Centre for Mission Studies
St. Philip and St. James Church
Woodstock Road
Oxford, OX2 6HR, UK
www.regnumbooks.net

British Library Cataloguing in Publication Data
A catalogue record for this book is available from the British Library

ISBN: 979-8-8898-3877-7
eBook ISBN: 979-8-8898-3878-4

Typeset by Words by Design

Cover developed by Words by Design based on a design by Patrick Knowles

The publication of this volume is made possible through the
financial assistance of Evangelische Mission Weltweit.

Distributed by Fortress Press in the US, Canada, India, and Brazil

Foreword

Elaine Storkey, PhD

BBC Broadcaster and Philosopher-Theologian, Oxford University; Past President of Tearfund and Past Executive Director of John Stott's London Institute for Contemporary Christianity; author of numerous works, including *Scars Across Humanity: Understanding and Overcoming Violence against Women*

I am enormously grateful to the editors for the commitment and work which has gone into this powerful volume. Every author has added invaluable chapters and the result is a book which opens new windows and lets more light into those vital areas crying out for justice. We are now in the third decade of the modern anti-trafficking movement. It is a movement which has grown within the church as well as amongst secular humanitarians. People fed on biblical revelation can readily understand the ubiquity of sin, and the destructive power of bondage. I wisdom and experience has grown rapidly, every new study bringing more exposure of corrupt systems of power, and the complex interweaving of vulnerability, poverty and the struggle for survival. I communities experiencing God's call to love-in-action in these areas also appreciate their secular counterparts and often experience a unique relationship with them. In that relationship, they have been challenged to be more authentically I in their own response to God's leading whilst recognizing that the call to justice is for all humankind.

This book therefore comes at a crucial time. It is a very deliberate attempt to encourage I reflection and action in what is increasingly an overwhelming task for us. Its authors are clear about what they have set out to do. It is not simply to provide another "discourse of experts and activists who recognize in sexual exploitation" although it certainly does that. It is more deeply constructed to help us to think and talk of God in relation to those issues; to provide a series of reflections, narratives and studies with theology at its very heart.

The outcome is this remarkable volume which brilliantly integrates insights and teachings from both the Hebrew Scriptures and the New Testament with what we recognize to be one of the great scourges of our age. It does this not by tagging theology on to a secular agenda, but by hearing the experiences of the powerless in Scripture, delving into issues of the kingdom of God, understanding the importance of lament, and reflecting on how God identifies and participates in the suffering of creation. The expository skills of many of the authors in this volume are well honed and a privilege to read. No attempt is made to ignore hermeneutical issues in applying Scripture today but throughout the book we find a readiness to question assumptions and practices and look critically at mistakes we might have made in the past.

The richness of the book lies also in the diversity of its authors. All of them are I with different backgrounds and insights who gently invite us to listen to their experiences and theological reflections, even when these differ from our own. Their chapters reveal a wide variety of callings and professions, written from within every continent. Stories from Ethiopia, India, Thailand, Cambodia, Sierra Leone, South Africa, and other countries offer a diversity of perspectives and voices. This in itself helps us to recognize what has often been the Western framing of the I anti-trafficking response and suggest ways we might reshape our thinking. The wealth of different writing styles adds to the diversity; some are natural storytellers, some are painstaking academics, others offer case studies, yet others are competent reporters and statisticians. Many share their work of a lifetime and reveal what they are still in the process of learning. To have so much expertise and experience in one volume is an enormous gift. To find each author speaking from a faithful engagement with the God disclosed in Jesus is true spiritual enrichment.

Those familiar with the social sciences will find familiar topics revisited by I thinkers. Social construction and issues of language feature prominently, not least in understanding sexual exploitation. Victimhood, trauma, survival, agency, gender and masculinity, and the need for dignity are revisited with professional skill and with pleas not to further distort reality by reinforcing stereotypes. The backcloth of consumerism and marketing are probed, where sex is not tied to an intimate relation but constructed as a marketed commodity with no commitment from the client other than payment. Holistic theological probing is evident throughout and we find ourselves rethinking freedom and forgiveness and what these mean in the lives of those who suffer.

In her introduction, Christa Foster Crawford offers us the opportunity to pause, and seize the chance to create new pathways for Christians on this journey that are more ethical, more empowering, more effective. It is an opportunity not to be missed. *Stepping Out of the Traffick* provides a resource for that which is second to none. I commend this outstanding work to you and pray that God will use it to bless you and draw you even further into this costly but valuable work of God's kingdom.

Foreword

Dan B Allender, PhD

Leading Thinker at the intersection of trauma, abuse, theology, and story; founder of The Allender Center and Founding President and Professor of Counseling Psychology, The Seattle School of Theology & Psychology; author of numerous works, including *Redeeming Heartache: How Past Suffering Reveals True Calling*

Glenn Miles and Christa Foster Crawford, with Bill Prevette, have produced a third volume to their human trafficking series. It is impossible to speak about this labor of love without resorting to superlatives. I know and love both Glenn and Christa and know a small portion of the losses and heartache they have endured to see this volume come to print. The labor to bring this edited work to life is majestic and herculean.

To do so during ongoing direct work with victims of trafficking, conducting research, working with vastly complex, often antithetical systems, along with personal heartache and loss while guiding this process to completion is beyond my comprehension. To say this volume is a labor of love is not sufficient; there is blood, sweat, and tears that permeate each page.

The book itself is equally breathtaking. Each article is rich tapestry of theory, theology, biblical acumen, and practicality. There is a core premise to the labor: praxis inevitably becomes destitute without returning to the *raison d'etre* that enervates the practice.

Addressing human trafficking in all its evil and horror would seem to be reason enough – it is not. As much as we are meant with every fiber of our being to say, "Hell, no" to all forms of evil, be it personal, familial, cultural, and systemic; nevertheless, merely standing in the way of harm is not enough.

We are meant to say, "Heaven, yes." As we stand against the kingdom of evil, we are even more so to lean into the kingdom of God to create and celebrate goodness. Each chapter in its own way, drawing from divergent theological frames of reference, is a work of art that offers ultimately a reflection on the goodness of God found in the person of Jesus Christ.

As Glenn and Christa suggest, you will likely not agree with everything that has been written. If you do, then you are not reading carefully. But the differences and disagreements are part of the beauty that no one can possibly hold all truth. This volume will inform and educate, but even more so, it will help you develop a richer and more beautiful grasp of how engagement with the truth of our Creator, Redeemer, and Sustainer can lead to the passion and perspective to keep doing this work until all things are made well.

The gift of this volume will be a banquet we feast at for years and years. It will be a reminder that we all would have despaired if we did not believe we would see the goodness of God in the land of the living.

Contents

Part II
Thinking Theologically about Sexual Exploitation

Part III
Raising Our Response to Sexual Exploitation

Dedication and Acknowledgements

We dedicate this volume to those who have committed their lives to the abolition movement, and especially to two of our contributors Heike Lippman and Siobhan Miles, *in memoriam.*

Heike Lippmann, our friend and fellow freedom fighter, died on 26 February 2022. Even after her cancer diagnosis (her sister writes) "She went her way boldly trusting in God, an act both cheerful and profound." Heike returned to Kyrgyzstan, a country she loved to serve until shortly before her death. Heike taught us that lament can be a powerful act of worship. She helped set solid theological foundations for work among people who are exploited and was passionate about helping us journey well on the long road to justice.

Siobhan Miles, beloved wife of Glenn and friend to many, died on 4 August 2016. She is still deeply missed. She was working on her PhD at the Oxford Centre for Mission Studies exploring some of the challenges in the way some Christian organisations portray victims/survivors. Siobhan was unable to complete her PhD, but with the help of Jill Reimer her writings and notes were converted into one of the chapters of this book. Siobhan was also involved in initiating the Chab Dai Butterfly Longitudinal Research Project in Cambodia which was widely published between 2020 and 2022.[1]

We also want to thank the founding editors, Bill Prevette and Francesca Nuzzolese. We are grateful for their vision, work, and sacrifice in birthing this book, and for allowing us to be part of bringing it to the finish line. We also want to acknowledge the contributions of Haddon and Hilary Wilmer, John Blevins, Laura Lederer, Carl Jylland-Halverson, and other global scholars who joined them in September 2014 to begin the conceptual framework for this book.

We express profound thanks to the chapter authors for their hard work, generosity of time, and patience over the many years it took for this book to come to print. We appreciate how they have wrestled thoughtfully with "The Triangle" of Sexual Exploitation, Theology and Response, and that they have freely shared their wisdom so that others can step out of the traffick to pause and better their response.

Thanks also to April Stouffler (Schiller) and Haddon Willmer for offering their services in editing early drafts of chapter submissions, and to Alexandra Jagelman for helping with edits during the final stretch.

Finally, thanks to the Regnum team who make this all possible, especially Tony Gray of Words by Design[2] who has worked us with us for more than ten years on all three volumes in this series, and Patrick Knowles[3] who has designed each of the covers.

---

[1] www.chabdai.org/butterfly.

[2] www.wordsbydesign.co.uk.

[3] www.patrickknowlesdesign.com.

Introduction: Why This Book?

Introduction to This Book

Christa Foster Crawford

We Need to Pause: Traffic Jams as Invitation

Everyone hates traffic jams. You're on your way to your destination, traveling along at a good speed, when suddenly: a sea of red brake lights ahead. You slow to a stop and are engulfed by countless cars filled with impatient drivers. Is this a momentary lull that's part of a recognizable traffic pattern or is there an unexpected occurrence ahead that could take minutes or even hours to clear?

No one likes to stop while they are going forward. It disrupts your timeline. It thwarts your momentum. But sometimes stepping out of the traffic is a good thing. If danger is ahead, then pausing before becoming part of a multi-vehicle pile-up is a blessing. If a rush-hour backup is ahead, then pausing is a good opportunity to explore a better alternate route. Pausing reminds us that it's not just the destination but also the journey that matters. How we get there is as important as getting there.

The same is true when it comes to addressing sexual exploitation and other forms of human trafficking. For the first two decades of the modern anti-trafficking movement we have been traveling along, reacting to an urgent and devastating problem, improvising responses as needs have arisen, hurling towards the final destination of Freedom. But have we paused to ask the questions that are essential to a successful journey?

What is Freedom?

Are we taking the right kinds of actions to get there?

What harmful detours or practices have we fallen into?

What better routes have we not yet discovered?

These are questions that the entire anti-trafficking movement must undertake, intentionally and collaboratively, in order to more effectively reach our goal of Freedom and avoid unnecessary traffic jams. But what do these questions about practice in the field of sexual exploitation have to do with theology?

To answer that question let's look at how I first came to work in the anti-trafficking field nearly 25 years ago.

Why Theology?

I first heard about human trafficking through reading Kevin Bales' book *Disposable People*.[1] It was a very academic book, filled with pages of graphs and statistics and footnotes. It wasn't sensationalist, it wasn't religious. And yet,

[1] Bales, Kevin. *Disposable People: New Slavery in the Global Economy*. (University of California Press, 1999).

when I set the book down and tried to go on with my daily life, I suddenly hit the floor in a pile of tears. It was a deeply spiritual moment.

I felt a very clear call from God to do something, but I did not think that responding had anything to do with my faith. I was a Christian and I was a lawyer, but my paradigms taught me that while my personal calling came out of my faith, my practice would come out of my profession. Even as I sought a position in a Christian law school as a platform for my anti-trafficking work, I did not realize that my Christian beliefs were integral to my call. I lacked the theology to recognize it.

Like many of our readers, I was raised in an evangelical denomination that really loved the Bible. And yet, somehow, I was never taught the hundreds of verses about God's justice. I was never told the overarching narrative about God's care for the marginalized and oppressed. And then I heard Gary Haugen speak. It was the early days of the International Justice Mission and Gary, its founder, told a crowd of Christian lawyers the harrowing story of standing in a blood-stained church in Rwanda investigating the genocide that had just taken place and how weeks later he stood on a crowded bus in the US haunted by the age-old question: "Where was God in the midst of great evil?" The answer he received was: "Where were God's people?" He then explained how lawyers were particularly suited to respond to injustice, confirming my personal call. But what I remember most about his powerful talk was its deep rooting in scripture – from the Pentateuch and the Prophets to the Psalms, from the Gospels to Paul and beyond.

Gary's was a prophetic voice, bringing God's words to life in a way I'd never experienced before. And once those words came alive, the implications for theory and practice have never stopped unfolding.

> Like the once-dry bones of Ezekiel, the vast collection of scriptures were no longer mere memory verses. Instead, they were a clarion call that echoed from the wilderness where God cared for the discarded servant-girl Hagar, to Egypt where God used Moses to deliver a nation from slavery. These scriptures kept crying out in 19th Century America, inspiring Harriet Tubman to risk her own freedom conducting her people from a prison of brutal inhumanity to a pasture where they could once again be counted as humans created in God's image. And these scriptures still speak today, motivating a new generation of abolitionists to respond, and providing guidance for what our response should look like.
>
> Like the once-dry bones of Ezekiel, the problem of modern slavery was no longer bare statistics. Instead, it took on flesh and blood of real people's lives. But as we learned to recognize sexual exploitation, the existence of labor exploitation became apparent as well. Understanding the supply- and demand-side causes muddled the line between exploited and exploiter and, suddenly, obscure Bible verses about usury and treatment of outsiders held up a mirror revealing ways we might be exploiters ourselves.
>
> Like the once-dry bones of Ezekiel, our desire to "do something" was no longer simply theoretical. Instead, meeting real people in the messiness of their stories introduced us to the complexity of the problem and the careful consideration required in crafting an effective, ethical response. Formerly abstract biblical principles about justice and mercy and humility became mandates that we could

choose to heed or ignore as we developed modes of responding to human trafficking.

What caused these dry bones to come to life, entwining the sinews of scripture and faith with the practicalities of understanding exploitation and how best to help people out of it? Over two decades of working with people who have been exploited, people who have exploited others, and organizations that seek to end exploitation, I have had to engage with, wrestle with, and be constantly willing to learn and grow in three areas:

- My **understanding of sexual exploitation and human trafficking** – from not even knowing it existed to recognizing the complex dynamics that keep people in bondage despite our best intentions.
- My **understanding of theology** – from noticing God's care for the oppressed in a handful of scriptures to learning to see God's restoration of shalom in the overarching narrative of the Bible.
- My **understanding of responding to exploitation** – from doing what has always been done to realizing the need to continually ask if what we are doing is working, learn from the experience of survivors, and bring together expertise from various sectors to innovate more effective solutions.

It is these three areas that this book seeks to address.

Introducing the Triangle

Together, these core concepts are referred to as "The Triangle."[2]

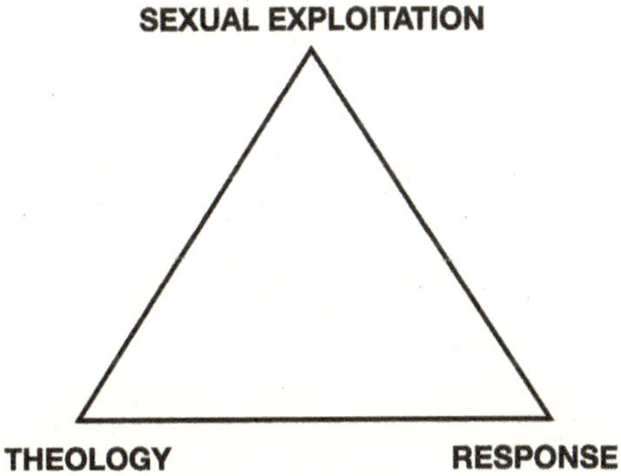

[2] The Triangle formed the intellectual framework of this book since its inception. An explanation of The Triangle in its original form is found in the Background of This Book by the book's founding editor, Bill Prevette. Note that while the three main points have been maintained, the terminology and nuances of the original conception have been modified and built upon by the current editors.

The Points of The Triangle

The first point in the triangle is the topic of this entire book series: **Sexual Exploitation**. What is it? What is it not? How are we to understand the problem? What happens when we misunderstand?

The second point is the reason this book series[3] exists: **Our Response**. How do we best address sexual exploitation, human trafficking, and related harms? What are the principles and practices that we should follow? What pitfalls must we avoid? What does success even look like?

This leads us to the final point: **Theology**. How do presuppositions from our faith impact how we understand exploitation and design our response? How can diving into the Bible and examining our beliefs shape the paradigms by which we approach the problem and our practice? How can failure to do so not only make us ineffective, but perhaps even unintentional perpetrators of harm ourselves?

The characteristics of each point of The Triangle (and the sections around which this book is structured) are summarized in the following chart:

SECTION OF THIS BOOK	GOAL	DESIRED IMPACT	PERSPECTIVE IN THE TRIANGLE
"See Sexual Exploitation in Scripture"	Redefine **Problem**	Better understand **Sexual Exploitation** (Exploitation, the Exploiters, the Exploited)	Sits more in **Scripture**
"Think Theologically about Sexual Exploitation"	Reconsider **Paradigms**	Better examine our **Theology** (Thinking and Talking about God)	Straddles **Scripture and Response**
"Raise our Response to Sexual Exploitation"	Revise **Practice**	Better carry out our **Response** (Disciplines and Services/ Concepts and Care)	Sits more in **Response**

Dancing Perspectives of The Triangle

The points of The Triangle are simultaneously interrelated and distinct.

While it is easy to plot these points on a one-dimensional drawing, in real life the distinctions are not so clear. The points of The Triangle are separate, but they are deeply integrated. They are not the same, but they are impossible to pull

---

[3]The first two volumes in the series are *Stopping the Traffick: A Christian Response to Sexual Exploitation and Trafficking* (Regnum 2014) and *Finding Our Way Through the Traffick: Navigating the Complexities of a Christian Response to Sexual Exploitation and Trafficking* (Regnum 2017).

neatly apart. Each point influences the other, influences the other, influences the other…

> How could our theological paradigm *not* drive our practical response to the problem as we understand it? And how could our understanding and practice *not* affect our theology?
>
> How could our understanding of exploitation *not* be connected to how we respond in light of our faith? And how could our theology and our response *not* shape our understanding of the problem?
>
> How could our experience in practice *not* transform how we understand the issue of exploitation and how we see exploitation in scripture? And how could our understanding of theology and the problem *not* impact our practice?

The Triangle is a dance, not a static form.

In one sense it is arbitrary to delineate discrete geometric points. But it is essential to do so. While the points are related they are also distinct, and unless we name each one we will be unaware of the influence – for good and for bad – that each has on the other(s).

Another way to think about The Triangle is that of perspective or starting point. A key priority of this book is integration.[4] The goal was not to have one set of chapters that looked at the problem, another that looked at the practice, and a third that looked at the paradigms. Rather, every chapter takes into consideration all three. And yet, each starts at a different place in The Triangle. Each approaches The Triangle from a different vantage point. When we encounter The Triangle from its different sides, our changed perspective changes our perceptions and understanding. And as with a kaleidoscope, every time we shift our perspective the image will never be the same. By recognizing this paradoxical nature and naming it, it is possible to see more clearly both the integration that makes for better outcomes as well as the dissonance that causes damage.

That said, it's often difficult to identify the starting point, to distinguish where the perspective is located. I found this particularly challenging in trying to order the works in this volume. Countless times I struggled to figure out whether a chapter started from the perspective of Practice or Paradigm or Problem. It's like what Justice Stewart said about pornography in a famous US Supreme Court case: "I know it when I see it." And yet the seeing is often illusive. The perspective that is clear in one moment suddenly blurs and becomes indistinguishable from another perspective in the next moment. Like a mirage in the desert, you are not sure if what you are seeing is really there, especially when it isn't, but even when it is. Seeing The Triangle both as a whole and as a sum of its parts became so challenging that I even considered abandoning it for an alphabetical arrangement of chapters instead. But that would have lost the unique perspective of each of The Triangle's facets and diminished the beauty of the dance.

---

[4] See Background of This Book.

On the other hand, arranging the chapters by their primary point in The Triangle risks over-delineation. Though they are separate they are also one; they are not just integrated, they are also iterative:

> Our theological assumptions drive our understanding of the problem and shape our response.
>
> At the same time, responding to exploitation causes us to see scripture in a new light, and both often result in a shift in our theology.
>
> And as our theology changes, we read scripture differently and are compelled to different actions.
>
> And so on and so on and so on….

The Triangle surely is a dance.

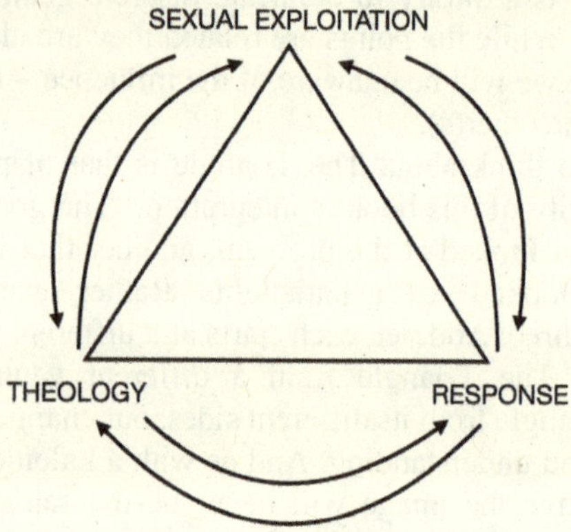

But dancing is not always easy. It is often awkward at first. We misstep. We get it wrong. We often avoid the dance for that very reason. Some may proclaim that there is only one way to do the dance and label all other steps as illegitimate. This can come from the "conservative" and the "progressive" side alike. Others may avoid the dance by declaring the dance itself out of bounds. They avoid the uncertainty by avoiding The Triangle altogether. Both approaches are a temptation, but we are grateful that that did not happen here with this book. We are thankful for the diverse contributors who accepted the invitation, vulnerable in their starting point, and risked making a misstep in one area so that we all could grow in each area. We are also thankful for readers who are willing to join the dance as well.

Getting Unstuck

So, what do triangles have to do with traffic jams anyway?

The purpose of this volume is to invite us to engage with the key question:

> How do we integrate the problem of Sexual Exploitation, and the practice of Responding to it, and the paradigm of Christian Theology so that we can more effectively end exploitation and cultivate the conditions for freedom?

This is a very important goal. But how do we get there? Chances are you have been stuck somewhere along the way. While brief interruptions present opportunities to avoid upcoming danger and make changes for greater success, being stuck prevents us from getting where we need to go to address urgent needs.

If we're stuck in a traffic jam, we have two choices: keep doing what we're doing or change what we're doing. Sometimes pausing in place allows the problem to clear and avoids wasted effort seeking alternative routes. But when what we're doing is not effective, we must change what we are doing. Maybe it's the route (we need to find a better course), maybe it's our preparedness (we need to research traffic patterns), maybe it's our decisions (we need to leave earlier next time), or maybe it's our methods (we need to take public transport).

The Triangle as a Lever of Change

How then do we get unstuck? We know that if we're stuck in mud and mire, keeping on doing the same thing the same way will only dig us in deeper. The same is true if we stick with the same box of practices, paradigms and problem-models we've always had if they are not working. Boxes keep us stuck. While they help contain a problem, they also put walls around our thinking, and a lid on our options for action.

We need a way out.

We need a lever. Levers provide a new angle. Instead of merely containing a problem like a box, levers dig into the problem and create a way for momentum to gain so that things can change. Levers allow us to explore a more insightful perspective, to discover a more accurate understanding of the problem, to develop a more effective solution.

The Triangle is a lever.

The Triangle helps us to get unstuck and to go forward. This dynamic, iterative process is demonstrated in the following "dance" involving our understanding of sexual exploitation (Problem), our theology about sexual exploitation (Paradigm), and our response to sexual exploitation (Practice).[5]

---

[5] There is no one single way that the "Triangle Dance" takes place. This example starts at the Sexual Exploitation point of The Triangle and makes a unique journey from there. There are other routes that could have been taken from the same starting point (e.g. going from Problem to Practice instead of Problem to Paradigm). Additionally, a different starting point could have been selected. So, while the process of engaging The Triangle remains the same, there are countless possible directions that it can take.

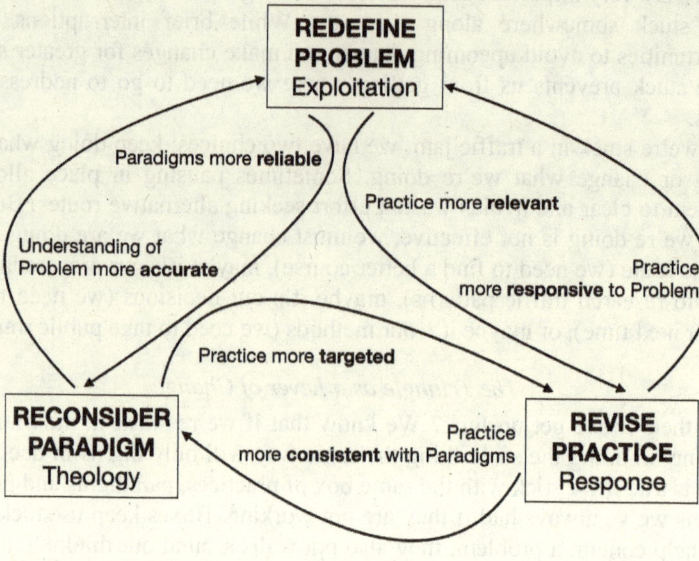

1. **Redefine Problem.** In responding to sexual exploitation, we quickly realize our need to better understand the Problem. As we learn to "See Sexual Exploitation in Scripture" we increase our understanding about exploitation (including exploiters and the exploited). When we Redefine the Problem, our *Paradigms can become more **reliable*** and our *Practice more **relevant***.

2. **Reconsider Paradigm.** As we better understand the Problem, we are led to better examine our theological Paradigms. As we "Think Theologically about Sexual Exploitation" we begin to recognize that our thinking and talking about God informs how we see the Problem and shapes how we respond in Practice. When we Reconsider our Paradigms, our *understanding of the Problem can become more **accurate*** and our *Practice more **targeted***.

3. **Revise Practice.** By examining our Paradigms, we are better able to evaluate and improve our Practice. As we seek to "Raise our Response to Sexual Exploitation" we consider how best to carry out our response through disciplines and services.[6] When we Revise our Practice, we try to ensure that our *responses are more **consistent** with our Paradigms* (e.g. they protect the image of God we say we believe in) and *more* **responsive** to the *Problem*.

4. **Reconsider Paradigm - Again.** Revising our Practice requires us to put our theology to the test. Applying our ideas in the real world reveals holes

---

[6] These terms are defined in the Background of This Book.

in our thinking and provides confirmation of theories that succeed. The Triangle invites us to again *Reconsider our Paradigms in light of our Practice.*

5. **Redefine Problem - Again.** Reconsidering our Paradigm requires us to reexamine how we think and talk about God in light of sexual exploitation. Is our theology (and the response that flows from it) based on flawed understandings of the Problem? The Triangle invites us to return to scripture to again *Redefine the Problem of sexual exploitation amidst evolving Paradigms.*

6. **Revise Practice - Again.** Redefining the Problem requires us to renew our understanding of exploitation, of those who exploit, and of those who are exploited. In turn, that understanding of the Problem must inform our response. The Triangle invites us to again *Revise our Practice to ensure that our disciplines and services are able to effectively address the Problem.*

7. **Repeat Entire Process.** As we Revise our Practice our experience will reveal additional knowledge and gaps in our understanding of sexual exploitation. As such, we should return to scripture to once again Redefine the Problem. As we engage in scripture our enhanced understanding will create new ways of thinking and talking about God and sexual exploitation. In response, we should again Reconsider our Paradigms. As our evolving theology creates practical implications for our response, we should once again Revise our Practice. *And so the dance continues….*

Limitations of The Triangle

The Triangle is a powerful tool, but the process of engaging it is not perfect. There are several things to consider.

First, unlike the other volumes in this series, the perspective of this book is specific to a Christian audience. The theology point of The Triangle is that of Christian theology, and each of the authors writes from the viewpoint of Christian faith. That said, we do hope that readers from other faiths or no religious faith will benefit from this book as well, in part by better understanding where Christians engaged in anti-trafficking work might be coming from. Such readers' outside perspectives can also help Christians better see where we might have gone off track or become stuck in our attempts to navigate the dance of The Triangle. Perhaps they will also be inspired to do similar reflection and analysis in their own contexts, and we can also learn from them. Readers from Abrahamic faiths can also offer different interpretations of commonly-held texts that can help Christian readers discover insights we haven't previously considered that might better inform how we understand exploitation, think about theology, and craft our practice.

Second, while this book is written from a Christian perspective it is important to recognize that there is no single Christian theology, and this book does not purport to represent one. The authors span a broad range of Christian belief and practice – some fundamentally different – though certainly not all traditions are represented. No one will agree with everything in this book, nor should they; nor do we. The point of the book is not to proclaim the "one" way to approach any of the points in The Triangle. Instead, we seek to present a variety of starting points in Christian tradition that can help us navigate in our own contexts. We pray that any disagreement with an author's theological beliefs or expression will not be seen as a barrier but an opportunity.[7] Readers are encouraged to wrestle not just with the questions of problem and practice but also with new paradigms within theology as well, especially from theologians who straddle multiple points on The Triangle (such as people who have been exploited or are members of people groups that have been enslaved). We hope that readers can learn from new perspectives even if they are not willing to adopt them, recognizing that unity does not require a flat homogeny but respects a beautiful diversity that will prayerfully lead to a more accurate understanding of the problem and a more effective response.

Speaking of diversity, this volume features chapters written by authors who are from or have lived in every continent. This provides much richness, and we hope future volumes will include even more diverse perspectives and voices. The authors also have a variety of experience, professions and writing styles, some more academic, some more down-to-earth; some readers will struggle with the first, while others may find the second a challenge. As you read, you will also be reminded that there is more than one single English language. We have retained the spelling, usage, and grammar of each author, so please don't think that we don't realize (or realise) that some pages appear riddled with misspellings or slightly-off word choice. We hope the exposure to unfamiliar communication styles (substantive, stylistic and linguistic) will help open our eyes to new ways of seeing and thinking as well.

Going forward towards Freedom

It's time to get unstuck and go forward. But to do so we must first take the time to pause, to reflect, to learn from the dancing perspectives of The Triangle.

Freedom matters. Faith also matters. And how well we do one affects how well we do the other.

What we do as Christians working against trafficking matters as well:

---

[7] For the most part, we have not sought to "fix" or harmonize theological language that may be problematic to some (e.g. pronouns for God). We have attempted to ensure that terminology related to sexual exploitation and practice centers personhood rather than problems (e.g. people in prostitution vs. prostitute or victim), but in some instances we have retained original language where extensive revision would interfere with the author's expression.

What we do matters for the anti-trafficking movement. People of faith have pioneered efforts to end exploitation for generations. What we do and how we do it shapes the course for others, both for good and for bad.

What we do matters for those who experience exploitation. Our failure to thoughtfully consider the best ways forward will be borne by those we seek to serve. Our failure to consider how to be more effective can itself become deeply exploitative.

What we do matters for ourselves and our colleagues. When the noble goal of Freedom justifies "by any means necessary" we begin to treat others as mere means instead of beings made in the image of God. How many more workers will we harm in our quest to "do good"? How much more damage will we do to ourselves?

What we do matters for the effectiveness of other Christians. Christians have enjoyed incredible influence in anti-trafficking, especially sex trafficking, even in countries where Christianity is a tiny minority. How well – or poorly – we do reflects not just on ourselves but also on other Christians, potentially impeding the willingness of governments and non-Christian NGOs to work with Christians in the future.

Most importantly, what we do matters for how others see God. It is vital for anyone to examine their paradigms, to better their understanding of the problem, and to continually improve their practice, bravely admitting where they've gone wrong, and committing to finding more effective ways. How much more so when our work is being done in the name of God; for it is not just our own reputation that is at stake but God's as well.

The effectiveness of our response matters greatly.

* * *

We have a moral imperative as our destination: Freedom – from a horror that impacts people in every area of their lives: emotionally, physically, economically, spiritually.

We have a profound starting point: Faith – embedded in our theology, in our understanding of the problem, in our confidence in our response.

And now, with this volume, we have a powerful way to get around the obstacles in our path: the lever of The Triangle.

But first, we must be willing to wait.

* * *

The goal of Freedom is in sight. But as we rush to get there we face major road blocks. Some give up in the face of the challenge and abandon the journey altogether, sometimes even losing their faith when it falls short of the demands of the task at hand. Some double down on their faith, even when it does not lead others to actual or metaphorical freedom, bulldozing through barriers meant to stop us from traveling down harmful paths. Others just get stuck, mired in the mud of a reality that no longer fits their beliefs, or in thinking that is incongruent with their actions. Denying the dissonance causes them to press harder on the gas, spinning the wheels deeper in mire, splattering mud on those they serve and those who have come to serve.

Very infrequently are most of us willing to take the opportunity to pause.

As we enter the third decade of the modern anti-trafficking movement, we encounter many abandoned vehicles and aborted tracks. Worse, there are entire thoroughfares that have been paved with good intentions that ignore the reality of the problem and are supported by anemic theologies that collapse in the face of complexity, leaving the route riddled with responses that are ineffective at best and harmful at worst.

And yet, for the most part, we continue to barrel on, resigned to an ever-rising number of exploited people, an ever-revolving door of disillusioned responders, and an ever-increasing pileup of naïve intentions gone wrong.

* * *

It's time to pause.

Instead of being stuck in the ways we've always done things, we have the chance to create new pathways that are more ethical, more empowering, more effective.

Instead of spinning our wheels or being immobilized at a crossroads, we have the chance to use The Triangle to re-consider where we are going and what is needed to get there.

Instead of doing the work of Freedom with a label of Faith pasted on top, or doing the work of Faith and pretending that it is positively affecting Freedom, we have the chance to integrate both in a way that can make each better and maybe even end exploitation in our lifetime.

* * *

So, let's choose to pause and Step Out of the Traffick, engaging The Triangle to discover better ways forward.

There's Freedom ahead if we do it well, of this we can surely have Faith.

About This Book

Glenn Miles, with Christa Foster Crawford

Attention, all! See the marvels of God!
He plants flowers and trees all over the earth, bans war from pole to pole, breaks all the weapons across his knee.
"Step out of the traffic! Take a long, loving look at me, your High God, above politics, above everything."

Psalm 46: 8-10, The Message

Readers might be surprised to learn that the title of this book is taken from scripture (Psalm 46: 8-10) which tells us to "Step out of the Traffic." Addressing trafficking is political. It involves governments and every department from justice to immigration, from labour to education. Yet this verse encourages us that God is all powerful and we should seek his loving mercy and justice above all else.

It is also good for us as practitioners to step out of the traffic for a while (Psalm 23), to pause and be with God, experiencing his rest and reflecting on God's heart of pure love for those we minister to and to us as the ministers.

But we're often too busy "doing the good work" to want to take the time to pause. When I decided to go to missionary training college, I wanted to do a one-year course because I wanted to get straight into the "real" work. The professors interviewing me wisely encouraged me to complete the full two-year training. They could see that I hadn't taken any shortcuts with the professional training I had done in preparation so I shouldn't take shortcuts with my theological and mission training either. I was grateful for their encouragement, and I have subsequently sought a balance in my practitioner and theological readings and understandings to be more holistic. Before I went to college I worked for a while in a Cambodian refugee camp in Thailand with YWAM. I was relieved and delighted when I got to college to realise that God really cared for the refugees and some of the most vulnerable people on the planet. God was right there behind my puny attempt at passionate service, and it was good to know that. It was reassuring. By pausing our "doing good work", we give the opportunity for God to change us so that we can do good work better.

How This Book Came About

This book has been a long time in the making. It has taken place over the turning of a decade and on at least three continents, with at least two sets of editors.

It is the third in a series of books[1] on identifying and wrestling with the problem of human trafficking and exploitation, particularly – but not exclusively – from a Christian perspective. But unlike the first two volumes, this book started out as a separate project with its own history. This book was birthed at the 2014 ICAP conference[2] when Bill Prevette and Francesca Nuzzolese invited a diverse group of Christian practitioners, scholars, and others to contribute to an edited volume addressing theology and response to sexual exploitation. While myself and series co-editor, Christa, assisted in initial planning meetings, Bill and Francesca served as lead editors, overseeing the framing and development of the book, including convening a group of practitioners, theologians, and scholars in Oxford, England later that year. (You can read more about the original framework of the book in the "Background of the Book" by Bill Prevette, and in the "Reflections on the Book" by Haddon Willmer.)

Great progress was made on the book under Bill and Francesa's leadership, including nearly-final forms of most of the chapters you hold in your hands – an amazing accomplishment given the full-time professional commitments of the editors and contributors (all of whom volunteer their labor). A few years in, Bill requested that Christa and I take the lead, making this book part of our existing series on Christian response to sexual exploitation and human trafficking, to which we gladly agreed.

But unfortunately, this book was deterred by forces beyond anyone's control: Major events in the lives of each of editor. Troubles with technology and logistics. Serious illnesses, and even death, of editors, contributors, and family members. A global pandemic that shut down the world.

This book experienced many seasons of involuntary Pause.

But despite the nearly-decade of challenges, we have persisted. While the delivery of the book has often been unsure, one thing was certain: The need to consider and cultivate what it means to engage in anti-trafficking work from a Christian perspective – in other words, how do we understand and reconcile the problem of exploitation and the practice of addressing it from the paradigms of Christian faith? (More on this in Christa's Introduction.)

We are honored to finally share with you the voices of experts from around the world, including survivors of exploitation, experienced practitioners, academics and theologians, and those who straddle in-between. We do not always agree with or endorse everything being said because we want to give voice to people from different contexts and churchmanships. But, if we are good practitioners, academics, and/or theologians then what we understand and believe to be right and true should evolve as we age and grow.

---

[1] Miles & Crawford, *Stopping the Traffick: A Christian Response to Sexual Exploitation and Trafficking* (Regnum 2014) and Crawford & Miles, *Finding Our Way Through the Traffick: Navigating the Complexities of a Christian Response to Sexual Exploitation and Trafficking* (Regnum 2017).

[2] International Christian Alliance on Prostitution.

How This Book is Structured

Anyone who has attempted to edit a book will know that what they end up with may be quite different from how it started and this is book no exception. However, there is a sense that what ended up in the volume was how it should be.

This volume invites us to pause and consider three key areas: Sexual Exploitation, Theology, and Response. Known as "The Triangle", the importance of each individually and together is explained in the Introduction by Christa, as well as the Background and Reflection by Bill and Haddon.

The book is organized around three parts:

- Part I: Seeing Sexual Exploitation in Scripture
- Part II: Thinking Theologically about Sexual Exploitation
- Part III: Raising Our Response to Sexual Exploitation

Part I: Seeing Sexual Exploitation in Scripture helps us to explore places in scripture where sexual exploitation, sexual harm, and other forms of exploitation/trafficking take place, and understand their relevance for those who have experienced harm. **Christa Foster Crawford and Bryon Lippincott** use the story of Tamar and Judah to demonstrate that unless we see what "The-God-Who-Sees" sees we will get our practice very wrong. They also provide guidance for how to see and do better. **Jennifer Singh** introduces us to a bible study method that comes out of theology from the margins and helps us understand how women in prostitution in Ethiopia read the story of Hagar as encouragement that God makes a way where there is no way. **Andrew J. Schmutzer** takes a deep dive into the story of Sodom and other sexual violence in Scripture to analyze striking patterns and similarities of sin. **David Tombs** demonstrates how the stripping of Jesus at the crucifixion involves sexual humiliation and abuse, and explores the implications that this theological insight has for practice. **Glenn M. Harden and Leslie Harley** bring an academic and a survivor perspective together to explore the meaning of authority throughout Scripture and contrast it with the misuse of authority in both sexual exploitation and aftercare. **Joni L. Middleton** shows us how the *imago Dei* (image of God) found in the book of Genesis and the New Testament reinforce the importance of dignity in our practice. **Tim Davy** engages with Psalm 10 to show us the implications of the *missio Dei* (mission of God) for the church in advocating for unaccompanied asylum-seeking children who are at risk of trafficking, abuse and exploitation. And finally, **Amanda Avila Kaminski** uses a literary analysis of Lamentations to introduce us to the practice of lament prayer as a way for exploited women to express their grief, anger, and protest at what has happened to them.

Part II: Thinking Theologically about Sexual Exploitation helps us to examine how we think and talk about God and sexual exploitation, and how this shapes our theology and our practice. **Leah Edwards** uses Kingdom of God theology to explore and challenge the motivations of Christian abolitionists. **Dan Pratt** explains unhelpful theologies of the cross and demonstrates how Black Saturday provides a middle space where God's presence can be experienced in suffering and trauma. **Siobhan Miles and Jill Reimer** examine stigma and reflect on how Christian NGOs have portrayed their clients in a way that may not always be dignifying. **Glenn Miles, Jarrett Davis and Hannah Sworn** look at how the story of Joseph's trafficking and exploitation challenges organizations that ignore the exploitation of boys and men, and presents research about the role of resilience and spirituality in providing services. **Heike Lippmann** explores theological implications of our consumer culture and its role as a root cause of human trafficking. Lastly, **Myrto Theocharous** examines themes of patriarchy and refuge to understand sex trafficking and the responsibilities of the people of God to respond.

Part III: Raising Our Response to Sexual Exploitation helps us to engage better in our disciplines and services as we seek to practice the gospel in the midst of sexual exploitation. **Vanntheary Lim, Glenn Miles and Channtha Nhanh** listen to what survivors in Cambodia have to teach us about the changing role of spirituality in recovery and how our responses can be more effective and less harmful. **Stephanie Goins** unpacks research on forgiveness from both academics and survivors, and offers forgiveness as a practice as a resource for people who have been exploited. **Genevieve James** introduces us to a toolkit that uses the story of David and Tamar to combat child rape. **Haddon Willmer** describes the particulars of a response that works with parents as agents of change and examines the issue of working with secular NGOs. **Carl Jylland-Halverson and Timothy Gaikwad** consider what scripture says about ministering to transgender people and provide principles for ministry using the case study of a ministry to *hijira* in India. Finally, but crucially important, **Samantha Miller and Glenn Miles** consider whether there is a place for forgiveness, healing and hope for perpetrators of sexual exploitation and trafficking.

What's Next

This book series has always sought to elevate diverse voices to speak to the tough questions faced in a Christian response to sexual exploitation and human trafficking. When the first volume, *Stopping the Traffick*, was published in 2014, there was very little written about the intersection of sex trafficking and how people addressed it from a Christian or theological perspective. That volume's authors challenged us to make sense of sexual exploitation in the context of our beliefs and the importance of networking together to make the most of our resources. It started by looking at addressing demand and reaching those in the margins, and ended with a call to network and collaborate better. The second volume, *Finding Our Way Through the Traffick*, explored the challenges of responding well, being careful in our language and assumptions, considering prevention and safeguarding, and responding holistically and safely in aftercare and reintegration. This third volume, *Stepping Out of the Traffick*, answers a request to get more theological whilst still learning from the grassroots.

So where do we go from here? In the future, we are interested in developing another volume that focuses on listening to the voices of survivors, including their reflections on their experiences and where God was in it all. As Tombs points out in his chapter in this volume, we need to learn from those who are experts of their own experiences. We look forward to sharing those conversations with you.

We also recognize the need to get voices out more quickly than the process of an edited book volume allows. Perhaps someone is interested in developing a journal or other vehicle that explores the practice and theology of sexual exploitation/trafficking. Maybe that someone is you! We must continue to think, individually and as a movement, about these important issues. Thankfully the number of people doing so is increasing all the time, but they need a place to share their work.

We look forward to what God has in store for the future as, together, we continue to explore the promise and the pitfalls of Christian response to sexual exploitation and human trafficking.

Background of this Book

Bill Prevette with Haddon Willmer

Sexual Exploitation, Theology, and Disciplines and Services: The "Triangle" Philosophy behind the Origins of this Book

In the autumn of 2014 a small group of practitioners, theologians, social scientists, and public heath scholars met together in Oxford, England with the intention of creating and editing a book that would integrate two themes: Sexual Exploitation and Theology. As a group, we were concerned that much of the Christian discourse addressing the questions and problems of sexual exploitation were leaving theology on the periphery of both theory and practice. Our initial discussions were both difficult and instructive. Some of the participants felt we needed a book that privileged theology, others stressed gender-based violence, others focused on the problems of patriarchy and misogyny in the church, a few wanted a book that drew on the voices of front-line practitioners. At the end of three days of working together and several intense conversations, we agreed we were committed to producing a useful book about sexual exploitation and Christian theology. We recognized this was an unusual combination and our task would require creativity and ingenuity. We further recognized that adapting the metaphor of a "Triangle" could help our contributors to hold themselves balanced between three important points: first, the phenomena of sexual exploitation; second, the disciplines & services responding to sexual exploitation; and third, engagement with Christian theology. Our intention in using the philosophy of The Triangle was to help shape the individual chapters of the book and give the overall outcome a coherent structure.[1]

How Does the Triangle Help Us to Achieve Our Common Purpose?

The guidelines we offered to our contributors were not designed to tell individual writers what they were to say or the methodology they were to use, let alone the conclusions they would come to. The Triangle was not offered as an abstract of the argument. Rather, The Triangle marked out a field in which those who were intent on producing this particular book agreed to work. The field was defined by three points, thus making a symbolic Triangle.[2] The Triangle enabled our writers to judge whether what they were writing was relevant – or not – to the

---

[1] Note that this background is written by the founding editors of this book and explains the original conceptual framework and structure. While the three main points of The Triangle have been maintained in the book you are now reading, the terminology and nuances have been built upon and modified by the current editors.

[2] There can be other triangles to facilitate work on other issues: see Bill Prevette, et al., *Theology, Mission and Child: Global Perspectives* (Regnum, 2014).

book. The Triangle served to remind us of the original *concern,* which generated the book and the *resources* and *obligations* with which we responded to them.

The three points of The Triangle can be summed up briefly:

- The phenomenon of *sexual exploitation*, including exploiters and exploited.
- The *disciplines & services* that seek to understand sexual exploitation better, and to diminish exploitation and care for the exploited.
- *Christian theology* – that is, thinking and talking of God in Christ by the Spirit.

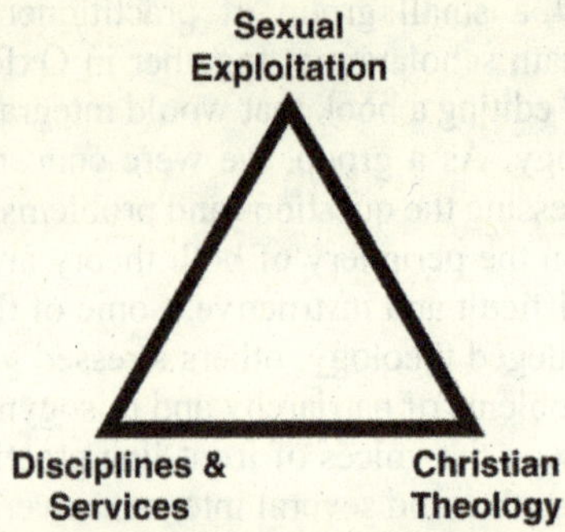

More about Each Point and How They Relate

The First Point: Sexual Exploitation

Sexual exploitation is the prime focus for this book. It is in itself a massive and evil reality embedded in, and not merely superficially on the surface of, the present fallen world. It is related in various ways to many other sorts of exploitation. To understand it, sexual exploitation needs to be viewed in its distinct identity and in its intimate and remote relationships. Sexual exploitation is not an impersonal force or a function of a "system." Like the "Powers,"[3] it has no being apart from the persons who are simultaneously caught and shaped in it, and who decide for it and enact it. People are both agents and victims in varying mixtures. The exploiters include procurers, pimps, traffickers and those who "buy sex", taking what they want without regard for the worth and dignity of those from whom they take (they think paying gives them a right: such is the exploitative mind which they share with the exploiters who think that their victims can be treated as mere material in trade). The exploited are many women and children – and an increasingly growing number of men and boys – whose vulnerabilities (including poverty, lack of social status, psychological issues, or just ordinary human virtues like curiosity, adventurousness, social connections,

---

[3] See Ephesians 6:12 and Walter Wink's *Naming the Powers: The Language of Power in the New Testament* (Fortress Press, 1984).

and sexuality.) are taken advantage of, rather than treated with respect, affirmation, and wise care.

Through our contributors' various essays, the book reports and illuminates the complex reality of sexual exploitation. This is the first point of The Triangle.

The Second Point: Disciplines & Services

The second point of The Triangle comprises two different but complementary ways of responding to sexual exploitation. On the one hand, seeking to uncover and understand it, and on the other hand seeking to respond to it, through caring for the exploited (sustaining, liberating and restoring them) and through curbing the exploiters and their destructive operations. We struggled to find a label for this point and agreed on "Disciplines & Services." Another way to think of this pole is "Theory & Practice" or "Research & Action." By "Disciplines", we mean the ways of investigating, understanding, and interpreting sexual exploitation. The term, Disciplines, is drawn from the academy, but good thinking about sexual exploitation is not confined to organized academic disciplines (anthropology, psychology, sociology, economics, philosophy, history, even theology); there are many other people who think honestly, intelligently, and usefully outside these boxes. Such thinkers are often found in what we label "Services", whose primary concern in engaging with sexual exploitation is action: Christian activists, police committed to catching and curbing exploiters, medical and social services caring for the exploited, educators helping to deter potential exploiters and build up vulnerable people, the media, which inform the wider public as a resource against sexual exploitation (at least potentially, if they resist the profitable temptation to titillate and sensationalise), the churches spasmodically, and many families. This is an incomplete listing of the wide phalanx of agencies which, at least to a degree, stand against exploitation and for the exploited. One of the issues we accept is the imperfection of all Disciplines & Services: their competence and reliability cannot be assumed. It is too common for them to make respectable professions on this subject while colluding with exploiters or being compromised in their own personal practice. We must not be misled by anything like a crude, simplified picture of the wicked exploiter; the poor, incapable victim; or the good and competent Crusader riding to the rescue.

This second point of The Triangle is a massive phenomenon in the world, though its financial resources probably do not match those of the exploiters.[4] A book that simply confined itself to the first point (Sexual Exploitation) would either glamorise and excuse the exploiters or be misery literature from the point of view of the exploited, and there would be no hope. But that is not how it is on the ground. Sexual exploitation provokes resistance striving to realise an alternative. This is not the only reason why this book sets the second point over

---

[4] Readers should always be wary of false precision. The sex trade is an underground industry, so any statistics presented that quantify the revenue from the trafficking of human beings should be understood only as estimates. For our purposes here, we recognize that the scale of human suffering defies quantitative measurement.

against the first. It is where we, as authors, stand. We, the writers of this book, are all located somewhere amongst the Disciplines & Services. We are neither exploiters nor exploited. We do not write about it from within the first-hand doing or the direct suffering of it.[5] We know much about sexual exploitation, often through intimate encounters, often through intense study, but there is still significant distance between us, the exploited, and the exploiters. This distance is both advantage and disadvantage. We may research and theorise, and yet fail to feel and to understand much about the reality. On the other side, distance gives us a chance to see sexual exploitation in a longer perspective and from more varied viewpoints than those who are imprisoned in its action and suffering. Thus, it is possible for the distanced to render useful service, so long as distance does not amount to passing by on the other side, to indifference and moralism, to condemning rather than giving help to move forward from the mess.

As we stand at this second point, we may be helped to be critically aware of what we know, how we know it, what the limitations of our knowing might be, and how we need to be helped by others, like those who know from experience. Only with them and for them can we move towards more truth.

We are not the only sort of people who discover within ourselves and our situation obstacles to facing the truth. The exploiters invent and practice exploitation, but they do not know what they are doing. They cannot because their deeds are evil, and they dare not come to the light. Their first-hand talk of what they do is shot through with euphemism, excuses, self-justification, and evasion. Any evidence exploiters provide about what is going on has to be suspiciously and imaginatively excavated – there might be some truth hidden somewhere, but they are not saying it plainly.

The exploited have the truth the exploiter denies because he does not respect the exploited. But they too have difficulty saying it. For some in the early stages of grooming, the truth is hidden by the initial adventure and excitement of it. Then, when the exploiter – who has alienated them from family and friends – controls them they do not tell because they do not expect an open hearing from anyone they have a chance of talking to. Sometimes, they resolve the issue by resigning themselves to their situation: "Evil be thou my good." Despair seems to be hard and realistic, against all do-gooding sentimentalities, but this realism is blind because it is incomplete. Hope against despair, resistance against resignation, are not merely healthy practical attitudes; they also give access to fuller truth.

We are more realistic, not less, when we look beyond the present prison, in hope; and when we risk building on hope, even though hope seems such a little frail elusive thing. Despair is powerful because in many situations it is easier than hope and resistance, but that does not make it true or the way to truth. Those who are distanced enough from exploitation not to be beaten down into resigned

[5] Editor's Note: While this may be true for most of the authors, some of the authors have experienced sexual exploitation and/or abuse, though only one author has revealed their experience in this book. Additionally, while none of the authors has been a professional exploiter, all of us have participated in exploitation (as consumers or otherwise) as the chapter by Lippman points out.

acceptance and despair can serve those who are in darkness. As the hymn, *The Servant Song* from Richard Gillard puts it:

> Brother, sister, let me serve you
> Let me be as Christ to you…
> I will hold the Christ-light for you
> In the night-time of your fear…

One reason why Disciplines & Services need to go together is that knowledge only comes from learning from and with the exploited and the poor, blind exploiters. And no one can decently get close to the exploited without acting to help them. Information is sterile without action: service is an indispensable way to get to know.

A key role of Disciplines & Services is, or could be, to hold open to the exploited and the exploiter a real, viable, good humanity, which they are not experiencing and find hard to believe in or hope for. This is very difficult in practice, because merely being *against* sexual exploitation doesn't guarantee that a person will be generous, hopeful, tactful – in short, *for* human beings. For example, police dealing with the exploited are often moralistic and condemnatory or seem to be so both in their language and in the measures they are able to take. So, it is good for our enterprise that Disciplines & Services are both represented in our contributors. But our contributors also demonstrate that Disciplines & Services are not always in agreement with each other. If disagreements can't be ironed out, let them at least be fertile.

Whether a Third Point?

We recognise that most discourse and action about sexual exploitation is carried on between these first two points: Sexual Exploitation and Disciplines & Services. But two points by themselves cannot be a triangle. Between them, they seem to have the essentials of the matter sewn up. So is another point to make a triangle needed? The problem and the search for solution are both there, the need and the help, the abuse and the protection.

We believe that the difference between a line that connects two points and a triangle helps us to see what is unusual about this book and why it has a distinctive contribution to make. We also understand why it might be dismissed by the people who run busily up and down the line between the first two points. This is especially so when the third point is "Theology", or "faith" with a strong identity, or straight out language and thought of God.

The Third Point: Theology

The third point of The Triangle is Theology. We choose theology – or talking and thinking about God – in our dealing with sexual exploitation because, in the first place, we are Christians. So we want to come to this task as whole persons, in integrity, and give it all we have got. We not only have concern and expertise, we also have faith: a substantial relation with God the Father through Jesus Christ in the Spirit, in whom our whole life is redeemed, being renewed, claimed and enabled to do God's will in the world with and for others. (Romans 12.1-2)

Secondly: theology, faith, and religion are important on the human scene. There are more people who believe in God and go to church or to a comparable gathering of faith people, than there are exploited and exploiters, and people in Disciplines & Services. The action of people of faith takes up space in the public square and in the private lives of millions of people. Religion is not unambiguously good. Some Christians are abusers and exploiters, some are apathetic bystanders, some are simplistic, impatient enthusiasts who imagine that short sharp bursts of activity dressed up in faith clothes will do what ordinary regular activities can't do – miracles. Gathering the forces available at this third point does not solve the problem; these forces will only help if they are modest and penitent, truthful about themselves and their limitations and open to learning.

We write as Christians,[6] for Christians[7] gathered at this third point and for those who are on their way towards faith, knowingly or not. For ourselves and for them, this book may be a stimulus to seeking and finding, because it will display Christian understanding and vision in the course of talking in informed, wise and constructive ways about sexual exploitation. The book is an act of solidarity with the exploited and cooperation within the Disciplines & Services. This solidarity and this cooperation is talked and walked in such a way that it becomes clear that this "Theology" requires to be seen as a *third* point. It has its own integrity. But by standing apart to be itself, it enlarges and strengthens the good that is done between the first two points of The Triangle.

Possible Challenges Raised by Our Reference to "The Triangle"

One of this book's biggest challenges to our thinking and imagination is that it calls us to think and talk of God in dealing wisely and responsibly with issues arising from sexual exploitation. If we fail here, the book will fall back into the conventional discourse of experts and activists who specialise in sexual exploitation. Therefore, this book is not a collection of conventional secular articles with one or two theological essays loosely attached. That solution would be an implicit confession that we as a group of Christians are practical secularists and don't find significant excitement or help in theology and don't have much idea of how to mix theology into the stew of living.[8]

In summary, The Triangle did not instruct the individual writers in what they have written, nor in how they should argue their cases. It simply marks out the territory in which we are working together and reminds us of the three major sorts of activity, community, and difficulty we are addressing. We have suggested that we all think and write within The Triangle, giving balance and weight to all three points, and letting our minds become a place where all three

[6] Editor's Note: As noted in the Introduction to this book, while having a common Christian faith, the authors do represent a variety of Christian traditions. We treasure that diversity and do not try to harmonize differences but rather display them for the reader to experience and make their own conclusions.

[7] Editor's Note: While this book is written from a Christian theological perspective, and therefore most relevant to Christians, we do hope that people from other faiths – or none – will read and benefit from this book.

[8] *Cf* Dietrich Bonhoeffer, letter of 21 July 1944 in *Letters and Papers from Prison.*

points meet each other. The outcome is a collection of varied essays which have a discernible coherence and relevance on Sexual Exploitation and Theology.

Works Cited

Bonhoeffer, Dietrich. *Letters and Papers from Prison.*

Prevette, Bill, C., Keith J. White, C. Rosalee Velloso Ewell, and D.J. Konz. *Theology, Mission and Child: Global Perspectives.* Oxford, UK: Regnum, 2014.

Wink, Walter. *Naming the Powers: The Language of Power in the New Testament.* Philadelphia: Fortress Press, 1984.

Reflections on this Book

Haddon Willmer

The varied chapters in this book share two key characteristics. First, they want sexual exploitation to end, the exploiters to be deterred and turned round, the exploited to be freed and healed, and societies, cultures and economies no longer to be conducive to it. This is the horizon of hope towards which the arguments and passion of these papers are looking, in company with the people and projects featured here. The horizon is far distant but it is enough that the direction of our travel and our duty are both clear and compelling. Second, they are written by Christians, seeking to see and respond to sexual exploitation in the light given by God in Christ.

In their practical engagement with sexual exploitation, Christians are bound to work with many wise and competent people who are content to leave anything that looks like religion to one side as an unhelpful complication. For many, faith is a private option, which brings them inward personal support, but they do not expect it to do enough to make a significant difference to their analysis of sexual exploitation and their action in response to it. So they do not initiate a close encounter between exploitation and theology. This book is born out of a conviction that such an encounter would be as useful as it is difficult. It calls for deliberate effort to do theology with one hand and to oppose sexual exploitation with the other. It is not surprising then that making this book has not been easy, for the organizers, editors, and authors.

The audience hoped for includes all who are concerned about sexual exploitation in any way – even including the exploiters themselves and the bystanders and those (unreliably) assured that "This doesn't happen in our town." Much in this book will be immediately accessible to people who experience sexual exploitation or merely learn about it from the newspapers. But theology does not get a hearing so readily.

Why Theology?

One obstacle on that way is the off-putting image that theology generally has. Politicians sometimes dismiss the ideas of their political opponents as "theology", not because God has been brought into the discussion, but because the talk has become complicated, practically irrelevant, merely clever. People immediately know what the politician is getting at, and if they ever go to church and hear a sermon, they feel the same. And even worse than the pulpit, university theology is often "academic" in the bad sense, a mystifying elite pedantry.

This dismissal is unfair to theology and stifles its potential usefulness. Why? Because it judges theology from occasional (though frequent) symptoms of disease, as though the body never was or could be anything but the cancer now found to be growing in it. Let us start with theology as a body in its beautiful healthy original elements, before any disease twists it. Theology is simply talking and thinking (*logos*) of God (*theos*). In its essential roots, it does not have to be an extended, abstracting learned discourse; rather it is free exploration, risking naivety and clumsiness to venture a meeting between situated human being and the living God: "Draw near to God, and He will draw near to you." (James 4:8)

Theology and Prayer

Jesus tells us: "When you pray, do not heap up empty phrases, speak to your Father who knows what you need before you ask." (Matthew 6:7) To pray, we only have to be human beings, alert to our context in the world, which is awesome, both in its manageable accessibility and in its disconcerting hidden reticence. We sense that we are beset by both good, life-giving and life-enhancing "powers beyond our own" and by menacing, even malevolent possibilities. We seek to make sense of ourselves in context, and to find ways of living well. We seek to know, respect, and have the supporting accompaniment of good powers. And so we pray, reaching outward from what we have and looking for help. Many more people pray than preach sermons, or speak about God. Praying has theological authenticity because it is not cluttered: indeed on its human side it consists largely in uncluttering, until our hand is empty and open to receive, unbusy and ready to be redirected. Prayer is simply human being talking to, and with, God: "God, if you are there, help me." "God be merciful to me, a sinner." "God, why have you forsaken me?" "Even so, come Lord." "*Dona nobis pacem*. Give us peace." "Make my way plain, before my eyes." "Lord, here I am, send me." "God, thank you." "Our Father, who art in heaven, hallowed be your Name…."

Theology rests on the acknowledgement of God as God. Christian faith is constituted by the recognition that "God is in Christ", and so confesses that "Jesus is Lord." Such confession can only be made in the humility and openness of prayer, where we give up all pretence that we are masterfully free to decide whether Jesus shall be Lord or not. Theology becomes cancerous when the human talker assumes defining control of the talk. Indeed, in our talking about God we easily become idol makers, so achieving nothing beyond mirroring ourselves in puppet-images that have no life in themselves and cannot bring us near the living God.

Whether prayer is a tentative entry into mystery, ready to find out what, or who, shows up, or is a peaceable conversation with a trusted Other, it cannot avoid being a little seed of theology that grows roots and shoots. "Help me" leads to specification of what is desired, or needed, and with it, some imaging of what the Helper must be like. The cry "Why have you forsaken me?" implicitly confesses: "We thought you were faithful and able" and thus confronts us with a choice between two questions that spawn more theology. The one: "Is God not here at all, or at least, not for me?" and the other: "If God is, but in this time and place is not giving the answer I think I need, or have a right to, what then is God doing? What is the meaning of his silence and absence? What is it now to have trust and hope?"

When what passes for theology ceases to be sensitive to questions and possibilities that arise in prayer (which is the most basic, simplest attempt to draw near to God in truth), it is losing its way, no matter how clever it may be. Or put it the other way around: the *theological* appreciation of any human discourse or chunk of life comes from looking for the prayer that is being prayed in it, openly or implicitly, precisely or vaguely. Discourse – in words and in practice – may be searched with the aid of many disciplines, all bringing some reality to light; to understand it theologically, find the prayer in it and then pray along with it.

Theology in Practical Context

This is how, on the human side of prayer, theology is seeded and may grow. But many who pray are not aware or interested enough to become self-conscious or publicly active as "theologians." Nevertheless, they do find that when they pray, they move outside themselves and are met in some way. Their requests may not be granted according to the terms in which they were made, but a conversation develops, and they are accompanied on the road of life in ways beyond their expectations. What they wanted for themselves is both sifted and enlarged by what the Other gives to them.

What God gives is more than a detachable gift, like the healing nine lepers got from Jesus that they could take away with them, and never look back. The tenth leper understood better the connection between giver and gift so he turned back to thank Jesus. (Luke 17) The younger son got the inheritance and left his father behind, until life brought him to himself, and he saw that the good part of his inheritance could not be detached and enjoyed without his being with the father. (Luke 15) To seek and to be finding the non-detachable gift is to get beyond being merely a needy, consuming recipient; it is to be drawn into close company with the Giver, and thereby, in turn, into being a giver.

The poor are not simply to have their needs supplied so that they can survive. They need to be able to *share in the giving*. The objection to "charity" is not that have-nots are dependent on the haves, but that charity rarely calls or enables have-nots to become more than recipients, with enough spiritual and material resources to be cheerful, open-hearted givers. Calculating charity (that makes sure people have just enough to get by on) fails because it has no practicable intention to call and equip recipients to be givers. Understand this, and we are moved on from praying, consumer-like prayers of "Lord, help me" to the prayer of a fellow-worker: "Lord, here I am, send me."

Theology is more than a theory about the power and goodness of God the bountiful provider. Such a theory embroils theology in theodicy, lamely defending God who does not appear to live up to the job specification that our neediness writes for him. Theology is not, however, a theory of provision, but a challenging and empowering call to courageous and generous living for others, in company with God who enters human living, suffering as God and human being together, taking responsibility for the mess as a helper and hopeful pathfinder. Theology thus is missiology – it articulates vision and understanding of what we human beings are called to do, starting from where we are now, in faithfulness to God who is faithful to us: We love, because He first loved and loves us; the love of Christ shapes, directs, and empowers us.

Theology in the Pages of this Book

Praying is the way into the treasury of talk about God which is found, for example, in the accumulation of Christian theology through the centuries and throughout the world. The chapters in this book dip into the treasury and deploy some of its treasures, showing how it inspires and informs responses to sexual exploitation. There is a search for resonances between the engagement of victims and perpetrators, bystanders and theorists, and themes and motifs of theology. Reading the Bible, praying in hope of the promise of God, loving genuinely according to the measure of God in Christ, being forgiven as we forgive, sharing the grace of God, learning to serve in the way and spirit of Christ, standing by God in the hour of his grieving: all this and more come into view in the reports and analyses of contemporary action against sexual exploitation found in the pages of this volume.

Part I

Seeing Sexual Exploitation in Scripture

Seeing What "The-God-Who-Sees" Sees: How Tamar "The Righteous Prostitute" Helps Anti-Trafficking Organizations to Recognize Dehumanizing Preconceptions and Resist Exploitative Depictions

Christa Foster Crawford and Bryon Lippincott

> "When Judah saw Tamar, he thought she was a prostitute because she had covered her face. So, he went over to where she was sitting and said, not realizing that she was his daughter-in-law, 'Come, let me sleep with you.'" Genesis 38:15-16 (Complete Jewish Bible)

Judah saw a prostitute.

He did not see a person. He did not see a woman. He only saw a *zanah*, a loose woman or an adulteress or a prostitute.[1]

He saw her and turned to her and said: "Come now, let me come in to you – let me have sex with you." And he did.

But this was not just any "loose woman." This was his daughter-in-law. His dead sons' wife, to whom he had broken his promise.

He saw a *zanah* and he used her for his own sexual gratification. And even in that most intimate of acts, he still did not see her for who she really was. He only saw what she could do for him. He did not see relations with another person. He only saw a transaction – she would have sex with him and he would pay her money, leaving his seal and staff as a guarantee.

Judah's friend also saw a prostitute.

Judah sent his friend Hirah to settle accounts and get his guarantee back.

Hirah looked for a prostitute. He did not look for a person. He did not look for a woman. He asked the men of the place: "Where is the *qedeshah* – the prostitute, possibly a temple prostitute – who was on the road at the fountain?" The men replied: "There hasn't been any *qedeshah* here."

When Hirah reported back to Judah that he could not find the *qedeshah,* Judah decided that keeping his reputation was more important than even the return of his goods. Judah told Hirah: "All right, let her keep the things so that we won't be publicly shamed."

Society also saw a prostitute.

---

[1] Most scripture quotations are based on the Complete Jewish Bible translation, with some New King James and other versions woven in. Hebrew transliteration and Strong's Reference are primarily from QBible [Available at: http://qbible.com/hebrew-old-testament/genesis/38.html]. Most definitions are from Brown-Driver-Briggs (Old Testament Hebrew-English Lexicon) accessed through QBible.

Three months later, Judah was told: "Tamar your daughter-in-law has been acting like a *zanah*. Behold, moreover, she is pregnant as a result of her *zenunim* [prostitution or adultery]."

They did not see a person. They did not see a woman. They only saw an unmarried female whose body revealed that she would bear a child.

They did not know that Judah had propositioned her on the side of the road. They only concluded that she must be a "whore." They did not know that Judah was the one who had impregnated her. They only concluded that she had committed adultery. They understood when Judah said: "Bring her out and let her be burned alive!" that the destruction of a "fallen woman" was a just response in their society.

* * *

A Prostitute; a Whore; an Adulterous Woman. That is what everyone in the story saw.

But God saw Tamar. God saw a woman. God saw a person.

By seeing a prostitute, Judah and his friends and his society could ignore Tamar's humanity.[2] She was only an object for Judah's pleasure; a threat to Judah's reputation; the cause of her own shame.

By seeing a prostitute, Judah and his friends and his society could ignore their own actions and absolve themselves of blame. She was the bad one. They were not culpable for her sin. The role they played in how she got there was of no concern. She was the one who should be punished. They could go on with their lives and never have to change.

But God saw Tamar. A Woman. A Person.

And, eventually, Judah did as well.

* * *

The story of Tamar is one of many stories where God sees people that no one else sees. Let's look at two other examples.

In Genesis 16, we see another woman whose potential for childbearing has made her a pawn in a family drama. Sarai, unable to conceive, sends her slave Hagar to her husband Abram. Offended and jealous, Sarai treats the pregnant Hagar harshly. Hagar flees to the desert wilderness where she encounters the Most High God at a spring in the road.[3] In a great reversal, the lowest person in the story is given the highest honor of being the first person to give a name to God. She calls God *El Roi*: The God Who Sees – The God Who Sees Me.

---

[2] "Judah abandons [Tamar], exploits her, and violates her because his desire to maintain power is greater than his desire to respect and honor human life" (George and Toyama-Szeto, 2015: 41).

[3] Genesis 16:7 "The angel of Adonai found her by a spring (*ayin*; also "fountain" or "eye") in the desert, the spring on the way (*derek*) to Shur." Note the parallel to Genesis 38:14 where Judah found Tamar "at the entrance to the fountain (*ayin*) which is on the way (*derek*) to Timnah." The significance of these words will be discussed below in the second act of the Tamar story.

While a woman is doing the unprecedented naming of God in the Old Testament, there is also an unprecedented naming of women in the New Testament. In Matthew 1, we see women in the genealogy of Jesus. To list a woman was unusual. To list five women[4] who had questionable sexual reputations was unheard of. Not only that, the first woman mentioned in the Matthew account is not Mary, the mother of Jesus, Sarah, the mother of Israel, or Eve, the mother of all. The first woman mentioned in the New Testament is Tamar herself; her contribution to Jesus' royal lineage the product of commercial adultery.[5]

God sees women. God sees women as people. God sees even "sullied" women as people made in the image of God and as not just worthy of respect as humans but also gives them the honor of being heroes in the story of the Bible, progenitors in the birth of the Messiah.

* * *

So, what did God see in Tamar? What did Judah eventually come to see?

In Genesis 38:6, we meet a person named Tamar. That's all that we are told about her, her name: "Judah took a wife for Er, his firstborn, and her name was Tamar." Tamar's story takes place in three acts. For the first act she does not have any lines or actions of her own; she is merely a prop. Her role in the story mirrored her role in society. Women had no status or rights outside of the men in their lives – first in relation to their fathers, then in relation to their husbands. They depended on them for everything: food, shelter, security, reputation.[6]

So, when Judah took Tamar to be the wife of his firstborn son, she became dependent on Judah's family. But Tamar's husband was wicked. Although we are not told how, it is possible (perhaps likely) that his malice extended to her. No matter how much abuse or neglect she experienced, Tamar had no choice but to endure.

And then her husband died. Now Tamar was a widow. Widows were even more vulnerable than daughters and wives because they no longer had a husband to care for them.[7] Thankfully society had a safety net for Tamar. As a wife, it was her role to produce offspring to extend the family line. But her husband had died before she had borne children. So, Judah told his second son: "Go and sleep with your brother's wife – perform the duty of a husband's brother to her and preserve your brother's line of descent" (v.8). Being forced to marry your husband's brother doesn't seem like a very liberating thing, but it ensured her position in the family and the protection that entailed. Once again, regardless of her desires, Tamar had no choice but to endure.

---

[4] Tamar, Rahab, Ruth, Bathsheba (as Uriah's wife), and Mary.

[5] Credit to David Lamb's book *Prostitutes and Polygamists* for additional details to this observation. (Lamb, 2015: 95).

[6] In Tamar's society, there are "few options for survival for women who are not married or part of a family" (George and Toyama-Szeto, 2015: 42).

[7] Tamar's "status in society denies her some of the opportunities and provision that she needs to flourish" (George and Toyama-Szeto, 2015: 40).

And then the brother also died. Now Tamar was a widow again. Even worse, she was a childless widow. The brother intentionally refused to perform his duty to impregnate her "so as not to give his brother offspring" because "he knew the child would not count as his" (v.9). Whether he did this out of financial reasons or merely jealousy is unknown;[8] but what is clear is that he had the power and choice to violate his duty to Tamar,.and Tamar had no choice but to endure.

And then her last hope died. Tamar was entitled to be married to the last remaining brother. But Judah refused. He knew that God had killed his first son because he was evil, and his second son because he did evil in refusing to fulfil his duty. Judah didn't want to lose his only remaining son, and so he sent Tamar home to her father's house with the shame that carried, the instruction to "stay a widow," and the empty promise of marriage to his third son when "he grows up" (a pretense according to the text). But regardless of whether Judah had any intention of fulfilling this obligation, Tamar remained bound. Although she was twice-widowed, she was not free to marry – even if someone was willing to have her (and why would they, since to anyone watching she was probably barren and certainly not successful in keeping a husband alive). Furthermore, society does not provide her "an advocate or opportunity to lodge a complaint. There is no system within which Tamar can seek justice for herself."[9] So, once again, Tamar's fate was dependent upon the willingness of the men in her life to fulfil their duty, and once again Tamar had no choice but to endure.

But in the second act, the story pivots. Tamar becomes an agent instead of an object. Beginning in verse 14, the language shifts. Tamar is no longer referred to in the passive sense as something the other characters act upon. Instead, she takes action herself. Time has passed and the third son is grown. But still, Judah fails to fulfil his personal promise and cultural duty to marry Tamar to him. This time instead of merely enduring, Tamar makes a choice to pursue the justice that has wrongly been denied to her. Tamar learns that Judah has gone up to Timnah to shear his sheep. So, Tamar takes off her widow's clothes, revealing her essence as a young woman who has endured more tragedy than most do in a lifetime. Tamar puts on a veil that completely covers her face, portraying to passersby that the person concealed is a prostitute. And then, Tamar sits down at a fountain and waits.

Tamar has done a lot of sitting in this story. In Hebrew, the verb is *yashab*, and has a variety of meanings including to marry, to dwell, to settle, to remain. She has married twice and has remained (*yashab*) a widow staying (*yashab*) at home with her father until Judah decides to fulfil his obligation to her (v.11). When he fails, she takes the only action she has in her power. She sits. This time her sitting is not passive waiting, but it takes on another connotation of the verb

---

[8] Theologian David Lamb argues for financial motives: "Onan was willing to 'go in to' Tamar, but he was reluctant to impregnate her because it would dramatically reduce his own inheritance, so he spilled his seed on the ground... Onan's sexual exploitation of Tamar, using her for his sexual pleasure while denying her the dignity of motherhood, was so displeasing to Yahweh that Onan was killed." (Lamb, 2015: 96).

[9] (George and Toyama-Szeto, 2015: 41).

yashab: to sit quietly in ambush as a judge. Let's take a closer look at these verses to see how this becomes the case for Tamar.

In this second movement of the story, Judah is now the one whose spouse has died. But the result of his loss is very different than what Tamar experienced. Verse 12 tells us: "In due time, Shua's daughter, the wife of Judah died. After Judah had been comforted…" The loss of Tamar's husbands brought her little comfort, and the broken promise of marriage to the third son left her in a limbo that would make her guilty of adultery were she with someone else.[10] She, not Judah, would pay the price for his betrayal. By contrast, Judah is not only free to visit a prostitute after his loss, he is bold enough to send his friend to get his belongings back afterwards.

Next, we are told that "After Judah had been comforted, he went up (*alah*) to be with his sheep-shearers (*gazaz*) in Timnah" (v. 12). Those facts are so important they are repeated in the next verse: "Tamar was told, 'Your father-in-law has gone up (*alah*) to Timnah to shear (*gazaz*) his sheep.'" What might be going on? Timnah means "assigned portion" and *alah* means "to ascend", both in a literal and figurative sense. Despite his widowerhood, Judah's assigned portion keeps going up; but because of her widowhood, Tamar's assigned portion has gone increasingly down. Furthermore, *gazaz*, or shearing sheep, has the figurative meaning of destroying one's enemy. Judah gets to choose to go be with his sheep shearers. By contrast, the men in her life have made choices which cause Tamar repeated loss and destruction.

It is in this context that Tamar sits (*yashab*) at the entrance to the fountain which is on the way (*derek*) to Timnah (v.14). *Derek* means road but has the figurative meaning of "course of life/mode of action." In choosing to sit in the road to *Assigned Portion*, Tamar is choosing a new *Course of Life*. In choosing to sit down (*yashab*) in the road that Judah is ascending, she is waiting quietly in ambush as a judge of the unjust course of life that Judah has chosen, which has resulted in the unjust deprivation of Tamar's assigned portion. Sometimes the only choice left to women is to sit.

The second act ends in verse 19 with: Tamar "arose (*quwm*) and went away. She took off her veil and put on her widow's clothes." In rising,[11] Tamar returns to her true identity – a woman who has been wronged, not (as Judah sees her) a wanton, adulterous prostitute.[12] In rising (*quwm*), she changes the course of Judah's ascent (*alah*) that has until that point always kept her down.

These important lessons of the story could be taught in a children's Sunday School class. But this second act reminds us why this story has relevance for

---

[10] "Adultery in this context – in Israelite society men could have more than one wife, but women could only have one husband – means sexual relations between a married or betrothed woman and a man other than her husband or betrothed." (Levine and Brettler, 2020: 188).

[11] *Quwm* means to rise, both literally and figuratively.

[12] We'll see this sentiment affirmed in the third act when Judah's friend went to find Tamar: "Hirah asked the people near where she had been, 'Where is the prostitute who was openly on the road at the fountain?' But they answered, 'There hasn't been any prostitute here.'" (v. 21).

people wrestling with the Triangle of Theology, Sexual Exploitation, and Response. Thus far, we've left out the important detail that Tamar sits in this quiet judgment seeking justice while dressed as a prostitute. We've left out the parts where Judah says, "Come, let me sleep with you," and Tamar replies, "What will you pay?", where Tamar takes his seal and staff as a guarantee, and where Tamar sleeps with him and conceives a child. Surely the moral of the Sunday School lesson must be that, although it was wrong that Judah violated his obligation, it was also wrong that Tamar broke hers. But, perhaps not.

* * *

We now turn to the final act of the story where Judah – and everyone else – eventually sees what God sees.

Judah sends his friend Hirah to find The Prostitute and deliver the young goat he promised in payment. Why is Judah suddenly eager to fulfil a promise when he failed to in the past? Perhaps it is more that he needs to retrieve the guarantee that he left behind. Judah's seal/signet ring and staff would have mattered greatly to him in society.[13] These however did not matter as much as the loss of his reputation if people realized that he lost them to a prostitute.[14] When Judah learns that The Prostitute could not be found, he says, "All right, let her keep the things, so that we won't be publicly shamed (*buwz*). I sent the kid[15] but you didn't find her" (v. 23). *Buwz* has the meaning of contempt, disrespected, despised, to be a laughing stock. Judah manages to avoid these things, but they are exactly what Tamar would have experienced in all the years that Judah reneged on his promise to send her his third son.

Although Hirah did not find Tamar, it is important to understand what he was looking for. When Hirah arrives at the fountain, he doesn't see what he expects to see. He expected to see a *qedeshah,* which is a female devotee, possibly a temple prostitute (v. 21). But this is different from what Judah saw, a *zanah*, one who has committed adultery, usually the female, also known as a "loose woman" or prostitute. It is also different from what Judah told Hirah to look for. Judah told Hirah to get his belongings back from the "woman's hand" (v.20). The Hebrew word here is *ishshah*, a generic word for woman that is used in the creation story in Genesis 2:22.[16] Hirah was told to go to a woman (a person made in the image of God with full humanity and declared by God as "very good" in

---

[13] "This exchange would be comparable today to someone giving away their driver's license and credit cards. To hand over all his valuables to a stranger like this must have meant he was really in the mood." (Lamb, 2015: 97).

[14] While it could be argued that Judah feared reputational loss in sleeping with a prostitute, this is contradicted by the fact that he had no problem in leaving his identifying seal with her, and that he sent his friend to publicly enquire about getting them back.

[15] Note the irony in the (English) pun that Judah was willing to send his kid (a young goat) but was still unwilling to send his kid (the son he had promised).

[16] There are two words for men and women used in the creation accounts in Genesis. In Genesis 1:26-31, the words are *zakar* (male) and *neqebah* (female). In Genesis 2:20-25, the words are *adam* (man) and *ishshah* (woman).

Genesis 1:31). At the core of her being, Tamar is a woman, but her identity has been defined by others in terms of her (perceived) sexual behavior: a prostitute, an adulteress, a wanton female. Our words determine what – and who – we see, as we shall discuss later in this chapter.

Three months pass and someone tells Judah what no upright man wants to hear: "Tamar, your daughter-in-law, has been acting like a whore (*zanah*) and is pregnant as a result of her prostitution/adultery (*zanuwn*)." (v.24) Judah responds: "Burn her alive!"[17] Once again, Judah sees a prostitute. He does not see a person. He does not see a woman. And, this time, it is not just a stranger on the road but his daughter-in-law of whom he rejects the humanity. He does not see her. Instead, he sees an adulteress, and a woman who is pregnant outside of marriage. He certainly does not see his own role in either of those actions, nor how his own broken promise is what brought her down that road.

But God sees something else.

God sees Judah's unrighteousness and injustice – his failure to fulfil his personal vow and societal duty by withholding his remaining son, among other wrongs.[18] God sees the unrighteousness and injustice of Judah's sons, one in refusing to impregnate her, the other in an unnamed form of evil. And God sees that Tamar's actions are a direct result of what the men in her life had failed to do in the context of a society that seemed to leave her no other options.

And yet, Judah continues to be blind. When Tamar is brought out to be killed, she sends a message to Judah: "I am pregnant by the man to whom these things belong. Determine (*nakar*) whose these are – the signet, the cords and the staff' (v.25). The verb *nakar* marks a turning point in the story. *Nakar* has a variety of meanings, including recognize, acknowledge, know, respect, discern, regard.[19] Each of these connotations will come into play.

At last, Judah sees what The-God-Who-Sees sees.

Judah sees his own wrong-doing. "Judah recognized (*nakar*) the items and acknowledged (*nakar*) they belonged to him" (v. 26). In the book of Genesis, the story of Tamar interrupts the story of Joseph, with many similarities between

---

[17] And yet, even this punishment is an injustice to Tamar under the biblical standard that would be later articulated in Deuteronomy, Leviticus and Numbers. One, this punishment requires the testimony of multiple witnesses. Two, it is a more extreme punishment than the law called for since she wasn't the daughter of a priest. (See Lamb, 2015: 98).

[18] Judah's life includes a long list of wrongs: "[Judah] gets off to a good start, since his name means "praise" (Gen. 29:35), but it quickly goes downhill from there. Judah is absent from the text until he proposes the scheme to his brothers to sell Joseph to slave traders (Gen. 37:27). He raises a batch of wicked sons. He deceives his daughter-in-law Tamar about giving her his third son, Shelah. He propositions Tamar, thinking she's a prostitute. He condemns her for sexual immorality when he is the only one guilty of that particular crime" (Lamb, 2015: 100).

[19] "Nakar", *Bible Study Tools* [Available online at: https://www.biblestudytools.com/lexicons/hebrew/kjv/nakar.html], [Last accessed: 7th October 2022].

them.[20] Here, Judah *nakars* his identity items, evidence of his mistreatment of Tamar; earlier Judah's father *nakars* Joseph's bloody robe, evidence of Judah's scheme to enslave his brother (Gen. 37:32-33). In both cases, Judah's complicity in someone else's exploitation is recognized (*nakar*).

Judah sees Tamar as a person. *Nakar* can mean scrutinizing or looking at intently and having respect and care for. Before, Tamar was just a faceless object in his line of vision; a pawn in his campaign to save his son. Now Judah sees her as a human being: one whom he has responsibility towards, one whom his own actions have harmed. While we are not told whether he finally gives Tamar his youngest son, we are told that "he did not sleep with her again" (v.26), properly respecting her bodily integrity, her reputation, and their relationship.

Judah sees Tamar's moral value – more so, her moral superiority. *Nakar* can also mean discern or acknowledge with honor. The third act ends with a stunning proclamation from Judah: "Tamar is more righteous[21] than I, because I didn't let her become the wife of my son" (v. 26). In this statement, Judah sees beyond the surface and perceives her true worth. Once seen as a "shameful whore", Tamar (whose name means date palm, a tree with a straight trunk) is now recognized as the upright, righteous person that her name connotes.[22]

Judah sees the impact of Tamar's righteousness on his own life and beyond. In the first two acts of the story, the unrighteousness acts of Judah and others brings Tamar down. As a woman caught in adultery, Tamar's actions would have brought shame to her family. But in a great reversal reminiscent of Jesus' Upside-Down Kingdom, Judah's knowledge (*nakar*) of Tamar's righteousness is the beginning of Judah's own reputation being restored. David Lamb explains:

> "[Tamar's] actions appear to be the catalyst for a massive transformation in the life of Judah, the ancestor of David and Jesus. All of his deeds so far in the text are evil – until clever Tamar sends back his signet ring, cord, and staff, prompting him to declare that she is more righteous than he. Apparently, his interaction with pious

---

[20] There are remarkable parallels in the story of Tamar and the story of Joseph (Judah's half-brother who is also Jacob's son). Here are a few of the most relevant. (1) Judah trafficks and exploits his family. His actions send Joseph into slavery (37:27); his inaction leads to Tamar's prostitution. (2) Fathers refuse to risk their remaining (youngest) son. Having lost his two older sons, Judah refuses to send Shelah to Tamar to save her from shame and harm; having lost Benjamin's only brother Joseph, Jacob refuses to send Benjamin to Egypt to help save the family from famine (42:4) and initially refuses to send him to secure release of his half-brother Simeon (42:38). (3) The exploited recognize and hide from their exploiters. Joseph pretends to be a stranger to Judah and the other brothers (42:7-8); Tamar's veil conceals her identity from Judah. (4) Those betrayed demand a surety from their betrayers. Joseph keeps Simeon to ensure that Benjamin is brought to him (42:19); Tamar demands Judah's identity documents to ensure payment. (5) Sureties reveal Judah's heart. The surety he gave Tamar exposes his selfishness in protecting his youngest son by failing to provide for her; later, Judah twice displays his selflessness in protecting his youngest half-brother by offering himself in place of Benjamin (43:9, 44:33). (6) Those who have been treated the most unjustly are the most righteous. Joseph provides abundantly for his brothers despite their betrayal (45:4-11); Tamar is declared righteous by Judah in the end.

[21] Interestingly, this is the same phrase that Saul says to David in 1 Samuel 24.

[22] BEMA Discipleship Podcast, Episode 15: Into the Pit.

> Tamar somehow transforms him. [Later in Genesis], Judah offers to become a slave in place of his youngest brother, Benjamin (Gen. 44:18-34). The person most responsible for Joseph's enslavement is thus also the person most responsible for Joseph's fraternal reconciliation. After his encounter with Tamar the pious prostitute, Judah morphs from being a prostitute-frequenting, slave-trading brother into a self-sacrificing, volunteer-to-be-enslaved brother. [...] And curiously, when it comes time for a father's final blessing, Jacob declares that not the oldest, Reuben, and not the favorite, Joseph, but the transformed slave-trader, Judah, is the one deemed worthy to receive a promise of an eternal royal dynasty (Gen. 49:10), a declaration which points forward first to David (2 Samuel 7), but then ultimately to Jesus, specifically to his royal genealogy, where Tamar appears first among females."[23]

Finally, a key tension in this story must be acknowledged and wrestled with: "Some may think Tamar's one-time gig as a prostitute would disqualify her from the ranks of the pious, and yet Scripture refers to Tamar exclusively in favorable terms. [...] Judah was unrighteous because he was selfishly attempting to fulfill his sexual desires. Tamar, however, was righteous because she was cleverly trying to honor her deceased husband Er, to continue his lineage, and to provide for herself so she wouldn't need to resort to prostitution as a lifestyle. She was a pious prostitute." (Lamb, 2015: 98). Despite being widowed and abandoned and dressing as a prostitute and sleeping with Judah and being pregnant and unwed, Tamar is acknowledged to be the most righteous person in the entire story. This messy outcome may present an abstract curiosity for most readers, but it highlights the crucial theological, conceptual and practical questions that Christians engaging with real-life people working in prostitution must wrestle with, and which The Triangle and this volume seek to inform.

* * *

What do we see when we see Tamar in the Bible? Do we only see The Prostitute? Or do we dare to see a "Righteous One" acting in the midst of an unjust existence to restore her family line and reorder the life of its patriarch?

What do we see when we see the Tamars in our lives? Do we only see their sinful actions and let that forever define them in the stories that we tell, whether that of "innocent victim" or "deserving whore"? Or do we dare to see them as God sees them, with the beauty of redemption displayed in the messy narratives of their lives (and ours)?

And if we so dare to learn to see as The-God-Who-Sees sees, how do we begin? This chapter – while certainly not providing all of the answers – seeks to help us understand how to approach these and other important questions.

Believing Is Seeing

Why did Judah and his society fail to see Tamar as a person with agency, value and worth? Why do we fail to see the full value and worth of people in

---

[23] (Lamb, 2015: 100).

prostitution today, even when we are trying to work on their behalf? In a very real way, what we believe is what we see. Our preconceptions about people and problems influence how we comprehend them and shape our responses.[24] "Prostitution is bad. Everyone in it wants to be freed." "Trafficked people are helpless victims. They need us to save them." "Perpetrators are evil. Driven only by greed, they will never change."

It is not that these beliefs are false, at least not completely. But what happens when what we believe isn't what we actually see? When what we see is not the full reality of what is going on?

Theology tells us how we are supposed to think about God and God in our world. Folk theology tells us how we really feel. If we are Christians working against sexual exploitation, there are many ways in which these feelings and beliefs come into conflict with reality.

We believe that all people are created in the image of God, but we see some people as worthy of our help ("true victims") and others as objects of our scorn ("juvenile delinquents" or "whores"). So, when those we serve return to prostitution again and again, we decide to focus on those who "really want our help" instead of walking with people over a journey of years.

We believe black and white edicts about sexuality, but we fail to see how complex nuances play out in a broken world. So, we portray our ministries in hyperbolic terms that amplify a war against evil and gloss over the moral messiness implicit in helping restore shattered Shalom.

We believe that there are sinners and saints, but we see others as the sinners and ourselves as the saints. So, when it comes to addressing root causes, we call out the overtly bad acts of traffickers and pimps, and rationalize our party's policies that increase vulnerability and ignore our desires that contribute to demand.[25]

These are not merely abstract hypotheticals. These are actual conversations that I've had with multiple ministry leaders, actual images on countless ministry websites, actual attitudes that I embody in my own choices as a citizen and consumer. I also saw these beliefs reflected in the cover of a popular Christian magazine. In 2007, *Christianity Today* had a cover story entitled "The Business of Saving Girls from a Life of Prostitution." It featured the work of Christians pioneering the use of real business to address the under-met need for sustainable economic alternatives for people leaving prostitution. A social business that I co-founded was one of the businesses profiled. A photographer came to our program and took pictures of our trainees learning a new profession. After the photoshoot, he looked through the hundreds of frames and proclaimed: "This is the cover

---

[24] "Descriptors, metaphors, and conceptual models can have a profound effect on both how we understand something and how we act" (Kandiah, 2019: 66).

[25] And even if we don't commit overt acts of injustice, our failure to speak out against unjust systems is also a form of injustice: "To live in a society where the built-in systems leave people poor, weak and looked down on and not to do anything about it is to engage in injustice, especially when we have the means – no matter how little – to speak out against the structures which create inequalities in our societies" (George and Toyama-Szeto, 2015: 43).

shot." It was a picture of young women radiant with the joy of being equipped with skills to help them build a future that was more hopeful than their past.

When the issue came out, the cover photo chosen by the publisher portrayed the complete opposite. The magazine saw what Judah saw: a Prostitute, a Whore. Instead of a thriving survivor from one of the organizations featured in the article, the cover showed a random young woman dressed in sexy black clothes; the implication that she was a prostitute, without any certainty that she actually was. She was not identifiable, which was good for her privacy, but she was also not portrayed as an actual person with dignity and worth: her body was blurry, the top of her head cut off by the masthead banner, she was merely another faceless object forever frozen in her sin and shame.

The cover also prominently featured the face of an innocent little girl. Nothing explicitly identified her as sexually exploited, but her proximity to The Prostitute and the words "RED-LIGHT RESCUE" in red above her head screamed that she was at risk of harm. Maybe six years old, her sad eyes stared at you with innocence and desperation; "Save me," they seemed to plead. Unlike the faceless woman, this was a face we all wanted to help. The cover suggested that this was a problem which could be easily solved without having to wrestle with the complexities of economics and agency; that there were root causes that had nothing to do with my stance on labor migration or women's empowerment or the products I buy. The problem was that this cover had absolutely nothing to do with the article that was inside.

We see what we want to see. And what we see reflects what we believe. Hope and dignity may be what we pray for, but those images do not sell as many magazines or generate as many web-based donations as the pictures that demonize the problem and simplify the solution. How might that cover image have been different if we were truly willing to see how The-God-Who-Sees sees? How might we be different? How might those we seek to serve?

What happens when we fail to see as God sees?

What happens when we fail to see the humanity and dignity and image of God in the people around us, in women, in any person working in prostitution?

What happens when we focus on the obvious evidence of their individual sin and ignore the "acceptable" things in society and our own lives that unintentionally increase their vulnerability or fuel demand for exploitation?

What are the subtle – and not so subtle – ways that our language defines and limits who they are and who they are allowed to be: objects of pity sitting helpless in their circumstances or actors in their own story with agency and capacity to arise?

What do we show others when we are given permission to share their stories? Do we present one-dimensional labels that reinforce stigma and shame, or do we portray full human beings, situated in complexity, with inherent dignity and worth?

What can we do better to see people as God sees them – as a reflection of God's own image – and how can we better communicate what that truly means to our ourselves, to our friends, to our supporters, and to society?

What we believe affects how we see. How we see the problem affects what we do to address it. And at the heart of both is the language that we use. In the second half of this chapter, Bryon examines how language matters and explores the implications that the way we *see* and *believe* and *speak* have for our *practice*.[26]

Words Matter

The questions raised by Christa thus far in this chapter underscore the need for us to understand how we as humans create and assign meaning to the world around us. How we create meaning and the individual and social effects of that process are a core component of ensuring that our communication (with ourselves and with others) is dignified and enhances the dignity and value of every person we encounter or communicate about.

There are a variety of theories regarding how we as humans engage in meaning-making. One of the most useful in understanding the role of language social interaction in meaning-making is the Social Construction of Reality Theory by Peter Berger and Thomas Luckman (1967). They theorize that our understanding of reality is socially constructed through our use of language and our social interactions with the people around us.

One of the core concepts of social construction theory and human communication is that we use mental shortcuts to process information faster. We develop labels and categories for different actions, physical objects, and even people. These shortcuts summarize our knowledge and influence our emotions and physical reactions to things we encounter. When looking for a screwdriver at the store, understanding it is a tool helps us know where to look. Suppose we had an accident while working with a screwdriver that bruised our knuckles in the past. In that case, we will likely associate the pain from hitting our knuckles with the word screwdriver and the sight of a screwdriver, even if it is a different screwdriver.

These mental shortcuts, or "typifications", according to Berger and Luckman (1967), are used constantly in our social interactions. These shortcuts can be helpful, for example when we meet an old friend, we associate a series of labels with that person. They can be a CEO, a lawyer, a tennis player, a golfer, and a musician all at the same time. In the context of that specific person, those typifications are personified by the qualities of that person. Their CEO title feels less powerful, aloof, and unreachable when they are a close friend. Their status as a lawyer brings an understanding of the hard work that they did to become a lawyer and the value of their skill in helping people receive justice in court.

However, the personalization and personification of these typifications that result from relationships decrease significantly the more social distance we perceive to be between the person we are labeling and us. If we do not know any CEOs, then the title or label of CEO is associated with general assumptions of

[26] Editor's Note: For additional consideration of these issues, see the chapter by Miles and Reimer elsewhere in this volume, as well as Parts II and III in Crawford and Miles, *Finding Our Way through the Traffick* (Regnum, 2017).

what CEOs are like absorbed by us from social interactions, movies, television, and other inputs. If we have just read an article about corporate greed and corruption, we're more likely to attach additional negative labels and emotions to a person we don't know who happens to be a CEO. Likewise, if a friend of ours recently had a court decide in favor of their opponent, we are more likely to associate negative stereotypes with a lawyer whom we do not know.

On the surface, these mental shortcuts or typifications seem harmless enough, merely a natural process which helps us quickly understand the world around us. However, our use of these shortcuts and stereotypes does not stop at understanding. We regularly convert these typifications into "objectifications" (Berger and Luckman, 1967). This conversion typically happens through the use of language. Labels and titles become loaded with meanings and experiences from our subconscious that are then projected through our tone and the context we use around these words. Objectifying a lawyer or CEO based on their role removes their personal traits and individual humanity, reducing their role to a social object. As these objectifications of roles are transferred from person to person and from generation to generation, they become more and more institutionalized and more entrenched. This process institutionalized the slur of "ambulance chasers" with the legal profession or the association of greed and excessive salaries and bonuses with the title of CEO over the last few decades.

So how does this relate to how we see people and human trafficking?

The typifications and objectifications that we utilize daily all start with language. They start with our inner dialogue, the thoughts in our heads. If we fail to recognize and control when and how we use these shortcuts and the embedded language that comes with them, we reduce our ability to truly see the people we meet and interact with.

There has been a much-needed shift in the anti-trafficking movement from the word "victim" to the word "survivor" when talking about people who have experienced exploitation, trafficking, or slavery. However, "survivor" is still a typification and objectification of a person based on their experiences. To be more specific, it is a typification and objectification of a person based on what is possibly the worst experience of their lives. (I say possibly because I believe it is presumptive to make assumptions about another person's life and what parts of it are good, bad, or worst.)

The label "survivor" has deep connections to many serious social problems and traumatic personal experiences. It instantly paints a picture of what a person could have endured.

According to Berger and Luckman (1967), there are more stages to the social construction process. The more typifications and objectifications are used in our inner dialogue and our conversations and social interactions the more they become legitimized by the volume of use and their adoption by the people around us. Over time, these shortcuts or stereotypes or projected identities become institutionalized; this means that their use and meaning becomes part of the social framework. Once this occurs, their definitions and the perceived roles of these identities are rarely disputed.

If we look back over the last twenty years of the anti-trafficking movement, we can see how this process has played out and can recognize the "understood realities" that have been institutionalized into the social framework of the anti-trafficking movement, specifically, "trafficking = sex trafficking" and "prostitution = sex trafficking", consequently resulting in the association of prostitution and sex trafficking with human trafficking survivors. The construction and acceptance of those equivalencies and the conversion of human trafficking survivors into a typified and objectified identity that instantly brings to mind sexual violence has been distributed and further institutionalized into the global cultural understanding of what human trafficking is and what a trafficked person looks like. Photos of women working in various situations in bars and other entertainment venues that cannot be proven to be trafficking situations are commonly associated with human trafficking on the websites of many anti-trafficking organizations.

Research has identified two distinct identities projected onto survivors. These are the personas most commonly used to describe potential trafficking victims and trafficking survivors. When reduced to their most basic elements, they are the innocent, virginal female child (any female under the age of legal consent or who can be perceived as under the age of legal consent) and the prostitute or "whore" persona.[27] The innocent, virginal female is portrayed as a sacred object to be protected from harm, the ideal portrait of virtue who is susceptible to the violent perversions of evil men.

The prostitute or "whore" is often portrayed as the person we don't want the young, innocent, virginal girl or woman to become. Gail Pheterson explains that the word prostitute in noun form is an identity, most often associated with females who "offer heterosexual sex [...] for money."[28] Pheterson further notes that, when used as a verb, prostitute refers to a person's activity that is used to drive "noncommendable", socially inappropriate outcomes. What is not noted in these definitions is that we, as a society, have legitimized and institutionalized the understanding that the noun form of the word carries the negative connotations of the verb form. Prostitute, as a noun or identity, carries with it the knowledge that the person is "noncommendable" and participates in inappropriate activities. My point here is not related to the legality or morality of prostitution. Instead, it is calling attention to the fact that combining the two meanings, noun and verb, creates a label or identity that is highly stigmatized. Pheterson also notes that women who "claim self-determination as prostitutes lose victim status and ideological sympathy",[29] resulting in further stigmatization.

Pheterson also found that men, when caught participating in the purchase of sex, were seldom "judged unworthy" in ways that affected their identities. On the other hand, women were "ostracized for *being* a whore". Women are

---

[27] (Baker, 2013; Brysk, 2009; Kamler, 2011).
[28] (Pheterson, 1993).
[29] (Pheterson, 1993).

stigmatized as "bad women" who are "spoiled". Women are bad because of who they are. Men are bad because of what they do.[30]

In a recently concluded ten-year longitudinal study of human trafficking survivors in Cambodia, Morrision *et al.* (2015) found that stigmatization of women with a history of prostitution or sex trafficking was pervasive. Rachel Mauro (2015) describes this stigmatized understanding of the differences between women and men as originating in part from a traditional Cambodian saying or proverb: "Men are gold, women are cloth." This saying implies that if a man does bad things, it cannot affect his identity or value. Gold can always be cleaned and polished and retain its value; a woman's value can easily be damaged as cloth is easily stained, ripped, and ultimately irreparable. The honor and dignity of her identity can easily be erased by her actions or by things that happen to her.[31]

I introduce this proverb to further illustrate that identity matters, that projecting identities associated with prostitution and sex trafficking onto women or associating these elements of negative identity with any human being has consequences.

These institutionalized identities of "prostitute" or "survivor" are subject to what Berger and Luckman (1967) describe as legitimization. While a person can attempt to define their own identity and enforce it within society, ultimately, their identity is subjective, at the mercy of the people in their community.

Berger and Luckman state it this way:

> By the very nature of socialization, subjective identity is a precarious entity. It is dependent upon the individual's relations with significant others, who may change or disappear. The "sane" apprehension of oneself as possessor of a definite, stable, and socially recognized identity is continually threatened, even if it remains relatively consistent in everyday interaction.[32]

Society decides what identities are legitimate and acceptable and enforces those rules. As beliefs, customs, and culture are institutionalized and legitimized, enforcement of social and cultural norms becomes necessary to maintain the social order.

Returning to our exploration of the prostitute or survivor identity, the actions that lead to this identity and even actions that are misidentified with this identity are easily recognized and quickly stigmatized to maintain social order and behavior standards. Link and Phelan (2001) conducted extensive research on stigma based on Erving Goffman's (1963) book on stigma. Goffman described stigma as an "attribute that is deeply discrediting and reduces the bearer from a whole and usual person to a tainted and discounted one." Fine and Asch (1988) describe stigma as "something in the person rather than a designation or tag that

---

30 (Pheterson, 1993).

31 I think it is important to note that Morrison found that these beliefs are being challenged more and more by younger generations and that the influence of these beliefs is weakening. It is also crucial for us to not demonize an entire country based on a single problematic idea; furthermore, this value is not unique to a single country and is more widespread that we would like to admit.

32 (Berger and Luckman, 1967).

others affix to the person."[33] Lester and O'Reilly (2021) found that stigma is "socially constructed" through social interaction and discourse.

Link and Phelan (2001) determined that the result of stigmatization was "loss of status, disapproval, rejection, exclusion, and discrimination. This discrimination is not just social. It is often all-encompassing, affecting every aspect of a person's life".[34] In short, the typifications that we use to make sense of our world can quickly become a person's identity; if that identity is counter to cultural norms, that person can be stigmatized, discriminated against, and actively oppressed based solely on how they are perceived within their community.

Speaking and Seeing and Doing

This brief introduction to the construction of meaning and identity through language and social interaction provides us with a basic understanding of one challenge faced by the anti-trafficking movement. As humanitarians, we long to see people freed from exploitation, trafficking, and slavery. We desperately want the world around us to care about the problem as much as we do. The problem is that the language we are using to cry for help and demand that people care affects the way we see and value the people we are desperate to help.

Solomon described this very dynamic in Proverbs 23:7: "As a man thinketh in his heart, so is he." As Christians, we love to project this on people who do "evil". It feels comfortable and normal to think about a trafficker in this light. We assume that their evil thoughts and perversions drive them to act out these evil thoughts and cause the immense harm we are trying to prevent. But I think this could just as easily be read "as a man perceives other people in his heart, so he will treat them."

We are looking for prostitutes, sex slaves, and victims that we can transform into survivors. Unfortunately, if that is what we are looking for, that is what we are going to find, and we will struggle to see them as anything else. We might help them move from prostitute or sex slave to survivor, but survivor still carries the baggage of the identity we assigned to them when we first went looking.

I think it might be helpful to visualize this in a different way. Take a break for a second, grab your phone or go to your computer and type the word "trafficking" in the search bar and get the image results that Google (or your chosen search engine) associates with trafficking. In my search, 12 of the 16 images depict violence against women or the purchase of sex from women who are physically restrained or locked behind bars. Unfortunately, these types of images are what the average person thinks of when they hear the word trafficking. As you look at the pictures from your search, chances are most of the images will depict women deprived of agency, women restrained, locked behind gates and bars, ropes, chains, and in isolation. While these visualizations may be accurate in extreme circumstances, the reality of trafficking is much more complex and nuanced. A

---

33 (Fine and Asch, 1988 as cited by Link and Phelan, 2001).

34 (Morrision et al., 2015; Dahal et al., 2015; Counts, 2014; Richardson and Laurie, 2019; Lazzarino, 2014).

woman who works in a bar in Bangkok is not necessarily a prostitute. A woman (or man) who is a prostitute in Phnom Penh is not always there against their will. A prostitute is not necessarily a sex slave. The common association of these images with trafficking also associates these images with survivors. When knowing a person is a survivor automatically associates them with sexual violence, it changes how we perceive them. Whether we are willing to admit it or not, how we perceive people affects how we treat them.

In our desperation to raise awareness of the problem, this is the identity we have projected onto survivors: imprisoned, battered prostitutes, and sex slaves[35] with no agency or ability to act in their own self-interest. This identity that we have built for survivors in an attempt to advocate for change is deeply harmful to our understanding of who each of these individual people are, male or female. We all know the anti-trafficking vocabulary, we have all seen the photos and the films, and many of us have helped create and mainstream the vocabulary, taken the photos, and produced the films. At the beginning of this chapter, we discussed how Judah only saw a prostitute, and that changed how he saw Tamar, what he expected from her, and how much (or how little) value he believed she had.

As an anti-trafficking movement, we have to reimagine and reform the language and the imagery we use to talk about human trafficking in general and how we talk about people who have been trafficked and exploited specifically. The language we use and the media we create significantly affect how our global society perceives people who experience exploitation, trafficking, and slavery. We need to embrace the reality that there are many aspects to every person's identity. A person can have experienced exploitation or trafficking and not choose to identify as a survivor. A person can choose to identify as a survivor and that can still be a small, even insignificant, part of their identity. They can still be a mother, a daughter, a leader, a chef, a musician, a designer, or any other identity they want to claim. We have a responsibility to see those other identities first in our thoughts and to share them first in our communications.

Toward a Better Way of Seeing, Speaking, and Doing

The questions I want to address with the rest of this chapter are:

- How can we stop ourselves from making the same mistake Judah made?
- How can we stop seeing prostitutes, slaves, and survivors and start seeing humans?

---

[35] As I edited this document, the grammar assist function repeatedly suggested that I change the words "slave" and "slaves". I chose to use this word because it is often used in anti-trafficking campaigns and by anti-trafficking organizations, and I wanted to point out the problems that it causes. The grammar assistant reminded me that slave and slaves "may be considered dehumanizing toward people subjected to slavery." Sadly, the grammar assistant functions in our software are more aware of the harmful effects of language than some anti-trafficking organizations who continually use these words in their marketing and donor communications.

- How can we see mothers, daughters, sisters, fathers, sons, brothers, students, farmers, businesswomen, nurses, doctors, mechanics, athletes, musicians, and leaders?

The short answer is that it starts with the language of our thoughts and our communication. The longer answer is unpacked below.

I want to focus on two key principles that can help guide us toward more dignified communication about human trafficking in general and about people who have been exploited, trafficked, or enslaved.

1. We must always be conscious of the assumptions we are making about people when we perceive them to be exploited or trafficked.
2. We must be intentional about how we influence others to perceive people who are exploited, trafficked, or enslaved.

We must always be conscious of the assumptions we are making about people when we perceive them to be exploited or trafficked.

Most of us use a smart phone now and use one or more of the many social media apps that allow us to communicate with the people around us personally and professionally. Therefore, most of us have seen or even used the ever-changing sets of filters that can change how we look in a photo as we take the picture. Some filters make your skin look soft, some add rabbit ears or cat ears on your head, others add glasses or make you look like you just joined a biker gang. When you use those filters to take a photo, they become part of the photo. They do not change who you are, but they can change how people who do not know you perceive you. They can cause other people to make assumptions about who you are and your identity.

The typifications we discussed earlier in this chapter function very much like these camera filters, except they are filters we project on others based on the few externally obvious things we know about them. If we are going to be conscious of how we see people, we need a way to turn these typifications or filters off, to intentionally choose to see people the way they want to be seen and understood.

Below is a series of questions that I feel can help us recognize and remove the filters that affect how we see and value the people around us.

- Do I know this person?
- Do I really know this person?
- What are the keywords that I am associating with this person?
- What assumptions am I making about this person based on their appearance, their job, or their actions?
- If I had to quickly describe this person or group of people with one word, what would it be?
- What would I say if I had to describe this person in one sentence?
- Does that word or sentence provide a complex understanding of who they are, or is it a generalization?
- Is the identity I am projecting on them honoring of their strength, agency, and ability to make decisions for themselves?
- Would the person I am describing be comfortable with that word or sentence becoming their entire identity?

- Would I be comfortable having the idea I am projecting on them as my only identity for the next year, five years, or possibly the rest of my life?
- Is this identity that I have projected onto this person harmful or stigmatizing? Would it adversely affect their social and economic well-being if it were made public?

We must be intentional about how we influence others to perceive people who are exploited, trafficked, or enslaved.

The questions above help us reflect on the way we see and perceive the people around us and are essential to improving our perceptions of people. Now, let us turn our attention to how we communicate about human trafficking and people who have experienced exploitation, trafficking, or slavery.[36]

We have talked a lot about identity and not projecting identities onto people. Looking at the last sentence of the paragraph above, you will notice that I have intentionally avoided using the words, prostitute, survivor, or victim. Instead, I wrote "people who have experienced exploitation, trafficking, or slavery." This phrasing frames exploitation as something that has happened to them and clearly differentiates it from who they are or their identity. Having said that, we still need to be careful about how we use words like exploited, trafficked, and enslaved. For many people worldwide, the mere perception that they may have experienced exploitation is stigmatizing and often leads to social and economic exclusion, discrimination, and oppression, as we discussed earlier.

I would like to close with another series of questions that I believe can help us filter the words we use and the media we create to advocate for the anti-trafficking cause. We definitely need to influence society, but the core of that influence must be a dignified understanding of the issue and a dignified representation of people who experience exploitation, trafficking, or slavery.

Essential questions to ask about our portrayal of the problem:

- Does what I am communicating reflect the complexity of the problem, or does it create an overly simple understanding that may be harmful to how people and the problem are perceived?
- Does my message reflect the opinions, understandings, and beliefs of the people I am trying to help? Does it acknowledge their worldview as valid and valuable and recognize their agency and right to self-determination?
- Am I using trigger words for an effect to increase outrage and sympathy in an attempt to drive donations?
- Am I using photos and videos that trigger a desired response in my audience? Would my clients want to be associated with those images as part of their identity?
- Would I want those images associated with an immediate family member's identity (not in the sense of modeling as an act of advocacy, but in the sense that those images are descriptive of their life and identity)?

---

[36] Additional resources in this task include "The Ethical Storytelling" website, available at: https://www.ethicalstorytelling.com and Parts II and III in the second volume in this series: Crawford and Miles, *Finding Our Way through the Traffick* (Regnum, 2017).

- Would the people I am serving use those words to describe themselves and their experiences?
- How am I visually portraying the problem and the people involved? Am I using images that allude to gender-based violence, sexual violence, or imprisonment?
- Does the media I am creating and sharing encourage others to see the people who have experienced exploitation as lacking agency, powerless to improve their situation or succeed without my help?
- Does my message, both in words and images, place me, my organization, or my audience in a place of power, and cast the people I serve as powerless?

In conclusion, we need to take the time to explore and investigate how we are thinking and our perceptions related to human trafficking and people who have experienced exploitation, trafficking, and slavery. We need to slow down and make an intentional decision about how we choose to see people and how we will influence others to think about these critical topics. We must expand our understanding of communication beyond a tool for fundraising and driving donations and recognize that we have a responsibility to ensure that people who have experienced exploitation and trafficking are seen for what they are: whole, complex human beings whose identity, value, and worth cannot be adequately summarized by words like prostitute, sex worker, survivor, or victim. Our communication must first and foremost affirm and convey the infinite value of each person with dignity and respect for the complexity of their lived experience.

And in so doing, may we help ourselves and others begin to see a little bit more of what "the God-Who-Sees" sees.

Reflection Questions

1. This chapter asked a lot of questions. Go back through and reread them. Which ones make you uncomfortable? Take some time to sit in that discomfort and ask yourself what God might be saying to you through that discomfort.
2. What do people who have been sexually exploited think about the themes in this chapter? Without putting extra work or emotional burden on them, seek out their voices, perhaps in already-published sources or with someone that you are in a trusted-relationship with. How do they think God sees them? How do they think you see them? What realities do they wish you could see about their lives? How would they like their stories to be portrayed? Be sure to compensate their input as you would that of other experts.
3. What challenges to your theology does the story of Tamar raise? What challenges to your understanding of sexual exploitation? What challenges to your practice? What will you do next in each of these areas as you wrestle with learning how better to see what The-God-Who-Sees sees?

4. In what ways does Seeing and Believing affect your Practice? What beliefs and ways of seeing do you need to change to better reflect complex realities?
5. What do you want others to see? What images do you communicate in your words and publications? How do they promote the image of God in the people you seek to serve? How do they impact their identity? In what ways can your images be improved to communicate more accuracy and dignity?
6. Chose a few practical recommendations from the end of the chapter to implement in your own work. How might you encourage your co-workers or colleagues from another organization to join you in this journey?
7. Seek out additional resources to help you learn more about this topic. The Ethical Storytelling website is a great place to start and is available at: https://www.ethicalstorytelling.com. In addition, the second volume in this series addresses the use of language and the concept of "story-pimping" (unintentionally re-exploiting the people we are seeking to help) – see Parts II and III in Crawford and Miles, *Finding Our Way through the Traffick* (Regnum, 2017).

Works Cited

Baker, C. "Moving Beyond 'Slaves, Sinners, and Saviors': An Intersectional Feminist Analysis of US Sex-Trafficking Discourses, Law and Policy". *Journal of Feminist Scholarship* 4(4), (2013): 1-24.

BEMA Discipleship Podcast. Episode 15: Into the Pit. [Available at: https://www.bemadiscipleship.com/15].

Berger, P. L., and T. Luckmann. *The Social Construction of Reality: a treatise in the sociology of knowledge.* New York: Doubleday, 1967.

Brysk, A. "Beyond Framing and Shaming". *Journal of Human Security* 5(3), (2009): 8-21.

Counts, P. A. "Self-concept and recovery: the effects of stigma on survivors of sex trafficking". *Theses and Dissertations* 516. Pepperdine University, 2014. [Available online at: https://digitalcommons.pepperdine.edu/etd/516\].

Crawford, C. and G. Miles. *Finding Our Way Through the Traffick.* Oxford, UK: Regnum, 2017.

Dahal, P., S. K., Joshi and K. Swahnberg. "We are looked down upon and rejected socially: a qualitative study on the experiences of trafficking survivors in Nepal". *Global Health Action* 8, (2015).

Fine, M. and A. Asch. "Disability beyond Stigma: social interaction, discrimination, and activism". *J. Soc. Issues* 44, (1988): 3-22.

George, A. and N.A. Toyama-Szeto. *God of Justice*. Downers Grove, IL: InterVarsity, 2015.

Goffman, E. *Stigma: Notes on the Management of Spoiled Identity*. Englewood Cliffs, NJ: Prentice Hall, 1963.

Jewell, D.H. "Red-Light Rescue: The Business of Saving Girls from a Life of Prostitution". *Christianity Today* 51(1), (January 2007): 29.

Kamler, E. "NGO Narratives in the Global Public Sphere". *The International Journal of Diversity in Organisations, Communities, and Nations* 11(2), (2011): 75-86.

Kandiah, K. "Church is a Family Not an Event". *Christianity Today* 63(1), (January/February 2019): 66.

Lamb, D.T. *Prostitutes and Polygamists: A Look at Love, Old Testament Style.* Grand Rapids, MI: Zondervan, 2015.

Lazzarino, R. "Between Shame and Lack of Responsibility: The Articulation of Emotions among Female Returnees of Human Trafficking in Northern Vietnam". *Antropologia* 1(1 N.S.), (2014): 155-167. [Available at: https://doi-org.libproxy.calbaptist.edu/10.14672/ada2014260%p].

Lester, J.N. and M. O'Reilly. "The Social Construction of Stigma: Utilizing Discursive Psychology for Advancing the Conceptualization of Stigma in Mental Health". *Stigma and Health, Advance Online Publication* 6(1), (2021): 53-61.

Levine, A.J. and M.Z. Brettler. *The Bible With and Without Jesus: How Jews and Christians Read the Same Stories Differently*. San Francisco, CA: HarperOne, 2020.

Link, B.G. and J.C. Phelan. "Conceptualizing Stigma". *Annual Review of Sociology* 27(1), (2001): 363.

Mauro, R. "Men are gold, women are cloth". The Cambodia Project. (2015). [Available at: https://womensvoicesofcambodia.wordpress.com/2015/04/11/men-are-gold-women-are-cloth/].

Morrison, T., S. Miles, L. Vanntheary, S. Phaly and B. Davin. *Stigma: Survivor Experiences and Perceptions.* Chab Dai Coalition. Phnom Penh, Cambodia, 2015.

Pheterson, G. "The Whore Stigma: Female Dishonour and Male Unworthiness". *Social Text* 37 (Winter 1994): 39-64.

Richardson, D. and N. Laurie. 2Returning to sexual stigma: post-trafficking lives". *British Journal of Sociology* 70(5), (2019): 1926-1945. [Available at: https://doi-org.libproxy.calbaptist.edu/10.1111/1468-4446.12707].

Making a Way When There Is No Way: Voices of Women in Prostitution in Ethiopia – A Theology of Lament

Jennifer Singh

Hareg's Story

> I must have been about thirteen. I got so tired of my mum's beating, so one day, I just ran away. I thought I had only gone so far and it got dark, and I started to cry. Then this guy came and kind of comforted me and he took me to his house and he raped me. He was going to visit his friend's house where they were having a wake, so after he raped me, he took me to that place and left me there for about seven to eight days. And every time he wanted to have sex, he would come and get me. One day, a lady from my mum's neighborhood was coming to visit the family and she saw me there, and she went back and told to my mum. The next night, my mum came with some guys, grabbed me, beat me. I didn't want to go home but I had no choice. I did not want to go home because of [my] mum beating [me] up. The difference here [in Ethiopia] is you cannot say "I do not want to." Here, someone decides for you. After being brought back, the beating got worse, so I ran away again. I started working again on the street, but working on the street is really hard because if you are not picked up by someone then you do not have any place to spend the night. Even when I would be picked up by a man, I would not negotiate, I would just go give the service and if he gives me money, fine. If he didn't, that was the beginning because I didn't know I could ask money for it. I just thought it was something you do.[1]

How does anyone begin to make sense of an experience like this, especially the one telling the story, my friend Hareg? Thirteen years old, running away from an abusive mother only to find yourself being offered refuge and comfort by someone who would, later, repeatedly rape you. Instead of the story becoming better, it only gets worse. Hareg entered the world of homelessness on the streets of Addis Ababa, the capital of Ethiopia: a perilous place for vulnerable young women.[2]

---

[1] *Unashamed: A Journey to Hope*, directed by Darren Kaualback (Toronto, Canada: Listen Up TV Productions, 2011), DVD. I assisted in the production of this documentary.

[2] A 1990 study conducted by the World Health Organization (WHO) estimated that 7% of all sexually active women in Addis Ababa were involved in prostitution. World Health Organization, "Preventing HIV among sex workers in Sub-Saharan Africa: A literature review" (Geneva: World Health Organization Press, 2011): 5.

Context of Prostitution in Ethiopia

A 2011 World Health Organization report determined that, in Africa, the average age of people involved in prostitution was between 25 and 30 years old, except in the urban areas of Ethiopia and Kenya where lower age estimates were found.[3] This is in line with previous research conducted in 2002 that found nearly 60% of "sex workers" identified in Ethiopia and Kenya were between 15 and 25 years old. Most respondents in that study stated that they had started commercial sex for economic reasons, thereby linking poverty and commercial sex.[4]

In addition, research conducted in the year 2000 with prostituted children in Addis Ababa revealed that children fled their homes for the streets of the capital city in order to escape early forced marriage, the inability to attend school, and abuse in the home.[5] My friend Hareg was one of these children, struggling to survive. Thankfully, Hareg's story does not end in a red-light district of Addis Ababa; but rather, continues to be lived in the compassionate embrace of a loving God.

Love Incarnated: Ellilta Women at Risk

How, then, did Hareg end-up in the arms of a loving God after years of surviving in street prostitution? She describes her awakening to the existence of God through her first encounters with Ellilta Women at Risk,[6] a faith-based organization (FBO) that has been journeying with women exiting a life of prostitution since 1996.

> Before I came to [Ellilta] Women at Risk, I never heard anything about God. Everything that I was hearing about God [when at Women at Risk] was a surprise to me because I didn't even know about God. I didn't even know I was created by God. [crying] There were so many times that I should have died. There were times when people wanted to kill me. There were times that people took a gun out on me. There were times when people tried to run over me [with a car]. But God protected me from all that, and that really amazed me, touched me. To rescue a person is very important because even Jesus gave the example of the shepherd leaving the ninety-nine and going and to find the one that was lost.[7]

Before Ellilta, Hareg had not understood that God could be personal or relational. Her first personal experience of God was as her protector, the one who defended and preserved her life. Hareg found her own story in that of the lost

---

[3] WHO, "Preventing HIV", 14.

[4] Family Health International-Ethiopia and Addis Ababa City Administration Health Bureau, "Mapping and Census of Female Sex Workers in Addis Ababa, Ethiopia", (Addis Ababa: Family Health International-Ethiopia, 2002): xi.

[5] Rahmet Abdella, James Hoot, and Selamawit Tadesse, "Seldom Heard Voices: Child Prostitutes in Ethiopia", *International Journal of Early Childhood* 38(2), (2000): 82.

[6] Since its inception, this local FBO has offered psycho-social, economic, educational, spiritual, and child-care support to over one thousand women who have expressed a desire to leave prostitution. See 'What We Do,' Ellilta International.org. www.ellilta.org/what-we-do/ (17th April 2018).

[7] *Unashamed: A Journey to Hope*, directed by Darren Kaualback (Toronto, Canada: Listen Up TV Productions, 2011), DVD.

sheep who was separated from the flock and rescued by Shepherd Jesus. Her views of God as a protector and Jesus as a shepherd are insightful and theological: they speak to the nature and character of God. Hareg was able to make sense of some of the most painful experiences of her life through grafting her story into the grand metanarrative that began when the Word was brooding over His creation, seeking to bring order to the chaos. The reason that Hareg was able to do this is because the Word incarnated itself through Ellilta and moved into her neighborhood.[8] Ellilta staff befriended Hareg while she was working in a bar and, through weekly visits, were able to gain her trust which eventually led to Hareg entering Ellilta's rehabilitation programme. Upon completing the programme, Hareg went on to raise an adopted daughter, to serve as a prevention officer at Ellilta, and to eventually become a teaching pastor in a local evangelical church.

Ellilta was established by an Ethiopian woman, Serawit Teketel Friedmeyer, who after an encounter with a woman engaged in prostitution began to visit one of the red-light districts in Addis Ababa on a weekly basis. Serawit never intended to start an FBO; however, after a few months of visiting and befriending women on the streets, listening to their stories and hearing their desire to find another way – anything other than prostitution – to earn an income for their families, she felt compelled to do something. Serawit discerned a sense of call by God to respond to the plight of these women and, after gathering a few like-minded people around her, Serawit started a small community which would eventually lead to an FBO that has assisted over one-thousand women and their children out of a life of prostitution since 1996.

Ellilta is not just a rehabilitation programme offering psychosocial support and vocational training to women seeking to exit prostitution; it is a compassionate community that initiates contact with women engaged in prostitution and develops a relationship with them, on the street, without conditions. Ellilta's staff exhibit the ability to love these women as sisters and to welcome them into a family created among the staff and the women they are helping. When a woman decides to join the programme, members of Ellilta's staff stand alongside her in one of the greatest transitions of her life. They listen to the entirety of her story, cry alongside her, share meals with her, care for her children, and provide her with the opportunity to feel like she is a part of a family again.

Ellilta humanizes these women through meaningful relationships. The staff does not engage in this process through reading a training manual or a theological textbook, but by being immersed in the lives of the women and their children, and bearing witness to the stories of indescribable grief, exploitation, pain, and suffering. The staff of Ellilta are able to relate to the women not because of their own educational backgrounds or skill-level, but because most of them know what it is to have been on the margins of society and to have experienced the Kingdom of God – the nearness and presence of Christ – in those places. The Ellilta staff know and live the story of God's in-breaking Kingdom in front of

---

[8] John 1:14. *The Message*.

these women. As a result of this, Ellilta staff are able to incarnate the love of Jesus Christ in unique, effective, and powerful ways that enable the women they are serving to make sense of their stories within the larger Biblical narrative, just like Hareg was able to do.

Why Theologize about Prostitution?

In 2014, I moved to Addis Ababa in order to conduct research on the situation of prostitution. Specifically, I wanted to investigate how women affected by prostitution, like my friend Hareg, were able to make sense of their lives within a theological context. My reasons for wanting to examine prostitution from a theological perspective was fueled by two facts. First, Ethiopia is a country in which religion, especially the Orthodox faith, plays a significant role in people's lives:

> Religion permeates morals, work, relationships […] whether they are Muslims, Orthodox Christians or others, [Ethiopians] share a deep conviction that there is a God who is creator of the heaven and earth.[9]

In a country where over 50% of the population identify themselves as Orthodox Christians,[10] and the Christian God is included in the process of how people attribute meaning to their lives, a theological investigation of how people understand God and His relationship to human exploitation seemed appropriate, especially working with those women who have been abused sexually.

Second, despite the fact that "commercial sex has been an important and attractive topic for sociological research in Ethiopia,"[11] Ethiopian scholar Bethlehem Tekola notes that often very little differentiation is made between the institution of prostitution and the practitioners of prostitution internally:

> While the voluminous literature on both of them [prostitution and women in prostitution] is the result of different perspectives and different judgements, the literature that seeks to understand them from within is amazingly thin.[12]

In order to address the gap in the field of sociological research on prostitution within the context of Ethiopia, Tekola says that:

> Any effort to enrich our understanding of the lives and concerns of the women behind commercial sex work in Ethiopia […] [should] shift the focus of research

---

[9] Vasianen in Alemayehu Mekonnen, *Culture Change in Ethiopia: An Evangelical Perspective* (Oxford: Regnum, 2013): 27.

[10] Gerald West and Musa Dube, *The Bible in Africa: Transactions, Trajectories and Trends* (Leiden: Brill, 2000): 253.

[11] Bethlehem Tekola cites the following studies on commercial sex work in Ethiopia since the 1960s: Mayor, 1962, 1963; Andargatchew, 1967; Lema, 1968; Laketch 1978, 1991; Banchiyeleku, 1984; Ayehunie, 1987; Mehret, 1990; Habtamu, 1991; Baardson, 1993; Kebede, 1993; Tamene, 1993; Atakilt, 1994; Gedu, 1995; Alemayehu, 1996; Aklilu 1998; Hussein, 1998; Seble 1998; Mulumebet, 2000; Bethlehem, 2000, 2002. See Tekola, *op cit.*, 39.

[12] Bethlehem Tekola, *Poverty and the Social Context of Sex Work in Addis Ababa: An Anthropological Study* (Addis Ababa: Forum for Social Studies, 2005): 35.

even more towards the women themselves to bring to the foreground their *emic* descriptions of life behind commercial sex.[13]

The voices of women affected by prostitution have not been privileged in the existing sociological research on prostitution in Ethiopia. I learned through the course of my own research that to ask a woman affected by prostitution to interpret her experiences of prostitution strictly within a sociological framework is unusual in the highly religious context of Ethiopia. Therefore, my research project sought to address this gap through listening to the voices of women who were affected by prostitution[14] as they interacted with Christian Scripture and entered into a process of theologizing about their lives. My purpose was to transcend the current categories of meaning-making available to women affected by prostitution and to hear, from their perspective, if or how they perceived God at work in their lives.

How to Theologize about Prostitution: Contextual Bible Study Method

In order to access the voices of the women, I chose Contextual Bible Study as the primary method for data collection. Contextual Bible Study allows for storytelling, which is a common mode of communication in many African cultures, and thereby allows for the stories of the text and the participants to intersect.[15] Research among vulnerable populations must seek out silenced voices;[16] Contextual Bible Study is specifically geared toward unearthing such voices. It is a method that has been utilized significantly by African contextual and African Womanist theologians, with particular reference to the HIV/AIDS pandemic. This approach has enabled the voices of those who are infected with, and affected by, HIV/AIDS on the African continent to contribute to a deeper interpretation of Christian Scripture in light of the situations of oppression they face.[17] Contextual Bible Study starts with the question: "How do the life experiences of the reader serve as a key for reinterpreting the Bible?"[18] This process requires sensitivity, as those who have been silenced in multiple ways

---

[13] Tekola, *Poverty and the Social Context of Sex Work*, 42.

[14] I chose to use the descriptor "affected by prostitution" because the research participants in the project were women who were engaged in prostitution at the time of the research and women who were in a rehabilitation program seeking to exit prostitution.

[15] Musa Dube's book *HIV & AIDS Bible: Selected Essays* (Scranton: University of Scranton Press, 2008) which outlines various ways of mainstreaming HIV/AIDS into theological education, includes teaching students how to lead Bible studies with those affected by HIV/AIDS in a manner that assists people to appropriate their situation to relevant Biblical texts. See especially her Chapter 3: 72.

[16] Julie Cwikel and Elizabeth Hoban, "Contentious Issues in Research on Trafficked Women Working in the Sex Industry: Study Design, Ethics, and Methodology", *The Journal of Sex Research* 42(4), (2005): 306-316; 309, [Available at: http://www.jstor.org/stable/3813783], [Last accessed: 10th October 2022].

[17] Dube, *HIV & AIDS Bible,* 72.

[18] Dube, *HIV & AIDS Bible,* 72.

have not previously been invited to explore and tell their life stories authentically. African Womanist theologian Musa Dube asserts that this hermeneutical point of view in the struggle against HIV/AIDS points toward reading and re-reading the Bible with a focus on saving life.[19]

This approach also reflects the commitment of South African theologian Gerald O. West to facilitate meaningful interactions with the Bible among marginalized people. West claims that "for a dialogue to take place between text and context, a real flesh and blood African reader is required."[20] In the process of appropriation, readers of Christian Scripture are empowered to bring their life experiences to bear on a particular biblical text.[21]

The Story of Hagar: Making a Way When There Was No Way

During the course of my research, I conducted twenty-six Contextual Bible Studies with various groups of women affected by prostitution, and explored nineteen Biblical stories. One of the first studies I conducted was on the story of Hagar found in the Book of Genesis in chapters sixteen and twenty-one. I selected the Hagar story for the following reasons: 1) previous readings of this text with single and widowed women in Africa had produced lively discussions and I anticipated the same might happen with these women; 2) Hagar was a housemaid to Abram and Sarai; therefore, I thought she might be a character that the women could possibly identify with, as a common story in Addis Ababa is that of a rural young woman travelling to Addis Ababa in search of a better life, being hired as a housemaid and, after experiencing abuse and/or exploitation at the hands of her employer, entering prostitution;[22] and 3) the use of Hagar among Womanist theologians in African American culture has produced a variety of ways to appropriate this text to women suffering from exploitation and abuse.[23]

The story of Hagar proved to be highly significant to my research because the greatest amount of data from the twenty-six Contextual Bible Studies was generated from this Biblical story. The Hagar story also had the unintended consequence of serving as a catalyst by which the women were able to share their stories of how they became involved in prostitution. I did not anticipate this outcome; however, the data demonstrated that this story helped the women to recount the various circumstances and situations they faced during their prelude into prostitution.

---

[19] Dube, *HIV & AIDS Bible,* 72.

[20] Gerald O. West, "Biblical Hermeneutics in Africa", in Diane B. Stinton (ed), *African Theology on the Way: Current Conversations* (London: SPCK, 2010): 1.

[21] West, "Biblical Hermeneutics".

[22] *Unashamed: The Journey to Hope* [DVD], Director D. Kaulback, Toronto, Canada, Listen Up TV Productions, 2011.

[23] According to Dolores S. Williams, African Americans have appropriated the Biblical figure Hagar to their lives for over two-hundred years. See "Hagar in African American Appropriation", in Phyllis Trible and Letty M. Russell (eds), *Jewish, Christian, and Muslim Perspectives* (Louisville: Westminster John Knox Press, 2006): 172.

Prelude to Prostitution:
Experiences of Leaving/Running, Confusion, and Loneliness

> When I left my aunt's place, there was no one that I knew and I didn't even know Amharic very well. I was very lonely, although there were so many people around, and I was hungry and I couldn't ask anyone for food. I slept out, and it is very difficult when you face something you haven't faced before in your life. I stood there [on the street] and I was confused. I considered myself being in one of the caves in my home place [rather] than in Addis. I felt very lonely even though there were people around me.[24]

This story was shared by one of the women participating in the Hagar Bible study in response to the question, "Have you ever felt in your life that you are in a desert? Not physically, but have you ever felt that there is nothing around you?"[25] When I originally drafted this question in my discussion guide for this study, I did not anticipate that some of the women would draw a parallel between a desert experience and the circumstances that preceded their entrance into prostitution in Addis Ababa; however, this is the time period that they chose to reflect upon when answering this question.

The young woman who shared the story above (who will now be called Saba) had been under the care of her aunt, and while she did not share the exact reasons as to why she left her aunt's home, her leaving resulted in her coming to an unfamiliar place: the streets of Addis Ababa. Although Saba was not objectively alone or isolated, she recounted her feelings of loneliness while in the midst of people around her: these were people to whom she could not communicate some of her most basic needs (food and shelter). This experience of loneliness while surrounded by people was significant for Saba, as she used the phrase "people around her" twice when recounting her story. With nowhere to go, Saba slept "out" (on the street) and she recalled the difficulties of confronting a situation she had never encountered before: "*It is very difficult when you face something in your life that you haven't faced before in your life.*"[26]

Saba's sense of bewilderment at her circumstances is captured in her use of the word "confused" when reflecting on her experience of standing on the street. Saba related her first days on the streets to a desert-like experience and admitted that she preferred living in a cave in the part of Ethiopia that she came from to standing on the streets of Addis Ababa engaged in prostitution. Saba's use of the word "confusion" is an appropriate descriptor when examining the factors that she had to cope with in her new surroundings: hunger, sleeping outside, and her inability to communicate with those around her. The mention of caves is notable as caves are predominantly located in the rural areas of Ethiopia. A cave in Saba's hometown seemed more hospitable in that moment than sleeping on the streets of Addis Ababa where she could not even communicate her need for food.

A sense of community characterizes life in Africa and this moves people, particularly women, to care for strangers, those who are sick and in need,

---

[24] Transcript of Hagar Session EWAR Women, 5/2/2016: 6, Addis Ababa, Ethiopia.

[25] Transcript of Hagar Session EWAR Women, 5/2/2016: 6.

[26] Transcript of Hagar Session EWAR Women, 5/2/2016: 6.

widows, the disabled, and others deemed vulnerable.[27] For this reason, it is understandable that Saba experienced an acute sense of loneliness and isolation after leaving her aunt's home. Despite being surrounded by many people, no one present on the street corner where she stood demonstrated the kind of care for Saba that would have communicated a sense of community to her. She had no relational ties to the people passing by her or any sense of place or belonging in this unfamiliar context. African cultures, by and large, tend to emphasize that "a human being is born into a human community, and that is what makes him or her human."[28] Saba was alone, and to be alone in the Ethiopian context can be interpreted as being a non-person.[29] Yet, loneliness is a universal human experience, one felt all the more keenly by anyone on the edge of society.

This equation of isolation with non-personhood is reflected in African Womanist Christian anthropology inasmuch as it takes African culture seriously and recognizes life as life-in-community.[30] Within the Ethiopian context, life-in-community is appropriated through the significant emphasis placed on greetings. Whether encountering a life-long friend, or a brand-new acquaintance on the street, greetings will usually last for several minutes, and these serve to convey the message, "I see you; therefore, you are human."[31] Failure to greet a person appropriately can be a source of great offense in Ethiopian culture.

When Saba recounted her experience of standing on the streets surrounded by people, she did not mention anyone approaching her and greeting her. This is an important omission because had someone greeted her, she would have experienced a sense of acknowledgement rather than of invisibility. Her repetition of the phrase "people around" underscores how confusing this experience was for her.[32] In Africa, it is rare for people to define themselves without reference to their immediate or extended family;[33] therefore, it is understandable that Saba experienced deep loneliness and confusion after leaving her aunt's home and finding herself on the streets of Addis Ababa.

Another woman that participated in a Hagar Bible study session (let us call her Fikir) shared the following story in response to the question, "Has any one of you been chased out of the house? Thrown out?":[34]

---

[27] Mercy Amba Oduyoye, *Introducing African Women's Theology: Introductions in Feminist Theology*, Mary Grey, Lisa Isherwood, Catherine Norris, Janet Wootton (eds) (Cleveland, OH: Pilgrim, 2001): 34.

[28] Oduyoye, *Introducing African Women's Theology*, 26.

[29] Participant observations from living in Ethiopia and conversing with my Ethiopian colleagues, 2014-2016.

[30] David Kirwa Tarus, "Theology of Social Transformation in the Theological Works of the Circle of Concerned African Women Theologians", *African Journal of Evangelical Theology* 33(1), (2014): 7.

[31] Participant observations from living in Ethiopia and conversing with my Ethiopian colleagues, 2014-2016.

[32] Transcript of Hagar Session EWAR Women, 5/2/2016, Addis Ababa, 6.

[33] Agbonkhianmeghe E. Orobator, "A Church in Dialogue as the Family of God", *e-Publications@Marquette* 1(1), (1995): 35.

[34] Transcript of Hagar Session Flamingo Women, 26/09/2015, Addis Ababa, 3.

> My uncle brought me to Addis [Ababa from Hawassa] promising that he will educate me, but he never sent me to school. He used to beat me daily then I run [to Hawassa] and began working in a house as a maid.[35]

The woman went on to share that after growing up in the town of Hawassa (southern Ethiopia) working as a housemaid, she met another uncle in that town and he sent her back to Addis Ababa to look for her brothers who were then working in Addis Ababa. When she found her brothers, they were not able to host her so she returned to the uncle in Hawassa. However, like the first uncle who brought her to Addis Ababa under the guise of educational opportunities, this second uncle also refused to send her to school. Fikir went on to say:

> Then I met a girl who was in the same kind of problem as I was, and we agreed to run away and be on the streets. We heard that there was a place around Kolfe [area of Addis Ababa] where women do business [prostitution]. So we went. When we got to the place, we asked the women and they told us there is a job. When we asked what we were supposed to do, they told us to stand at the door and "do short or overnight". I had no idea what they were talking about but my friend did. She had been in the business before. At first, I decided not to do such a business but the woman [pimp] encouraged me and taught me how to do it, so I became one of them. I used to give every coin I made to that woman [pimp] because I was young and did not really know money.[36]

After several journeys characterized by running between Hawassa and Addis Ababa, Fikir found herself unable to secure a permanent dwelling with family members or a means for attending school. Fikir recounted running to Addis Ababa with another young woman facing a similar predicament. The two girls decided to go to a red-light area in Addis Ababa; however, based on how she told her story, it seemed that Fikir lacked clarity regarding the type of "business" that was being practiced in this part of town: "*we asked what we are supposed to do*."

A common theme that emerged throughout several of the Bible study sessions I conducted was the women admitting that, before becoming involved in prostitution, although they had heard about prostitution and that it was a way to earn an income, they were unaware of what prostitution actually entailed: exchanging sexual acts for payment. This explains why Fikir described having to ask the pimp what she was supposed to do: "*stand at the door and do short or overnight.*"[37] Fikir spoke of her confusion regarding what was being asked of her, "*I had no idea what they were talking about*"[38] and once she received clarification, she was resistant to take up her new "job". However, due to the necessity of meeting her basic needs as a homeless young woman on the streets of Addis Ababa, Fikir reluctantly became "*one of them*".[39] Fikir's confusion about what prostitution entailed is highlighted in her reference to giving all the proceeds she earned to the pimp, "*I used to give every coin I earn to that woman*

---

[35] Transcript of Hagar Session Flamingo Women, 26/09/2015, Addis Ababa, 3-4.
[36] Transcript of Hagar Session Flamingo Women, 26/09/2015, Addis Ababa, 4.
[37] Transcript of Hagar Session Flamingo Women, 26/09/2015, Addis Ababa, 4.
[38] Transcript of Hagar Session Flamingo Women, 26/09/2015, Addis Ababa, 4.
[39] Transcript of Hagar Session Flamingo Women, 26/09/2015, Addis Ababa, 4.

[pimp] *for I was young and did not really know money.*"[40] Fikir's story suggests that a significant degree of confusion marked her entry into prostitution.

Discussion of Leaving/Running, Confusion, and Loneliness

Leaving/running, confusion, and loneliness are themes that Saba and Fikir highlighted as they related their stories of entry into prostitution to Hagar's foray into the desert. Saba and Fikir described the streets of Addis Ababa (where they began prostitution) as a place where they experienced hunger, homelessness, linguistic challenges, and confusion as to what *shekela* (which is the Amharic translation for doing business) actually meant. Similar to Hagar, both women left familiar places for an unknown destination: neither Saba nor Fikir had premeditated plans to engage in street prostitution, just as Hagar had not planned to find herself near a spring in the desert (Genesis 16:7) or the Desert of Beersheba (Genesis 21:14).

Womanist Theologian Dolores Williams argues that leaving and running in the Hagar story are emblematic of risk tasking: "She [Hagar] takes the risk rather than endure more brutal treatment by Sarai [...] she has run off into the wilderness as a lone woman without family support or protection."[41] Hagar finds herself running and alone just like Saba and Fikir. Phyllis Trible commends Hagar for "taking command of her own life under the threat of Sarai." One is left to ponder if running "for safety" means "taking command" of the situation. Both Williams and Trible interpret Hagar's running as an action of survival, an attempt to preserve her life. While Saba was not forthcoming about why she left her aunt's home, it is clear that both Saba and Fikir were seeking survival on the streets of Addis Ababa after leaving their families.

Williams notes how African American women resonate with the themes of survival-struggle, poverty, and oppression that are highlighted in Hagar's story and that "God helped them make a way out of no way."[42] Williams notes that "God is not only involved in the women's survival struggle, but also that God supports their struggle for life, which making a way suggests."[43] Williams' interpretation can be applied to Saba and Fikir's stories as "trying to make a way"' when they found themselves on the streets of Addis Ababa, trying to figure out how to engage in prostitution. Both women sought to secure the basic means of life when they found themselves outside their families, the traditional African unit tasked with sustaining life.[44] This sort of thinking and analysis invites more theological questions. Women in this sort of situation are desperate, and go to any length to survive, to hang on in hope of something turning up, or

---

[40] Transcript of Hagar Session Flamingo Women, 26/09/2015, Addis Ababa, 4.

[41] Dolores S. Williams, "Hagar's Story: A Route to Black Women's Issues", in *Sisters in the Wilderness: The Challenge of Womanist God-Talk*, (Maryknoll, NY: Orbis Books, 1993): 19-20.

[42] Dolores S. Williams, "Hagar in African American Biblical Appropriation", in Phyllis Trible and Letter Russell (eds), *Hagar, Sarah, and Their Children: Jewish, Christian, and Muslim Perspectives* (Louisville, KY: Westminster John Know Press, 2006): 177.

[43] Williams, "Hagar in African American Biblical Appropriation", 177.

[44] Orobator, "A Church in Dialogue", 24.

not. Does describing their action as "seeking to secure the basic means of life" represent the will and mercy of God?

When theologizing about the contentious issue of HIV/AIDS, African theologians have stressed the sanctity of life and that as a result of God being the Creator of life, life is good and should be made good when it is threatened by evil.[45] Therefore, actions taken to protect life such as undergoing Anti-Retroviral Treatments (ARTs) by those infected by HIV/AIDS are encouraged. Saba and Fikir's turn to prostitution as a means of survival is not be analogized to taking ARTs; rather, the point being made is that precisely because life is considered sacred, in the case of these two young women, actions such as prostitution can be viewed as an attempt to preserve their lives when they faced life-threatening circumstances such as hunger, homelessness, and a lack of family. Hagar's foray into the desert was precipitated by Sarai's harsh treatment;[46] she was fleeing the person who threatened her life. Hagar fled twice to a desert, a place known for its inhospitable climate and limited means for preserving life; in the end, Hagar resigns herself to death. Saba and Fikir equated desert experiences in their lives with finding themselves on the streets of Addis Ababa, places where they encountered loneliness and confusion about what was entailed in prostitution, the means of survival available to them in that moment.

Conclusion

The story of Hagar provided an access point for Saba and Fikir to explore their stories of how they entered into a life of prostitution, without being intrusively asked by an outsider to disclose the painful details of their prelude to prostitution. Theologically speaking, Saba and Fikir related their stories to a desert experience, one of being alone and confused. The extensive theological work that has been done by both African American and African Womanist theologians on the Biblical story of Hagar gives space for Saba and Fikir's survival stories to be read as a story of *making a way when there was no way.*[47] This is a helpful interpretation when trying to transcend the current theological categories of meaning-making within the Ethiopian context, where unfortunately, prostitution is predominantly interpreted as a sin and therefore the fault of the woman.[48] This theological categorization of prostitution as sin only serves to produce stymied and ineffective (or non-existent) responses to these women who are just trying to make a way when there is no way. When prostitution is described by those

---

[45] Lovemore Togarasei, "Christian theology of life, death and healing in an era of antiretroviral therapy: reflections on the responses of some Botswana churches", *African Journal of AIDS Research* 9(4), (2010): 433 .

[46] The Hebrew word (*'nh*) used for "afflict" in Genesis 16:7, has a strong connotation and is the same word used to characterise the suffering of the entire Hebrew population in Egypt, the land of bondage. See Trible and Russell, *Hagar, Sarah, and Their Children,* 13.

[47] Dolores S. Williams, "Hagar in African American Biblical Appropriation", 177.

[48] Refer to the chapter by Andrew J. Schmutzer who argues that prostitution can be seen as sin, but not be blamed on the woman alone or primarily.

living through this experience as making a way when there is no way, it spurs the potentiality for others, particularly those who consider themselves followers of Christ *to find a way when there is no way*. Ellilta's interpretation of prostitution in this manner has resulted in hundreds of Ethiopian women and their children being companioned on their journey out of the desert for over twenty-three years.

My friend Hareg was able to revisit the horrific circumstances leading to her entry into prostitution by identifying Ellilta as the Shepherd in her narrative who came and found her, the Word who incarnated itself and moved into her neighborhood. Hareg found her story in the Kingdom story that was shared with her and incarnated in her midst through the community of Ellilta. This empowered her to walk out of a life of prostitution and to forge a different way, a redemptive way, that included raising an orphaned child and walking alongside other women seeking to make a way when there was no way. Theologizing about prostitution may not solve this scourge directly; however, it is one way of allowing women affected by prostitution and those involved in trying to help to these women make sense of their dehumanizing experiences, locate God's redemptive presence in the darkness, and pursue the process of making a way when there is no way.

Reflection Questions

1. In your context, do those who are sexually exploited often end up on the streets at risk of prostitution because of violence in the home which made them run away? How do you think they could relate to the story of Hagar and how could you use that story to support them?
2. Could those in your context relate to the idea of a desert experience and/or "making a way when there is no (other) way"? How could you encourage them emotionally and spiritually to think differently in the future?
3. How can your ministry/church provide a kind and supportive community for people who are desperately lonely and isolated from their community, which is exacerbated due to their sexual exploitation.
4. We are told that "the story of Hagar provided an access point for Saba and Fikir to explore their stories of how they entered into a life of prostitution, without being intrusively asked by an outsider to disclose the painful details of their prelude to prostitution." How might the Contextual Bible Study method be useful in your context? See the Ujamaa Centre for Community Development & Research website for details.[49]

[49] The Ujamaa Centre for Community Development & Research, *Doing Contextual Bible Study: A Resource Manual* (2015) [Available online at:

5. The chapter raises an uncomfortable theological question: "Women in this sort of situation are desperate, and go to any length to survive, to hang on in hope of something turning up, or not. Does describing their action as 'seeking to secure the basic means of life' represent the will and mercy of God?" Read the story of Hagar in light of this question. What answers come to mind (however tentative or uncertain)? What questions remain? Now read the story of Tamar in Genesis 38 with the same question in mind. How does this inform or change your answer? See the chapter by Crawford and Lipponcott elsewhere in this volume for a further exploration of these themes.
6. The chapter concludes with the observation that "this theological categorization of prostitution as sin [and therefore the fault of the woman] only serves to produce stymied and ineffective (or non-existent) responses to these women who are just trying to make a way when there is no way." How does our theology affect our understanding of sexual exploitation and influence our practice? How might exposure to the work of theologians from marginalized communities or the non-dominant culture change the way that we do "The Triangle" (i.e. see sexual exploitation in Biblical texts, think theologically about sexual exploitation, and practice the gospel in the midst of sexual exploitation)?
7. The chapter also states that "When prostitution is described by those living through this experience as making a way when there is no way, it spurs the potentiality for others, particularly those who consider themselves followers of Christ to find a way when there is no way." How might personal experience and deeper understanding of sexual exploitation affect our theology and our practice? What theological contributions can sexually exploited people in your context make based on their experience? How can you encourage them to share their thinking and amplify their voices?
8. Finally, what does it mean practically to "find a way where there is no way"? What are the risks to our theology, our understanding of sexual exploitation, and our practice of wrestling with this question? What can be gained? How can honest engagement with The Triangle help us to find new ways in all of these areas?

---

http://ujamaa.ukzn.ac.za/RESOURCES_OF_UJAMAA/MANUAL_STUDIES.aspx], [Last accessed: 10th October 2022].

Works Cited

Primary Sources: Contextual Bible Study Transcripts

Transcript of Hagar Session EWAR Women, 5th February 2016, Addis Ababa, Ethiopia.

Transcript of Hagar Session Flamingo Women, 26th September 2015, Addis Ababa, Ethiopia.

Secondary Sources

Abdella, Rahmet, James Hoot and Selamawi Tadesse. "Seldom Heard Voices: Child Prostitutes in Ethiopia". *International Journal of Early Childhood* 38(2), (2000): 81-85.

Cwikel, Julie, and Elizabeth Hoban. "Contentious Issues in Research on Trafficked Women Working in the Sex Industry: Study Design, Ethics, and Methodology". *The Journal of Sex Research* 42(4), (2005): 306-316. [Available at: http://www.jstor.org/stable/3813783], [Last accessed: 10th October 2022].

Dube, Musa W. and Musimbi R.A. Kanyoro. *Grant Me Justice! HIV/AIDS and Gender Readers of the Bible*. Maryknoll, NY: Orbis Books, 2005.

Family Health International Ethiopia and Addis Ababa City Administration Health. *Mapping and Census of Female Sex Workers in Addis Ababa, Ethiopia.* Addis Ababa: Family Health International Ethiopia, 2002.

Mekonnen, Alemayehu. *Culture Change in Ethiopia: An Evangelical Perspective.* Oxford: Regnum Books International, 2013.

Oduyoye, Mercy Amba. *Introducing African Women's Theology: Introductions in Feminist Theology*. Mary Grey, Lisa Isherwood, Catherine Norris and Janet Wootton, Eds. Cleveland, OH: The Pilgrim Press, 2001.

Orobator, Agbonkhianmeghe E. "A Church in Dialogue as the Family of God". *e-Publications@Marquette* 1(1), (1995).

Tarus, David Kirwa. "Theology of Social Transformation in the Theological Works of the Circle of Concerned African Women Theologians". *African Journal of Evangelical Theology* 33(1), (2014).

Tekola, Bethlehem. *Poverty and the Social Context of Sex Work in Addis Ababa: An Anthropological Perspective*. Addis Ababa: Forum for Social Studies, 2005.

Togarasei, Lovemore. "Christian Theology of Life, Death and Healing in an Era of Antiretroviral therapy: Reflections on the Responses of Some Botswana Churches". *African Journal of AIDS Research* 9(4), (2010): 433.

Trible, Phyllis. *Texts of Terror: Literary-Feminist Readings of Biblical Narratives*. Philadelphia, PA: Fortress Press, 1984.

Unashamed: The Journey to Hope [DVD], Directed by D. Kaulback, Toronto, Listen Up TV Productions, 2011.

West, Gerald O. "Biblical hermeneutics in Africa". In Diane B. Stinton, Ed. *African Theology on the Way: Current Conversations.* London: SPCK, 2010. Accessed pre-publication version from Google Scholar 9th May 2016.

West, Gerald O. and Musa Dube, Eds. *The Bible in Africa: Transactions, Trajectories and Trends*. Leiden: Brill, 2000.

Williams, Dolores S. "Hagar in African American Appropriation". In Phyllis Trible and Letty M. Russell, Eds. *Jewish, Christian, and Muslim Perspectives*. Louisville, KY: Westminster John Knox Press, 2006.

Williams, Dolores S. "Hagar's Story: A Route to Black Women's Issues". In *Sisters in the Wilderness: The Challenge of Womanist God-Talk*. Maryknoll, NY: Orbis Books, 1993.

World Health Organization. *Preventing HIV Among Sex Workers in Sub-Saharan Africa: A Literature Review*. Geneva: World Health Organization Press, 2011.

STRIKING PATTERNS OF SIN IN NARRATIVES OF SEXUAL VIOLENCE

Andrew J Schmutzer

> "All memories are communal [...] individuals do not remember alone but as members of a group." Miroslav Volf[1]

We presently live in a time of Victim Olympics. Our global community seems infatuated with sexual trauma. While the literature may be more sophisticated, it is not necessarily holistic or interested in the faith dynamic.[2] This current climate causes numerous results. While some needed language has been normalized, the dialogue persists in isolating pathologies from personhood, "flattening" suffering for true victims. This trauma culture craves a political identity more than personal healing.[3] Clearly, in the absence of transcendent faith, all that remains is politics. What has been lost is the way that sexual victimization connects various social groups in increasingly toxic ways. Unfortunately, the addressing of sexual victimization is often more about building a platform of protest than committing oneself to a pilgrimage of healing.

Sexuality may be personal, but it is never private. Discussions of sexual violence have struggled for some time to build a holistic view of such violence. Either physicalism takes over, in which the human person is reduced to an actor in a material world, or social constructs can loom so large that personal agency is lost and individuals become merely a product of power plays they are helpless to resist.

This chapter explores some familiar biblical stories of sexual violence to illustrate how evil progressively shapes reality, colonizing itself through destructive social interactions that increasingly tear apart the relational ecosystem.

---

[1] Miroslav Volf, *The End of Memory: Remembering Rightly in a Violent World.* Grand Rapids, MI: Eerdmans, 2006: 99.

[2] A good illustration is the best seller by Bessel Van Der Kolk, *The Body Keeps the Score: Brain, Mind, and Body in the Healing of Trauma* (New York, NY: Penguin Books, 2015).

[3] There is a growing trend to ban many classic princess characters of fairy tales as passive victims of aggressive (white) men who assault them without getting consent before they kiss them. Weaponizing an ancient genre is not going to aid healing for anyone, and, we will also lose the role of the imagination in mythology. See, for example, Thomas Moore, "The Need for Myth, Ritual, and a Spiritual Life," in *Care of The Soul: A Guide for Cultivating Depth and Sacredness in Everyday Life* (New York, NY: Harper Perennial, 1992), 203-229.

Sin's Organic Continuum

The Bible does not separate the *act* of sin from the *effects* of sin that organically follow. In other words, there is a deed-consequence continuum that is operating, which is very evident in stories of sexual violence. These stories and the violence in them should not be read in isolation from their larger context. Accounts of sexual violence actually participate in shared social realms, maturing into ever-expanding consequences.

In the Old Testament, the Hebrew term *'awon* is insightful in such stories of sexual harm. The word focuses on the natural relationship between a deed and its consequence and, if left alone, the inevitable maturation of such an act into guilt, and ultimately into a totality of consequences (cf. Deuteronomy 19:15; Amos 3:2; Psalm 103:3).[4] Various meanings can be highlighted from *'awon*:

- "bend" → deed and consequence
- "being crooked" → fate, punishment
- "being twisted, perversion, being perverted" → resulting state, completion.[5]

The insight here is not what defines an improper act per se, but how sin creates a real circumstance that lingers in the world until it comes to fruition. Unfortunately, the nature of sin's impact on the person's environment – its almost independent afterlife – means that even forgiveness is often unable to stop the ongoing effects of sin.[6] Evil has a multidimensional nature to it which is not halted with forgiveness, nor is evil simply rendered inoperative.[7] Alistair McFadyen explains sin's distorting effects on the entire person, including faith:

> Sin is hence, not so much free choice, as spiritual disorientation of the whole person at the most fundamental level of life-intentionality and desire [...] In all our relations, we live out an active relation or misrelation to God, we enter the dynamic of worshipping God or other forces and realities. Sin is therefore living out an active misrelation to God.[8]

Sin Twists Perceptions and Decisions

Reality is twisted and perverted by sin. In other words, there is a trans-generational dynamic, one very evident in King David's power-rape of Bathsheba, and the ensuing moral failure within his own house (2 Samuel 11-13) – yet David was forgiven!

These ongoing effects reflect: (1) children impacted by their parents' sins, (2) creating conditions that negatively affect the options available to the children, (3) predisposing the children toward certain choices, (4) that then contribute destructively to their present identities. Children now perpetuate their parents'

---

[4] Knierim, "*'awon*, perversity," *Theological Lexicon of the Old Testament*, 2:864.

[5] Knierim, "*'awon*, perversity," 2:863-64.

[6] Biddle, *Missing the Mark*, 118.

[7] Biddle, *Missing the Mark*, 95.

[8] McFadyen, *Bound to Sin*, 221, 223.

behaviors.[9] This is the relational ecosystem in which sin, in general, and sexual violation, in particular, live on.

God watches over the moral calculus, from which sin grows in the relational ecosystem (Psalms 38:4; 40:12). So God tells Abraham that the Promised Land must wait until the sin of the Amorites bring forth needed expulsion as a consequence: "for the sin [*'awon*] of the Amorites is not yet mature" (Gen. 15:16). In this way, God holds generations accountable, not unfairly for their ancestors' sins, but for their solidarity with their ancestors' actions. So *'awon*-sin, while not inherited as legal guilt, is reflected in the disposition to extend parental attitudes, habits, beliefs, and relational patterns, "I will repay your sins [*'awonot*, King Jehoiakim] and your ancestors' sins [*'awonot*, his children] together" (Is. 65:6-7); "They have returned to the sins [*'awonot*] of their ancestors" (Jer. 11:10; cf. Mt. 23:36; Lk. 11:51).

God Intervenes to Protect His Creation

The Creator who formed the world is also the Warrior who preserves its order. Whenever God steps into the mess of sinful people, there is inevitable "destruction" that results in the process of restoring order to his creation.[10] When "all flesh" (Gen. 6:7) corrupts its way in the created order, God intervenes to judge and restore. Following the Flood, powerful forces are allied against Abraham who has been called by God as a counterforce against global deterioration, and as an agent of blessing in God's redemptive program.[11] This is the larger backdrop to one of the greatest examples of divine judgment – the story of Sodom (Gen. 19).

Abraham is God's agent for "all nations on earth" (Gen. 12:3), ensuring that "righteousness" (*tsedaka*) and "justice" (*mishpat*) prevail on the earth (Gen. 18:19). This is the lead-up to the Sodom story. In reality, the behavior of those who live in Sodom and Gomorrah actually bears on the well-being of God's entire created order.[12] As Creator, God works in "righteousness," for the "good" of his creation (Gen. 1:31). It is significant that the king who rules in Psalm 72 is held up before God so that his reign might be characterized by divine righteousness and justice (Psalm 72:1). This includes the king's obligation to defend the interest and cause of the poor: "May he judge your people with righteousness, and your poor with justice" (72:2). They pray that, "the mountains yield prosperity (*shalom*) for the people, and the hills righteousness" (72:3). *Shalom* works in concert with righteousness. In verse 7, the prayer expresses hope that righteousness would flourish and "peace" (*shalom*) to abound, including lush vegetation and crops (72:6, 16).

As we turn our attention to four key stories of sexual violence, it is the Sodom story that we will look at most closely. Notice how righteousness and justice are woven into the Sodom story, beginning in Genesis 18:16, when Abraham's visitors depart, they "looked down toward Sodom," shifting the direction of the

---

[9] Biddle, *Missing the Mark*, 120, 121; cf. Isa. 65:6-7; Jer. 11:10; 36:31.
[10] Creach, *Violence in Scripture*, 73.
[11] Blenkinsopp, "Abraham as Paradigm," 233.
[12] Creach, *Violence in Scripture*, 75.

story. God takes Abraham into his confidence, divulging his plans to Abraham (18:19), since he is God's prime agent to teach his family and so that "all nations on earth will be blessed" (18:18). The hospitality, energy, and feast that Abraham prepares for his guests stands in counterpoint to the angels' reception in Sodom. These cities are in violation of the cosmic requirements for justice, righteousness, and the defense of the needy. We can now set the Sodom story in the train of other stories of sexual violence.

Cycles of Destruction Around Sexual Violence

In a recent study of Old Testament rape narratives, Frank M. Yamada uses a literary and rhetorical approach to analyze the narratives of Genesis 34 (Rape of Dinah), Judges 19 (Rape of Levite's Concubine), and 2 Samuel 13 (Rape of Tamar). These stories, Yamada claims, reveal "explicit thematic or functional connections between them" when read alongside each other.[13] He finds that these "stories betray similar elements, development, and outcome," namely: (1) rape, (2) that leads to excessive male violence, (3) and culminates in social fragmentation.[14] While this is helpful, I believe more can be observed.

A Type-Scene of Sexual Violence

Yamada's findings supply further biblical demonstration for the organic spread of sin within the relational ecosystem. In fact, I would argue that eight to ten elements are so consistent in biblical stories of sexual violence that they form a *type-scene*.[15] A type-scene is a kind of literary repetition that uses a programmatic sequence of speech and behavior in analogous situations (e.g., in English: "In a land, far, far away…").[16] Biblical type-scenes are not used for the mundane issues of life. Instead, type-scenes are employed for "crucial junctures in the development of the narrative."[17] Two common type-scenes are *betrothal scenes* (Gen. 24:10-61; 29:1-20; Ex. 2:15b-21)[18] and *annunciation stories* (Gen. 18:1-15; Judges 13; 1 Sam. 1; 2 Kings 4:8-37).[19]

Why would authors use the predictable elements of type-scenes? They used these literary scenes to draw on the expectations of the audience, through a

---

[13] Yamada, *Configurations of Rape*, 11.
[14] Yamada, *Configurations of Rape*, 6, 2.
[15] For definitions of type-scene, see Savran, *Telling and Retelling*, 7; though a classic treatment is Alter, *The Art of Biblical Narrative*, 47-62.
[16] Other standard kinds of repetition are key word (*Leitwort*), motif, theme, and sequence of actions (see Alter, *The Art of Biblical Narrative*, 95-113).
[17] Alter, *Art of Biblical Narrative*, 51.
[18] The betrothal type-scene uses the following sequence: man or servant journeys to a foreign land, encounters a young marriageable woman at a well, either draw water, the female party hurries home to declare the stranger's arrival, the betrothal is finalized in the context of a meal.
[19] Other kinds of type-scenes include: (1) the trial in the wilderness, (2) the revival of the dead child, (3) rivalry between the barren and fertile wife, (4) the hero's journey from his homeland to a foreign country, (5) and sibling rivalry.

"literary contract." The authors' didactic goals and literary convention merge, forming "matrices against which the past must be understood."[20] Possibly started in oral form, it is important to realize that both the narrator and the audience recognize this sequence of elements. The texts I've collated here could even be described as "type-plots" because of the *amount* of text involved, entire chapters, in some cases. Greater time coverage, however, actually occurs in Abraham's annunciation type-scene as he and Sarah struggle in their long wait for the promised son (cf. Gen. 15:1-6; 18:1-15).

Thus, stories of sexual violence can be read *collectively*, not just as isolated accounts that divulge horrific facts. For our purposes, I only wish to identify reoccurring themes shared by these narrative stories that construct a large type-scene. I've placed Yamada's three thematic observations in the table below along with nine additional themes I've observed.[21] I've also added Genesis 19 (Attempted Rape in Sodom) as a fourth text, but one which confirms the profile of these very themes, if not setting the pattern for other scenes that follow.

Sexual Violence in Type-Scene

Reoccurring Themes (by verse)	**Gen. 19 Attempted Rape in Sodom**	**Gen. 34 Rape of Dinah**	**Judg. 19-20 Rape of Levite's Concubine**	**2 Sam. 13 Rape of Tamar**
1) Traveling Guest(s) in a City	1-3	1	19:15	
2) Violation of Hospitality Code	4-5	2, 7	19:15	8-11
3) Hostile City Residents	4-11	2, 23	19:22	
4) Night Evoking Danger	2-4		19:15-16, 20	
5) Threatened Male Gang Rape	5		19:22	
6) Door as Symbol of Personal Space	6, 9-11		19:22, 25-26	17-18
7) Rape of Female		2	19:24-25	14
8) Male-Male Violence	9, 11	25-26	Chapter 20	28-29
9) Political Turmoil	13-28	13, 30	20:1	20, 30-36
10) Social Fragmentation	31-38	30	20:20	20, 22, 37-39
11) Absence of God		34:1-31	19:1-30	1-39
12) Narrator's Moral Assessment	16, 29	7	23, 30	13:12; cf. 12:9

This collation reveals an intensifying profile of themes that reverberate between these texts. Themes 1-6 reveal some antecedent moral, domestic, and cultural patterns that lead up to the female rape, excessive male violence, and social fragmentation – Yamada's core three (7, 8, 10). Collective shame and honor are very evident here. What begins with traveling strangers ends with people sexually violated, entire communities socially estranged or even physically destroyed.

Largely using the narrative of Genesis 19 – that Yamada does not address – I will briefly comment on a few of these themes: 1 (traveling guests), 2 (violation

[20] Merrill, "History," in *Cracking Old Testament Codes*, 104.

[21] This analysis of thematic elements draws from the following literature: Hendel, et al., "Gender and Sexuality," 71-91; Younger, *Judges/Ruth*, 30-40, 349-66; and Yamada, *Configurations of Rape*, 133-40.

of hospitality code), 6 (door symbolism), 11 (absence of God), and 12 (narrator's moral assessment).

A Closer Analysis of the Sodom Account

The Sodom account in Genesis 19 invokes several key themes. The manner in which travellers encounter the city gate, whether welcoming or ominous, sets a *judicial* tone for the entire narrative. Such stories use menacing meetings of various kinds (cf. Gen. 19:1-2; Judges 19:15). In addition, the *door* signals a deeper threshold. In the case of Lot, he is a keeper of both boundaries (i.e., city gate, house door), vital barriers for vulnerable people. The door can signal a *personal space*, a gateway to a far more private world, "at our door is every delicacy" (Song of Songs 7:13b; cf. 8:9). In these larger type-scenes noted above, space is more than social, it is "theatrical" space, where character is revealed and shapes the destiny of others. This is hardly mere architecture. Such portraits establish the legal versus illegal space or the private versus public continuum. Proverbs 5, for example, is a highly developed allegory of the public versus private reality intended sexual expression, "do not go near the door of her house [...] should your springs overflow in the streets?" (Proverbs 5:8b, 16a).

In this way, movement itself is thematized – infused with symbolic meaning – within a threefold analogy: (1) entering the city gate, (2) passing through the door of a house, (3) and followed by the threat of sexually penetrating the male or female body.[22] What the male citizens of Sodom demand is coercive sex with the vulnerable visitors. In the Old Testament, homosexual sex is a capital offense (Lev. 18:22; 20:13).[23] In the Sodom narrative, sexual violence threatens every group, from the "male" bodies of guests, to Lot's daughters, and finally Lot himself (19:5, 8, 9; cf. v. 36). Breaching so many boundaries is not only hostility, but it festers into greater waves of violence, fueling social disintegration, and finally, creating vandalism of community shalom.[24] Ronald Hendel sums up various elements of our discussion:

> The attempted violation of the house by the men of Sodom is the very image of rape [...] In all narratives of sexual violence in the Bible, doors and entryways are central concepts in establishing narrative space – marking a clear boundary between inside and outside – and the site of violation is always on the rapist's own territory.[25]

In a passage like Proverbs 5:15-23, it is not surprising that the domestic and moral spaces merge. Here, boundaries are constructively used of sexual exclusivity, highlighting the private versus public motif using a progression of liquid imagery: "cistern" (v. 15a), "well" (v. 15b), "springs" (v. 16a), and "fountain" (18a).

---

[22] Hendel et al., "Gender and Sexuality," 78.
[23] Waltke, *Genesis*, 276.
[24] Plantinga, *Not The Way It's Supposed to Be*, 30.
[25] Hendel et al., "Gender and Sexuality," 80, citing Shemesh, "Biblical Stories of Rape Narratives," 315-344.

In the larger stories, rape – an abhorrent misuse of power – is both crime and catalyst, enflaming further brutalities. Notice that the sexual violation never initiates or concludes these type-scenes. What happens to aliens and strangers is the antithesis of the command to "love them as yourself" (Lev. 19:34). So this theme catches the reader off guard when the residents of Sodom identify Lot as an "alien" playing the "judge" (Gen. 19:9). They then threaten to "treat you worse" than the two guests. In such narratives, sexual violence is the symmetrical opposite of hospitality.[26] Abraham was also such an "alien," but he knew how to broker peace and cooperation (Gen. 14:17-20). Those who treat Abraham poorly court disaster (Gen. 12:17). Hospitality was the most elemental form of human righteousness, especially for the stranger.[27]

The Lot narrative is not a simple example of violating the hospitality code, however. There is also the culpability of attempted male gang rape by "all the men" of the city (Gen. 19:4), which seems to offer the legal evidence of wickedness that the angels are there to find (Gen. 18:20-21). According to Jerome F.D. Creach, the "residents of Sodom saw the vulnerable guests as merely victims to abuse."[28] Observe that the narrator has already hinted at the city's destruction (Gen. 13:10), as well as their on-going wickedness (13:13).[29]

Further, God is aware of the "outcry" *against* Sodom, according to Mark Boda, "cries for help from those who have been abused" (18:20-21).[30] This is legal language in the status of "legal complaint, requesting deliverance," and Abraham knows when to intercede for others like a prophet (Gen. 20:7).[31] God states, "How great the outcry against Sodom and Gomorrah and how very grave their sin!" (18:20). For this reason, God resolves, "I *must* go down and see" (Gen. 18:21).[32] Significantly, this is *before* the angels arrive at the city. "Outcry" is used of the shrieks of oppressed people (Gen. 4:10; 27:34). God heard the same "outcry" when his people were oppressed in Egypt (Ex. 2:23; cf. 3:7, 9). The nation of Israel is charged: "You shall not wrong or oppress a resident alien, for you were aliens in the land of Egypt" (Ex. 22:21). Shortly after, God commands the nation: "you shall love the strangers" (Deut. 10:19). Elsewhere, love is only commanded for God.[33] Clearly, the welcome of the male population left much to be desired, but the men's express purpose "to know" (idiom for sexual

---

[26] I agree with Bill T. Arnold that arguments focusing primarily on the city's poor hospitality have more to do with contemporary sexual politics (*Genesis*, 184; contra Carr, "Genesis," 36).

[27] Mann, *The Book of the Torah*, 53.

[28] Creach, *Violence in Scripture*, 77.

[29] Sodom's wickedness becomes an *archetype* for various kinds of evil, both treatment of poor and sexual violation (see Isa. 3:9; Jer. 232:14; Lam. 4:6; Zeph. 2:8-9; 2 Pet. 2:6; Jude 7). God also challenges Israel to a new level of social ethics, precisely because his nation knows what it is like to be an "alien" (cf. Deut. 24:17-22).

[30] Boda, *A Severe Mercy*, 26, n.26. S. Lasine argues that Judges 19 employs the Genesis 19 text ("Guest and Host in Judges 19," 40).

[31] Bruckner, *Implied Law in the Abraham Narrative*, 91-92.

[32] This reflects God's self-determination to take an action, using a Hebrew cohortative of *resolve* "I must" (Arnold and Choi, *A Guide to Biblical Hebrew Syntax*, 65).

[33] Nelson, *Deuteronomy*, 137.

intercourse, 19:5, 8, 9; cf. 24:16) Lot's "guests," pushes the moral compass of this text beyond just a breach of hospitality laws to coercive sex in an attack on strangers who are due hospitality.[34] Lot also understood this premium placed on hospitality, but Sodom had skewed Lot's personal morals. The offer of his daughters, "who have not known a man" (18:8), shows just how twisted his thinking had become.

The thorough nature of God's judgment is not only evident in the later intertextual references to Sodom and Gomorrah (e.g., Jude 7), but by three additional points in the text of Genesis 19.[35] First, the very plant life was also destroyed; "what grew on the ground" (Gen. 19:25) was also listed among the victims. Creation suffers, too, because "the social, moral, and geo-physical spheres are intricately connected."[36] The environment also suffers the effects of judgment. Second, Lot's wife is directly associated with salt, which reflects an ancient practice of scattering salt to condemn a place to perpetual barrenness and desolation (e.g., Deut. 29:23; Judges 9:45). Third, the destruction of Sodom and Gomorrah employs many terms and phrases taken from the destruction of the Flood narrative (e.g., "from the LORD," "from the heavens," "to rain," "to keep alive seed," etc.). In both cases, an epidemic moral perversion only marks one family for survival and a male survivor becomes drunk, and is somehow sexually violated by his own offspring.

Observations on Other Type-Scenes of Sexual Violence

In addition to the Sodom account, key themes are also invoked in the accounts of the rape of Dinah, Tamar, and the Levite's concubine. If one is alone, one risks being robbed or worse (Lk. 10:25-37; 2 Cor. 11:26). Not surprisingly, hospitality is implicitly tied to sexual danger, and the other texts of sexual violence illustrate this.[37] Tamar's story demonstrates a form of this: "And Tamar took the bread she had prepared and brought it to her brother Amnon in his bedroom" (2 Sam. 13:10b). As a grotesque meal – analogous to the Baptist's head served on a banquet platter – "the host in Judges 19 offers the Gibeahites the concubine and his daughter" as substitutes for his male guest.[38] The rape of the concubine (Judges 19) is rhetorically placed in a context of religious, social, and moral decline, "In those days there was no king in Israel; every man did what was right in his own eyes" (Judges 17:6 [Chap 19] 21:25 RSV).[39] How true: the

---

[34] Longman III, *Genesis*, 238.

[35] Not including significant writers, like Philo, the biblical text variously refers to the Sodom story to indict: a lack of justice (Isa. 1:9-10; 3:9), idolatry (Deut. 32:15-43), arrogant disregard for the poor (Ez. 16:49-50), and sexual perversity (Jude 7); see Philo, *On Abraham* in *The Works of Philo*; translated by C.D. Yonge (Peabody, MA: Hendrickson, 1993): 411-444.

[36] Creach, *Violence in Scripture*, 78.

[37] Hendel et al., "Gender and Sexuality," 79. How serious must Jerusalem's sin be when her transgressions merit the punishment of Sodom (Isa. 1:9; Jer. 23:14; Ez. 16:48-49; Mt. 10:15; Lk. 10:12; 2 Pet. 2:6-8).

[38] Younger, *Judges/Ruth*, 359.

[39] Yamada, *Configurations of Rape*, 134.

concubine dies "with her hands on the threshold" of the door, what should have been for her a "safe zone" (Judg. 19:26). In fact, the host's words shockingly reveal his own moral conditioning, "do to them what is good in your own eyes!" (Judg. 19:24, author's translation).

For Tamar, Amnon uses the door initially to *isolate* a culinary nurse, then to *exclude* the shamed (2 Sam. 13:17, 18). By contrast, the well-ordered Hebrew home was intended to be God-fearing, with the very doors testifying to God's law and family *shalom* (Deut. 6:9; cf. Ex. 13:9; Mt. 23:5).

The type-scene in the Dinah story contains a rare expression of what Robert Alter calls "narrated monologue."[40] This is the narrator's own moral assessment or judgment: "They were shocked and furious, because Shechem had done an outrageous thing against Israel by sleeping with Jacob's daughter – a thing that should not be done" (Gen. 34:7b; cf. Judges 19:23; 2 Sam. 13:12). Alter observes:

> This entire clause is a rare instance in biblical narrative [...] the narrator conveys the tenor of Jacob's sons' anger by reporting in the third person the kind of language they would have spoken silently, or to each other. It is a technical means for strongly imprinting the rage of Jacob's sons in the presence of their father who has kept silent and, even now, gives no voice to his feelings about the violation of his daughter.[41]

God's own silence or absence is also a theme in this profile. In the Dinah story, for example, it is significant that God's name is entirely withheld from a narrative of rape, deceit, and wholesale murder (Gen. 34), only to reappear in chapter 35 with "God" [10x], "El Bethel" [1x], "El-Shaddai" [1x], a divine audience (35:13), and eight occurrences of the names "Bethel" and "Israel."

Conclusion and Implications

We can observe several points from our study, not only in terms of method, but also in the practical pastoral implications.

First, when it comes to working with large type-scenes, which we find in narratives of sexual violence, so much of the story is driven by strategic repetition.

> [This] may well reflect the "oral" beginnings of many such biblical narratives, given that the mechanical limits of oracular storytelling – the necessity for plot to be committed entirely to memory, without the aid of external apparatus, and then faithfully retold – engenders a heavy reliance on shared knowledge between a storyteller and his audience, and the conventions which capitalize on such knowledge. In this sense, the well-worn formulaic conventions used by the storyteller provide a means of enhancing memory and simplifying the details of the story [...] *type-scenes act as a kind of oral shorthand, a means of covering familiar ground quickly*, without getting lost in detail. A story can thus be told as a series of

[40] Alter, *The Five Books of Moses*, 190.
[41] Alter, *The Five Books of Moses*, 190.

> set scenes rearranged in a different order and filled out with different personages, places and objects.[42]

In the words of Leland Ryken, "We do not have to memorize lists of narrative 'rules,' but we do have to develop the right 'antennae' by which to receive what these stories have to communicate."[43] Sexual violence as a type-scene reminds us that we are all travellers, just as the biblical characters. There is an "epic-ness" that enjoins us all in these sober stories. Biblical travellers, like us, are in transit for spiritual reasons – life never stands still.

Second, these type-scenes carry an abiding message: sexual violence can and does live on in families and social structures of society. Environment is not destiny, but environment is a predisposing factor.[44] The complex actions of biblical characters are codified in type-scenes of sexual violence. These stories collect numerous themes that highlight the heinous sexual acts; actions which, in turn, reverberate far beyond their own contexts to warp the realities in which others act. In the words of Mark E. Biddle:

> One sees sin lingering in the world, distorting perceptions, offering inauthentic possibilities, skewing the system, perpetuating itself [...] forgiveness granted the first sinner in the chain of causation (e.g., David) is sometimes, sadly, unable to interrupt the sequence if the seeds sown in the environment have already taken root in the lives of others.[45]

This continuum of sin has been demonstrated through significant similarities in these four Old Testament narratives. These stories place sexual violence on a large and public stage using the reading lens of type-scenes. If this is correct, we must read such biblical accounts as the layered relational ecosystem that they are.

Third, there is a unique theological profile that emerges from these texts of sexual violence. The organic continuum of sin works with *antecedent conditions* in its socio-religious environment as: cause → effect → further cause.[46] Part of the teaching lesson intensified in these stories is that unless sin is checked, the continuum naturally "matures" into further results (Gen. 15:16; Rom. 1:18-32). "Sin, as a continuum, twists reality and passes on this contorted system as an antecedent reality to those who come after, limiting their freedom to perceive reality properly and, thus, also their freedom to choose rightly."[47] Some injury outlives the act of wrongdoing. The pernicious nature of violence wrapped in sexuality creates a complex social carnage that destroys the very fabric of society, a layered social fabric that is needed to bring healing. To understand and address sexual violence, a fuller spectrum of sin's *afterlife* must be faced, which explains the social embeddedness, intrafamilial customs, trans-generational patterns, and internalized beliefs.[48]

---

[42] Gartner-Brereton, *The Ontology of Space*, 34; emphasis added.
[43] Ryken, *Words of Delight*, 51.
[44] Biddle, *Missing the Mark*, 135.
[45] Biddle, *Missing the Mark*, 130.
[46] Biddle, *Missing the Mark*, 131.
[47] Biddle, *Missing the Mark*, 128.
[48] Schmutzer, "A Theology of Sexuality and its Abuse," 125.

Fourth, when the autonomous *self* – so prized in Western cultures – remains unaccountable or when some consequences of evil are minimized because the harm was "unintentional," then that act is placed beyond the realm of redemption.[49] Increasingly, "the nexus of sin and its consequences – its afterlife in the everyday world – has no place in the popular Christian mind."[50] In an era when sex trafficking blankets our globe, understanding the dynamics at work illustrated in a type-scene of sexual violence is more than just important: it is a powerful mirror of the human heart.[51] *Our stories are not just personal they are frighteningly connected.* There are realities that we can neither see nor control.

Fifth, Abraham's complaint that he puts to God still rings true for people of faith today, namely, that the wicked would not determine the fate of the righteous (Gen. 18:23). Self-care may be an important lifestyle, but no intervention for others will ever occur without risk. The pain of victimization acutely felt by some must become a dangerous incursion undertaken by many if we are to police our own communities and increasingly complex urban centers. One of the tasks of the righteous in any community is the prophetic role of prayer for God's blessing to cover the world (cf. Gen. 20:7), for the Creator remains concerned with his creation.[52] God's people are still a healing presence in the roughest of our cities, the world over.[53] They always have been, and they always will be.

Sixth, for those skeptics who still believe that the God of the Old Testament is an "angry monster," the Sodom story in Genesis 19 has an ironic response with some lessons of its own. Among these significant lessons are the following:

- God is not deaf to the cries and violence in our cities;
- God investigates accusations thoroughly;
- God takes serious questions, seriously, when we ask;
- God uses objective witnesses, even where they are not recognized;
- God involves faithful people in his judgments and mission;
- God displays active compassion for the suffering;
- God prioritizes mercy over wrath, even for the weak and confused.

"Because of the LORD's compassion for him […] they brought him out and left him outside the city" (Gen. 19:16). God still rescues the weak and vulnerable, if one is willing to follow.

---

[49] Biddle, *Missing the Mark*, 97.

[50] Biddle, *Missing the Mark*, 117.

[51] Phrase from J. G. Herder, *The Spirit of Hebrew Poetry*, translated by E. Marsh (Burlington, VT: Edward Smith, 1833), 1:228.

[52] Provan, *Discovering Genesis*, 140.

[53] Longmann III, *Genesis*, 244.

Reflection Questions

1. Explain how sexual violence can, in fact, be a symptom of other "forces" in life that are already skewed and damaged. How does this relate to the cause-effect nature of the organic continuum of sin described in this chapter?
2. In the biblical story of Sodom, why is poor hospitality alone too shallow of an explanation to explain God's judgment? What other elements do people often overlook in Genesis 19?
3. What are some destructive trans-generational patterns of sexual violence that you have witnessed? What can be done to address them? What insight does the type-scene approach provide?
4. Popular faith today rejects the connection between forgiveness and consequences. What do you believe is driving this disconnect? What is true forgiveness? What does true righteousness (*tsedaka*) and justice (*mishpat*) require?

Works Cited

Alter, Robert. *The Art of Biblical Narrative*. New York, NY: Basic Books, 1981.

——. *The Five Books of Moses: A Translation with Commentary*. New York, NY: W.W. Norton & Company, 2004.

Arnold, Bill T. and John H. Choi. *A Guide to Biblical Hebrew Syntax*. Cambridge: Cambridge University Press, 2003.

Arnold, Bill T. *Genesis*. The New Cambridge Bible Commentary. Cambridge: Cambridge University Press, 2009.

Biddle, Mark E. *Missing the Mark: Sin and Its Consequences in Biblical Theology*. Nashville, TN: Abingdon, 2005.

Blenkinsopp, Joseph. "Abraham as Paradigm in the Priestly History in Genesis." *Journal of Biblical Literature* 128 (2000): 225-241.

Boda, Mark J. *A Severe Mercy: Sin and Its Remedy in the Old Testament*. Siphrut 1. Winona Lake, IN: Eisenbrauns, 2009.

Bruckner, James K. *Implied Law in the Abraham Narrative: A Literary and Theological Analysis*. Journal for the Study of the Old Testament Supplementary Series 335. Sheffield: Sheffield Academic Press, 2001.

Carr, David M. *Reading the Fractures of Genesis: Historical and Literary Approaches*. Louisville, KY: Westminster John Knox Press, 1996.

Creach, Jerome F.D. *Violence in Scripture*. Interpretation Resources for the Use of Scripture in the Church. Louisville, KY: Westminster John Knox Press, 2013.

Gartner-Brereton, Luke. *The Ontology of Space in Biblical Hebrew Narrative: The Determinate Function of Narrative "Space" within the Biblical Hebrew Aesthetic*. London: Equinox, 2008.

Hendel, Ronald, Chana Kronfeld, and Hana Pardes. “Gender and Sexuality”. In Ronald Hendel, Ed. *Reading Genesis: Ten Methods*. Cambridge: Cambridge University Press, 2010, 71-91.

Herder, J.G. *The Spirit of Hebrew Poetry*. Translated by E. Marsh. Burlington, VT: Edward Smith, 1833.

Knierim, Rolf. “*‘awon*, perversity”. In E. Jenni and C. Westermann, Eds. *Theological Lexicon of the Old Testament*. Volume 2. Translated by M.E. Biddle. Peabody, MA: Hendrickson, 1997: 862-866.

Lasine, S. “Guest and Host in Judges 19: Lot’s Hospitality in an Inverted World.” *Journal for the Study of the Old Testament* 29 (1984): 37-41.

Longmann III., Tremper. *Genesis*. The Story of God Bible Commentary. Grand Rapids, MI: Zondervan, 2016.

Mann, Thomas. *The Book of the Torah*. Atlanta, GA: John Knox, 1988.

McFadyen, Alistair I. *Bound to Sin: Abuse, Holocaust and the Christian Doctrine of Sin*. Cambridge: Cambridge University Press, 2000.

Merrill, Eugene H. “History”. In D. Brent Sandy, Ronald L. Giese, Jr, Eds. *Cracking Old Testament Codes: A Guide to Interpreting the Genres of the Old Testament*. Nashville, TN: Broadman and Holman, 1995.

Nelson, Richard D. *Deuteronomy: A Commentary*. Old Testament Library. Louisville, KY: Westminster John Knox Press, 2002.

Plantinga, Jr, Cornelius. *Not the Way It’s Supposed to Be: A Breviary of Sin*. Grand Rapids, MI: Eerdmans, 1995.

Provan, Iain. *Discovering Genesis: Content, Interpretation, Reception*. Discovering Biblical Texts. Grand Rapids, MI: Eerdmans, 2016.

Ryken, Leland. *Words of Delight: A Literary Introduction to the Bible*. 2nd Edn. Grand Rapids, MI: Baker, 1992.

Savran, George W. *Telling and Retelling: Quotations in Biblical Narrative*. Bloomington, IN: Indiana University Press, 1988.

Schmutzer, Andrew J. “A Theology of Sexuality and Its Abuse: Creation, Evil, and the Relational Ecosystem”. In A. J. Schmutzer, Ed. *The Long Journey Home: Understanding and Ministering to the Sexually Abused*. Eugene, OR: Wipf & Stock, 2011: 105-135.

Volf, Miroslav. *The End of Memory: Remembering Rightly in a Violent World*. Grand Rapids, MI: Eerdmans, 2006.

Waltke, Bruce K. *Genesis*. Grand Rapids, MI: Zondervan, 2001.

Yamada, Frank M. *Configurations of Rape in the Hebrew Bible: A Literary Analysis of Three Rape Narratives*. Ed. Hemchand Gossai. Studies in Biblical Literature, 109. New York, NY: Peter Lang, 2008.

Younger, Jr., Lawson K. *Judges/Ruth*. NIV Application Commentary. Grand Rapids, MI: Zondervan, 2002.

CRUCIFIXION AND SEXUAL ABUSE: A THEOLOGICAL RESOURCE FOR ADDRESSING SEXUAL EXPLOITATION

David Tombs

Please be aware that this chapter contains graphic descriptions of sexual and other violence.

Introduction

The Bible is always read with a context in mind.[1] Assumptions are made about the original social context of the text and these are most often derived – consciously or otherwise – from the current social context of the reader or critic. In recent decades, the positive value of recognizing these connections has been advocated by contextual theologies in Latin America and elsewhere. Although some critics have rightly cautioned against superficially equating contemporary social contexts and the biblical world, those committed to a contextual approach have maintained that, when used appropriately, a serious engagement with current social contexts can offer insights into the biblical context and hence into neglected aspects of the biblical text.[2]

One area where I believe that shared similarities between past and present contexts can be most usefully investigated is the political arena of state terror and the use of torture for this end. Latin American military regimes used terror in the 1970s and 1980s to create fear and promote fatalism throughout the whole of society. An understanding of this provides a context to recognize Roman crucifixions as instruments of state terror. Furthermore, Latin American torture practices involved deliberate attempts to shame the victims and undermine their sense of dignity. Physical torture and assaults were often coupled with psychological humiliation in attempts to end the victim's will to resist, or even to live. Sexual assaults and sexual humiliation are a particularly effective way to do this, and are commonplace in torture practices past and present.

---

[1] See Fernando F. Segovia, "Jesus as Victim of State Terror: A Critical Reflection Twenty Years Later". This is available in David Tombs, *Crucifixion, State Terror, and Sexual Abuse: Text and Context* (Dunedin: Centre for Theology and Public Issues, University of Otago, 2018): 22-31; OUR archive [Available at: http://hdl.handle.net/10523/8558], [Last accessed: 11th October 2022].

[2] For one of the most sophisticated and sustained developments of a contextual hermeneutic, see Clodovis Boff, *Theology and Praxis: Epistemological Foundations* (Maryknoll, NY: Orbis Books, 1987 [1978]). Boff's approach recognizes both the similarities and differences between the contemporary Latin American context and the biblical world.

This chapter[3] argues that torture practices can offer a deeper understanding of Roman crucifixion as a form of state terror which included sexual abuse. The analysis below draws on Latin American reports, but a similar reading could be offered through attention to torture in many other contexts, including torture and prisoner abuse at Abu Ghraib.[4]

To raise the question of sexual abuse in relation to Jesus may at first seem inappropriate. However, the Gospel accounts indicate a striking level of public sexual humiliation in the treatment of Jesus, and even this may not disclose the full horror of Jesus' torture before his death. Although this may be a very disturbing suggestion at first, at a theological level, a God who has identified with the victims of sexual abuse can be recognised as a positive challenge for contemporary Christian understanding and response. At a pastoral level, it could help sensitize people to the experiences of those who have suffered sexual abuse and, in some cases, might even become a healing step for the victims themselves.

Crucifixion and State Terror

Military coups in the 1960s and 1970s installed military regimes in Brazil (1964-85) and throughout the Southern Cone of Latin America (Chile, 1973-89; Uruguay, 1973-85; and Argentina, 1976-83). During these years, state-sanctioned human rights abuses including torture, assassinations, and disappearances were commonplace. Likewise, in the 1980s, the authoritarian governments in Guatemala and El Salvador were involved in some of the most brutal campaigns of repression the region has known. The transition to democracy in Brazil and the Southern Cone countries and the peace treaties in El Salvador (1992) and Guatemala (1995) have prompted official investigations into human rights abuses during the repression. Published reports from these

---

[3] Material in this chapter was first presented in the paper David Tombs, "Biblical Interpretation in Latin America: Crucifixion, State Terror, and Sexual Abuse" in the Biblical Hermeneutics Section at the Society of Biblical Literature International Conference, 20th July 1998, Krakow, Poland. It was first published in a longer version as David Tombs, "Crucifixion, State Terror, and Sexual Abuse", *Union Seminary Quarterly Review*, 53 (Autumn 1999): 89-109. This abridged version of the article was first published under a Creative Commons license in Portuguese as David Tombs, "Crucificação e abuso sexual", *Estudos Teológicos* 59(1), (July 2019): 119-32, and subsequently republished under a Creative Commons license in English, French, Spanish and German. Source material is used with permission under a Creative Commons license from David Tombs, "Crucificação e abuso sexual", *Estudos Teológicos* 59(1), (July 2019): 119-32. [Available at: http://dx.doi.org/10.22351/et.v59i1.3579], [Last accessed: 11th October 2022]. The abridged version has been slightly revised for publication in this collection.

[4] On state terror and sexual abuses in Latin American torture in the 1970s and 1980s, see further discussion in Tombs, *Crucifixion, State Terror, and Sexual Abuse: Text and Context.* On reading crucifixion in light of the torture at Abu Ghraib, see David Tombs, "Prisoner Abuse: From Abu Ghraib to The Passion of The Christ" in Linda Hogan and Dylan Lehrke Dylan (eds), *Religions and the Politics of Peace and Conflict*, (Princeton, NJ: Princeton Theological Monograph Series, 2009): 179-205.

countries offer detailed documentation that make grim reading on the years of terror endured by the civilian populations.[5]

Any understanding of the political and social dynamics of these countries during this time must address the widespread use of state terror to support and enforce the illegitimate power of military regimes. Terror was an effective means in enforcing brutal authoritarianism through a culture of fear.[6] Fear "persuades" people that it is better to endure injustices fatalistically rather than to resist them. The arrest and torture of "suspects" by the police and military in Latin America cannot be adequately explained in terms of the threat they might have posed or the need to elicit information from them. Rather, they should be understood as intended to paralyze a society's willingness to resist. In addition to targeting the victims themselves, disappearances, torture, and executions were intended to terrorize a public audience.

In a similar way, Roman crucifixion was more than the punishment of an individual. Crucifixions were instruments within state terror policies directed at a wider population in the ancient world.[7] As acts of terror against potentially rebellious people, the Romans principally used crucifixions against slaves and other subjected peoples who might challenge Roman authority.[8] One of the clearest illustrations of the use of crucifixion to inspire terror is provided by Josephus' description of the treatment of those who attempted to flee Jerusalem during the siege by Titus in 70 C.E.:

> Scourged and subjected before death to every torture, they were finally crucified in view of the wall. Titus indeed realized the horror of what was happening, for every

---

[5] These include: Archdiocese of Sao Paulo, Torture in Brazil: A Report by the Archdiocese of São Paulo (New York: Vintage Books, 1986); National Commission on Disappeared People, Nunca Más: A Report by Argentina's National Commission on Disappeared People (Boston and London: Faber and Faber, 1986); National Commission on Truth and Reconciliation, Report of the Chilean National Commission on Truth and Reconciliation (Notre Dame, IN: Centre for Civil and Human Rights, Notre Dame Law School, 1993); Truth and Reconciliation for El Salvador, From Madness to Hope: The Twelve Years War in El Salvador: Report of the Truth Commission, 1992-93 (New York: United Nations, 1993).

[6] See the collection of essays that explore this from different disciplines in Juan E. Corradi *et al.* (eds), *Fear at the Edge: State Terror and Resistance in Latin America* (Berkeley and Los Angeles, CA: University of California Press, 1992). On the use of torture to promote terror, see Elaine Scarry, *The Body in Pain: The Making and Unmaking of the World* (Oxford: Oxford University Press, 1987).

[7] For a brief history of crucifixion, see the classic work by Martin Hengel, *Crucifixion in the Ancient World and the Folly of the Cross* (Philadelphia, PA: Fortress Press; London: SCM Press, 1977 [German orig. 1976]).

[8] Crucifixion was rarely used against Roman citizens and even these infrequent occasions were to punish lower classes rather than the aristocracy. On the use of crucifixion by the Romans, see the classic work by Hengel, *Crucifixion*. For recent treatments see Raymond E. Brown, *Death of the Messiah* (New York: Doubleday, 1994): 945-52, and the exhaustive bibliography, pp. 885-87; Stephen D. Moore, *God's Gym: Divine Male Bodies of the Bible* (New York: Routledge, 1996); and Gerard S. Sloyan, *The Crucifixion of Jesus: History, Myth, Faith* (Minneapolis, MN: Fortress Press, 1995).

> day 500 – sometimes even more – fell into his hands.... But his chief reason for not stopping the slaughter was the hope that the sight of it would perhaps induce the Jews to surrender in order to avoid the same fate. The soldiers themselves through rage and bitterness nailed up their victims in various attitudes as a grim joke, till owing to the vast numbers there was no room for the crosses, and no crosses for the bodies. (*War* V. 446-52)[9]

The effectiveness and security of the Roman troops in Palestine was ultimately based on the legions in Syria and – if necessary – elsewhere in the Empire. The relatively small force in Palestine were able to maintain order because they were backed by an assurance of severe reprisals if serious rebellion broke out. The combination of moderate presence and massive threat was usually enough to preserve the so-called "peace" of the *pax Romana*.

The mass crucifixions with which the Romans responded to major incidents conveyed the message of fearful retaliation with a terrifying clarity. Josephus describes how in 4 B.C.E. Varus (governor of Syria) responded to the upheaval caused by the inept rule of Herod's son Archelaus with the crucifixion of 2000 "ringleaders" of the troubles (War II. 69-79 [75]). The census revolt when Quirinius was governor of Syria (6-7 C.E.) and Coponius procurator of Judea (6-9 C.E.) also met with widespread reprisals (*War* II. 117-18; Ant. 18.1-10). Josephus also records that, when Cumanus (procurator of Judea 48-52 C.E.) took a number of prisoners involved in a dispute, Quadratus (governor of Syria) ordered them all crucified (*War* II. 241). Likewise, when Felix (procurator of Judea, 52-60 C.E.) set out to clear the country of banditry, the number that were crucified "were too many to count" (*War* II. 253). Josephus also records how in the build-up to the revolt in 66 C.E., Florus (procurator 64–66 C.E.) raided the Temple treasury and then – because of the disturbance that followed – scourged and crucified men, women and children until the day's death toll was 3600 (*War* II. 305-08).

Individual crucifixions should be understood within this political context. Even if only one victim was crucified, the execution had more significance than the punishment of an individual victim. Crucifixion was an important way in which the dire consequences of rebellion could be kept before the public eye. Individual crucifixions served to remind people of the mass crucifixions and other reprisals which the Romans were all too ready to use if their power was challenged.

There are few detailed descriptions of how crucifixion took place – the Gospels provide the fullest description in ancient literature – but the picture that emerges fits the profile of public state torture very well.[10] The victim was tied or nailed to a wooden cross to maximize their public humiliation: a contrast of the

---

[9] The English translation Josephus, *The Jewish War* (trans. G.A. Willon; Harmondsworth: Penguin Books, rev. ed. 1970 [1959]) is used here and for all other passages cited below.

[10] Analysis of how crucifixion was used in the ancient world is complicated by the close relationship between crucifixion, impalement and the hanging of bodies (which might be carried out either before or after death). That the New Testament writers can move easily between crucifixion and hanging on a tree is shown in Galatians 3:13; Acts 5:30; 10:39.

shame of the victim with the might of imperial power. The Romans displayed the victim on a roadside or similar public place. Crucifixion was a protracted ordeal that might last a number of days, a sustained attack on the dignity of the human spirit as well as the physical body.[11] The shame for Jews was further heightened by the belief that "anyone hung on a tree is under a curse" (Deut. 21:23), a curse that Paul refers to in relation to Jesus' crucifixion in Galatians 3:13.

Crucifixion and Sexual Abuse

Testimonies to torture in Brazil, Argentina, Chile, Central America and elsewhere consistently report stripping and sexual abuse as part of torture.[12] In Brazil, torture by electric shock invariably included shocks to the genitals.[13] The same focus on the genitals was shown in Argentina. The preferred instrument for administering electric shocks in Argentina, *la picana* (a small electrified prod), is itself highly suggestive of the sexual element in this torture.[14] Its use in the rape and sexual abuse of women has been well documented and at least two Argentinean male victims also witness to how this abuse eventually led to anal rape.[15]

For a reading of crucifixion, two elements of these torture practices deserve particular attention. First, as we shall see, sexual assault and humiliation were standard practices in Roman state torture practices; sexual abuse was standard

[11] During crucifixion, it is likely that all control over body functions would have failed. The following account of electric shock torture in Argentina by Nélson Eduardo Dean suggests how humiliating the consequences of this would be: "During the application of electricity, one would lose all control over one's senses, such torture provoking permanent vomiting, almost constant defecation, etc."; National Commission of Disappeared People, *Nunca Más*, 39.

[12] Further examples are included in Tombs, *Crucifixion, State Terror, and Sexual Abuse*.

[13] "… he was tortured naked, after taking a bath, while hanging on the parrot's perch where he received electric shocks from a magneto [small electric generator] to his genital organs and over his whole body." (José Milton Ferreira de Almeida); Archdiocese of Sao Paulo, *Torture in Brazil*, 17.

[14] On the sexualized use of the *picana* and other sexual aspects in Argentinean torture, see Francisco Graziano, *Divine Violence: Spectacle, Psychosexuality, and Radical Christianity in the Argentine 'Dirty War'* (Boulder, CO and Oxford: Westview Press, 1992), especially 153-58.

[15] The rape of women during torture has been well documented but recorded instances of the rape of men are less frequent. The frequency with which male prisoners were subjected to some form of rape is hard to determine. However, it is clear that rape was sometimes used to torture men as well as women. Dr Liwski, whose extended testimony starts the *Nunca Más* report, describes his treatment in detail: "Another day they took me out of my cell and, despite my [previously tortured] swollen testicles, placed me face-down again. They tied me up and raped me slowly and deliberately by introducing a metal object into my anus. They then passed an electric current through the object. I cannot describe how everything inside me felt as though it were on fire" (Dr Norberto Liwski) (*Nunca Más*, 20-26 [24]).

rather than unusual or exceptional. Second, the awareness of a victim's sexual humiliation among a wider public was often an important part of this humiliation.

Against this background, the crucifixion of Jesus may be viewed with a disturbing question in mind: to what extent did the torture and crucifixion of Jesus involve some form of sexual abuse? The testimonies from twentieth-century Latin America create hermeneutical suspicions that merit careful examination of the Gospels to see whether there is any evidence that this was the case.

To explore this question further, it is helpful to distinguish between sexual abuse that involves only sexual humiliation (such as enforced nudity, sexual mockery and sexual insults) and sexual abuse that extends to sexual assault (which involves forced sexual contact, and ranges from molestation to penetration, injury, or mutilation). I will argue that the Gospels clearly indicate that sexual humiliation was a prominent trait in the treatment of Jesus and that sexual humiliation was an important aspect of crucifixion. If this is the case, the possibility of sexual assaults against Jesus will also need to be considered. In the absence of clear evidence to decide this one way or another, I will suggest that what has proved so common in recent torture practices cannot be entirely ruled out in the treatment of Jesus.

Crucifixion in the ancient world appears to have carried a strongly sexual element and should be understood as a form of sexual abuse that involved sexual humiliation and sometimes sexual assault. Crucifixion was intended to be more than the ending of life; prior to actual death, it sought to reduce the victim to something less than human in the eyes of society. Victims were crucified naked in what amounted to a ritualized form of public sexual humiliation. In a patriarchal society, where men competed against each other to display virility in terms of sexual power over others, the public display of the naked victim by the "victors" in front of onlookers and passers-by carried the message of sexual domination. The cross held up the victim for display as someone who had been – at least metaphorically – emasculated.[16] Depending on the position in which the victim was crucified, the display of the genitals could be especially emphasized. Both Josephus and the Roman historian Seneca the Younger attest the Romans' enthusiasm for experimentation with different positions of crucifixion.[17] Furthermore, Seneca's description suggests that the sexual violence against the victim was sometimes taken to the most brutal extreme with

---

[16] 1 Samuel suggests that emasculation and sexual assault were also recognised practices at an earlier time in Israel's history. On emasculation, see 1 Samuel 18:27: "David rose and went along with his men, and killed one hundred of the Philistines; and David brought their foreskins, which were given in full number to the king, that he might become the king's son-in-law." On the fear of sexual-assault, see 1 Samuel 31:4: "Then Saul said to his armor-bearer, 'Draw your sword and thrust me through me with it, so that these uncircumcised may not come and thrust me through, and make sport of me.'" I am grateful to John Jarick for pointing these out to me.

[17] On Josephus *War* V. 452 (see above); Seneca, *To Marcia on Consolation* 20.3, records: "I see crosses there, not just of one kind but fashioned in many ways: some have their victims with head down toward the ground; some impale their private parts; others stretch out their arms on their crossbeam" (cited in Hengel, *Crucifixion*, 25).

crosses that impaled the genitals of the victim. This practice might never have been the case in Palestine – and there is no evidence that suggests it happened to Jesus – but at the very least, it suggests the highly sexualized context of violence in which Roman crucifixions sometimes took place.

The sexual element in Roman practices was part of their message of terror. Anyone who opposed the Romans would not only lose their life but also be stripped of all personal honor and human dignity. It is therefore not surprising that the Gospels themselves indicate that there was a high level of sexual humiliation in the way that Jesus was flogged, insulted, and then crucified. From evidence of the ancient world, it seems that flogging the victim in public whilst naked was routine. Mark, Matthew, and John all imply that this was also the case with the flogging of Jesus.[18] Likewise, as noted above, crucifixion usually took place whilst the victim was naked and there is little reason to think that Jesus or other Jews would have been an exception to this.[19] If the purpose were to humiliate the victim, full nakedness would have been particularly shameful in the Jewish context.[20] Furthermore, prior to crucifixion, Jesus was handed over to

---

[18] Although Mark 15:15, Matthew 27:26 and John 19:1 are not explicit on this (and Luke does not mention a flogging), the sequence of events they describe strongly suggests it. Mark and Matthew (who have the flogging at the end of the trial) and John (who has the flogging midway through the trial) each report that, immediately after the flogging, Jesus was handed over to the Roman soldiers to mock him. All three present the first act of mockery as the soldiers dressing Jesus in a crown of thorns and a purple cloak (Mk. 15:17), purple robe (Jn. 19:2) or scarlet cloak (Mt. 27:28). There is no mention in Mark of needing to strip him before doing so, but it is explicitly stated in Matthew 27:28. By contrast, both Mark 15:20 and Matthew 27:31 explicitly mention that, after the mocking, he is stripped of the garb and his own clothes are put back on him for the procession to Golgotha. Brown notes that the usual custom outside Palestine was for the condemned man to be paraded naked to execution but that exceptions to this in Palestine may have been a concession to Jewish scruples on public nakedness (see Brown, *Death of the Messiah*, 870). It is possible that this sensitivity was especially high within the limits of the holy city.

[19] This is clearest in John 19:23-24 which records that, after putting Jesus on the cross, the soldiers took his clothes to divide amongst themselves and that these included his undergarments for which they cast lots so as not to tear it. The synoptic Gospels (Mk. 15:24, Mt. 27:35 and Lk. 23:34) are a little vaguer and simply refer to the division of his clothes by lots. In a careful assessment of the evidence, Raymond Brown offers cautious support for the likelihood of full nakedness. Although Brown reports that the evangelists are not specific on the matter, and that they might not have known for sure, he offers three reasons that would support the view that Jesus was fully naked (Brown, *Death of the Messiah*, 952-53).

[20] On the deliberate humiliation of enemies by genital exposure, see 2 Samuel 10:4-5 which describes how David's envoys were seized by Ha'nun and sent back with their beards half shaved and their garments cut off "in the middle at their hips". Jewish sensitivity over insulting displays of the body is also shown in a disaster which occurred during the time that Cumanus was governor (48-52 C.E.). Josephus reports that a soldier on guard on the Temple colonnade during the Feast of Unleavened Bread lifted his tunic, bent over indecently and exposed himself to the crowds below whilst making indecent noises (*War* II. 223-27). Fearing a riot in the commotion that followed,

a cohort of Roman soldiers to be further humiliated (Mk. 15:16-20; Mt. 27:27-31; Jn. 19:1-5).[21] All the Gospels apart from Luke report that the Roman soldiers mocked Jesus by placing a crown of thorns on his head (Mk. 15:17; Mt. 27:29; Jn. 19:2) and clothing him in a purple (Mk. 15:17; Jn. 19:2) or scarlet (Mt. 27:28) garment.[22] The texts also mention that the soldiers spat at Jesus (Mk. 15:19; Mt. 27:30), struck him with a reed (Mk. 15:19; Mt. 27:30), and mocked him with verbal taunts (calling him King: Mk. 15:18; Mt. 27:29; Jn. 19:3) and symbolic homage (kneeling before him, Mk. 15:19; Mt. 27:29).[23]

Based on what the Gospel texts themselves indicate, the sexual element in the abuse is unavoidable. An adult man was stripped naked for flogging, then dressed in an insulting way to be mocked, struck and spat at by a multitude of soldiers before being stripped again (at least in Mk. 15:20 and Mt. 27:31) and re-clothed for his journey through the city – already too weak to carry his own cross – only to be stripped for a third time and displayed to die whilst naked to a mocking crowd. When the textual presentation is stated like this, the sexual element of the abuse becomes clear: the assertion is controversial only in so far as it seems startling in view of usual presentations.[24] The sexual element to the torture is downplayed in artistic representations of the crucifixion that show Jesus wearing a loincloth. These images distance us from the biblical text, perhaps because the sexual element has been too disturbing to confront.

Although it is vital to acknowledge the sexual humiliation that is revealed in the text, what the texts might conceal may also be significant. There may have been a level of sexual abuse in the *praetorium* that none of the Gospels immediately disclose. This suspicion is prompted by the testimonies from Latin

Cumanus sent for heavy infantry but this triggered a panic, and Josephus claims that 30,000 were crushed to death as they tried to escape.

[21] For Mark and Matthew, this happens at the end of the trial and both mention it taking place in the *praetorium*. For John, the mockery takes place during the trial and it appears to have been done within Pilate's headquarters (18:28).

[22] Luke places the mocking of Jesus rather earlier in the story at a point that is unlikely to have involved Roman soldiers. According to Luke 22:63-64, the mockery takes place prior to the trial before the Jewish elders. The mocking, beating, blindfolding and challenges to prophesy (Luke makes no mention of spitting) were carried out by the men who were holding Jesus overnight before the trial in front of the Council. Presumably, these were members of "the crowd" mentioned as capturing him in Luke 22:47. Mark 14:65 and Matthew 26:67-68 also report that Jesus was spat at, struck and challenged to prophesy, but they put this immediately after the Council had condemned him, rather than before, and say it was carried out by members of the Council themselves. John does not mention any parallel treatment associated with the questioning by the High Priest (Jn. 18:19-24).

[23] In addition, Matthew 27:29 also mentions placing the reed in Jesus' right hand prior to striking him. Although John makes no mention of a reed, John 19:3 records Jesus being struck.

[24] This paper is primarily concerned with how the texts present events. The picture of abuse that they present is historically very plausible but further assessment of textual historicity will not be attempted here. In view of the shame and embarrassment that would have been associated with sexual abuse, it is probable that the Gospels understate it rather than exaggerate it.

America presented earlier. Whilst the testimonies from Latin America do nothing to directly establish the historical facts of crucifixion in Palestine, they are highly suggestive for what may have happened within the closed walls of the *praetorium*.[25]

Both Matthew and Mark describe Jesus as being handed over weakened and naked – already a condemned man without any recourse to justice – to soldiers who took him inside the *praetorium* and assembled the other troops.[26] Both Gospels explicitly state that it was the whole cohort (*speira*) of Roman soldiers – over five hundred men – that was assembled together to witness and participate in the "mockery." This probably included a significant number of Syrian auxiliaries who might have viewed their Jewish neighbors with particular hostility.[27] In view of the testimonies to gang rapes that are given by victims detained by security forces in the clandestine torture centres of Latin America, this detail of overwhelming and hostile military power sounds a particularly disturbing note.

Many in the Roman cohort would have experienced the fears and frustrations of military life in an occupied country, which could have generated an awkward inner tension of omnipotence and powerlessness. As representatives of imperial Rome, the soldiers collectively exercised almost unlimited power. On the other hand, each individual soldier was at the bottom of a long chain of Roman hierarchical command and would also have felt their individual powerlessness on a daily basis. The instinctive response to such powerlessness is often to impose one's own power forcefully on those who are even less powerful. Individual soldiers had very little freedom or personal choice to act on this, however, and often their interactions with local people would reinforce their feelings of powerlessness and frustration. The common soldier would often have

---

[25] The privacy of the *praetorium* (whether Pilate's palace or the Antonia fortress) means that the details of what transpired inside are inevitably circumstantial and would probably not have been known even at the time. Furthermore, even if it was believed that Jesus had been sexually assaulted in the *praetorium*, the absence of this in the Gospel accounts is hardly surprising. Apart from the distance of years and the desire to pass over a shameful event, the Gospels are usually seen as notably biased in excusing the Romans for Jesus' trial and death.

[26] Despite the attempts of the Gospels to excuse Pilate from blame, if rape did take place in the *praetorium*, presumably it would only have done so with Pilate's positive approval or knowing indifference. It is quite possible that Pilate deliberately handed Jesus over to be sexually assaulted by his soldiers as part of the crucifixion sentence. Such an action might have served to reinforce his own status as a triumphant lord who was able to sexually vanquish his victims through the actions of his underlings. Richard Trexler notes that a Roman master might find it more insulting to have his slaves rape his adulterous wife's young suitor rather than to rape the youth himself; Richard Trexler, *Sex and Conquest: Gendered Violence, Political Order, and the European Conquest of the Americas* (Cambridge: Polity Press, 1995): 22.

[27] Josephus suggests that, at least whilst Felix was procurator (52-60 C.E.), the majority of the Roman garrison in Caesarea were raised in Syria and they readily sided with the Syrian inhabitants of Caesarea in a civil dispute against its Jewish citizens (*War*, II. 266-270 [268]).

to suffer without taking immediate revenge when faced by lack of co-operation, disrespect or barely concealed hostility. The resentment created by this situation would normally have been held in check by military discipline and the fear of military superiors who wished to avoid unnecessary trouble wherever possible. Nonetheless, the aggressive urge to vengeance would remain close to the surface and could give rise to extreme violence when superiors were willing to turn a blind eye or sanction its expression on a sacrificial victim. The desire to take out the frustrations and brutalities of military life through sexual violence has given rise to atrocities throughout history.

Josephus' account of the Siege of Jerusalem (*War*, V. 420-572) suggests that the comparisons between the ancient world and twentieth-century Latin American torture practices may be appropriate. Josephus' description of how the Jewish militants inside Jerusalem tortured the civilian population in the search for food provides a graphic insight into sexual tortures at the time: "Terrible were the methods of torture they devised in their quest for food. They stuffed bitter vetch up the genital passages of their victims, and drove sharp stakes into their seats" (*War*, V. 435). Although the actual historicity of Josephus' claims can hardly be taken for granted (since Josephus was writing for a Roman audience and his exaggerations and vested interest in casting the Jewish rebels in a poor light affects his testimony throughout his account), it nonetheless suggests that the sexualized tortures of twentieth-century Latin America might correspond quite closely to their first-century Mediterranean equivalents. Likewise, Plato's description in the *Gorgias* of a hypothetical crucifixion (preceded by torture and castration whilst on the rack) indicates that castration might have taken place prior to crucifixion in at least some parts of the ancient world.[28] Furthermore, the historian Richard Trexler has claimed that the anal rape of male captives was "a practice notoriously rife in the ancient world."[29] In view of this background, it is important to ask whether the fraternal and respectful kiss of greeting in the Garden of Gethsemane might have set events in motion that led to some form of sexual assault in the *praetorium* of Pilate.[30]

The privacy of the *praetorium* makes it unrealistic to expect a definitive answer on what exactly happened inside. Nonetheless, the suspicions raised by the experiences of those who have suffered under recent Latin American regimes suggest that a question mark needs to be put against the completeness of the

---

[28] *Gorgias*, 473C, cited in Sloyan, *The Crucifixion of Jesus*, 16.

[29] Trexler, *Sex and Conquest*, 20. According to Trexler, "in the Ancient Greek world [...] the premier sign of male dependence was to be anally or orally penetrated by another male without, at least fictively, being able to resist", 33; he continues, "Seneca [...] declared that 'bad army officers and wicked tyrants are the main sources of rapes of young men'", 34. In this context, even the widely held assumption that the soldiers forced Jesus to wear scarlet/purple clothing for solely political mockery might be reconsidered. Dressing a male victim in bright clothing might also have been a prelude to sexual assault (cf. Trexler, *Sex and Conquest*, 34).

[30] This might also have implications for the question of why Judas had profound feelings of regret and repentance for his actions (Lk. 22:3-5; Mt. 27:3-5). Judas may not have anticipated the full implications of his betrayal and, if the argument here is correct, his despair and shame would be easy to understand.

Gospel narratives at this point. There is a possibility that the full details of Jesus' suffering are missing from the Gospel accounts. Whereas the texts offer clear indications of sexual humiliation, the possibility of sexual assault can only be based on silence and circumstance. However, it should be remembered that although a distinction in sexual abuse between humiliation and assault is helpful, there can also be considerable overlap between them and the two tend to go together. In sexual torture, sexual assault is a form of sexual humiliation *par excellence* and sexual humiliation often rests on the threat of physical or sexual assault. What form of sexual assault – if any – might actually have taken place may be impossible to determine but the possibility needs to be recognised and confronted more honestly than has happened so far. To shed light on this, further historical investigation into the treatment of condemned prisoners by Roman soldiers and the treatment of Jesus in particular is obviously required.[31] However, if further historical research is to be done, it is appropriate to pause and ask what positive purpose these lines of enquiry will serve.

When Did We See You Naked? Applying Theology to Practice

Given the concern in this volume for a theological response to trafficking and sexual exploitation, it is important to ask how recognition of the sexual abuse of crucifixion might contribute to an effective theological response to sexual exploitation. What difference does this past make to the present, beyond correcting the historical record? Adapting the question posed by Jon Sobrino, and other liberation theologians in Latin America, how might it help to "take the crucified down from the cross"?[32]

When the article on which this chapter is based was first published, it concluded with a brief reflection of avenues that theologians, biblical scholars, and churches might explore in response to some of the issues raised.[33] In particular, it identified Jesus' words in the parable of judgement in Matthew 25:31-46 as a biblical invitation to consider how acknowledgment of Jesus' experience might provide practical help to contemporary victims of torture and sexual abuse. It suggested that recognition of sexual abuse in the treatment of Jesus could bring a liberating and healing message to the women, children, and

---

[31] See David Tombs, *The Crucifixion of Jesus: Torture, Sexual Abuse, and the Scandal of the Cross* (London: Routledge, in preparation). On the Roman background, see especially: Judith P. Hallett and Marilyn Skinner (eds), *Roman Sexualities* (Princeton, NJ: Princeton University Press, 1997); Craig A. Williams, *Roman Homosexuality: Ideologies of Masculinity in Classical Antiquity* (Oxford: Oxford University Press, 1999).

[32] Jon Sobrino, *Jesus the Liberator* (Maryknoll, NY: Orbis Books; Tunbridge Wells, Burns & Oates, 1993); Sobrino, *The Principle of Mercy: Taking the Crucified People from the Cross* (Maryknoll, NY: Orbis Books, 1994); see David Tombs, *Latin American Liberation Theology* (Boston and Leiden: Brill, 2002): 280-81.

[33] Tombs, "Crucifixion, State Terror, and Sexual Abuse" 108-109; see further, Jayme R. Reaves and David Tombs, "#MeToo Jesus: Naming Jesus as a Victim of Sexual Abuse", *International Journal for Public Theology*, 13(4), (2019), 387-412.

men of Latin America and elsewhere who have also been abused. It suggested that the acceptance that even Jesus may have suffered evil in this way can give new dignity and self-respect to those who continue to struggle with the stigma and other consequences of sexual abuse. A God who through Christ is to be identified with the hungry, the thirsty, the stranger, the naked, the sick, and the imprisoned (Mt. 25:40), is also to be identified with those suffering abuse and torture in the contemporary world. For reasons of space, it is beyond the scope of this chapter to develop at any length the theological and pastoral implications of how recognition of the sexual abuse of Jesus might impact on a Christian response to sexual exploitation. Nonetheless, some of these opportunities can be briefly suggested, and many of these have been developed further in recent work.[34]

Victims of sexual trafficking are subjected to a wide range of degrading and violent sexual practices. Whilst it would be wrong to equate these practices in a simplistic way with the sexual torture of political detainees, it would be equally wrong to imagine that the mistreatment of prisoners by the Romans in the first century, or mistreatment under military regimes in the twentieth and twenty-first century, have no points of contact with violence of sexual exploitation. It is better to see these as different examples of a broader continuum of sexual violation and abuse.[35] Sexual violence in trafficking can take different forms, and it should be remembered that in addition to serving clients, victims of sexual trafficking are often subjected to other forms of physical and sexual mistreatment by those who control and exploit them.[36] In some cases, this mistreatment constitutes torture, or the threat of torture, or the forced witnessing of torture against others. The sexual abuse and torture of Jesus is therefore relevant to any theological work on sexual exploitation.

Furthermore, at a theological level, confronting the possibility of sexual abuse in the passion of Christ might deepen Christian understanding of God's solidarity with the powerless. Sexual abuse is a destructive assertion of power and control. It shows the sinful impulses and degrading consequences that distorted power can generate in human society. An important element in Christian doctrine has been that Jesus confronted the power of evil and suffered death on the cross as a result.

At a Christological level, this understanding of crucifixion offers insights into a fuller Christian understanding of a God who is in real solidarity with the powerless and suffers the worst evils of the world. An *a priori* judgement that Jesus did not, and could not, suffer sexual abuse may accompany an unexamined assumption that Jesus was not in fact fully human, a form of the docetic heresy

---

[34] See Jayme R. Reaves, Rocío Figueroa, and David Tombs (eds), *"When Did We See You Naked?": Acknowledging Jesus as a Victim of Sexual Abuse* (London: SCM Press, in preparation); David Tombs, "Confronting the Stigma of Naming Jesus as a Victim of Sexual Violence", in Clive Pearson (ed), *Enacting a Public Theology* (Stellenbosch: SUNMeDia, 2019), 71-86.

[35] On sexual violence as a continuum, see Liz Kelly, *Surviving Sexual Violence* (Cambridge: Polity, 1988).

[36] See, for example, the documentary on Svay Pak, Cambodia, *The Pink Room* (directed by Joel Sandvos, 2011).

which denies the real form of Jesus' physical suffering. Refusal to accept that Jesus *could* have been sexually abused suggests a refusal to accept Christ's full incarnation into human history. To say that Jesus could not have been vulnerable to the worst abuses of human power is to deny that he was truly human at all.

Another way to deny the true humanity of Jesus would be to jump quickly to resurrection so as to avoid the reality of crucifixion.[37] The crucifixion must be read alongside resurrection but this does not mean that the suffering of the cross is not real or does not matter. Faith in resurrection affirms that the cross is not the final word, but this does not mean that the reality of the cross can be ignored or sanitized. It is only when the scandalous nature of crucifixion is understood that the shocking good news of proclaiming Christ as both crucified and risen can be fully grasped.

The view of crucifixion presented here – that Jesus was a victim of sexual abuse in the sexual humiliation he underwent and he may even have been a victim of sexual assault – is disturbing. Some Christians may instinctively wish to dismiss and reject reading the texts this way, or deride this reading as offensive and scandalous.[38] It has even been described as blasphemous. This can make discussion of these issues difficult but it also offers a valuable opportunity for learning. It is important to ask what might lie behind this resistance and these reactions. Part of the answer is likely to be a lack of familiarity with both the biblical texts and the cruelty of Roman punishments. There has been reinforced by an over-reliance on the highly sanitized version of crucifixion which has been handed down over the centuries, especially through Christian art. However, the strong reactions that the idea often provokes suggests that it is not just a lack of familiarity. Something deeper and more instinctive is going on. Responses to seeing Jesus this way often suggest a tacit assumption that, if Jesus was a victim of sexual abuse, then he is lessened by it. He is seen as less worthy of worship or devotion.[39] This response is not always expressed in an explicit way but it seems to lie beneath the surface of many negative reactions. This offers an opportunity for discussion of the stigma associated with sexual abuse and sexual exploitation and the ways that victims are stigmatized.

At a pastoral level, one of the benefits of exposing this stigmatizing attitude in relation to Jesus is that it can be examined and discussed more widely. People who are not fully aware that they might carry such negative attitudes to victims of sexual abuse can become more conscious of the complexity in their responses. Responses to recognizing Jesus as a victim of sexual abuse which are initially negative can thereby be used as self-learning opportunities for considering appropriate responses to sexual abuse more generally. The best learning comes when people discover this for themselves rather than just hearing it. Such self-learning allows for a long-term transformation in values and attitudes.

---

[37] Shelly Rambo, *Spirit and Trauma: A Theology of Remaining* (Louisville, KY: Westminster John Knox Press, 2010).

[38] Tombs, "Confronting the Stigma of Naming Jesus as a Victim of Sexual Violence", 84-85.

[39] Reaves and Tombs, "#MeToo Jesus", 407-12.

The project "When Did We See You Naked?" at the University of Otago seeks to understand how the recognition of Jesus as a victim of sexual abuse might provide support and resilience for survivors and also contribute to wider change within church and society. The project's interviews in 2018 with seven survivors of institutional church abuse suggest that four of the interviewees felt that the experience of Jesus was helpful to them, but three did not see it as relevant.[40] This suggests that although there is no easy or simplistic solution, there is nonetheless good reason for more work with survivors to discover more about how and why some survivors see it as helpful and some do not. This may also help to develop new ways to discuss the issue with survivors in ways that are more likely to be helpful.[41] Extending this discussion to survivors of sexual exploitation, with appropriate care and attention to safe-guarding and ethics in the research involved, would add a further dimension to this work and offer insights into what might work for survivors.

Perhaps the most important finding from these interviews is that, although the survivors themselves have different views on whether this idea is helpful them and others, there is a strong consensus that recognizing Jesus as a victim of sexual abuse is important for the church.[42] Survivors of sexual abuse often report experiencing negative and judgmental attitudes from other people, even though most Christians would deny holding them.[43] A bible study on Matthew 27:26-31 is currently in preparation to explore how the stripping of Jesus is presented in the text and the responses that readers have to this when they are encouraged to discuss what it might mean.[44]

---

[40] Rocío Figueroa and David Tombs, "Recognising Jesus as a Victim of Sexual Abuse Responses from Sodalicio Survivors in Peru", *Religion and Gender* 10 (2020): 57-75. It should be noted that the study is too small to draw any universal conclusions. Futhermore, the work discussed here is primarily descriptive (recording what interviewees reported) rather than prescriptive (offering our own suggestions), or interventionist (exploring a transformative change). Subsequent interviews with female survivors have also suggested a split between those who found it personally helpful and those who don't but, in this second study, the split was more in favor of those who found it helpful. See Rocío Figueroa and David Tombs, "Seeing His Innocence, I See My Innocence: Responses from Abused Nuns to Jesus as a Victim of Sexual Abuse" (Discussion Paper; Centre for Theology and Public Issues, University of Otago, 2020).

[41] See David Tombs, "Unspeakable Abuse and Forgiveness", *Doctrine and Life* 61(6), (July-Aug 2011): 16-27 (24-26) on the shame, anger, and self-blame which some survivors report.

[42] Figueroa and Tombs, "Recognising Jesus as a Victim of Sexual Abuse Responses from Sodalicio Survivors in Peru", *Religion and Gender* 10(1), (2020): 57-75.

[43] See Tearfund, *Silent No More: The Untapped Potential of the Worldwide Church in Addressing Sexual Violence* (Teddington, Middlesex: Tearfund, 2011); David Tombs, "Silent No More: Sexual Violence in Conflict as a Challenge to the Worldwide Church", *Acta Theologica* 34(2), (December 2014): 142-60. [Available at http://dx.doi.org/10.4314/actat.v34i2.9], [Last accessed: 11th October 2022].

[44] The bible study was developed in 2019 as part of a collaboration with the Ujamaa Centre at the University of KwaZulu-Natal, South Africa. See especially Gerald West, "Jesus, Joseph, and Tamar Stripped: Trans-textual and Intertextual Resources for

Conclusion

The dynamics of state terror in Latin America, and in other countries, can be a fruitful starting point for insights into the crucifixion. An awareness of human rights abuses in Latin America can yield important insights into the political context and full horror of Jesus' experience. The role of crucifixions in the production and maintenance of state terror and the element of sexual abuse in Roman practices require further investigation. The Gospels indicate a high level of public sexual humiliation in the treatment of Jesus, and the closed walls of the *praetorium* present a disturbing question about what else might have happened inside. This understanding of crucifixion offers an opportunity to develop a deeper theological response to sexual abuse and a better pastoral response to sexual exploitation.

Reflection Questions

1. Spend a few minutes considering what you have read in light of your work with survivors and any sexual humiliation or abuse you may have experienced yourself. What feelings and thoughts come to the surface? Please reach out to a trusted advisor if needed.
2. How did you first react to the idea that Jesus was a victim of sexual humiliation and may have experienced sexual abuse? How do you think other Christians might react?
3. Does your reaction offer any insight into the stigma that might be associated with sexual abuse and sexual exploitation?
4. How might acknowledging Jesus as a victim of sexual abuse have value for survivors at a personal level? How might it be important for others in the church? How might you utilize the insights from this chapter in a bible study with those who have experienced sexual humiliation and/or sexual abuse in a way that might be helpful for their healing process?

Works Cited

Boff, Clodovis. *Theology and Praxis: Epistemological Foundations.* Maryknoll, NY: Orbis Books, 1987 [1978].

Figueroa, Rocío and David Tombs. "Recognising Jesus as a Victim of Sexual Abuse Responses from Sodalicio Survivors in Peru". *Religion and Gender* 10(1), (2020): 57-75.

Figueroa, Rocío and David Tombs. "Seeing His Innocence, I See My Innocence: Responses from Abused Nuns to Jesus as a Victim of Sexual

---

Engaging Sexual Violence Against Men" in Reaves, Tombs and Figueroa (eds), *When Did We See You Naked? Jesus as a Victim of Sexual Abuse* (London: SCM Press, 2021).

Abuse". Discussion Paper; Centre for Theology and Public Issues, University of Otago, 2020.

Graziano, Francisco. *Divine Violence: Spectacle, Psychosexuality, and Radical Christianity in the Argentine 'Dirty War'*. Boulder, CO and Oxford: Westview Press, 1992.

Hallett, Judith P. and Marilyn Skinner, Eds. *Roman Sexualities.* Princeton, NJ: Princeton University Press, 1997.

Josephus. *The Jewish War.* Trans. G.A. Willon. Rev. Edn. Harmondsworth, London: Penguin, 1970 [1959].

Kelly, Liz. *Surviving Sexual Violence.* Cambridge: Polity, 1988.

Rambo, Shelly. *Spirit and Trauma: A Theology of Remaining.* Louisville, KY: Westminster John Knox Press, 2010.

Reaves, Jayme R. and David Tombs. "#MeToo Jesus: Naming Jesus as a Victim of Sexual Abuse". *International Journal for Public Theology* 13(4), (2019): 387-412.

Reaves, Jayme R., Rocío Figueroa, and David Tombs, Eds. *"When Did We See You Naked?": Acknowledging Jesus as a Victim of Sexual Abuse.* London: SCM Press, in preparation.

Segovia, Fernando F. "Jesus as Victim of State Terror: A Critical Reflection Twenty Years Later". In David Tombs, *Crucifixion, State Terror, and Sexual Abuse: Text and Context.* Dunedin: Centre for Theology and Public Issues, University of Otago, 2018: 22-31; [Available at: http://hdl.handle.net/10523/8558], [Last accessed: 11th October 2022].

Sloyan, Gerard S. *The Crucifixion of Jesus.* Minneapolis, MN: Augsburg Fortress Publishing, 1995.

Sobrino, Jon. *The Principle of Mercy: Taking the Crucified People from the Cross.* Maryknoll, NY: Orbis Books, 1994.

Sobrino, Jon. *Jesus the Liberator.* Maryknoll, NY: Orbis Books; Tunbridge Wells, Burns & Oates, 1993.

Tearfund. *Silent No More: The Untapped Potential of the Worldwide Church in Addressing Sexual Violence.* Teddington, Middlesex: Tearfund, 2011.

Tombs, David. *The Crucifixion of Jesus: Torture, Sexual Abuse, and the Scandal of the Cross.* London: Routledge, in preparation.

Tombs, David. "Confronting the Stigma of Naming Jesus as a Victim of Sexual Violence". In Clive Pearson, Ed. *Enacting a Public Theology.* Stellenbosch: SUNMeDia, 2019: 71-86.

Tombs, David. "Silent No More: Sexual Violence in Conflict as a Challenge to the Worldwide Church". *Acta Theologica* 34(2), (December 2014): 142-60. [Available at http://dx.doi.org/10.4314/actat.v34i2.9], [Last accessed: 11th October 2022].

Tombs, David. "Unspeakable Abuse and Forgiveness". *Doctrine and Life* 61(6), (July-Aug 2011): 16-27 (24-26).

Tombs, David. "Prisoner Abuse: From Abu Ghraib to The Passion of The Christ". In Linda Hogan and Dylan Lee Lehrke, Eds. *Religions and the Politics of Peace and Conflict.* Princeton, NJ: Princeton Theological Monograph Series, 2009: 179-205.

Tombs, David. *Latin American Liberation Theology.* Boston, MA and Leiden: Brill, 2002.

Trexler, Richard. *Sex and Conquest: Gendered Violence, Political Order, and the European Conquest of the Americas.* Cambridge: Polity Press, 1995: 22.

Williams, Craig A. *Roman Homosexuality: Ideologies of Masculinity in Classical Antiquity.* Oxford: Oxford University Press, 1999.

Sexual Exploitation and the Meaning of Authority

Glenn M Harden and Leslie Harley

The following chapter contains brief references to sexual assault, rape and suicide.

Introduction

This chapter explores the intersection of sexual exploitation, political theory, and biblical theology around the idea of *authority*. A biblical understanding of authority will inform our practice to end and heal sexual exploitation. From both the scriptures and political theory, we argue that authority is a relation which depends on trust, not coercion. We define *an authority* as an actor who has both the power to act (that is, freedom) and to originate and perpetuate meaning, and, because of these characteristics, has relationships with others who conform their beliefs and conduct to those desired by the authority. The Biblical understanding of all legitimate authority is rooted in the authority of God *which always uses creative power for the good of others (that is, love) and is willing to subject godself to suffering to this end.* Sexual exploitation is a perversion of authority where the authority is bent toward self-aggrandizement and domination of others. Moreover, this perversion of authority undermines meaning through its contestation with God's authority that has invited us into the story God has originated. In particular, we will see how the worldly authorities of family, church, marketplace, and state betrayed Leslie. We examine the scriptural portrayal of authority – both worldly authority and God's authority – so that we can better understand the relationship between suffering and the proclamation of good news, which not only offers healing to victims but calls human authorities to use their powers for the good of others. Finally, we conclude with some suggestions for Christian mission.

First, however, a word about who we are and why we write. Glenn is an American political scientist, theologian, and activist against human trafficking. Leslie, a Costa Rican, is a survivor of sexual exploitation. We want our conversation about Christian mission in the context of sexual exploitation to include both non-survivors and survivors. The good news we proclaim must really be good news, not just for the healthy, but for victims and survivors, so it is necessary to listen to their stories and learn from them. Herein, we will share some of Leslie's personal experiences with sexual exploitation. These stories are meant to illustrate the actual interplay between authority and victim, so that those of us who have not experienced these things might better understand these dynamics. Leslie is much more than the stories we share here, but, in this regard, is a *survivor* who brings to the church a perspective we who are non-survivor activists need to hear. Finally, we are also aware that our perspectives are still limited; Leslie cannot speak for all survivors, but only from her experiences.

The Meaning of Authority

The meaning of the word "authority" is contested in political theory. While it will not help us to wade in too deep into the debates surrounding its meaning, I do want to highlight a few concepts that we will use to define authority in this chapter. First, authority is a kind of *relationship* between two or more actors. Authority is part of the social world; it requires community.[1] Moreover, it presupposes a kind of *inequality* in the relationship: one actor possesses something that the other does not. Consider how the authority of the doctor for the patient depends on an unequal knowledge of medicine. Or consider the first authority in one's life: the one who teaches the child to talk. Authority here is an unequal relation between one who can speak and the one who must submit in order to acquire speech.

Following Hannah Arendt, the authority relation needs to be distinguished from both coercion and persuasion.[2] Authority is not just anything that causes obedience. The threat of violence does *not* make one an authority. Nor does persuasion, which requires appealing to a common authority – such as science or scripture – to succeed. By way of example, Arendt adds: "A father can lose his authority either by beating his child or by starting to argue with him, that is, either by behaving to him like a tyrant or by treating him as an equal."[3] Rather, *trust* is the foundation that calls forth obedience to authority. This trust may be derived from some common epistemological ground – a common understanding of science, for example, or it may be derived from a history of trustworthiness in which the one who is recognized as an authority has proven faithful and true. Consider Jesus' prayer at Gethsemane: "not my will, but yours be done" (Lk. 22:42). Here Jesus' expressed desire is to not suffer, but his belief in God's faithfulness enables him to conform his conduct with God's call to lay down his life, contrary to his immediate desire to avoid suffering. Jesus surrenders his judgment to God's authority and obeys. Note that by emphasizing trust and trustworthiness in the authority relation, we are de-emphasizing the language of duty and rights. Legitimate authority – that authority to which we owe obedience, and which has a right to ask for submission – depends on the authority's trustworthiness grounded in an experience of faithfulness in acting toward our own good.

The reflections on political theory briefly described above are part of a long-standing conversation that shapes the language in which the scriptures are written. But it is fair to ask: in what sense does the idea of authority described above conform to the expression of authority in scripture? Do the scriptures understand authority as a relation that depends on trust, not coercion or persuasion?

In scripture, the Greek word for authority is *exousia* (ἐξουσία) and has two main senses: First, *exousia* means *power over*, whether derived from the office or the internal characteristics of the actor. This power means that the actor is free

---

[1] Zambrano, "Authority, social theories of," 1-2.
[2] Arendt, *On Violence*, 45.
[3] Arendt, *On Violence*, 45.

with respect to the decisions that they can make regarding the thing or person over which they have power. The second sense of authority has to do with *rights* derived especially from creation or origination. For example, the potter has *exousia* over the clay (Rom. 9:21). This corresponds to the Latin word *auctoritas* from which the English words *authority* and *author* are derived. In Roman thought, *auctoritas* was grounded in the idea of initiating or perpetuating something – and that something is, at its heart, a story which gives meaning to people's lives. Roman *auctoritas* perpetuated the Roman tradition, the meaning of what it meant to be Roman.[4]

The concept of God's *exousia*, then, is not merely the raw power and freedom to control things, but, more importantly, this idea of being the source of all stories – the source of meaning.[5] At the end of Revelation, we find "Blessed are those who wash their robes, so that they will have the *exousia* to the tree of life and may enter the city by the gates" (Rev. 22:14). Here, *exousia* is normally translated "right", but let us clearly understand this as a ruling right – the right of the potter to do what he wants with the clay. The promise for those that wash their robes is that they, too, will have authority over life. This is an extraordinary promise, especially in light of Genesis 3:22 which declares that humans were driven out of paradise in order to prevent them from seizing the tree of life. The difference between the human relation with the tree of life (that is, with life itself) in Genesis and Revelation has everything to do with the difference between coercion and authority.

What of persuasion? Do we not see Jesus trying to persuade us to follow him? Jesus does invite us to share in the reign of God, but the appeal is to "come and see". We do need to learn that God is faithful and desires our own good, but the only one who can demonstrate that to us is God, so ultimately God's appeal to us is as *an* authority. When he teaches the scriptures, Jesus teaches as if he is the author of them – as if his words have the same authority. Indeed, the early church's recognition of the Trinity has everything to do with their experience of Jesus *as* divine authority, not an experience of Jesus as one persuading them that he was the Messiah by appealing to some higher authority.

The fundamental source of authority is creation, and creation is always linked to meaning. Scripture declares that God is the sole creator of all that is, that God is the Word (*logos*), and that we are created in the image of God. That God is so closely linked to speech – to language – suggests strongly that God is the ultimate source of all meaning for, without language, we have no stories, and without stories, no meaning. Consider how coercion through fear and violence seeks to silence its victims' voices: the abuser puts his hand over the mouth of his victim to keep her quiet. Leslie, in her experience of abuse, became used to shutting up. This is evil in action – it is the attempt to dominate the victim so thoroughly that their story is destroyed.

---

[4] Furedi, "Bringing Historical Dimensions into the Study of Social Problems: The Social Construction of Authority."

[5] For more on the connection between stories and meaning, see Harden, *The Sex Trade, Evil, and Christian Theology*; Stump, *Wandering in Darkness*; and Singer and Salovey, *The Remembered Self.*

But God is not this way; indeed, God wants to open our voices, to "sing a new song" (e.g., Ps. 96:1). One of the unique aspects of the Jewish faith was that God had called them into a story shared with God. God spoke and created the world. God spoke and created us. God spoke and gave us the Law. And then came Jesus who "taught as one having authority, not as the scribes" (Mt. 7:29). God is the one who rightly possesses authority and rightly demands our obedience. And Jesus came proclaiming that God's *reign* had begun.

This reign of God invites us to participate with God in God's story, to be who we really are – a people made in God's image, who are loved by God, and who also create and tell stories. Throughout scripture, those who submit to God's reign are promised authority to reign with God – we see this in the Psalms as well as in Revelation. We are meant to have and exercise authority, to share in the life of God.

But what does God's authority look like? This is a key question. For *we* are too apt to seize authority by force – that is, to use violence or the threat of violence to control others. This is not God's way revealed in the way of Jesus who received the blow rather than give it, although he claimed to possess the authority to call down a legion of angels. Jesus understood his authority – that is his freedom, power, and creativity – to require not domination, but suffering. God's victory is made possible by way of the Suffering Servant.[6] We will later return to the way of Jesus because the way of suffering is problematic for those who do suffer in that it might be used to perpetuate their suffering rather than liberate them. For now, considering the foregoing discussion, we define an *authority* as an actor who has both the power to act (that is, freedom) and to originate and perpetuate meaning, and, because of these characteristics, has relationships which call forth from others an obedience grounded in faith. Furthermore, the Biblical understanding of all legitimate authority is rooted in the authority of God who always uses authority for the good of others (that is, in love) and is willing to subject godself to suffering to this end. Through an authority's acting in and for our good, we come to trust the authority, and so the authority relation is legitimized. Where one who is in a position of authority rejects self-sacrifice or uses coercion to achieve self-aggrandizing ends, the authority relation is illegitimate.

Yet, it should be obvious that human authorities fail, at least partly, in acquiring this legitimacy through self-sacrificial love. Indeed, sexual exploitation demonstrates the betrayal of authority to its calling of love. We now turn to Leslie's story to illustrate how the worldly authorities of family, church, marketplace, and state failed her.

---

[6] See Bright, *The Kingdom of God: The Biblical Concept and Its Meaning for the Church.*

Sexual Exploitation and The Betrayal of Worldly Authority

Family

My parents were an abusive, absentee father and an abusive, authoritarian mother. Physical, emotional, verbal, and sexual abuse shaped my feelings and my mind during my childhood and adolescence. I was sexually abused by my father from a very young age, perhaps only two or three years old. According to the vague recollection, it was probably repeated abuse. I have no way of knowing how often the abuse occurred when I was such a little girl. But the abuse would reoccur each time my father returned home, so I have detailed memories of that horror from the ages of seven to thirteen years.

Why did I submit to my father's abuse? Why did I keep silent?

I kept silent because I loved my father. After he abandoned me for the first time, at three years of age, I began a lifelong search for men's love. I missed my father and, simultaneously, I feared he would come back and hurt me again. I longed for him and dreaded him. Today, I still carry the same hole and the same fear, although I have not seen my father in more than four decades and he is probably dead. As a young woman, I sought comfort from older men who gave me attention yet only wanted to use me. In the process, I learned that "love" was a painful and costly thing.

I kept silent because I was afraid. My body has its own memory of my father's abuse. It was a horrific experience, more than I can explain with words. I clearly remember the sound of my heart beating in a dark place. Since then, in the silence of the night, the sound of my own heart beating terrifies me. It is as if Death is there, standing ready to devour me. Even today, it is a trigger for panic attacks. Even today, I sleep with a light on. Every day since then, I have been afraid.

I kept silent because, as a child, I could not have told anyone, even if I had wanted to, because I did not understand what was happening. My father told me not to tell anybody about the abuse, he said that it was "our secret". And silence was a way of forgetting what happened, of putting distance between myself and the pain.

We have seen how authority is something distinct from coercion, but how could I have known what true authority looked like? For me, authority was always connected to fear. Sexual abuse deeply wounded me. How can I express it in words? It disrupted the trust I might have had in *any* authority. It has affected all the relationships in my life. It led to a deep distrust of pastors, other authority figures, other men, and God. I have lived my life in guilt, shame and unworthiness, for this was what the voice of my father said to me: You are worthless and unloved. And underneath it all, I have had a tremendous repressed anger, much of it focused on God for allowing the abuse to take place.

Before my father abandoned us the first time, he and my mother had a violent argument; they were fighting about something I didn't understand, but I knew it was about me. I felt terror and guilt. Today, the pieces of the puzzle are finally joined in their correct places, and I realize that my father's sexual abuse was the real cause of my parents' first separation. Yet, even today, my mother denies that anything ever happened, to my continued distress and frustration. Why in the face of one parent sexually abusing a child, does the other parent remain silent?

Unfortunately, there was no real emotional connection between my mother and my sister and me; the only emotions that seemed to be present were intimidation, fear, and control. My mother was a harsh authoritarian figure to be feared and obeyed rather than a loving mother. Like my father, the voice of her authority in my life was one of rejection.

Church

During high school, I had an intense spiritual life. Those days were a time of peace. Christ called me to follow Him, and I did. I went to school at a monastery, and there my soul found joy and hope. I was a respectful and disciplined girl, taught to submit my life to the sisters' authority; after all, they were God's authority to me. I especially gave my obedience to the Master Sister. I surrendered all my dreams, my desires, and my will to achieve the precious honor to be called the bride of Christ, his unconditional slave.

Then my father came back home again. I was on vacation from school at the time. Taking advantage of my mother's absence, my father raped me. This event blew my mind and my heart to pieces; I lost all my dreams. I didn't tell anyone what happened. I don't remember speaking about it to anyone at all, having made the conscious decision to never speak about it or how it made me feel.

The monastery was then not merely a place of peace; it became a refuge where I hid my deepest pain. Finally, my father left home for the last time, and my parents divorced. But the nuns would not allow me to become a nun as my profession due to a rule that disqualified daughters of divorce, considering them as lacking in qualities that made for successful nuns. For me, this meant God had abandoned me in my deepest hour of need. The church's voice of authority had rejected me and, at the age of 16, I felt as if God had rejected me as well.

The Marketplace

The authorities in the marketplace – those institutions that shape our vocation and our labor – were no better than family or church. Rather than offering me fulfillment, I was horribly exploited and trapped in prostitution for more than ten years. It began with a man I met in the university who deceived me and ultimately abused me. I was hungry for love, and I had learned well how to submit. I was the perfect prey for that man. He isolated me from my friends and family. He asked me to perform risky erotic fantasies for him. My brokenness was the key for him to take from me what he desired.

One night, he took me to a bar and told me to prostitute myself. I had been prepared for this, it seems, for my whole life. It was as if I was running toward that moment; all moments of pain, humiliation, and abuse were joined together, giving birth to a prostitute that unforgettable night: her name was Daniela. Changing my name was very symbolic and significant; it was not just to maintain anonymity. I hated the person who I was; I did not want to be Leslie any more. But over time, I would come to hate Daniela in the same way.

I became trapped. In Hesse's *Steppenwolf*, a book that has been deeply influential for me, the main character writes: "While out walking, Steppenwolf comes across an electric sign: "MAGIC THEATER. ENTRANCE NOT FOR

EVERYBODY. FOR MADMEN ONLY!"[7] As in the Magic Theater, my sanity was the price to enter into prostitution. Like the Steppenwolf, I was isolated and suicidal; my main conflict, as his, was my inability to separate myself from reality. I was living in two prisons simultaneously: my body and the world of prostitution. I hated them, but I couldn't escape from either of them. I was alienated and isolated. I was like the Steppenwolf: a loner, a castaway desolate at the mercy of the waves of an absurdity greater than mine. Even today, thinking about that time, I tend to lose my mind. Every night for all those years, I paid a high price to enter that bar where I prostituted myself; every day, I surrendered my sanity, dignity, identity, and freedom in that marketplace.

All of those around me exploited me: the guards, the managers, the clients. One night, I was with a client and, when I left the room, a security guard was waiting for me. He forced me to enter another empty room and asked me to do the same thing I had been doing with the client. And so, I learned on that day that we were observed by hidden cameras all the time. The guard hurt me a lot, and then threatened me, saying that nobody would believe me if I told someone what happened that night. Again, the silencing. I was helpless and assaulted all the time; I had no power even over my own body. I was observed on cameras like a circus animal. Every day, I was degraded more and more.

The clients had the power that money gives. Moreover, they had the powers of intimidation, manipulation, and blackmail. Negotiating the price for my body tore up something inside of my soul. It seems that buying sex is less blameworthy than selling it. The clients could remain hidden in their normal life. For me, leaving with a stranger and going to an isolated place was like playing Russian roulette. On two occasions, someone threatened me with a gun. On another occasion, a client nearly strangled me to death. And if this was not enough, I also survived two overdoses – one of which was caused by a client who put something in my drink; the other was my fault. Every client I met could be my death.

I am a survivor.

In the marketplace, I was for sale. The authority of money told me what I was worth – and to be sellable at all meant I was not really worth anything. Those that made money from us and those that bought us did everything in their power to degrade us, to silence us, to break us, to turn us into things rather than people.

The State

In Costa Rica, prostitutes do not have support in the law. If someone is caught working in prostitution without a health card, the penalties could include time in prison. The law punishes prostitutes for jeopardizing the public health – that is, the health of the clients. While prostitutes face the constant threat of violence and abuse, crimes against them are unenforceable. The duties and penalties point in just one direction, to the prostitutes. There are no duties or penalties for clients.

Prostitutes are especially vulnerable to police violence, as police officers can threaten victims with arrest or stage an arrest and then sexually assault victims. In theory, the police combat human trafficking, organized crime, and corruption. However, in actual practice, the police easily become another source of danger

[7]Hesse, *Steppenwolf.*

for prostitutes. Late at night, patrols frequently drive around night clubs, bars, and brothels. Not all police are corrupt, but some of them are sharks seeking prey. Some want money, so they ask for a bribe from underage girls, or foreign ones without passports, or Costa Rican girls without health cards, rather than taking them to jail. They have the power to decide the future of those girls. Women of color, drug users, and individuals with criminal records are especially vulnerable. Some police also want to have free sex as a price for the prostitute's silence. Police have impunity; even if the girl is underage, the police are not accountable for breaking the law.

When present, the authority of the state tells the victim that she is worthless. The law is not there to protect her. But her abusers are safe.

The Scriptural Admonitions to Respect Worldly Authorities

We have followed Leslie's experiences of the worldly authorities in her life – her family, the church, the marketplace, and the state. What we have seen is that at every level, the worldly authorities betrayed her. In English, one may be "*in* authority" and one may be "*an* authority". For the former, authority is something external to the actor – the source of the authority is the position or office. The claim to obedience is based on the office, not the person. In the latter, authority is something internal to the actor – the source of authority is dependent on the mutual recognition of some inequality, and the claim to obedience is based on this recognition, not the office.[8] Of course, the two ways of thinking about authority can be united when one is placed *in* authority because one is *an* authority. This distinction helps us see how those *in* authority may betray their calling to be *an* authority, as they did in Leslie's life. For Leslie, authority was always connected to coercive power and the fear that it generates.

Consider how these scriptural admonitions sound to Leslie: "Let every person be subject to the governing authorities; for there is no authority except from God, and those authorities that exist have been instituted by God. Therefore, whoever resists authority resists what God has appointed, and those who resist will incur judgment" (Rom. 13:1-2). And "children, obey your parents in the Lord, for this is right" (Eph. 6:1-2).

To one who believes that authority *is* a coercive power that produces fear, then God, too, is a coercive power who produces fear. If God commands us to obey these authorities to our destruction, then God is responsible for our destruction. This is a problem because it strikes at the heart of God's character. It matters because the "good news" may not sound good if it is reinforcing the voices of degradation like those that Leslie experienced.

Given our previous definition of authority, the reliance on coercive power to produce fear for the purposes of destruction is simply not legitimate authority. If one is *in* authority but acts contrary to one's calling as *an* authority, then one loses legitimacy. Illegitimate authority stands in sharp contrast to scriptural authority; indeed, it stands under God's judgment.

---

[8] Friedman, "On the concept of authority in political philosophy."

By betraying Leslie, by speaking what is false about her belovedness, and by seeking to silence and destroy her – ultimately to demean her very existence, the people and institutions in Leslie's life that were in place of authority over her, became instruments of raw power. They lost legitimacy. When the scripture admonishes us to submit to worldly authorities – even when it asks slaves to submit to their masters – it is *not* asking us to submit to raw, destructive power which is bent on destroying us.[9]

Admonitions to submit to worldly authorities do mean that these powers can operate as legitimate authorities grounded in trust rather than fear. Parents *can* teach and encourage their children. Markets *can* dignify labor. States *can* protect their people. And the church *can* proclaim good news to the poor. Inasmuch as worldly authorities accrue their power from trust rather than violence and operate in service to those under their authority, they contribute to God's purposes in the world and we ought to obey them. Yet, just as "an unjust law is no law at all,"[10] we must resist voices of destruction from illegitimate authority.

To show that God is not the greatest coercive power among a host of worldly powers, all committed to self-aggrandizement, and ultimately destruction, let us turn again to the authority of God as revealed in scripture, especially in the person of Jesus Christ.

The Authority of Jesus Christ

We find authority on every page of the Bible. The deeply rooted struggle against idolatry is a struggle over authority; the proclamation of the good news is an invitation to submit to God's authority. Central to the preaching of Jesus, the "kingdom of God", which Bright argues is "the total message of the Bible,"[11] is just such an invitation. Early in his ministry, Jesus read in the synagogue the passage from Isaiah: "The Spirit of the Lord is upon me because he has anointed me to bring good news to the poor; he has sent me to proclaim release to the captives and recovery of sight to the blind, to let the oppressed go free, to proclaim the year of the Lord's favor" and declared that this scripture had been fulfilled in him (Lk. 4:18-21). In his speech, he "spoke as one with authority" (Lk. 4:32), as if here, among us, had appeared the one who had the right to shape God's story, to give history its meaning.

How did Jesus use his authority? Women who were shamed and marginalized by society recognized in Jesus one who would not betray them. The woman who had been menstruating for twelve years was "unclean" and thus, unable to fully participate in society. She had faith in Jesus. Touching him should have made *him* unclean, but instead of doing so, the power of God healed her and she became clean. Wherever in scripture those who are shamed come to Jesus for healing, Jesus heals them and removes their shame. Note how the authority of Jesus also included power: power to heal, not destroy. The unclean are made clean. The shamed have their shame removed.

---

[9] There is, in this, the seeds to undermine slavery as a system, of course.

[10] Augustine, *On Free Choice of The Will*, Book 1, § 5.

[11] Bright, *The Kingdom of God*, 7.

The woman caught in adultery was brought before Jesus to judge her, to pronounce the penalty of stoning. And what a judgment it was! For Jesus told the crowd that the one without sin should cast the first stone. To their credit, the crowd then dispersed. But remember, there was one without sin there – and that was Jesus himself. Jesus had the authority and the power to cast the first stone and to destroy the woman. But what does he say? "I do not condemn you. Go and sin no more." Jesus used his authority, not to destroy, but to *reclaim* the meaning of her life and to restore her freedom to not sin.

Jesus lives and his work continues. Leslie tells of how Jesus found her:

During my last year in prostitution, I often wanted to commit suicide. The last night, in the bar where I had been working for more than ten years, I was desperately crying. I had decided to end my life. I clearly remember that at dawn, I took the phone to call somebody that could help to carry out my suicide plan. I dialed a taxi driver's number, but something weird and miraculous happened: the person that answered my call was not the driver but my sister Katherine. She had come to Christ a year before and had been praying for me as she knew that something really bad had been happening to me. When I heard her voice, I started crying and asked her to come for me.

That morning, I told my sister the whole truth about my job. (At home, everybody believed that I had been working as a receptionist in a hotel.) My sister took me to her pastor and after a prayer, I came back to Jesus' arms. God, in his power, healed me instantly from drugs, alcohol, and cigarette addiction, and from that morning until today I am free of those things and the desire to do them. Since that day, I devoted my life to Jesus. Since that day, I have lived in sexual purity. I dedicated my time to take care of my children, to serve God, to do my job, and to study theology.

According to my enemy's plan, according to all the voices of the so-called authorities in my life, I shouldn't be here right now. But I live, and I am a witness to God's power and love. I am an ambassador of God's goodness. I am a trophy of his grace. I am running on my journey of healing. Being alive is a precious gift of God's grace.

The Problem of the Suffering Servant for the Suffering

In defining a biblical view of authority, we have argued that Jesus models authority in his role as the Suffering Servant. Rather than using coercive power to destroy us for our sin, Jesus lets the coercive power break across him. He receives the blow so that we might not. And he calls us to be like him; to take up our cross and follow him.

One difficulty with the idea of the Suffering Servant whom we are to emulate is the question it raises about the suffering of the victim of sexual exploitation. If God the Father demands that his Son be abused, then what are we to say to the victim of abuse? Should we recommend that they endure their abuse, as Jesus did?

Absolutely not.

First, whatever we make of the atoning sacrifice of Jesus, if we believe that the gospel is to proclaim continued captivity and torture, then we have clearly misunderstood it.

Second, and especially pertinent here, Jesus suffered and died, not as one without power, but as the rightful and authoritative King.[12] What Jesus is exemplifying for us is not how the oppressed should endure, but *how rightful authority should act*. That is, legitimate authority is willing to sacrifice itself on behalf of its people. The death of Jesus is a judgment on the earthly powers who executed him – it demonstrates their illegitimacy. It shows them to be idols and false gods, those who depend on fear. Yet at the same time, it shows them what they might become. And, indeed, many in authority do act in self-giving, even self-sacrificial ways on behalf of their people – not only do stories of parents risking or sacrificing their lives for their children abound, but many of our most admired heroes were people in authority who gave their lives on behalf of others, people like Martin Luther King, Jr or Raoul Wallenberg.

When Jesus promises that we who follow him will be made rulers with him, we must understand that we will rule in the manner of Christ, not in the manner of the world. Our ruling authority will go hand in hand with obedience in self-giving love. To those of us who have authority and wish to follow the way of Christ, this means we must choose the path of suffering for and with the oppressed.

Does this mean that the suffering of the victim is not also found in the suffering of Jesus? No. The suffering of Jesus does many things, and one of those is that it hallows all suffering. Remember, the promise of Christ is that we might have authority over the tree of life. That is, all that we suffered – all that was destroyed – might be brought to life and might be incorporated into the great story of God. What was dead can be made alive again in Christ.

And what of the survivor? The one who has suffered – are they called to enter the suffering of others? Are they called to now act with authority to proclaim good news to the captive and to suffer on their behalf even though their own journey has been one of suffering?

God can and does call survivors into this work. As a survivor, Leslie writes: First, I can share with the oppressed a common understanding of what it means to be trapped in the sexual-exploitation world and the deep suffering of this kind of slavery. I am one who can gain the trust of the victims because of my own suffering. And *because I have suffered*, I can humbly speak with authority to their situation. Second, I am a witness of God's redemption. I am a living miracle. I am no longer a slave, but God's child. I can be the voice of the silenced victims. I can show how God's love has broken the silence. As a witness, I can tell others of God's divine and precious mercies and of the power of his love to cleanse, deliver, heal, and comfort the tormented soul. My testimony is part of the great story of God, and my life has meaning in the calling to help the oppressed through sacrificial love. God made a way for me to pass on to the other side of the abyss. Now, I can be a bridge between the victims and God's hand extended through ministries which are working with the victims.

---

[12] Wright, *How God Became King.*

God sends broken people to proclaim good news. Consider the Samaritan woman at the well: she was a shamed woman, although we know not the source of her shame. Jesus, a good Jew, should not have been speaking to her. Yet Jesus struck up a conversation with her that is extraordinary for its theological sophistication. By the end, the woman – who had been shamed – becomes a missionary, preparing the way for the good news of Jesus Christ.

Yet Leslie again: What if I am not ready to help others? What if I'm never ready? What if I commit suicide? I have a fear of failure, a fear of disappointing God. Being a survivor in this life means walking in that space between healing and brokenness, between the "now" and "not yet" of the kingdom of God. Being a survivor is not about what one feels, but what one has endured. Sometimes, the concept of "survivor" can paint a misleading picture of victimhood and healing, silently promoting a vision of superhumans who have overcome their traumas and surpassed their overwhelming anguish to proudly proclaim that they're not defined by their past traumatic events. But, having passed through a deadly peril, a survivor fully understands their precarity and their fragility. They may never feel safe again in this life. The awareness of the proximity of death may continue to threaten the meaning of their life.

The Apostle Paul was a survivor, declaring to the Corinthians that he and his companions had been "utterly, unbearably crushed", and that they had "despaired of life". And while they were delivered from one peril, they remained in danger and were deeply conscious of their weakness, depending on God to "continue to rescue" them.[13] Jesus, too, is a survivor – the one who died and rose again. His broken body was healed, and his scars took on new meaning. The resurrection is therefore good news for the survivor because it offers hope that we will be saved even in our uttermost weakness – in death. Nor will death continue to threaten the meaning of our lives; death loses its sting. But on this side of resurrection, the survivor walks in between two deaths – the death from their past trauma and their future physical death. The scripture promises healing and salvation, but the fulfillment of this promise is in the future. So, we find that many survivors vacillate between proclaiming the gospel of hope and being overwhelmed by their trauma in despair. Others may find this inconstancy so troubling that, like Job's friends, they would prefer that survivors "stick to the script" of one who overcomes. In so doing, the non-survivor demonstrates an unwillingness to suffer with the suffering survivor. Despite the threat that unhealed trauma of another may pose to our faith, we ought to help the survivor carry their burdens and let their help carry our own. In this way, together, we better approximate how rightful authority acts when it suffers for and with others.

In our final section, we explore the implications of our theological reflection on authority for our mission to victims of sexual exploitation.

---

[13] 2 Corinthians 1:8-11. NRSV.

Implications for Mission

Our reflections on political theory and theology are meant to inform our practice. If what we have presented here is true, then what does that suggest for our engagement with the worldly authorities and their victims?

First, let us recognize that victims may misunderstand authority. Given a history of abuse, they may believe that authority relies on coercive power and that authorities – in families, communities, churches, and the marketplace – are self-aggrandizing and destructive. We have argued here that this is not what worldly authorities need to be, and it is not what God's authority is like.

This means that we in Christian mission to the exploited must act in the way of Christ and not the way of coercive power. The authority of the kingdom of God will not come through control or coercion, but through faithful presence and love, and a willingness to suffer with and on behalf of victims. We must not fall into the habit of thinking about victims as if they are things. They are people, beloved by God. One of the dangers of a "rescue" mentality is that we see people as objects to be saved. We need to resist the temptation to fall into patterns of self-aggrandizement. Our mission is not to make us feel self-important but to proclaim the coming of the day of God's favor.

We must call the worldly authorities to live in the way of God and serve those who are under their authority. Parents, teachers, police, managers, lawmakers, pastors, church leaders – almost all of us hold some authority. We must rule in the way of Christ. Our voices of authority must say what is right about people – that they are of infinite worth. We recognize that in many cases, the individuals who comprise the worldly authorities are not Christian. No matter. God's calling for them is still to reject self-aggrandizing power.

It is not enough to make the appeal of social change to individuals alone. We must also work for social change – for ordering the way society is structured so that markets dignify labor and states protect their people. Recall that the year of jubilee that Jesus proclaimed for the poor was a year in which wealth was redistributed; debts were forgiven; captives released; property returned to its original owners. Even though we do not bring about the kingdom of God – it is something God must do – the call of the kingdom means we are not listless or without hope. Using the wisdom God has given us and listening to the Spirit, we may call our society's institutions to act on behalf of the poor and broken, so that they are better able to fulfill their divine purposes. The church community itself ought to be a model for the world where the "first shall be last and the last shall be first." In many communities, Christians not only work to change social institutions from the outside, but also from the inside through self-giving, even self-sacrificial, public service.

Furthermore, we must be the church in submission to the authority of Jesus Christ. We must obey him. Jesus says our work is this: "to believe" – and this is not mere intellectual assent, but the work of the heart. We must trust that the work of Christ – that of the Suffering Servant – is indeed how the world is changed, how we are changed. It is so tempting to fall back on coercive power – to control rather than love. In Leslie's testimony, she spoke of how a Catholic order rejected her because her parents were divorced, and how she felt as if God had rejected her. We must not think that reliance on moralistic rules is a temptation for some Catholic orders alone. Indeed, too many of us in the church value just such a reliance on moralism – too many of us believe the poor deserve to be poor, believe the prostitute deserves their fate, believe that punishment and shame will make people better. This isn't the way of Christ.

As the church, we must ask ourselves: is what I proclaim today good news to the poor? Is it good news to the little girl who was raped repeatedly by her father? Is it good news to the victim of prostitution? To the drug addict? To the violent felon? If the answer is no, then we have somehow misunderstood the gospel. Instead, let us submit ourselves to the authority of God's reign, and let it shape our mission to the broken world.

Finally, we want to consider the role of survivors in our mission. As Leslie has taught us, survivors are able to speak with authority where non-survivor activists are not. As God heals survivors, survivors can become agents for healing. Our paramount example is Jesus Christ who takes what is broken and heals – we proclaim this about him whenever we celebrate the Eucharist. But just as the kingdom of God is both "now" and "not yet", we must walk in the tension between the healing that is and the healing that is yet to come. And please hear me friends: this is not a reality for survivors alone – for no survivor can bear it alone. Non-survivor activists must come alongside survivors and share the weight of the pain and the shame. Not only must we recognize that survivors continue to face crushing despair or social anxiety which can – in our minds – limit the effectiveness of practical ministry, but we must be willing to enter that despair ourselves. We proclaim the good news of Jesus Christ and the coming of his kingdom, yet we do so as a broken people, survivor and non-survivor activists together, who are sometimes crushed by the betrayal of worldly authority. Ultimately, it is a call to faith – to trust the God as revealed in Jesus Christ knows our suffering and will save us, that he who "will not break a bruised reed or quench a smoldering wick until he brings justice to victory" will tenderly love us, even should we take our own lives in despair. This frees us to love others without having to control them, but it also exposes us to doubt. And that is why we need each other.

Reflection Questions

1. Do you have a positive, neutral, or negative emotional response to the word "authority"? Whom do you associate with this word?
2. How have authorities helped you grow? How have they abused their power and harmed you?
3. Besides government and family, what authorities shape the meaning of our lives? When and how do these authorities encounter victims and survivors of sexual exploitation? What can be done to reform authorities that are harmful?

4. Can authorities act in the way of God by giving themselves for others? Can you think of examples of authorities that act in the way of God?
5. Is the message proclaimed in our churches good news to the victim of sexual exploitation? What messages of false authority and false power perpetrate the causing of harm and the experience of victimization?
6. How does your church exemplify the acting as an authority in the way of God? How does it call on other authorities to act in this way?
7. What are some ways in which individuals and organizations that care for exploited and trafficked people (intentionally and unintentionally) exercise authority in an unhelpful and ungodly way? What can be done to prevent this?
8. How can survivors be encouraged in understanding the true meaning of authority, both in recovering from the illegitimate exercise of authority over them, as well as in growing in their own realms of authority as people with value, worth, and dignity?

Works Cited

Arendt, Hannah. *On Violence*. Boston, MA: Houghton Mifflin Harcourt, 1970.

Augustine. *On Free Choice of The Will*. Indianapolis, IN: Hackett, 1993.

Bright, John. *The Kingdom of God: The Biblical Concept and Its Meaning for the Church*. New York: Abingdon Press, 1953.

Friedman, Richard B. “On the concept of authority in political philosophy”. *Authority* (1990): 56-91.

Furedi, Frank. “Bringing Historical Dimensions into the Study of Social Problems: The Social Construction of Authority”. *Qualitative Sociology Review* 11(2), (2015): 94-108.

Harden, Glenn M. *The Sex Trade, Evil, and Christian Theology*. Eugene, OR: Wipf and Stock, 2016.

Hesse, Hermann. *Steppenwolf*. London: Penguin, 2012.

Singer, Jefferson A., and Peter Salovey. *The Remembered Self: Emotion and Memory in Personality*. New York; London: Simon and Schuster, 2010.

Stump, Eleonore. *Wandering in Darkness: Narrative and the Problem of Suffering*. Oxford: Oxford University Press, 2010.

Wright, Tom. *How God Became King: The Forgotten Story of the Gospels*. New York: HarperCollins, 2012.

Zambrano, Eduardo. “Authority, social theories of.” Prepared, by invitation, for *the International Encyclopedia of the Social and Behavioral Sciences*, 2001.

KINTSUGI FOR A BATTERED SOUL: ENHANCING AND RESTORING HUMAN DIGNITY AFTER SEXUAL EXPLOITATION

Joni L Middleton

While volunteering with an anti-trafficking organization in Kolkata, India, I learned about *chai.* I am a tea drinker, and the fragrantly spiced tea and milk concoction could bring a smile to my face on the hottest and most frustrating of days. I would follow my nose or look for a small pile of pottery shards to find the nearest tea stall. The tea was served in small brown clay cups meant to be thrown on the ground after the tea was consumed, but I often took my little cups home to hold paper clips, coins, and flowers.

Through the years and in numerous training sessions, I have used those small cups to illustrate the way sexual exploitation fractures a person's dignity. If I throw the cup to the floor, it will break, but I don't have to leave the pieces scattered on the floor. I can gather them up and try to glue the cup back together. If I was in Japan, I could take the shards to a specialist potter to repair the cup with a method called *kintsugi.* The potter uses gold, silver, or platinum to fuse the shards together, creating veins of the precious metal across the original pot, cup, or plate. Rather than throwing the shards of pottery away, the potter repairs the piece, creating a new work of art. Often, the repaired pot increases in beauty and worth.

Kintsugi seems an appropriate way to illustrate the shattering of human dignity that occurs with sexual exploitation. During my first years involved in anti-trafficking work, I often heard individuals and organizations state that they were restoring the dignity of trafficking survivors. I heard the phrase often enough to begin a reflective journey into what we mean when we say we are "restoring the dignity of trafficking survivors."[1] I also recognized that I was daily interacting with individuals who described their dignity as battered, bruised, broken, and/or lost. It seemed that something needed to be restored and *kintsugi* provided a hope-filled search for me to explore dignity restoration.

---

[1] I have worked with survivors of trafficking for sexual purposes and survivors of sexual exploitation. For the purposes of this essay and the book's theme, I will use the term *sexual exploitation* rather than *human trafficking* or *trafficking.*

What Is Human Dignity?

When I began exploring our meanings for the phrase "restoring the dignity" of sexual exploitation survivors,[2] I had no idea that I had jumped into a contemporary quagmire of debate surrounding the term's relevance and usage in modern thought. In the past century, the advocates and activists for various issues have invoked human dignity as a validation for their positions on bioethics,[3] proselytism,[4] human trafficking[5] and especially, human rights.[6] The modern cornerstone for human dignity resides in *The Universal Declaration of Human Rights* (1948) where the Preamble and Article 1 establish "their faith" in the "dignity and worth of the human person".[7] This has resulted in a conflation and/or confusion between human dignity and human rights. The use of the term *human dignity* has significantly increased since World War II, but "the meaning and substance of the term [has] become vague and contested".[8] Ruth Macklin and Stephen Pinker, in their scathing remarks concerning the President's Council on Bioethics report,[9] called the term *dignity* "useless"[10] and "stupid"[11]. Professor Pinker says, "the problem is that 'dignity' is a squishy, subjective notion, hardly up to the heavyweight moral demands assigned to it".[12] John Witte Jr. states that the "concept of human dignity has become ubiquitous to the point of cliché – a moral trump frayed by heavy use, a general principle harried by constant invocation".[13] The popularity of using *human dignity* to describe the work against sexual exploitation only adds to its overuse as a self-evident and self-perpetuating term. The challenge for Christian practitioners and organizations will be to maintain a God-centric definition as the wider culture moves closer to a self-centric definition of human dignity.

Faith-based organizations and Christian practitioners have a unique opportunity to re-engage the biblical and theological roots undergirding human dignity and to apply their understanding to the development of dignity-infused policies and practices. We can counter Pinker's "squishy, subjective notion" of dignity with intentional reflection. Donna Hicks describes how an understanding of dignity and violations to dignity could resolve conflicts, provide safety, and create new opportunities to be vulnerable together.[14] Archbishop Emeritus

---

[2] Although I will primarily be referring to female survivors of sexual exploitation and sex trafficking, I do not mean to infer that men, boys, and transgenders are not sexually exploited nor that survivors of other forms of human trafficking (labor, organs, and reproductive purposes) do not suffer from indignity.

[3] (Kaas, 2002; Foster, 2011)

[4] (Bickley, 2015).

[5] (Lagon, 2008; Aston *et al.*, 2013).

[6] (Carozza, 2008).

[7] (United Nations, 1948).

[8] (Soulen and Woodhead, 2006).

[9] (Schulman, 2008).

[10] (Macklin, 2003).

[11] (Pinker, 2008).

[12] (Pinker, 2008: 1).

[13] (Witte, 2003).

[14] (Hicks, 2011).

Desmond Tutu, who worked with Hicks in Northern Ireland, says that dignity "made reconciliation possible".[15] Soulen and Woodhead reject the idea that we must "rely upon unexamined secularized notions of human dignity, or to reject dignity altogether as an unbiblical and therefore unhelpful concept."[16] Rather, we can see the "imperative [...] that those of us who follow Jesus reaffirm our biblical vision of human dignity in the face of confusing public discourse."[17] A rigorous reflection at the theological, sociological, and praxis levels may provide new opportunities for faith-based organizations and Christian practitioners to see the dignity of sexually-exploited people enhanced, invigorated, and healthy.

Thinking Theologically about Human Dignity

Archbishop Tutu describes dignity as "that inalienable God-given right of all humankind."[18] His statement reveals a deeper theological undergirding to the term that may include status or rank,[19] but also reveals its magnanimous origin in God. All humans have dignity. We carry that image with and in us. When we get it right, we reflect God's greatest characteristics of love, holiness, patience, truth, faithfulness, goodness, justice, mercy, grace, truth, and wisdom.[20] When we get it wrong, we look to ourselves and our own interpretations of who we are. We succumb to pride[21] and create an image less than what God intended.

Being created in God's image (*imago Dei*) provides a subset of characteristics which set us apart from the rest of creation. In fact, the Psalms identify humans as the pinnacle of God's creation (Psalm 8:4-8). We are eternal. We have free will and volition. We are autonomous. We think rationally. We experience our surroundings as separate from us. We recognize our own personalities and the impact of our actions on others and our environment. We may be a conglomeration of cells working together, but we recognize that we have existence and inherent value. Yet, we must recognize that our dignity cannot be separated from God creating us in His image. He establishes the worth of human beings. Our secular definitions fall short in their defining qualities of autonomy, reason, capability, and innateness because they are based solely in human existence. Genesis chapters 1 and 2 remind us that God intended humans to carry and reflect his image, not their own sense of the human image. When we forget that our image is from God, we err on the side of the diminished and marred image that sin's influence has left us.

---

[15] (Hicks, 2011).
[16] (Soulen and Woodhead, 2006).
[17] (Richard Stearns cited in Darling, 2018).
[18] (Hicks, 2011).
[19] Exodus 28:2,40; Job 30:15; Proverbs 5:9; 31:25 in the *New International Version.* Additionally, Genesis 49:3; Job 40:10; Habakkuk 1:7; I Timothy 3:4, and Titus 2:7 in the *English Standard Version.* The *King James Version* adds Esther 6:3; Ecclesiastes 10:6; 2 Peter 2:10; and Jude 8 to the list.
[20] (Wilkin, 2018).
[21] (Tinder, 2003).

Based on the early Genesis account of human creation, human dignity seems to exist within a collaborative and intersecting space between our identity as created in the image of God (the *imago Dei;* Gen. 1:26-27*)*, our placement in a family and community (Gen. 1:26-8; 2:4-25; 4:1-2), and our purposeful work (Gen. 1:28-30; 2:15-20; 1 Cor. 15:58). In each of these three domains, we carry and reflect God's character and image and develop our sense of personal identity and dignity. If we adopt an approach based on the inherent value of a human in his/her/their own interpretation and expression of humanness, we create a self-perpetuating and potentially narcissistic view of human dignity, reminiscent of the ancient Greek sin of *hubris*. Our formula for human dignity becomes "I am human; therefore, I have value and worth. I have value and worth; therefore, I am human." Rather, when our theological expression of human dignity is based and embedded in *imago Dei*, we do not validate ourselves, God does.

The contemporary quagmire about human dignity arises because the Edenic description of human dignity contrasts sharply with the impact of a sin influenced post-Edenic world. The first two chapters of Genesis portray and assume a God-based and God-created human dignity. Adam and Eve reflect their intact and unbattered human dignity in Genesis 2:25 when "the man and his wife were both naked and were not ashamed."[22] Unfortunately, Genesis 3:9-11 shows the quick devolution into shame and the first bruises on human dignity:

> But the Lord God called to the man and said to him, "Where are you? And he said, "I heard the sound of you in the garden, and I was afraid, because I was naked, and I hid myself." He said, "Who told you that you were naked? Have you eaten of the tree of which I commanded you not to eat?"

Consequently, nakedness becomes a divining rod for the state of human dignity in the biblical record. Numerous examples in Scripture identify shame and humiliation with nakedness to illustrate the indignity suffered after the Fall.[23] Before the Fall of humans and the entrance of sin into the world, innocence and unabashed confidence in God's presence mark a dignity-rich human life. After

---

[22] All Scripture references are from the *English Standard Version* unless otherwise noted.

[23] Noah cursed his son Ham and his descendants because Ham "saw the nakedness of his father" and did not cover him like his brothers did (Gen. 9:20-27). David's servants suffered humiliation when Hanun sent them home with half their beards shaved and their garments cut to expose their hips (2 Sam. 10:4-5; 1 Chron. 19:4). Isaiah walked "naked and barefoot" for three years to illustrate how Assyria would lead Egyptian and Cushite captives away from their lands (Isa. 20:2-5). When the chiefs of Ephraim rescue Syria's Judean captives, they quickly clothed "all who were naked among them" (2 Chron. 28:15). God includes nakedness in His threats and judgments for Israel's and Judah's disobedience (Dt. 28:48; Hos. 2:3,9: Nah. 3:5; Mic. 1:8,11). Idol worship is linked with prostitution and nakedness (Lam. 1:8; Ez. 16:7, 22, 36-37; 18:7, 16; 23:10, 18, 29). God includes the covering up of nakedness as a righteous act in the true fast (Isa. 58:7; see also Mt. 25:35-46). Jesus includes clothing the naked as an element of inheriting the kingdom of God (Mt. 25:34-40). Robes of righteousness washed in the blood of Jesus become the only adequate way to cover the shame and humiliation of post-Edenic nakedness (Job 29:14; Rev. 7:9-14; 22:14).

the Fall, the association of shame, embarrassment, and humiliation with nakedness clearly identifies the damage rendered to human dignity.

God also created the first humans to live together. He says that "it is not good for Adam to be alone" (Gen. 2:18), so he makes an *ezer* (a strong helper, a warrior companion).[24] Eve becomes Adam's companion and confidante, joining him in the Garden of Eden to exist, live, and work together in harmony and purpose. Together, they experience themselves, each other, their environment, and God in wholeness and without impediment. The Bible clearly states their nakedness is without shame. They are healthy and whole. They share intimacy with each other and with God. They work together to maintain and expand God's creation. Genesis 1:29 says that God specifically tells them to multiply, fill the earth, and subdue it. In the first chapters of Genesis and in the Garden of Eden, we see two humans living with a healthy identity, intimate relationships, and purposeful work. Their dignity is intact.

Unfortunately, the events of Genesis 3 happen. Satan, in the form of a serpent, appears to Eve and asks her, "Did God really say [...]?" From that moment forward in the biblical record, we see humanity in a fallen state. Sin has entered their existence and radically changed their sense of themselves, each other, the environment, and God. That space where they knew no shame is gone. The effect of that moment and decision alters their reality. They are ashamed to be themselves in the presence of God and try to hide from him. The rest of the biblical record identifies the resultant battering and bruising that human dignity suffers. Sins abound. Atrocities occur. Hiding from God's presence becomes normalized.

Into this normalized human experience of indignity, Christ enters bearing His divinity and his humanity. Matthew records the angel's message to Joseph that Mary's child was Holy Spirit-conceived and would save people from their sins (Mt. 1:19-21). Paul declares that Christ came "while we were still sinners" and died for us (Rom. 5:8). Humanity did not have to "clean up their act" before God's plan of redemption would unfold. Rather, Matthew highlights in his genealogy how Christ came into the midst of people bearing battered and bruised dignities from the effects of sin.[25] Survivors of sexual exploitation would especially understand the indignities and alienation the five women included in Matthew's genealogy experienced: Tamar who disguised herself as a temple

---

[24] The concept of the *ezer* could be an empowering Bible study to do with female survivors. For women and girls who have been subjugated in sexual exploitation, the strong military imagery associated with the *ezer* could be empowering and inspiring to their self-identity as created in the image of God. For male sex buyers, the imagery and study could help to reawaken a sense of co-operation and partnership with females rather than oppressive domination. See the following books by Carolyn Custis James: *The Gospel of Ruth, Half the Church,* and *When Life and Beliefs Collide* for a theological study and application of the concept of the *ezer*.

[25] Editor's Note: the chapter by Crawford and Lippincott elsewhere in this volume examines the story of Rahab and the inclusion of these 5 women in Jesus' genealogy.

prostitute to bear a son for the family (Gen. 38)[26], Rahab the prostitute hiding the spies in her inn (Joshua 2), Ruth the Moabite widow gleaning in the fields for food, needing protection from the men (Ruth 2:8-9), Bathsheba who was summoned to King David's bedroom (2 Sam. 11), and Mary who conceived a child outside marriage (Mt. 1:18-25). These women suffered indignity but, later in the same chapter (Mt. 1:23), Matthew presents Jesus as both Savior and Immanuel (God with us).

The gospels clearly present Jesus Christ as the perfect, walking-around image of God who is both divine and human. Throughout His story, Jesus interacts with people who carry marred images of God and whose dignity bears many scars and bruises. His earthly parents are a carpenter and his young fiancée. Shepherds are the first visitors to Jesus' baby crib. His travelling crew includes fishermen, a tax collector, a Zealot, some Roman women, common village people, children, and possibly a formerly prostituted woman. He spends enough time with people of less esteem that he's criticized for being "a glutton and a drunkard, a friend of tax collectors and sinners!" (Lk. 7:34). He heals men, women, and children of blindness, deafness, bleeding issues, leprosy, demons, a fever, and even death. He feeds people who have travelled to hear him speak. He saves a woman from a public stoning for adultery. He waits at a well to meet the Samaritan woman. He shows no preference for high-ranking Jews over other Jews, Samaritans, and Romans, nor adults over children. He treats people with kindness and respect. He lives a dignity-rich and dignity-enriching life, but then he suffers the greatest indignity of his day – betrayal, public beating,[27] dragging a cross through the streets of Jerusalem, mockery, and crucifixion. As he is dying, he experiences alienation and cries out, "My God, my God, why have you forsaken me?" (Mt. 27:46). Women announce his resurrection. He appears to travellers on the road to Emmaus and then to his disciples hiding from the authorities.

Jesus Christ's encounters with people reveals his ability to make people feel welcomed and valued, to return vulnerable people to their faith community and families, and to transform laborers into purpose-filled workers (Jn. 21:15; Acts 1-4). Each time, he interacts with a leper or a tax collector, he gives a glimpse into the restoration of human dignity through his compassion. The woman caught in adultery stands up and walks away from her accusers. The Good Samaritan reflects the image of God to the beaten and injured Jewish traveler on the road to Jericho. The Prodigal Son realizes he has a better life in his father's house. The Gadarene tomb-dweller, the lepers, the Samaritan woman at the well, and the woman with the issue of blood realize they can return to a belonging life in their communities. The Son of God as Son of Man shows us how to treat one another with dignity and how a battered dignity can be restored.

---

[26] Normally, I would not use the term "prostitute" to identify a person, but it highlights the cultural indignity these women suffered.

[27] David Tombs (1999) draws comparisons between the trial and crucifixion procedures of Jesus Christ with those of historical Roman and contemporary Latin American prisoners. Survivors of sexual exploitation would certainly understand the sexual humiliation of Jesus standing naked or in minimal undergarments during the trial and crucifixion.

Paul's message continues developing a Christology around the crucified Savior and the unifying Lord. In Romans and Galatians, he describes the impact of sin on humans and their dignity, emphasizing how it separates them from God and changes how they reflect God's image through "debased minds" (Rom. 1:28-32) and the "works of the flesh" (Gal. 5:19-21). The indignities that humans experience because of their sin-influenced world are changed with the death of Christ. Through the death and resurrection of Christ and the transforming power of the Holy Spirit, humans can once again reflect God's image back to Him and to their fellow human beings in a healthy manner through the fruit of the Spirit and righteous living.

Paul also identifies the unifying nature of Christ in that humans are all sinful and in need of Christ. The new faith community demonstrates renewed and transformed relationships in their fellowship with one another (Acts 4:42-46). Paul describes their unity in Christ in Galatians 3:26-29:

> [...] in Christ Jesus you are all sons of God, through faith. For as many of you as were baptized into Christ have put on Christ. There is neither Jew nor Greek, there is neither slave nor free, there is no male and female, for you are all one in Christ Jesus. And if you are Christ's, then you are Abraham's offspring, heirs according to promise.

Not only does Christ save people from their sins and provide a path away from the indignities those sins cause, but He wipes out the boundaries and distinctions that divide people from one another. Humans are no longer slaves but free sons and heirs through the work of Christ (Gal. 4:6-7). Their union in Christ empowers them to live a new and transformed life (Gal. 5:1). The redemptive and salvific work of Jesus makes the restoration of human dignity possible.

The Impact of Sexual Exploitation on Human Dignity

There is a growing body of research[28] identifying the physical, psychological, social, and spiritual impact of sexual exploitation on human beings. Beyond the obvious impact of sexually transmitted illnesses, sexually exploited individuals endure sleep and food deprivation, inadequate shelter and clothing, little access to healthcare, and the social isolation of stigma and traumatic relationships. Many victims describe grooming behaviors and a long list of dignity violations which diminish their sense of autonomy and volition occurring before, at the onset of and throughout their sexual exploitation.[29] Within the understanding of human dignity as existing in a conjoined space between being created in the image of God, experiencing mutuality and companionship in family and social relationships, and expressing gifts, talents, skills, and abilities through purposeful work, we see three significant impacts of sexual exploitation on a

---

[28]See Farley's research at https://prostitutionresearch.com/?sfid=5318&_sfm_author=Melissa%20Farley /; Miller, 2007; Greenbaum, 2015; Ottisova, 2016; Litam, 2017.

[29] (Long, 2014).

person's dignity: a diminished personhood, fractured relationships, and degraded work.

Diminished Personhood through Objectification and Dehumanization

Immanuel Kant argued that humans are an end not a means. Yet, at its core, sexual exploitation contends that humans are a means and an object. Sexual exploitation takes a human person, and in Pygmalion fashion, reshapes her into the image desired in prostitution and pornography. Pimps or madams may prescribe a "uniform" for identification purposes or to play a role. In one area of Paris, Chinese women in street prostitution wear black dresses with stilettos and long black hair. On a road in Madrid, a pimp dresses his youngest girls in a bra, thong, and stilettos (even in frigid weather). In Kolkata, the teenaged girls of certain brothels wear t-shirts and jeans. In Anchorage, escort services advertise role-playing activities with specific costumes. The wardrobe, makeup, hair color, grooming, and body enhancements (through hormones, injections, and/or surgeries) are used to diminish the exploited person to a sexually-enhanced object or a fantasy role.[30]

Dehumanization and objectification are further advanced through the power imbalances inherent in sexual exploitation. Farley describes the imbalance where sex buyers have both the "social and economic power to hire" a prostituted individual (Farley 2003).[31] She loses her volition and autonomy when the goal of sexual exploitation "is to ensure that one person does *not* use her personal desire to determine which sexual acts do and do not occur – while the other person acts on the basis of his personal desire."[32] The objectification and dehumanization of the prostituted woman maintains an inequality of sexuality in prostitution and pornography, reducing her to "a sexualized puppet" or a "sex toy".[33]

Through the processes of grooming, costuming, and domination, the exploited person loses a large part of her identity and potentiality. Confiscated identity documents and changed personal details (name, age, appearance, hometown, nationality, and social media passwords) bolster the pimp's control, eradicating her "sense of personal identity".[34] Jones concludes that the process of dehumanization and control "leaves victims stripped of their natural personalities, and with no sense of identity other than being a woman who cannot trust, cannot control her anger and cannot understand life without abuse". One American survivor recounted, "I never knew the person I could be."[35] The garish recreation of the exploited person to reflect the ideals and fantasies of sex buyers seeks to usurp and diminish her reflection of God and his character. Her enlarged

---

[30] Prostituted transgender people maintain a rigorous regimen which may include any combination and repetition of hormone replacement, waxing, skin treatments, hair extensions, collagen implants, cosmetic surgeries, and sex reassignment surgery.

[31] (Farley, 2003).

[32] (Farley, 2003, citing Davidson, 1998).

[33] (Farley, 2003; Friedman, 2005).

[34] (Jones, 2009).

[35] (Friedman, 2005).

and heavily altered body parts, gestures, and demeanor create a caricature of a human person.

Fractured Relationships through Isolation and the Intense Hierarchy of Pimps and Sex Buyers

Increasingly, humans, especially those in Western cultures, are living in isolation.[36] They make "friends" on social media, conduct video conferences, and work remotely, even before the impact of the COVID-19 epidemic. The breakdown of the extended family and the rise of two-parent incomes has increased both wealth and economic vulnerability. Often children are left alone to care for themselves, creating a social and relational void easily manipulated and/or exploited. Into that void, pimps expertly identify vulnerable individuals through a predatory method identified as the grooming process. Mariah Long (2014) identifies the basic stages of grooming as targeting a vulnerable victim, filling a need, isolation, beginning abuse, and then maintaining control. Isolation, the physical and psychological distancing of someone from their relational network, has a long and effective history of being used to break down the resolve of a person in order to extract information or coerce a specific behavior.[37] As more individuals face social isolation and loneliness in the wider culture, the exploiter can profit from the resultant vulnerability and then expertly use the isolation of migration, competition, violence, long working hours, and separation from the person's normal social relationships for their own exploitative purposes.

An exploited individual's social relationships are then further damaged through the hierarchy and power dynamics of commercial sex. The pimp, at the top of the hierarchy, enforces his power position through physical and psychological violence, demanding absolute obedience from the prostituted person and toward the sex buyer. Jones maintains that the goal of the daily rapes and beatings a victim may experience are "to wipe out any trace of resistance".[38] In the process, she loses her autonomy and volition, but combined with isolation and/or abuse, she also loses the normal familial and social relationships intended to protect her.

The isolation and an eroticized version of hierarchy allow sex buyers and pimps to enjoy a greater sense of "male supremacy".[39] The reduction of her sexuality and her sexual skill to an economic transaction obliterates the intimacy, consent, and commitment of a mutually satisfying relationship intended to help her thrive. She is no longer the *ezer* God created her to be. She is now a subordinate to be dominated.

---

[36] As I finish writing this chapter, I experienced France's mandated stay-home measures during the 2020 COVID-19 health crisis. It will be interesting to read the upcoming research on the impact of the enforced physical distancing on sexual exploitation survivors and the wider population. See de Jong et al (2006), Cacioppo et al (2011), and Biordi and Nicholson (2013) for the impact of social isolation on humans.

[37] (Lucas, 1976; Hopper and Hidalgo, 2006; Biordi and Nicholson, 2013).

[38] (Jones, 2009).

[39] (Davidson, 1998, location 3366).

Degraded Work through Commodification, Hazardous Work Expectations, and Human Rights Abuses

In 2008, the United Nations Office on Drugs and Crime (the UNODC) created a public service announcement called "Work Abroad," depicting an employment notice which stated the job's scope, characteristics, and expectations juxtaposed against the realities of commercial sex. The words did not match the images. Instead of a job providing a good salary, most of the money was returned to the employer. Instead of a safe working environment, employees had a dingy room with a single bed. Instead of meeting new people, employees met sex buyers. Melissa Farley's nine-country study (2003) illustrated the effects of this duplicity. The study's participants identified and exhibited the effects of commodification, dehumanization, hazardous work environments, and human rights abuses. They suffered accelerated levels of rape, sexual assault, and other acts of violence before and during their entry into prostitution. Prostituted women in her study experienced PTSD at the same or higher rates as combat veterans.[40] General health issues included STIs (sexually transmitted infections), menstrual complications, neurological problems, joint pain, gastrointestinal symptoms, and emotional issues.

Farley's study catalogued the physical and psychological realities prostituted individuals experienced in their exploitative situations. One survivor of strip club prostitution described a long list of behaviors which would normally constitute workplace infractions and human rights violations:

> The job required her to tolerate verbal abuse (with a coerced smile), being grabbed and pinched on the legs, buttocks, breasts, and crotch. Sometimes, this resulted in bruises and scratches on her thighs and arms and breasts. Her breasts were squeezed until she was in severe pain. She was humiliated by customers ejaculating on her face. She was physically brutalized, and her hair was pulled as a means of control and torture. She was severely bruised from beatings and frequently had black eyes. She was repeatedly beaten on the head with closed fists, sometimes causing concussions and unconsciousness. From these beatings, her jaw was dislocated, and her eardrum was damaged. Many years later, her jaw is still dislocated. She was cut with knives. She was burned with cigarettes by customers who smoked while raping her. She was gang raped. She was raped individually by at least twenty men at different times in her life. Rapes by johns and pimps sometimes resulted in internal bleeding.[41]

Another survivor states that she imagined her experience was similar to those who had been in concentration camps, describing it as a "real deep pain, an assault to my mind, my body, my dignity as a human being".[42] One survivor stated that "you just give them [the sex buyer] what they want and pray they don't kill you".[43] Most commercial sex survivors do not have the opportunity to report job-related safety violations or receive worker's compensation for their physical and psychological injuries. They are expected to continue working in

---

[40] (Farley, 2003: 37).

[41] (Farley, 2003).

[42] (Jeffreys, 2006).

[43] (Farley, 2017).

whatever conditions, under whatever circumstances, and with whomever buys sex from them.

Commodification reduces a prostituted individual to her economic status. She is a product to supply a demand, a part of the market structure where her only value is in the amount of money she brings to her pimp or manager. Her needs and desires are irrelevant to the market demands for sexual experiences and novelties. Rather than using her personal gifts and talents to do purpose-filled work, she must satisfy a long line of sex buyers. One sex buyer said, "For me, being with a prostitute is not a relationship. It's like having a cup of coffee, when you're done, you throw it out".[44] For a sexually exploited person, the three purpose-filled sexual commands God gave Adam and Eve in the Garden of Eden to "be fruitful and multiply and fill the earth" (Gen. 1:28) degrade to the realities of fulfilling the sexual desires and fantasies of sex buyers and pimps. She and the relational intimacy of sex become the consumable product.

What Should Our Praxis Look Like?

Good praxis[45] with sexual exploitation survivors usually conforms to a victim-centered, trauma-informed, rights-based approach. The blending of these approaches helps provide survivors with our best efforts to accompany them on their healing journey. An intentional look at human dignity and how it influences this blended approach, can provide a theological foundation for Christian practitioners and faith-based organizations to collaborate their victim-centered trauma-informed rights-based approach. As Christian practitioners, we acknowledge God's ultimate place in a survivor's healing journey. We encourage survivors to engage their unique healing journey because they are individuals created in God's image. God cares about them, their experiences, and their restoration to his intended purposes. Understanding trauma and how it affects survivors enables practitioners to consider a holistic approach to healing that includes physical, psychological, social, and spiritual restoration. Creating legal and social services to empower a survivor, helping her know her rights, helps her to see her value in the wider society. The interconnectedness of a survivor's identity, relationships, and work help create space where God can restore her dignity.

Enhancing and Restoring Human Dignity in Survivors of Sexual Exploitation

Unfortunately, the effects of commercial sex on a survivor have a profound influence on her perception of human dignity. She may not see herself as created in the image of God, but we can interact with her in ways that remind her of her humanness and her value. She can begin to realize that her dignity has always been there because it is from God and based in his character. Her experiences have not diminished her value in God's sight. Rather than starting with her victimhood, her trauma, or her rights, we start with God and his own character.

---

[44] (Farley, 2015).

[45] "Practice"; in other words, the Response part of our Triangle.

A focus on human dignity will also benefit our organizational practices and policies as we provide programming approaches that emphasize human dignity. Jesus said that we should treat others as we would like to be treated (Mt. 7:12); therefore, we can aspire to be "agents of dignity" in our work with survivors of sexual exploitation.[46] The example of Jesus imaging God in his humanity and Paul's description of the fruit of the Spirit provides a short catalog of the characteristics which can guide our interactions with survivors: "love, joy, peace, patience, kindness, goodness, faithfulness, gentleness, self-control" (Gal. 5:22). We must build a safe environment where she can embrace the healing journey without fear of indignity. The practitioners and organizations can model dignity-enhancing practices in their work, like confidentiality, ethical storytelling, and participation. Restoring human dignity is more about creating an environment in which a survivor can re-imagine and realize what her human dignity looks like in Christ.

Recognizing the Scars of Indignity

Donna Hicks (2011) has developed a dignity model for working with conflict resolution. She found that the "emotional undercurrent" that can derail negotiations was often "the result of primal insults to dignity". Hicks developed a model to help conflicting parties identify the essential elements of dignity: (1) acceptance of identity, (2) inclusion, (3) safety, (4) acknowledgement, (5) recognition, (6) fairness, (7) benefit of the doubt, (8) understanding, (9) independence, and (10) accountability.[47] Hicks also identifies ten temptations to violate dignity: (1) taking the bait, (2) saving face, (3) shirking responsibility, (4) seeking false dignity, (5) seeking false security, (6) avoiding conflict, (7) being the victim, (8) resisting feedback, (9) blaming and shaming others to deflect your own guilt, and (10) engaging in false intimacy and demeaning gossip.[48] Helping practitioners and survivors recognize these dignity elements and violations could counter the effects of dehumanization, commodification, control, objectification, and isolation.[49] Practitioners can use discussion topics, art therapy sessions, and prayer to help the survivor express herself. The aim is to decrease the amount of coercion, force, and manipulation she has experienced in order to increase her awareness of her own human dignity.

Belonging in a Community

In Carolyn Custis James' discussion of Eve's creation as the *ezer* Adam needed, she notes that Eve's gifts, skills, and abilities do more than add purpose to

---

[46] (Hicks, 2011).

[47] (Hicks, 2011).

[48] (Hicks, 2011).

[49] Practitioners could develop a curriculum and learning activities to discuss the 10 Essential Elements of Dignity and the 10 Temptations to Violate Dignity. The lessons could include a short Bible study, reflective questions, small group discussions, and/or counseling sessions to help a survivor regain a sense of her own dignity being restored. She may want to identify the violations to dignity she experienced. The goal would be to help her come to a place where she can recognize that she has value and can treat others with respect.

Adam's work.[50] Together, they build a family and community. We often speak of God creating humans for social relationships, but it goes beyond just having relationships. It speaks to the fundamental intent of God to create humans to thrive with a healthy human dignity. Individually, they could grow and mature into self-awareness and the ability to reflect God's nature. Corporately, their personal identity deepens and thrives in social relationships and work. Reflecting God back and forth in community allows a greater understanding of God and his character. Each relationship reveals a new perspective. Left alone, Adam would have known God well, but with Eve, his perspective doubled. With additional family members and then neighbors, their understanding of God grew exponentially. Living in community would not be simply an exercise in abolishing loneliness, but a deeper walk with God through both individual and corporate interactions.

After decades as a psychologist, Dr Larry Crabb realized his clients needed more than he could offer them in their counseling sessions. He recognized that the problem beneath their struggles and psychological problems was a "disconnected soul".[51] They needed a healing community, the church.[52] Dr Crabb wondered how local Christians could develop more profound connections with one another where "the truest part of one soul meets the emptiest recesses in another and finds something there, when life passes from one to the other".[53] If Christian practitioners and survivors do the difficult work described above in identifying dignity scars and dignity-violating behaviors, they may begin to embrace the mutual humility and vulnerability needed to create the connection Dr Crabb describes.

Our work must intentionally consider the impact of community and changing communities on survivors. Restoring dignity includes more than building empowerment, raising awareness about rights, and criminalizing perpetrators. A survivor's dignity must heal personally as she reflects God's image through her selfhood, autonomy, and volition. We help survivors "to stand on their own two feet," but not alone. Beth Grant reminds us that "independence is not the goal. Interdependence is".[54] A survivor's individualism must exist within a community, preferably a faith community where she can find a "'family that loves, supports, mentors, and disciples" her.[55] As Grant and Crabb suggest, she stands best surrounded by scores of other feet. She needs the solidarity, faith, skills, and relationships of others. Due to her numerous betrayals and separations from family and communities, she may respond with isolation and withdrawal, but the steadfastness and patience of practitioners and other believers reflect God's faithfulness and character back to her. Belonging cannot be optional. It must be essential.

---

[50] See Footnote 6 for James' discussions about the *ezer* in her books.

[51] (Crabb, 1997).

[52] Ryan Klassen (2008) suggests that it "is only relationality that provides an adequate foundation for the dignity of [...] humans" (p. 101).

[53] (Crabb, 1997).

[54] (Grant, 2014).

[55] (Grant, 2014).

Engaging with Purposeful Work

Work, and especially purposeful work, helps encourage a healthy sense of dignity. Not only does work involve social relationships and a community, it also allows humans the opportunity to reflect God's character through creativity, care, and intellectual stimulation. Miroslav Volf defines work as:

> […] honest, purposeful, and methodologically specified social activity whose primary goal is the creation of products or states of affairs that can satisfy the needs of working individuals or their co-creatures or (if primarily an end in itself) activity that is necessary in order for acting individuals to satisfy their needs apart from the need for the activity itself.[56]

In Genesis 1:26-31, we see Volf's definition of work in action as God turns the creation over to Adam and Eve to nurture and steward. Their work requires manual labor and intellectual organization. They make decisions and solve problems. They maintain the Garden of Eden to sustain their needs for food, water, oxygen, and shelter. Their work has purpose as it meets their needs and provides a space where they can interact with God.

One of the challenging areas for practitioners and organizations working with survivors of sexual exploitation is helping them to find adequate and sustainable work. Survivors who entered sexual exploitation as minors or refugees often experience an eruption in their formal education, requiring a "catch-up program" and/or language acquisition. The effects of trauma can severely impact learning, resilience, coping skills, and attention span.[57] In some countries, survivors have a criminal record, making the job search even more complicated. Assessing vocational readiness and providing access to services in job skills training, strengths assessment, catch-up educational programs, and business mentorships can help survivors nàvigate the complexities and difficulties of moving into a new job.

In 1999, I joined a local organization working with women and children in the largest red-light district in Kolkata, India. I spent ten years with that organization and in a network with several other organizations, two of which created businesses for women exiting prostitution. Freeset (www.freesetglobal.com) began in 2001 with twenty women making jute bags before expanding into onsite screen printing, organic cotton t-shirts, and fashion accessories. Sari Bari (www.saribari.com) started consulting and providing training for local organizations to make quilts from recycled saris using kantha stitching. In 2006, they started their own business, and added other textile items. Both businesses started with unskilled workers and provided the necessary training for their products. They soon realized they needed to provide other services. Today, Freeset offers literacy classes, childcare, budgeting, and debt management along with job training, and eventually, a full-time job. Sari Bari also offers job training prior to a full-time job and includes wellness checkups for the women, school

---

56 (Volf, 2001).

57 Trauma profoundly impacts learning which could slow down the process of transitioning to sustainable work. For research on trauma and learning, see Kerka, 2002; Janik and Daniel, 2005; Perry, 2006; Cusick et al, 2011; Carrion and Wong, 2012;, Middleton, 2015; Shapiro, 2018.

support for their children, health insurance, and retirement benefits. Both businesses have modeled practices which have impacted positively on the dignity of their workers in identity, community, and work.

Conclusion

Working with Donna Hicks to bring peace in Northern Ireland, Archbishop Emeritus Desmond Tutu says their "sense of dignity" provided success. He gives a description of how dignity undergirded and inspired their work bringing peace to a conflict zone.

> Dignity not only sustains but also energizes and enables. It accomplishes great things. If lifts the fallen and restores the broken. When the recognition of the good in the other is shared, it is the sense of personal dignity given that can bring peace to situations of potential conflict. People's awareness of their own dignity, their sense of worth, is the only answer to the inertia of an everyday life ruled by feelings of uselessness. How wonderful it would be if we all, every one of us, became agents of dignity, purveyors of the truth that this God-given dignity is the birthright of all.[58]

As Christian practitioners and faith-based organizations, we have an opportunity to think intentionally about the theology, sociology, and praxis behind a holistic approach to the restoration of a survivor's sense of dignity. Rigorous inspection and identification of how our practices impact a survivor's identity, community, and work[59] could help us develop more precise dignity-affirming and dignity-enhancing practices.

I started the chapter describing *kintsugi* pottery. Our Christian faith provides the foundation for our work and a shared experience with survivors. We are all broken individuals. We have experienced the salvation of Jesus to pick up those shards and put them back together to form a "new creation" (2 Cor. 5:17). We have known the times when we had no answers and had to step back to let God do what he wanted to do. Our experiences help us navigate with survivors along their healing journey. We have good practices to help survivors exit their exploitative situation, but ultimately, the Father's love, the suffering of Jesus, and the renewal of the Holy Spirit cement the shards of their dignity and ours back together. Together, we can reflect the image of God better as we work to enhance a survivor's sense of personal identity and value, surround her with healthy social relationships and interconnectedness, and renew her engagement with purpose-filled work.

---

[58] (Hicks, 2011).

[59] One of Miroslav Volf's statements particularly challenged me concerning the dignity of certain types of work. He discussed the dehumanizing aspects in some jobs where workers are denied freedom and creativity due to "tyrannical managers" (2001: 40). He illustrated the dehumanizing of creativity with assembly line work. "True, at the peak years of assembly line production, only 5 to 6 percent of the work force in industrialized nations worked on the assembly line. Yet it must be a cause of concern when a minority of workers is forced to perform, day-in, day-out, a few simple operations. Such work is an assault on human *creativity* and is dehumanizing" (2001: 39).

Reflection Questions

1. How do you understand the meaning and importance of dignity? In what ways can dignity be impacted by sexual exploitation? In what ways does dignity remain inherent/intact regardless of circumstances?
2. How practically can dignity be restored in how the exploited person views themselves? How can dignity be restored in how others view and treat the exploited person? How can dignity be respected in our practices as caregivers? In what ways do our programs and practices promote the dignity of survivors (e.g. agency, autonomy, protection)? In what ways do they diminish/undermine dignity?
3. Recall Donna Hicks' dignity model described in the final section of this chapter. In what ways can those elements of dignity and temptations to violate dignity have biblical and practical applications to our response to sexual exploitation and our interactions with survivors? How do we ethically build dignity-affirming relationships when our professional standards encourage maintaining an objective distance?
4. Recall Miroslav Volf's statements about the dehumanizing nature of certain types of work found in the conclusion to this chapter. What types of jobs, beyond hazardous and dangerous, might not be conducive to enhancing the dignity of a survivor of sexual exploitation? How can we ensure that our programming does not inadvertently cater to those types of work? What does it mean for work to be dignifying? How can we help survivors be better prepared to enjoy dignifying work?

Works Cited

Aston, J.N. and V.N. Paranjape. "Victims of human trafficking: a human rights perspective". *SSRN* [online] (22nd March 2013). [Available at: http://dx.doi.org/10.2139/ssrn.2237914], [Last accessed: 13th October 2022].

Bickley, P. "The problem of proselytism" [online]. *Theos Think Tank.* London: Theos, 2015. [Available at: https://www.theosthinktank.co.uk/cmsfiles/archive/files/Problem%20of%20Proselytism%20web%20version.pdf], [Last accessed: 13th October 2022].

Biordi, D.L. and N.R. Nicholson. "Social isolation. Chronic illness: Impact and intervention". [online] (2013): 85-115. [Available at: https://www.semanticscholar.org/paper/Social-Isolation-Biordi-Nicholson/67b7cf4a9d1aeacc000a11f617a4dda83e396256?p2df], [Last accessed: 13th October 2022].

Cacioppo, J.T., L.C. Hawkley, G.J. Norman, and G.G. Berntson. "Social isolation". *Annals of the New York Academy of Sciences* [online], 1231(1),

(August 2011): 17-22. [Available at: https://www.ncbi.nlm.nih.gov/pmc/articles/PMC3166409/], [Last accessed: 13th October 2022].

Carozza, P.G. "Human dignity and judicial interpretation of human rights: A reply". *European Journal of International Law* [online], 19(5), (2008): 931-944. [Available at: https://academic.oup.com/ejil/article/19/5/931/505548], [Last accessed: 13th October 2022].

Carrion, V.G. and S.S. Wong. "Can traumatic stress alter the brain? Understanding the implications of early trauma on brain development and learning". *Journal of Adolescent Health* [online], 51(2), (2012): S23-S28. [Available at: https://doi.org/10.1016/j.jadohealth.2012.04.010], [Last accessed: 13th October 2022].

Crabb, L. *Connecting: Healing for ourselves and our relationships – a radical new vision* [Kindle]. Nashville, TN: W Publishing Group, 1997.

Cusick, L., B. Brooks-Gordon, R. Campbell, and F. Edgar. "'Exiting' drug use and sex work: Career paths, interventions and government strategy targets". *Drugs: Education, Prevention and Policy* [online], 18(2), (2011): 145-156. [Available at: https://doi.org/10.3109/09687631003776901], [Last accessed: 13th October 2022].

Darling, D. *The Dignity Revolution: Reclaiming God's Rich Vision for Humanity*. [Kindle]. Purcellville, VA: The Good Book Company, 2018.

Davidson, J.O.C. *Prostitution, Power, and Freedom* [Kindle]. Cambridge, UK: Polity Press, 1998.

de Jong Gierveld, J., T. Van Tilburg, and P.A. Dykstra. "Loneliness and social isolation". In: A.L. Vangelisti and D. Perlman, Eds. *Cambridge Handbook of Personal Relationships*. New York: Cambridge University Press, 2006: 485-500. [Available at: https://pdfs.semanticscholar.org/67bc/66d9f7d27349de61b163bdddd8b6557d15ae.pdf], [Last accessed: 13th October 2022].

Farley, M., J.M. Golding, E.S. Matthews, N.M. Malamuth, and L. Jarrett. "Comparing sex buyers with men who do not buy sex: New data on prostitution and trafficking". *Journal of Interpersonal Violence* [online], 32(23), (2017): 3601-3625. [Available at: https://journals.sagepub.com/doi/10.1177/0886260515600874], [Last accessed: 13th October 2022].

Farley, M. *Prostitution, Trafficking and Traumatic Stress*. Binghamton, NY: The Haworth Maltreatment & Trauma Press, 2003.

Farley, M. "Risks of Prostitution: When the person is the product". *Journal of the Association for Consumer Research* [online], 3(1), (2018): 97-108. [Available at: https://doi.org/10.1086/695670], [Last accessed: 13th October 2022].

Freeset. "Who we are" *Freeset Website.* Kolkata: Joyya, 2020. [Available at: https://freesetglobal.com/about-us], [Last accessed: 13th October 2022].

Foster, C. *Human Dignity in Bioethics and Law.* [Kindle]. Oxford: Hart, 2011.

Friedman, S.A. *Who is There to Help Us?: How the System Fails Sexually Exploited Girls in the United States: Examples from Four American Cities*.

New York: ECPAT-USA, 2005. [Available at: https://static1.squarespace.com/static/594970e91b631b3571be12e2/t/5977b5ded7bdce9b3785afab/1501017567091/WHO-IS-THERE-TO-HELP-US-How-the-System-Fails-Sexually-Exploited-Girls-in-the-United-States-Examples-from-Four-American-Cities-.pdf], [Last accessed: 13th October 2022].

Grant, B. *Courageous Compassion: Confronting Social Injustice God's Way* [Kindle]. Springfield, MO: My Healthy Church, 2014.

Greenbaum, J., J.E. Crawford-Jakubiak, and Committee on Child Abuse and Neglect. "Child sex trafficking and commercial sexual exploitation: Health care needs of victims". *Pediatrics* [online], 135(3), (2015): 566-574. [Available at: https://doi.org/10.1542/peds.2014-4138], [Last accessed: 13th October 2022].

Hicks, D. *Dignity: The essential role it plays in resolving conflict*. [Kindle]. New Haven: Yale University Press, 2011.

Hopper, E. and J. Hidalgo. "Invisible Chains: Psychological coercion of human trafficking victims". *Intercultural Human Rights Law Review* [online], 1 (2006): 185-209. [Available at: https://pdfs.semanticscholar.org/faf8/80204a8b1e06f6107c0f1da51c2065041643.pdf], [Last accessed: 13th October 2022].

James, C. C. *The Gospel of Ruth: loving God enough to break the rules*. [Kindle]. Grand Rapids, MI: Zondervan, 2008.

James, C.C. *Half the Church: Recapturing God's global vision for women*. [Kindle]. Grand Rapids, MI: Zondervan, 2010.

James, C.C. *When Life and Beliefs Collide: How knowing God makes a difference*. [Kindle]. Grand Rapids, MI: Zondervan, 2002.

Janik, M.D. and S. Daniel. *Unlock the Genius Within: Neurobiological trauma, teaching, and transformative learning*. [Kindle]. Lanham, MD: R&L Education, 2005.

Jeffreys, S. *The Idea of Prostitution*. [Kindle]. North Melbourne: Spinifex Press, 2006.

Jones, A.A. "Post-traumatic stress disorder and victims of human sex trafficking: A perpetuation of chronic indignity". *Intercultural Human Rights Law Review* [online], 4 (2009): 317-354. [Available at: https://www.stu.edu/wp-content/uploads/sites/5/2019/04/4-17Jones.pdf], [Last accessed: 13th October 2022].

Kaas, L.R. *Human Cloning and Human Dignity: The report of the President's council on bioethics*. [Kindle] New York: PublicAffairs, 2002.

Kerka, S. "Trauma and adult learning". *ERIC Clearinghouse on Adult Career and Vocational Education*. 2002. [Available at: https://www.ohioteachered.org/Conference_Fall_2017/Presentations/ERIC_Trauma_and_Adult_Learning.pdf], [Last accessed: 13th October 2022].

Klassen, R. "A Review of God and Human Dignity – Edited by R. Kendall Soulen and Linda Woodhead". *International Journal of Systematic Theology*, 10(1), (2008) [online]. [Available at: https://www.academia.edu/2121625/God_and_Human_Dignity_Edited_by_

R._Kendall_Soulen_and_Linda_Woodhead], [Last accessed: 14th October 2022].

Kraynak, R.P. and G. Tinder. *In Defense of Human Dignity: Essays for our times.* Notre Dame, IN: University of Notre Dame Press, 2003.

Lagon, M.P. "Trafficking and human dignity". *Policy Review* [online], 152 (2008): 51-61. [Viewed 3 March 2020]. Available from: http://faculty.une.edu/cas/jgarrett1/110Lagon.pdf

Litam, S.D.A. "Human Sex Trafficking in America: What Counselors Need to Know". *Professional Counselor* [online], 7(1), (2017): 45-61. [Available at: https://eric.ed.gov/?id=EJ1159657], [Last accessed: 14th October 2022].

Long, M. "Basic stages of grooming for sexual exploitation". *End Slavery Now Website.* 22nd September 2014. [Available at: http://www.endslaverynow.org/blog/articles/basic-stages-of-grooming-for-sexual-exploitation], [Last accessed: 14th October 2022].

Lucas, E. W. "Solitary confinement: Isolation as coercion to conform". *Australian & New Zealand Journal of Criminology* [online], 9(3), (1976): 153-167. [Available at: https://doi.org/10.1177%2F000486587600900304], [Last accessed: 14th October 2022].

Macklin, R. "Dignity is a useless concept: It means no more than respect for persons or their autonomy". *BMJ: British Medical Journal* [online], 327(7429), (2003): 1419. [Available at: https://doi.org/10.1136/bmj.327.7429.1419], [Last accessed: 14th October 2022].

Middleton, J. L. *Trauma and learning in human trafficking survivors.* Springfield, MO: Assemblies of God Theological Seminary, 2015. [Unpublished item].

Miller, E., M.R. Decker, J.G. Silverman, and A. Raj. "Migration, sexual exploitation, and women's health: a case report from a community health center". *Violence Against Women* [online], 13(5), (2007): 486-497. [Available at: https://doi.org/10.1177%2F1077801207301614], [Last accessed: 14th October 2022].

Ottisova, L., S. Hemmings, L.M. Howard, C. Zimmerman, and S. Oram. "Prevalence and risk of violence and the mental, physical and sexual health problems associated with human trafficking: an updated systematic review". *Epidemiology and Psychiatric Sciences* [online], 25(4), (2016): 317-341. [Available at: https://doi.org/10.1017/S2045796016000135], [Last accessed: 14th October 2022].

Perry, B.D. "Fear and Learning: Trauma-related factors in the adult education process". *New Directions for Adult and Continuing Education* [online], 110, (2006): 21-27. [Available at: https://eric.ed.gov/?id=EJ760423], [Last accessed: 14th October 2022].

Pinker, S. "The Stupidity of Dignity". *The New Republic*, 28 (May 2008): 28-31. [Available at: http://www-management.wharton.upenn.edu/raff/documents/2009/Pinker_New_Repub.pdf], [Last accessed: 14th October 2022].

Sari Bari. "Learn more about freedom & opportunity" [online]. *Sari Bari Website.* 2020. [Available at: https://saribari.com/pages/mission], [Last accessed: 14th October 2022].

Schulman, A. "Human dignity and bioethics: Essays commissioned by the President's council on bioethics". *Government Printing Office.* Washington D.C.: The President's Council on Bioethics, March 2008. [Available at: https://bioethicsarchive.georgetown.edu/pcbe/reports/human_dignity/chapter6.html], [Last accessed: 14th October 2022].

Shapiro, S., R. Farrelly and M.J. Curry, Eds. *Educating Refugee-Background Students: Critical issues and dynamic contexts.* [Kindle]. Bristol, UK: Multilingual Matters, 2018.

Soulen, R.K. and L. Woodhead, Eds. *God and Human Dignity.* [Kindle]. Grand Rapids, MI: Wm. B. Eerdmans, 2006.

Tombs, D. "Crucifixion, state terror, and sexual abuse". *Union Seminary Quarterly Review* 53 (Autumn 1999): 89-109. [Available at: https://ourarchive.otago.ac.nz/handle/10523/6067], [Last accessed: 14th October 2022].

United Nations. *Universal Declaration of Human Rights*. Paris: United Nations General Assembly, 1948. [Available at: https://www.un.org/en/about-us/universal-declaration-of-human-rights], [Last accessed: 14th October 2022].

United Nations. "Work Abroad", *YouTube Video*. United Nations Office of Drug and Crime, (25th November 2008). [Available from: https://www.youtube.com/watch?v=9HWmR6psHn8], [Last accessed: 14th October 2022].

Volf, M. *Work in the Spirit: towards a theology of work.* [Kindle]. Eugene, OR: Wipf and Stock, 2001.

Wilkin, Jen. *In His Image: 10 ways God calls us to reflect his character* [Kindle]. Wheaton, IL: Crossway, 2018.

Witte, Jr. John. "Between Sanctity and Depravity: Human dignity in protestant perspective". In: R.P. Kraynak and G. Tinder, Eds. *In Defense of Human Dignity: Essays for our times.* Notre Dame, IN: University of Notre Dame Press, 2003: 119-137.

CONNECTING A MISSIONAL READING OF PSALM 10 WITH THE TRAFFICKING, ABUSE, AND EXPLOITATION OF UNACCOMPANIED ASYLUM-SEEKING CHILDREN IN EUROPE

Tim Davy

Introduction

> Why, O Yahweh, do you stand far away?
> Why do you hide in times of distress?
> In arrogance the wicked hotly pursue the afflicted;
> may they be caught in the schemes they have devised! (Psalm 10:1-2)

> They risk detention, rape, forced labour, beatings or death. Yet, tens of thousands of children, many of them unaccompanied or separated, are making the dangerous refugee and migrant journey in the hope of finding safety or a better life in Europe. They are fleeing brutal violence, abject poverty, drought, forced early marriage, untold hardship or lack of prospects and hope in dozens of countries in Africa, Asia and the Middle East.[1]

How might the Bible help the Church to respond to the wicked and calculating cruelty of those who exploit unaccompanied asylum-seeking children (UASC) caught up in the current European refugee crisis?

In this chapter, I attempt an answer to that question by bringing together three elements. The first reflects the crisis of context alluded to in the above quote, this "time of distress" to borrow the psalmist's language. In the midst of the turmoil and suffering of the European refugee crisis, many UASC are being targeted, abused, and exploited. The second element is to craft a biblical response to this harrowing phenomenon by taking a biblical text, in this case Psalm 10, and explore how it might shape the Church's theology and practice when responding to the plight of UASC. The third element is my use of a "missional hermeneutic" to connect the biblical text and current context.

In line with the purposes of this volume, difficult and complex issues require an interaction between deep, reflective thinking and applied imagination. It is my hope and prayer that this chapter will serve as an example of how we can engage with the Bible to promote and inform the advocacy work of the Church amongst and on behalf of exploited children. I also hope that it will demonstrate how facing up to a current contemporary crisis may also lead to an enriched understanding and appreciation of the Bible and mission, by sensitizing us to

[1] United Nations Children's Fund, *Danger Every Step of the Way: A Harrowing Journey to Europe for Refugee and Migrant Children* (UNICEF, June 2016), 2.

experiences all too familiar to the people of the Bible and our suffering neighbors.

It will soon become evident why I have chosen Psalm 10 as my text, which seems particularly apposite when wrestling with the callous and calculated exploitation of UASC. Ian Stackhouse has rightly observed that engaging prayerfully with the book of Psalms points us to the needs of others and draws us into life as it is:

> Sometimes when I am praying a psalm a face will appear; someone for whom this Psalm describes actual experience. Other times the words of the Psalm sound for all the world like the latest news bulletin from Kosovo, or the Congo, and so, in a strange way, the ancient liturgy helps me to be more up-to-date than I would otherwise be. Precisely because the world hasn't changed much, and human experience is awful a lot of the time, praying the Psalms, far from representing a retreat into private interiority, is an advance onto the concourse of life.[2]

As I will show, Psalm 10 faces up to the cruel injustices of the wicked towards the vulnerable. It is unflinching in its insistence on treating these as urgent matters of prayer before a God who, although he might not seem to be attentive, will act decisively in the end. In our reading of Psalm 10, the faces that will appear are the unaccompanied children and young people caught up in the European refugee crisis.

I begin with a brief orientation to the plight of UASC, and then examine the approach of missional hermeneutics, before turning my attention to Psalm 10. To conclude the chapter, I then draw out three missional themes that emerge from the discussion that are particularly prescient for the Church's thinking and practice of working with and for vulnerable and exploited children.

The Exploitation of Unaccompanied Asylum-Seeking Children

In recent years, the continent of Europe has seen a significant rise in the number of people fleeing war and persecution from a variety of countries, not least Eritrea, Afghanistan, Syria, and Iraq.[3] Between 2015 and 2017, for example, around 180,000 UASC claimed asylum in EU member states.[4]

Amongst the many vexing issues raised by the current refugee crisis in Europe is the way in which the desperate and vulnerable are being exploited by unscrupulous individuals and networks. In 2016, the UK's Anti-Slavery

[2] Ian Stackhouse, *The Day is Yours: Slow Spirituality in a Fast-Moving World* (Milton Keynes, UK: Paternoster, 2008): 95.

[3] See, for example, Tim Davy and Mark Walley, "Unaccompanied Asylum Seeking Children: Shaping a Church Response", *Kirby Laing Institute of Christian Ethics*, Ethics in Brief paper, 22.5 (Cambridge: KLICE, 2017). [Available at: https://kirbylaingcentre.co.uk/wp-content/uploads/2021/01/22.5EiBDavyandWalley.pdf], [Last accessed: 14th October 2022].

[4] The European Commission's Eurostat website reported 88,300 in 2015, 63,300 in 2016, and 31,400 in 2017. Of course, this does not account for children who are not recorded in the asylum system.

Commissioner stated that "the migration crisis is clearly being used by human trafficking networks to target and brutally exploit the most vulnerable."[5]

Europol, the European police agency, has noted an overlap between criminal gangs already active in human trafficking who were also active in smuggling refugees into Europe.[6] For example, a survey of 9000 refugees arriving into Europe found "strong evidence of predatory behaviour by smugglers and traffickers and the kinds of enabling environments within which trafficking and associated forms of exploitation and abuse thrive."[7]

UASC are understood to be amongst the most vulnerable to exploitation. As a House of Lords report put it:

> Unaccompanied migrant children are, of course, particularly vulnerable to all these problems. Many of them face poverty, war or persecution in their countries of origin. During their journey to, or through, the EU, they are particularly vulnerable to smugglers or traffickers, as well as to sexual abuse. According to Ms. McNeill, doctors in Save the Children's Italy programme "found that 50% of the children they are dealing with have an STI [sexually transmitted infection]. That is evidence of them being sexually exploited in transit."[8]

The same report listed "vulnerability to sexual violence, sexual exploitation and trafficking" as one of the problems facing UASC.[9] Indeed, "Those who have not made it into the system are extremely vulnerable and, we would argue, the most vulnerable of all."[10]

Alarmingly, in early 2016, Europol made a conservative estimate that at least 10,000 UASC had gone missing since arriving in Europe.[11] Although there would have been a variety of reasons for losing track of them in official records, it is feared that a significant number may have already have been, or may end up being, victims of exploitation. More recently, the sexual exploitation of children crossing the Italian-French border has been noted by *The Guardian*: "The minors, mostly from sub-Saharan Africa, are being forced to perform sex acts if they cannot afford the €50-€150 asked by drivers in exchange for a lift across

---

[5] Kevin Hyland, UK Anti-Slavery Commissioner, quoted in International Organization for Migration, "Abuse, Exploitation and Trafficking: IOM Reveals Data on the Scale of the Danger and Risks that Migrants Face on the Mediterranean Routes to Europe" (IOM, 18th October 2016). https://sdg.iisd.org/news/iom-data-highlight-migrants-vulnerability/.

[6] Cited in Mark Townsend, "10,000 Refugee Children Are Missing, says Europol", *The Guardian*, 30th January 2016. [Available at: https://www.theguardian.com/world/2016/jan/30/fears-for-missing-child-refugees], [Last accessed: 14th October 2022].

[7] Townsend, "10,000 Refugee Children".

[8] House of Lords European Union Committee, "Children in Crisis: Unaccompanied Migrant Children in the EU" (2016), 11.

[9] House of Lords European Union Committee, "Children in Crisis", 11.

[10] Kristy McNeill, oral evidence to the committee. [Available at: http://data.parliament.uk/writtenevidence/committeeevidence.svc/evidencedocument/eu-home-affairs-subcommittee/unaccompanied-minors-in-the-eu/oral/31318.html], [Last accessed: 14th October 2022].

[11] Townsend, "10,000 Refugee Children".

the border […] The children are also being offered food or shelter in return for being abused."[12]

We see, then, that the European refugee crisis is characterized by large numbers of people, including children, brought to the brink of vulnerability and beyond.

This is the context in which Christians, working with and advocating for vulnerable and exploited children, are reading their Bibles. We come to the text with an urgency and a pain, seeking recognition and hope in these desperate times of distress.

However, before moving to a reading of Psalm 10, I need to provide an outline of my approach for bridging the biblical text and the contemporary context, and how this might inform and energize Christian action in the light of God's mission.

Missional Hermeneutics: Development and Definitions

As I seek to frame it, a missional reading of a biblical text is one that seeks to interpret Scripture in the light of the mission of God. It is an approach to biblical interpretation that has gained increasing currency over the last two decades and offers, I believe, an important and urgent contribution to the way the Church reads Scripture and frames our mission thinking and practice accordingly. While it is beyond the scope of this chapter to account for the scholarly conversation in detail, I highlight three themes upon which I will build my missional approach to Psalm 10.[13]

Such is the rich potential of the approach, there are a number of lines of enquiry that a missional reading could pursue. George Hunsberger has helpfully mapped out several broad themes that reflect the emphases of scholars in this field, including (but not limited to) (1) the relationship between the text and the *missio Dei* (the mission of God), (2) the way in which the text forms the people of God for our participation in the *missio Dei*, and (3) the way in which the reading community's missional context shapes our reading of texts.[14] A brief expansion on these is needed in relation to our chapter.

---

[12] Angela Guiffrida, "Migrant Children Sexually Exploited to 'Pay' For Italy-France Crossing, Says Charity", *The Guardian*, 29th July 2018. [Available at: https://www.theguardian.com/world/2018/jul/29/migrant-children-sexually-exploited-in-italy-france-crossing], [Last accessed: 14th October 2022]. This article was picking up on a 2018 report by Save the Children Italy, "Piccoli Schiavi Invisibili 2018." [Available at: https://www.savethechildren.it/cosa-facciamo/pubblicazioni/piccoli-schiavi-invisibili-2018], [Last accessed: 14th October 2022].

[13] For a recent overview of the development of missional hermeneutics, see Michael Goheen's essay, "A History and Introduction to a Missional Reading of the Bible", in Michael Goheen (ed), *Reading the Bible Missionally* (Grand Rapids, MI: Eerdmans, 2016): 3-27.

[14] George Hunsberger, "Mapping the Missional Hermeneutics Conversation", in Michael Goheen (ed), *Reading the Bible Missionally* (Grand Rapids, MI: Eerdmans, 2016): 45-67.

Relationship to the Missio Dei

Most missional hermeneutics scholars understand the Bible to be an unfolding "grand narrative" of God's mission to reconcile the whole of creation to himself. As such, each text may be examined to establish how it contributes to the depiction of that narrative and the God whose purposes that narrative describes. As such, Chris Wright, for example, can suggest,

> a missional hermeneutic will work hard to read any text in the Old Testament canon within this overarching narrative framework, discerning its place within that framework, assessing how the shape of the grand narrative is reflected in the text in question, and conversely, how the particular text contributes to and moves forward the grand narrative itself.[15]

Elsewhere I have sought to refine that question, to ask not simply how a text fits into and moves forward the progression of the story, which predisposes us to looking at texts that fit within the chronological plotline of the narrative.[16] Nevertheless, taking in a more general line of "how does this text relate to the *missio Dei*?" enables us to consider, in our case, a Psalm more helpfully. Wright's point that we should ask how the shape of the *missio Dei* is "reflected" in the text is also valuable as it broadens our attention beyond simply chronological placement to consider the *nature* of that "big story." Richard Bauckham's expansion on this theme is important in the context of a text like Psalm 10 and is worth quoting in full:

> The gospel does not come to each person only in terms of some abstracted generality of human nature, but in the realities and differences of their social and economic situations. It engages with the injustices of the world on its way to the kingdom of God. This means that as well as the outward movement of the church's mission in geographical extension and numerical increase, there must also be this (in the Bible's imagery) downward movement of solidarity with the people at the bottom of the social scale of importance and wealth. It is to these – the poorest, those with no power or influence, the wretched, the neglected – to whom God has given priority in the kingdom, not only for their own sake, but also for all the rest of us who can enter the kingdom only alongside *them.*[17]

We must heed Bauckham's words when discussing UASC: children with names, faces, stories, hopes and fears, experiencing suffering and exploitation that is anything but "abstract and general." We will bring to Psalm 10 the question: how this text relates to and reflects the existence and nature of the *missio Dei*, within which the marginalized play so crucial a role.

---

[15] Christopher J.H. Wright, "Mission and Old Testament Interpretation", in Craig G. Bartholomew and David J. H. Beldman (eds), *Hearing the Old Testament: Listening for God's Address* (Grand Rapids, MI: Eerdmans, 2012): 184.

[16] See my forthcoming book, *The Book of Job and the Mission of God: A Missional Reading* (Eugene, OR: Pickwick).

[17] Richard Bauckham, *Bible and Mission: Christian Witness in a Postmodern World* (Milton Keynes, UK: Paternoster Press, 2003): 53-54. His italics.

Formative Function of the Text

Emerging particularly from the work of Darrell Guder on the New Testament, this approach builds on the idea that the Scriptures have a formational function in the life of the people of God, shaping and equipping the faithful readers of the text to participate more fully in the mission to which we have been called. As Guder puts it:

> The New Testament writings were addressed to communities already in mission; the purpose of the canonical Scriptures was (and is) to enable them to continue that mission. The Scriptures are thus the warrant for the church's mission by engaging their situations, their challenges, and their struggles.[18]

Others have rightly observed the point that this approach can also be applied to audiences (original and contemporary) of the Old Testament, and have demonstrated this effectively with their subsequent readings.[19]

Put briefly, this line of enquiry will ask the reader of Psalm 10 to consider how that text might contribute to the shaping and equipping the people of God as we participate together in God's mission. More specifically, how does the text equip the Church to work amongst and on behalf of UASC?

Missional Context of the Reader

Building on an assumption of the Church's call to participate in the *missio Dei*, Michael Barram has alerted us to the need to own the "social locatedness" of our reading contexts.[20] By this, he means that all readers are situated within (and shaped by) a specific social location and this context will shape the kinds of questions, concerns, and sensitivities we bring to our reading of Scripture. He advocates for, "an approach to biblical texts that privileges the missiological 'location' of the Christian community in the world as a hermeneutical key"[21] and, as such, he is interested in how texts "functioned missionally in their original contexts" and how they might, "inform and equip the *contemporary* Christian community for its mission."[22] Reflecting on Barram's approach, Wright helpfully comments,

> Contexts count. And theology must be done in the process of missional engagement with each context, seeking to be both faithful to the text and the doctrinal tradition it embodies, and relevant to the context and the committed praxis for which it calls.[23]

---

[18] Darrell Guder (ed), *Missional Church: A Vision for the Sending of the Church in North America* (Grand Rapids, MI: Eerdmans, 1998): 223.

[19] See, for example, writings from Wright, from Goheen, and from Davy.

[20] See his influential essay, Michael Barram, "The Bible, Mission, and Social Location: Toward a Missional Hermeneutic", *Interpretation* 61(1), (2007): 42-58, [Available at: https://doi.org/10.1177/002096430006100106], [Last accessed: 14th October 2022].

[21] Barram, "Social Location", 42-43.

[22] Barram, "Social Location", 49. His italics. I lack the space to discuss the nuances of Barram's approach more fully. His is a more reader-centred approach than many of his fellow missional hermeneutics scholars, although not, in my view, an extreme form of postmodern biblical interpretation.

[23] Wright, "Mission and OT Interpretation", 187.

For the purposes of this chapter, I am defining the social location as the refugee crisis in Europe, which has been used by unscrupulous people to exploit vulnerable unaccompanied children caught up in the crisis. As such, our reading of the Psalm will make much of the mutually experienced "times of distress" owned in Psalm 10:1 and in our review of the plight of UASC.[24]

This "owning" of the context allows us not to distort the meaning of biblical texts but to be sensitized to what is already there, and to imagine with greater depth and possibility the implications of the text for the Church and world.

Following the death of his son, Nicholas Wolterstorff reflected, "I shall look at the world through tears. Perhaps I shall see things that dry-eyed I could not see."[25] Those who work with and advocate for vulnerable and exploited UASC come to the Bible reading it through tears of sorrow and anger. Perhaps we will see things in Psalm 10 that dry-eyed we could not see?

Moving towards Psalm 10: Reading the Psalms Missionally

Reflecting on the relationship between the Psalms and mission is not a new phenomenon only brought about by the emergence of missional hermeneutics.[26] However, to set my work on Psalm 10 in its scholarly context, it is worth noting some of the themes that have emerged in some recent "missional" approaches to the Psalter.

Michael Goheen, for example, suggests that:

> The psalms nourish *faithfulness* in all its dimensions, so that Israel might be an attractive display people […] In the midst of the land, before the nations, Israel's worship celebrates the one true God and his mighty deeds in history […] Israel's identity and self-understanding, its role and calling in the midst of the nations, are constantly celebrated and nourished by its liturgy.[27]

While Goheen is correct in setting the Psalter within the universal scope of God's purposes, he does not allow space to develop the discussion to account more for the "negative" psalms. As Psalm 10 illustrates, a significant amount of Israel's liturgy prayed and sung before the watching world was filled with cries of pain and lament.

---

[24] While I would not say that our reading location "creates" meaning in the text, I do think that an attuned awareness and ownership of our reading context makes us more attentive readers, and more likely to apply the insights of the text in meaningful and appropriate ways.

[25] Nicholas Wolterstorff, *Lament for a Son* (Grand Rapids, MI: Eerdmans, 1987): 26.

[26] As evidenced, for example, in James R. Rohrer's article, "The Psalms in Nineteenth-Century Mission Theology", *Scottish Bulletin of Evangelical Theology* 34(2), (2016): 172-187. See further examples in James Chukwuma Okoye's *A Light to the Nations: A Mission Theology of the Old Testament* (Maryknoll, NY: Orbis Books, 2006) and Walter C. Kaiser, *Mission in the Old Testament: Israel as a Light to the Nations*, 2nd edition (Grand Rapids, MI: Baker Academic, 2012).

[27] Michael Goheen, *A Light to the Nations: The Missional Church and the Biblical Story* (Grand Rapids, MI: Baker Academic, 2011), 57-58. His italics.

Mark Boda's treatment of mission in the Psalter has a special interest in the kingship of Yahweh as "foundational to the theology of the nations in the Psalms."[28] As such, he provides a detailed outline of ways in which Yahweh's reign is established, celebrated, located, exhibited, and challenged.[29] He then examines the overall structure of the final form of the Psalter, picking up on "a development of the theme of Yahweh, king, people, and the nations."[30]

Relevant for our purposes, in the detail of his discussion, Boda does reference Psalm 10 at certain points; for example, noting Yahweh's capacity to subdue his enemies and exercise justice.[31] However, perhaps more could be said about the role the Psalms of lament play in a missional reading of the Psalms. Whilst Boda is right in claiming that "everlasting praise to Yahweh is the *telos* of this book" (p. 31, his italics), might the struggling of the psalms of lament (however they are or are not resolved) exhibit, for a moment at least, a challenge to the legitimacy or credibility of God's reign?[32]

One final element of Boda's treatment is worth noting as it connects the reign of God with a call to serve the exploited, and speaks into themes closely tied to Psalm 10:

> if the evidence of God's rule is seen in his exercise of justice, it is imperative that this be evident in the missional enterprise. Any mission worthy of God is one that seeks for the establishment of the justice of God alongside the proclamation of his reign. This means that where the gospel of the kingdom is proclaimed, the vulnerable and powerless will be protected and defended.[33]

Such a sensitivity to the social obligations brought about by the proclamation of Yahweh's rule will play an important part of my approach to Psalm 10.

In his treatment on the Psalter, Brian Russell picks up on similar themes to Goheen and Boda, such as praise, Yahweh's kingship, and the way in which the psalms shape "the identity and ethos of God's people."[34]

Particularly striking in Russell's treatment is the way in which he discusses the harsh realities of living faithfully in the world, including the value of lament. He is worth quoting at some length to attend to his point:

> laments or prayers for help dominate the landscape of the Psalms. They are the most common type of prayer found in the Psalter [...] The assumptions of a lament are that the pray-er's present circumstances do not line up with the abundant life of God's kingdom and that God can do something about it. These complaints arise from a deep trust and faith in God; but this faith is matched by the desperation of the pray-er's circumstances. God's missional people need laments because our

---

[28] Mark J. Boda, "'Declare His Glory among the Nations': The Psalter as Missional Collection", in Stanley E. Porter and Cynthia Long Westfall (eds), *Christian Mission: Old Testament Foundations and New Testament Developments* (Eugene, OR: Pickwick, 2010): 24.

[29] Boda, "Declare His Glory", 14-27.

[30] Boda, "Declare His Glory", 36.

[31] Psalm. 10:16, 17-18; Boda, "Declare His Glory", 16, 20.

[32] Boda, "Declare His Glory", 31. His italics.

[33] Boda, "Declare His Glory", 39. His italics.

[34] Brian D. Russell, *(re)Aligning with God: Reading Scripture for Church and World* (Eugene, OR: Cascade, 2016): 57-61: 57.

> Genesis 3-11 world remains broken and lost […] Missional communities need to reflect deeply on the reality that laments heavily dominate the initial eighty-nine psalms in the Book of Psalms. Learning to rely on God by remembering to bring all needs and even all complaints to the God who loves his people is critical for a dynamic and missional faith.[35]

It seems to me that this is a helpful approach, and I would simply want to add that, in line with Stackhouse's observation previously, the psalms of lament provide us with a way not only to process our pain, but also tutor us in the pain of others. This, I would argue, is critical as we advocate for others for whom these experiences are a daily reality. Thus, as we advocate for others, we live, in Russell's words, "as a missional people as clues to the good future that God has promised. Yet, God's people live in *anticipation* of this and so face the realities of a broken world."[36]

As I hope the preceding discussion has demonstrated, a missional approach opens up and alerts the reader to ways of reading the Bible that enable an encounter between text and context, which will shape not only how we think about mission in a broken world, but also how we go about fulfilling our role in that mission.

Three Questions to Bring to Our Text

We now arrive at Psalm 10. It would not be possible to pursue every possible line of enquiry offered by missional hermeneutics. I propose instead to approach Psalm 10 by giving a basic orientation to the Psalm, and then carrying out an exegesis of each of its main sections. Through this, I will draw out three missional reflections based on an encounter between the text of Psalm 10 and the context of the exploitation of UASC caught up in the European refugee crisis. These three reflections revolve around the following questions:

1. How does Psalm 10 relate to and reflect the existence and nature of the *missio Dei*? Put another way, how does this text declare God's kingship in a world that witnesses the exploitation of UASC?
2. How does Psalm 10 obligate, energize, shape, and equip the Church to work amongst, and advocate for, vulnerable and exploited UASC?
3. How does an attentiveness to the exploitation of UASC sensitize our reading of Psalm 10?

---

[35] Russell, *(re)Aligning with God*, 59.

[36] Russell, *(re)Aligning with God*, 59. His italics. For more on lament and mission see Cathy Ross, "Lament and Hope," *Anvil* 34(1), (February 2018) [Available at: https://churchmissionsociety.org/resources/lament-and-hope-cathy-ross-anvil-vol-34-issue-1], [Last accessed: 14th October 2022]. See also Tim Davy, *Book of Job*.

Psalm 10

Orientation to the Psalm

Psalm 10 clearly exhibits features associated with "lament", such as complaint, a plea to God, and prayer against an enemy.[37] In broad structural terms, the psalm opens with an initial cry and complaint (vv. 1-2), followed by a lengthy description of the attitudes and actions of the wicked (vv. 3-11). The psalmist then summons God's reign (vv. 12-15), and concludes with a celebration of that reign (vv. 16-18).

It seems likely that Psalms 9 and 10 were originally a single literary unit, forming an acrostic poem with common themes and vocabulary.[38] There is no consensus concerning the dating of the Psalm, although the final form may reflect post-exilic concerns of "complaint and confidence."[39] Peter Craigie points to the difficulty of interpreting a text that was once joined to its neighbor but is now separated, although his suggestion of maintaining an awareness of two levels of interpretation, one where Psalm 10 is part of the preceding poem, and one where it is distinct, is helpful.[40] Partly due to space, with Craigie, I will attempt to examine the unique text of Psalm 10 on its own terms, while being sensitive to the close connection with Psalm 9.[41]

We begin, then, with the Psalm's opening cry and complaint.[42]

Initial Cry and Complaint (Psalm 10:1-2)

1 Why, O Yahweh, do you stand far away?
Why do you hide in times of distress?
2 In arrogance the wicked hotly pursue the afflicted;
may they be caught in the schemes they have devised!

These verses set the scene: all is as it ought not to be. Yahweh's apparent absence, inattentiveness, and distance are set alongside the unwelcome presence

---

[37] Tremper Longman III, *How to Read The Psalms* (Leicester: IVP, 1988): 27; cf. Glen Pemberton, *Hurting with God: Learning to Lament with the Psalms* (Abilene: Abilene Christian University Press, 2012): 30.
[38] J. Clinton McCann, "Psalms" in Leander E. Keck (ed), *New Interpreter's Bible Commentary*, Volume 3 (Nashville, TN: Abingdon Press, 2015): 328; Craig G. Broyles, *Psalms* (Peabody, MA: Hendrickson, 1999): 74.
[39] McCann, *Psalms,* 328.
[40] Peter C. Craigie, *Psalms 1-50* (Waco, TX: Word, 1983): 117.
[41] Walter Brueggemann, for example, reads the end of Psalm 9 and beginning of Psalm 10 as asking God "to do again what was earlier celebrated [i.e., in 9:1-18], to pursue and execute judgment against the exploiters"; "Psalms 9-10: A Counter to Conventional Social Reality" in Patrick Miller (ed), *The Psalms and the Life of Faith* (Minneapolis, MN: Fortress, 1995): 223. Cf. Steven Croft, who sees Psalms 9-10 as a festal psalm in which there is a movement from the celebration of God's international reign to a plea for God to exhibit that same rule against the wicked within Israel; Steven J.L. Croft, *The Identity of the Individual in the Psalms* (Sheffield: JSOT Press, 1987): 108-113.
[42] Note: The translation is my own, although I am indebted to the ESV in particular.

and attentiveness of the wicked. Just when he is needed most, Yahweh's lack of movement is contrasted with the fierce pursuit by the wicked of the afflicted.[43]

The psalmist finds this situation vexing in the extreme. Why is God not present for the afflicted? The contrast with Psalm 9:9 is evident: not only is Yahweh failing to be a "stronghold in times of distress" (9:9), he cannot even be found.[44] Yahweh does not hide the oppressed but hides himself, leaving a vacuum of presence, attentiveness and protection, and allowing the wicked to intrude into that space:

> The prospect for the well-being of the vulnerable in social relations depends on the initiative, attentiveness, and activity of Yahweh [...] By 10:2, the poem has made clear that everything in social relations depends on the presence or absence of Yahweh. When Yahweh is absent, social relations will take their inevitably destructive course, which the weak cannot resist. When Yahweh is present, as Yahweh may be because of urgent petition, conventional destructive relations are overcome and new social possibilities may emerge.[45]

Concluding his initial cry and complaint, the psalmist then issues an opening shot, calling on Yahweh to bring poetic justice to the wicked: may their scheming be their undoing.

The Psalm speaks to the seemingly overwhelming questions raging around the exploitation of UASC caught up in the refugee crisis. The "Why?" needs to be asked, screamed even. The "Why?" is an essential tool in the work of the people of God: we are allowed – obligated, even – to cry to God on behalf of the suffering.

Why does God let this happen? Why a refugee crisis at all? Why does God seem so hesitant to attend to the vacuum into which traffickers and other exploitative adults have stepped so eagerly? "Enter in!" we cry. "Appear! Attend! Wade in and leave no room for those who exploit!" Articulating absence, telling the story of God's seeming inattentiveness is part of our faithful calling.

Complaint about the Attitudes and Actions of the Wicked (Psalm 10:3-11)

> 3 For the wicked has boasted about the desires of his heart,
> and the greedy curses and renounces Yahweh.
> 4 In pride the wicked does not seek him;
> all his thoughts are, "There is no God."
> 5 His ways prosper at all times;
> your judgments are high above him;
> as for all his foes, he scoffs at them.
> 6 He says in his heart, "I shall never be shaken;
> from generation to generation I shall not meet disaster."

In the first part of the complaint, the psalmist builds up a picture of the arrogance of the wicked. In thought and speech, the wicked displays a remarkable disregard for God. We are given an insight into his inner life, which he makes public by boasting of "the desires of his heart" (v. 3). He is greedy, godless and proud,

[43] Craigie, *Psalms 1-50*, 123.
[44] McCann, "Psalms", 330; Brueggemann, "Psalms 9-10", 224.
[45] Brueggemann, "Psalms 9-10", 224.

imagining that he is beyond the reach of divine retribution or human competition. He curses and spurns Yahweh, declaring, "There is no God." This is a strange assertion, given he later addresses God in the second person (v. 13). Perhaps it can be said that his life is now oriented around a denial of God's ability or intention to interrupt and intervene, and so the wicked sees God as functionally irrelevant, employing a kind of "practical atheism."[46] His self-confidence extends beyond the present to the distant future: he cannot envisage a time when he will be called to account for his deeds. Such "dismissals of God are assertions of self-sufficiency and autonomy"; as such, he need not hold back from all that he wants to do.[47]

> 7 His mouth is full of cursing, deceit and oppression;
> under his tongue are trouble and wickedness.
> 8 He sits in ambush in the villages;
> in hiding places he slays the innocent;
> his eyes watch stealthily for the hapless;
> 9 he lies in wait in hiding places like a lion in his thicket;
> he lies in wait to seize the afflicted;
> he seizes the afflicted when he drags him into his net.
> 10 Crushed, he is brought low,
> the hapless fall by his might.[48]
> 11 He says in his heart, "God has forgotten,
> he has hidden his face, he will never see."

If verses 3-6 tell us about the overall life-stance of the wicked, the following verses reveal the social implications of his attitudes. The layering of terms in verse 7 give us a disturbing portrait of the depths and range of his manipulative thoughts and speech.[49] Indeed, his speech does more than just describe: "One of his chief weapons is the tongue, whose varied techniques of intimidation and confusion are suggested in the long catalogue of verse 7."[50]

With no regard for the One above or the ones around him, the wicked plans and plots, schemes and lies. He is focused on his goal: to exploit the weak. His is no mere empty talk; like a lion waiting patiently and deliberately, he is a callous and calculating opportunist. Rather than coming to the helpless person's aid, he uses their helplessness to his advantage, playing on their weakness and vulnerability.

Goldingay points out the dangers inherent in a rural setting:

> The villages might be dangerous because they lack walls to keep out wild animals, and there is nothing wrong with being a hunter. Such a person protects the

---

[46] Craigie, *Psalms 1-50*, 124; Derek Kidner, *Psalms 1-72* (Leicester: IVP, 1973): 71; John Goldingay, *Psalms: Volume 1: Psalms 1-41* (Grand Rapids, MI: Baker Academic, 2006): 180.

[47] Brueggemann, "Psalms 9-10", 225.

[48] Cf. Goldingay, *Psalms 1-41*, 181: "Broken, he sinks down, the wretched fall by his might [*or*, The wretched are broken, sink down, fall by his might." His italics.

[49] There may even be a hint of "pleasurable taste and genuine delight" for the wicked in his words; Craigie, *Psalms 1-50*, 125.

[50] Kidner, *Psalms 1-72*, 71.

community by hiding, keeping watch, and slaying. But this hunter is hiding in order to keep watch for vulnerable people and slay them.[51]

Like Yahweh in the psalmist's estimation (v. 1) the wicked hides from the afflicted. The psalmist has accused Yahweh of hiding and staying hidden, far away and inattentive. Not so the wicked, who fill Yahweh's absence with their own unwelcome presence, breaking cover and preying upon the weak, dragging them away, and perhaps out of sight. With no one protecting them, the afflicted are crushed, left broken and empty, unable to stand up to the might of their oppressor. All they can do is capitulate to the horror that awaits them.

Goldingay, again, points to the pathos in these verses, which offer "painfully repeated accounts of the event – the wretched keep falling into the net before our eyes. The power of the 'hunter' is too much for them."[52]

A striking reflection on the speech of the wicked is offered by Brueggemann, who observes that the wicked themselves are not allowed to speak, but rather their words are reported by the psalmist.[53] He sees this as a "remarkable rhetorical strategy", which reverses the normal speech-power dynamic, where the powerful wicked are used to being in control of their own speech and, crucially, the speech of others as well.[54] When the wicked are in control of the discourse, they are able to "manipulate social processes, social symbols, social communication, and social decision-making in ways that further victimize the weak."[55]

By robbing the wicked of a direct voice, the psalmist subverts the typical and systemic public discourse:

> What has happened in this poem is that the wicked have *lost their control of the social conversation.* They no longer decide what will be uttered or who will speak; now, perhaps for the first time, the strong are at the mercy of the weak, who are free to construe conflicted social dynamics in a very different way. Instead of the usual self-justifying, mystifying ideology of the wicked, we now get a critical exposé of the actions and intentions of the wicked. Their actual intent is now placed in their own mouths as a harsh self-indictment.[56]

Despite this potential subversion, the passage ends with a verse of seeming despair, as if the afflicted ones' imagination submits once again to that of the wicked: "The wicked have imagined God away, and the poor now accept that verdict. The world without God [...] is a hopeless world for the poor."[57]

Perhaps no one is prepared to speak aloud what is going on. Perhaps God has not noticed this travesty, or does not care. This is what the wicked assumes, and his victim fears.

For those working with and on behalf of exploited UASC, the psalmist directs our attention in several ways. Even if overstating the case, Brueggemann's

---

[51] Goldingay, *Psalms 1-41*, 181.
[52] Goldingay, *Psalms 1-41*, 181.
[53] Brueggemann, "Psalms 9-10", 226.
[54] Brueggemann, "Psalms 9-10", 226.
[55] Brueggemann, "Psalms 9-10", 226-227.
[56] Brueggemann, "Psalms 9-10", 226. His italics.
[57] Brueggemann, "Psalms 9-10", 229.

framing of the psalm as subversion of the social conversation is evocative. Stories must be heard, collated, and retold; what is hidden must be exposed. We have a role to play in subverting the assumptions and speech of those who exploit. We have a role to play in enabling their victims to have the final word. To call attention to exploitation is to articulate its unacceptability and move others to action.

Of course, this is not just about speech. Identifying and articulating the motives, means, and mechanisms by which exploitation happens (as seen in vv. 7-11) could contribute to countering that exploitation. Even if small steps, such work can lead to greater awareness, policy change, and practice on the ground.

The intense vulnerability of the afflicted in the psalm finds parallels with UASC. Theirs is a dangerous vulnerability with multiple layers of risk associated with their journey. While displaying remarkable agency in making the journey at all, they are also severely at risk in the absence of those who will help, and the presence of those who will exploit.

Summoning God's Reign (Psalm 10:12-15)

12 Arise, O Yahweh!
O God, lift up your hand!
Do not forget the afflicted!
13 Why does the wicked renounce God
and say in his heart, "You will not call to account"?
14 But you do see, you do pay attention to trouble and vexation,
to take it into your hands;
to you the hapless abandons himself;
you have been the helper of the fatherless.
15 Break the arm of the wicked and evildoer;
call his wickedness to account until you find none.

The circumstances of the psalmist (or of those for whom he is advocating) seem hopeless. Yet the psalm now turns to utter a word of "inexplicable hope – surely rooted in an unquenchable sense of Yahweh as a third party in social relations."[58] Verse 12 represents a key moment in the Psalm with a call for Yahweh to take action, smash the assumptions and hold of the wicked, and transform the fortunes of the afflicted. The psalmist has brooded long enough and decides to throw off his despair: "he is going to arise and face the enemy and asks God himself to arise with him."[59] In this echo of a battle cry, he calls on God, who alone is able to conquer, to exert his strength to protect the afflicted and purge the wicked.[60]

The wicked boasted that Yahweh was indifferent to the oppression of the poor, evidenced by his apparent inattentiveness. He declared that God had "forgotten" and did not see his deeds (v. 11), and would not hold him to account (v. 13). As long as Yahweh remains disinterested, the wicked are safe. The psalmist, however, is consumed by a vision of Yahweh's attentiveness and

---

[58] Brueggemann, "Psalms 9-10", 230.
[59] Craigie, *Psalms 1-50*, 125.
[60] Craigie, *Psalms 1-50*, 125. He notes Numbers 10:35 as an example of a military association of this phrase.

intervention. He charges God to reverse the boasts of the wicked: "Forget not the afflicted", he pleads (v. 12). This appears to rouse his memory and stir his confidence, issuing in an emphatic statement: "You *do* see."[61] Yahweh does indeed pay attention to the trouble and vexation.

Moreover, Yahweh will take this knowledge and do something with it. He will involve himself and provide the help that is needed by the helpless. Those who are abandoned and helpless now commit or "abandon" themselves to Yahweh.[62] The fatherless, an archetypal figure of helplessness and vulnerability, now finds their help in Yahweh. Yahweh rescues them from the clutches of the wicked by breaking his power and hold over them. He gives them a new freedom and a new belonging. Simply put, this is who Yahweh is (Psalm 68:5). They are safe because they belong to Yahweh; they are safe because Yahweh is calling the wicked to account (*contra* the claim of v. 13b) and putting all things right.

As such, these verses recall attributes and actions of Yahweh celebrated in Psalm 9 (see, for example, vv. 9-12) and calls on Yahweh to do it again in this new situation.[63]

As the psalmist cries, so do we. Not just "Why?" but "Do it again!" For those of us working amongst and on behalf of exploited UASC, we use the psalm to call on God to arise, to take action. Despite our questions and lament, we look to God and call to him in trust and hope. Our outrageous, seemingly precarious position is that God does pay attention, does care, is present, is involved, is at work. He is a God to whom all can abandon themselves. This is no mere triumphalism; although wrestling deeply with when and how this will happen, he is a God who will put all things right.

Celebrating God's Reign (Psalm 10:16-18)

16 Yahweh is king forever and ever;
the nations perish from his land.
17 You hear the desire of the afflicted, O Yahweh;
you will strengthen their heart; you will incline your ear
18 to execute justice for the fatherless and the oppressed;
so that man who is of the earth may terrify no more.

The psalm finishes with a declaration and celebration of Yahweh's benevolent and attentive rule. In 10:6, the wicked had boasted that *his* reign of terror would last forever, yet now set alongside the eternal rule of Yahweh this ridiculous claim is exposed for the folly it is. Far from lasting, the desires of the wicked (v. 3) will become a distant memory; it will be the desires of the afflicted that will last. They will have hope because Yahweh is on the throne. This reference to Yahweh's everlasting kingship seems to recall the Exodus, when the enthroned

---

[61] McCann notes the emphatic use of the Hebrew pronoun, "you"; "Psalms", 330.
[62] Cf. Kidner, who sees this "abandonment" to Yahweh as expressing "trust even more completely, because more personally, than the similar saying, 'commit your way to the Lord' (37:5)." *Psalms —72*, 72.
[63] Broyles, *Psalms*, 77–78.

Yahweh countered seemingly impossible opposition to establish freedom for the oppressed whose cries he heard.[64]

Yahweh has seen the plight of the afflicted (v. 14) and he hears their desires (v. 17). He will see to it that the weak, the vulnerable and the exploited will witness that for which they so desperately yearn: a new life freed from terror and marked by the justice of the eternal king.

The psalm concludes, but without a simple fix. As Broyles helpfully summarizes:

> Psalm 9-10 presents a powerful appeal to God. It neither retreats from reality, using God's promises as a security blanket, nor rejects God's promises in view of the lamentable reality. Rather, it sets the contradictions side by side and leaves their resolution to God.[65]

And while the psalmist and the afflicted wait for this resolution, they receive renewed "energy, courage, hope, and imagination" to withstand the current onslaught.[66] Where this leaves UASC is not easily resolved. Perhaps this awkward juxtaposition leaves the reader to consider how we might be moving towards or away from the implicit challenge.

Conclusion and Missional Themes

To conclude my missional reading of Psalm 10, I want to revisit the three questions highlighted earlier in the chapter.

Theme 1: Psalm 10 and the Mission of God

How does Psalm 10 relate to and reflect the existence and nature of the *missio Dei*? Put another way, how does this text declare God's kingship in a world that witnesses the exploitation of UASC?

Psalm 10 does not progress the chronological storyline of the *missio Dei*, but it does tell us (or scream at us) about the kind of world in which the story of God's mission is being played out. The psalm illustrates starkly the tension between the proclamation of the kingship of Yahweh alongside the seeming absence of that rule, with Yahweh being seen both as *a* (even, *the*) contributing factor to the thriving of the wicked, but also the ultimate answer to the protection of the vulnerable.

The identity and declared purposes of God are never in doubt for the psalmist. He knows who Yahweh is and what he is committed to. Indeed, similar to Job, this is what drives the complaint when it appears that Yahweh is not following through on those commitments.[67] And so, in effect still waiting for a response, the psalmist calls God to account, to fulfil his mission to deliver, restore, and put right. He is desperate to see the justice and righteousness of Yahweh's rule worked out in the mess of his broken world. This *missio Dei* is being worked out

---

[64] Cf. Exod. 15:18; Goldingay, *Psalms 1-41*, 183; Craigie, *Psalms 1-50*, 126.
[65] Broyles, *Psalms*, 78.
[66] Brueggemann, "Psalms 9-10", 232.
[67] On this, see Tim Davy, *Book of Job*; see also John H. Walton, *Job*, Kindle edition (Grand Rapids, MI: Zondervan, 2012): 36.

in a world in which the wicked exploit and the vulnerable suffer. Somehow Psalm 10 holds together an unswerving depiction of some of the worst cruelties with a trust that Yahweh does indeed "see", and will set right. This articulation of the concrete detail of ambush, stealthy eyes and snatching the poor, brings discussion of the *missio Dei* into the realm of the concrete. Talking about the "big picture" of God's mission can lead to abstraction. Psalm 10 reminds us that brokenness, beauty, and the renewing of all things will happen in space and time, to people with names and faces, broken bodies, traumatized minds, and lost opportunities. It is an archetype of situations that continue today and so the text provides multiple ways for the people of God to continue to respond.

Theme 2: Psalm 10 and the Formation of God's People

How does Psalm 10 obligate, energize, shape, and equip the Church to work amongst and advocate for vulnerable and exploited UASC?

In the midst of (to borrow Broyles' phrase) the "lamentable reality" of the exploitation of UASC, Psalm 10 models the need to tell the story of these young people. It confronts us with the pain of those suffering exploitation, and models an attempt to make sure the wicked do not go quietly about their business. Psalm 10 challenges us to keep attending to their stories, to keep lamenting over their suffering, to keep hoping that God will put things right, to keep speaking up and speaking out, and to keep working with and on behalf of UASC.

Psalm 10 can act as a means of voicing the anger and frustration of those caught up in, or supporting those caught up in, the refugee crisis. This attentiveness to the vexing questions of faith and suffering should be allowed to breathe. But Psalm 10 also charges us to carry hope alongside, or as part of lament, and insists on God's intervention. As the people of God pray this ancient prayer, we must also take up the call to work out justice and righteousness with and on behalf of UASC. As such, the psalm exposes the contemporary Church, confronting us with the extent to which we are doing just such work.

Theme 3: Psalm 10 and More Sensitized Reader-Practitioners

We have seen how the text can shape the reader for our participation in mission. But how might our participation in mission shape how we approach and appreciate the Bible? That is, how does an attentiveness to the exploitation of UASC inform or sensitize our reading of Psalm 10?

Put bluntly, for those working with and on behalf of UASC through NGOs, church-based community projects, or more secular settings (or a mixture of these), how can we read Psalm 10 without thinking of what we have heard? Our experiences inevitably shape how we think about such texts. The exploitation of UASC gives our reading of these ancient texts a renewed urgency, a bluntness and shared yearning with the psalmist for God to notice and for justice to be done. Following Stackhouse's point about praying the Psalter, Psalm 10 becomes current and faces, names, and conversations appear as we read passages like verses 7-10.

Perhaps we might say that, as readers of this psalm, we are more ready to read and enter into it because the UASC with whom we spend time have tutored us by their pasts and their presence. While, of course, this is not the reason we seek to engage with UASC, there is a mutuality that means that with them and because of them, our engagement with the Bible becomes more painful, more true, and more urgent. We read, pray, and act more closely aligned with the purposes of the psalmist, and with the questions and commitments of the God whom it both accuses and celebrates.

Reflection Questions

1. Is your church tradition comfortable with the idea and practice of lament? What happens when we fail to lament?
2. What are some practical ways that lament can lead to action?
3. How is lament part of and essential to our understanding of theology, sexual exploitation, and response? What happens when we fail to consider the role of lament? How can we better incorporate lament?
4. Do you give yourself time and space to lament on behalf of the children and vulnerable people you work with? If not, what practical steps could you take?
5. Pray through Psalm 10 with specific children and vulnerable people in mind. Name them as you pray.

Works Cited

Barram, Michael. "The Bible, Mission, and Social Location: Toward a Missional Hermeneutic". *Interpretation* 61(1), (2007): 42-58. [Available at: https://doi.org/10.1177/002096430006100106], [Last accessed: 16th October 2022].

Bauckham, Richard. *Bible and Mission: Christian Witness in a Postmodern World.* Milton Keynes: Paternoster Press, 2003.

Boda, Mark J. "'Declare His Glory among the Nations': The Psalter as Missional Collection". In Stanley E. Porter and Cynthia Long Westfall, Eds. *Christian Mission: Old Testament Foundations and New Testament Developments.* Eugene, OR: Pickwick, 2010.

Broyles, Craig G. *Psalms.* Peabody, MA: Hendrickson, 1999.

Brueggemann, Walter. "Psalms 9-10: A Counter to Conventional Social Reality. In Patrick Miller, Ed. *The Psalms and the Life of Faith.* Minneapolis, MN: Fortress, 1995.

Craigie, Peter C. *Psalms 1-50.* Waco, TX: Word, 1983.

Croft, Steven J.L. *The Identity of the Individual in the Psalms.* Sheffield: JSOT Press, 1987.

Davy, Tim and Mark Walley. "Unaccompanied Asylum-Seeking Children: Shaping a Church Response". *Kirby Laing Institute of Christian Ethics*, Ethics in Brief paper, 22.5. Cambridge: KLICE, 2017. [Available at: https://kirbylaingcentre.co.uk/wp-content/uploads/2021/01/22.5EiBDavyandWalley.pdf], [Last accessed: 16th October 2022].

Davy, Tim. *The Book of Job and the Mission of God: A Missional Reading.* Eugene, OR: Pickwick, 2020.

Goheen, Michael. "A History and Introduction to a Missional Reading of the Bible". In Michael Goheen, Ed. *Reading the Bible Missionally.* Grand Rapids, MI: Eerdmans, 2016.

Goheen, Michael. *A Light to the Nations: The Missional Church and the Biblical Story.* Grand Rapids, MI: Baker Academic, 2011.

Goldingay, John. *Psalms: Volume 1: Psalms 1-41.* Grand Rapids, MI: Baker Academic, 2006.

Guder, Darrell, Ed. *Missional Church: A Vision for the Sending of the Church in North America.* Grand Rapids, MI: Eerdmans, 1998.

Guiffrida, Angela. "Migrant Children Sexually Exploited to 'Pay' For Italy-France Crossing, Says Charity". *The Guardian*, 29th July 2018. [Available at: https://www.theguardian.com/world/2018/jul/29/migrant-children-sexually-exploited-in-italy-france-crossing], [Last accessed: 16th October 2022].

House of Lords European Union Committee. "Children in Crisis: Unaccompanied Migrant Children in the EU". 2016.

Hunsberger, George. "Mapping the Missional Hermeneutics Conversation". In Michael Goheen, Ed. *Reading the Bible Missionally.* Grand Rapids, MI: Eerdmans, 2016.

International Organization for Migration. "Abuse, Exploitation and Trafficking: IOM Reveals Data on the Scale of the Danger and Risks that Migrants Face on the Mediterranean Routes to Europe". IOM, 18 October 2016. http://unitedkingdom.iom.int/abuse-exploitation-and-trafficking-iom-reveals-data-scale-danger-and-risks-migrants-face

Kaiser, Walter C. *Mission in the Old Testament: Israel as a Light to the Nations.* 2nd Edn. Grand Rapids, MI: Baker Academic, 2012.

Kidner, Derek. *Psalms 1-72.* Leicester: IVP, 1973.

Longman III, Tremper. *How to Read the Psalms.* Leicester: IVP, 1988.

McCann, J. Clinton. "Psalms". In Leander E. Keck, Ed. *New Interpreter's Bible Commentary.* Volume 3. Nashville, TN: Abingdon Press, 2015.

Okoye, James Chukwuma. *A Light to the Nations: A Mission Theology of the Old Testament.* Maryknoll, NY: Orbis Books, 2006.

Pemberton, Glen. *Hurting with God: Learning to Lament with the Psalms.* Abilene: Abilene Christian University Press, 2012.

Rohrer, James R. "The Psalms in Nineteenth-Century Mission Theology". *Scottish Bulletin of Evangelical Theology* 34(2), (2016): 172-187.

Russell, Brian D. *(re)Aligning with God: Reading Scripture for Church and World.* Eugene, OR: Cascade, 2016.

Stackhouse, Ian. *The Day is Yours: Slow Spirituality in a Fast-Moving World.* Milton Keynes: Paternoster, 2008.

Townsend, Mark. "10,000 Refugee Children Are Missing, says Europol". *The Guardian.* 30th January 2016. [Available at:

https://www.theguardian.com/world/2016/jan/30/fears-for-missing-child-refugees], [Last accessed: 16th October 2022].

UNICEF, *Danger Every Step of the Way: A harrowing journey to Europe for refugee and migrant children*, June 2016.

Walton, John H. *Job.* [Kindle]. Grand Rapids, MI: Zondervan, 2012.

Wolterstorff, Nicholas. *Lament for a Son.* Grand Rapids, MI: Eerdmans, 1987.

Wright, Christopher J.H. "Mission and Old Testament Interpretation". In Craig G. Bartholomew and David J. H. Beldman, Eds. *Hearing the Old Testament: Listening for God's Address.* Grand Rapids, MI: Eerdmans, 2012.

SCANDALOUS PRAYER: LAMENT AS PROTEST IN AN INTERTEXTUAL READING OF LAMENTATIONS 1 AND 2 AND THE DOCUMENTARY FILM *PRAY THE DEVIL BACK TO HELL*

Amanda Avila Kaminski

Introduction

Situations of conflict dramatically escalate the risk of sexual and gender-based violence.[1] During the 1994 genocide in Rwanda, combatants raped between 250,000 and 500,000 women.[2] The early 1990s saw between 20,000 and 50,000 females sexually violated in the Bosnia-Herzegovina war.[3] In the peril of internal displacement during the eleven-year armed conflict in Sierra Leone, militants sexually attacked 50,000-64,000 women.[4] The United Nations estimated that forty females suffered as victims of rape each day in the Second Congo War in South Kivu, Democratic Republic of Congo.[5] Armed aggressors often utilize tactics of terror among civilians and deploy sexual violence as a military strategy. Soldiers target women and girls as a method of humiliation, domination, and force. The threat for women and children in combat zones and the insecurity of displacement create immediate and long-term risks due to the prevalence of human trafficking, prostitution and sex crimes, and the lingering damage of institutionalized violence, unaddressed wartime injustices, and exclusion of females from formal peace processes.[6] The stigma of sexually transmitted

---

[1] For more information on violence and other human rights violations in conflict settings, see the comprehensive content in the searchable database, https://www.beyondintractability.org/. E.g., Michelle Maiese, "Human Rights Violations", in Guy Burgess and Heidi Burgess (eds), *Beyond Intractability* (Conflict Information Consortium, University of Colorado, Boulder, 2003) [Available at: https://www.beyondintractability.org/essay/human-rights-violations], [Last accessed: 16th October 2022].

[2] UN Special Rapporteur to the Commission on Human Rights, "Report on the Situation of Human Rights in Rwanda" (E/CN.4/1996/68) para 16.

[3] Jeanne Ward, "Bosnia and Herzegovina", in *If Not Now, When?: Addressing Gender-based Violence in Refugee, Internally Displaced, and Post-Conflict Settings*. (New York: Women's Refugee Commission, 2002): 81.

[4] Physicians for Human Rights, "Executive Summary", *War-Related Sexual Violence in Sierra Leone: A Population-based Assessment* (Boston/DC: Physicians for Human Rights, 2002): 3.

[5] Claudia Rodriguez, 'Sexual Violence in South Kivu', *Forced Migration Review*, 2007 (27): 45.

[6] The UN Entity for Gender Equality and the Empowerment of Women documents many women and children being abducted by armed groups and subjected to multiple

diseases, unwanted pregnancies, and psychological traumatization persists in the wake of combat. It is compounded by the establishment of inequitable systems that further castigate females by restricting their access to education, denying their rights to land, and disregarding their contributions to new patterns of governance and nation-building.

But sexual assault, exploitation, and sex slavery do not occur only in unstable and violent political territories. For example, survivors of sex trafficking in the United States report that an alarmingly large number of them were part of the foster care system.[7] The literature unequivocally shows that children who have been sexually abused experience greater vulnerability to sexual exploitation, particularly through prostitution.[8] According to the 2020 World Population Review, 35% of women worldwide experience some form of sexual harassment, and only 40% of rape survivors report violations. Even fewer seek the help of law enforcement with the percentage lingering around 10%![9] Only 0.04% of survivors of human trafficking cases are identified, leaving this vulnerable group of 4.8 million "hidden figures [of a virtually invisible] crime."[10]

---

forms of abuse, and exploitation, including sexual slavery. The data also shows that in the eleven UN negotiations for which there is sufficient data, a mere 8% of participants were female and only 3% were signatories to agreements, indicating a disparaging view of women's roles as peacemakers despite the fact that they continue in perilous situations to feed their children, care for the injured, and maintain the cohesion of their family unit" [Available at: https://www.peacewomen.org], [Last accessed: 16th October 2022].

[7] United States Department of State, "2019 Trafficking in Persons Report", (Washington D.C: United States Department of State Publication Office of the Under Secretary for Civilian Security, Democracy, and Human Rights, June 2019). [Available at: https://www.state.gov/wp-content/uploads/2019/06/2019-Trafficking-in-Persons-Report.pdf], [Last accessed: 16th October 2022].

[8] Heather J. Clawson, Nicole Dutch, Amy Solomon, and Lisa Goldblatt Grace, "Human Trafficking Into and Within the United States: A Review of the Literature," Office of the Assistant Secretary for Planning and Evaluation 30th August 2009, (Washington D.C.: U.S. Department of Health and Human Services, 2009). [Available at: https://aspe.hhs.gov/report/human-trafficking-and-within-united-states-review-literature#Trafficking], [Last accessed: 16th October 2022].

[9] World Population Review, "Rape Statistics By Country 2020", *World Population Review Website,* [Available at: http://worldpopulationreview.com/countries/rape-statistics-by-country/], [Last accessed: 16th October 2022].

[10] International Labor Organization, "Forced Labor, Modern Slavery, and Human Trafficking",*ILO Website,* September 2022 [Available at: http://www.ilo.org/global/topics/forced-labour/lang--en/index.htm], [Last accessed: 16th October 2022]; United Nations Office on Drug and Crime, "Monitoring Target 16.2 of the United Nations Sustainable Development Goals", *UNODC Website*, [Available at: https://www.unodc.org/documents/research/UNODC-DNR_research_brief.pdf], [Last accessed: 16th October 2022]; Californians Against Sexual Exploitation, "What is Human Trafficking", *Case Act Website*. 2012 [Available at: http://www.caseact.org/wp-content/uploads/2012/07/Prop-35-Human-Trafficking-Fact-Sheet.pdf], [Last accessed: 16th October 2022]; Human Rights First, "Human Trafficking by the Numbers", 7th January 2017, https://humanrightsfirst.org/library/human-trafficking-by-the-

What resources exist to liberate populations experiencing such terror? How might trauma-aware spirituality catalyze survivors and their allies to break cycles of violence and exploitation, to acknowledge risks and root causes, and to reconnect and thrive in post-trauma situations?

As a theologian and faith-based non-profit practitioner, I believe that the lived practice of faith can serve a key role in the emotional, cognitive, spiritual, and social healing of survivors of rape and trafficking. However, I am disturbed by texts in the Bible that entrench violence against women and institutional patterns of religion that sacralize hegemonic practices of injustice and abuse. Sarojini Nadar argues that the "rape [and trade] of women especially within the biblical literature and its subsequent endorsement by biblical writers and interpreters alike is a great cause for concern."[11] The marginalization of female voices in the holy text, the unchallenged economic and political exchange of women's bodies in biblical narratives, and the silence of God in sacred stories that involve sexual assault demand a transformed reading of Scripture for the resilience of survivors and the awakening of allies. African theologian Mercy Oduyoye insists that biblical passages like these must be exposed, challenged, deconstructed, and liberated by biblical interpretation rather than being skimmed over, ignored, or sanctioned.[12] The poems of Lamentations 1 and 2 offer an opportunity for a trauma-informed reading of a problematic biblical text.

This chapter offers an intertextual treatment of a powerful form of Hebrew prayer called lament to demonstrate how this type of prayer practice empowers the vulnerable to regain their voice and dignity in the wake of sexual assault or exploitation. Further, this chapter will demonstrate how prayer is not only personal but also social, political, physical, and spiritual. Lament engages the Divine in an honest struggle that demands justice and brings the praying person's brokenness to the Redeeming God without sanitizing the suffering one's confusion, anger, or concerns about God's complicity or inaction. Further, prayer in this tradition goes beyond the spiritual and emotional dimension of praxis by redressing grievances, naming offenses, and seeking to reestablish new social connections in the wake of the total wreckage experienced in trauma.

From the fusion of my horizons – training those involved in post-war processes of peacebuilding, teaching trauma awareness and resilience in theological formation, and developing a Christian spirituality that protects and empowers vulnerable populations – the text of Lamentations 1-2 presents a disturbing image of YHWH as the God who perpetrates violence against Woman Zion. The personified city cries out to YHWH and to passersby about her

---

numbers/#:~:text=An%20estimated%2024.9%20million%20victims,in%20state%2Dimposed%20forced%20labor.

[11] Sarojini Nadar, "Texts of Terror: The Conspiracy of Rape in the Bible, Church, and Society: A Reading of Esther 2:1-18", in Isabel Apawo Phiri and Sajorini Nadar (eds), *African Women, Religion, and Health: Essays in Honor of Mercy Amba Oduyoye* (Maryknoll, NY: Orbis, 2006): 78.

[12] Mercy Amba Oduyoye, "African Women's Hermeneutics", in E. Schüssler Fiorenza (ed), *The Power of Naming: A Concilium Reader in Feminist Liberation Theology* (Maryknoll, NY: Orbix, 1998), as cited by Nadar, 78.

suffering only to be shamed, devalued, and disregarded. The sacred text haunts and disturbs the reader:

> My eyes waste with tears; my bowels are in ferment;
> My bile is poured out on the ground because of the breaking of the daughter of my people;
> As the child and the infant are fainting in the streets of the city.
> To their mothers they say, "Where is the corn and the wine?"
> As they faint like the mortally wounded in the streets of the city,
> As their lives are poured out on the breasts of their mothers? (Lam. 2:11-12)[13]

This harrowing scene of biblical poetry comes to life in the opening moments of the award-winning film, *Pray the Devil Back to Hell.*[14] Real-time video footage and post-war interviews document the mobilization of the Women's Peace Initiative of Liberia during the bloody battle between Charles Taylor's regime and the warlords of Liberians United for Reconciliation and Democracy (LURD) from 1989 to 2003.[15] A mother, five months pregnant, flees with her children, aged three and two. The sound of gunshots rings out as Taylor's forces descend on her small village. For seven hours, this heroic woman walks with her babies until they reach her parents' home:

> It was hell on earth. My three-year-old [...] sweat pouring off his body [says] to me, "I wish for a piece of donut [...] I am so hungry." I am sitting there thinking "Where am I going to get a piece of donut for this three-year-old?" The anger built up again; the pain was there [...] "Nuku, I don't have a piece of donut to give you." He said, "I know. I just wish for a piece of donut." Liberia has been at war for so long that my children have been hungry and afraid their entire lives.[16]

A Liberative Approach to Reading a Troubling Biblical Text: Sexual Assault and Exploitation in Lamentations 1-2 and the Spiritual-Political Resilience Offered by Lament

Patrick Miller states that "narrative contexts function to literalize poetic metaphor."[17] The stories of the 2,500 "ordinary mothers, aunts, grandmothers, and sisters" gathering together to pray for peace in Liberia concretizes the careful

---

[13] The translation of Lamentations 1-2 used in this chapter comes from Kathleen O'Connor, *Lamentations & The Tears of the World* (Maryknoll, NY: Orbis, 2002). I chose the first two poems of the five-poem series in the biblical book in order to the limit the scope of my analysis.

[14] Gini Reticker, and Abigail E. Disney, *Pray the Devil Back to Hell* (Sausalito, CA: Rocco Educational Film Distributors, 2009).

[15] This film will be treated as a text throughout the course of this chapter through analysis of the documentary's stories, voices, prayers, and images. Anytime the Women's Peace Initiative of Liberia is referenced, the quotes or narratives come directly from the film.

[16] For more information on Gbowee, see Nobel Women's Initiative, "Leymah Gbowee, 2011, Liberia", [Available at: https://www.nobelwomensinitiative.org/leymahgbowee], [Last accessed: 16th October 2022].

[17] Patrick Miller quoted in Samuel Balentine, *Prayer in the Hebrew Bible* (Minneapolis, MN: Fortress, 1993): 218.

acrostic structure of Lamentations 1-2. Miller notes that embedding a lament in a story helps elucidate how the three-dimensional address of the prayer forms a unified complaint. To understand how a prayer can be directed simultaneously to the self, to the enemy and the community, and to God, a plot "helps us to see how these faces hold together and make sense."[18] This fundamental threefold structure of Woman Zion's lament and of the Women's Peace Initiative of Liberia prayer protest will act as the hermeneutical key to my intertextual reading. While an historical-critical approach can uncover possible details about the original context in which Lamentations may have been written or compiled,[19] this chapter will employ a liberative approach to question the brutal violence and irresponsiveness of God implicit and explicit in the three-dimensional prayer of chapters 1-2 of Lamentations. This trauma-informed reading seeks to determine whether such offensive charges against YHWH and such abhorrent images of suffering can be beneficially appropriated in women's spirituality, particularly by survivors of sexual exploitation. Can the reading of the first two chapters of Lamentations serve redemptive spiritual purposes for contemporary women? How might women, especially those who have suffered the horrors of abuse, rape, trafficking, war crimes, starvation, grief, and loss, use this text in a way that empowers them? Are the brutal depictions of God abusing Zion, and the pictures of the vulnerable Woman Zion being exploited as a conquest of war too savage for use in 21st century liturgy? Does this text hold revelatory power to awaken resistant spirituality in victims of sexual exploitation and to elicit faithful action by allies of trafficked persons?

Allowing this biblical text to interact with the documentary *Pray the Devil Back to Hell* will demonstrate how the practice of lament functions as protest. I will interrogate the grammar of both texts' complaints in order to argue that the three-dimensional structure of lament, as an address (1) to self, (2) to enemy/community, and (3) to God, gives a clue to how the prayer tradition itself empowers the petitioner(s) toward autonomy while also enabling resistance against disparate adversaries. I will begin by analyzing four features of biblical lament and demonstrating how they work in the film. Showing how this Hebrew prayer form functions in the context of the Women's Peace Initiative of Liberia will allow the reader to see scandalous prayer as political critique, faith development, personal empowerment, and prophetic re-imagination. Then, using imagery analysis, the feminization of the city of Zion will heighten the problem of divine inaction and intensify the changing face of the enemy. This intertexual

---

[18] Patrick Miller, "Trouble and Woe: Interpreting the Biblical Laments", *Interpretation* 37(1), (1983): 32–45: 40.

[19] For more on this see the history and authorship section of Dianne Bergant, *Abingdon Old Testament Commentary Series – Lamentations* (Nashville, TN: Abingdon Press, 2003): 16-18; see also Maria Häusl, "Lamentations: Zion's Cry in Affliction", in Luise Schottroff and Marie-Theres Wacker (eds), *Feminist Biblical Interpretation: A Compendium of Critical Commentary on the Books of the Bible and Related Literature* (Grand Rapids, MI: Wm. B. Eerdmans, 2012): 334-344; and Leannn Snow Flesher, "Lamentations", in Catherine Clark Kroeger and Mary J. Evans (eds), *The IVP Women's Bible Commentary* (Downers Grove, IL: InterVarsity Press, 2002): 392-395.

reading will exemplify how women, especially those who suffer or stand in solidarity with the afflicted, can powerfully utilize lament as a tactic of resistance and a practice of trauma healing.

The Four Features of Lament as Protest: A Biblical Invitation to Grief and Resistance

Claus Westermann defines four characteristics of this Hebrew prayer form.[20] They include (1) the dialogic Hebrew relation to God in prayer, (2) poetic meter, (3) standard movement from complaint through petition to thanksgiving, and (4) a three-fold structure of address.

Dialogic Hebrew Relation to God in Prayer

Firstly, Westermann notes that in the dialogical relationship between God and humanity in the Hebrew Bible, the "call of distress" or the "cry out of the depths" constitutes a central substance of the exchanges between humans and God.[21] He calls the language about one's suffering in the Hebrew Bible "lamentation of affliction" and notes that this is a way in which the people of the Old Testament tradition related to their life in the midst of confusion, feelings of abandonment by God, attack by enemies, disaster, and pain. Lament reaches out for life: "it is the only possibility in life left for [the sufferer] as long as [s]he has breath."[22] Thus, the contemporary Christian tendency to restrict or sanitize scandalous prayer from faith formation or to present visceral outcries of divine questioning as "faithless" breaks with a prophetic strand of *faithful* engagement with the God of the Hebrew Bible.

Like Daughter Zion whose gasps from her pain consist of only a few words ("YHWH, look and see my affliction"), Leymah Gbowee, leader of the Women's Peace Initiative of Liberia, in her own prayer of desperation simply utters: "God, please." In the face of rape, displacement, and hunger, what more can be said?

> Taylor had absolute power and total control over the finances of the country. Life was bad; it was miserable. People couldn't even afford a cup of rice. Taylor had his private army […] We lived in fear. It was like you go to bed and you pray you would have something different the next day: that the killing would stop, that the hunger would stop. Saying, "God please."

Westermann identifies that lament carries the suffering to God, who is the giver of life and breath, the promise of peace, and the hope for redemption. Thus, even as the complaint accuses a Sovereign God of threatening the petitioner's existence, the prayer itself demands the attention of the Divine and engages both parties anew in a covenantal relational exchange. Introducing this practice among survivors of rape or trafficking encourages people who have lived through trauma to engage the Divine in a way that does not silo suffering or cause feelings of shame in honest existential questioning. Rather, it enables grief to

---

20 Claus Westermann, "Role of the Lament in the Theology of the Old Testament", *Interpretation* 28(1), (1st January 1974): 20-38.

21 Westermann, "Role of the Lament", 22.

22 Westermann, "Role of the Lament", 22.

take its proper place in the process of healing and welcomes outrage, mourning, numbness, or aggression before God.[23]

Beau Harris and Carleen Mandolfo note two additional facets of Lamentations' dialogical nature. The first highlights the constant shift of voices.[24] Various perspectives help to tell the story of suffering and devastation from multiple angles. The Narrator of Lamentations gives context and plot to the prayers of Daughter Zion, weaving together a descriptive fabric while still making the story unspecific and thus adaptable to various situations. Where Daughter Zion offers first-person prayer language from the position of the sufferer, the dialogical voice of the Narrator roots the story in a larger depiction of human cruelty and divine action. Similarly, the structure of *Pray the Devil Back to Hell* employs the storylines of many interviewees to feature the myriad forms of suffering generated by Taylor's war. Together, the cast of characters constructs a more holistic picture of the atrocities of the civil conflict. Differing points of view enable a multifaceted picture of the protest to come into relief. Natives of Monrovia, displaced women in camps, leaders of the campaign for peace, quiet petitioners, mothers, daughters, wives, mobilizers, Christians, and Muslims add their diverse voices.

Another dialogical feature of Lamentations refers to Daughter Zion's "talking back" to the prophetic threat of God's divine punishment of sin.[25] The prophets in the Hebrew Bible warn about God's judgment for sin, which may come through war, death, famine, or conquest. Lamentations offers a response by God's covenanted people from the despair of the ash and destruction. The rebuttal of Daughter Zion declaims the situation as unjust and oppressive and decries the severity of the situation, condemning the violence as inappropriate no matter the trespasses she committed. Daughter Zion inveighs against God's retribution: she insists that "suckling infants [going] into captivity" (1:5), "women eat[ing] their children" (2:20), "the child and the infant fainting in the streets of the city" (2:11) could never be a reasonable or justifiable punishment, especially not by a loving God. Similarly, the women of the film condemn the dehumanizing tactics of the warring factions, both of whom claim to be fighting to establish good governance for the nation. When asked about the root causes of the conflict, Gbowee simply replies, "Power, money, ethnicity, greed; but

---

[23] Literature from the field of racial healing has recognized the power of lament. See e.g. Brenda Salter McNeil, Eugene Cho, and J. Derek McNeil, *Roadmap to Reconciliation: Moving Communities into Unity, Wholeness and Justice* (Downers Grove, IL: IVP Books, 2016);
Brenda Salter McNeil and Rick Richardson, *The Heart of Racial Justice: How Soul Change Leads to Social Change* (Downers Grove, IL: IVP Books, 2009); Soong-Chan Rah, *Prophetic Lament: A Call for Justice in Troubled Times* (Downers Grove, IL: IVP Books, 2015).

[24] For more on the dialogical voices in the form of Lamentations 1-2, see Jill Middlemas, "Speaking of Speaking: The Form of Zion's Suffering in Lamentations", in Mark J. Boda, Carol J. Dempsey, and LeAnn Snow Flesher (eds), *Daughter Zion: Her Portrait, Her Response* (Atlanta, GA: Society of Biblical Literature, 2012): 39-54.

[25] Carleen Mandolfo, *Daughter Zion Talks Back to the Prophets: A Dialogic Theology of the Book of Lamentations* (Atlanta, GA: Society of Biblical Literature, 2007).

there is nothing in my mind that should make people do what they did to the children of Liberia." In their protests, both the biblical Woman Zion and the historical women of the Liberian Peace Initiative denounce their current reality and demonstrate that the ends do not justify the means. By talking back, they reclaim the power to redress their grievances.

Poetic Meter

The second form-critical characteristic of lament highlights the rhythmic, poetic structure of the poetry.[26] Westermann likens the language, tone, and feel of this prayer tradition to the voice of the oppressed in the midst of their plight: a wail. During a visit to the internally displaced persons camps in Monrovia, one woman of the Liberian Peace Initiative responds to the abject poverty and the hopelessness of the women saying, "we just broke down and cried because there was no outlet for the [distress and outrage]." In suffering, lament is the only appropriate response to grief. Lament is a poetic cry intended to combine the pain of one's inmost being with the power of weeping to evoke compassion in one who hears. Therefore, the rhythmic prayers function to appeal simultaneously to God for mercy and to the oppressor or society through its throbbing cadence.

The *qinah*, or lament meter, indicates the pulsing arrangement of the verses in the poetic structure. This dominant rhythmic pattern is an elemental feature of the genre. The lines fall into two distinct parts, which make up the tempo. The first part is longer than the second. As one beat corresponds with each word or set of words, each line develops in a 3 + 2 pattern. This irregularity of beats forms something like a sob, a choke, or a gasp for breath, indicative of mourning, sorrow, and affliction.[27] This pattern has also been described as a limping meter, one that is fading out in exhaustion or death.[28] Kathleen O'Connor writes:

> With the alarming cry of a funeral dirge, the narrator demands our attention in the poem's opening verse […] The "how" is a bitter declaration that death has occurred, but as Naomi Seidman observes, it also implies interrogation – "How could this happen to beloved Zion?" […] To convey the breath-stopping shock of the catastrophe, Seidman proposed the opening ["how"] "be pronounced with a catch in the throat."[29]

This literary trait comes to life during the footage of the Liberian women's network protest in Accra, Ghana in 2003 when Taylor and the rebels of LURD

---

[26] Westermann, "Role of the Lament", 23.

[27] Bergant, *Lamentations,* 18.

[28] Some commentators challenge the identification of *qinah* as a characteristic feature of lament because not every line fits this distinctive poetic form. However, Bergant notes a high percentage of verses that use this meter. Further, she argues for unity in the entire book of Lamentations, which give the entire collection a *qinah* beat of 3 + 2. The similar structure of poems one to three in Lamentations and the diminutive movement of poems four to five of the collection give the entire oeuvre a limping feeling. Bergant suggests that this artistic choice by the editor makes the book one elongated lament, which stretches in anguish through its third chapter and then falls and gasps into a sorrowful end, 18-21.

[29] O'Connor, *Lamentations*, 19.

are finally convinced to come to the table for peace negotiations. The women continue fasting and praying in their signature white garb inspired by their imagination of the biblical narrative of Esther, who sat clothed in sackcloth and ashes during her own period of prayer and political advocacy. Half of the protesters remain in the fish market in Monrovia daily participating in sit-ins while the other half travel to Accra and mobilize refugee women to join in their demonstration of prayer at the peace talks. "We are their conscience sitting out here. We are calling to their conscience to do the right thing and the right thing now is to give women and their children the peace they so desperately need." When the news breaks that Charles Taylor has been indicted for war crimes in Sierra Leone, a violent backlash in Monrovia breaks into full-scale war: a missile hits the American embassy where many refugees are housed; Taylor's supporters begin a campaign of rape and murder claiming that without him there is no Liberia. Far from their families, the women in Accra feel even more powerless and afraid: "My son called me and said, 'We just dug a mass grave and we are burying hundreds of them [...] we are enclosed and can't get out. How will we find food?'" The film shows the women weeping and singing, their voices breaking with uncontrollable emotion, their prayers dissolving into groans and cries.

The metric pattern of Lamentations 1-2 follows a more formalized and edited style than the ad-hoc songs of the women in Accra. The formal text artistically captures the all-encompassing nature of grief. The first line of each verse correlates with the respective alphabetic letter in successive order forming a careful acrostic. Dianne Bergant notes that such precision clearly demonstrates skill and creativity, which, although it restricts the flow of the verse, nonetheless serves a significant theological purpose. Commentators have suggested the following possible functions:

a. The acrostic aids in memorization.
b. The poetic structure reaching from "A to Z" embodies the intended comprehensiveness of the content.
c. The acrostic functions to mirror the total range of human despair and grief.
d. The extreme emotion of the poem expresses the chaos of the situation and seeks some control and order within the confines of the acrostic pattern.[30]

The acrostic design of Lamentations embeds the poem into the memory of Israel and allows the range of the lyrical device along with the tempo to express more than the words alone can convey. This creative expression of remembrance and reflection on a people's traumatic history offers practitioners and ministers working in post-traumatic healing processes a powerful example of a critical stage in recovery: memorializing.[31]

---

[30] Bergant, *Lamentations*, 14-15.

[31] See the Strategies for Trauma Awareness and Resilience (STAR) training resources from Eastern Mennonite University for more on stages and activities for building resilience after trauma. [Available at: https://emu.edu/cjp/star/toolkit], [Last accessed: 16th October 2022].

The Women's Peace Initiative of Liberia employs a similarly anamnestic power in their song of lament: "We want peace, No more war [...] Our children are dying [...] We are tired of running." During the footage of the peace talks, some of the delegates and participants are recorded whistling the tune as the women successfully weave their way into the consciences of their representatives through musical agency. This practice gave the women unity and connection in the joining of their voices, poetic power to invade the memory of their adversaries, and aesthetic expression of their mourning and desires.

Movement from Complaint through Petition to Thanksgiving

The third notable characteristic of lament highlighted by Westermann – movement from complaint to petition to thanksgiving – remains poignantly absent in Lamentations. Westermann claims that the psalms of lament never end with jeremiad but move into thanksgiving and praise as an act of faith and a response to God's faithfulness. He avers that this resolution mirrors the relationship with YHWH:

> There is not a single [one] that stops with lamentation. Lamentation has no meaning in and of itself. That it functions as an appeal is evident in its structure. What the lament is concerned with is not a description of one's sufferings [...] but with the removal of [it]. The lament appeals to the one who can remove suffering. The transition is evident in the fact that the lamentation flows into petition (to secure God's attention and intervention) – or, that petition follows lamentation.[32]

However, the poems of Lamentations defy Westermann's standard form suggesting that there is prophetic power to the mere expression of suffering and theological import in refusing to move toward praise before the praying subject is ready.[33] These biblical poems validate the role of lament on its own as a spiritual practice when resolution or theological absolution remain far off. The mood of the text in Lamentations never moves past despair to faith, confidence, trust, or adoration. The voices of chapters 1 and 2 remain in a state of weeping and accusation against God.[34] Daughter Zion refuses Westermann's demand for

---

[32] Westermann, 26.

[33] Some scholars disagree with my basic premise that the practice of resistant spirituality captured in these chapters offers a positive theological resource for those living in the midst of trauma. Some challenge the notion that struggling against God is a legitimate biblical theology. By focusing on the aberrant and infrequent versus that express hope or trust in the Divine in Lamentations, most notably the few words of the Strong Man character from the center of Lamentations 3, some interpreters have missed the opportunity to find within the Scriptures a form of religious praxis that takes seriously women's voices and lived experience. For an incredible feminist interpretation of Lamentations which argues that the remaining poems do not ascend toward a climax of hopeful praise but instead die off in exhaustion and extremity, see O'Conner, *Lamentations & The Tears of the World.*

[34] Again, see O'Conner for her insistence that this remains true for the entire collection of poems. See esp. her explanation of why the Strong Man's famous refrain in Lamentations 3, "The steadfast love of YHWH never ceases for his mercies... are new every morning. Great is your faithfulness," actually reflects a desperate effort to remind God and to remind himself of their relationship from the pit of despair. Within the larger

lament to be a temporary stop *en route* to praise; she sits in her suffering and remains unmoved until God acts or her community responds or she unsettles her feelings of helplessness to discover her own power and agency. However, her prayer invites the Narrator, passersby, and God to look upon the extent of her suffering as a corrective to their negligence and callousness. The very form of her weeping prayer acts as protest, reclamation of autonomy, and social critique.

Petition to God is made in only a few verses of Lamentations 1 and 2. In chapter 1, only four verses image Daughter Zion beseeching God to "look" at her suffering, "hear" her cry, and recognize the evil of her enemy. Only one verse in chapter 2 depicts Daughter Zion beckoning God to "look" at what God has done to her.

> YHWH, look at my affliction for the enemy has made himself great. (1:9)
> YHWH, look and pay attention for I have become worthless! (1:11)
> Look, YHWH, I am in anguish, my bowels are in ferment… (1:20)
> Hear how I am groaning; there is no one to comfort me… (1:21)
> Let all their wickedness come before you and deal severely with them as you have dealt severely with me… (1:23)
> Look, YHWH, and pay attention to whom you are acting so severely. (2:20)

The tenor of the complaint resounds throughout the accompanying verses, but the cry to God is singular: "Pay attention to me, YHWH: look; see; hear!" With Westermann, who confidently claims that "lamentation has no meaning in and of itself," the reader is left to wonder: what is the point of such a violent collection of prayers? How can these cries yield meaning without a response from YHWH? How can the faith-filled petitioner reconcile the seeming Divine indifference? Inviting these unresolved questions into a trauma-informed prayer practice gives space in the spiritual life for acknowledging the extent of a survivor's suffering and the inexplicability of experiences of extremity and terror. Stigmatizing such expressions in prayer as faith-less or dogmatically inaccurate has been the mistake of too many theologians and practitioners. Encouraging this resistant form of prayer remains a key purpose of this chapter. And seeing its efficacy for the Liberian women demonstrates how it works for community-building, recovery, personal dignity, political organizing, and peacemaking.

Three-Fold Structure of Address

The final form-critical feature offers a hermeneutical key for my thesis about lament as resistance. Westermann defines the three-dimensional address in the petitions of lament as constitutive of the grammar of this prayer tradition. The

---

narrative context of poem 3, this singular verse which interpreters have clung to for a hint of praise in an otherwise mournful book reflects the whiplash of a sufferer trying to make sense of God and God's promises while experience God's silence and the realities of trauma, possibly at God's hand. This exclamation is less a cry of praise than an unsuccessful attempt to convince God and the petitioner himself of a covenant that seems beyond repair. The remainder of the chapter insists that Adonai does not see and then that Adonai does see and therefore must bring recompense and justice. Poems 4 and 5 fade off with even greater despair.

protest takes multiform aim: "it is directed toward God (an accusation or complaint against God), toward other men [sic] (a complaint against an enemy), and toward the lamenter himself (I-lament or We-lament)."[35] Thus in one unified act of grievance, Daughter Zion addresses the personal, social, political, and divine structures of her life in a heart-wrenching wail against all the powers that have brought her to the present place of suffering. This innate connection between one's theological, individual, and communal worlds in prayer uncovers a distinctly Hebrew mindset evidenced throughout the whole of the Hebrew Bible.[36] This unique aspect of lament clearly arises in the first two chapters of Lamentations. The practice seamlessly weaves together self-address, demand for social accountability, and negotiation of covenantal terms and power dynamics between the prayer and God.

The process of the Narrator's reformation from Lamentations 1 as distant storyteller to Lamentations 2 as empathetic advocate demonstrates the efficacy of the multiform address. The Narrator begins with a somewhat detached omniscient perspective describing the suffering Woman Zion:

> How lonely she sits the city once great with people!
> She has become like a widow, she who was once great among the nations.
> A princess among the provinces, she is now in forced labor. (1:1)
> Bitterly she weeps in the night and her tears are upon her cheeks. (1:2)
> And departed from Daughter Zion is all her splendor…(1:6)
> …When her people fell by the hand of the foe and there was no one to help her, her enemies saw her and laughed at her collapse. (1:7)

The Narrator takes on the role of accusing Daughter Zion of her sin and naming her transgression as the source and cause of her misery:

> Jerusalem has sinned grievously; therefore, she has become an unclean thing.
> All who honored her make light of her, for they see her nakedness.
> Indeed, she herself groans and turns away. (1:8)

When Daughter Zion finally finds her voice in 1:12, she fluidly moves between addressing YHWH and accusing onlookers of their apathy:

> YHWH, look and pay attention for I have become worthless! (1:11)
> Is it nothing to you who pass by on the way? Pay attention and look! (1:12)
> Listen, I beg you, all peoples and see my pain. (1:18)
> Look, YHWH, I am in anguish (1:20).

When Chapter 2 opens, the Narrator, a representative of Zion's social audience, remains unaffected by Zion's plea. They go about the task of describing how Adonai brought destruction upon Daughter Zion (2:1-10). Then in what Kathleen O'Connor entitles "The Narrator's Conversion," something changes, and the Storyteller becomes enraged at the pain and despondency of Zion[37] As in the case of many first responders in disaster relief, the Narrator is moved by the unbearable suffering and wretchedness of the conflict zone and begins to vomit (2:11). The Narrator can no longer stand at a distance. First

---

[35] Westermann, "Role of the Lament", 27.
[36] Westermann, "Role of the Lament", 28.
[37] O'Connor, *Lamentations*, 35.

responders describe the smell of death and the emotion of uncovering bodies amid the chaos of the living searching for their loved ones in the wreckage.[38] The bodily response can cause dizziness, nightmares, hysteria, melancholy, and vomiting.[39] The Narrator who previously looked at Woman Zion with judgment and disdain, accusing her of adultery (1:19) and likening her to a menstrual rag (1:17c), now says to her, "What can I liken to you that I may comfort you, O Virgin Daughter of Zion?" (2:13). The Storyteller has been moved to compassion and solidarity by the cries of Daughter Zion. They no longer mock her, nor do they rehearse Zion's sins; rather, they encourage her not to give up in her protest (2:18c) and instruct her in resistance (2:19). Hearing Zion's lament and seeing her clearly transforms this member of Daughter Zion's community; the prayer itself creates new social relations.

Leymah Gbowee reports a similar transformation among the actors at the peace negotiations during a poignant moment of the film. For months, through torrential rains and 100-degree heat, females, young and elderly, sit outside the meetings quietly praying, singing, watching their husbands' murderers and daughters' rapists eating, drinking, and rubbing elbows with important people while their families at home starve and suffer. Infuriated, the women link arms and sit at the doors of the building where the negotiations are underway vowing that they will not allow anyone to exit until an agreement is signed. Footage shows Gbowee weeping and screaming, "Let them go without food until they've made a decision. They can feel what our children have felt." The security guards arrive threatening to arrest the women for "obstructing justice." They begin to wail and cry, and in an act of protest, Gbowee begins to disrobe. In the Liberian culture, to see your mother naked is a curse and evokes shame and humiliation in the audience. As Gbowee begins to undress, she juxtaposes her volitional exposure with the horrific brutality of the men inside who have been systematically undressing someone's mother and violating someone's wife for greed and power.

In an ironic moment that highlights the multidimensional audience of lament, the same police who were trying to arrest the women for their demonstration, moved by their lament, begin to alert them to breaches in their blockade saying: "You have to send some women to the window because some delegates are

---

[38] IFRC, *Management of Dead Bodies After Disasters: A Manual For First Responders* (Washington, DC: Pan American Health Organization, 2006), [Available at: http://www.ifrc.org/docs/idrl/I967EN.pdf], [Last accessed: 16th October 2022]. For more on the trauma suffered by first responders, see Alexander Klein, "First responders after disasters: a review of stress reactions, at-risk, vulnerability, and resilience factors", *Prehosp Disaster Med* 24(2), (March-April 2009): 87-94.

[39] Carolyn Yoder calls this "secondary trauma" in *The Little Book of Trauma Healing: When Violence Strikes and Community Security Is Threatened* (New York: Good Books, 2005): 14. The various forms of trauma (singular event, continuous, collective, generational/historical, secondary, participation-induced) that scholars have parsed out demand a consideration of how practices of lament could facilitate healing spaces and dialogic rituals for various actors in situations of extremity to tell their stories, name their fears and loss, and move toward integration.

escaping." When a warlord in frustration and hunger attempts to break through their line by kicking at the women's backs, the former Nigerian President and Moderator of the negotiations disgraces the perpetrator saying, "Get back inside and sit down. If you were real men, you wouldn't kill your women." Thus, this prayerful protest stirs the watching political figures to recalibrate the system to consider the women's complaint. In the film, Gbowee notes how the mood of the peace talks suddenly, dramatically changed "from gay and happy to sober and serious." After the blockade, even the international community threatens to pull funding if an agreement does not occur in the two-week period demanded by the women.

Walter Brueggemann notes the political and structural dimension of lament. He writes that the prayer tradition "shifts the calculus and redresses the redistribution of power between the two parties, so that the petitionary party is taken seriously and the God who is addressed is newly engaged in the crisis in a way that puts God at risk."[40] He asserts that the articulation of injustice by the sufferer constitutes a form of power. The loss of such an oppositional type of prayer threatens "theological monopoly" through the engenderment of "docility and submissiveness" which re-enforce the socio-political and economic status quo.[41] For contemporary spirituality, Brueggemann warns that the removal of lament from the life of liturgy and personal practice jeopardizes firstly, personal participation in redemptive activity, and secondly, resistance to injustice through verbal complaint and social challenge.

Brueggemann's articulation of ego-strength development in the process of lament builds the case for the lament as self-address. As the suffering human experiences empowerment through verbal expression, she regains her dignity, her individuality, and her power of agency.[42] He writes:

> where there is lament, the believer is able to take initiative with God and so develop over against God the ego-strength that is necessary for responsible faith. But where the capacity to initiate lament is absent, one is left only with praise and doxology […] the believer is nothing […] the outcome is a "false self", bad faith which is based in fear and guilt and lived out as resentful or self-deceptive works of righteousness.[43]

Schmidt, Delekat, and Beyerlin all frame the lament in juridical terms illuminating the way in which lament raises questions "in terms of social goods, social access, and social power."[44] Brueggemann further outlines four ways in which the prayer of lament complains:

---

[40] Walter Brueggemann, "The Costly Loss of Lament", *Journal for the Study of the Old Testament* 36 (1st October 1986): 59.

[41] Brueggemann, "The Costly Loss", 60.

[42] Brueggemann, "The Costly Loss", 60-1.

[43] Brueggemann, "The Costly Loss", 62.

[44] H. Schmidt, *Das Gebet der Angeklagten im Alten Testament* (BZAW 49; Giessen: A. Töpelmann, 1928); L. Delekat, *Asylie und Schutzorakel am Zionheiligtum* (Leiden: Brill, 1967); W. Beyerlin, *Die Rettung der Bedrängten in den Feindpsalmen der Einzelnen auf institutionelle Zusammenhänge untersucht* (FRLANT, 99; Göttingen: Vandenhoeck and Ruprecht, 1970), as presented by Brueggemann in his analysis of juridical language in lament Psalms.

1. The present arrangement of life is unjust.
2. The present arrangement of life cannot remain the same.
3. In the present arrangement, I need change; I will not allow this to stay this way.
4. God you must change this present arrangement.[45]

This schema demonstrates the multiple levels of engagement in lament: personal, divine, social, structural, economic. The address of the complaint speaks to the community, the structures that arrange the life she protests, the self, and the Divine who upholds it all. Brueggemann notes that "while the cry is addressed to Yahweh, it is clear that the cry is not merely a religious gesture but has important and direct links to social processes."[46] Thus, in the language of lament in Israel, the function is juridical action to judge, to protest, and to re-establish the marginalized in the course of social reform. Brueggemann warns that the loss of lament strips the petitioner of both her authentic relation to God and her personal agency in transformation, writing "where God's dangerous availability is lost because we fail to carry on our part of the difficult conversation; where God's vulnerability and passion are removed from our speech, we are consigned to anxiety and despair and the world as we now have it becomes absolutized."[47]

Imagery Analysis: The Feminization of Daughter Zion and the Silent, Abusive God

The horrors of the post-war poetry in Lamentations come alive in the narrative of the Liberian Peace Initiative. But perhaps even more sobering are the disturbing images depicted metaphorically in Lamentations and literalized in the lives of the women in countless historical moments. This chapter now turns to an intertextual analysis of the feminized, sexualized, and abusive imagery of the two texts examined in this interpretation to further investigate the proposed thesis of lament as a prayer of resistance.

Feminized Imagery

In Hebrew, the word for city is a feminine noun often personified through a female figure.[48] City laments offer imaginative space where reality can be experienced metaphorically.[49] The gendered language helps to elucidate the

[45] Brueggemann, "The Costly Loss", 62.
[46] Brueggemann, "The Costly Loss", 63.
[47] Brueggemann, "The Costly Loss", 64
[48] John J. Schmitt, "Israel and Zion – Two Gendered Images: Biblical Speech Traditions and Their Contemporary Neglect", *Horizons* 81(1), (1991): 18-32.
[49] For more on this see F. W. Dobbs-Allsopp, *Weep, O Daughter of Zion: A Study of the City-Lament Genre in the Hebrew Bible* (Rome: Editrice Pontificio Istituto Biblico, 1993); Donna Lee Petter, "The Book of Ezekiel: Patterned After A Mesopotamian City Lament?" PhD diss., University of Toronto, 2009, 45-63; *Lamentations Anchor Bible*

city's function as mother to its inhabitants and provider and sustainer for its dwellers. The personification of Daughter Zion feminizes the suffering of the city in a single character who is described in various female roles: widow, princess, mother, lover, daughter, virgin. Christl Maier notes how the feminization of the city in this genre allows the author to emphasize the loss and grief felt concerning the ruined status of Jerusalem through the exploitation of the social vulnerability that women bore in the patriarchal society of ancient Israel.[50] The city once full of people is now a widow, lonely, without her children. The princess Zion once cloaked in majesty has now been stripped and shamed by her pursuers, overtaken and desolated by the hand of her foe, cast into exile and forced into hard servitude. In these positions, the female Zion now finds herself powerless, in need of legal protection: a woman once married is now widowed and childless; a princess has been captured and made subject to a powerful foe.[51]

Abusive Imagery

Violence in Lamentations 1-2 also takes on personhood, surrounding the center square and dominating Woman Zion. Assault takes on not only spatial existence but also movement, suggesting that "time and space are subject to the effects of violence."[52] The identification of the city as a breeding ground of brutality, deceit, and oppression is juxtaposed against its intended function as a walled mechanism of defense. The "I" of the text is both the place and object of violence, relating the language particularly powerfully to women who have experienced sexual assault.

Furthermore, the inside of the walls of the city are imaginatively envisioned as the heart of the land, the center of its cultural and religious life. The penetration of the city walls then strikes at the very heart of the "I" of the text. The heart, the very self of the figure, has been violated. "This is not a historically identifiable occupation of a historically identifiable city; rather, the image of the city is the part of the topography of violence, metaphorically expressed by means of the [lament's] spatial structure."[53] Ulrike Bail draws a comparison in her intertextual reading of Psalm 55 with Judges 19 and Genesis 19 where the heart

---

71, 2nd rev. ed. (Garden City: Doubleday, 1992), 32-9; W. C. Gwaltney, "The Biblical Book of Lamentations in the Context of Near Eastern Lament Literature," in W.W. Hallo, et. al. (eds), *More Essays on the Comparative Method: Scripture in Context II* (Winona Lake, IN: Eisenbrauns, 1983): 191-211; and Thomas F. McDaniel, "Alleged Sumerian Influence upon Lamentations", *Vetus Testamentum* 18(2), (April 1968): 198-209.

[50] Christl M. Maier, *Daughter Zion, Mother Zion: Gender, Space, and the Sacred in Ancient Israel* (Minneapolis, MN: Fortress Press, 2008): 145.

[51] Maier, *Daughter Zion,* 145.

[52] Bail, Ulrike, "The Psalms: 'Who Is Speaking May Be *All* That Matters'" in Schottroff, Luise and Marie-Theres Wacher (eds.) *Feminist Biblical Interpretation: A Compendium of Critical Commentary on the Books of the Bible and Related Literature* (Eerdmans 2012).

[53] Bail, 259.

of the city, that is the market place, is struck with violence.[54] Similarly, the text of the Liberian Women's Peace Movement also saw the marketplace as central to the story. This economic center, which for the community signified jobs, food, social exchange and commercial opportunity, now stood still as the women's sit-ins exposed it as a violent place of murder and rape.

Sexualized Imagery

The language in city lament of being "surrounded" intimates the threat of rape. The language of the city being penetrated and violated clearly images a scene of sexual assault. Bail writes, "The limits of the city, like the limits of the body, have not been respected. Like the city, the body of a woman can be conquered, taken over, plundered and destroyed." This is the powerful metaphorical parallel between the vision of a city being ravaged and the experience of a woman in rape. The characterization of the city as a woman and a daughter heightens the shock and horror of the adversary's physical and sexual assault on Zion. The inhabitants of the city have been murdered or carried away leaving the surviving mourner, also usually a female role in Hebrew society, wailing in grief and shock as she contemplates the blood on the streets of the city and remembers when they used to be filled with singing and religious celebrations (1:4, 7). The poetic language mingles the breaching of the city walls by the enemy with the graphic imagery of a woman being violently undressed and violated. In 1:3, the enemy overtakes her in her distress; in verse 5, the foes have become her head; in verse 10, the enemy stretches out his hands over all the woman's precious things and invades her sanctuary.

Between these political images of a nation overtaking the personified city comes the visceral depiction of the vulnerable woman suffering public humiliation and sexual violence. Alan Mintz demonstrates how the language of sexual intercourse in this text depends upon a correlation between the woman and the city, the body and the temple, the female genitals and the sanctuary.[55] The image of the conquerors invading the fortressed walls becomes vehemently sexualized as Daughter Zion is stripped and raped:

> Jerusalem has sinned grievously; therefore, she is an unclean thing.
> All who honored her make light of her, for they see her nakedness.
> Indeed, she herself groans and turns away.
> Her uncleanness is on her skirts; she did not remember her future;
> She has fallen terribly. There is no one to comfort her. (Lam. 1: 8-9 a)

The exposure of the woman's broken body in public view conjures horrifying images of denigration and indignity. Some scholars have argued that the comments about the fluids in her skirt imply ritual impurity associated with menstruation, signally her ritual impurity and thus her status as a woman

---

[54] Bail, 249.

[55] Alan Mintz, "The Rhetoric of Lamentations and the Representations of Catastrophe", *Prooftexts* 2 (1982): 1-17.

scorned, cut off from holiness, and removed from others.[56] However, with Kathleen O'Connor, I find it much more convincing that the fluids come from the intercourse her enemy has forced upon her based on the context preceding and following.[57] The metaphorical body of the feminized city becomes an object of defilement and ignominy. After having her nakedness exposed in plain sight, the mortified victim groans and turns her face away (1:8). Verse 9 articulates her sense of no longer being able to even imagine her future. So great is her suffering and loss in the wake of this event that she can no longer dream of a time to come. Not only has the enemy attacked her in the most grotesque way. He has also stolen her hope and pillaged her future.

Finally, left alone with no one to comfort her, she turns to YHWH and addresses the Divine directly for first time in Lamentations: "YHWH, look at my affliction, for the enemy has made himself great!" (1:9c) She intensifies her prayer and dejection in verse 11: "YHWH, look and pay attention for I have become worthless!" (1:11c) Between these two succinct prayers, she utters a description of the enemy spreading out his hand on her "precious things" marked by a political correlative of the nations "coming into her sanctuary" (1:10). If the metaphor of sexual assault carries through these verses equating the "precious things" of verse 10 with Daughter Zion's genitals, then the image of verse 11 continues the offensive storyline with the desperate, starving people of the city giving away their "precious things" in exchange for food and survival. If the metaphoric schema of Mintz extends to these verses, then the enemy has not only defiled the temple by entering the sanctuary but has also confiscated the treasured ornaments of worship. The liturgical and symbolic tools that Israel uses to perform her religious observances have been plundered, leaving the Chosen Nation's identity hanging in the balance. The symbolic parallel must not go unnoticed to fully digest the poignancy and discomfiture of this image. In the same way that the very identity of the worshipping community has been destroyed by the pillaging of the temple, so too has the dignity and selfhood of Woman Zion been disfigured by this traumatic incident. Worse, the seat of Woman Zion's identity – now violated, decimated, and exposed – has become an economic resource commercially exploited. Raped and reduced to trading sex for survival, the city appears in the most traumatized state imaginable. These are the images into which the second short prayer of Daughter Zion resounds. Groaning and wailing at her lost sense of self, the victim calls herself worthless (1:11c).

In the film, the women recognize the sexualized war tactics of both parties in the conflict. They shrewdly begin to leverage this in protest. First, they begin to reclaim their power and mobilize, using their physical bodies to make their complaints known. Like Daughter Zion begging for a witness to her suffering, the women ask themselves, how can we get Taylor to see us and recognize what

[56] Maier, *Daughter Zion,* 147; Adele Berlin, *Lamentations: A Commentary* (Louisville, KY: Westminster John Knox, 2002), 53-59; Frederick W. Dobbs-Allsopp, "Raising Zion in Lamentations 2", in B. F. Batto and K. L. Roberts (eds), *David and Zion: Biblical Studies in Honor of J. J. M. Roberts* (Winona Lake, IN: Eisenbrauns, 2004).

[57] O'Connor, *Lamentations,* 22.

he is doing to the mothers and children of his own people? Thousands of females respond by making their complaint known through sitting together in strategic locations of commercial life and political activity.

After days of praying, singing, and sitting, they advance their counterattack by answering the sexualized tactics of war with a sex fast. They reason that since both sides are raping and abusing somebody's wife, sister, mother, or daughter, all the women should voluntarily unite and refuse to let anyone have sexual satisfaction. Until their men, whether committing or condoning these assaults, acknowledge the way their jockeying for power had played itself out on women's bodies, the women assert their autonomy and agency by taking back their own bodies as sites of resistance.

> We decided to have a sex strike. We have power as a woman: deny the male sex. Men were the perpetrators of violence so whether out of commission or omission you were guilty […] The husbands were now praying equally with them and the end of the war meant the beginning of enjoyment.

Bail notes that the "true achievement" of the lament as prayer is the woman's ability to avert her gaze from the destruction and pain of violence, to rediscover her own voice, to reconnect with her own body and self, and to begin to articulate her own future again. "No one hears my cries" is a grievance often articulated by victims of rape and one utilized by the Liberian women and Woman Zion in their short prayers.[58] Kathleen O'Connor argues that the weeping of Daughter Zion persists not due to loss of her glory and splendor, as the Narrator's supposes, but because no one sees her, because she has no comforter, and because she has lost sight of her future.[59] Woman Zion not only expresses her sense of devaluation from the sexual violation but also suffers from the silence and irresponsiveness of God and the lack of protection or intervention of her social network. Daughter Zion fluctuates between beseeching a distant God and a hardened community to pay heed to her suffering. In the midst of such negligence, lament alone has the capacity to be "a living witness to a pain that knows no release."[60] The experience of sexual violence can breed a sense of powerlessness, but the potency of the lament unleashes the petitioner's agency to name the atrocity, accuse the perpetrator, reclaim imaginative capacity, and declaim an end to the violence. As prayer, these acts also implore God, the Almighty, to invert the oppressive structure of dominance, to ease divine judgment, to remove anger, to be true to covenant promises. Language itself becomes a means of exercising authority. The very act of lament catalyzes latent potentiality for transformation and liberation.[61] If subjectivity is shaped by language, then the cry of lament empowers the one who has experienced the denigration of sexual objectification and victimization to reclaim her self-esteem

---

[58] O'Connor, *Lamentations,* 244.
[59] O'Connor, *Lamentations*, 26-7.
[60] Mintz, "Rhetoric", 3.
[61] Quoting Konrad Raiser, Bail says that the naming of violence in the form of lament grants strength to the one suffering and "in this way the lament itself becomes a source of liberation," 242.

and autonomy.[62] The complaint itself enables her to reclaim her value, redefine her identity in relation to God, and redress the grievances she names against her multiform enemy.[63] But who is the enemy, especially if she accuses God of divine punishment and God remains unmoved? As the petitioner pitches her complaint against a changing audience – structures, society, political enemies, God – who is her foe?

Enemy Identity

The sources of Daughter Zion's suffering in Lamentations 1-2 change as fluidly as her accusations. While the first half of chapter 1 presents Woman Zion being attacked by former friends (1:2, 8), enemies (1:4, 7), pursuers (1:3), and the nations (1:10), the second half paints a starkly different picture. In 1:12, God, not the nations, emerges as the enemy who has killed the inhabitants of the city: an abusive husband beating Daughter Zion until her bones burn (1:13); a captor binding her with the rope of her sins and tying her down (1:14); and a killer crushing the blood of Zion's warriors like grapes in a winepress (1:15). Using corporeal imagery, the assault against the vulnerable Woman Zion appears gruesome and inexcusable at the hand of God: "her feet are fettered, her bones burning, she lies on her back, her neck feels like it is bound by ropes, her heart is overturned, her eyes are full of tears, and her spirits are low."[64] The face of the foe transfigures from one-time friend, to enemy, former lovers, to pursuer, and finally to YHWH. This metaphoric shifting provides ample space for survivors to relate their own experiences to Daughter Zion's.

Pray the Devil Back to Hell offers a poignant parallel as the women struggle to truly determine their enemy in the complex system of sexual crime, enslavement, and murder. Neighbors, sons, and relatives were joining either the army or the rebel forces. Both sides were sexually attacking innocent women, murdering wives' husbands before their eyes, dragging away children to make them into child soldiers, and looting homes. The adversary could not easily be distinguished as Taylor recruited kids as young as six, drugging them and training them to kill and plunder for his political gain:

> It was just bad […] you didn't know who was who because they were all dressed in the same outfit. They would leave the front because they wanted to loot because they wanted to rape […] they would come to your house and pull you out and take everything even your shoes from your foot.

Both the Liberian Women's Peace Initiative and Woman Zion carry their grievances against the enemy to God, simultaneously accusing the Divine for the evil at hand and decrying God's nonintervention. Prayer emboldens sufferers to reassert their sense of self, to accuse their adversary, and to complain to God for

---

[62] For more on the effects of sexual assault including pregnancy, PTSD, sleep disorders, eating disorders, self-mutilation, depression, and identity disorders, see "Effects of Sexual Violence", *Rape, Abuse & Incest National Network Website*, [Available at: http://www.rainn.org/get-information/effects-of-sexual-assault], [Last accessed: 17th October 2022], and Bail, 261.

[63] Bail, 257.

[64] Maier, *Daughter Zion*, 149.

the inexplicable horrors surrounding them. The protest implicit to lament aims to stir the women to action, to accuse and condemn the physical perpetrators, and to implicate a cruel, unmoved God for withholding Divine intervention. But even as the prayer form rages in despair, it also seeks to reestablish new covenant relationships.

YHWH's frequent activity in the life of Israel further exacerbates the silence of God in Lamentations, impelling the interpreter to ask: how can we reconcile the powerful Hebrew God with the violence raging in Lamentations 1-2? Why has YHWH not comforted Woman Zion in the wake of such an unspeakable violation?[65] Marjo Korpel and Johannes de Moor analyze the speech patterns of God in the Hebrew Bible and note that 1,882 verbs and nouns characterize God as speaking, while 29 verbs and nouns specify God's silence.[66] They observe that God's inactivity in the Hebrew Bible particularly emerges in scenes of savage violence and instances of rape.[67] What could possibly explain YHWH's seeming callous indifference to such situations of cruelty?

Mandolfo and Beau posit that perhaps the Divine is left baffled and stunned by the devastation God is witnessing. "Perhaps God is silently ashamed of letting things get out of hand."[68] Shame is certainly the response that fits most concretely with the narrative of the Women's Peace Initiative of Liberia. Taylor recognizes that the women's protests were a humiliation, and he challenges his female opponents saying, "Nobody is going to get in the streets to embarrass my administration." However, after months of sit-ins, sex fasts, and prayer demonstrations in strategic locations in the course of his political envoy, Taylor caves to the pressure and agrees to attend the summit at Accra. Once there, the warlords ease into their new luxurious accommodations having traded in the hunger and fighting in the bush for the luxury of fine hotels, well-cut suits, and political schmoozing. The irascible women respond with a final act of degradation and defiance by evoking the most humiliating form of female physical protest: intentional public disrobing as an act of defiance against the combatants' hidden ploy of rape and molestation. In response, the Moderator publicly shames the Liberian militants for their abuse against women further heightening the men's humiliation. The women's scandalous prayer and protest finally chastens their men into reaching an agreement in just two weeks: Taylor is exiled to Nigeria, UN Peacekeeping forces take over security in Monrovia, and a transitional government begins ruling toward democratic elections.

---

[65] Beau Harris and Carleen Mandolfo, "The Silent God in Lamentations", *Interpretation: A Journal of Bible & Theology* 67(2), (April 2013): 138.

[66] Marjo C. A. Korpel and Johannes C. de Moor, *The Silent God* (Leiden: Brill, 2011): 35.

[67] Harris and Mandolfo, "The Silent God", 140; see also Leah Schulte and Tammi Schneider, "The Absence of the Deity in Rape Scenes of the Hebrew Bible", in Ingolf U. Dalferth (ed), *The Presence and Absence of God, Religion in Philosophy and Theology* 42 (Tübingen: Mohr Siebeck, 2009): 21-33.

[68] Harris and Mandolfo, "The Silent God", 142.

Conclusion: A Trauma-Informed Spirituality of Lament as Resistance

In the film, when the women return from Accra, streams of children welcome them in the streets singing their chant: "We want peace. No more war. Our children are dying. We are tired of running." Their song of lament is transformed into a liturgical victory song. The intertextual reading offered in this chapter demonstrates the power of lament as a corrective to sexual violence, injustice, slavery, and war. The brutal depictions of rape and exploitation, the images of an abusive God, and the shifting face of the enemy pose challenges for the use of this prayer tradition in contemporary trauma-informed spirituality.[69] The struggle between the immanence and silence of God and the interdependence of human and divine action elucidated in this form of prayer empower petitioners with a multidimensional complaint that articulates the pain of suffering and simultaneously galvanizes acts of resistance.[70] The power of Lamentations as a site of revelatory encounter with God is its ability to move back and forth "between literal expression and imaginative force."[71] Lamentations inspires a practice of prayer suitable for those in the midst of distress, violence, threats from enemies, and seeming abandonment from God. These prayers, although disturbed and difficult, have invaluable potential to yield a strong sense of being seen, heard, and understood for those who find themselves in literal situations which are imaged in the biblical text. Further, as communal prayers and sources of theological formation, these scandalous prayers can stir conviction and outrage and catalyze action for justice among those reading the prayers from a position of comfort, unawareness, power, or safety.[72] This religious practice also serves as a strategy for resilience and healing following traumatic experiences including but not limited to sexual violence and trafficking.

May the image of the liberated children of Liberia singing the prayer song of their mothers symbolize the potency of this prayer tradition for a spirituality of fighting with God for their covenant, struggling against unjust structures, and transforming enemies into new communities of peace.

---

[69] Claus Westermann also mourns the loss of the lament tradition in the liturgy and worship of Western Christendom and warns of its effects, Westermann, "Role of the Lament", 25.

[70] Patrick Miller explains that the agency of God in the Hebrew mindset creates a major problem since God is both immanent and sovereign. "God is the source of his or her internal suffering as well as the source of its resolution," Miller, *Trouble and Woe,* 36.

[71] Miller, *Trouble and Woe,* 40.

[72] For more on reading the text of Lamentations 1-2 as survival literature see Tod Linafelt, "Surviving Lamentations", in Athalya Brenner and Carole Fontaine (eds), *Feminist Companion to Reading the Bible: Approaches, Methods and Strategies* (Sheffield: Sheffield Academic, 1997): 344-357.

Reflection Questions

1. Reading Lamentations 1-2, how do you feel? What questions, concerns, or memories does this biblical text conjure for you? Have you heard this text used in spiritual formation or liturgy? How have you or others in your tradition made sense of these difficult images? What scares you about this text? What inspires you about this text? Is there a way you can imagine it being meaningful to your own faith? Is there a way you can imagine this text offering meaning to victims of trafficking and sexual violence?
2. Pray with the text of Lamentations 1-2 using the story of the Women's Peace Initiative of Liberia to concretize the metaphor. What do you notice? What troubles you, makes you angry, or moves you? What do you think about the Liberian women's tactics of prayer and resistance? What situations of injustice or violence in your own history, community, or ministry make you want to weep? What makes you angry? What do you mourn or grieve? Journal some of your thoughts and prayers into a lament. Feel free to share with others or sit with this practice for the next week. If you notice yourself remembering personal or secondary traumatic experiences, please speak with a trusted therapist, counselor or advisor. Invite your spiritual practice into that therapeutic space as a spiritual resource.
3. How might you use the practice of lament for developing a trauma-informed and resilient spirituality for yourself? With a small group? What situations in your ministry or in your social location need communal lamentation? What resources could you use to create an experience of communal lament? What would a communal lament look like in your faith community or organization?

Works Cited

Aichele, George, and Richard G. Walsh. *Screening Scripture: Intertextual Connections Between Scripture and Film*. Harrisburg, PA: Trinity Press, 2002.

Balentine, Samuel. *Prayer in the Hebrew Bible: The Divine-Human Dialogue*. Minneapolis, MN: Fortress, 1993.

Bergant, Dianne. *Lamentations*. Abingdon Old Testament Commentary Series. Annotated Edn. Nashville, TN: Abingdon Press, 2003.

—. "'êkāh: A Gasp of Desperation (Lamentations 1:1)". *Interpretation: A Journal of Bible & Theology* 67(2), (April 2013): 144-154.

Berlin, Adele. *Lamentations: A Commentary*. Louisville, KY: Westminster John Knox, 2002.

Boase, Elizabeth. "The Characterisation of God in Lamentations". *Australian Biblical Review* 56 (2008): 32-44.

Boda, Mark J., Carol J. Dempsey, and LeAnn Snow Flesher, Eds. *Daughter Zion: Her Portrait, Her Response*. Atlanta, GA: Society of Biblical Literature, 2012.

Brenner, Athalya and Carole R. Fontaine, Eds. *Wisdom and Psalms* Vol. 2 of *The Feminist Companion to the Bible*. Sheffield: Sheffield Academic, 1998.

Brueggemann, Walter. "The Costly Loss of Lament". *Journal for the Study of the Old Testament* 36 (1st October 1986): 57-71.

Disney, Abigail E. and Gini Reticker. *Pray The Devil Back To Hell.* Sausalito, CA: Roco Films Educational, 2008.

Dobbs-Allsopp, F.W. *Weep, O Daughter of Zion: A Study of the City-Lament Genre in the Hebrew Bible*. Rome: Editrice Pontificio Istituto Biblico, 1993.

—. "Raising Zion in Lamentations 2". In B.F. Batto and K.L. Roberts, Eds. *David and Zion: Biblical Studies in Honor of J.J.M. Roberts*. Winona Lake, IN: Eisenbrauns, 2004.

Flesher, LeAnn Snow. "Lamentations". In Catherine Clark Kroeger and Mary J. Evans, Eds. *The IVP Women's Bible Commentary*. Grand Rapids, MI: InterVarsity Press, 2002: 392-395.

Guest, Deryn. "Hiding Behind the Naked Women in Lamentations: A Recriminative Response". *Biblical Interpretation* 7(4), (1st October 1999): 413-448.

Gwaltney, W.C. "The Biblical Book of Lamentations in the Context of Near Eastern Lament Literature". In W.W. Hallo *et al.*, Eds. *More Essays on the Comparative Method: Scripture in Context II.* Winona Lake, IN: Eisenbrauns, 1983: 191-211.

Harris, Beau and Carleen Mandolfo. "The Silent God in Lamentations". *Interpretation: A Journal of Bible & Theology* 67(2), (April 2013): 133-143.

Häusl, Maria. "Lamentations: Zion's Cry in Affliction". In Louise Schottroff and Marie-Theres Wacker, Eds. *Feminist Biblical Interpretation: A Compendium of Critical Commentary on the Books of the Bible and Related Literature*. Grand Rapids, MI: Wm. B. Eerdmans, 2012: 334-344.

Hillers, Delbert R. *Lamentations Anchor Bible* 71, 2nd Rev. Ed. Garden City: Doubleday, 1992.

Klein, Alexander. "First responders after disasters: a review of stress reactions, at-risk, vulnerability, and resilience factors". *Prehosp Disaster Med* 24(2), (March-April 2009): 87-94.

Knut M. Heim. "The Personification of Jerusalem and the Drama of Her Bereavement in Lamentations". In Richard S. Hess and Gordon J. Wenham, Eds. *Zion: City of God*. Grand Rapids, MI: William B. Eerdmans, 1999: 129-170.

Korpel, Marjo and Johannes C. de Moor. *The Silent God.* Leiden: Brill, 2011.

Linafelt, Tod. "Surviving Lamentations". In Athalya Brenner and Carole Rader Fontaine, Eds. *Feminist Companion to Reading the Bible: Approaches, Methods and Strategies*. Sheffield: Sheffield Academic, 1997: 344-357.

Maier, Christl M. *Daughter Zion, Mother Zion: Gender, Space, and the Sacred in Ancient Israel*. Minneapolis, MN: Fortress Press, 2008.

Mandolfo, Carleen. *Daughter Zion Talks Back to the Prophets: A Dialogic Theology of the Book of Lamentations*. Atlanta, GA: Society of Biblical Literature, 2007.

McDaniel, Thomas F. "Alleged Sumerian Influence upon Lamentations". *Vetus Testamentum* 18(2), (April 1968): 198-209.

McKenzie, Steven L. and Stephen R. Haynes, Eds. *To Each Its Own Meaning, Revised and Expanded: An Introduction to Biblical Criticisms and Their Application*. Rev. Exp. Ed. Louisville, KY: Westminster John Knox Press, 1999.

Miller, Patrick. *Trouble and Woe: Interpreting the Biblical Laments, Interpretation: A Journal of Bible & Theology* 37 (1983): 32-45.

Mintz, Alan. "The Rhetoric of Lamentations and the Representations of Catastrophe". *Prooftexts* 2 (1982): 1-17.

O'Connor, Kathleen M. *Lamentations and the Tears of the World*. Maryknoll, NY: Orbis Books, 2002.

Petter, Donna Lee. "The Book of Ezekiel: Patterned After A Mesopotamian City Lament?" PhD Diss., University of Toronto, 2009.

Schmitt, John J. "Israel and Zion – Two Gendered Images: Biblical Speech Traditions and Their Contemporary Neglect". Horizons 81(1), (1991): 18-32.

Schulte, Leah and Tammi Schneider. "The Absence of the Deity in Rape Scenes of the Hebrew Bible". In Ingolf U. Dalferth, Ed. *The Presence and Absence of God, Religion in Philosophy and Theology* 42. Tübingen: Mohr Siebeck, 2009: 21-33.

Vento, Johann M. "Violence, Trauma, and Resistance: A Feminist Appraisal of Metz's Mysticism of Suffering Unto God". *Horizons* 29(1), (Spring 2002): 7-22.

Westermann, Claus. "Role of the Lament in the Theology of the Old Testament". *Interpretation* 28(1), (1st January 1974): 20-38.

PART II

THINKING THEOLOGICALLY ABOUT SEXUAL EXPLOITATION

Exploring Kingdom of God Theology in Anti-Trafficking Work

Leah Edwards

Introduction

Some chapters in this volume have been situated in the passion and dedication that Christian anti-trafficking workers devote to their organizations and communities. The harsh, and complex realities of front-line work are well-known within the faith-based anti-trafficking community, as significant time and scant resources are spent attempting to address the needs at hand. Outside of the faith-based community, however, Christian anti-trafficking work is often categorized as zealous, emotive, and highly engaged with vulnerable individuals. This chapter will take time to explore a more reflective aspect of anti-trafficking work, by considering the theological motivations that energize front-line anti-trafficking workers and advocates. The theology of the Kingdom of God will be employed as an analytical concept that will help to understand the motivations behind evangelical Christian anti-trafficking work, and is vital for seeing how this work is framed and positioned. Within the Kingdom of God theology, a thematic analysis will be used to explore the overarching construct of justice. Particular attention will then be given to those Kingdom principles identified as being a voice to the voiceless and father to the fatherless within the anti-trafficking context.

Building on the limited scholarly work presented below, I will argue that current uses of the Kingdom of God theology negates individual agency, appears as maternal or paternalistic, and has a limited understanding of justice. In response to these findings, I will propose that a broader understanding of Kingdom of God theology can assist Christians involved in the anti-trafficking movement to look beyond divides of morality, and work towards justice that is both structural and individual. By employing a Kingdom of God theology that acknowledges the structural inequalities that contribute to sexual exploitation, recognizes the dynamics of racial and class power held by Western anti-trafficking organizations, and values the incredible amounts of agency possessed by the individuals in anti-trafficking programming, a radical re-writing of the Christian anti-trafficking narrative is made possible. Furthermore, through continual reflective re-evaluation of personal motivations, anti-trafficking front-line workers, advocates, and volunteers can embody this theological and rhetorical shift.

Situating the Understanding of Faith-Based Anti-Trafficking Organizations

Christian communities, or networks centered on social causes, have unique relationships with their secular counterparts. Since the increased focus on trafficking and sexual exploitation beginning in the 1980s, scholars have noted the relationships forming between evangelical Christians and radical feminists. Bernstein (2007, 2010) and Shih (2008) are two of the many scholars who have labeled this trend as a relationship of "strange bedfellows," to highlight the uncharacteristic partnerships formed in pursuit of creating and implementing abolitionist anti-trafficking policies. While Christians became highly involved in anti-trafficking advocacy and awareness raising, few empirical studies have explored the motivations and understanding of faith-based organizations. Specifically, empirical studies directed at Christian anti-trafficking organizations are scarce. Shih (2016), after interviewing and observing anti-trafficking awareness and prevention training with *Not for Sale*, argues that "vigilante rescue" initiatives fuel harmful criminal justice actions against vulnerable sex workers or prostitutes. Additionally, Shih (2018) argues for the acknowledgement of the imbalances of racial and class power in global anti-trafficking organizations where the labor of non-white women from lower socioeconomic backgrounds (i.e. rehabilitated victims of trafficking) are taken advantage of by white, Western charities who use the "anti-trafficking" products produced to create a rehabilitation industry.

Kamler (2013) researched how a non-government organization working in Northern Thailand constructed narratives from survivor's stories of trafficking and exploitation, as heard in their workplace. This study argues that non-government organizations need to acknowledge the power dynamics of being the "voice" for vulnerable women, and the influence these dynamics place on the dissemination of anti-trafficking information to policy and public discourse. Frame (2017), in South-East Asia, investigated to what extent faith influenced the ways of working with clients at an anti-trafficking organization that provided post-trafficking services. Frame argues for organizations to acknowledge the unique contexts that organizations are situated in when considering how faith-based organizations operate as either different or similar to secular counterparts. In relation to public health concerns, Ahmed and Seshu's (2012) case study of a sex worker collective in India found that the conflated narrative of sex work and human trafficking, by neo-abolitionists, was negatively impacting the lives of the sex workers and public health programming, by the organization.

More generally, Limoncelli (2016) empirically studied self-identified anti-trafficking non-government organizations through reports, Internet searches, and anti-trafficking networks. Limoncelli noted the methodological challenge of identifying anti-trafficking organizations as there is "no centralized mechanism by which to identify and count NGOs globally",[1] and argues that more work is needed to develop collaborative systems for sharing information. Limoncelli also argues that scholars need to acknowledge that the relationship between state

[1] (Limoncelli, 2016: 318).

actors and charity organizations is often complex, with contradictory interests and policies.

The work of Yvonne C. Zimmerman, an American Methodist theologian who focuses on gender, has contributed significantly to the critical analysis of American evangelical Christians and how their anti-trafficking initiatives have intersected with American public and foreign policy. In her body of work, Zimmerman (2010, 2016) writes extensively on the constructions of morality and the historical Christian response to moral injustices, drawing connections to the conservative approaches taken by the Bush Administration. A key focal point in Zimmerman's work is the passing of the 2000 Trafficking Victims Protection Act in the United States. This legislation and its effect on the global response to human trafficking gave specific attention to issues of sexual exploitation, with minimal expansion of the definition to include instances of labor exploitation. Zimmerman argues that this policy, under the conservative government of George Bush Jr., showcased the neoliberal Christian belief that the state is best used as a punitive mechanism for detainment and prosecution of traffickers, with added legal backing from trafficking-focused policy.[2] Through her historical analysis Zimmerman writes that, as the anti-trafficking movement grew in the late 1990s in the United States, the discourse was heavily shaped by the historical movements of advocating for persecuted Christians and against pornography.[3] When Christians responded to the global discussion surrounding trafficking, the Christian anti-trafficking discourse perpetuated the focus on vulnerable, poor women to be protected from exploitation.[4] Campbell and Zimmerman (2014) specifically noted that, in this era of advocacy, the issues of labor exploitation and injustice were quickly overshadowed by the moral concern around sex and sexual exploitation.

In summary, the empirical literature devoted to exploring and understanding faith-based organizations is limited and continually emerging. This chapter aims at contributing current findings to questions surrounding how Christian anti-trafficking agencies situate their approach to trafficking.

Methods

This chapter employs a theological, thematic analysis of the primary data that focuses on the Kingdom of God principles identified by research participants. This analysis is positioned in the understanding of the Kingdom of God by N.T. Wright and the writing of Bill Johnson, as participants identified his work as a key influence in their personal theology and Christian work. The theological texts that will be referenced are Wright's *Surprised by Hope* (2008) and Johnson's *When Heaven Invades Earth: A Practical Guide to a Life of Miracles* (2003). The material for this chapter is based on the author's PhD field research in the Middle East and in the United States that followed a qualitative

[2] (Zimmerman, 2016; Campbell and Zimmerman, 2014).
[3] (Zimmerman, 2011).
[4] (Shih, 2015).

ethnographic methodology. This methodology utilized observations, key informant interviews, and semi structured interviews with the founders of two Christian anti-trafficking organizations and safe house residents. The first organization, Hope Project,[5] was globally situated with a strong American support base. The second organization, Truth Project,[6] was located in the Middle East with workers from the United States, East Africa, and the Middle East. Truth Project operated safe houses within an urban environment, where vulnerable female, economic migrants and survivors of human trafficking were provided shelter, assistance with securing (relatively) safe employment in domestic work, and access to the Christian community in the city. The Truth Project was an unregistered charity and faced instances of harassment by police for operating and assisting vulnerable migrants. For this reason, the organization operated covertly and was very concerned with the risks associated with their work. This chapter is based on four months of fieldwork with the organizations, where interviews and observations were conducted.

The Rhetoric and Construction of the Kingdom

Cultural Approaches

The Christian anti-trafficking sector is highly reliant on Christian language that engages with the Bible and evangelical or charismatic understandings of communication with God. Furthermore, when speaking to anti-trafficking workers, Christian expressions and metaphors are often the primary method of explanation for the decision to work in the field. During the data analysis period for the thesis, I was confronted with the frustrating question of "Why do Christian anti-trafficking workers go through all the challenges to do this work?" This question led to a re-read of the data to consider the deeper motivations behind anti-trafficking leaders' organizational decisions. Within the context of conducting Christian anti-trafficking programming in the Middle East, missionaries are confronted with the complexities of migration, gender, and ethnicity. These tensions are situated within a political environment of government fear and control. Further investigation of the motivations of the faith-based workers in this study showed that the primary reasoning behind their anti-trafficking work was a belief that God had asked them to do it. This belief was predicated on a theology that prioritizes the active voice of God within Christians' lives. Within the Christian community, a presentation of personal motivation based on an affirmation of God's calling is often sufficient for a justification. However, when attempting to communicate this logic to secular actors or institutions, a deeper look into the theological understanding of what God requires, and the work that Christianity prioritizes, is needed. The following section will explore how the faith-based anti-trafficking organizations presented the rhetoric and discourse of the Kingdom of God.

---

[5] A pseudonym.

[6] A pseudonym.

The rhetoric of a Kingdom of God theology, and of missiology, was evident in the organizations' publications and online presence, where the Kingdom of God was presented as having the power to transform people and communities. In the field, it was observed in conversations with the organizational leaders that the deep desire to see cultural change in the treatment of women and vulnerable groups was rooted in the belief of a Kingdom culture. The phrase "Kingdom culture" is an overarching term for how Christians can live within a Godly influenced culture of honor and respect that believes in the love of God. Furthermore, this situation of the Kingdom believes in Christians displaying and connecting to the power of God. Johnson writes, "Our mandate is simple: raise up a generation that can openly display the raw power of God."[7] Johnson's interpretation of the Kingdom of God is rooted in a desire to see and empower Christians to be involved in supernatural experiences. This position appears to be informed by Johnson's study of revivalist movements and his personal experiences of supernatural encounters. This theological and personal faith position is represented in the global church yet is not considered to be a dominant voice in the Protestant evangelical church.

Returning to the work of Wright, neither project questioned the economic or political implications of globalization and capitalism when considering women's motivations to migrate. The leaders acknowledge poverty as a motivating concern but do not challenge the norm of capitalism and the economic stratification it has created. Wright directly writes to this fallacy of justice in his theology on the "kingdom of God."[8] The work of both organizations is aligned with Wright's critique of American (or Western) groups who are willing to travel to struggling countries to do (short-term) mission work but who are unwilling to challenge the practices of large monetary organizations or governances and the exploitations they encourage. Wright desires to see the Kingdom of God on earth yet pushes for a more nuanced and political understanding of this. The anti-trafficking leaders in this study embodied Johnson's call and saw their role as being active, engaged, and requiring a dual mentality. A dual mentality allows the actor to stand outside the realm of justice as perceived within "our present context", and engage in justice that stems from the Kingdom of God. In connection with the construct of God as powerful and active, both program leaders acknowledged the active work of the Holy Spirit and demonic spiritual forces. In lengthy conversations with the Middle East project leader, where the roots of trafficking and gendered oppression were explored, spiritual forces were acknowledged as contributing to violent and oppressive practices. This was observed following the discussion of "honor crimes."

Honor crimes are generally understood as violent acts (e.g. murder, forced marriages, forced abortion) enforced or committed by the male members of a family to ensure the "honor" of a family.[9] Dishonor is commonly viewed as being brought onto the family by a female member who committed an act that induces

---

[7] (Johnson, 2003: 27).
[8] (Wright, 2008).
[9] (Dogan, 2014; Accad, 2000).

shame (e.g. suspicion or act of sexual promiscuity, pre-marital pregnancy, fraternizing with men).[10] As the Middle East project leader presented experiences of working with women and honor-related violence, and explained how the cultural cycles and norms continued from her perspective. The project leader explained her perspective of the spiritual challenges local women faced when speaking to women who believed that "the only way to come near to Allah is to be intentionally so full of shameful humility, [and] always conscious of how imperfect you are so you can't even dare to approach Allah." The rhetoric and positioning of Kingdom culture appeared to be in direct juxtaposition to this perspective. The vision for providing support services to vulnerable migrant women and local women caught in shame and honor violence was presented by the safe house leader as having a "safe house where [a woman] can just come in and get soaked, blasted, loved on, set free and redeemed." This impassioned language connects to the core tenet of the Kingdom of God, where transformation and the power of God are seen in action.

In the face of societal and cultural norms that were situated in a value system that prioritized shame and honor dynamics over the Western mentality of right and wrong, the Kingdom of God rhetoric drew out questions of how to operate in different contexts. The observations conducted with the project leaders highlighted the diverse understandings of how to operate in belief of the Kingdom of God within the context of the Middle East. As missionaries experience surveillance and harassment within the region, two approaches to this reality were observed. The first reality observed was that the approaches to the context appeared to be highly connected to the chosen leadership styles of the program leaders. The leader of Project Hope employed a "top down" method to leadership that prioritized action and authority, and he was often not questioned for his style of delivery or interactions with those around him. This style of leadership was common throughout Western Christianity through patriarchal understandings of Christian leadership.[11] When traveling with the leader of Project Hope, questions were raised over his Western style of interacting with local women and safe house residents. The observed response in these situations was positioned within the explanation that, when in the Kingdom of God, we are above the social and cultural conventions of our present contexts. This response was highly questioned by those around him. Additionally, further instances were observed where the leader's identity as an American was used as a way of presenting controversial opinions without the threat of reproach. He commonly employed phrases in conversations such as "I live in the Kingdom [of God] so there is no offense." Due to the leader's position of power within a Christian community, he appeared to be given free rein on presenting his cultural understanding of the Kingdom of God from a Western perspective. The leader's well-known spiritual position, and the supposed spiritual power coupled with his brash Western presentation, was observed to be problematic throughout the research project.

---

[10] (Dogan, 2014; Accad, 2000).

[11] (Held Evans, 2014).

When discussing how the project leader chose to interact with survivors of trafficking in the attempt to exhibit the "goodness" of a father figure through providing hugs or being in close physical proximity to the women, his assistant stated that "[He] has a unique spiritual call for this, that is why we don't let other volunteers do what he does." Beyond the ethical challenges presented in these observations, the use of spiritual authority as a tool for acting without contest aligns with a top-down leadership approach. In addition, it appeared that the project leader attempted to embody a perceived identity of being a father, rather than use the scripture as a theological guide. This approach to top-down leadership is diametrically opposed to the teachings of Jesus where the meek, broken, and those considered to be last will be first (see Matthew 5). Finally, the use of spiritual exceptions in leadership behavior creates vulnerabilities for the abuse of physical and spiritual power that are only intensified by dominant Western Christian culture.

Conversely, the leader of Project Truth appeared to position her leadership with advocacy, empowerment, and awareness for the people and situations surrounding her. When traveling, the leader of Project Truth appeared to be highly informed by her embedded position and was attentive to surroundings, gendered situations, and security risks being taken. When discussing risks in program decisions, the project leader reflected: "Others may think I am operating in fear but I'm not. It's just the reality of [this country]." The project leader appeared to be in a contentious position where the logistical decisions of operating a covert organization that works with vulnerable individuals was criticized by other Christian actors outside of the context. The Truth Project was not a registered entity with the government as NGO organizations are not allowed in the country and Christians are highly distrusted and often surveilled by law enforcement. In this tension, the leader of Project Truth appeared to live by the principles of the Kingdom of God and enact Kingdom culture while ensuring the safety of those in her care.

Examples of this were observed in the process undertaken to gain access to the fieldwork location. The leader of Project Truth was extremely cautious of how the presence of foreigners in proximity to the women in the safe house could jeopardize their lives and the broader Christian community. For this reason, all leadership and management of operations related to the safe house were placed in the hands of either other migrants who had a long-standing history with the leader of Project Truth or a few key individuals who were Christian religious minorities of the region. When approached by Project Hope to bring in a group of Westerners to visit the project and visit other regions of the country where Project Truth worked, the leader of Project Truth refused them access. This decision was observed to have a negative affect on the working relationship between the programs and highlighted the differences in risk appetite between the organizations. This tension also highlights the degree to which anti-trafficking leaders believe in the power of God to protect and sustain their efforts. While the Project Truth leader had experienced intense challenges related to safety and security in the region – where she credited the protection and power of God as the sustaining influence – she remained cautious with her organizational approaches. While each individual anti-trafficking organization faces different risks and challenges, the differences presented in the findings of the research highlight the need for reflexive practice when employing spiritual justifications for action or inaction. For anti-trafficking actors supporting or managing within a top-down structure, the findings of this research suggest a collaborative and respectful relationship with leaders embedded in the front lines of practice.

Individualism and the Kingdom of God

Moving forward from the observations of how culture and context are approached from a Kingdom mentality the themes of individualism and relationality were observed within the field site. Generally, within Western Christianity, there is a focus on the individual relationship one has with Christ and a belief that within this relationship there is a "call" on a person's life to accomplish a variety of physical or spiritual goals in life. Within the anti-trafficking movement this has become embedded into the rescue and rehabilitation narrative, where the individual stories of survivors are used as examples of positive outcomes. The example of this is often seen in the supposed success of helping an individual woman leave a situation of exploitation while not considering how this affects her nuclear and extended family and broader community. While this research does not question the theology of each individual person being granted a unique call of God, it does call to attention the Western framing of the Christian anti-trafficking response. During the time in the field with the Western anti-trafficking leaders and a local pastor, this construct was discussed when attempting to determine the most appropriate types of economic empowerment programming. The conversation included below was recorded in my field notes following a group meeting with Astrid, the administrative secretary for Project Hope. The conversation occurred as follows:

> Astrid continued to discuss how Project Hope does not want the women to settle for jobs like cleaning if that is not what God created them to be. She said that women who are fully "healed" would need a halfway house and skills before moving on [...] She stated her opinion that African women were "imprisoned" in the country for the type of work available.

Various layers of relational and individualistic understandings applying to vulnerable migrants and trafficking survivors can be found within this exchange. Astrid's concern for women to find employment that is empowering is not inherently wrong, yet this mentality is rooted in an understanding of women's lives from an individual perspective. A resident of the safe house described what it meant to work abroad as "working for others," rather than working for oneself. Hence, vulnerable migrants and human trafficking survivors must be seen in a relational capacity, where the responsibilities and obligations of others (i.e. family, social or ethnic networks) are placed at a higher importance than their own personal desires. This connects to the construct of the Kingdom of God in how anti-trafficking organizations construct individuals, and the networks they are connected to, within their organizational programming. If anti-trafficking organizations continue to construct an individualized victim identity for survivors of trafficking or vulnerable migrations, their assistance will have limited effect. Organizations must also wrestle with the physical and theological realities that while there can be stories of survivors of exploitation being "restored" and empowered like seen in the story of Joseph, there are many women that will instead suffer the social and physical injustices like those seen in the rape of Dinah (Gen. 34) or the story of Tamar (Gen. 38). Further empirical understandings of the motivations behind the construction of faith-based restoration or aftercare services are needed to understand this intersection. Nevertheless, critical insight is needed to construct anti-trafficking approaches that assist the individuals within their organizational reach, while understanding the broader networks connected to the individual's experience.

Constructs of Justice

The need for a nuanced understanding of the Kingdom of God for the individual, and for a relational network, is highlighted in the constructs of justice. The following section will serve as a bridge into the final discussion section of this chapter, where the work of Wright (2008) and Johnson (2003) will be critically examined. As the Kingdom of God is built around the manifestation of God on earth through Christ's followers and the transformation of those in their paths, a critical review of anti-trafficking justice is required. First, within the context of the fieldwork experiences that inform this data, "criminal justice" was not of prime importance for the vulnerable migrants in the safe house. Conversely, the needs of survival, safe working environments, and the right to remain in the nation appeared to be of higher importance. This is counter to the Christian anti-trafficking narrative that prioritizes a criminal justice response for survivors.[12] While the safe house residents acknowledged the hardships experienced as African migrants in the Middle East, the persecution for their Christian faith, and the protracted insecurities on the horizon, they did not appear to question the need for the abuses of their pasts to be justified through the legal system. Furthermore, in a context where they had no legal opportunity to present situations of injustice to a legal system, the Western constructs of anti-trafficking justice – via the prosecution of traffickers or workers' rights – were unavailable. With legal or criminal justice out of reach, the discussion of anti-trafficking leaders focused on the application of social justice. Ironically, the early church was situated under the empire of Rome and was of low social standing.[13] Within this situation of vulnerability, the early disciples of Jesus and the churches under Paul's leadership advocated and assisted other vulnerable individuals as presented in the New Testament. Social justice is constructed as having a societal impact; this aligns with the desire of Christians to see social transformation through the Kingdom of God.

The organizations positioned their social justice work as a key component to the Kingdom of God. Returning to the biblical language of being a "voice to the voiceless" and a "father to the fatherless", the organizational leaders situated

---

[12] (Shih, 2016).

[13] (Mattson, 2018).

themselves as necessary actors in enacting justice. The concept of social justice and Kingdom of God theology intersects with the life and teachings of Jesus. Mattson argues that the prophecies that led up to the life of Jesus and his ministry on earth highlight an example for Christians as to how they are to regard the poor and vulnerable as an act of worship.[14] In modern Christianity, social justice movements have been characterized by generosity, becoming increasingly involved in the development sector, and acknowledging the importance of human rights within a Christian worldview.[15] Additionally, with the theological foundation, religious justice for persecuted Christians was a key motivator in providing services in a region where Christianity is either illegal or in the minority. The view of God as a "liberator" and "protector" also guided the understanding of freedom within the Kingdom of God. Through a construction of trafficking that prioritized gender and ethnicity, social justice was seen as a method to assist women in gaining a place in the society where patriarchal and racist structures of society need to be challenged. However, what was not recognized within the Kingdom of God theology approach to justice was the need for economic justice for the larger networks that trafficking survivors or vulnerable migrants were connected to.

The discussion section of this chapter will outline the work of Wright (2008) and Johnson (2003) as it relates to the position of Kingdom of God theology related to anti-trafficking. The first half of this article has presented evidence of the diversity found in the ways that anti-trafficking leaders position their motivation for anti-trafficking work within Kingdom of God theology. However, while faith-based anti-trafficking approaches are vigilant to personalized assistance, this may result in an individualistic construction of survivor's lives, thus negating their role in broader social networks. The following section will argue for a broader understanding of the Kingdom of God theology that considers structural inequalities (i.e. race, class, gender) contributed by Western societies as areas where economic justice is needed as a part of enacting the Christian faith. This chapter will then conclude with the call for a re-writing of the Christian anti-trafficking narrative with a focus not solely on the individual victims affected but with attention given to the global structures supporting the cycles of violence and economic need.

Reconsidering the Kingdom of God in Anti-Trafficking Work

As the research that informs this chapter set out to understand the key motivations for faith-based organizations, the underlying constructs of religion, politics, and economics are of prime importance. The following section will present the theological understandings of the Kingdom of God as found in two different presentations of Western evangelical theology. Bill Johnson (2003) was selected because of the importance this text holds for workers in the spiritual formation of anti-trafficking work. Johnson's work has been highly influenced by the work of North American theologians and teachers (e.g. The Toronto

[14] (Mattson, 2018).

[15] (Paras, 2014; Carson, 2015).

Revival, Jack Hayford, Liardon, 2000). The work of N.T. Wright (2008) was then included to highlight the differences in Western theological voices, as his work is situated in a European context. Each work will be discussed in turn.

Bill Johnson's Construction of the Kingdom

To begin, Johnson's construction of the Kingdom of God places agency and opportunity into the daily lives of individuals in order that they are triumphant in their faith. Johnson writes: "We were born to rule – rule over creation, over darkness – to plunder hell and establish the rule of Jesus wherever we go by preaching the gospel of the Kingdom".[16] The acknowledgement and use of the spiritual authority Christians have to bring the restoration to the world is a central tenet of Johnson's construction. The primary opposition to Christians' reclamation work is sin, which is anything that separates an individual from the holiness of God. Johnson teaches that alongside ruling with the authority of Christ to bring about the Kingdom of God, Christians are to be "focused on exposing and undoing the works of the devil".[17] The primary ways Johnson considers Christians to be involved in bringing about the Kingdom rest on the power of prayer, living a life that exhibits the power of the Holy Spirit (i.e. the supernatural/miraculous), and living a life aligned with the Kingdom of Heaven rather than the cultures of the world. Johnson teaches that the primary way Christians are to exhibit their power and their difference is through signs and wonders that show the glory of God, and the presence of sin. Power and difference would then be exhibited in repentance, and the receiving of forgiveness, which would then strengthen the broader Christian community. Johnson argues for Christians to consider the Kingdom to be "now" and not to subscribe to teaching that constructs a weak church and Kingdom of God reserved to heaven.

Johnson's rebuke of weak Christianity and a weak church results in his construct of the Kingdom being presented as militarized and forceful in the Spirit. He employs the rhetoric of "battle," "war," and "invasion" when presenting how Christians are to engage with spiritual forces and gain territory for the Kingdom. He challenges Christians to move into a power relationship with God where the supernatural power of the Spirit is actively sought out and engaged. With the enactment and use of supernatural power, Johnson believes that this will show the secular world that God is alive and active and affirms His glory. In order to bring forth the supernatural power of God, Johnson calls for Christians to "pursue Him with reckless abandon" and have a purpose filled life of prayer, studying scripture, living in Christian community, and practicing the gifts of the Holy Spirit.[18] Throughout the text, Johnson provides anecdotal stories of experiences within his life where the power of God manifested and he saw the Kingdom of God advanced. He positions this approach to the Kingdom of God as resulting "in a glorious church, further revelation of the knowledge, and a

---

[16] (Johnson, 2003: 32).
[17] (Johnson, 2003: 32).
[18] (Johnson, 2003: 102).

mature man".[19] In conclusion, Johnson's articulation of the Kingdom of God is situated in the desire for personal Christian change and spiritual understanding of the supernatural power of God. In this presentation, the implications for the broader communal and societal Christian encounters are not fully developed in concrete examples. The generalities of how the Kingdom of God intersects with broader social injustices require further development of Johnson's work.

N.T. Wright's Construction of the Kingdom

Wright constructs the Kingdom of God as "the sovereign rule of God (that is, the rule of heaven, of the one who lives in heaven), which according to Jesus was and is breaking into the present world, to earth".[20] This understanding of the Kingdom highlights the rule of God in the context of his reign as the Alpha and Omega, while connecting this power to the everyday circumstances of a Christian's experience. This dynamic supports Wright's construction of the Kingdom narrative through the Bible, where followers of God are commanded to redeem the contexts they inhabit. Wright explains this dynamic by reviewing the relationship that God had with the nation of Israel in the Bible. Wright creates a construct of the Kingdom from the Old Testament as follows:

> [God] did not want to rescue humans *from* creation any more than he wanted to rescue Israel *from* the Gentiles. He wanted to rescue Israel *in order* to rescue humans *in order that humans might be his rescuing stewards over creation*. That is the inner dynamic of the Kingdom of God.[21]

In this relationship dynamic, Wright identifies the core of what is considered to be God's mission. The dynamic is centered on Christians believing that Jesus' resurrection from the dead began a reclamation process that will be in progress, with the assistance of the Holy Spirit, until Christ's return where He will make all things new. In this current period of working to bring the Kingdom of God to earth, Wright believes that "God intends his wise, creative, loving presence and power to be *reflected* – imaged, if you like – into his world *through* his human creatures.[22] In acknowledging that Christians are to reflect these attributes of God within their lives, the reclamation process becomes embodied and intimate. Christians are then required to carry this Kingdom mentality and responsibility into the situations and contexts that require redemption and reclamation.

In this process of reflection and reclamation, a diversity of responses are found. Wright suggests that one of the many reasons why Christians have not come to fully understand the Kingdom of God is rooted in the lack of understanding that the Kingdom of God is not simply the afterlife in heaven. Wright also recognizes that the phrase "Kingdom of God" has been hijacked for campaigns of political, social, and moral agendas within the church. Wright explicates the historical and theological tendencies of fundamental groups to subscribe to dualistic thinking where the world is too corrupt to assist and that the only thing for Christians to do is wait for the return of Christ. This

---

[19] (Johnson, 2003: 181-183).
[20] (Wright, 2008: 201).
[21] (Wright, 2008: 202).
[22] (Wright, 2008: 207).

construction of Christianity uses mission as a way to comfort the poor and disadvantaged, yet not to question the global economic and political structures that create systemic poverty and injustice. Wright summarizes social justice as being based on the assumption that "if Jesus is the true revolutionary then the single main Christian task is to build the Kingdom here on earth through social, political, and cultural revolution."[23] While he acknowledges the good that has been accomplished by Christian organizations, he questions how much of the modern advancement for justice is connected to the work of Christians or to other groups.

Wright takes outright political positions with his construct of the Kingdom. This positioning is firmly fixed on dismantling the structures of global debt and economic subjugation. With the specific mention of slavery and of the Wilberforce era, Wright puts forth that, while sex is an important issue, the "present system of global debt is the real immoral scandal, the dirty little secret – or rather the dirty enormous secret – of glitzy, glossy Western capitalism" is an issue of greater urgency.[24] Wright continues to strongly state that the Kingdom of God is not to be conflated with the Kingdom of the West, with specific mention to conservative Christianity in the United States. This critique strongly resonates with the work of Zimmerman (2016) and the argument that American evangelicals are overly preoccupied with issues of morality while structural oppressions are ignored.

In conclusion, Wright "insists[s] on [an] inaugurated eschatology, on a radical transformation of the way we behave as a worldwide community, *anticipating*, the eventual time when God will be all in all even though we all agree things won't be complete until then".[25] This anticipation of justice, the pursuit of beauty and the power of evangelism are central to Wrights' construction of the Kingdom of God in Christian life. Wright is critical of Christians who do not connect the power imbalances of Western nations to the injustices they feel called to respond to. In this critique, Wright politicizes the Kingdom of God and challenges Christians to shift from the "band aid" or "feel good" approaches to mission.

The Kingdom of God and Anti-Trafficking Work

Returning to the empirical data of how Kingdom of God theology was utilized by anti-trafficking leaders, the works of Wright (2008) and Johnson (2003) highlight the diverse approaches within evangelical theology. The observed use of the Kingdom of God theology in the field resonated with Johnson's call to see Christians actively engaged in transforming and operating with the power of God. The anti-trafficking leaders positioned themselves as workers of the Kingdom and as bringing forth a Kingdom culture. Within the context of the anti-trafficking organizations they represented this resulted in highly passionate, individualized-assistance programming. This chapter argues that the Kingdom of God theology, as presented by Wright (2008), could assist workers in re-

---

[23] (Wright, 2008: 215).

[24] (Wright, 2008: 217).

[25] (Wright, 2008: 222).

centering their practice to address issues of justice from a social and structural level. Wright (2008) and Johnson (2003) do intersect by earnestly calling for Christians to realize that they are a part of revolutionizing the current world and to not passively wait for the coming of Christ.

Nevertheless, as Christian anti-trafficking work is focused on individuals, the larger socio-economic and political landscape must not be forgotten. The Kingdom of God embodies elements of struggle in the tension of being called to wait for the return of Christ while being the hands and feet of Christ to those in need. Anti-trafficking workers must consider the need to reflect the power of God into oppressive economic structures. This requires a reflective practice that acknowledges how evangelical anti-trafficking initiatives can be tethered to Western government political and economic imposition. Furthermore, the attempted aftercare interventions and creation of anti-trafficking businesses need to ensure that their business practices do not contribute to the commodification of labor and the continued control of vulnerable individuals' lives. Christian anti-trafficking workers, regardless of their stance on prostitution, must work with local, regional, and global organizations and governance to improve vulnerable individuals access to meaningful, sustainable, safe employment. This argument acknowledges that poverty and economic instability is not the single reason for trafficking and the exploitation of labor; it is a key contributor to the labor insecurities faced in post-colonial and post-socialist regions.

Kingdom of God theology requires a personal application of the belief that God is working and calling Christians to redeem situations of sin and injustice. Within the context of the personal constructions of the Kingdom of God by Western anti-trafficking workers, critical reflection of how the Western identity intersects with anti-trafficking efforts is required. Christians who feel a personal call of God to address human trafficking have to situate their engagement within "uncomfortable histories" and the current realities.[26] The uncomfortable histories in the Christian social justice narrative connect to the exploitation enacted in the name of God and mission. The current realities of a sharp political divide that supports patriarchal, racist, and sexist structures yet employing the name of evangelical Christianity needs to be recognized. Personal calling and the sense of divine connectivity is a spiritually intimate experience. However, the consequences of acting on these belief sets has far-reaching consequences for the individual, those being assisted, and the context in which the interactions are occurring. Western, white Christians must recognize the impact of their "race"/ethnicity, social class power, and political entanglements associated with Western interventionism and neo-liberal politics. Furthermore, the politicization of anti-trafficking work requires a political understanding of the Kingdom of God. Christian anti-trafficking organizations and leaders must challenge the constructs of anti-trafficking assistance to conceptualize a response that is powerful, biblical, and reflective. While the Kingdom of God theology is positioned to bring heaven to earth, it must be brought into all spheres and layers of society. While this chapter cannot provide definitive answers, a call for

---

[26] (Paras, 2014).

reflection and openness to understand the politicized nature of anti-trafficking is presented.

Conclusion

In conclusion, faith based anti-trafficking workers need to remain attuned with the presentation of the Kingdom of God. Within the context of the Middle East, the cultural dynamics of context remain of great importance when an embedded approach is required. In the application of Kingdom of God theology, in viewing vulnerable migrants or trafficking survivors, an understanding of their position within social networks is crucial. While attending to the needs of the individual, the larger struggles of regional economic instability or economic oppression must not be lost. This chapter has argued that Western anti-trafficking workers must remain attentive and reflexive when considering how class and race contribute to paternalist anti-trafficking. The individual agency and the location in social networks of trafficking survivors must remain at the forefront of faith-based anti-trafficking work. Finally, Kingdom of God theology has the potential of looking beyond moral divides and strengthening social and economic justice approaches. A radical shift within the mainstream faith-based anti-trafficking community is needed to recognize the power of structural inequalities that contribute to exploitation and violence and that a Christian response is required on this societal level.

Reflection Questions

1. How do Western cultural understandings of the Kingdom of God affect cross-cultural anti-trafficking work? How can we become aware of them and not be constrained by them?
2. What types of social, political, and economic injustice do survivors of trafficking face? Why is it important to address these issues? What are the barriers?
3. How can Christian anti-trafficking workers learn from the perceived successes and failures of helping survivors reintegrate into society through a Biblical lens?
4. Through what channels and methods can Christians interested in anti-trafficking work engage with the political nature of the Kingdom of God to address exploitation? What are the benefits? What are the limits, if any?

Works Cited

Accad, E. "Sexuality and Sexual Politics: Conflicts and Contradictions for Contemporary Women in the Middle East". In P. Ilkkaracan, Ed. *Women and Sexuality in Muslim Societies*. Istanbul: Women for Women's Human Rights – New Ways, 2000: 37-50.

Ahmed, A. and M. Seshu. "'We Have the Right Not to Be "Rescued"...': When Anti-Trafficking Programmes Undermine the Health and Well-Being of Sex Workers". *Anti-Trafficking Review* 1(1), (2012): 149-165.

Bernstein, E. "Militarized Humanitarianism Meets Carceral Feminism: The Politics of Sex, Rights, and Freedom in Contemporary Anti-Trafficking Campaigns". *Signs* 36(1), (2010): 45-71.

Bernstein, E. "The Sexual Politics of the 'New Abolitionism'". *Differences* 18(3), (2007): 128-51.

Campbell, L.M. and Y.C. Zimmerman. "Christian Ethics and Human Trafficking Activism: Progressive Christianity and Social Critique". *Journal of the Society of Christian Ethics* 34(1), (2014): 145-172.

Carson, M. *Setting the Captives Free: The Bible and Human Trafficking*. Eugene, OR: Cascade Books, 2015.

Doğan, R. "Different Cultural Understandings of Honor That Inspire Killing: An Inquiry into the Defendant's Perspective". *Homicide Studies* 18(4), (2014): 363-388.

Held Evans, R. "Patriarch and Abusive Churches". [online] *Rachel Held Evans Blog* 14th March 2014. [Available at: https://rachelheldevans.com/blog/patriarchy-abuse], [Last accessed: 17th October 2022].

Johnson, B. *When Heaven Invades Earth: A Practical Guide of a Life of Miracles*. Shippensburg, PA: Destiny Images, 2003.

Kamler, E. "Negotiating Narratives of Human Trafficking: NGOs, Communication and the Power of Culture". *Journal of Intercultural Communication Research* 42(1), (2013): 73-90.

Liardon, R. *God's Generals: Why They Succeeded and Why Some Failed.* [Reprint edition 17 December 2000]. New Kensington, PA: Whitaker House, 2000.

Limoncelli, S. A. "What in the World Are Anti-Trafficking NGOs Doing? Findings from a Global Study". *Journal of Human Trafficking* 2(4), (2016): 316-328.

Mattson, S. "Social Justice is a Christian Tradition – Not a Liberal Agenda". *Sojourners*. [online] 8th November 2018. [Available at: https://sojo.net/articles/social-justice-christian-tradition-not-liberal-agenda], [Last accessed: 17th October 2022].

Paras, A. "Between Missions and Development: Christian NGOs in the Canadian Development Sector". *Canadian Journal of Development Studies* 35(3), (2014): 439-457.

Shih, E. "The Price of Freedom: Moral and Political Economies of the Global Anti-Trafficking Movement". PhD Thesis. University of California, Los Angeles, CA: 2015.

Shih, E. "Not in My 'Backyard Abolitionism'". *Sociological Perspectives* 59(1), (2016): 66-90.

Shih, E. "Duplicitous Freedom: Moral and Material Care Work in Anti-Trafficking Rescue and Rehabilitation". *Critical Sociology* 44(7-8), (2018): 1077-1086. [Available at: https://doi.org/10.1177/0896920517751589], [Last accessed: 17th October 2022].

Zimmerman, Y.C. "From Bush to Obama: Rethinking Sex and Religion in the United States Initiative to Combat Human Trafficking". *Journal of Feminist Studies in Religion* 26(1), (2010): 79-99.

Zimmerman, Y.C. *Other Dreams of Freedom: Religion, Sex, and Human Trafficking.* Oxford: Oxford University Press, 2016.

Modern Slavery, Trauma, and Holy Saturday: Theological and Pastoral Responses

Dan Pratt

Introduction

This chapter explores modern slavery and human trafficking within the context of the United Kingdom. It outlines the UK's recent Modern Slavery Act and describes the characteristics and extent of modern slavery within the UK. In addition, it describes two case studies where Christians encounter people impacted by modern slavery which have implications for the Church.

It will then explore theological responses to modern slavery through the lens of trauma and Holy Saturday in the Passion narrative. Exploring Shelly Rambo's work, *Spirit and Trauma,* Holy Saturday will be examined as a "Middle Space" for survivors of modern slavery and trauma.

These learnings can be applied to pastoral responses through three frameworks that emerge: Living the Middle-Space, Presence, and Witness.

Christians and the Church Encounter Modern Slavery and Human Trafficking

Case Study #1: Richard's Story

Richard's story emerges from the church-pioneering context among rough sleepers, addicts and vulnerable people in Southend-on-Sea, Essex, that eventually became a church community known as 57 West.[1] It is rooted within Contextual Theology, "a Christian interpretation of life that is conscious of its circumstances."[2] Within this context, Christians encountered individuals who had been exploited and abused.

> Richard[3] became homeless in his early twenties while suffering with poor mental health. He was housed by a well-known homeless charity in the North of England. One day, he was called to the charity's reception and was offered a job by a traveller family. In return for labour, Richard would receive money, accommodation, and travel. Richard accepted the job and travelled with the family to Spain.
>
> Richard's work involved paving and tarmacking people's driveways in Spain, France, and the UK. Richard frequently worked fourteen to eighteen hours each day. Days off were rare. He was barely paid. Accommodation was in a caravan,

---

[1] 57 West is a member church of the Baptist Union of Great Britain. See website at: www.57west.org.uk. [Last accessed: 18th October 2022].

[2] S. Bergmann, *God in Context: A Survey of Contextual Theology* (Aldershot: Ashgate, 2003): 4.

[3] Shared with permission and name changed.

shared with the large dog of the family. Sometimes he was fed only a sandwich a day. His health suffered. Although Richard tried to escape, he and his family were threatened. He was told "we know where your family live." He stayed.

The family used Richard's identification documents many times without his knowledge or permission. Companies were set up in his name in Spain, France, and Austria. These companies would take out financial loans not to be repaid. Expensive equipment and cars were rented and not always returned. The police arrested Richard in France. He was sent to prison for the crimes his captors committed. Having served two years in prison, he was released and it was the first time he was able to get away from his captors in twenty years. Richard returned to Southend and was homeless once more. He started attending 57 West's community meal. Eventually he became housed with a homeless charity. He is trying to rebuild his life.

Unfortunately, Richard's case is not an exception. Stories from other rough sleepers share similarities of Richard's story: treated as slaves, exploited for labour, and forced to commit criminal acts for the financial gain of their exploiters. Sometimes these men were sexually and physically assaulted as a means of control and domination by the captors. Exploitation occurred for years and decades at a time. In some cases, these individuals were let down by charities and faith organisations who enabled them to meet their would-be exploiters. Encountering these survivors, it is essential to reflect theologically and pastorally on these contexts of exploitation and trauma as well as the extent of modern slavery and human trafficking within the UK.

Modern Slavery and Human Trafficking in the UK

Within the UK, the National Crime Agency estimates that there are tens of thousands of victims of modern slavery. Previous estimates of 10,000-13,000 victims in the UK were found to be the "tip of the iceberg."[4] The Global Slavery Index estimates there are 136,000 victims of modern slavery in the UK.[5] The UK's The Modern Slavery Act came into effect in 2015. It identifies modern slavery as "holding a person in slavery or servitude or requiring a person to perform forced or compulsory labour."[6] This includes "securing services by force, threats or deception."[7] The Act categorizes offences of Slavery, Servitude and Forced or Compulsory Labour and Human Trafficking. The Equality and Human Rights Commission explains these offences.[8] Slavery is defined as

---

[4] BBC News, "Modern slavery and trafficking 'in every UK town and city'", 10th August 2017. [Available at: www.bbc.co.uk/news/uk-40885353], [Last accessed: 18th October 2022].

[5] Global Slavery Index, "United Kingdom", *Global Slavery Index Website* [Available at: https://www.globalslaveryindex.org/2018/findings/country-studies/united-kingdom/], [Last accessed: 18th October 2022].

[6] *Modern Slavery Act 2015*, Chapter 30: 1 [Available at: http://www.legislation.gov.uk/ukpga/2015/30/pdfs/ukpga_20150030_en.pdf], [Last accessed: 18th October 2022].

[7] *Modern Slavery Act,* 3.

[8] Equality and Human Rights Commission, "Article 4: Freedom from slavery and forced labour", *Equality and Human Rights Commission Website,* [Last updated: 3rd June

"when someone actually owns you like a piece of property." Servitude is defined as being "similar to slavery – you might live on the person's premises, work for them and be unable to leave, but they don't own you." Forced Labour "means you are forced to do work that you have not agreed to, under the threat of punishment."

The Modern Slavery Act defines trafficking as when a "person arranges or facilitates the travel of another person ("V") with a view to V being exploited."[9] The United Nations Palermo Protocol expands the definition of trafficking in persons as "the recruitment, transportation, transfer, harboring or receipt of persons, by means of threat or use of force or other forms of coercion, of abduction, of fraud, of deception, of the abuse of power or of a position of vulnerability or of the giving or receiving of payments or benefits to achieve the consent of a person having control over another person, for the purpose of exploitation."[10]

Those who are kept in modern slavery are often forced to use their bodies for labour, sex, forced criminality, or organ donation against their will. They may feel that they are not able to trust health professionals or the police or those who would like to help them. They may be deceived or frightened into handing over money, identification documents or their mobile phones. Some are UK nationals, while others are economic migrants or migrants who lack legal status.

The UK's National Crime Agency[11] highlights that there are several broad categories of exploitation linked to human trafficking, including forced labour, sexual exploitation, domestic servitude, organ harvesting and forced marriage. Child-related crimes are also included such as child sexual exploitation, forced begging, illegal drug cultivation, organized theft, and related benefit fraud.

Modern slavery is a low-risk and high-reward crime. Individuals can be exploited many times over, resulting in great financial gain for their captor. Due to the hidden nature of the crimes, it is often difficult to find victims and catch perpetrators. Some victims don't identify themselves as victims due to their being manipulated and developing attachments to their captors. Others live in fear of their captors. Without a victim coming forward to give evidence, it is difficult to catch and prosecute perpetrators. People who come from contexts of poverty, with limited opportunities or other vulnerabilities, are often preyed upon by exploiters. Modern slavery is therefore attractive to criminals due to the low risk of prosecution.

In 2009, the UK government set up the National Referral Mechanism (NRM) to which potential cases are referred and through which victims can access relevant support. Statistics from the NRM for 2021 highlight that 12,727 people

---

2021], [Available at: www.equalityhumanrights.com/en/human-rights-act/article-4-freedom-slavery-and-forced-labour], [Last accessed: 18th October 2022].

[9] *Modern Slavery Act*, 3.

[10] United Nations, *Protocol to Prevent, Suppress and Punish Trafficking in Persons* (Palermo Protocol), Article 3, 2000, [Available at: https://www.osce.org/odihr/19223?download=true], [Last accessed: 18th October 2022].

[11] National Crime Agency, "Modern Slavery and Human Trafficking", *National Crime Agency Website*, https://www.nationalcrimeagency.gov.uk/what-we-do/crime-threats/modern-slavery-and-human-trafficking], [Last accessed: 18th October 2022].

were identified as potential victims of slavery and referred into the NRM in 2021, the highest number of referrals ever received.[12] These potential victims of trafficking were from 130 different nationalities. The report highlights that UK, Albanian and Vietnamese nationals were the most commonly reported potential victims, with nationals from the United Kingdom accounting for 31%.

Children, due to their vulnerability and need for care and protection, are at great risk from traffickers, especially when support and care is lacking. Children are particularly vulnerable to exploitation by individual opportunists, traffickers, organised crime groups, or people who should protect them. Of the 12,727 people identified as potential victims of slavery in 2021, 5468 were minors.[13]

The Global Slavery Index estimates that 136,000 people were living in modern slavery in the UK in 2016.[14] This estimate reflects a prevalence rate of 2.1 victims for every thousand people in the country. According to these statistics, if the national average is applied to a town of 30,000 people there would be an estimated 66 people exploited in modern slavery. Applied to a city of 1 million, there would be an estimated 2,200 people exploited in modern slavery. It is therefore an imperative for the Church to be able to identify potential victims of modern slavery as well as help and support survivors who are re-building their lives.

Case Study #2: Stella's Story

Stella's story came to light through Ella's Home, a charity in the UK which provides support, care and long-term accommodation for survivors of sexual exploitation and their families.[15]

> Stella grew up in an abusive family in Columbia. Yet, she had a dream to make something of her life and move far away from them. She worked hard so that she could study accounting and have a professional career. Partway through her studies she became very unwell and had to undergo major treatment. All her savings went to pay her medical bills and when she recovered, she was unable to carry on with her studies having no resources to do so. She met someone who said they could help her get work to pay the bills quickly. Stella knew it wasn't what she wanted to do but it was a means to an end. Little did she know that at that point she would lose her freedom.
>
> For the next decade, Stella was at the mercy of pimps who moved her to Italy and then between countries in Europe, finally reaching the UK. She was sold for sex and kept under the control of her pimps. During those years, Stella attempted to escape twice. Each time, she was captured and severely punished for her boldness.

---

[12] UK Home Office, "Modern Slavery: National Referral Mechanism and Duty to Notify statistics UK, end of year summary 2021", *UK Government Website*, 3rd March 2022. [Available at: https://www.gov.uk/government/statistics/modern-slavery-national-referral-mechanism-and-duty-to-notify-statistics-uk-end-of-year-summary-2021], [Last accessed: 18th October 2022].

[13] Home Office, "Modern Slavery".

[14] Global Slavery Index.

[15] Ella's Home, See website for more information at: www.ellas.org.uk, [Last accessed: 18th October 2022].

One day, however, a new opportunity of freedom presented itself and she made a run for it. She ran until she couldn't run anymore.

Eventually, she was picked up by the authorities. She was terrified but came to realizes that she was safe. Stella was referred to the Medaille Trust who provide safe-houses for survivors of trafficking. This was the first time in a decade that Stella felt truly safe. Stella was moved into longer supportive accommodation at Ella's Home where she has continued her journey of freedom. Through Stella's brave testimony, she helped to imprison some of those who had exploited her.[16]

Implications for the Church and Christian Practice

The experiences of Stella, Richard and others who have been trafficked raise questions regarding how we as churches and communities can respond. The National Crime Agency states that "ordinary members of the public are coming into contact with victims of modern slavery in their everyday lives." As the Church works with vulnerable people through food banks, crèches, homeless shelters, we are in a prime position to be able to encounter and help survivors of modern slavery. For instance, within the Baptist Union of Great Britain, 47 churches were surveyed regarding their contact with those who had been exploited through modern slavery.[17] 19% of those churches had knowingly encountered survivors of modern slavery. The percentage is even higher when it includes churches who unknowingly come into contact with survivors. Our churches are increasingly encountering people who have been victims of abuse and exploitation. Within pastoral work, it is becoming increasingly common to journey alongside those who have experienced great suffering and trauma. In order to minister and serve more effectively, we need increased understanding of the experiences of victims and survivors of modern slavery. There is, therefore, a need to develop our theological and pastoral responses to suffering and trauma. To this we now turn our attention.

Trauma, Holy Saturday, and "Middle Space": Theological Responses to Modern Slavery and Human Trafficking

How can the reality of trauma and the concepts of Holy Saturday and "Middle Space" shape our theological and pastoral understanding of modern slavery and human trafficking?

Trauma

Professor Shelly Rambo in *Spirit and Trauma*, states that traditional redemption narratives of the cross and the resurrection are insufficient, often overly focusing on the victory of the cross.[18] Indeed, Rambo notes that, "the redemptive narrative

---

[16] Together Free, "Sexual Exploitation", *Together Free Website,* [Available at: https://www.togetherfree.org.uk/sexual-exploitation], [Last accessed: 18th October 2022].

[17] Survey completed by the author among Baptist Churches within the Eastern Baptist Association, UK.

[18] S. Rambo, *Spirit and Trauma: A Theology of Remaining* (Louisville, KY: Westminster John Knox Press: 2010): 6.

of cross and resurrection is often read in a linear fashion in which life (resurrection) is victorious over death."[19] Christian triumphalism rushes to the proclamation of Easter and to its claims of new life and resurrection. Many sermons preached in churches jump immediately from death to life, glossing over what is between. Life conquers death. Victory and good news are sought, while not adequately addressing suffering. Well-meaning theologies promote redemption as a kind of fantasy, turning us away from, rather than towards, the complexity of human life, especially extreme suffering and exploitation. While this outlook can provide a sense of promise and hope, the linear reading of death ending and new life being ushered in can run into difficulty.

For those who have experienced and are experiencing trauma, these theologies can be particularly unhelpful. When responding to suffering around us, we are increasingly aware that phrases such as "it'll be alright in the end" can have little meaning and comfort for those experiencing trauma. But this raises questions about our theology of salvation and redemption, particularly relating to death and resurrection.

The Collins dictionary defines trauma as a "severe shock or very upsetting experience, which may cause psychological damage."[20] Judith Herman in her foundational book *Trauma and Recovery* writes, "Traumatic events are extraordinary, not because they occur rarely, but rather because they overwhelm the ordinary human adaptations to life. Unlike commonplace misfortunes, traumatic events generally involve threats to life or bodily integrity, or a close personal encounter with violence and death."[21] Focusing on the impact of trauma on an individual, Herman writes "Traumatic events produce profound and lasting changes in physiological arousal, emotion, cognition, and memory. The traumatized person may experience intense emotion but without clear memory of the event, or may remember everything in detail but without emotion. She may find herself in a constant state of vigilance and irritability without knowing why."[22]

Although a traumatic event can take place once, trauma results in the person re-living the trauma in the present. Victims and survivors of modern slavery are often held captive for weeks, months and years, subject repeatedly to degrading abuse. When a survivor has escaped their captivity, those experienced events remain and persist with the person. Death and new life are experienced as a pendulum swinging between the two, mixing both realities. Binaries disappear as death and life oscillate and merge. Rambo writes, "trauma is an open wound. For those who survive trauma, the experience of trauma can be likened to a death. But the reality is that death has not ended; instead, it persists"[23] This raises questions about theological narratives of death and resurrection.

---

[19] Rambo, *Spirit and Trauma*, 4.
[20] Collins Dictionary, "Trauma", [Available at: https://www.collinsdictionary.com/dictionary/english/trauma], [Last accessed: 18th October 2022].
[21] J. Herman, *Trauma and Recovery* (New York: Basic Books, 1992): 33.
[22] Herman, *Trauma and Recovery,* 34.
[23] Rambo, *Spirit and Trauma*, 4.

Within some contextual theologies and theologies of liberation, the experience of pain and suffering becomes the hermeneutical lens to explore theology and themes of redemption and healing.[24] The lens of suffering and trauma casts the relationship between death and life in the Christian narrative in a much more complex light.[25] Trauma studies challenges us to think about recovery differently and in turn help us to revisit redemption. "Trauma teaches us there is no clean break from the past, of death behind and life ahead. Trauma tells us that death returns, haunting the life that follows."[26]

Rambo proposes that redemption should be found in the "Middle Space" or the figurative site in which death and life are no longer bounded. This Middle Space enables theological reflection to be done in the space between death and life in the pendulum moving between the two. For Rambo, "The good news of Christianity for those who experience trauma rests in the capacity to theologize this middle."[27] This Middle Space is found not on Good Friday, or Easter Sunday, but on Holy Saturday.

Holy Saturday

The Passion narrative is a description of immense suffering. For those who witnessed the brutal torture of their beloved Jesus, trauma would be experienced in what they saw and in what they remembered of the event. For Christ, the suffering was immense, culminating in separation from God. Jesus breathes his last breath and as the Apostle's Creed indicates "he descended into hell." Much speculation surrounds the mystery of Holy Saturday and Christ's experience. Most agree that it was a time of extreme abandonment, forsakenness, and extreme loneliness and trauma.

Rambo writes, "Holy Saturday reveals a distinct landscape of suffering that cannot be understood exclusively in terms of the passion; neither can it be interpreted in relationship to resurrection."[28] For Rambo, "Holy Saturday is a pivotal part of this divine love story. It narrates divine love at its least discernable point – between death and resurrection, in the recesses of hell."[29] Rambo notes that Holy Saturday and Christ's descent into hell, the place devoid of love, "is a testimony to the persistence of love in utter forsakenness and abandonment."[30]

Perhaps it is this point in the Gospel narrative that is most pertinent to the estimated 136,000 people in the UK who are currently being kept in slavery. In their hellish situations of extreme abandonment and forsakenness, Holy Saturday's possibility of love at its least-discernible point, in the recesses of hell,

---

[24] For example, refer to: L. Boff, *When Theology Listens to the Poor* (San Francisco, CA: Harper and Row, 1970); L. Boff, *Cry of the Earth, Cry of the Poor* (New York: Orbis Books, 1997); J.H. Cone, *God of the Oppressed*, Revised Ed. (New York: Orbis Books, 1997); G. Gutiérrez, *A Theology of Liberation, History, Politics, and Salvation*, Sister Inda, C. & Eagleson, J. Translators. (New York: Orbis Books, 1973).

[25] Rambo, *Spirit and Trauma*, 11.

[26] Rambo, *Spirit and Trauma*, 156.

[27] Rambo, *Spirit and Trauma*, 8.

[28] Rambo, *Spirit and Trauma*, 46.

[29] Rambo, *Spirit and Trauma*, 55.

[30] Rambo, *Spirit and Trauma*, 53.

gives an alternate redemption narrative. Is God with the 136,000? Do they have an awareness of God's presence and love in their very real contexts of hell?

In exploring theological and pastoral responses to modern slavery, it is essential to question what persists between death and resurrection. This leads us to the following questions: When trauma occurs, where is God? And: Where is salvation and redemption in the midst and aftermath of abuse and exploitation? To respond, we will turn our attention to several theologians.

Theologian Jurgen Moltmann's bold interpretation of the crucifixion states that God does not stand outside of the events of the cross but rather experiences the suffering. "The Son suffers in his love being forsaken by the Father as he dies. The Father suffers in love the grief of the death of the Son..."[31] Not only Christ experiences suffering and trauma through the crucifixion and Holy Saturday, but also the Trinity. Moltmann expands his view of God suffering through the cross, highlighting that the suffering and death of humankind is experienced by God. "There is no suffering which in this history of God is not God's suffering, no death which has not been God's death in the history of Golgotha."[32]

This is further explored by Professor Paul Fiddes who writes, "in Christ God participated to the utmost in the human predicament, and has never journeyed farther into the depths of his creation."[33] In journeying into the depths and suffering of his creation, the relationship within the Trinity suffers. This relational suffering is expressed by Fiddes, "When Jesus is recognized as the Son of God, the cross must mean that the alienation and brokenness of the world enters right into the relationships that form the being of God."[34]

The trauma and suffering of the world is consequently experienced by God. God is present with those experiencing trauma. Not detached, but present and suffering with. This has implications for victims and survivors of modern slavery such as Richard and Stella. The brokenness and evil of their captivity and consequent trauma is experienced by God. God is not detached, but present in the survivor's trauma. God is present in the trauma of what Rambo describes as that which "shatters all current knowledge of the world and alters the way of operating within it."[35] The extent that the victim is aware of God's presence is something only they can testify to. Only they can say if their conscious experience of captivity is affected by God's presence.

Richard shares an awareness of God in the midst of extreme danger when he was driving a lorry loaded with heavy building materials. He was working for his captors when the brakes of the lorry failed:

> On one occasion, I was going down a mountain. It went around a bend and onto two wheels. It seemed to stay like that for a lifetime. I don't know if it was God. I am a bit of a religious person. It seemed to take a lifetime, but it fell back down

[31] J. Moltmann, *The Crucified God* (London: SCM Press, 1974): 56.

[32] Moltmann, *The Crucified God*, 255.

[33] P.S. Fiddes, *Past Event and Present Salvation* (London: Darton, Longman & Todd: 1989): 56.

[34] Fiddes, *Past Event*, 57.

[35] Rambo, *Spirit and Trauma*, 4.

> onto its four wheels. I thought I was dead. Scared is not the word. I'm not saying there's another being that saved me, but how I survived those three occasions, I still don't know. Maybe somebody else was deciding, "should I be kept alive, or should I not"?" Trying to save me for better days maybe.

During extreme danger, Richard has a sense of God's presence and intervention in his situation. Fiddes states, "Any doctrine of the atonement which is in continuity with the ministry of Jesus will therefore make the involvement of God in human life the central factor. Through Jesus, God participates in the situation of those oppressed by every kind of sin and evil."[36] God embraces the brokenness and alienation of humankind within himself, within the nature of the Trinity. The God-head is therefore united within suffering, experiencing trauma and atonement. In this way, God identifies and participates in the suffering of creation. The Crucifixion and Holy Saturday narrative therefore finds God in the midst of the human context, thereby being present with those who experience past and present suffering. This is evident in the example of the witnesses of Jesus' crucifixion.

Rambo writes, "Attributing theological significance to the middle involves resisting the forward pull of the Christian narrative, from death to life. The middle suspends this forward movement and, in so doing, provides a necessary witness to the struggles of living in a persisting storm of the aftermath."[37] The storm and trauma of Holy Saturday would be real for Mary, Jesus' mother; for Mary Magdalene; and for the disciples. They were witnesses to the torture and brutal death of their beloved Jesus. The immediate witnessing of these events would cause trauma. Perhaps like soldiers returning from war, who witness atrocities, sights and smells could trigger memories flooding back to the present. For those witnesses, where was God when Jesus breathed his last, and where was God during Holy Saturday?

Mark's Gospel tells us: "With a loud cry, Jesus breathed his last" (Mk. 15:37).[38] Rambo proposes that this breath is "carried on the breath and in the bodies of those who move in the aftermath of death."[39] The word describing Spirit in the Christian Scriptures in the translation from Hebrew to Greek is *Pneuma,* meaning breath. Is it possible that as Christ breathes his last breath on the cross, this breath, the Spirit, *Pneuma*, is "carried on the breath and in the bodies of those who move in the aftermath of death"? For Rambo, Christ's breath or *Pneuma* is shared with the witnesses of those at the cross.

When Christ dies, they are not left without a God presence. The Spirit is with them.

The Spirit is the force of life pulsing through all things. "In Him we live, move and have our being" (Acts 17:28). Holy Saturday attests to the painful position between life and death. Amidst a day of hell, where for the witnesses death is experienced in the midst of life, the Christ-breath, the Spirit, was present silently between death and resurrection.

---

36 Fiddes, *Past Event,* 56.
37 Rambo, *Spirit and Trauma*, 138.
38 New International Version Bible.
39 Rambo, *Spirit and Trauma*, 120.

Application: Living the Middle Space, Presence, and Witness

To conclude, three applications will be highlighted exploring Holy Saturday through a lens of trauma, specifically relating to modern slavery. These will include the importance of 1) enabling survivors to live the "Middle Space", 2) the Church being "Present" with survivors of modern slavery, and 3) the Church bearing "Witness" of exploitation within communities.

Making Space for Middle Space

Firstly, the importance of Holy Saturday highlights the need for a Middle Space to be lived out by survivors of trauma and those who accompany them. For Christians who journey with survivors of modern slavery, whether they be counsellors, ministers or befrienders, there is a need to be aware of how we live informed by sacred and redemptive stories. How are these stories told? What remains untold? Glossing over uncomfortable stories within our societies or church traditions glosses over oppression, violence, and injustice. The Truth and Reconciliation Commission in post-Apartheid South Africa gave witness to this need not to gloss over pain. Instead, it gave opportunity for memories of past suffering and oppression to be told.

Herman writes, "In order to escape accountability for his crimes, the perpetrator does everything in his power to promote forgetting. Secrecy and science are the perpetrator's first line of defence."[40] For Rambo, redemption narratives that smooth over the trauma of Holy Saturday are "tied to a larger smoothing over of oppression, violence and the injustices of history."[41] When we don't allow space for remembering and for stories of injustice to be told, we are acting contrary to the healing process. For those experiencing death through trauma in life, there must be space for these memories and stories. Freedom and space must be granted to live between life and death.

Just as the Trinity experienced suffering and death in the death of Christ, so they experience the suffering of those held in captivity. For the victims and survivors of modern slavery, only they can give witness to God's presence with them in the midst of extreme suffering and trauma. It is their witness that will testify if they experienced love's persistence in extreme abandonment, severe shock and sometimes psychological damage. As the survivor slowly comes to term with their trauma, this witness may take years to surface, or sometimes not at all. Indeed, there may be cases where the survivor is never able to come to terms with their trauma and life may become too unbearable to live.

Within the survivor's lived experience, it is only the survivor who gives testimony to whether they sensed the Spirit, the *Pneuma,* breathing within them and being present in the midst of abuse. Only the survivor can testify to "what persists between death and resurrection?" Richard, who was held captive for twenty years, was asked if he ever sensed God with him in the midst of captivity. Richard reflected on the times that he was put in the most danger and replied, "the two times when I nearly died, someone was there looking after me". In both

---

[40] Herman, *Trauma and Recovery,* 8.

[41] Herman, *Trauma and Recovery*, 129.

those times, Richard describes God altering his circumstances and enabling him to get out of those life-threatening situations. Upon finding freedom, Richard states, "God works in mysterious ways. You can never see him. But I sense that God is with me saying 'Richard's had enough. I'll help him out'".

It is from places of abandonment and trauma that those who have lived their lives during Holy Saturday testify to previously unheard experiences of God's presence and love and perhaps silence. These have the potential to give rise to new stories of redemption. As Christ suffered in humiliation at the hands of a godless world, Christ gives dignity and hope to those who experience pain and death as we wait for the full outworking of Christ's victory over death, sin, and injustice. It is a nuanced redemption. Not the triumphant, "Life has conquered death" redemption, but a more subtle redemption of love and the Spirit's presence when life and death co-exist on a pendulum.

Choosing to Be Present

Secondly, just as those at the foot of the cross on Good Friday chose to be present in the midst of extreme suffering, so too, the Church can choose to be *present* in communities that experience exploitation and suffering. Being present in the midst of suffering requires making a choice to be present in the midst of suffering and darkness. The Church has a choice to look away, or to be present in the darkness for the sake of the least, the lost, and the most vulnerable. As John reminds us: "The Light shines in the darkness, and the darkness has not overcome it" (Jn. 1:4-5).[42]

There are many ways for the Church to be present. Churches must upskill their leaders and congregants to respond to modern slavery. This may include partnering with antislavery organisations who can deliver awareness training. There are a number of Christian and non-Christian organisations that offer trainings and workshops on to what modern slavery is and how to safeguard against it.

Churches can also ensure that they "slavery-proof" their existing ministries among vulnerable people. This can be done through ensuring that modern slavery is included within Church's safeguarding processes and engrained within the culture of the Church. A number of denominations in the UK have now written specialist safeguarding material for their Churches to respond to modern slavery.

For Churches who would like to engage more actively in responding to modern slavery on their doorsteps, community mobilization and Antislavery Partnerships are an effective way to engage. The Church of England's response to modern slavery through The Clewer Initiative, and their Hidden Voices course, is mobilizing the Church to respond through community engagement. The course develops skills around victim identification and care.[43] Across the UK, well-established and emerging antislavery partnerships exist to bring

---

[42] New International Version Bible.

[43] The Clewer Initiative, available at: www.theclewerinitiative.org.

statutory services, law enforcement, and the third sector (including faith groups) together to combat local forms of modern slavery.[44]

For Churches responding to modern slavery on their doorstep, there may be a cost for Christ-followers, as extreme suffering is encountered. These stories of suffering will transform those who are not willing to look the other way. Jesus calls his followers through the Parable of the Good Samaritan to love and care for those who suffer, even when costly. Indeed, following the two greatest commands of loving God and our neighbor[45] includes loving those who are exploited, abused and often hidden. Just as those present at Christ's death would carry the trauma of Good Friday into Holy Saturday and beyond, are we also willing to be impacted by the darkness and suffering around us?

By being present in the midst of suffering, the Church opens itself up as a place of safety and refuge to vulnerable people in crisis. Churches have a sense of vocation to serve the poor and vulnerable within our communities. Existing social justice projects (including food banks, homeless projects or serving among poor families) are uniquely positioned to develop relationships of trust. For those who have been exploited within modern slavery, Churches may be the first place they turn to when they have an opportunity.

Survivors may not want to go to the police or social services. They want to find freedom on their own terms, without being subject to grueling questioning and potentially being forced to re-live the trauma before they are ready. Charities are finding that Churches and other voluntary organisations are often the first places that survivors of modern slavery turn to for help. Churches have the capacity to develop relationships of trust with those perhaps who are only looking for a free meal. Through that love and trust shown, exploited people may find safety and freedom to share their stories. Sensitive and open-ended questions have helped people to be able to share stories of exploitation. Without being present, neither these stories nor possibilities for helping would not have emerged.

Bearing Better Witness

Thirdly, through *witnessing* what happens among the vulnerable in our communities, we are able to testify against exploitation and oppression. Just as the disciples of Christ bore witness to the trauma of Good Friday, the church bears witness to the trauma experienced within our communities. Just as the disciples of Christ testified to the atrocities of the cross, so the church can testify to the traumatic realities of those they journey with who are carrying their own crosses.

Indeed, our faith communities are well placed in the community at the grassroots level. We are present in the midst of poverty, suffering and trauma. This creates opportunities to spot the signs of modern slavery around us. Police

---

[44] Refer to The Human Trafficking Foundation and Nottingham University's Rights Lab for further information: https://www.humantraffickingfoundation.org/nncf, http://iascmap.nottingham.ac.uk [Both last accessed: 18th October 2022].

[45] Mark 12:30-31.

have expressed their need for the wider community to share intelligence about exploitation as it is witnessed. Community-based intelligence is essential in stopping modern slavery and human trafficking.

Through Churches and charities working in partnership with the police, we can help overcome the disconnection that lets modern slavery and trafficking thrive. Of course, this requires sensitivity and wisdom. When relationships of trust have developed and survivors begin to share their stories, the first option must always be for the victim/survivor to have the power to tell their story. In cases where survivors refuse to go to law enforcement, it may be possible for them to share crimes committed against them anonymously. For Churches, there is a safeguarding responsibility to report activities where the person's life or the lives of others are in danger. With crimes relating to modern slavery, this can often be the case. We do not however want to break the confidence of those who are entrusting us with personal information. Consent from the victim/survivor must always be sought first and if consent is denied, then sharing information with the police about that person anonymously may be a way to help protect the identity of the survivor.

There are many people who belong to churches and actively engage in community life and witness what occurs among the vulnerable. To name a few, there are health care professionals (often going into people's houses), teachers (observing if kids are being recruited for drug running), and rubbish collectors (who can observe who is residing in houses and any suspicious rubbish/trash they throw out). There is also an opportunity to observe the houses and flats on our street. Have they been taken over for use as a brothel or for cannabis cultivation? Churchgoers and grassroots organisations have a grassroots view on our communities. Churches have many people ready to be sensitized to the signs of modern slavery around them, and to know how to respond and share community intelligence with the police or Modern Slavery Helpline[46] if they encounter something amiss.

For example, following a "Spotting the Signs of Modern Slavery" workshop, a retired church member saw something in his neighborhood that made him feel uncomfortable. He observed that a privately-rented house across the road from his house was suspicious. He saw two women being taken into the house. Following this, different men were frequenting the house. The women did not come out of the house. If we had observed this, what would we do in that situation? The retired church member reported his suspicions to the local police. The police investigated and the women were found and safeguarded. The house was being used as a "Pop-up Brothel", where residential houses or apartments are rented for short periods of time for the purposes of supplying women, men, or children to paying customers for sex. The retired church member in this scenario witnessed a scenario that made him feel uncomfortable. Rather than denying that witness and the potential trauma of the two women, he testified to what he had seen. This resulted in the safeguarding of the two women and the perpetrators prosecuted. Witness is essential in curbing exploitation within our communities.

---

[46] In the UK, the helpline is 0800 012 1700.

Conclusion

Modern slavery and human trafficking are impacting most communities within the UK and in many other parts of the world. For survivors of modern slavery, such as Richard and Stella, there is the challenge of experiencing freedom, while also experiencing ongoing captivity lived through their trauma. Rambo's Middle Space of Holy Saturday offers the Church and survivors of modern slavery a theological resource to live life while experiencing death. It suggests that the Spirit of God is a present Spirit, bearing witness to the trauma and darkness. Pastoral responses emerge through living in that Middle Space between life and death.

Perhaps in this precarious place of Holy Saturday, as the pendulum swings between life and death, exists a new expression and experience of love and God's breath. It is in this Middle Space, that just as the Spirit of God is present and bears witness, so too can the church be present and bear witness to the exploitation surrounding her. In this darkness, it is possible that the Church will know that God is already present, inviting us to join in Jesus' mission of "setting the oppressed free."[47]

Reflection Questions

1. To what extent does our understanding of the death and resurrection of Christ influence how we minister to those who have experienced trauma, who have an "open wound", and who have not yet experienced "resurrection"?
2. To what extent within our own life and in our ministry among the exploited do we allow the "Middle Space" of Holy Saturday for remembering injustice and enabling these stories to be told?
3. How can we help churches and charities choose to be present in communities and with people who experience exploitation and suffering? Who can we partner with to up-skill and empower churches, charities and non-government organizations to walk alongside those who suffer?
4. What practical steps could be taken to "slavery-proof" our churches or charities from exploitation? Are safeguarding policies in place to address modern slavery and human trafficking? Are these policies embedded within our organizations, and are volunteers and staff fully trained?

---

[47] Luke 4:18, New International Version Bible

Works Cited

BBC News, "Modern slavery and trafficking 'in every UK town and city'". *BBC News Website*, 10th August 2017. [Available at: www.bbc.co.uk/news/uk-40885353], [Last accessed: 18th October 2022].

Bergmann, S. *God in Context: A Survey of Contextual Theology.* Aldershot: Ashgate, 2003.

Equality and Human Rights Commission. "Article 4: Freedom from slavery and forced labour", *Equality and Human Rights Commission Website*, [Last updated: 3rd June 2021], [Available at: www.equalityhumanrights.com/en/human-rights-act/article-4-freedom-slavery-and-forced-labour], [Last accessed: 18th October 2022].

Fiddes, P.S. *Past Event and Present Salvation.* London: Darton, Longman & Todd: 1989.

Global Slavery Index. "United Kingdom". *Global Slavery Index Website* [Available at: https://www.globalslaveryindex.org/2018/findings/country-studies/united-kingdom/], [Last accessed: 18th October 2022].

Herman, J. *Trauma and Recovery*. New York: Basic Books, 1992.

Modern Slavery Act 2015. Chapter 30: 1 [Available at: http://www.legislation.gov.uk/ukpga/2015/30/pdfs/ukpga_20150030_en.pdf], [Last accessed: 18th October 2022].

Moltmann, J. *The Crucified God.* London: SCM Press, 1974.

National Crime Agency. "Modern Slavery and Human Trafficking". *National Crime Agency Website.* [Available at: https://www.nationalcrimeagency.gov.uk/what-we-do/crime-threats/modern-slavery-and-human-trafficking], [Last accessed: 18th October 2022].

Rambo, S. *Spirit and Trauma: A Theology of Remaining.* Louisville, KY: Westminster John Knox Press: 2010.

Together Free. "Sexual Exploitation". *Together Free Website.* [Available at: https://www.togetherfree.org.uk/sexual-exploitation], [Last accessed: 18th October 2022].

UK Home Office. "Modern Slavery: National Referral Mechanism and Duty to Notify statistics UK, end of year summary 2021". *UK Government Website.* 3rd March 2022. [Available at: https://www.gov.uk/government/statistics/modern-slavery-national-referral-mechanism-and-duty-to-notify-statistics-uk-end-of-year-summary-2021], [Last accessed: 18th October 2022].

United Nations. *Protocol to Prevent, Suppress and Punish Trafficking in Persons* (Palermo Protocol), Article 3, 2000. [Available at: https://www.osce.org/odihr/19223?download=true], [Last accessed: 18th October 2022].

Picture This: How Christian Organizations Envision and Portray Survivors of Sexual Exploitation and Trafficking[1]

Siobhan Miles and Jill Reimer

Background

Foreign Aid to Cambodia

Cambodia has long been at the receiving end of vast amounts of foreign aid from bilateral, multilateral, and non-governmental (NGO) sources. Increasingly, the goodness of this assistance is under question.[2] Nevertheless, aid continues to be targeted at many aspects of economic development, protection of human rights, and basic social services. The focus of this assistance evolves in response to real and perceived changes in the political, economic, natural, and social environment. One aid sector that has been particularly dynamic over the past two decades is "anti-trafficking." International NGOs have been active in Cambodia since the early 1990s assisting people (primarily girls and women) whom they regard as having been trafficked for sex and/or sexually exploited.[3] There is a distinct lack of clarity or consistency on how "human trafficking" and "anti-trafficking" are defined. "Trafficking" is often conflated with sexual exploitation, commercial sex work (prostitution), and labour migration.

Anti-Trafficking Work in Cambodia

Debate rages about the extent and scope of human trafficking in Cambodia, and particularly "sex trafficking." Estimates of the numbers of females who are "victims of sex trafficking" varies widely, with published numbers ranging from 20,000 to 100,000.[4] One of the reasons that it is difficult to quantify is that the contours are continually morphing. As attention and visibility (domestic and international) have increased, so those who benefit must change the way they work:

---

[1] This article has been adapted from the following article with the permission of the authors and the publishers: Miles, S., Miles, G., Reimer, J., Umrani, A., & Stenersen, M. (2024). "'What We Say Is What You See': Portrayal by Christian Faith-Based Organizations of Female Survivors of Sexual Exploitation and Trafficking in Cambodia," *Journal of Human Trafficking*, 1-15. https://doi.org/10.1080/23322705.2023.2281871.

[2] (Ear, 2013).

[3] (Keo, 2014). This is based on their understanding that (forced) prostitution can be regarded as one form of human trafficking.

[4] (Steinfatt, 2011).

> Traditionally, traffickers have subjected women and girls to sex trafficking in *brothels, bars, and massage parlors; however, in an attempt to better conceal their crimes, some traffickers have changed tactics and now exploit victims in hotel rooms and private apartments, making them harder [...] to detect.*[5]

What is not disputed, however, is that trafficking of girls and women for prostitution is still a serious problem in Cambodia.[6] Cambodia remains "a source, transit, and destination country for men, women, and children subjected to forced labor and sex trafficking".[7]

Many of the NGOs within the anti-trafficking sector intentionally identify themselves as Christian.[8] These Christian Faith-based Organisations (CFBOs) provide a range of services to their beneficiaries[9] (children and/or adults, usually women and girls) in residential and/or community-based settings. According to their respective ethos, each CFBO emphasizes a particular combination of services including counselling, psycho-social care, spiritual care, formal or non-formal education, skills training, alternative employment, and legal support.[10] However, while the nature of support and services may vary, there is startling conformity among CFBOs in their public portrayal of their beneficiaries and limited appreciation for the voice and perspective of the women and girls themselves in that portrayal. Rather than countering the deception that characterizes human trafficking and exploitation, the rhetoric of anti-trafficking CFBOs in Cambodia extends that betrayal and perniciously adds a particular "Christian" flavor which runs counter to Biblical principles of individual human dignity, equality, and free will.[11]

---

[5] (TIP, 2016: 7).

[6] (TIP, 2016, p. 121-123).

[7] (TIP, 2016: 119). Editor's Note: At the time of publication in 2022, Cambodia was downgraded to Tier 3 (the lowest ranking) for failing to fully meet minimum standards to eliminate trafficking after three years on the Tier-2 watch list. Office To Monitor And Combat Trafficking In Persons, "2021 Trafficking in Persons Report: Cambodia", *U.S. Department of State Website*. 2021. [Available at: https://www.state.gov/reports/2021-trafficking-in-persons-report/cambodia/], [Last accessed: 18th October 2022].

[8] (MoSVY, 2011).

[9] Use of the word "beneficiary" rather than "client" is intentional, and used consistently throughout this chapter regardless of how the CFBOs themselves refer to the people they assist. It is distinctly counter to current development discourse to use the word "beneficiary" as it implicitly suggests lack of agency and a one-way movement rather than the mutuality that international development aid now encourages. However, given the definition of "client" as someone who benefits from "professional services" (NGOs do not necessarily meet professional standards nor do beneficiaries pay for NGO assistance) and that "client" is also commonly used to describe the person who buys sex from prostitutes, the word "beneficiary" is preferable.

[10] (Miles et al., 2013).

[11] Editor's Note: For additional consideration of these issues, see the chapter by Crawford and Lippincott elsewhere in this volume, as well as Parts II and III in Crawford and Miles, *Finding Our Way through the Traffick* (Oxford: Regnum, 2017).

The Research Setting

This chapter analyses the discourse of 11 anti-trafficking CFBOs in Cambodia about their beneficiaries to their selected stakeholders, contrasting it with self-representation by the women. These particular CFBOs were selected because they were named by 18 Cambodian women whose life stories, gathered over a 3-year period, were the focus of the researcher's work. Each woman had at some time worked as a prostitute and was subsequently associated with one or more of the 11 anti-trafficking CFBOs.[12] The study revealed a sharp contrast between how women define themselves (how they "make sense" of their own lives vis-à-vis their experience with prostitution) over and against how they are defined by society, family, and CFBOs in regards to their involvement in prostitution, CFBO assistance, significant relationships, and spirituality/faith. This chapter describes the differences in the realms of experience with prostitution and CFBO assistance.

Why Are Women/Girls Involved in Prostitution?

Perhaps the most frequent concept promulgated in formal and informal communication by anti-trafficking CFBOs about the women and girls they assist is that the women/girls are "victims" – lacking agency, lacking choice. One CFBO director, a psychologist with years of experience working in Southeast Asia and Cambodia with women and children involved in prostitution, described her understanding of why women in Cambodia become involved in prostitution. Her ideas[13] were echoed by many of the other CFBOs in this study:

> My view of it all is that I only ever met one girl in Cambodia who went into sex work who had no regrets. Every other girl I've counseled over the years has told me that they regretted it. Most said they were forced into prostitution and they were physically and emotionally abused, humiliated and cheated.
>
> These are the girls' words. I'm not just coming in as a Westerner and judging against sex work because I don't happen to like it. Based on what girls have told me over the years I consider all [my emphasis] women in sex work and prostitution to be victims of sex work, sex slavery, and sex-trafficking. (Interview with expatriate female founder, CFBO #4, 28/08/2013)

This discourse renders the women/girls as a monolith – passive victims, people without freedom or agency or power or intellect sufficient to resist.[14] This theme of powerlessness is highlighted in the CFBO director's use of the term "girls" rather than "women" to describe the people her organization assists, thereby legitimizing her opinion as fact (girls are children, not yet fully developed, and thus require an adult's protection, care, support, decisions). Further, such a blunt rendering does not account for individual experience, and,

---

[12] All names have been changed to protect the identity of these women.

[13] Although this director referred to her beneficiaries as "girls," in actual fact, her program worked with older teens and women over the age of 18 years of age.

[14] (Barry, 1995; Farley, 2004; MacKinnon, 1993).

more importantly, ignores much larger national and global realities that constrain the parameters within which agency and choice can be exercised.

Another senior CFBO staff member who had worked in Cambodia for more than a decade echoed similar views, focusing on "real choice" in the context of coercive practices:

> [...] one of the questions I have is when our beneficiaries first started doing prostitution did they actually have a real choice in the matter or were they victims? Some of them were as young as 13 and I don't believe they made a decision for themselves! They were too young.
>
> I do believe some women working in karaoke are there only for the singing but I think most are forced into sex services. They are forced either because the customers rape them, or the owners force them. (Interview with expatriate male staff, CFBO #8, 14/08/2013)

This simplistic explanation paints a picture of the beneficiaries as innocent victims coerced by distant strangers – customers and establishment owners, a rendering that does not account for cultural and political factors nor for (national and global) structural factors. In fact, the "deception" may well have occurred before the women/girls even set out for the karaoke club, a result of socio-cultural norms which mandate the elevation of "family honor" over individual autonomy and well-being and value males over females.[15] The point here is that CFBO portrayals of "victims" tend to be individualized, generalized, and reflective of prevailing ideologies of power and privilege. As Eichler notes, "This individualization within the anti-trafficking discourse depoliticizes the phenomenon – which is deeply entangled in global political economy – and limits a nation's responsibility to tackle worldwide inequality."

Cultural Variance: Defining "Victim"

The word "victim" is frequently employed by organizations working with women, and especially by anti-trafficking groups. According to Van Dijk (2008), the etymological origins of the English term "victim" is derived from the Latin word *victima*, used for sacrificial animal or "sacrificed one." Therefore, a "victim" is blameless and passively bears an injustice. Theoretically, then, in a Western context, this "blamelessness" should, and almost always does, elicit compassion from others.

However, that is not the reality in Cambodia. In contrast to expatriate staff views of their beneficiaries as "victims" deserving of support and sympathy, several of the women participating in this study experienced harsh stigmatization and blame. Rather than being treated as blameless and innocent victims, these women are regarded in Cambodian society as immoral or "broken" (*srey kouc*) according to prevailing social norms in Cambodia. And this peculiar socio-cultural rendering may also be at odds with how the women perceive themselves. One CFBO staff member shared that the beneficiaries of his organisation regarded suffering as their "fate" (*karma*). While they would not have chosen such a fate, they considered suffering as a normal part of life – that is, to experience (unjust) situations which cause suffering (CFBO #8, 14/08/2013).

---

[15] (Reimer, 2006).

Thus, it is evident that in the Cambodian context, these women/girls are regarded by their compatriots as neither icons of vulnerability, nor people in need of particular sympathy or attention. Rather, they are objects of scorn and ridicule, even sub-human.[16]

CFBOs as a Stand-In for God

It is interesting to note that the primary target of the messages produced by CFBOs are, largely, not intended for a domestic (Cambodian or even Asian) audience. Rather they are meant to appeal to (evangelical) Christians in Western countries who (are/will/could be) sympathetic to the promulgation of redemption of humanity. The use of distinctly Christian concept/words such as "mission", "ministry", "church", and "pray" are noteworthy:

- "Join us in our mission to eradicate sex-slavery in Cambodia! We need support from our friends around the globe."[17]
- "Stayed informed about our ministry sign up email updates." and "Every purchase you make is an investment in freedom."[18]
- "Engage your church…" and "We are always interested in people who want to pray for us and for Cambodia."[19]
- "Give donations and pray."[20]

This equation of the CFBO with God / God's plan for humanity, and subsequent appeal for Christians to respond with praying and financial giving serves to trivialize the situation at hand – it removes the focus from systemic problems and global complexities to immediate action that might assuage the audience's conscience.

CFBOs also commonly used slavery metaphors[21] and war rhetoric to describe their struggle against sex trafficking. For instance, some described their beneficiaries as "prisoners of war."[22] One CFBO described Cambodia as "ground zero" [23] and another described their efforts as "Christ's church fighting the

---

[16] (Jacobson, N.D.).

[17] http://daughtersofcambodia.org/, quote from 02/03/2014, last accessed: 18th October 2022.

[18] https://raphahousc.org/takc-action, quotc from 02/03/2014. [Editor's note: By 2022, the language on the website has somewhat changed, as has the domain: https://rapha.org/ways-to-give, last accessed: 18th October 2022].

[19] http://ratanak.org/get-involved/take-action/, quote from 02/03/2014. [Editor's note: A similar sentiment is expressed at time of publication at https://www.ratanak.org/get-involved/pray/ including praying for the whole of Cambodia].

[20] http://agapewebsite.org/get-involved/give/, quote from 02/03/2014. [Editor's note: By 2022, again the language has fully changed].

[21] (Bales, 2012).

[22] https://www.destinyrescue.org/nz/blog/tony-kirwan-where-are-the-dads/, accessed 10/05/2015. [no longer active].

[23] 'Looking Back' https://www.ijm.org/transformcambodia/ accessed 26/02/2016. [no longer active] According to the Urban Dictionary, the term "ground zero" was first used following the atomic bombing of Hiroshima in which an estimated 80,000 deaths occurred from the explosion and an additional 60,000 deaths occurred from radiation

ground war on sex-trafficking in Cambodia."[24] One CFBO described its founder as hearing "[…] the call to arms" and referring to its staff as "foot soldiers."[25] Another described themselves as "ordinary people who became unlikely heroes in fighting evil…"[26] One CFBO website emotively asserted they were committed to "fighting to end trafficking in our lifetime"[27] and that "[…] as long as sex-trafficking and child sexual exploitation exist in our world, we will continue to fight and be advocates on behalf of the enslaved and vulnerable."[28] At the same time, this CFBO also warned the war will not be won unless there are more people on their side of the battle: "Until there are more people determined to stand and fight for these kids than there are people willing to sell and abuse them, we will not win."[29]

The broad strokes with which war rhetoric is used make it difficult to actually understand who the "enemy" is, and therefore to suggest effective ways to defeat the enemy. And it suggests that "might makes right," that God imbues the CFBO with "might" therefore, the CFBO will be victorious.

Theological rhetoric aside, such simplistic CFBO portrayals of the issues at hand and the women/children in their care align with the dominant secular discourse of victims needing rescue. Such messaging does not significantly contribute to combatting human trafficking.[30] Instead, it unhelpfully "advocates a simple 'do something now' approach that […] neglects the necessary structural changes and fails to offer sustainable and respectful solutions for those affected by exploitation."

The addition of this theological dimension compounds this error, as CFBOs (perhaps unwittingly) equate their role with God's for the redemption of humanity:

- [We] exist to Rescue, Restore, Protect, Empower and be a Voice for the Voiceless.[31]
- Our sole purpose is to offer a new life of freedom to victims of sex-trafficking and sex-exploitation in Cambodia.[32]

---

poisoning. http://www.urbandictionary.com/define.php?term=ground+zero, accessed 01-04-2016.

24 http://agapewebsite.org/, accessed 04/04/2014. [Now https://aimfree.org/].

25 "Foot soldiers" connotes the embodiment of people willing to do "active and difficult work for an organization or cause" http://www.merriam-webster.com/dictionary/foot%20soldier.

26 https://www.destinyrescue.org/us/who-we-are/our-history/, accessed 10/05/2015 [no longer active].

27 http://www.destinyrescue.org/us/who-we-are/our-history/ accessed 5/23/13, https://raphahouse.org/accessed 02-02-2015 "end the evil of sex-trafficking" http://freedommandate.agapewebsite.org/, accessed 01-11-2015 [no longer active].

28 https://www.destinyrescue.org/us/who-we-are/our-history/, accessed 10/05/2015 [no longer active].

29 https://www.destinyrescue.org/nz/blog/tony-kirwan-where-are-the-dads/, accessed 10/05/2015 [no longer active].

30 (Kepadoo, 2015).

31 https://www.destinyrescue.org/us/who-we-are/mission-statement/, accessed, 14/2/2014 [no longer active].

32 http://daughtersofcambodia.org/, quote from 13/11/13.

- Our purpose is singular; we restore broken lives [...] we do whatever it takes for as long as it takes to restore life in all its fullness.[33]
- Her hope was not in a government or politicians, but in a Christian non-profit powered by Jesus' Church.[34]

In reality, while the CFBOs can undoubtedly offer social services, it is disingenuous for them to equate themselves with the God who is the author of human redemption and, through their advertising, to conflate their work with that of God.

The Problem of Language, Labels, and Stigma

Agamben criticizes groups that claim to speak on behalf of women in prostitution, asserting that they reduce women to "voiceless bodies" and "object(s) of mere survival."[35] The claims made about the nature of problems may or may not accurately reflect the realities, understandings and experiences of these problems and thus serves to constrain rather than to promote solutions.[36] Moreover, ascribed labels within these various frames may not accurately reflect how those who are actually affected by "the problem" perceive themselves).[37] Allowing for the fact that it may be acceptable to interrogate the objectivity of how a person defines themself, integrity nevertheless demands that such questioning should be done in dialogue with the person and not in a way that excludes the person.

CFBO portrayals in the public sphere[38] not only contrasted sharply with how the women viewed themselves; but these portrayals were sometimes directly harmful to the women. While most of the CFBO staff interviewed expressed awareness that the prevailing social stigma against women involved in prostitution was distressing and disconcerting for those women, they did not actually apply this understanding to their own organization's public portrayals of the women. It is a tragedy, and betrayal of Christian values of human dignity and of justice, that in this public portrayal the women ostensibly "being rescued" and "redeemed" by CFBOs are through advertisement of CBFO "good works" actually re-rendered "for sale" although to a different set of "clients."

---

[33] https://hagarinternational.org/international/, quote from 02/04/2014.

[34] http://freedommandate.agapewebsite.org/, 01/11/2014 [no longer active].

[35] (Agamben, 1998).

[36] (Best, 1990).

[37] (Brubaker, 2000). Ascribed labels are social constructions, determined by the perceptions of those who have the power to ascribe or reject labels, and the experiences of those affected by those labels (Goffmann, 1963; Greer, 2007; Walklate, 2006). Thus, Brubaker (2000) asserts how one identifies oneself (self-understanding) and how one is "identified" by others may vary greatly according to situation and context.

[38] In this chapter, CFBO portrayals in the public sphere include their rhetoric and images they publish including: their websites, open Facebook pages, YouTube, blogs, Twitter, leaflets, bulletins, menus, signs, and their merchandise.

Beneficiary Voices

One of the women who expressed her anxiety about CFBO depictions of beneficiaries worked in a CFBO's social enterprise restaurant. As Sophal's English language skills improved, she realized that the leaflets and signs written in English stated that all its employees were "former sex workers." The CFBO apparently aimed to motivate people to "do good" (i.e., support the CFBO enterprise) by marketing what should have been a confidentiality – the information that all employees were "former sex workers." Upon realizing how she and her peers were being advertised, and thus recognizing that all the customers who came into the restaurant would be aware that she formerly worked as a prostitute, Sophal felt very exposed and vulnerable.

> While I think anti-trafficking organizations are good because they help us, still I think they do not know how much they hurt us. In our culture, honor and dignity is really important and that is why most women who stop doing sex work want to keep their past stories a secret.
>
> However, when customers read our CFBO leaflets and look at the images, it means people I never met before already know I used to be a sex worker.
>
> I think foreigners, who are mostly Christians, pity us. However, when Cambodians read these leaflets, I can see they look down on me and blame me for my past. To them I am *srey kouc*. (#92, 20/02/2014)

By publicly advertising their employees as "former sex workers", in effect this CFBO very publicly and indiscriminately disclosed their past and, at a minimum, put all employees in a position of "stigma by association".[39] Sophal astutely observed that while foreigners may have regarded the staff as "victims" deserving of pity, Cambodians instead saw *srey kouc*, that is women deserving blame and judgement for immoral behaviour. In fact, Sophal wanted neither pity, nor disdain: she simply desires control over her own story – both her history, and the future she would write.

The other woman who recognised how she and her peers were being defined by a CFBO outlined two problems resulting from the content of the CFBO public materials. The first was Sreymom's personal experience of being stigmatized at school. When classmates discovered she was sponsored by a CFBO, they looked up the organization on-line, and found that it assisted "victims of sex-trafficking." Eventually, although the sponsoring CFBO advocated against mistreatment, Sreymom had to leave that school to ensure her physical safety.

> One rich girl looked up our organization on the Internet and learned my shelter helps girls who have been trafficked into prostitution. After she found this out, she spread lots of mean gossip about me around the school. She told everyone that I was a sex worker.
>
> Everyone, even some teachers started calling me srey kouc. I was so ashamed. When I tried to explain, some kids beat me up. After a while of this, [the CFBO] moved me to another school because I was not safe. (#42, 17/05/2013)

The concern that Sreymom raised was the fact that many CFBOs feature actual beneficiaries on their websites and in other public media such as videos

---

[39] (Pryor, Reeder and Monroe, 2012).

for awareness-raising or fund-raising. Several of Sreymom's peers at the CFBO had been in these videos, their story and faces splashed across the internet. Although, in theory, each of the women who were featured likely provided consent, Sreymom's view was that these women felt compelled or obligated to agree because they were in a situation of utter reliance upon the CFBO. Although her friends had been reassured by the CFBO that their images would only be viewed by people who wanted to help victims of sex trafficking (i.e. Western Christian audiences in Western countries), based on Sreymom's own experience, she did not see how this could be true. Quite the opposite, Sreymom directly experienced stigma and oppression as a direct result of such public portrayals. Sreymom feared that her friends might also be targeted and bullied as a result of being featured in CFBO promotional materials: "Anyone and everyone can get on the internet. It is not just for people in America; whether people are sympathetic is not relevant. Anyone can see the internet."

Defining the Concept of "Social Stigma"

Much of the vast literature about the concept of "stigma" uses Goffman's classic definition; stigma is considered: "an attribute that is deeply discrediting [...] a special kind of relationship between an attribute and a stereotype".[40] Stigmatized people are reduced "from a whole and usual person to a tainted, discounted one".[41] Stigma can also be defined as devaluation based on difference, or social deviance.[42] Stigma is a social construct rather than an inherently discreditable attribute. In other words, stigma does not reside in the person but rather in the social context.[43] Yang *et al.* agree, asserting that the moral experience of stigma is "what is most at stake for actors in a local social world."[44] While stigma appears to occur in every culture and society,[45] it varies in degree and quality over distinctive periods of time as a result of dynamic political and social discourses.

Contemporary Stigma in Cambodia

Cultural constructions of gender are dynamic, consisting of on-going tensions between traditional, ideal, and actual realities – not only in Cambodia, but certainly in Cambodia.[46] Although societies and customs are nuanced, varied and in a constant state of evolution traditional views of Cambodian women remain strong today.[47] The predominant formal and informal discourse about women in Cambodia explicitly and implicitly references the *Chbab Srei*[48] (literally: *law for*

---

[40] (Goffman, 1963: 4).
[41] (Goffman, 1963: 3).
[42] (Crocker, Majo and Steel 1998).
[43] (Hebl and Dovidio, 2005).
[44] (Yang *et al.*, 2007: 1525).
[45] (Link *et al.*, 2004).
[46] (Aveling, 2012).
[47] (Brickell, 2011).
[48] Also anglicized as Chbap Srey.

females) as the primary code of conduct for all women, married or not.[49] This so-called "law" instructs women to uphold family honor by maintaining chastity,[50] obeying their husbands, and ensuring the appearance of family/matrimonial harmony regardless of reality.

In accordance with the *Chbap Srey*, women are expected to adhere to antiquated notions of an ideal (virtuous) Khmer woman (*srey krup leak*). The virtuous Khmer woman is industrious, subservient to males, sexually naive, never seeks to attract male attention and, when unmarried, always a virgin. When married, she is faithful, obedient and dutiful.[51] "A woman cannot be a virtuous woman if there exists the possibility that she has been sexually promiscuous".[52] For this reason, women who appear to have contravened the ideal prototype of a good and virtuous Cambodian woman, such as women involved in prostitution, are considered "broken" and "spoiled" (*srey kouc*)[53] regardless of the circumstances that led to their involvement and male culpability notwithstanding.

When the term *kouc* which in English translates to "broken," "spoiled," or "damaged")[54] is applied to *srey* which translates as "female" in English, it holds very negative connotations.[55] Generally, the term is applied to sexually promiscuous women and those who have lost their virginity outside of marriage, or had multiple sexual partners; and to woman involved in sex work.[56] There are multiple examples of "bad women" *(srey* KTV – entertainment workers in a karaoke bar; or *srey* beer – women serving in a beer garden) but there is no equivalent for "bad men".[57]

Stigma in Lived Experience

The women in this study consistently reflected upon their fears of being despised and shamed by others.[58] The following reflection exemplifies this tension.

---

[49] (Ledgerwood, 1996).

[50] (Jacobson, 2008).

[51] (Galabru, 2007).

[52] (Ledgerwood, 1996).

[53] (Derks, 2004: 2014).

[54] Tome (1967) defines *kouc* as "broken" or "damaged" and provides several examples of its use. When the term *kouc* is applied to *jehdt* (heart), *koh jhed'* (broken heart), it connotes an emotional sense of sadness, grief, feelings of loss or disappointment. When *kouc* is applied to *lahn* (car), *lahn kouc* (broken car) denotes an automobile that is not functioning properly according to its intended purpose. When *kouc* is applied to *kone* (child), *kone kouc* (bad child), it means a child characterized as behaving in naughty, disobedient, or rebellious ways.

[55] (Derks, 2008).

[56] (Maher *et al.*, 2015).

[57] (Jacobson, personal email 11th July 2014).

[58] As a collectivist shame/ honor-based culture, most women feared that they and their families would be despised and looked down upon. Although Benedict's (1946) work comparing Japanese Shame vs. Western Guilt has been criticized as simplistic, it must be noted that there is a corpus of research highlighting the importance of shame in Asian and more collectivist cultures (Crystal, 2001).

> People in our society think that if one fish in a basket stinks, then all the other fish stink [...] People in my community always look down and spread bad gossip about [the prostitute]. They think we are all bad and immoral *srey kouc*. They don't know our suffering and they make our suffering worse by blaming us.
>
> No one in my community knows my past story and every day I live in fear that I will be found out. I fear that my husband and his parents will reject me. I fear that people will look down on my children because their mother is *srey kouc*.
>
> Living with this secret causes me so much pressure and I fear one day being found out. (Interview with participant #99)

This woman had apparently internalized for herself the identity of *srey kouc*. Although she appears to be resistant to identifying with the term (e.g. "They think we are all bad and immoral [...] they don't know our suffering"); she also seems to have (unwittingly) capitulated to social pressure to see/feel herself in those terms since she does refer to herself as *srey kouch*.

CFBO Awareness of Social Stigma

Some CFBO staff did express an awareness of the reality of stigma as something adversely affecting their beneficiaries. However, the fact that few (if any) CFBOs actually accounted for this in their intervention design suggests that they did not fully grasp the power of shame to influence people's lives, behavior, decisions in the Cambodia context.

Srey Kouc – *A Gendered Double Standard*

One Cambodian CFBO staff member strongly expressed her views about the concept of *srey kouc*. Although she personally had never experienced prostitution or any form of sexual violence, in her work she had counselled many women with such experiences. As a compatriot, having lived in Cambodia her entire life, this woman expressed empathy with women who have been commercial sex workers.

> I think our culture is not fair to women. Our society has double standards between men and women. We value women who are sexually pure, which means women must remain virgins until marriage and then faithful afterwards.
>
> However, for men it does not seem to matter; they have sex with prostitutes, girlfriends and mistresses on the side. But for women, this matters. Everyone looks down on the promiscuous woman, and stigmatizes the sex worker for selling sex. She is despised, disrespected and shunned because they think she is impure and a very bad person. People see her life as worthless, and they call her Srey Kouc.
>
> This thinking is so different from our organization's way. We listen to our beneficiaries' stories and see they have suffered a lot in their lives. They deserve our pity not our scorn. (Interview with Cambodian female staff, CFBO # 4, 20/09/2013)

From this woman's standpoint as a Cambodian female, she expressed frustration with her own culture's biased and discrepant gendered expectations, particularly regarding chastity and promiscuity. Although she did not clarify her specific understanding of "suffering" (whether it was their experience of prostitution and/or bearing the label of *srey kouc*, or other hardships in their lives) in this CFBO staff member's opinion, these women clearly deserved pity and care, not stigma and blame.

Social Stigma: Women as Victim or Villain?

An expatriate male CFBO director expressed his frustration with how his organization's beneficiaries were treated by their communities when they attempted to return to their home communities. His CFBO considered all their beneficiaries to be victims of prostitution, thus not at fault and certainly not *srey kouc*. Despite the CFBO ostensibly treating the women with dignity and respect, the reality was however, that when the women and girls returned to their original communities, they were immediately stigmatized as *srey kouc*.

> The bottom line is that these girls, when they go through therapy, they learn they have inherent value. We try to communicate to them that they are not trash and they are not at fault for what happened to them. Being forced into prostitution and sexually exploited is a crime. These girls are victims of this. We don't blame the victims, do we?
>
> But the truth is, from a cultural standpoint, back in society, they are trash. We haven't changed the community; we haven't changed the culture of Cambodia. After they leave us, our social workers follow up every month to check up and encourage them. They have observed and overheard people's gossip referring to our former beneficiaries as srey kouc and other bad names. Society blames and stigmatizes our girls.[59] (Interview with expatriate founder/director, CFBO #1, 06/11/2013)

What's Missing?

Conspicuous by its absence is the concept of justice in CFBO portray of issues and solutions to sex trafficking. None of the CFBOs analyzed here seriously address systemic issues, apart from blaming "culture" and "poverty" for trafficking, but leaving them so ill-defined as to not enable resolutions. None of the CFBO implicated men nor discussed the demand side of the prostitution equation. None referenced domestic or global inequalities.

The solutions proffered by the CFBOs are inconsistent with the lived reality of the Cambodia context. Not one of the CFBOs actually addresses underlying gender discrimination and social issues, which makes it very difficult for women who have worked in prostitution to be "reintegrated" or to achieve genuine social (re)integration.

---

[59] Similar to the earlier interview, this director referred to beneficiaries usually as "girls" and sometimes as "women", although in fairness it should be noted that this organization worked with both groups. It was common for all CFBO expatriate staff interviewed to refer to their female beneficiaries as "girls" despite most beneficiaries are women. This perhaps indicates a deeply held view that many Western Christians have, of females as diminutive, inferior, not equal to males, needing protection.

CFBO Portrayals of Underlying Causes and the Ideal Enemy

Blaming Poverty

CFBOs explicitly stated their understanding of underlying causes of sex trafficking in Cambodia. Among the 11 CFBOs under review, 10 discussed economic/structural poverty, social norms, inadequate educational opportunities, and limited job opportunities for poor women in Cambodia.[60] Five CFBOs reasoned that poor families in Cambodia were vulnerable to injustices, because societal structures favored the rich and socially powerful. They reasoned that poor, uneducated girls ended up in sex work and prostitution "because they lack other options."[61]

One CFBO explained how poor families were particularly vulnerable to foreign pedophiles and sex tourists who "prey upon parents to sell their children."[62] "Some people are so poor, they're even willing to sell their own children into the sex trade to survive – and [our organization] isn't ok with that."[63] In all these portrayals, the abstract notion of "poverty" is depicted as the enemy. While poverty is most certainly one dimension of the cause of human trafficking in Cambodia, it is worth pointing out that the vast majority of poor people in Cambodia – and globally – do not sell their children. It is worth asking the question – why is human trafficking / prostitution / sexual exploitation considered a viable option?[64]

Blaming Cultural Norms

Two CFBO portrayals were comparable to the "*Srey laor neak*" ideal that women must remain chaste, regardless of circumstance. These two CFBOs wrote about how losing one's virginity made women (and girls) vulnerable to sex trafficking. They explained that women and girls who have lost their virginity, either by choice, rape or sexual abuse, were more at risk of ending up in prostitution because their value decreased as a result of transgressing culturally defined sexual mores.[65] There is absolutely no mention made of or aspersion cast on the perpetrator of the violence against these women and girls. This understanding of culpability echoes the earlier account of the gender-double-standard described by the female Cambodian CFBO staff.

Blaming Parents

It is common for CFBOs to attribute causation to poor parenting and distorted cultural norms. Several CFBOs explained how parents and the custom of filial piety were "distorted" and contributed to the sex trafficking of children in Cambodia.[66] "Parents use filial piety against their children, for evil, and for

---

[60] (Bolton *et al.*, 2008).
[61] https://raphahouse.org/, accessed 10/02/2014 [no longer active].
[62] http://ratanak.org/, accessed 11/01/2014 [no longer active].
[63] https://www.destinyrescue.org/us/who-we-are/our-history/, quote from 10/05/2015.
[64] (Reimer, 2006).
[65] https://raphahouse.org/, quote from 10/02/2014.
[66] http://ratanak.org/projects/exploitation/, quote from 01/01/2015.

selfish gain."[67] A CFBO explained that while some girls and young women daughters might appear to choose to do sex work, in fact, "Cambodian culture requires girls to pay their parents for being born"[68] and thus, through prostitution, some daughters are sanctioned to help to support their families financially.

Several CFBOs that used slavery as a descriptive motif also asserted that parents were either tricked or otherwise unwittingly "sold their children into prostitution," or they did it intentionally, emphasizing their view that these were bad parents.[69] One CFBO view is clearly explained in a blog entitled "Money Hungry parents".

> Sadly, the odds are this kid's father played a role in her being here. He is most likely sitting at home drinking whiskey, gambling or doing drugs, all paid for by his daughter's flesh.[70]

CFBOs cast parents as enemies of the women and girls in care in at least two distinct ways. In the first instance, parents are shown to be greedy, selfish, and knowingly abusive of the cultural norm of filial piety.[71] In the second instance, parents are painted as being too weak and incapable of protecting their children: "We wrestle for the destinies of these precious kids from the ones who should [their parents] be protecting them in the first place." This CFBO further challenged "*all of the people living in the West to be their mothers and fathers*":

> I know that I or one of my team is the closest thing so many of these kids will *ever experience to the love of a father* […] *to all of us living in the West* […] *these kids need each of us to step up and be their mothers and fathers, their brothers and sisters!*[72]

At first glance, this CFBO's sentiment may seem to be a reflection of Kingdom values; but on deeper reflection, it smacks of neocolonialism and deeply engrained western cultural superiority.

Blaming the Khmer Rouge Legacy

Several CFBOs highlighted the negative impact of the Khmer Rouge legacy on their beneficiaries' parents. This is not surprising, as most scholars and survivors of the Khmer Rouge period agree that virtually all Cambodians who directly lived through this time experienced some degree of trauma.[73] Not surprisingly then, in their public space, several CFBOs attributed the cause of trafficking to

---

[67] https://www.destinyrescue.org/nz/blog/tony-kirwan-money-hungry-parents/, accessed, 08/07/2015 [no longer active].

[68] http://daughtersofcambodia.org/, quote from 09/01/2014.

[69] https://raphahouse.org/, quote from 10/02/2014.,
http://ratanak.org/projects/exploitation/, quote from 01/01/2015.
https://www.destinyrescue.org/nz/blog/tony-kirwan-money-hungry-parents/, quote from 08/07/2015 [no longer active].

[70] https://www.destinyrescue.org/nz/blog/tony-kirwan-money-hungry-parents/, quote from 08/07/2015 [no longer active].

[71] Daughters.

[72] https://www.destinyrescue.org/us/blog/tony-kirwan-where-are-the-dads/, quote from 10/05/2015 [no longer active].

[73] (Kinzie *et al*., 1984).

the destructive Khmer Rouge legacy on Cambodian society and family. The "decimation of the family"[74] has meant, "kids had to raise themselves, and they haven't had good role models."[75] The Khmer Rouge legacy left a "moral vacuum"[76] in which the "darkest side of human nature was left unchecked."[77]

> The family unit was systematically torn apart during the Killing Fields revolution [...] This has a large impact on the children of these survivors. Parents suffering, untreated, from post-traumatic stress disorder can fail to provide necessary safety for children at risk of being trafficked, and sometimes become desperate enough to sell their own children into situations of exploitation.[78]

In contrast to portraying parents as the enemy victimizing their own children, this portrayal of parents who survived the Khmer Rouge era instead transforms them into victims themselves. Parents are portrayed as being damaged psychologically and thus unable to protect their children from trafficking. In this way, they also merit sympathy and support rather than blame.

Blaming Victimhood

In contrast to the above externally-driven rescue approaches, one of the CFBOs, described how beneficiaries in their program were able to "free themselves." Despite depicting sex workers as formerly forced into sex work as children and then entrapped, this CFBO argued that women later exited brothels on their own accord. Such women self-referred into their CFBO. The CFBO described this as "victims saving themselves."[79] The CFBO saw its "sole purpose as offering a new life of freedom"[80] to not return to sex work by providing skills, training and alternative employment with their social enterprises.

> We have developed a unique model where sex workers come directly to our organization from brothels by their own choice [...] even though they are victims entrapped in sex slavery, they are already motivated to change their lives [...] and set themselves free [...] We give them a steady income so they can walk away from the sex industry and we provide them the therapeutic services they need to leave the sex industry behind emotionally.[81]

Ironically, although the CFBO speaks of women exercising personal agency and "saving themselves", still the dominant image is of women requiring assistance, women running to the care of others and being unable to independently care for themselves.

---

[74] http://agapewebsite.org/, quote from 12/02/2015.
[75] http://agapewebsite.org/, quote from 12/02/2015.
[76] http://ratanak.org/projects/exploitation/, quote from 01/11/2015.
[77] http://ratanak.org/projects/exploitation/, quote from 01/11/2015.
[78] http://ratanak.org/projects/exploitation/, quote from 01/11/2015 and http://agapewebsite.org/, quote from 12/02/2015.
[79] http://daughtersofcambodia.org/, quote from 01/02/2014.
[80] http://daughtersofcambodia.org/, quote from 01/02/2014.
[81] http://www.endslaverynow.org/daughters-of-cambodia.

A Different Sort of Frame

It is possible to imagine a world where CFBOs treat and portray their beneficiaries with dignity and respect. In contrast to the emotive depictions and narrative of "slavery" used by CFBOs, one CFBO in Cambodia, which uses human rights as a way to frame its discourse, simply described beneficiaries as "victims of trafficking" and "victims of sexual exploitation." This CFBO did not describe beneficiaries as slaves or women who had been tricked or trapped, nor did they use any images depicting these notions.

Another CFBO went further than this and in the public sphere did not even refer to trafficking or to their beneficiaries. Their public description of beneficiaries was breathtaking in its brevity and simplicity: "[Our] non-profit organization […] empowers and skills Cambodian women".[82] Staff from this CFBO unanimously spoke about the importance of strict confidentiality and treating their beneficiaries with dignity, which they defined in part as taking great care to not disclose their beneficiaries' past experiences even by association.

> The reason why we don't put stuff on our website, advertise, or let people know the girls we work with were formerly sexually exploited and sex trafficked is because it's not dignifying. That's the biggest thing for us […] this is about their new life so we don't want any reminders of their old life so […] it feels gossipy. We've got girls who have been through programs from other places and they are too embarrassed to show people the certificates they have earned from their programs because if they show that certificate then everyone knows about their past and what they have come out of […] we don't want them to be embarrassed to say "this is where I work." We really believe in upholding their confidentiality and dignity. (Interview with expatriate female staff, CFBO #3, 29/03/2013)

This CFBO stands in marked contrast to the other ten. They are able to sell their products and raise the necessary funds to operate without portraying their beneficiaries/ employees as "victims" or "slaves." They do not even advertise themselves as a "social enterprise." Rather the emphasis is on providing a quality service that attracts adequate business to make a profit, money which is then used to pay for the support services they provide to the women in care. This CFBO does not capitalize on the vulnerability of their beneficiaries: it is doing good, well.

Conclusion: Two "Victims" Make Sense of CFBO Portrayals

By and large, all CFBO staff expressed an understanding of the tensions with which women lived in terms of societal stigma, and the priority to maintain their "secret" in order to divert and manage this stigma. Despite having this awareness, however, in portraying beneficiaries as "victims" and by drawing attention to their past, CFBOs which used a slavery or sex work framing actually disempowered the very women they purportedly seek to empower. What is an even more egregious violation of these women's basic rights, these CFBO

---

[82] Respecting and agreeing to their request for confidentiality, I do not provide their website link.

exacerbate the possibility that the women will be stigmatized as a direct result of their portrayal of the women in their care.

This chapter highlights the tensions experienced by two women participating in my research by the way they and their pasts have been used by the CFBO. Although CFBOs claimed their purposes were to assist and restore women victimized by prostitution, CFBO portrayals were blatantly exposing them to societal stigma by association, while the women themselves were seeking to control their own stories about their past involvement in prostitution and thus manage societal stigma.

The first woman spoke about how important it is in Cambodian culture to be treated with dignity and honor. Ironically, she felt dishonored by the CFBO assisting her. Because of her dependency on the CFBO for employment, and the obvious power differential, this woman has reasoned herself into accepting this tension: "*I understand my organization wants to help us. They need money to do this and they get it through foreigners' pity. The leaflets seem to make them feel sad for us.*" (#92, 20/02/2014). However, this woman also recognized that the leaflets/portrayal did not generate sympathy among Cambodian patrons of the restaurant. As reflected in her own words, this woman was cast within a particular anti-trafficking frame that made it difficult to live in her local reality.

Similarly, the second woman expressed her concerns that CFBO portrayals were potentially detrimental, yet she reasoned that because she benefitted from their assistance, she would simply endure the hardship they caused her. She particularly worried some of her friends who featured in CFBO videos might later regret their decisions. In her analysis, she compared CFBO videos to pornographic videos as in both cases, the subjects of the videos had been coerced and would thereby face a lifetime of stigma due to the loss of control of their story and their image.

This exploration reveals that the majority of CFBOs use anti-trafficking discourse which consistently characterizes their beneficiaries as "coerced" and "victims." In addition, they apply the notion of "enemy" to parents as well as to more abstract notions of culture and poverty. In the women's local realities, these depictions are derogatory; rather than offering explanation or engendering sympathy, they rather are likely to cause social stigma to be directed to the women and to their families.

It is encouraging to see that some CFBOs do treat their beneficiaries with dignity and respect – both in public renderings as well as in programming. The portrayals by these CFBOs are not emotive, and they avoid inadvertently disclosing their beneficiaries' pasts. They exemplify careful, Christian conduct. Given the negative repercussions of women being associated with prostitution in Cambodia, it is absolutely imperative that CFBOs pay much closer attention to the way they advertise their work and portray their beneficiaries. Failure to do so will continue to jeopardize the future of the very people they seek to help, and likely having extending negative implications for future generations.

In summary, the 18 women who participated in this study see themselves in a very different way than they are portrayed by CFBOs. One woman, for instance, wanted to be a lawyer one day and to "*advocate for others who have been trafficked.*" (Woman #18). Another wanted to run a stall in the market, selling clothes; to be an upstanding Christian; and to get married (Woman #29). A third said, "*I want to lead a quiet life as a "normal woman" and not srey kouch. I want to give my daughter the education I never had and opportunities I have never had.*" (Woman #92). Another was very pragmatic in her hopes for the future: "*I want to become financially independent of my husband in case he divorces me or dies. To do that I want to own my own beauty salon business.*" (Woman #91). Of all non-profits, it is most incumbent upon Christian organisations to recognize the individuality, personal agency, and basic human rights of the women they are "serving."

Reflection Questions

1. Think about the ways that Christian Faith Based Organizations have framed the problems of human trafficking and sexual exploitation and the types of responses they have designed. What theological assumptions and understandings underlie those framings and responses? How do the depictions and solutions affirm Biblical principles about dignity and other core values? How do they undermine them instead?
2. Imagine that you were a young Cambodian woman who had been trafficked by her parents to work in a brothel and then spent a year in a Christian NGO "rescue shelter" before being employed at that NGO's coffee shop. After working there for a few months, you are told that the advertisements for your coffee shop declare: "This enterprise is staffed by women who have been sexually exploited." How do you think you would feel? What would you do when you found out this information? What would make it difficult for you to challenge the coffee shop manager/leadership?
3. Why do you think it is that among anti-trafficking organizations, Christian organizations are more likely than secular organizations to clearly show or advertise the exploitation of their clients and/or staff? What, if any, theological assumptions or motivations are behind this?
4. What reasons/justifications (theological and otherwise) do organizations that communicate to the general public about the background/exploitation of their clients or staff have for sharing this confidential information publicly? Do you agree with their rationale?
5. Some people argue that Western NGOs have a "double standard" in that they operate in a low-income country very differently than they could operate in their own home country in terms of representation of their work. Do you think that the laws and standards of an organization's home country should influence the

operations of that organisation in a different context? If so, why? And if not, why not?

Works Cited

Agamben, Giorgio. *Homo Sacer: Sovereign Power and Bare Life*. Redwood City, CA: Stanford University Press, 1998.

Aveling, N. "Critical Engagement with Whiteness: Beyond Lecturing on the Evils of Racism", In Barry Down and John Smyth, Eds. *Critical Voices in Teacher Education: Teaching for Social Justice in Conservative Times*. New York: Springer, 2012: 111-123.

Bales, Kevin. *Disposable People: New Slavery in the Global Economy*, Revised Edition. Berkeley, CA: University of California Press, 2012.

Barry, Kathleen. *The Prostitution of Sexuality: The Global Exploitation of Women.* New York: New York University Press, 1995.

Best, Joel. *Threatened Children: Rhetoric and concern about child victims.* Chicago, IL: University of Chicago Press, 1990.

Bolton, Paul, Sara Nadelman and Teresa Wallace. "Qualitative Assessment of Trafficked Girls in Cambodia". World Vision 23. Phnom Penh: Johns Hopkins University, Boston University, World Vision, 2008.

Brickell, Katherine. "'We don't forget the old rice pot when we get the new one': Discourses on Ideals and Practices of Women Contemporary Cambodia". *Signs* 36(2), (Winter 2011): 437-462.

Brubaker, R. and F. Cooper. "Beyond 'identity'". *Theory and Society* 29 (2000): 1-47.

Crocker, J., B. Major and C. Steele. "Social stigma". In D.T. Gilbert, S.T. Fiske and G. Lindzey, Eds. *Handbook of Social Psychology*. 4th Edition, Vol. 2. Boston, MA: McGraw-Hill, 1998: 504-553

Derks, Annuska. "Broken Woman (Srey kouc)". In Erik Harms, Joshua Barker and Johan Lindquist, Eds. *Figures of Southeast Asian Modernity.* Honolulu: University of Hawai'i Press, 2014.

—. *Khmer Women on the Move: Exploring Work and Life in Urban Cambodia*. Honolulu: University of Hawai'i Press, 2008: 258.

—. "The Broken Women of Cambodia". In Evelyne Micollier, Ed. *Sexual Cultures in East Asia: The Social Construction of Sexuality and Sexual Risk in a Time of AIDS.* London: RoutledgeCurzon, 2004: 127-55.

Doezema, Jo. *Sex Slaves and Discourse Masters: The Construction of Trafficking.* London: Zed Books, 2010.

Ear, Sophal. *Aid Dependence in Cambodia: How foreign assistance undermines democracy*. New York: Columbia University Press, 2013.

Eichler, Maya. "Private Security and Gender". In Rita Abrahamsen and Anna Leander, Eds. *Routledge Handbook of Private Security Studies.* Abingdon: Routledge, 2016.

Farley, Melissa. "'Bad for the Body, Bad for the Heart': Prostitution Harms Women Even if Legalized or Decriminalized". *Violence Against Women* 10(10), (2004): 1087-1125. [Available at:

https://doi.org/10.1177/1077801204268607], [Last accessed: 19th October 2022].

Fawthorp, Tom and Helen Jarvis. *Getting Away with Genocide? Elusive Justice and the Khmer Rouge Tribunal.* London: Pluto Press, 2004.

Galabru, Kek. *Violence Against Women: How Cambodian Laws Discriminate Against Women.* Phnom Penh: CAMBOW The Cambodian Committee of Women, 2007.

Goffman, Erving. *Stigma: Notes on the Management of Spoiled Identity.* Englewood Cliffs, NJ: Prentice Hall, 1963.

Hebel, M.R. and J.F. Dovidio. "Promoting the 'social' in the examination of social stigmas". *Personality and Social Psychology Review* 9(2), (2005): 156-182.

Jacobson, Trudy. *Lost Goddesses: The Denial of Female Power in Cambodian History*. Copenhagen: NIAS Press, 2008.

Jacobsen, Trudy. "Misogyny, Malice, and Male Privilege in Cambodia: The Cbpab Srei [c.1800]". *Journal of Southeast Asian Studies* (2016).

Kempadoo, K. "The Modern-Day White (Wo)Man's Burden: Trends in Anti-Trafficking and Anti-Slavery Campaigns". *Journal of Human Trafficking* 1 (2015): 8-20.

Kennedy, D. "Selling the distant other: humanitarianism and imagery – ethical dilemmas of humanitarian action". *The Journal of Humanitarian Assistance* (1st February 2009).

Keo, Chenda. *Human Trafficking in Cambodia.* London, New York: Routledge, 2014.

Keo, Chenda, Thierry Bouhours, Roderic Broadhurst and Brigitte Bouhours. "Human Trafficking and Moral Panic in Cambodia". *The Annals of the American Academy of Political and Social Science* 653(1), (2014): 202-24.

Kinzie, David J., R.H. Fredrickson, Ben Rath and Jenelle Fleck. "Posttraumatic stress disorder among survivors of Cambodian concentration camps". *The American Journal of Psychiatry* 141(5), (1984): 645-50.

Ledgerwood, Judy. "Politics and gender: negotiating conceptions of the ideal woman in present day Cambodia". *Asia Pacific Viewpoint* 37 (1996): 139-52.

Link, B.G., L.H. Yang, J.C. Phelan and P.Y. Collins. "Measuring mental illness stigma". *Schizophrenia Bulletin* 30(3), (2004): 511-541.

MoSVY – Cambodia. *With best intentions: A study of attitudes towards residential care in Cambodia.* Phnom Penh, Cambodia: Ministry of Social Affairs, Veterans & Youth, 2011.

MacKinnon, Catharine A. "Prostitution and Civil Rights". *Michigan Journal of Gender & Law* 1 (1993): 13-31.

Maher, Lisa, Thomas Dixon, Pisith Phlong, Julie Mooney-Somers, Ellen Stein and Kimberly Page. "Conflicting rights: How the prohibition of human trafficking and sexual exploitation infringes the right to health of female sex workers in Phnom Penh, Cambodia". *Health and Human Rights* 17(1), (2015): 102-113.

Miles, Siobhan, Sophal Heang, Vanntheary Lim, Phally Sreng and So Dane. "The Butterfly Longitudinal Research Project: A Chab Dai study on (Re-)

integration: Researching the lifecycle of sexual exploitation & trafficking in Cambodia: End of Year Progress Report 2013". Phnom Penh: Chab Dai, 2013.

Pryor, J.B., G.D. Reeder and A.E. Monroe. "The infection of bad company: stigma by association". *J Pers Soc Psychol* 102(2), (Feb 2012): 224-41.

Reimer, J.K. *At What Price Honour? Research into domestic trafficking of Vietnamese (girl) children for sexual exploitation, from urban slums in Phnom Penh.* Phnom Penh, Cambodia: Chab Dai, 2006. [Available at: https://static1.squarespace.com/static/55a81f9be4b01a30079bb9d3/t/581284fb197aea56cf609c63/1477608709210/At+What+Price+Honour.pdf], [Last accessed: 19th October 2022].

Steinfatt, T.M. "Sex trafficking in Cambodia: fabricated numbers versus empirical evidence". *Crime Law Soc Change* 56, (2011): 443-462. [Available at: https://doi.org/10.1007/s10611-011-9328-z], [Last accessed: 19th October 2022].

Tome, I.K.M. *Dictionaire Cambogien.* Phnom Penh: L'Institut Bouddhique, 1967 [1888].

US Department of State. *Trafficking in Persons Report June 2016.* Washington D.C: United States Department of State Publication Office of the Under Secretary for Civilian Security, Democracy, and Human Rights, 2017: 121-123. [Available at: https://2009-2017.state.gov/j/tip/rls/tiprpt/2016/index.htm], [Last accessed: 19th October 2022].

US Department of State. *Trafficking in Persons Report July 2022.* Washington D.C: United States Department of State Publication Office of the Under Secretary for Civilian Security, Democracy, and Human Rights, 2022. [Available at: https://www.state.gov/wp-content/uploads/2022/04/337308-2022-TIP-REPORT-inaccessible.pdf], [Last accessed: 19th October 2022].

Weitzer, R. "The Social Construction of Sex Trafficking: Ideology and Institutionalization of a Moral Crusade". *Politics & Society* 35(3), (2007): 447-475. [Available at: https://doi.org/10.1177/003232920730431], [Last accessed: 19th October 2022].

Yang, Lawrence H., Arthur Kleinman, Bruce G. Link, Jo C. Phelan, Sing Lee, Byron Good. "Culture and Stigma: Adding moral experience to stigma theory". *Social Science and Medicine* 64(7), (April 2007): 1524-1535.

The Story of Joseph and What We Can Learn about Trafficking, Sexual Abuse, and Resilience of Young Men

Glenn Miles, Jarrett Davis and Hannah Sworn

Introduction

The problem of sexual abuse and the exploitation of boys and young men is often absent from the attention of the media, the awareness of the church, and the assistance of helping organizations. However, this problem is present not only in our modern-day context, it can also be found in the pages of the Bible. How to better understand – and respond to – this problem will be the focus of this chapter, with perspectives from biblical reflection on the experiences of Joseph, findings from the discipline of social science drawn from research with service providers, and an examination of the role of spirituality and resilience in survivors.

This chapter will look at the story of Joseph and how he was trafficked into slavery by his brothers, and later sexually abused and humiliated by the wife of his boss. This will challenge the way sexual exploitation and trafficking has been addressed by faith-based organizations, which has focused predominantly on women and girls. Secondly, this chapter will survey research from South-East Asia that provides evidence of how this disparity happens and will demonstrate that males should not be ignored. Finally, this chapter will look at the role of spirituality and resilience, based on evidence from research conducted with sexually exploited men in Manila into how their spirituality helped their resilience in a way that is not so dissimilar Joseph's story.

Scope and Focus

The authors are not in any way suggesting that female sexual abuse and exploitation should be dismissed or minimized, but that the amount of resources (including funding, research, government and NGO support including Faith Based Organizations) should be devoted to males in proportion to the level of exploitation and abuse they experience.

The research considered is mainly from Cambodia, Thailand, and the Philippines where the religious contexts are Theravada Buddhism and Christianity/Catholicism. South Asia has not been included due to cultural differences between the regions.

There are a large number of Christian FBOs working on anti-trafficking and anti-sexual exploitation issues, the majority of these non-profits work exclusively or mainly with women and girl beneficiaries. This reflects the exclusionary and conservative cultural attitudes of organizations, service providers, and donors working in South-East Asia towards males as victims of exploitation.

Gender Differences

Many organizations and individuals working in development believe that girls and women require "more care and attention" than males. Grieger notes this as "an instance where a young man's very maleness and perceived (greater) agency works against him".[1] Many stakeholders working in the human rights sector paint a polarized picture, where males are perpetrators of crimes and women and children the victims. Grieger found that an NGO working with young men in Chiang Mai, Thailand was told by others in the NGO community that these men were not "real" victims and that they would only "steal from you and lie to you. Nothing good comes from those boys".[2] This outdated and reductionist conception of victimhood may be one of the reasons that the majority of both programming and research on sexual violence in the region exclusively focuses on women and children.[3] As Hilton et al. succinctly note in their seminal qualitative explorative research on the sexual abuse of boys in Cambodia:

> The vast majority of local contemporary academic discourse also contributes to what may be described as the "feminization of victimization", creating the impression that boys are invulnerable, rarely abused, less seriously affected when they are and/or more likely to be abusers of others than victims.[4]

This view is illustrated in the Cambodian proverb: "A girl is like a piece of white linen: when it is soiled it is ruined forever. Whereas a boy is like a piece of gold: if dropped in the mud it can be easily washed clean." This proverb emphasizes the vulnerability of girls and their lack of agency and resilience. For boys, it assumes that they are able to get up, dust themselves off, and continue on as if nothing has happened. This implies boys are resilient and lacking in vulnerability, juxtaposed as the opposite of girls. In reality, boys can be just as vulnerable as girls, but are often less likely to seek help because they don't want to be seen as weak. Furthermore, they are often less likely to be offered help because they are assumed to be inherently strong.

The Role of Media

The notion of male sexual exploitation is commonly trivialized in media and popular culture. Hollywood films such as "*Magic Mike*", as well as popular *telenovellas* and soap operas in South Korea, Philippines, and Japan have glamorized the use of male escorts and sex workers and ascribed an inherent agency to males who sell sex. Males in the sex trade are presented as manly, aggressive, and in control of their bodies. Males who remove their clothes on stage are thought to demonstrate pride or self-confidence at their willingness to expose their bodies. There is a continuing subtext of agency and power, which

---

[1] (Grieger, 2012: 57).
[2] (Grieger, 2012: 60-61).
[3] (Piper, 2005: 209).
[4] (Hilton *et al.*, 2008: 8).

presents a caricature of masculinity and neglects the experiences of the individuals involved. The experience of females is commonly the inverse of this. Females who trade sex are more likely to be seen as dirty or downtrodden. They are less likely to be seen as willing participants but are more likely to be seen as the victims of social economics.

The media, along with many international development agencies and organizations, continue to propagate the stereotype of the "acceptable" victim, making it increasingly hard to "recognize the exploitation of those who do not fit this (vulnerable female) archetype [...] their status as exploited individuals is delegitimized".[5] This is somewhat due to the role of the media, especially as it is used by NGOs that sensationalize the exploitation of young girls and women who are portrayed as passive and innocent victims of the violence inflicted upon them by the patriarchal societies they live in. In his article on the trafficking of men and boys, Jones describes this "powerful traditional narrative used by media personalities and commentators to describe human trafficking through sensationalized accounts of heinous male predators molesting female captives, while ignoring the significant number of male victims of forced labor and sex trafficking".[6]

Inaccurate Images of Victimization

This "idealized" image and the stories associated with it "sell" to donors because they are simple and lend greater publicity and funding opportunities to the organizations involved. A more complex picture of exploitation, where many individuals with diverse identities are victims of institutionalized patterns of exploitation with no obvious scapegoat to blame for the perpetration of these crimes is arguably less glamorous and might be seen as "simply too complex for most audiences to process".[7] In this way, the image of the male victim is very different from the female one and is often "too problematic to be understood" as it does not "meet the criteria of how a victim should act or look".[8] These attitudes towards male survivors of sexual violence not only contribute to greater silence and isolation of these individuals (which, in turn, can often leave them open to re-exploitation) but also present a narrow picture of exploitation that misleads many into thinking this type of exploitation does not exist. This in no way discounts or denies the seriousness of the exploitation of women and girls, as Hilton *et al.* explain clearly in the preface to their research:

> The existence of this study does not assume or imply that recognition, resources, services and protection for girls and women are adequate – for that is clearly not the case. It is hoped, however, that by recognizing and highlighting issues for males, this study may expand our understanding of the culture of sexual abuse and rape and contribute positively to the well-being of all victims and survivors of sexual abuse, whatever their identity.[9]

---

[5] (Grieger, 2012: 60).
[6] (Jones, 2010: 1144).
[7] (Grieger, 2012: 57).
[8] (Grieger, 2012: 58).
[9] (Hilton *et al.*, 2008: 5).

In this context, the qualitative nature of this research is particularly important. As Mahdavi and Sargent note, these groups of "problematic victims" have been generally "excluded from the opportunity to contribute their own narratives to the programmatic paradigms into which they have been scripted".[10] Giving sexually exploited males a chance to tell their own stories in their own words is essential as "[p]ractical policy responses to exploitation [...] cannot be crafted unless the reality is known – and that knowledge can only be learned from those directly affected".[11] In order to inform best practices in current and future service provision (both prevention and aftercare) for boys and men, it is crucial to listen to their accounts of abuse and the circumstances around these incidents as well as their specific needs for recovery and rehabilitation. In their 2008 study, Hilton *et al.* found that their respondents offered a rich and creative range of responses regarding what they wanted from their families, support staff, and authorities in order to have a positive recovery experience.[12]

Many participants stated that they needed caregivers to believe them, respect their confidentiality, and show them kindness and patience. Many NGO staff who were also interviewed saw boys as difficult, aggressive, and disobedient compared to generally "compliant and well behaved" girls, responding reactively to this behavior rather than seeking and addressing the root cause of it in a non-judgmental manner.[13] When discussing the commercial sexual exploitation of boys in Vietnam, UNICEF states that:

> specialized care and protection measures are required which address the reception and administrative procedures for boys and their recovery and reintegration requirements. Boys equally deserve community care options and will require separate accommodation facilities. And, just as with girls, it is not satisfactory to place boys in centres for drug addicts or alongside children with other needs (child orphans or children with disabilities). Boy victims of commercial sexual exploitation require the same level of specialized support as girls.[14]

Recognizing the Abuse and Exploitation of Boys and Men: A Biblical Reflection

In this section, we will consider how the story of Joseph illustrates the vulnerability of males as well as females to abuse, exploitation, and trafficking, and note parallels that are relevant to the modern-day exploitation of boys and men.

But first, we cannot look at prostitution without also considering the injustice of poverty. Scripture is clear that those who have resources should provide for those who do not and that we are accountable to God to ensure that the rights of the poor and vulnerable are met. Although many abolitionists do not like the term

[10] (Mahdavi and Sargent, 2011 as cited in Grieger, 2012: 4).

[11] (Grieger, 2012: 9).

[12] (Hilton *et al.*, 2008: 87-88; 107-109; 116-117; 123).

[13] (Hilton *et al.*, 2008: 156-157).

[14] (UNICEF and MOLISA, 2011: 54).

"sex work" because it implies choice alongside other forms of work, the reality is that many of the people involved in prostitution do so because their body is the only commodity left for them to sell. Due to the assumptions applied to the male gender, it may seem unthinkable to many heterosexual men that they might be in a position where they would need to sell themselves as sex objects to those willing to pay for it. However, this is the reality for many men – both those who identify as homosexual and those who identify as heterosexual – not because they enjoy it or because they have a real choice, but because they and their family need to survive and options available to them to earn money are restricted to things that are undesirable and dangerous.

In 1 Corinthians 6:15, we are reminded that our bodies are members of Christ. We are persuaded that it is never appropriate for a member of Christ to unite with a prostitute because they will become one body with her/him; the two become one flesh (6:16). Earlier in the chapter, male prostitutes and "sodomites" are listed among the wrongdoers who will not inherit the Kingdom of God (6:9). It is of interest that Paul nevertheless is speaking out to members of the Corinthian church which would have included male prostitutes and "sodomites", which assumes they are present and not rejected from being a member of the church. Bearing in mind the previous comment about poverty, it is also of note that greed is also on the list of wrongdoers. Forcing someone to prostitute themselves or someone else due to the poverty you have created and your greed is arguably more morally wrong than the person who has to do sex work to survive.

Now we can turn to the story of Joseph itself. In Genesis, Joseph was sold by his brothers for 20 pieces of silver to the Ishmalites (Midianite traders) to become a slave in Egypt (Gen. 37:12-36). Back then, as well as in the present-day, families must be carefully considered for their potential involvement in the trafficking of children.[15] Joseph was stripped of the beautiful garment that had been given to him by his father, likely as a way to humiliate him and symbolically take away the favor given to him. His brothers took the garment dipped in the blood of an animal as false "evidence" to their father that Joseph had been killed.

Although victimhood in sexual abuse is generally assumed to be of females by males, the story of Joseph is an example where this is turned on its head. The victim of trafficking is a young man who, like a number of people who are trafficked for other reasons, became embroiled in a situation where he was sexually harassed and abused, but in this case by the wife of his wealthy master, Potipher (Gen. 39). Potipher was captain of the palace guard, an officer of Pharaoh, the king of Egypt. Echoing Joseph's childhood, Potipher's wife grabbed hold of his robe given to him by her husband and pulled it off him as he ran away from her, using it as false "evidence" that he had raped her. These two stories of Joseph being stripped of his robes should be read in conjunction with David Tombs' chapter addressing the nakedness of Christ, found earlier in this volume.

Certainly, many prostituted young men (and women) are longing for someone to provide what they see as the security of a wealthy country/home, and for them to be taken away from their situation of poverty by a rich man or woman as in

---

[15] (Gozdziak, 2010; Rafferty, 2007; Reid *et al.*, 2015).

the Hollywood movie "*Pretty Woman.*" Sadly, these situations might appear to be in the best interest of the person in the beginning but there are many examples where the situation becomes abusive and exploitive later on. We can only speculate what might have happened to the well-built and handsome Joseph had he agreed to provide regular sexual services to Potiphar's wife. Although he may have made the right decision morally, choosing to not adhere to her demands had severe negative consequences whereby he ended up in jail. Our research in Cambodia has made us aware of young men being hired by lonely, wealthy women married to senior government ministers and businessmen but see very little of them. Research on this phenomenon is more prevalent in Africa than Asia.[16] More research is needed but, as it involves people of wealth and power, evidence is well hidden.

Understanding the Abuse and Exploitation of Boys and Men: A Review of the Research

Now that we have seen a picture of males as victims in the story of Joseph, we will turn to an examination of the problem in the modern context, based on a literature review of sexual violence against boys and men in Southeast Asia.

Regional

In a review of the literature on sexual abuse of children in the region, UNICEF estimates the prevalence of child sexual abuse of boys in East Asia and the Pacific to lie between 3%-16.5%, with this prevalence being slightly higher for males than females in low-income countries in the region compared to middle- and high-income countries.[17] However, the report clearly outlines the various methodological issues with this type of meta-analysis, including underreporting, varying definitions of sexual abuse, and varying measuring systems.

In a more recent meta-analysis of studies on child maltreatment in East Asia and the Pacific, Fang *et al.* found child sexual abuse rates for males to be 16.46% in low-income countries, 14.58% in lower-middle income countries, 4.79% in upper-middle income countries, and 3.09% in high-income countries.[18] However, there are also extensive methodological issues with grouping data according to these World Bank income brackets as well as with analyzing data from such diverse studies.[19]

A survey of men, women and children receiving post-trafficking services in Cambodia, Thailand, and Vietnam found that 14.6% of male respondents reported experiencing sexual violence prior to migrating, and 2.6% of males

---

[16] (Barthelemy Kuate-Defo, 2004).
[17] (UNICEF, 2014: 14).
[18] (Fang *et al.*, 2015: 154).
[19] (Fang *et al.*, 2015: 157-160).

reported experiencing forced sex while in the trafficking situation.[20] Only one male respondent in the study was trafficked for sexual purposes.[21]

World Vision found that the majority of respondents in their study across Thailand, Cambodia, Vietnam, and Laos "felt that girls were generally seen to be more vulnerable to abuse than boys", and sexual abuse was not seen as a real threat to or "something that could happen to boys".[22] Furthermore, most participants viewed sexual abuse as something committed by those outside of the family and community, "especially where the sexual abuse of boys was concerned".[23] The report identified these attitudes as leading to male victims feeling shame in reporting abuse and their reports not being taken seriously, recommending that "more attention should be paid to the sexual abuse of boys, which is less known and has been less researched, especially as boys are more vulnerable due to increased stigma surrounding homosexuality".[24]

Cambodia

Child sex offenses by foreign pedophiles has been a significant issue in Cambodia, with local NGO Action Pour Les Enfants (APLE) reporting that 61.6% of victims of child sex offenses from 2003-2013 were boys abused by foreign preferential offenders.[25] The Johns Hopkins University Protection Project also notes that Western men are typically involved in street pedophilia in Cambodia, targeting mainly underage boys.[26] Due to the high visibility of this issue, research on the sexual exploitation of boys in Cambodia generally focuses on this area.

In a study on street-based child sexual exploitation by foreigners (both tourists and residents) in Phnom Penh and the beachside town Sihanoukville, Keane interviewed a group of child survivors of sexual exploitation, the majority of whom were males, which reflected the high number of cases (80%) involving boys that their partner NGO APLE had received prior to the study.[27] Because of the demographics of the research, the following findings concern a majority male group of survivors. The study identified a number of risk factors in the families of sexually exploited children: the death of one parent and/or parental separation/divorce, large families with many siblings, alcoholism, domestic violence, debt, parents with no or low paying menial jobs, lack of parental education, and rural to urban migration.[28] Furthermore, only 38% of the children were regularly attending school at the time of abuse, and those not attending school or who never had were more likely to be living or working on the street and using drugs. Particularly noteworthy was that 38% of the child survivors who were currently or previously using drugs regularly were male, and 70% of

---

[20] (Zimmerman *et al.*, 2014: 3-4).
[21] (Zimmerman *et al.*, 2014: 31).
[22] (World Vision, 2014: 70; 72).
[23] (World Vision, 2014: 70;).
[24] (World Vision, 2014: 12; 72).
[25] (APLE, 2014: 10).
[26] (John Hopkins University Protection Project, 2007: 108).
[27] (Keane, 2006: 6).
[28] (Keane, 2006: 13).

these were “already using drugs before the time that they were first sexually exploited”.[29] The author identified drug use as “a significant factor enhancing the vulnerability of children to sexual exploitation”.[30] Grooming was experienced by half of the children, often by an “uncle” or godfather figure who would provide food and shelter “to develop a relationship of trust and control” – the children had no expectation that this relationship would lead to sex.[31] Children with a background of family violence and instability were noted to be “more prone to falling victim to a cycle of abuse and more open to grooming techniques”, as they were eager to engage with a person showing them attention, kindness, and giving them gifts, all generally out of their ordinary experiences.[32] Twenty-seven per cent of the participants had also watched pornography with an offender.[33]

A more recent study focusing solely on street-working boys in Sihanoukville found that 47% of respondents knew other boys who had been asked for sexual services by foreign adults, and 17% knew of boys who had been asked the same by locals.[34] Thirty-eight per cent of the participants surveyed reported being sexually touched by an adult and 26% of this group stated that the perpetrator had “gone further than just sexually touching them” (it is also significant that 22% declined to respond to this question).[35] Fourteen per cent of the participants reported having been “physically forced to do something sexual”, and 46% had been shown pornographic materials by mostly foreign adult tourists.[36] Respondents who didn’t have any family members as caretakers were significantly more likely to have exchanged sexual services for food, money and/or gifts and those who had migrated from rural areas were more likely to have experienced all forms of sexual exploitation.[37] Participants who had reported sexual exploitation were more likely to have felt “shame, self blame, numbness, and suicidal thoughts”, and were more likely to use drugs and alcohol.[38]

Although much of this research focuses on foreigners as perpetrators of child sex offences, APLE states that: “the issue of child sexual exploitation in Cambodia is much more country based than international based. Exploitation perpetrated by Cambodian nationals accounts for a far greater percentage of abuse in Cambodia than that perpetrated by foreigners”.[39]

Prior to 2008, there was fairly limited information on sexual violence against boys and men outside of the realm of street-based exploitation by foreigners.

[29] (Keane, 2006: 14).
[30] (Keane, 2006: 15).
[31] (Keane, 2006: 17).
[32] (Keane, 2006: 17).
[33] (Keane, 2006: 18).
[34] (Davis and Miles, 2014: 24).
[35] (Davis and Miles, 2014: 25).
[36] (Davis and Miles, 2014: 26).
[37] (Davis and Miles, 2014: 34; 36).
[38] (Davis and Miles, 2014: 40-41).
[39] (Renault, 2006: 12).

Miles and Sun found that more boys had experienced direct genital touching by an adult than girls, both after the age of nine (18.9% of boys and 13.5% of girls) and before the age of nine (15.7% of boys and 13.3% of girls).[40] This data was attributed to the cultural practice of touching a male child's genitals to soothe them or show affection, a practice that Hilton *et al.* found that boys do not like and find embarrassing and shameful.[41] Furthermore, in Miles and Sun's study, a higher number of boys (1.8%) reported a direct experience of child rape than girls (0.6%).[42] In focus-group discussions, children said that rape never happens to boys.[43] A 2004 government study found that 1.9% of boys reported being raped compared to 51.2% of girls.[44]

One of the most valuable contributions to the literature in South-East Asia on sexual violence against men and boys is Hilton *et al.*'s 2008 qualitative study on the sexual abuse and exploitation of boys and young men in Cambodia. Forty boys and young men shared their experiences with and views on sexual violence with researchers, who also interviewed over 100 staff from a "range of NGOs and service providers, including social workers, counsellors, carers, managers, team leaders, directors and lawyers".[45] The study set out not just to explore the experiences of these boys and service providers, but also to understand their needs for recovery and for providing better assistance to boys respectively. The study found that although most of the boys and young men had been abused by foreigners, "a significant number had been sexually abused by Khmer adults or other children or adolescents".[46] Abuse of boys was found to be treated with inadequate attention and seriousness due to cultural beliefs that Cambodians don't abuse boys, that abuse is not harmful if money is exchanged, that "it is impossible for a boy and a man to have sex", and that "it is only abuse if the boy ejaculates".[47] A recurring theme throughout the study was the denial of victim status to boys, who are expected to be strong enough to protect themselves from abuse and/or able to recover from abuse easily due to normative expectations of masculinity. The study identified a number of important risk factors from the data collected, including poverty, separation/divorce of parents, death of a parent/sibling(s), domestic violence, street-involved living, lack of access to education, and bullying/violence from older boys and gangs. These are similar to those identified by Keane, discussed above.

Boys who had experienced abuse often became "the target of discrimination, mocking and jokes from people in the community, resulting in further isolation and marginalisation",[48] as well as lacking options for income generation, resulting in some boys becoming more vulnerable to repeat abuse. The sexual

---

[40] (Miles and Sun, 2005: 28).
[41] (Hilton *et al.*, 2008: 118).
[42] (Miles and Sun, 2005: 29).
[43] (Miles and Sun, 2005: 25).
[44] (The Ministry of Education, Youth and Sports, UNICEF and UNESCO, 2004 as cited in UNICEF, 2012: 48).
[45] (Hilton *et al.*, 2008: 8-11).
[46] (Hilton *et al.*, 2008: 8-9).
[47] (Hilton *et al.*, 2008: 8).
[48] (Hilton *et al.*, 2008: 9).

abuse experienced by these boys resulted in painful and damaging physical effects, as well as psychological impacts including "shame and loss of honor [...] fear of repercussions of disclosing or being discovered, confusion relating to sex, sexuality and gender, self-blame, feelings of isolation [...] nightmares, wanting to commit suicide and use of drugs".[49]

Older MSM-identifying[50] respondents discussed experiences of being sexually abused as children as well as recent instances of sexual abuse, rape and violent gang rape. Participants shared invaluable information on their needs for support and help, with many identifying basic provisions of "physical and emotional safety, confidentiality, to be accepted and not judged and to receive empathy and respect [...] The need for protection, affection, love and a sense of belonging", and "help with education and work".[51] Other respondents "wanted society to take the protection of boys seriously and recognize that they too are vulnerable to abuse and feel great shame and loss of honor".[52]

A general lack of knowledge on and awareness of sexual abuse of boys was found among the service providers interviewed in this study, although rural service providers were significantly more unaware than those in urban sites. A severe deficit in coordination and collaboration in the response to this issue both within and between organizations was identified, leading to boy victims being ignored or lost track of. While a small handful of staff members demonstrated understanding and awareness of this issue, they were often "isolated from each other" and "expressed frustration and helplessness" surrounding the lack of understanding of the behavioral problems of boy survivors by their peers.[53] This was also discussed by survivors, who wanted "helpers and supporters to be gentle rather than shout or be violent when they do something wrong".[54] Basic training on the abuse of boys was identified as a major need, as well as the development of "male friendly approaches for engaging boys and specific tools and ideas for helping them build relationships" and support for and networking between staff members working with boys. Lack of donor awareness on this issue as well as competition and lack of communication between organizations were also identified as barriers to addressing this issue sufficiently.

Importantly, Hilton *et al.* identified a number of instances of abuse that had taken place in pagodas by monks and others residing in or near the temple.[55] This issue was further highlighted by a February 2016 article in the *Southeast Asia Globe* on the topic of child abuse in pagodas that drew on Hilton *et al.*'s research and other recent cases of sexual abuse perpetrated by monks in Cambodia.[56] The article discusses the vulnerability that pagoda settings create by offering

---

[49] (Hilton *et al.*, 2008: 9).
[50] MSM is an abbreviation for "males who have sex with males" and includes a variety of sexualities, including those who identify as heterosexual.
[51] (Hilton *et al.*, 2008: 10).
[52] (Hilton *et al.*, 2008: 10).
[53] (Hilton *et al.*, 2008: 10).
[54] (Hilton *et al.*, 2008: 10).
[55] (Hilton *et al.*, 2008: 96-97; 102; 108; 112).
[56] (Hutt, 2016).

"overwhelmingly boys – temporary residence and an education that poorer, provincial Cambodians cannot often afford" without sufficient child protection measures. The issue is further exacerbated by a lack of dialogue and action on this issue by monks, who failed to broach the topic at the annual congress of Buddhist monks in December 2015, despite the high-profile nature of recent cases of pagoda-based abuse coupled with Hilton *et al.*'s revealing findings. A respondent in a study by World Vision also reported knowing of a seven-year-old boy who was raped by a monk, who was arrested but subsequently released upon payment of a bribe to the police by his family.[57]

There have also been a few studies on male masseurs in Cambodia and their vulnerability to and experiences of sexual violence. The pioneering study on this topic was carried out in Phnom Penh from 2010 to 2011 and found that 13% of the male masseurs surveyed had been forced to have sex against their wishes, although this finding is limited by different understandings and definitions of "coercion" and "force" held by different participants.[58] The study also found that just over 30% of respondents' first sexual experiences had been forced, and that this was more likely if their first sexual partner was male.[59] In later research conducted by Davis and Miles on young males employed in massage parlors in the northern city of Siem Reap, 62% of those working in mixed-gender massage establishments reported having been forced or coerced into sex, compared to 28% in male-to-male massage establishments who experienced the same.[60] The authors posit that this is because sexual services are not as implied in mixed-gender establishments and sexual services are not commonly offered, leading to greater rejection of sexual advances by male masseurs working there. Furthermore, males working in mixed-gender establishments were less educated, experiencing more economic hardship and younger than those in male-to-male massage parlors.

World Vision's qualitative study on attitudes and beliefs regarding child sexual abuse found that respondents in Cambodia felt the idea of homosexual intercourse to be inappropriate, meaning that boys "could be vulnerable to abuse or hesitate to report abuse if they had been raped by a man".[61] Respondents also generally felt that sexual abuse of boys couldn't really happen and that Cambodian men don't commit these crimes, but rather that foreigners were the perpetrators of such crimes.

When conducting a study on male to female transgender individuals in the Phnom Penh sex industry, Davis *et al.* found that 55% of respondents reported experiencing forced or coercive sex (and knew of other transgender persons who also had experienced this) and 32% had experienced gang rape.[62]

---

[57] (World Vision, 2014: 68).
[58] (Miles and Blanch, 2011: 39).
[59] (Miles and Blanch, 2011: 34).
[60] (Davis and Miles, 2013a: 62-63).
[61] (World Vision, 2014: 49).
[62] (Davis *et al.*, 2014: 26).

Philippines

Davis and Miles contributed two studies to the topic of sexual violence against men and boys in the Philippines. Their 2013 baseline study on male masseurs in the Metro Manila area discussed the taboo nature of sexual abuse of boys and the blame of boys for their abuse, which is seen as a sign of weakness or homosexuality, leading to low levels of reporting due to fears of stigma and discrimination.[63] The authors explored how masculinity is often equated with heterosexuality and being "tough, macho, not showing emotion, having libido, and making a family", although a man is able to have a same sex relationship without jeopardizing his masculine identity as long as he fulfills normative masculine characteristics and roles.[64] The study found that 38% of male masseurs surveyed reported having experienced forced or coerced sex and that 33% stated they were aware of other male masseurs experiencing forced sex.[65] During qualitative interviews participants described coercion via violence, physical force, bribery, verbal abuse, and threats of complaining to the management regarding the masseurs' performance. There was also some indication that some of the respondents' first sexual encounters had been coercive – despite their insistence that they were consensual – due to the very young ages (the youngest being three and six years old) or circumstances around them, for example being with teachers as a minor.[66]

Davis and Miles' 2015 baseline study on the vulnerabilities of street-involved boys to sexual exploitation in Manila found that 76% of respondents said that they knew other boys who had been asked for sexual services by adults, most of whom were local and opportunistic.[67] Sixty-five per cent of participants disclosed experiencing some form of sexual abuse, the most common form of which was being shown pornography by an adult (49%), followed by sexual touching (47%) and further abuse including forced intercourse and oral sex (27%).[68] Revealingly, only six (12%) of the boys in this study had ever sought help for an incident of abuse, and two of these were turned away where they sought help.[69] While most of the sexual exploitation was opportunistic and/or a result of "survival sex", there were a few instances where a third-party broker was involved.[70] Sleeping on the street and social networking were both identified as factors associated with higher vulnerability to sexual abuse.[71]

In a study on intimate partner violence, 64.6% of females and 42.3% of males reported being sexually coerced by their partner. The author specifically notes that "young men can also be victims of sexual coercion", with one respondent commenting that:

---

[63] (Davis and Miles, 2013b: 5-6).
[64] (Davis and Miles, 2013b: 6-7).
[65] (Davis and Miles, 2013b: 19).
[66] (Davis and Miles, 2013b: 28).
[67] (Davis and Miles, 2015: 28-31).
[68] (Davis and Miles, 2015: 41).
[69] (Davis and Miles, 2015: 35).
[70] (Davis and Miles, 2015: 42).
[71] (Davis and Miles, 2015: 43).

> young men like me, are also victims of sexual coercion […] But our sufferings are often unheard especially if it has been done by a woman. People believe that with or without coercion it is always the man who wins. But this is not true.[72]

This and other qualitative interviews with male victims were particularly rich, with respondents reporting feeling "angry, shocked, afraid and remorseful".[73] Mechanisms of bribery in sexual coercion were significantly more common in intimate partner violence against young men compared to women.[74]

A study on adverse childhood experiences and health-risk behaviors among adults found that 4.5% of males and 6% of females had experienced sexual abuse by an adult or someone five years older than them before the age of eighteen, suggesting a fairly close prevalence rate between the two genders.[75] These individuals (of both sexes) were twelve times more likely to engage in early sex and five times more likely to attempt to commit suicide.

Thailand

Although the literature relating to sexual violence against boys and young men in Thailand is limited, a number of NGO research reports and academic studies touch on this subject in various ways. There are a few reports by the Thai government on reported numbers of child sexual abuse and of children receiving medical services for abuse in hospitals; however, no distinction is made between male and female children and thus they have not been included in this review.

Child sex tourism, which often involves young boys, has received a large amount of attention in Thailand, and also provides some insight into the exploitation of boys. ECPAT estimates 60,000 minors to be involved in prostitution in Thailand, and noted that the majority of victims of alleged traveling child sex offenders arrested between 2007-2008 were boys and young men between the age of twelve and twenty years old.[76] The report also identifies Pattaya and Phuket as areas where child sex tourism continues to be prevalent.[77] In ethnographic qualitative research on underage sex workers in a Thai urban slum, half of the participants of the study were boys.[78] Although the majority of attention on commercial child sexual exploitation lies with foreign offenders, ECPAT notes in its 2011 Global Monitoring report that "demand of sex services from children does not only come from foreigners but also from locals".[79] The report references "gender norms" and the inability of authorities to act in these cases as contributing factors towards the "tolerance" of this form of demand,

---

[72] (Serquina-Ramiro, 2005: 488).
[73] (Serquina-Ramiro, 2005: 487; 491).
[74] (Serquina-Ramiro, 2005: 492).
[75] (Ramiro, Madrid and Brown, 2010: 847).
[76] (ECPAT, 2013: 13-14).
[77] (ECPAT, 2013: 14).
[78] (Montgomery, 2001).
[79] (ECPAT, 2013: 13).

suggesting that these cases could be significantly more widespread than previously thought, despite the low attention they receive.[80]

A few studies on child sexual abuse also address sexual abuse of boys. In a study of youth in Northern Bangkok, Jirapramukpitak, Prince and Harpham found that 4.9% of male respondents had reported experiencing sexual abuse before the age of sixteen, almost the same percent as females, suggesting there is little difference in abuse prevalence rates between genders in this area.[81] Conflictingly, a 2008 qualitative study of sexual abuse of children in Thailand included four boys who were victims of "substantiated cases of child sexual abuse" – this very low participant sample in comparison to the fifty-six girls interviewed in the research is problematic.[82]

A small handful of studies offer more relevant information on the sexual exploitation of young men and boys in Thailand. A 2005 study on forced sex among MSM in Bangkok, Chiang Mai, and Phuket (sampling participants over the age of fifteen working in entertainment venues, parks, saunas, street locations and male-sex work venues) found that 18.4% of participants "reported a history of forced sex".[83] Of this group, 83.8% were forced by someone they knew, 67% had been forced more than once and 55.1% had experienced the first occurrence of forced sex during adolescence. Most participants had also been forced by a man and without the use of a condom, and those who had experienced forced sex were more likely to use drugs. The highest number of participants reporting having experienced forced sex was in Phuket, where participants were also more likely to have been forced before the age of eighteen compared to participants from Bangkok or Chiang Mai. Respondents reporting sex role identification as "bottom" or receptive partner were also more likely to have experienced forced sex.

Another revealing finding was that transgender participants were most likely to have experienced forced sex compared to male sex worker participants. The researchers speculate that "male sex workers, as a group, adhere more to the male heterosexual role and thus less subjected to gender-role conforming social and sexual pressure." They suggest that "Thai men who perceived themselves to be female or transgender may, in fact, take on traditional gender roles of a Thai woman in both the private and public contexts, and hence may be more prone to forced sex from their male partners".[84] Because this study is venue-based, the results may not be reflective of the experiences of those outside these venues and its cross-sectional nature means causal inferences cannot be drawn from the data.[85] It is also worth considering the above findings of van Griensven *et al.* and Manopaiboon *et al.* in this respect, both of which found sexual coercion to be higher in self-identifying homosexual and/or bisexual male participants. Guadamuz *et al.* also note that research on "the cultural meanings of identities

---

[80] (ECPAT, 2013: 13).
[81] (Jirapramukpitak, Prince and Harpham, 2005 as cited in UNICEF, 2012: 51).
[82] (Trangkasombat, 2008).
[83] (Guadamuz *et al.*, 2011: 259-261).
[84] (Guadamuz *et al.*, 2011: 264-265).
[85] (Guadamuz *et al.*, 2011: 265).

and gender norms and their relationships to sexual domination, power and control and the spaces (e.g., public, private/intimate, virtual) where these domains transpire in the context of sexual health risks is desperately needed".[86]

Grieger contributes a comprehensive and nuanced qualitative study on the human trafficking and commercial sexual exploitation of young ethnic Akha men in Chiang Mai to the literature on male sexual exploitation. Although the study does not focus specifically on sexual violence, Grieger found that two of his twelve participants described experiencing sexual violence from clients while undertaking sex work in Chiang Mai.[87] Interestingly, a number of participants noted that they had more frequently heard of Thai male sex workers attacking or beating their expatriate clients, while a few others stated that they hadn't been victimized by their *farang* (Western) clients, with one young man even saying that "If they're going to hurt me I'll hurt them first. The guys who come to the bar look like tough men but since they're gay, when we go to the room, they act like a girl." It is important to consider these findings in relation to most of these participants preferring or mainly engaging with foreign clients rather than Thai ones, as they are generally less or not aware of Thai social hierarchy.

A survey of male entertainment workers in Chiang Mai between the ages of fifteen to thirty-five found that two respondents' first sexual encounters were forced by an adult female perpetrator while they were between fifteen to sixteen years of age, and 21% of all first sexual experiences qualified as adult-to-child sexual abuse.[88] The study also found that one in four respondents had experienced forced/coerced sex by clients, with six participants (12%) reported that this happens "always", one stating that this happens "very often" and four reporting this happening "sometimes".[89] Bar-based sex workers were not only younger but were also found to experience significantly higher instances of forced sex than the overall group, with three out of four participants reporting forced sex compared to one in four overall. Over half (60%) of participants reported experiencing unwanted sexual touching within the last year, mostly perpetrated by clients, with one third stating that it happens "always" and 11% "often." However, a limitation to this study is that respondents only participated from entertainment venues that allowed the researchers permission to interview workers from their establishments – the authors note that "four-out-of-five show-bars denied the research team access to employees with many massage parlors doing the same".[90] Furthermore, these results rely on what may be considered unreliable self-reporting data collection methods.[91] Other literature also suggests that male sex workers are "frequently victims of physical and sexual violence from their customers (men)" primarily because customers feel the need to "prove they are the dominant man in the situation, prove they have more power and are tougher".[92]

---

[86] (Guadamuz *et al.*, 2011: 265).
[87] (Grieger, 2012: 110-112).
[88] (Miles, Glotfelty and Davis, 2013: 26).
[89] (Miles, Glotfelty and Davis, 2013: 30).
[90] (Miles, Glotfelty and Davis, 2013: 20).
[91] (Miles, Glotfelty and Davis, 2013: 21).
[92] (Cameron, 2006: 57-58).

A qualitative study by World Vision on the beliefs, attitudes, and knowledge of children and adults in Laos, Vietnam, Cambodia and Thailand towards child sexual abuse found that respondents in Chiang Mai saw the sexual abuse of boys to only be a problem for other countries as they had never heard of such issues in their circles.[93]

Overcoming Abuse and Exploitation of Boys and Men: The Role of Resilience and Spirituality

The final task of this chapter is to examine the provision of services in light of the story of Joseph, towards the goal of addressing the problem of sexual exploitation.

Despite the generally negative research findings presented in the literature review, our research conducted in the Philippines with men involved in prostitution demonstrates that even those who have been sex trafficked and abused can and do develop the resilience reflected in the story of Joseph who went on to become a significant leader.[94]

We chose to explore the spiritual wellbeing of the respondents because of the numerous studies that indicate spiritual wellbeing as playing a core role in developing resiliencies among vulnerable people groups.[95] Given the strong influence of Catholicism and Christianity on the Philippine context, the Spiritual Well-Being Scale (SWBS)[96] was introduced to understand what role, if any, perceptions of God were playing in the existential realities of males in sexually-exploitive careers in the Philippines. An understanding of the respondents' sense of themselves was further desirable because it facilitated a mutual exploration of their spiritual and psychological assets, inviting both the respondents and researchers to go beyond awareness of the negative elements of the respondents' experience to view, perhaps with new eyes, the positive.[97]

We hypothesized that the respondents' greatest vulnerabilities and resiliencies would lie within the social capital they possessed within their respective communities. Given our assumptions about the expectations of highly religious societies in the Judeo-Christian tradition, we hypothesized finding a low self-esteem coupled with a high sense of shame and guilt among respondents. We further hypothesized that feelings of connection with God would be, at best, limited. Specifically, and pointedly, we were concerned about their place within their families and in the church, two institutions posited to be central within Filipino life.

---

93 (World Vision, 2014: 49).

94 Editor's Note: For more on the spirituality of survivors of sex trafficking, see the chapter by Lim, Miles and Nhanh elsewhere in this volume.

95 (Davis and Hill, 2012; Smith, 2011; Kass, 2007).

96 (Paloutzian and Ellison, 1982).

97 (Green, 2006).

Affiliation

Of those professing religious affiliation (n=45), the majority, or 82% of respondents indicated affiliation with Catholicism, 9% with other various Christian denominations, 6% indicated Indigenous, and other religious traditions and 2% (or one person) indicated affiliation with Islam. These findings among male masseurs almost exactly mirrored the general religious landscape of the Philippines. Outside of the family, the church remains, it seems, the most pervasive institution in Filipino society.

Regarding affiliation as a construct of spirituality – that is, affiliation as it refers to a person's belief that they are loved and cared for by God and that they experience a positive relationship with God – 54% state that they strongly feel that they receive strength and support from God. An almost equivalent percentage (52%) strongly believe that God is interested in them personally. Forty percent of the respondents strongly feel that they have a satisfying prayer life.

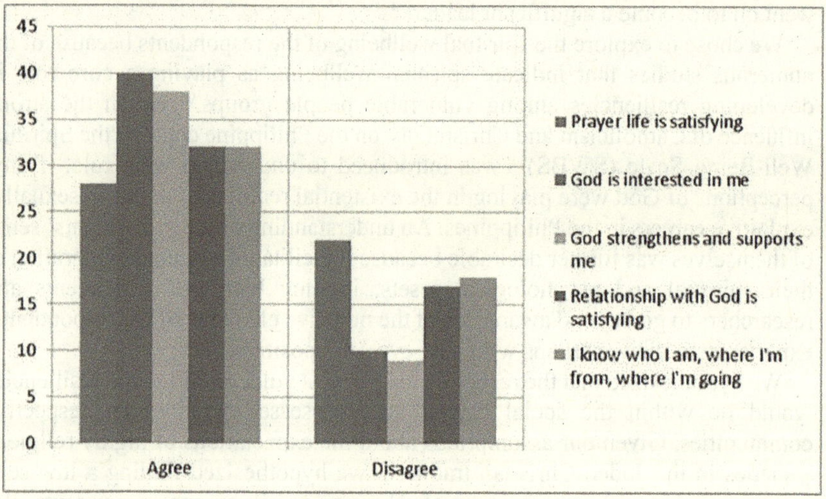

Figure 1: Alienation

Social Capital in the Church

Every respondent in this study received moderate to high scores on this scale, meaning this population has a relatively good sense of spirituality. All respondents indicated not only having "a faith" but also that it played an important role in their sense of self. Notably, although they felt that their faith played a significant role in allaying their sense of guilt, it did not have the same effect on their sense of shame. As such, the church was not acknowledged amongst these respondents as a place of nurturing community.

Church attendance however, and the regular practice of personal prayer seemed to be consistent with the respondents' respective religious traditions. While researchers in this study anticipated finding instances of guilt and shame associated with attendance in their respective places of worship, this assumption proved to be true of only a minority. The majority of respondents indicated worship to be, in some sense, healing. They used descriptions such as "lightened, free, feeling forgiven", etc. to describe their feelings after leaving their respective places of worship, and seemed to indicate these feelings to be their primary impetus for the pursuit of worship.

Given the societal (religious) stigma and discrimination associated with the overt expression of the sexuality explored here, one wonders at the high sense of spiritual wellbeing possessed by the respondents. Perhaps the priority that meaning-making takes when one has to grapple with "differentness" may be presumed to have some effect, and may be a more plausible explanation for the high levels of spiritual awareness indicated by this group, as is often ascribed to people within LGBT communities.[98]

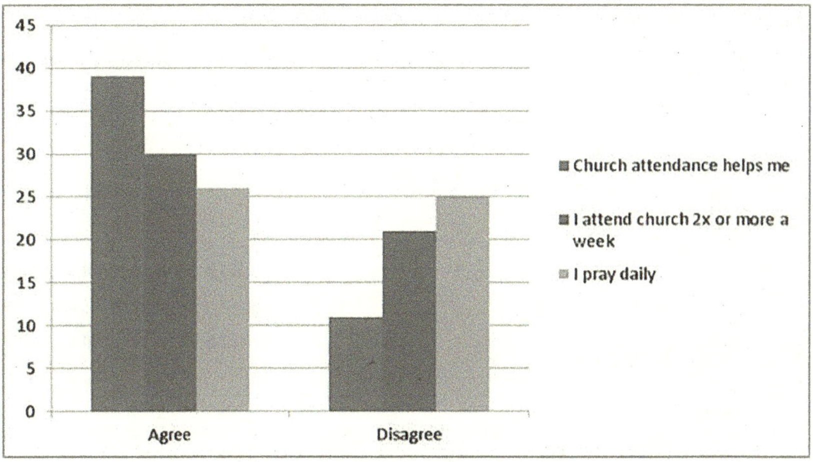

Figure 2: Religious Coping Strategies

Social Capital in Their Families

For a majority of the respondents, either their families or their housemates were aware of their involvement in the sex industry. Where it did not negatively affect intimacy, the respondents felt valued as husbands, fathers, brothers, and relatives who supported the nuclear and extended family financially as expected, even though such support cost both the individual respondents and their families their presence. The fact that so large number of these respondents indicated an active functioning in heterosexual marriages may explain this unique situation. By and large, the average MSM in this survey does not feel alienated from his family, despite admission of an awareness of complications it posed to intimacy with their wives and lovers.

[98] (McNeill, 1988; Williams, 2011).

Dissatisfaction with Life

With regard to their perceptions of their present life situations, 42% strongly affirm that they are enjoying themselves and generally do not experience their lives as full of conflict or unhappiness. Thirty-two percent strongly disagree. The locus of their dissatisfaction however is the financial uncertainty of their situation.

Of those that responded to questions exploring their orientation to the future (n=45), 80% feel strongly that their lives have purpose, and that purpose is tied to providing for their dependents. As such, it appears, the respondents may circumvent the stigma of their work by rationalizing its role in helping them fulfill what they perceive to be their financial obligations to their dependents. As indicated earlier, between 80-98% of the respondents functioned in most of the socially prescribed roles of heterosexual males while simultaneously functioning within the MSM sub-culture, with admittedly manageable dissonance between the two identities.

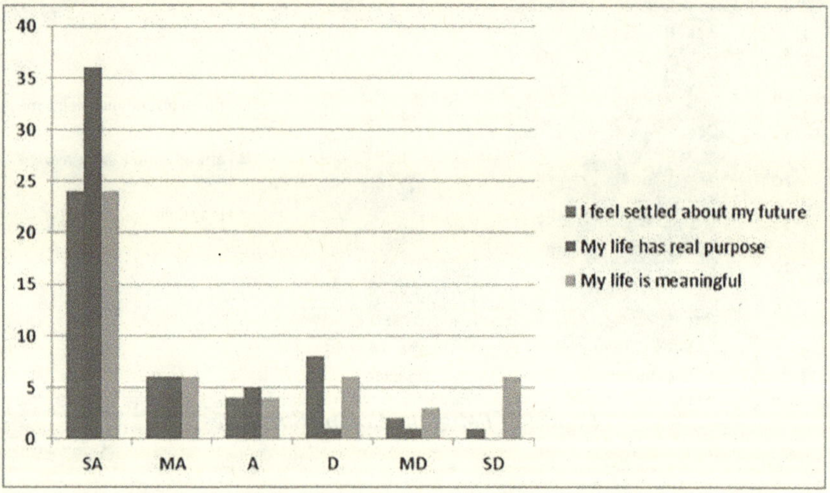

Figure 4: Dissatisfaction with life (future orientation)

Conclusions

No respondents scored low on the SWBS overall. During data collection and initial analysis, we felt that these high self-evaluations could have been due to the euphemistic nature of Philippine culture and that respondents might have been simply responding with idealistic, religiously-pleasing answers, rather than answers which they felt to be true. In further analysis, we compared the final spiritual results of male masseurs in Manila, with published SWBS results of other people groups from varying cultures, faiths, socio-economic groups, and educational levels. While there were a few apparent similarities within some isolated cases, only one group had near statistically identical results, a study amongst sexually-abused outpatients. Male masseurs in Metro-Manila were found to be within one percentage of all scales and subscales, including standards of deviation of this group as shown below.

Male Masseurs in Metro Manila (N=51)	**Sexually-Abused Outpatients (N=50)**
RWB - Mean: 46.54; SD: 12.28	RWB - Mean: 46.46; SD: 11.48
EWB - Mean: 40.62; SD: 11.85	EWB - Mean: 39.26; SD: 10.5
SWB - Mean: 87.17; SD: 23.41	SWB - Mean: 85.82; SD: 19.61

Perhaps these similarities reiterate the importance of recognizing vulnerability, but also the potential for resilience in persons who live under sexually-exploitive circumstances despite the distinctly different manifestation of said vulnerabilities.[99]

Reconsidering the story of Joseph: he had gone through a series of difficulties, becoming a slave and being whisked off to Egypt. After the traumatic experience of false accusation by Potipher's wife, he then goes to jail and works his way out because he explains Pharaoh's dreams to him and ends up getting promoted to become the second most powerful person in the land. In our research, we have the story of the boys who surprisingly indicate having an intimate relationship with God. Then, in the challenges of their work and marginalization, they may actually become stronger through it and stronger in their relationship to God. Perhaps this connects them to the story of Joseph.

Rather than writing them off because they are tainted and have "no more use", we should see their acquired resiliency. Those who prove themselves worthy should, like Joseph, be offered leadership positions to have an impact on society.

It is of interest that Hard Places Community in Cambodia[100] have worked with a number of previously exploited young men and many are now in impressive positions of leadership in their work, supporting new boys as they grow.

Reflection Questions

1. How can we increase the awareness of ourselves and others that boys and young men can be vulnerable as well as resilient?
2. What lessons can be learned from the story of Joseph that are relevant to the abuse, exploitation, and trafficking of boys and young men in your context?
3. What can we do to strengthen families to reduce the risk of them trafficking members of their own family?
4. How can we work with spirituality to make it an effective part of the process of developing resilience and leadership?

[99] (Valente, 2005; Dube *et al.*, 2005).

[100] "Punlok Thmey Men", *The Hard Places Website.* [Available at: http://thehardplaces.org/punlok-thmey-men/], [Last accessed: 20th October 2022].

Works Cited

Alola Foundation *Trafficking in East Timor: A Look into the Newest Nation's Sex Industry*. Dili: Alola Foundation, 2004.

APLE. *Investigating Traveling Child Sex Offenders: An Analysis of the Trends and Challenges in the Field of Child Sexual Abuse and Exploitation in Cambodia*. Phnom Penh: Action Pour Les Enfants, 2014.

Cameron, L. *Sex Workers, Transgender People & Men Who Have Sex with Men: Thailand.* Sexual Health and Rights. Open Society Institute, 2006.

Choo, W., M. Dunne, M. Marret, M. Fleming and Y. Wong. "Victimization Experiences of Adolescents in Malaysia". *Journal of Adolescent Health* 49(6), (2011): 627-634.

Davis, J. and G. Miles. "The Lingha Boys of Siem Reap: A Baseline Study of Sexually-Exploited Young Men in Siem Reap, Cambodia". *Journal of Loyola school of theology* 27(1), (2013a): 27-72.

Davis, J. and G. Miles. *Hidden in Plain Sight: A Baseline Study of Sexually Exploited Male Masseurs in Metro Manila*. Manila: Love 146, 2013b.

Davis, J. and G. Miles. *"I want to be brave": A Baseline Study on the Vulnerabilities of Street-Working Boys to Sexual Exploitation in Sihanoukville, Cambodia*. Phnom Penh: Love 146 and M'lop Tapang, 2014.

Davis, J., H. Lippman, G. Miles, T. Morrison, Z. Miles, V. Hem, C. Sokun, P. Song and E. Isaac. *More than Gender: A Baseline Study of Transgender Persons in the Phnom Penh Sex Industry (Book)*. Sixth Annual Interdisciplinary Conference on Human Trafficking. Lincoln, NE: Love 146, 2014.

Duong, L. *Children in Prostitution in Hanoi, Hai Phong, Ho Chi Minh City and Can Tho: A Rapid Assessment*. Bangkok: International Labour Organization, 2002.

ECPAT. *Protection of children against sexual exploitation in tourism.* Bangkok: ECPAT and Ministry of Foreign Affairs of the Netherlands, 2013.

Fang, X., D. Fry, D. Brown, J. Mercy, M. Dunne, A. Butchart, P. Corso, K. Maynzyuk, Y. Dzhygyr, Y. Chen, A. McCoy and D. Swales. "The burden of child maltreatment in the East Asia and Pacific region". *Child Abuse & Neglect* 42 (2015): 146-162.

Gozdziak, E.M. "Identifying Child Victims of Trafficking: Toward Solutions and Resolutions". *Criminology & Pub. Policy* 9(2), (2010): 245-255.

Grieger, M. *Challenging Conventional Wisdom: Sex Work, Exploitation, and Labor Among Young Akha Men in Thailand*. Master of Arts. George Washington University, 2012.

Guadamuz, T., W. Wimonsate, A. Varangrat, P. Phanuphak, R. Jommaroeng, P. Mock, J. Tappero and F. van Griensven, F. "Correlates of forced sex among populations of men who have sex with men in Thailand". *Archives of Sexual Behavior* 40(2), (2011): 259-266.

Hilton, A., K. Sokhem, N. Socheat, O. Syphat, S. Channy, S. Sothearwat, T. Ponarry, L. Vibol and M. Dalin. *"I Thought it Could Never Happen to Boys": Sexual Abuse & Exploitation of Boys in Cambodia – An Exploratory Study*. Phnom Penh: Hagar and World Vision, 2008.

Hutt, D. "Holy Sin: Child Abuse in Cambodia's Buddhist Pagodas". *Southeast Asia Globe*. 5th February 2016. [Available at: https://southeastasiaglobe.com/holy-sin-child-abuse-in-cambodias-buddhist-pagodas/], [Last accessed: 20th October 2022].

IJM. "Trafficking Ring Run by Thai Monk Crumbles with Leader Behind Bars". *International Justice Mission*. 2015. [Available at: https://www.ijm.org/news/trafficking-ring-run-by-thai-monks-crumbles-with-leader-behind-bars], [Last accessed: 20th October 2022].

Jackson, P. and G. Sullivan. "A Panoply of Roles: Sexual and Gender Diversity in Contemporary Thailand", In P. Jackson and G. Sullivan, Eds. *Lady Boys, Tom Boys, Rent Boys: Male and Female Homosexualities in Contemporary Thailand*, 1st ed. New York: Harrington Park Press, 1999.

Jackson, P. "Male Homosexuality and Transgenderism in the Thai Buddhist Tradition", In W. Leyland, Ed. *Queer Dharma: Voices of Gay Buddhists*, 1st ed. San Francisco, CA: Gay Sunshine Press, 1997.

Jones, S. "The Invisible Man: The Conscious Neglect of Men and Boys in the War on Human Trafficking". *Utah Law Review* 4, (2010): 1143-1188.

Keane, K. *Street-Based Child Sexual Exploitation in Phnom Penh and Sihanoukville: A Profile of Victims*. Phnom Penh: Action Pour Les Enfants, 2006.

Komolvadhin, N. *New Economy and Gender Relations in Thailand: The Implications of the Internet*. Ph.D. London School of Economics and Political Science, 2008.

Logie, C., P. Newman, J. Weaver, S. Roungkraphon and S. Tepjan. "HIV-Related Stigma and HIV Prevention Uptake Among Young Men Who Have Sex with Men and Transgender Women in Thailand". *AIDS Patient Care and STDs* 30(2), (February 2016): 92-100.

Lyttleton, C. *Endangered Relations*. Boca Raton: CRC Press, 2000.

Manopaiboon, C., P. Kilmarx, K. Limpakarnjanarat, R. Jenkins, S. Chaikummao, S. Supawitkul and F. van Griensven. "Sexual coercion among adolescents in northern Thailand: Prevalence and associated factors". *Southeast Asian Journal of Tropical Medicine and Public Health* 34(2), (2003): 447-457.

Miles, G. and H. Blanch. *What about boys? An initial exploration of sexually exploited boys in Cambodia*. Phnom Penh: Chab Dai, The Hard Places Community, First Step, Love 146, 2011.

Miles, G. and V. Sun. *Stop Violence Against Us! Summary Report*. Phnom Penh: Child Welfare Group, Tearfund, World Hope and World Vision Cambodia, 2005.

Miles, G., E. Glotfelty and J. Davis. *Boys for Baht? A Baseline Study on the Vulnerability of Male Entertainment Workers in Chiang Mai, Thailand.* Love 146 and Urban Light, 2013.

Montgomery, H. *Modern Babylon? Prostituting Children in Thailand.* New York: Berghahn Books, 2001.

Paloutzian, R.F. and C.W. Ellison. "Loneliness, Spiritual Well-Being and the Quality of Life", In L. A. Peplau and D. Perlman, Eds. *Loneliness: A*

Sourcebook of Current Theory, Research, and Therapy. New York: John Wiley and Sons, 1982: 224-237.

Piper, N. "A Problem by a Different Name? A Review of Research on Trafficking in South-East Asia and Oceania". *International Migration* 43(1-2), (2005): 203-233.

PRADET Timor Lorosa'e and UNICEF East Timor. *An Investigation on Child Abuse and Commercial Sexual Exploitation of Children (CSEC) in East Timor*. Dili: PRADET, 2002.

Pradubmook-Sherer, P. "Prevalence and correlates of adolescent dating violence in Bangkok, Thailand". *Journal of Sociology and Social Welfare* 36(1), (2009): 9-37.

Rafferty, Y. "Children for sale: Child trafficking in Southeast Asia". *Child Abuse Rev.* 16(6), (2007): 401-422. [Available at: https://doi.org/10.1002/car.1009], [Last accessed: 20th October 2022].

Ramiro, L., B. Madrid and D. Brown. "Adverse childhood experiences (ACE) and health-risk behaviors among adults in a developing country setting". *Child Abuse & Neglect*, 34(11), (2010): 842-855.

Reid, J. A., J. Huard and R.A. Haskell. "Family-facilitated juvenile sex trafficking". *Journal of Crime and Justice* 38(3), (2014): 361-376. [Available at: https://doi.org/10.1080/0735648X.2014.967965], [Last accessed: 20th October 2022].

Renault, R. *Survey on Street-Based Child Sexual Exploitation in Cambodia: Overview of 7 Provinces*. Phnom Penh: Action Pour Les Enfants, 2006.

Shytov, A. *Indecency on the Internet As a Challenge to Thai Law*. [online] Thailand Law Forum, 2016. [Available at: http://www.thailawforum.com/articles/indecency-challenge-thailaw.html], [Last accessed: 20th October 2022].

Serquina-Ramiro, L. "Physical Intimacy and Sexual Coercion Among Adolescent Intimate Partners in the Philippines". *Journal of Adolescent Research* 20(4), (2005): 476-496.

Thanh Nguyen, H., M. Dunne and A. Vu Le. "Multiple types of child maltreatment and adolescent mental health in Viet Nam". *Bulletin of the World Health Organization* 88(1), (2010): 22-30.

The Protection Project. *International Child Sex Tourism: Scope of the Problem and Comparative Case Studies*. Baltimore, MD: Johns Hopkins University, 2007.

Trangkasombat, U. "Sexual abuse in Thai children: a qualitative study". *Journal of the Medical Association of Thailand* 91(9), (2008): 1461-1467.

UNICEF. *Child Maltreatment: Prevalence, Incidence and Consequences in the East Asia and Pacific Region.* Strengthening Child Protection Systems Series. Bangkok: UNICEF EAPRO, 2012.

UNICEF. *Violence against Children in East Asia and the Pacific: A Regional Review and Synthesis of Findings*. Strengthening Child Protection Systems Series. Bangkok: UNICEF EAPRO, 2014.

UNICEF and MOLISA. *An Analysis of the Commercial Sexual Exploitation of Children in Selected Provinces and Cities of Viet Nam*. UNICEF and the Ministry of Labour, Invalids and Social Affairs, 2011.

van Griensven, F., P. Kilmarx, S. Jeeyapant, C. Manopaiboon, S. Korattana, R. Jenkins, W. Uthaivoravit, K. Limpakarnjanarat and T. Mastro. "The Prevalence of Bisexual and Homosexual Orientation and Related Health Risks Among Adolescents in Northern Thailand". *Archives of Sexual Behavior* 33(2), (2004): 137-147.

World Vision. *Sex, Abuse, and Childhood: A study about knowledge, attitudes and practices relating to child sexual abuse, including in travel and tourism, in Cambodia, Lao PDR, Thailand and Vietnam*. Melbourne: World Vision Australia, 2014.

Wongnorkaew, A. "Ex-monk held for sex abuse". *Bangkok Post*. 30th January 2016. [Available at: http://www.bangkokpost.com/news/general/845584/ex-monk-held-for-sex-abuse], [Last accessed: 20th October 2022].

Zimmerman, C., L. Kiss, N. Pocock, V. Naisanguansri, S. Soksreymom, N. Pongrungsee, K. Sirisup, J. Koehler, D. Thuy Dung, V. Nguyen, B. Dickson, P. Dhavan, S. Rathod and R. Borland. *Health and human trafficking in the Greater Mekong Subregion: Findings from a survey of men women and children in Cambodia, Thailand and Viet Nam*. Geneva; London: International Organization for Migration and London School of Hygiene and Tropical Medicine, 2014.

"Too Much Is Not Enough": A Theological Reflection on Consumer Culture

Heike Lippmann

Human trafficking and commercial exploitation of sex and labor don't happen in a vacuum but within cultures that are driven and informed by certain mindsets. It's important to uncover these mindsets and to respond to their claims. Theology can help with this. Theology is about knowing God and his story within our world. It deals with the complexities of real life. It helps us to see the world differently and to find our place in God's bigger story. God's story is our dwelling place. It's the story that really matters. Theology helps us to break through the claims of cultural ideologies that there is no reality outside of the dominant mindsets, in this case the claims of consumer culture. It offers alternatives that actually give life. The way things are now is not the way things have to be. We trust and hope in the God who created and redeemed this world and who makes all things new!

A Sense of Entitlement

A few years ago, I spent six months in Asia working alongside people who are fighting human trafficking and commercial exploitation. During this time, I was exposed to a kind of poverty that I hadn't seen before. Life reduced to its bare minimum! That left a deep impression and changed the way I looked at life back in Europe. Returning to Europe actually felt depressing. I was overwhelmed by the overabundance of stuff available in shopping malls or in online shops. There was more than enough and yet people complained as if they lacked the bare essentials. In one of those moments of frustration, I asked my sister how she would describe the dominant mindset in our Western culture. She said, "Everything has to be available to me at all times and ideally it shouldn't cost anything." What makes it worse is that we actually believe that we are entitled to this lifestyle. It's like we are saying, "My need is my right, and as long as I pay for these needs to be met, everything is alright."

That bothered me and I couldn't shake it off anymore. I realized that this lifestyle might be pleasant for some, but it ignores all the people who pay the price for it. So much of what we consume is produced by people who are exploited in their "work setting." Just take a closer look at the fashion industry, smartphone production, meat/agriculture industries, or the sex industry to see more clearly. I started having conversations with the people around me about this, which was interesting at best and frustrating at worst. Of course, there are initiatives and ideas to depart from the consumer madness. Some people expressed concern, but quite often I heard: "This is just how the world works.

It's complex and complicated. We can't change it. It's like fighting windmills." I don't believe that this is true.

On the following pages, I will take a brief look at what consumer culture is about, how it relates to human trafficking and commercial exploitation and how scripture deals with its claim that no matter how much we have, there is never enough.

Consumer Culture

Before focusing on what consumer culture looks like on an everyday level, I'd like to put it into the context of what I call the "exploitation narrative." I believe that human trafficking and commercial exploitation are relational issues. That means they are expressions of how individuals, groups of people, or segments of society relate to and impact each other. The exploitation narrative is shaped by the values and beliefs that nurture and drive these relationships.

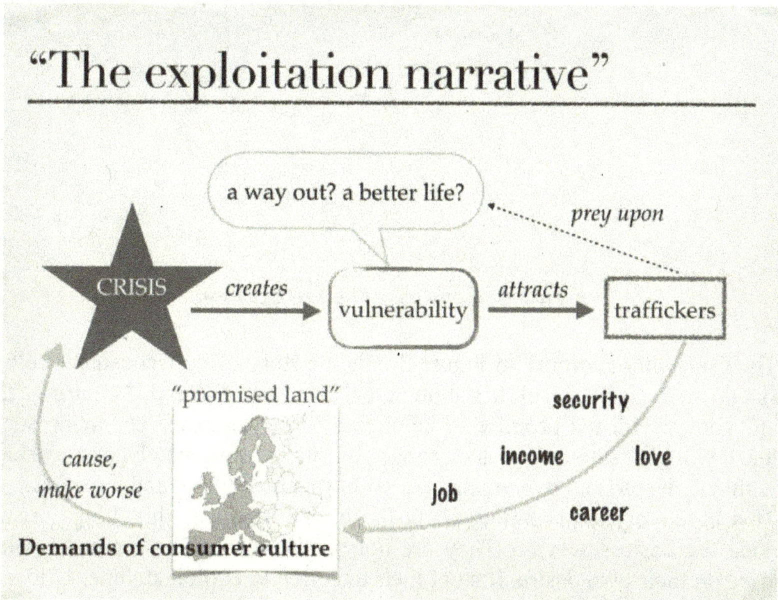

Figure 1: The Exploitation Narrative Mind Map

The mind map in Figure 1 illustrates how it works. There are many crises in today's world, often man-made – caused by war, economics, and personal factors, for example. These crises make people vulnerable to exploitation. Traffickers prey upon their desperation to find a way out, promising a better life in the "promised land." These false promises create false hopes in those who are desperate. Their ability to hope is abused before they even reach the "promised land" where they will be used to meet the demands of consumer culture. These demands often cause or exacerbate the crises people are trying to escape. Consumer demand also drives exploitation. It is fueled by mindsets and beliefs.

These mindsets are like the soil or the breeding ground in which exploitation can flourish or even go unnoticed because we are numbed to its reality.

Figure 2: Consumer Culture Cartoon

The Consumer Cartoon[1] in Figure 2 tells the story of how consumer culture works on an everyday level. It's about a real or perceived need. Acquiring "this thing" comes with the promise of belonging to the in-crowd or having social status. It will give satisfaction and change your life. Unfortunately, once we have "this thing", it starts all over again. We go for the next thing, and the next…

This little story says nothing about those who produce "this thing" or who provide the desired service. They are not on the radar. The person is solely focused on their own desire. It's not their intention to exploit anyone. It doesn't even cross their mind that they are part of a bigger reality.

Broadly defined, in consumer culture what you do and how you are valued and defined revolves around the consumption of stuff. Well-being and identity are measured by the capacity to purchase. And even though there is too much of everything (just think about the thousands of tons of foodstuff thrown away every year), it never seems to be enough!

Scarcity is key to this mindset. Markets only value what is scarce. "Scarcity is the deep belief that no matter how much we have, it is not enough. Therefore,

---

[1] Source unknown.

more scale and growth is always required. Grow or die. The system of scarcity feeds on itself."[2]

This ideology has captured our imagination and we are made to believe that there is no life outside of it.

The question, "Is it enough?" is not new at all. It's as old as humanity. We already find it on the first pages of the bible. Revisiting Genesis 3 is helpful to understand the desire behind the question.

"It's Not Enough" ... in Paradise?

Reflections on Genesis 3: 1-7

As human beings, we are created in the image of a relational God – Father, Son and Holy Spirit. We only have life in relationship with God and with each other, and we are supposed to be good stewards of creation. Adam and Eve lived in the abundance of paradise and yet the serpent found a way to attack them: "Is what you have and who you are really enough? You know you could be more. God knows that you would be just like him. That's why he denies you the fruit of that tree." In today's language, we would call that "fake news."

The aim of the attack was to destroy Adam and Eve's trust in God's goodness. They lived in a garden that was supposed to be their home where they could find abundant life. There was everything they needed. Now they feared that if they received life solely out of their relationship with God it would not be enough. The serpent suggested, "Why wait until you receive life when you can just grab it and have it at your own disposal?" The god the serpent introduced was a rival who restricts them. This god is not good, not generous, not giving but greedy and manipulative.

Against this god or without him, they had to acquire as much life as possible. The consequence is that humankind took the place that belonged to the relational God and what was promised to them as gain by the serpent led into the exact opposite. They were robbed of their humanity.

The refusal to find life in community with God or with each other leads to self-isolation and self-centeredness. Striving for this kind of autonomy is destructive to the life we seek because we can only be fully human in community with God and with one another. Otherwise, life turns out to be "not enough" because something finite cannot fulfill the deepest longing for love, life and happiness. Therefore, sin is ultimately a lie. Instead of life, the sinner puts himself into the sphere of death. Death in Scripture is more than just physical death. Death is the realm of futility, hopelessness, emptiness, and nothingness, with physical death as the obvious sign that in the end striving for life without "the other" was for nothing.[3]

This isn't only a private matter but it also affects the way people live together in society. Slander, betrayal, disloyalty, rivalry, corruption, and exploitation are

---

[2] Peter Block, Walter Brueggemann and John McKnight, *An Other Kingdom: Departing the Consumer Culture* (Hoboken, NJ: John Wiley & Sons, 2016): 2.
[3] Gisbert Greshake, *Der Dreieine Gott* (Freiburg: Herder, 2007): 326-328.

a few obvious symptoms of this. The intensification of negative behaviors and attitudes leads to societies where true community is unattainable. Mistrust and the fear that "there won't be enough for me" and that "I will miss out if I don't fight for myself and only myself" aren't ingredients for a society where people can thrive and flourish. Sin becomes systemic. It's not a label for some and not for others.

The result: Even too much is not enough. We are driven to the ultimate consumerism of consuming each other!

Living from a Place of "Enough"

Reflections on Jesus' parable of the wheat and the weeds (Matthew 13:24-30)

In this parable, Jesus describes a wheat field that an enemy has sowed with weeds. When the wheat sprouted, the weeds did as well. In response, the workers wanted to pull out the weeds. The owner had a different plan.

At first glance, it might not seem like this parable has anything to do with our theme. However, it addresses the issue of systemic evil, scarcity, and a way to live through the realities we are facing today.

In Jesus' time, wheat was basic food. When there was no harvest, people wouldn't eat. The harvest was often threatened by circumstances: war, weather, animals. The attack in this parable can only be seen as an act of deliberate sabotage. The only purpose was to destroy the livelihood of the people. The weeds looked very similar to the wheat until they were about 10 centimeters high. Before that height, there was no way to see a difference. The weeds also produced grains. However, they were not fit for consumption. If they got mixed in with the wheat, people could get sick or even die if they ate too much of it. In this parable, Jesus talks about matters of life and death.

The shock of the workers is understandable, but the response of the field owner is not very comforting: "An enemy did this." This implies that the whole field was affected. The owner acknowledges that this was an evil act. Evil in scripture is everything that stands against God and against life.

It is striking that the owner neither minimizes the threat nor panics. The threat is real and it is shocking, but he holds the tension without being torn apart by it. His workers probably wanted to stay close to him in this challenge so his way could rub off on them. But first they were scared into action. They were good people who were willing to do overtime in order to immediately remove the weeds. All they wanted was to save the harvest in order to save the lives of their people.

But the owner says, "No." He is cautious because he takes seriously what's going on under the surface. There is a real limit to what we can see or perceive. The roots are entangled, and tearing out the weeds would destroy the wheat as well. Discernment is difficult if not impossible. Isn't that true for many things in life that look so similar but are very different: faith and superstition, humility and false modesty, being carefree and being reckless, real love and softness or compliance, real hope and empty promises, collaboration and using or taking advantage of others.

With his "No" the owner says that timing is important. He says "no" for the sake of the harvest and not because he wants evil to grow. He doesn't say: "This is just how the world works. You better get used to it." Nor does he say that we should leave the world to the criminals. What he's asking for is engagement in authorized ministry instead of unauthorized action.

The workers' question-behind-the-question is: "Will there be enough nourishment for the wheat if we don't take out the weeds?" This takes us back to the concept of scarcity and the question: "Is it enough?"

With this parable, Jesus says: "Yes, there is enough. Despite the hostile circumstances there will be a harvest." The world doesn't only consist of weeds. The wheat grows too.

There is a temptation to think that if the one grows the other automatically diminishes. Sometimes it might be very difficult to answer the question of whether things get better or worse. The parable is an invitation to hold the tension like the field owner does – to celebrate God's reign in the world and the good that is growing, and to lament the evil systems that are still powerful in our world. We do that in the knowledge that one is temporary (the weeds) and one is lasting (the wheat). This way we become agents of hope as we walk with our God who created and redeemed the world and who is in charge of the future.

Meditation: On Generosity[4]

On our own, we conclude:
there is not enough to go around
we are going to run short
of money
of love
of grades
of publications
of sex
of beer
of members
of years
of life
we should seize the day
seize our goods
seize our neighbor's goods
because there is not enough to go around
and in the midst of our perceived deficit
you come
you come giving bread in the wilderness
you come giving children at the 11th hour
you come giving homes to exiles
you come giving futures to the shut down
you come giving easter joy to the dead
you come – fleshed in Jesus.

---

[4] https://www.goodreads.com/quotes/1042357-on-generosity-on-our-own-we-conclude-there-is-not.

and we watch while
the blind receive their sight
the lame walk
the lepers are cleansed
the deaf hear
the dead are raised
the poor dance and sing
we watch
and we take food we did not grow and
life we did not invent and
future that is gift and gift and gift and
families and neighbors who sustain us
when we did not deserve it.
It dawns on us – late rather than soon –
that you "give food in due season
you open your hand
and satisfy the desire of every living thing."
By your giving,
break our cycles of imagined scarcity
override our presumed deficits
quiet our anxieties of lack
transform our perceptual field to see
the abundance
mercy upon mercy
blessing upon blessing.
Sink your generosity deep into our lives
that your muchness may expose our false lack
that endlessly receiving we may endlessly give
so that the world may be made Easter new,
without greedy lack, but only wonder,
without coercive need but only love,
without destructive greed but only praise
without aggression and invasiveness…
all things Easter new…
all around us, toward us and by us
all things Easter new.
Finish your creation,
in wonder, love and praise.
Amen.

(Walter Brueggemann)

Reflection Questions

1. Where do you see the consumer-mindset in action in your heart, your work, and your everyday life? What could living and working from a place of "enough" look like for you?
2. How do consumer culture, the exploitation narrative, and scarcity contribute to human trafficking and exploitation in your context? What role does your own involvement play?

3. What theological lessons can we draw from Matthew and Genesis to help us be more responsible consumers and not participate in unethical consumerism?
4. What practically can be done, at the individual and societal levels, to counter consumer culture and its exploitative impact? What steps will you take today to become an agent of hope to the people around you?
5. How do people involved the sex industry relate to consumer culture? For example, some sex buyers think: "It's just an exchange: I need sex and the other person needs money." What does this mindset reveal about consumer culture? Are people and sexuality just items to be used and discarded?

Works Cited

Block, Peter, Walter Brueggemann and John McKnight. *An Other Kingdom: Departing the Consumer Culture*. Hoboken, NJ: John Wiley & Sons, 2016.

Brueggemann, Walter. "On Generosity". *Good Reads Website*. [Available at: https://www.goodreads.com/quotes/1042357-on-generosity-on-our-own-we-conclude-there-is-not], [Last accessed: 22nd October 2022].

Greshake, Gisbert. *Der Dreieine Gott.* Freiburg: Herder, 2007.

Zimmer, Siegfried. "Das Gleichnis vom Unkraut unter dem Weizen". *Worthaus Website.* 22nd June 2014. [Available at: https://worthaus.org/worthausmedien/das-gleichnis-vom-unkraut-unter-dem-weizen-mt-1324-30-4-5-2/] [Last accessed: 22nd June 2022].

Becoming a Refuge: Sex Trafficking and the People of God[1]

Myrto Theocharous

Introduction

In his book *The Rise of Christianity*, Rodney Stark speaks about the pagan emperor Julian who admonished his pagan priests to match the morality of the Christians in works of charity. Stark notes that:

> there was little or no response because there were no doctrinal bases or traditional practices for them to build upon. It was not that Romans knew nothing of charity, but that it was not based on service to the gods. Pagan gods did not punish ethical violations because they imposed no ethical demands – humans offended the gods only through neglect or by violation of ritual standards.[2]

People often ask me, "How does biblical scholarship match with ministry to trafficked women?" And my response is that it is precisely biblically based doctrine that animates social ministry and, conversely, social ministry is where biblical doctrines come to life. For example, the doctrine that every human being is made in the image of God is what we cling to when we speak to a girl in a brothel. Not when we find ourselves among respectable equals who are *clearly* image bearers to us, but when we find ourselves among "lessened" humans, "dehumanized" humans, who look nothing like divine icons.

Even issues regarding biblical history are morally tested here: Why is it important that the Exodus was a *physical historical* exodus of actual bodies and not a spiritual tale? Why is it so important that Jesus' resurrection is a *bodily* resurrection and not a mere spiritual reality? A denial of the physicality of these stories carries the danger of anesthetizing the church to the importance of the physical along with our spiritual mission and would thus be morally suspect. Insisting on the historicity and physicality of these stories binds us with an inescapable social responsibility. If bodies mattered in Scripture and these stories are not simply allegories of spiritual truths, then bodies matter today and the church is unable to rest in a world where bodies are used, abused, or raped.

Also, systematic categories such as the divine attributes must "hit the ground." For example, God's omnipresence is to be reflected by His church, meaning that we, as His body, must *also* be "everywhere," not shying away from certain areas

---

[1] A version of this chapter first appeared in the *Journal of the Evangelical Theological Society* 59(2), (2016): 309-22. Used with permission of *JETS* (editor Dr Andreas Köstenberger).

[2] Rodney Stark, building on MacMullen, *The Rise of Christianity: How the Obscure, Marginal Jesus Movement Became the Dominant Religious Force in the Western World in a Few Centuries* (San Francisco, CA: Harper Collins, 1997): 83-88.

as if there was such a thing as profane territory. Divine presence infuses the space that was once regarded "unclean." A brothel *can be* a temple where prayers and offerings can be lifted up to God, as Malachi expresses: "in every place incense will be offered to my name" (Mal. 1:11). This is often a reaction we get from the girls and women in the brothels: "We cannot pray in here. There is no way God has anything to do in this place." But omnipresence is to be acted out. So, yes, anti-trafficking work *is* doctrinally grounded, whether one is aware of its doctrinal roots or not.[3] Likewise, human trafficking can be doctrinally based. Joe Carter wrote recently that the Islamic State has theological justification for the rape of young girls and they consider sexual slavery of apostate women to be a sign prefiguring the Day of Judgment.[4] All our beliefs against human trafficking are not disconnected articles of faith: they emanate from our God's very essence. He is the God who brings people *out* of trafficking, out of slavery.

Biblical Refuge: "*bet ab*" Ethics

In the Old Testament, God manifests Himself as a refuge for Israel (Ps. 46:2) and a refuge for the poor (Ps. 14:6), but at the same time, He ascribes responsibility for this security and protection of the most vulnerable to His people, predominantly through the institution of the בית אב (*bet ab*, in English "House of a Father").[5] The House of a Father was probably the most significant structure dictating life in ancient Israel and whoever was found lacking a close association to a בית אב (*bet ab*) was most vulnerable and in need of special protection. The emphasis given by the Old Testament to orphans, widows, foreigners, Levites and even runaway slaves reveals God's intention that the father's house should be a place of refuge for those in need. Repeated exhortations in Scripture, as well as God's "soft spot" for the poor,[6] show that the boundary lines of the patriarchal house (or patrocentric house) were constantly pushed further and further so that the security enjoyed by the nuclear family would extend outwards.[7]

The more "inclusive" the בית אב (*bet ab*), the more justice would cover the land of Israel. The more inward and restricted the patriarchal house, the more displeased the Lord would be with his people, as the needs of the most vulnerable

---

[3] Humanitarianism is itself a "form of faith." See Luke Bretherton, "Poverty, Politics, and Faithful Witness in the Age of Humanitarianism," *Interpretation* 69(4), (2015): 447-459.

[4] Joe Carter, "9 Things You Should Know About Islamic State," *The Gospel Coalition*, 14th November 2015, [Available at: http://www.thegospelcoalition.org/article/9-things-you-should-know-about-islamic-state], [Last accessed: 22nd October 2022].

[5] See for example the significance of this structure in texts such as Genesis 12:1 and 1 Samuel 22:1 and the addressees of the Decalogue in Exodus 20 and Deuteronomy 5. Cf. the study of J. David Schloen, *The House of the Father as Fact and Symbol: Patrimonialism in Ugarit and the Ancient Near East,* Studies in the Archaeology and History of the Levant 2 (Winona Lake, IN: Eisenbraus, 2001).

[6] Ex. 22:22-23; Dt. 10:18; Ps. 68:5; 146:9, etc.

[7] E.g. Dt. 10:18-19; 27:19; Is. 1:17; Zech. 7:9-10; Ez. 16:49; 18:5-9; Jer. 22:16.

remained unattended. Women, especially, would find themselves in danger of being exploited, and often turning to prostitution as the only means left for survival.[8] Individualistic moral judgments about such women could easily miss the societal neglect that led them to such a plight.

Biblical principles regulating the בית אב (*bet ab*) were not relevant only for a time when Israelite society was regulated by heads of households, but they also formed the criteria for prophetic indictment by figures such as Amos, Micah and Isaiah.[9] These principles are adapted for changing circumstances in Israel, holding accountable whoever had enough power to regulate justice in the land (e.g. kings, officials, the elite; e.g. see Ez. 22).[10] This testifies to the adaptability of these moral principles and their continuing relevance under any socio-economic and political regime. The driving biblical demand is the same throughout: the most vulnerable people in our world must be secure. בית אב (*bet ab*) values are binding on us and our households but they cannot be restricted to the sphere of the private. As with the prophets, these values form the ground of our critical stance against larger institutions, systems, and powers operating in our world.

One should be careful to differentiate between Israelite patriarchy and the ideals expressed in *biblical* patriarchy. The goal of this chapter is neither to defend nor to object to a patriarchal model. I am suggesting that biblical values that came to control, critique, and regulate Israelite patriarchy, when properly and responsibly extracted from Scripture, are binding for the Church whatever the social model it operates in. Biblical patriarchy offers values that can inspire *both* men and women to image God as a refuge for the victims of one of the biggest challenges of our world today: human trafficking. I shall attempt, at various points in this chapter, to show how these values can penetrate into the way we think about human trafficking.

Applying the "Triangle" to Sex Trafficking

What does Christian theology and Christian care have to teach us about how we can understand and respond to sex trafficking?

In this chapter, I focus on sex trafficking, not because other forms are less condemnable, but primarily because this is the area I am mostly involved with in ministry and where many of my Greek Bible College students do their internships. Our street work takes place in the center of Athens, in the red-light districts but also in brothels, bars, cheap hotels, etc., where trafficked victims are most likely to be found. We approach them, have coffee with them, try to get to know them, and eventually let them know that we can help them escape.

---

[8] See Daniel I. Block, "Marriage and Family in Ancient Israel", in Ken M. Campbell (ed), *Marriage and Family in the Biblical World* (Downers Grove, IL: IVP, 2003): 51.
[9] E.g. Amos 2:6-8, Mic. 2:1-2, Is. 1:17, 23.
[10] Richard Horsley, "You Shall Not Bow Down and Serve Them: Economic Justice in the Bible", *Interpretation* 69(4), (2015): 417-419.

But our opponent is formidable. The actual revenue generated by sex trafficking is almost five times greater than that of labor trafficking, making sex trafficking the most lucrative form of exploitation by far.[11]

Traffickers have various methods of enslaving people in sex trafficking, and this is where poverty plays a decisive role. They will promise a high-paying job (for instance, domestic work), with good benefits and reasonable working conditions, and in this way induce them into taking employment.[12] Given their often-miserable circumstances in their country of origin, they will take the risk for a better life abroad and the opportunity to send some money to their families as well. We know that in the U.S. massage parlors are often fronts for prostitution. Many of the Asian girls and women who work there, once brought into the country, are told that they owe a large amount of money to the owner and they will have to work in order to repay it, not only by performing massages but also through sex work. Refusal means rape and severe beating.[13]

Traffickers will also spend time courting the girls and women, promising them marriage in order to get them to follow.[14] A small number of them *do* know ahead of time that they will be working in prostitution, although they do not know the oppressive conditions they are entering. For this reason, the UN Protocol holds that initial consent or the signing of contracts is irrelevant since deception about the *conditions* of the work has been used in order to achieve such consent.[15]

Numerous structural factors contribute to sex trafficking, such as social inequality, market downturns, and attitudes to gender. In this chapter, I will focus on three factors: Legal, Poverty, and Demand, with some observations on the profile of the client.

---

[11] Of course, people enslaved in other forms of trafficking are often exploited sexually as well: "Female victims of forced or bonded labor, especially women and girls in domestic servitude, are often sexually exploited as well." Some child soldiers, both male and female, are often sexually abused and are at high risk of contracting sexually transmitted diseases. U.S. Department of State, *Trafficking in Persons Report*, 8. In 2001, it was estimated that within U.S. borders, profits from sex trafficking were approximately seven billion dollars annually, but this estimate is very conservative as the U.S. population increasingly engages in sex trafficking, McCabe and Manian, (eds), *Sex Trafficking*, 148. According to the International Labor Organization (ILO) in 2014 the annual profits per victim were 21,800 dollars for sexual exploitation compared to 4,800 dollars for a victim of labor trafficking. See Belinda Luscombe, "Inside the Scarily Lucrative Business Model of Human Trafficking", *Time Magazine Website,* 20th May 2014. [Available at: http://time.com/105360/inside-the-scarily-lucrative-business-model-of-human-trafficking/], [Last accessed: 22nd October 2022].

[12] Sally Cameron and Edward Newman, "Trafficking in Humans: Structural Factors", In Sally Cameron and Edward Newman (eds), *Trafficking in Humans: Social, Cultural and Political Dimensions* (Tokyo; New York; Paris: United Nations University Press, 2008): 39.

[13] Kara, *Sex Trafficking*, 179-182.

[14] See for example the Carreto family case in Kara, *Sex Trafficking*, 192.

[15] United Nations, *Treaty Series: Treaties and International Agreements Registered or Filed and Recorded with the Secretariat of the United Nations* Volume 2237. A-39574, Article 3 (New York: United Nations, 2005): 344.

Legal

After widespread abolition of institutional slavery globally in the 19th century, the League of Nations and later the United Nations Organization began to address a form of slavery that was less formal, less public, and harder to detect than institutional slavery: human trafficking.[16]

Six successive treaties were signed to address the problem with the last one being the 2000 UN Anti Human Trafficking Protocol.[17] In order to combat human trafficking and forced labour, the Trafficking Victims Protection Act (TVPA) was passed by the U.S. Congress in October 2000, signed by president Clinton,[18] and later reauthorized by Presidents Bush and Obama.[19] Out of the

---

[16] Christal Morehouse, *Combating Human Trafficking: Policy Gaps and Hidden Political Agendas in the USA and Germany* (Wiesbaden: VS Verlag, 2009): 25-26.

[17] The first two treaties (the 1904 International Agreement for the Suppression of White Slave Traffic and the 1910 International Convention for the Suppression of the White Slave Traffic) were signed prior to the establishment of the League of Nations and four treaties followed later (the 1921 International Convention for the Suppression of Traffic in Women and Children [1921 Anti Human Trafficking Convention], the 1933 International Convention for the Suppression of the Traffic in Women of Full Age [1933 Anti Human Trafficking Convention], the Geneva Convention of 1949 for the Suppression of the Traffic in Persons and of the Exploitation of Others [1949 Anti Human Trafficking Convention] and the 2000 United Nations Protocol to Prevent, Suppress and Punish Trafficking in Persons, Especially Women and Children, supplementing the United Nations Convention against Transnational Organized Crime [2000 UN Anti Human Trafficking Protocol]). Morehouse, *Combating Human Trafficking*, 26-27.
Various parameters such as ethnicity, age and consent as well as gender were gradually refined. For example, it was not until 1949 that both genders began to be viewed as possible trafficked victims (Morehouse, 31-32). The impact of the adoption of the UN Protocol has been remarkable, since, today, more than 150 countries have become a party to the Protocol. This means that countries are in the process of updating their legal framework to better address this crime and they are also monitored to ensure that the Protocol is implemented allowing for no cultural variations whatsoever, U.S. Department of State, *Trafficking in Persons Report*, July 2015, [Available at: http://www.state.gov/j/tip/rls/tiprpt/2015/], [Last accessed: 22nd October 2022], 11, 20.

[18] U.S. Department of State, *Victims of Trafficking and Violence Protection Act of 2000*, Public Law 106-386. 28th October 2000. [Available at: http://www.state.gov/j/tip/laws/61124.htm], [Last accessed: 23rd October 2022].

[19] U.S. Department of State, *U.S. Laws on Trafficking in Persons*, see all at: http://www.state.gov/j/tip/laws/index.htm [Last accessed: 23rd October 2022].
Reauthorizations of the Act allowed for prosecution against the involvement of US citizens with sex trafficking abroad. This included child sex tourism, with more than 500 arrests since 2003 of U.S. citizens travelling to Asia to have sex with children, but also to address other forms of slavery such as the scandal of 35000 workers trafficked from several South Asian and Middle Eastern countries to work on U.S. military bases in Iraq. Siddharth Kara, *Sex Trafficking: Inside the Business of Modern Slavery* (New York; Chichester: Columbia University Press, 2009): 193-196. Cam Simpson, "Officer Says Iraq Firms were Slow to Return Passports", *Chicago Tribune,* 22nd June 2006, [Available at: http://articles.chicagotribune.com/2006-06-22/news/0606220181_1_human-trafficking-passports-foreign-workers], [Last accessed: 23rd October 2022].

TVPA grew the Trafficking in Persons Report, which ranks various countries according to their compliance in tackling human trafficking. The report categorizes countries into tiers from fully compliant (Tier 1) to noncompliant (Tier 3). The latter are then subject to sanctions by the U.S. government.[20]

In these instruments, human trafficking has been generally defined as "the act of recruiting, harboring, transporting, providing, or obtaining a person for compelled labor or commercial sex acts through the use of force."[21] Participation in any of these stages constitutes a crime of human trafficking, which can have many different purposes, including sex trafficking, forced labor, debt bondage, domestic servitude, and child soldiering.[22]

For most countries, previous to this, there were no specific national laws prohibiting trafficking in persons as "a crime that encapsulates deception, transportation, coercion and exploitation as a broad process. Trafficking issues have been and often are approached as an issue of illegal immigration and prostitution rather than illegal detention or coercion."[23] When we speak with trafficked girls and women in the streets of Athens, they will spot the police patrolling the area and, instead of running to them for rescue, they immediately run to hide because they know that if they are caught by the police they will immediately be charged with illegal prostitution and given the status of an illegal immigrant. On these grounds, the authorities will then deport them by force back to their country, in effect delivering them right back to the hands of their traffickers. These women are completely trapped within the legal system which treats them as criminals instead of offering protection. The structure of the laws themselves is problematic and must be examined to see who they ultimately protect. How just is a legal system in which a victim is doubly victimized?

Governments are often keen to punish certain crimes not seeing that often a much more serious crime is "lurking in the shadows." We have such examples in the Old Testament where *Israelite* patriarchy rushes into criminalizing the innocent. In Judah and Tamar's story, where the patriarch is ready to implement judgment, the voice of *biblical* patriarchy demands a court ruling that goes beyond the obvious to the much more serious offense: the neglect of the widow by this patriarchal house. Actually, executing the law would have resulted in Tamar's double victimization. Christians operating under בית אב (*bet ab*) ethics will go beneath the surface of simplistic categories of crime such as "illegal immigration," because, as in the cases of so many trafficked victims, by applying

---

[20] Melissa Goss, "Closed for Business: The Fight Against Human Trafficking", *The Christian Century* 129(21), (2012): 13; Linda Bales Todd, "The U.S. Takes on Trafficking", *The Christian Century* (11th August 2009): 25.

[21] U.S. Department of State, *Trafficking in Persons Report*, 7.

[22] U.S. Department of State, *Trafficking in Persons Report*, 7-8.

[23] Edward Newman and Sally Cameron, "Introduction: Understanding Human Trafficking", In Sally Cameron and Edward Newman (eds), *Trafficking in Humans: Social, Cultural and Political Dimensions* (Tokyo; New York; Paris: United Nations University Press, 2008): 6. See also Kimberly A. McCabe and Sabita Manian (eds), *Sex Trafficking: A Global Perspective* (Plymouth: Lexington Books, 2010): 152.

this law we actually cooperate with traffickers instead of protecting the weakest in our midst on whom they prey.

The security of the mistreated is fundamental to בית אב (*bet ab*) ethics as the law in Deuteronomy 23:15-16 (unique in the ancient world) demonstrates with respect to the runaway slave. While the law of the ancient Near East (ANE) dictates that the right thing to do is to return a runaway slave to his/her master or country, biblical law breaks away from this norm and forbids such a "deportation." Giving asylum to such refugees was a distinctive of Israelite law marking them apart from all other nations. Biblical patriarchy places more weight on the victim's motives for fleeing, rather than the rights of the master, and the patriarchs are obliged to offer protection and secure residence to the victim.[24] Daniel Snell notes that "if consistently applied, such a prohibition would have eroded the entire institution of slavery."[25]

In the US, Germany, and perhaps other countries, granting legal residence to human trafficking victims is currently dependent on the victim's cooperation in prosecuting human traffickers. Granting a victim long-term residence is an exception, not the rule. Most victims are subject to repatriation after they have made their contribution to the prosecution and those who refuse to aid the prosecution (always due to severe traumatization or fear of the trafficker and their associates) are never given access to residence in their country of exploitation. Yet both the US and Germany claim to take a victim-centered approach to combating trafficking. One explanation for this contradictory policy is that "some policy makers assert that granting legal residence as a victim's right would lead to a large increase of immigration and to large-scale fraud."[26] While this may be true, no serious deterrent against human trafficking is given and that contributes to the increase of the crime. If one compares human trafficking to a case of drug trafficking, the sentence for slavery is perhaps ten years, while distributing a kilo of heroin may carry a life sentence.[27]

Now, it is worth comparing these laws with the biblical runaway slave law, each in their own contexts. Biblical patriarchy sees its primary role as being a place of refuge for vulnerable people in danger. While, in the ANE, the temple

---

[24] See the discussion on fugitive slaves in David L. Baker, *Tight Fists or Open Hands? Wealth and Poverty in Old Testament Law* (Grand Rapids, MI; Cambridge: Eerdmans, 2009): 130-135.

[25] Daniel C. Snell, "Slavery in the Ancient Near East", In Keith Bradley and Paul Cartledge (eds), *The Cambridge World History of Slavery.* Volume 1: The Ancient Mediterranean World (Cambridge: Cambridge University Press, 2011): 18.

[26] Morehouse, *Combating Human Trafficking*, 51. Extradition is important in the case of traffickers: Due to the global nature of human trafficking, national governments have to overcome national sovereignty limitations in order to investigate, access and prosecute perpetrators who operate in multiple countries. When national governments do not agree to extradite suspected human traffickers and to exchange the necessary information to facilitate extradition, then the international nature of the crime becomes an advantage for the perpetrator. National borders become a protective shield behind which the perpetrator can hide. In such a case globalization and the freedom of movement mutate into instruments of oppression and human rights abuse. (Morehouse, 57).

[27] McCabe and Manian, *Sex Trafficking*, 152.

could have this role as a refuge one could run to for protection from their masters, in the case of these refugees the entire land of Israel functions as a sanctuary offering permanent asylum![28]

Poverty

Poverty is one of the main reasons, if not the primary reason, for the flourishing of human trafficking in terms of the vulnerability of the victims. Poverty is what motivates people to consider migration.[29] Both real and relative poverty are strong enough motivators for migration and both expose people to the dangers of trafficking. Relative poverty is the perceived inequalities which arise through economic comparison, an inevitable process in our current reality of globalization.[30] Whether we are aware of it or not, our comforts, beautiful homes, cars and electronic gadgets contribute to the formation of people's self-perception as poor. We create "perceived" poverty which is just as powerful and alluring for dangerous risk-taking as is real poverty. In other words, the "American dream" has its victims.

When Ezekiel writes his incredible three chapters (26-28) against the city of Tyre for its excessive wealth, arrogance and economic injustices, one gets the sense that he is describing the world of today. Actually, Tyre, one of the richest cities in antiquity, is also the one condemned by the prophets for human trafficking (e.g. Amos 1:9, Joel 4:6, Ez. 27:13). The hubristic excesses did not leave the prophets indifferent; they seem to regard injustice as endemic to wealth accumulation, or rather, wealth concentration.[31]

While many humanitarian organizations respond to poverty through philanthropic donation or acts that often serve the public image of celebrities, such responses "emphasize rather than bridge the distance between giver and receiver and too often leave intact the structures of inequality."[32] Luke Bretherton reminds us that *kenosis* or renunciation (i.e. ongoing surrendering of idolatrous ties to property, kinship, comfort and status for the sake of meaningful relationships to God and neighbor) is entirely absent in secular humanitarianism, but it is a mark of the Christian.[33] Or, it *ought* to be! בית אב (*bet ab*) ideas of justice *presuppose* an identity of absolute identification with the receiver (e.g. Dt. 15:15: "Remember that you were once slaves in the land of Egypt and the LORD your God redeemed you! That is why I am giving you this command"

---

[28] Daisy Yulin Tsai, *Human Rights in Deuteronomy: With Special Focus on Slave Laws*, BZAW 464 (Berlin; Boston: De Gruyter, 2014): 66.

[29] Cameron and Newman, "Trafficking in Humans: Structural Factors", 22.

[30] Cameron and Newman, "Trafficking in Humans: Structural Factors", 25.

[31] Agrarian Mediterranean societies of the ancient world considered wealth to be limited in quantity, thus becoming rich was generally understood to have happened through corruption. For a full analysis of wealth perceptions see, Brian S. Rosner, *Greed as Idolatry: The Origin and Meaning of a Pauline Metaphor* (Grand Rapids, MI: Eerdmans, 2007): 116-121.

[32] Bretherton, "Poverty, Politics, and Faithful Witness in the Age of Humanitarianism", 451.

[33] Bretherton, "Poverty", 451.

[NLT]; 24:18). Victims of sex trafficking are not mere recipients of our charity but they are our most treasured guests at our table.

Demand and the Client

Persistent demand, of course, is the beginning and the end of human trafficking. A few years ago, the discussion of human trafficking began to focus more on the client. Various studies have shown that anyone can be a client of prostitution.[34] In the streetwork of Athens, I witnessed groups of young boys coming to the brothels, old men who could barely walk up the stairs, Greeks, immigrants, Christians, Muslims, sober people, drunk people, low-wage poor-looking people as well as wealthy, handsome, successful men in their suits, pulling up their expensive car on the side of the street, paying for their quick service and heading back to work. Men who would literally step out of church, visit the brothel, and then return to their pews.

The first significant study on the client was conducted in the US back in the 1940s, and showed that, at the time, two thirds of the men contacted had paid for sex at least once in their lives and 15-20% were regular clients of prostitutes. In Britain, around the same time, the number of men who had purchased sex at least once in their lives was 1 in 4.[35] Some shared characteristics of the client surfaced, such as the need for dominance and/or affection, the (at least partial) awareness of exploitation, and the related neutralization techniques.[36] Neutralization techniques are things clients tell themselves in order to justify their use of trafficked victims. The clients neutralize their guilt, as many interviews have shown, by saying that even though they suffer, the girls/women get good incomes and they can also send some cash to their families. The clients also believe that they are not the ones responsible to check whether the woman is legally or freely there and even if they knew that she was forced into this business it would not deter them from buying.[37]

---

[34] Studies conducted in various EU countries with differing policies towards prostitution now show that "clients of trafficked prostitution are likely to be ordinary men (professionals and workers, married and single, high and low educated, young and elderly persons); in other words, they are *transversal* to all social classes and do not represent a particular deviant group of individuals." Andrea Di Nicola *et al.* (eds), *Prostitution and Human Trafficking: Focus on Clients* (New York: Springer, 2009): 3-4. Also, Πάολα Μοντζίνι, *Εμπόριο Γυναικών: Πόρνεία, Μαστροπεία και Εκμετάλλευση* (Αθήνα: Εκδόσεις Μελάνι, 2007); trans. Φωτεινή Ζέρβου (Roma: Donzelli editore, 2002): 30.

[35] Nicola *et al.* (eds), *Prostitution and Human Trafficking*, 6. In the 1970s, two distinct studies have shown that the majority of clients were married and aged between 30 and 60, and that a large number of them purchased sex when away from home (Nicola *et al*, 6). Editor's Note: See elsewhere in this volume and in the previous books in this series for updated information on demand.

[36] Nicola *et al.* (eds), *Prostitution and Human Trafficking*, 232.

[37] "All of them are exploited. However, they also have good incomes. They can have good clothes and can send money home to their families. Of course they don't like the life, but they also get some benefits." (Italian client).

What pushes men to commercial sex? Earlier studies thought of the purchase of sex as a form of psychopathology until this was disproved in the 1980s and 1990s.[38] In 2005, Ben-Israel and Levenkron focused on three macro-categories of motives inducing men to seek commercial sex: biological reasons connected to the "inner" nature of men, individual psychological factors, and social and supra-individual elements.[39]

The biological theory, which regards the male sexual impulse as an instinct as uncontrollable as the need for food or drink, in contrast to women who are thought to have a weak sexual impulse, is now deemed outdated as studies have shown the controllability and the importance of social and cultural factors in the characterization of this male "need."[40] It must be said that this is an area where the church's teaching on personal moral purity has played a positive role.

Among the psychological factors, there is the fantasy of a dirty, degraded sexual object devoid of human qualities. There is the need for "real" manhood which demands the submission of female to the male, and also the desire for different kinds of sex not obtainable within the relationship with a regular partner.[41] "Prostitution is an industry in which fantasy is an important part of the product,"[42] and it is the force of this fantasy that causes many of the customers to consider the fact that a woman is not voluntarily a sex worker as *part* of the attraction. This testifies to the formidable powers of the male fantasy. While most clients would recognize the wrongness, the injustice, the dehumanization of women in this industry, it is paradoxically this objectification that attracts them and keeps them compliant to this evil. Even in the case of pornography, where many people are aware of the direct relationship between sex trafficking and the pornographic industry, they persist in blocking justice out of their heads and continue to feed this oppressive business.[43] Jesus responds to this

---

"Of course I don't ask for the residence permit. It doesn't matter to me if they have it or not. If tomorrow they are kicked out into the street, bad luck. I have nothing to do with it." (Dutch client).
"If I could differentiate [between forced and voluntary…] it would probably not influence my choice. Because if I like the girl, I would ask her to join me in the room. It is totally wrong of course." (Dutch client).
"I do it because of the excitement, but also because of the addiction. Meeting a prostitute doesn't involve demands, and you get to do other stuff than in your relationship." (Swedish client). Nicola *et al.* (eds), *Prostitution and Human Trafficking*, 232.

[38] Nicola *et al.* (eds), *Prostitution and Human Trafficking*, 10-13.

[39] Summarized by Nicola *et al.* (eds), *Prostitution and Human Trafficking*, 13.

[40] Hanny Ben-Israel and Nomi Levenkron, *The Missing Factor: Clients of Trafficked Women in Israel's Sex Industry* (Jerusalem: Hotline for Migration Workers and The Hebrew University, 2005): 18.

[41] Ben-Israel and Levenkron, *The Missing Factor*, 18-21.

[42] Cameron and Newman, "Trafficking in Humans", 33.

[43] McCabe and Manian, *Sex Trafficking*, 150, 152-153. See also Michelle Lillie, "The Connection Between Sex Trafficking and Pornography", *Human Trafficking Search Website,* 14th April 2014. [Available at: https://humantraffickingsearch.org/the-

schizophrenic world by going straight to the heart of the problem. He tightens the law against adultery in Matthew 5:27-28 by demanding justice in one's fantasy realm, taking biblical patriarchy to another level. Biblical patriarchy refined has to execute justice in *every* realm, *even* in the territory of human imagination.

Social theories have pointed out the massive "exodus" of sexuality in all forms of social media and the use of primarily women's sexuality for advertisements of various products, thus connecting sexuality with consumerism.[44] Sex has been increasingly constructed "more as a marketed commodity than an expression of intimate relations"[45] so the clients have fully adopted the identity of the consumer, paying for the merchandise, demanding consumer satisfaction, and leaving the scene when the transaction is completed. We tend to think of women as the ultimate consumers, but actually, in the US, approximately 60% of internet purchases involve the porn industry.[46]

What is dangerous about the consumer identity is that a consumer will rarely ask questions about the supply chain leading up to the transaction. His only concern is getting the most out of the lowest-priced product. In fact, the clients prefer to maintain their traditional role of the ignorant buyer; they want to be invisible, anonymous and free of any culpability.[47] Assuming a "consumer" identity is morally evasive because consumers do not feel responsible for the journey of the product. They do not ask "who collected the raw materials" or "who put the pieces together" or "how the product was transported to the shop." It is the responsibility of the seller to worry about all this. Carrying this consumer attitude into the sex industry allows these layers of separation to ease one's conscience.[48]

This attitude is directly opposed to בית אב (*bet ab*) ethics. It is interesting that even in ancient Babylonian law, it was the responsibility of the buyer to establish the legal status of a slave. It was the client's loss if the slave was sold illegally, i.e., if they were stolen. As David Baker shows, several laws consider someone who buys a slave to a thief if he cannot establish the identity of the seller or has no witnesses or contract to verify the purchase.[49] Of course, these laws are there to protect the legal owners of the slave but at the same time, and especially for Israel, they seek to ensure that the sale of this person did not result from kidnapping. As I have argued elsewhere, kidnapping was a serious crime in the ANE and a capital crime in Israel. Forced enslavement (outside special circumstances of war or service for a crime) was abominable to Israelite identity, which was constructed against their former status of being Egyptian slaves.

---

connection-between-sex-trafficking-and-pornography/], [Last accessed: 23rd October 2022].

[44] Μοντζίνι, *Εμπόριο Γυναικών*, 34-38.

[45] Ben-Israel and Levenkron, *The Missing Factor*, 22.

[46] Μοντζίνι, *Εμπόριο Γυναικών*, 68.

[47] Μοντζίνι, *Εμπόριο Γυναικών*, 39.

[48] See how layers of separation are added in the human trafficking recruitment in U.S. Department of State, *Trafficking in Persons Report*, July 2015, 14-15.

[49] Baker, *Tight Fists or Open Hands?*, 114; Daisy Yulin Tsai, *Human Rights in Deuteronomy*, 136-138.

God's law holds his people responsible for exposing forced enslavement of citizens and not participating in any way in the benefits of such enslavement.[50] In most countries today, the buyer is still considered outside the criminal chain of human trafficking, but in 2000 the UN Protocol opened the way for the criminalization of the client.[51]

We tend to think that prostitution exists because it satisfies a particular physical need in men, but this is only partially true. Prostitution is the reflection of an existing relational problem between men and women and rests on a particular definition of gender identity in our societies. It is being observed that prostitution has become a safe space where the male feels secure about his performance in relating to the opposite gender. He experiences absolute freedom from the burden of commitment and responsibility. Resorting to paid sex may be interpreted as a form of temporary satisfaction and affirmation of male domination over the female.[52] One of the clients interviewed said:

> Being able to choose without being rejected, this ability just by itself brings great satisfaction, so then you don't have to invest too much in the performative side of things. It is beautiful being able to choose like a feudal lord and being absolutely certain there will be no rejection from the other side.[53]

Other clients feel that the status of male superiority is being threatened in our age. They feel that feminism is destroying traditional hierarchies and that the battle for equality places more and more demands and expectations on males.[54] Prostitution becomes, then, an escape, a vacation from reality. A forty-year old client returning from a "royal" holiday in Thailand said: "In Thailand I found a very good woman which I [...] rented for a week [...] 'choice' was no longer a factor, only the satisfaction in possessing, not so much a woman, but a slave."[55] In a 2001 study, it was pointed out that sexual tourists consider the prostitutes that they meet abroad to be women who have accepted their "role" of subjugated beings who must satisfy men's sexual needs.[56] This ideal of having a submissive woman is *central* to the identity of the client. Therefore, Christian discourse about the submission of women, leadership, and headship of men must be nuanced and sensitive so as not to merely affirm primitive instincts.

---

[50] See Myrto Theocharous, "Stealing Souls: Human Trafficking and Deuteronomy 24:7", In Jason DeRouchie, Jason Gile and Kenneth J. Turner (eds), *For Our Good Always: Studies on the Message and Influence of Deuteronomy in Honor of Daniel I. Block* (Winona Lake, IN: Eisenbrauns, 2013): 495-509.

[51] Morehouse, *Combating Human Trafficking*, 61.

[52] Μοντζίνι, *Εμπόριο Γυναικών*, 26-27.

[53] Μοντζίνι, *Εμπόριο Γυναικών*, 27.

[54] Emancipation of women is a major factor that encourages the demand for prostitution, Nicola *et al.*, *Prostitution and Human Trafficking*, 231.

[55] Μοντζίνι, *Εμπόριο Γυναικών*, 28.

[56] Nicola *et al., Prostitution and Human Trafficking*, 13.

Redemption and Hope

Biblical patriarchy is accountable for everything that happens "within the gates," and is the guarantor of the flourishing of the vulnerable. The alertness to the cry of the oppressed demanded of the patriarchal house is uncompromised. The patriarchal house must be vigilant in seeking rather than being passively "present". This is evident in Deuteronomy 22:24, the law forbidding the punishment of a woman if a sexual act takes place in a field, because she may have cried out and no one would have heard her. What this law presupposes is that a woman *inside* the town is safe. She can cry out and people will hear and respond and rescue. It presupposes that windows and doors are wide open, ears and eyes are alert to see and hear any occasion where a victim might need help! This is how safe a town was expected to be. Of course, we live in towns and cities today, but do we really live among others in such a way that their cry can be heard? Women continue to cry out in our cities but could it be the case that the Church has moved out of hearing distance? Has the Church removed itself to such a distance that the cry of those who are hurting cannot be heard anymore?

What is happening "within our gates"? In Texas, sex trafficking victims have been discovered, the vast majority of whom were actually U.S. citizens.[57] In Portland, a city called by some "the national hub for child sex trafficking," underage girls have been found working in the city's strip clubs.[58] In Atlanta, girls as young as ten are housed and prostituted by their traffickers.[59] And let's not forget boys. 50% of victims in New York were found to be boys.[60] Where do these children go once discovered? Who discovers them? Christian organizations all over the US and internationally are becoming increasingly mobilized.[61] The fact is that approximately one-third of trafficking victims in the U.S. are discovered not by the police but by individual citizens[62] – citizens with "ears" tuned in to the cries, imaging God who "hears our cries."

In all this, the Church must be cautious not to snatch people out of their current state by force.[63] A balance must be observed. In Athens, we are very careful to win the trust of the women gradually (not in short-term missions but through long-term commitment) and empower them into a state where they express their desire for freedom themselves. They need to bake their own unleavened bread,

---

[57] Associate Baptist Press, "Texas Enacts Law to Aid Human-Trafficking Victims", *The Christian Century* 126 (2009): 17.

[58] Katelyn Beaty, "Portland's Quiet Abolitionists: Leading the Liberal City's Efforts to Halt Child Trafficking is a Network of Dedicated Christians. Just Don't Go Advertising It", *Christianity Today* 55 (Nov 2011): 28.

[59] Jane O. Hansen, "Selling Atlanta's Children: What Has and Hasn't Changed", *CNN* 18th July 2015, [Available at: http://edition.cnn.com/2015/07/17/us/child-sex-trafficking-update-hansen/], [Last accessed: 23rd October 2022].

[60] Jerome Elam, "The Story of One. Trafficked Boys: Vandalized Innocence Hidden in Plain Sight", http://www.commdiginews.com/life/trafficked-boys-vandalized-innocence-hidden-in-plain-sight-26356/. [Last accessed: 1st August 2018].

[61] Some of these are mentioned by Goss, "Closed for Business", 13.

[62] Kara, *Sex Trafficking*, 195.

[63] Bretherton says that loving concern often produces "modes of domination." "Poverty, Politics, and Faithful Witness in the Age of Humanitarianism", 448.

prepare their own bitter herbs, and brush the blood on their doorposts as active participants in their own deliverance.[64]

Conclusion

I will close with an excerpt from our last newsletter:

> As we entered the brothel, there was Lena [...] right away she asked if we had brought her a Bible. When I said yes, her face lit up [...] Natasha helped her understand where to start and how to read God's Word. Lena was listening carefully and was getting more and more excited with every word [...] [She] told us how thrilled she was to read and get to know the loving Father and Savior Jesus Christ. She recognized she needed to repent and to find God in a more personal way. When we asked her how we could pray for her or if she wanted us to pray *with* her, in seconds she was down on her knees. We all got down with her. Lena was touched by the Holy Spirit, she could not stop crying. Her tears were tears of sadness, repentance and joy, all at the same time. This image of three girls kneeling down in a brothel and praying, opening the Scriptures and sharing with Lena just stayed with me. The brothel is not that ideal place one would want to kneel in, but in that moment, we were so consumed by the Holy Spirit, none of us realized where we really were.[65]

The work is hard, slow, and low in numbers. But we are not doing this work because of the high numbers and spectacular successes or the numerous miracles we witness. We do it because of the miracle that happened *to* us and that *these girls and women* get to witness: the miracle is getting to see people leaving their comfort and warm homes to go and seek them out in cold and filthy streets; the miracle is seeing a Church that "was, is and is coming" towards them instead of withdrawing from them and abandoning them in their bondage; the miracle is meeting people who choose to touch them and embrace them without disgust or meaning harm; the miracle is seeing people who long to talk to them out of genuine interest and not in order to manipulate them for their own gain; the miracle is people who are able to look at them, regard them and treat them as the divine sacred icons of the invisible creator instead of as objects of merchandise. Witnessing a church that tells them "we are the same, you and me, both of us guests in the Father's House, but I refuse to enter it alone without taking you along with me" is the miracle of God, our refuge.

---

[64] There are cases where women have been "rescued" against their will. An Indian NGO has been accused of such actions and the women themselves escaped from the center where they had been placed post-"rescue". Cameron and Newman, "Trafficking in Humans", 34.

[65] Email conversation with anonymous ministry volunteer on 7th July 2014.

Reflection Questions

1. How does understanding the biblical concepts of refuge and *bet ab* ethics affect your theological and practical understanding of trafficking, exploitation and related issues?
2. How do legal, economic and demand factors play out in your context? How can a better understanding of *bet ab* ethics and other theological concepts in this chapter help to better address these factors?
3. What attitudes, theologies, or prejudices prevent Christians and the Church from hearing the cry of the vulnerable and engaging actively with anti-trafficking work? What are some ways one could work on altering these attitudes, theologies, or prejudices in your church? Think of practical ideas.
4. Sex trafficking is not the result of an uncontrollable sex drive but of a problematic view of gender, as well as fractured gender relations. Research the gender biases that exist in your society/community, both in and outside of the church, and reflect on the factors that feed and perpetuate them.

Works Cited

Associate Baptist Press. "Texas Enacts Law to Aid Human-Trafficking Victims". *The Christian Century* 126 (2009): 17.

Baker, David L. *Tight Fists or Open Hands? Wealth and Poverty in Old Testament Law.* Grand Rapids, MI; Cambridge: Eerdmans, 2009.

Beaty, Katelyn. "Portland's Quiet Abolitionists: Leading the Liberal City's Efforts to Halt Child Trafficking is a Network of Dedicated Christians. Just Don't Go Advertising It". *Christianity Today* 55 (Nov 2011): 28.

Ben-Israel, Hanny and Nomi Levenkron. *The Missing Factor: Clients of Trafficked Women in Israel's Sex Industry.* Jerusalem: Hotline for Migration Workers and The Hebrew University, 2005.

Block, Daniel I. "Marriage and Family in Ancient Israel". In Ken M. Campbell, Ed. *Marriage and Family in the Biblical World.* Downers Grove, IL: IVP, 2003.

Bretherton, Luke. "Poverty, Politics, and Faithful Witness in the Age of Humanitarianism". *Interpretation* 69(4), (2015): 447-459.

Cameron, Sally and Edward Newman. "Trafficking in Humans: Structural Factors". In Sally Cameron and Edward Newman, Eds. *Trafficking in Humans: Social, Cultural and Political Dimensions.* Tokyo; New York; Paris: United Nations University Press, 2008.

Carter, Joe. "9 Things You Should Know About Islamic State". *The Gospel Coalition*, 14th November 2015, [Available at: http://www.thegospelcoalition.org/article/9-things-you-should-know-about-islamic-state], [Last accessed: 22nd October 2022].

Goss, Melissa. "Closed for Business: The Fight Against Human Trafficking". *The Christian Century* 129(21), (2012): 13.

Hansen, Jane O. "Selling Atlanta's Children: What Has and Hasn't Changed". *CNN* 18th July 2015, [Available at: http://edition.cnn.com/2015/07/17/us/child-sex-trafficking-update-hansen/], [Last accessed: 23rd October 2022].

Horsley, Richard. "You Shall Not Bow Down and Serve Them: Economic Justice in the Bible". *Interpretation* 69(4), (2015): 417-419.

Kara, Siddharth. *Sex Trafficking: Inside the Business of Modern Slavery.* New York; Chichester: Columbia University Press, 2009.

Lillie, Michelle. "The Connection Between Sex Trafficking and Pornography". *Human Trafficking Search Website,* 14th April 2014. [Available at: https://humantraffickingsearch.org/the-connection-between-sex-trafficking-and-pornography/], [Last accessed: 23rd October 2022].

Luscombe, Belinda. "Inside the Scarily Lucrative Business Model of Human Trafficking". *Time Magazine Website,* 20th May 2014. [Available at: http://time.com/105360/inside-the-scarily-lucrative-business-model-of-human-trafficking/], [Last accessed: 22nd October 2022].

McCabe, Kimberly A. and Sabita Manian, Eds. *Sex Trafficking: A Global Perspective.* Plymouth: Lexington Books, 2010.

Μοντζίνι, Πάολα. *Εμπόριο Γυναικών: Πορνεία, Μαστροπεία και Εκμετάλλευση.* Αθήνα: Εκδόσεις Μελάνι, 2007. trans. Φωτεινή Ζέρβου. Roma: Donzelli editore, 2002.

Morehouse, Christal. *Combating Human Trafficking: Policy Gaps and Hidden Political Agendas in the USA and Germany.* Wiesbaden: VS Verlag, 2009.

Newman, Edward and Sally Cameron. "Introduction: Understanding Human Trafficking". In Sally Cameron and Edward Newman, Eds. *Trafficking in Humans: Social, Cultural and Political Dimensions.* Tokyo; New York; Paris: United Nations University Press, 2008.

Nicola, Andrea Di *et al.* Eds. *Prostitution and Human Trafficking: Focus on Clients.* New York: Springer, 2009.

Rosner, Brian S. *Greed as Idolatry: The Origin and Meaning of a Pauline Metaphor.* Grand Rapids, MI: Eerdmans, 2007.

Schloen, J. David. *The House of the Father as Fact and Symbol: Patrimonialism in Ugarit and the Ancient Near East.* Studies in the Archaeology and History of the Levant 2. Winona Lake, IN: Eisenbraus, 2001.

Simpson, Cam. "Officer Says Iraq Firms were Slow to Return Passports". *Chicago Tribune,* 22nd June 2006. [Available at: http://articles.chicagotribune.com/2006-06-22/news/0606220181_1_human-trafficking-passports-foreign-workers], [Last accessed: 23rd October 2022].

Snell, Daniel C. "Slavery in the Ancient Near East". In Keith Bradley and Paul Cartledge, Eds. *The Cambridge World History of Slavery.* Volume 1: The Ancient Mediterranean World. Cambridge: Cambridge University Press, 2011.

Stark, Rodney. *The Rise of Christianity: How the Obscure, Marginal Jesus Movement Became the Dominant Religious Force in the Western World in a Few Centuries.* San Francisco, CA: Harper Collins, 1997.

Theocharous, Myrto. "Stealing Souls: Human Trafficking and Deuteronomy 24:7". In Jason DeRouchie, Jason Gile and Kenneth J. Turner, Eds. *For Our Good Always: Studies on the Message and Influence of Deuteronomy in Honor of Daniel I. Block.* Winona Lake, IN: Eisenbrauns, 2013: 495-509.

Todd, Linda Bales. "The U.S. Takes on Trafficking". *The Christian Century* (11th August 2009): 25.

Tsai, Daisy Yulin. *Human Rights in Deuteronomy: With Special Focus on Slave Laws.* BZAW 464. Berlin; Boston, MA: De Gruyter, 2014.

United Nations, *Treaty Series: Treaties and International Agreements Registered or Filed and Recorded with the Secretariat of the United Nations* Volume 2237. A-39574, Article 3. New York: United Nations, 2005.

U.S. Department of State. *Trafficking in Persons Report*, July 2015. [Available at: http://www.state.gov/j/tip/rls/tiprpt/2015/], [Last accessed: 22nd October 2022].

U.S. Department of State. *Victims of Trafficking and Violence Protection Act of 2000*, Public Law 106-386. 28th October 2000. [Available at: http://www.state.gov/j/tip/laws/61124.htm], [Last accessed: 23rd October 2022].

U.S. Department of State. *U.S. Laws on Trafficking in Persons.* [Available at: http://www.state.gov/j/tip/laws/index.htm [Last accessed: 23rd October 2022].

Part III

Raising Our Response to Sexual Exploitation

"*Though No-One Understands My Feelings, But There Is God*" Journeys of Faith for Survivors of Sex Trafficking in Cambodia

Vanntheary Lim, Glenn Miles and Channtha Nhanh

The Butterfly Longitudinal Re/Integration Research project is a unique study of more than 100 survivors of human trafficking, sexual exploitation, and abuse in Cambodia. The 10-year-long study is "one of the longest running trafficking survivor research projects in the world" as the Chab Dai Butterfly Project Website says. It was launched by Chab Dai Coalition in 2010, with a variety of reports on the findings published between 2010 and 2020. Many of the reports relate to specific themes involved in residential aftercare and reintegration. This chapter presents certain research findings from one of those thematic reports: "Children of the Wood, Children of the Stone: The Journeys of Faith for Survivors of Trafficking" (2020). This chapter was written by the authors of that report and draws heavily from it. References to "the study" refer to the full report and/or the overall Butterfly Project.

Objective

This chapter presents the perspective and experiences of survivors of human trafficking and sexual exploitation regarding their spirituality/faith journey. The full study, "Children of the Wood, Children of the Stone", addressed both Buddhist and Christian spirituality. However, the focus of this chapter is on the Christian faith that many (but not all) participants developed during their time in faith-based shelters and community programs.

The research questions of the study are:

1. What is the participants' understanding of faith/spirituality?
2. How has their faith/spirituality impacted their life and personal restoration?
3. How has their faith/spirituality impacted their relationships/impact on others/society?

At the time of writing, the Butterfly Longitudinal Re/Integration Research (BLR) project was in its tenth year. The project began in 2010 when members of the Chab Dai Coalition and practitioners working in anti-human trafficking in Cambodia desired to understand the long-term impact of their programs on survivors leaving their program. 15 members of Chab Dai agreed through a rigorous terms-of-agreement process to allow access to their clients. Recruitment of participants for the research took place in 2010-2011, with 128 child and adult survivors making up the participant pool. At that time, 14 members of the Chab Dai coalition offered residential aftercare services, however, some of them no longer do so.

The research study was designed to be longitudinal, exploratory, broad, and descriptive with a mixed-methods approach. Of the original 128 participants, 80% are female and 20% male. The original age range at the beginning of the study was between 6 and 30 years old. 72% of the cohort are ethnic Cambodians and 13% Vietnamese.

One of the biggest challenges to the project was the high potential for attrition as participants lives were often transitory, involving chaotic environments and frequent moves, sometimes to hard-to-locate locations. However, by 2019, despite distance and time difficulties, the research team had been able to maintain contact with more than 90 of 128 original participants; 52 of whom were present each and every time data was collected between 2011-2019.

Over the duration of the study, the associate partner organizations evolved and changed and the participants also needed to prepare for re/integration. This research has sought to listen to the voices of participants and understand both positive and negative aspects of the re/integration process to look at both the vulnerabilities and resilience of the participants.

The long-term nature of the research enables reflections of their experiences to be better understood. The hope has been that this can inform programs, policy and wider debates, locally, regionally and globally. Over the years, there has been dialogue with partners and stakeholders through round-table discussions, annual reports, and confidential feedback on issues of concern to individual organizations.

One of the major benefits of this approach has been an evolving trust and disclosure over the ten years. Frequent contact by caring researchers has led to deep friendships with the participants. As a result, researcher effect cannot be denied. However, the deep trust developed between participants and the researchers has meant that the information is rich and reflections thoughtful. In one sense, it also means that the research is more ethical, because it becomes something that is about a relationship rather than about being used as a tool to get information. Some of the participants have told the researchers that they are able to be open to them more than anyone else.

Ethics

The National Ethics Committee, situated in the Royal Government of Cambodia Ministry of Health, approves the Butterfly Longitudinal Research project annually. The project also adheres to the United Nations UNIAP ethical standards for research with trafficking victims.

Abiding by research ethics and confidentiality protocols, the research project team are always mindful about participant and data confidentiality; no personal identification information has been revealed, either during participant interviews or in reports and publications. None of the names in this paper are the actual names of the participants.

Methodology

The data in this chapter was gleaned from interviews conducted between 2011-2017, including interviews of 85 participants in 2017 which focused on their current beliefs and the impact of these on their lives. The information was sorted into different categories to determine patterns and similarities in the data analysis. The results section allows the reader to directly listen to the voices of survivors. We have not excluded comments that are negative towards different faiths.

One of the huge advantages of this longitudinal study is the way the research team have developed close relationships with the participants over the ten years. Although this level of relationship will likely have affected the results, the depth of responses reflects a degree of honesty that is impressive.

Limitations

One's spiritual journey changes all the time as one interacts with others and gains (or does not gain) a deeper understanding of a greater power beyond the everyday. It is not easy to articulate things about spirituality, especially for participants who are not aspiring to be religious leaders and who may have a limited spiritual/religious vocabulary.

Participants have been involved in a variety of Christian settings during their time in shelters or aftercare programs as well as in the churches they attended after leaving their programs. While all the programs in the study had different denominational or non-denominational emphases, all of them were Christian NGOs with mainly Christian staff and therefore a Christian culture.

Had this been a one-off survey conducted shortly after participants left their aftercare programs, we might be more cautious about positive comments about their experiences. However, most of the responses were made some time after participants left their programs. In addition, the ten-year time frame of the research study has made their relationships with the research staff stronger and the responses are therefore likely to be more honest. The long history of confidentiality has also reduced participants' concern that someone is going to lose face if they are honest in their responses.

Due to confidentiality concerns, we were not able to give more detailed descriptions of the lives of the participants beyond their own quotations.

Making Sense of Life for the Participants

Although the wider cultural-religious context in Cambodia is predominantly Buddhist, over the past decade, it has largely been Christian NGO groups who have taken a leading role in addressing prostitution and sexual exploitation.[1]

In light of this, what does it mean and how does it matter to these survivors' sense of understanding about their experiences of exploitation:

---

[1] (Delaney and Scharff, 2010; Jordanwood and Lim, 2011).

- that they are the second and third generation following the Khmer Rouge period when all religion was forbidden?
- that they have been raised in a post-conflict society?
- that following their negative experiences they encountered Christian influences largely through Christian Faith-Based Organizations (CFBOs)?
- that they live in a context of a wider dominant Buddhist milieu?
- that, whilst they live in a neo-liberal culture that is ever modernizing and changing, still there are traditional cultural beliefs, values and practices such as marked gender differences, expectations and filial piety where children are expected to work for their parents?

Hierarchy, Respect for Elders, and Rules for Women

Cambodia has a strong hierarchical structure with the king, who has always been seen as a demigod, at the top. This hierarchy is also associated with *kharma* – a fatalistic attitude that means that those with power and money feel entitled to it and those who are poor may feel that it is their lot and that change is not possible. The cultural norm of respect for elders gives value to people in authority but it can also make children more vulnerable and voiceless. Children feel obligated to pay gratitude by obeying their parents and serving them (filial piety). This has positive aspects including sharing of tasks in the needs of the household and continuing care from children when parents (including participants) age. But it also has negative implications, for instance when some parents (intentionally and unintentionally) pressure their children to work in exploitative ways. The traditional rules for women (*Chbab Srei*) encourage women to be subservient and obedient to their partners and could be interpreted as making allowances for their partner's misdeeds. Although there are also rules for men (*Chbab Pros*), they are not so well known and therefore not followed/adhered to.

Roots of Christianity in Cambodia

Christianity has a long but fractured history in Cambodia. The book *The Cathedral in the Rice Paddy* by Fr. Francois Ponchaud documents 450 years of the Catholic church in Cambodia.[2] Although present since the 16th century, it is now in a rebuilding stage, having been almost completely wiped out during the Khmer Rouge era and later anti-Vietnamese persecution. The history of the Protestant church is described in the book *Killing Fields Living Fields* by Don Cormack as more recent, being "first planted among rice farmers" in the mid-1920s.[3] Christians make up a small fraction of the overall population, with Protestants around 2.5% and Catholics around 0.5% according to some estimates.

Christian NGO Impact

While the number of national Christians is small, the work of Christian NGOs has had an outsized role in Cambodia. Historically focused on health and social

---

[2] (Ponchaud, 1990).

[3] (Cormack, 2009).

care, Christian Faith-Based Organizations were involved in refugee camps in the aftermath of the Khmer Rouge genocide and more recently have taken a prominent role in the anti-trafficking movement. Although several CFBOs had previously been caring for people in prostitution for years, in 2005, the issue of sexual exploitation of children was brought to international attention through a documentary by American news media entitled "Children for Sale." Featuring covert video footage from the International Justice Mission, a Christian NGO headquartered in the United States, images from a brothel rescue were broadcast around the world and created deep concern among the public in the US, Australasia and Europe. The US State Department took this issue to a new level and human trafficking became a major target for them. In addition, a number of Christians were inspired to do something. Since then, with support from Chab Dai Coalition, more than 50 Christian organizations committed themselves to address sex trafficking in Cambodia and provide support for survivors.

Christianity and Spiritual Abuse

Chab Dai have gone to some length to ensure that all organizations working with survivors have policies to protect children and vulnerable people from harm. This includes protection from spiritual abuse where children might be forced or pushed to believe something without fully understanding. Christians should be encouraged to understand where they stand in the debate and to be clear about their boundaries, for instance, when what Christians are doing is spiritual abuse and when it is simply holistic care that takes into consideration the spiritual needs of children.[4]

Christian Values on Dignity, Respect, and Love

According to child-rights expert Judith Ennew, "spiritual nurture rather than conversion must be the core of faith-based activities [...] One human right is not to have the existence of a spiritual dimension is regarded as a delusion or neurosis [...] Spiritual lives of children must be neither abused nor distorted through power relationships."[5]

The Bible upholds values of dignity, respect, and love for all human beings because they are made in the image of God (Gen. 1:27).[6]

David Hay and Rebecca Nye identify 4 major responsibilities which can be applied to any faith:

- To help children keep an open mind;
- To explore with children different ways of perceiving the world;
- To encourage children's awareness of their own spirituality and that of others;
- To become aware of social and political dimensions of spirituality.[7]

---

[4] (Ennew, 2015).
[5] (Ennew, 2015).
[6] For more on this, see the chapter by Joni Middleton elsewhere in this volume.
[7] (Hay and Nye, 2006).

In this research, all these aspects have been explored.

Results

Participant's Experience of Beliefs

In 2012, 80 of the participants said that they were primarily Christian in their faith compared to 26 primarily Buddhist. By 2017, just 43 said they were primarily Christian and the number who considered themselves to be primarily Buddhist were 33. It is noted that the identity recorded here is according to what the participant said; not by the degree of their faith practice in their daily life. Some who claimed themselves belong to either Christian or Buddhist do not necessarily practice it all the time.

These figures should be read with discernment, as the impact of faith appears to be much broader. In fact, some of the responses below do not provide definitive answers. Some participants have clearly been influenced by Christian faith but do not consider themselves to be Christian. More about this is included in the Discussion section.

About the Quotes from Participants

These results have been organized into categories but they have been left without comment so that the reader is able to immerse themselves solely in the voices of the participants, free from commentary of the researchers. The authors' interpretation is in the Discussion section and the reader can thus decide if they think it is an acceptable interpretation or not.

Quotes about Reflections and Practice on Teachings of Beliefs of Christianity

God created everything and he loves everyone.

> God created the plants and the birds and helps them to grow up and how much more does he love us as human beings. (Nary)

God teaches us not to discriminate or look down on others.

> Jesus teaches us not to discriminate to anyone else. Even if we clean the bathroom or clean up dog shit we are doing it to serve God. God told me not to look down on the dirty person. Last night a man's hand was bleeding and I got my olive oil to put on him. I didn't feel bad. I think God won't allow his disease to spread to me. Some people don't like it and are scared of blood and they were afraid of getting the disease from him but I remember God's word not to discriminate and I just helped them. I just follow God's command. Even the garbage collectors or beggars I brought fruit salad for them. I bought two bottles, keep one for myself and one for them. (Nary)

God teaches us to help others and not expect return.

> When I help someone, I don't expect anything back from them. I support the family who need things. I help them with my heart. I do not take the interest from those who want a loan. Some people took advantage of poor people. (Champa)

God teaches us not to worry.

> In the Bible God said not to worry about tomorrow so I don't worry about tomorrow. I told my friends not to worry. God will never leave you. I encouraged them about God. I had arguments with some people but I don't hate them. God wants us to love our enemies. I was always the one to start talking with them ahead with humble behavior. (Maly)

> I sometimes feel discouraged but I encourage myself. Job had a very difficult life but he endured it. Just in a blink of an eye, ten of his children died and he had a lot of property and it was destroyed. I don't have property and I don't need to worry. (Kanya)

God teaches us to forgive and to love.

> I learnt about love from God. I was taught about love from the Bible and that I need to forgive others. I think about this every day. I have more love than at that time when I did not believe in God. It is still difficult for me to forgive, including anger when we had the problem and then we just confess. I think that the wrong-doer needs to meet me first and then I can forgive. But God does not want me to be like this; God wants us to move ahead but even though I have tried, I can't do it yet because I am still angry with the person. We only understand our feelings. You think you are right and they think they are right. I easily get angry and aggressive. It is my attitude and I need to reduce it. But I also have love in my feelings and I try to talk about good things. (Malis)

God teaches us not to be envious of others.

> I told my partner that I don't care if we make money or not. I said, "Honey I am happy with what God gives me." Before I got so jealous even of my own siblings but now I never care about this. I never feel greedy anymore. Even though my sister got a car, I am not sad about this. (Kanya)

Walk the narrow path with God.

> I will work with God seriously. I would not walk in the wide path as that is the world and goes to the lake of fire. I will walk on the narrow path which is with God and to heaven. (Suon)

God teaches us to confess our sins to him and He answers us.

> God helps me to try the best. If I do the mistake then I need to make adjustments. I always confess my sins to God. When I am faced with difficulties God answers me. It is important for me in my daily life [...] I found my true God. (Suon)

Jesus forgives our sins (but it is hard to love our enemy).

> They told us that even though I have committed sins if I believe in Jesus these sins will be forgiven. God taught us to love our enemy. God told us that if someone is persecuting us then we should be happy with it but I think it is impossible for me. I could not do it. (Visal)

When I have a problem with stress or anger, I can talk to God by praying.

> When I have a problem I can use my Bible knowledge to practice and I don't feel stress in my heart. God teaches to not get angry with other people even if they speak badly against us and we need to forgive them. We don't just think it's difficult – we need to forgive them. If I obey God, I feel relaxed in my heart. (Danith)

God understands me and is with me.

> I think that when I face the issues in my life, I could pray to God and ask for God's help. He knows the problems in my life, even though no-one understands my feelings but there is God. He is near me. I think God helps me a lot. (Nimul)

Attitude changed, no longer gossips.

> I decided myself. I wanted to learn about God. I changed my attitude a lot. I changed to do better. I did not gossip about other people like before. (Leng)

More calm and respectful and loving, less violent, aggressive and angry.

> I learned from the Bible that I shouldn't speak impolitely and should respect others. Before I came to the shelter I was an aggressive person and didn't listen to others. When I had an argument I didn't talk with them easily and used violence instead. I was still young at the time. Later I spoke and communicated with others in a more tolerant way. (Chea)

Don't react to meanness. Better able to control my feelings. More patient. Don't harm others.

> I feel that my relationship is closer to God and my faith is much stronger than before. I don't care what other people say and the most important thing is that I know how to control my feelings. I don't think much or compare myself to other people or anything else. Before I used to compare myself and get jealous of those who got warmth from their families but now I don't have that feeling anymore. I just think that if Jesus is true and God and the only one who loves me. (Phalin)

> I never harm other people. In every situation in my life I always have God with me. I give all my burdens to God and can solve the situations for me. (Romdaul)

God never gives up on me. He helps me.

> I had a weak faith before but now it is strong. I feel close to God. I want to go to church. I know God is great. God never gives up. God always helps me. (Maly)

I experience love from faith which helps me survive when I don't experience it elsewhere.

> Most people have love from four ways. Love from lover. Love from friends. Love from family and love from faith. If we lack these we cannot survive. I do not have love from family, lover or friends I have only from faith which makes me to survive right now. I hope in faith a lot. (Phala)

Peace, safety and protection.

> Recently, when I was walking home late at night 1-2am it was so quiet and there were only people who use drugs. I was scared but I prayed, "Jesus I am afraid the drug people might hurt me" When I said that the light turned on and an aunty came out. Then I was able to walk home with joy. Since then I am happy because I used to be the girl who was always afraid of ghosts. (Nary)

No more fear of death.

> I do not fear to die as I know that God does not give up on me. If I die I will go to be with God. God always responds to me so I think God will not go away from me. (Champey)

God saved me from suicide.

> When I faced difficulties I accused God who gave me the trouble but I still believe and respect Him. I then said sorry to God. I said I wanted to walk with God even if I faced persecution or difficulties. Even if some people give me lots of money to

make me change my belief I would not change it. I sometimes think too much. Once I wanted to stab myself to death. I then thought again and I put the knife down though my hand was bleeding. I realized that if I killed myself I couldn't go to heaven. Even though I have done many good things if I kill myself God will not forgive me. God has given me the body and life and my parents also gave me my body so I should not do that. I thought that if I died I would be out of sorrow as Buddhists think but those who live are full of sorrow so I did not want that. My faith helped me until now. If I did not have faith I would be sitting with the ghosts and not you [the interviewer] now. (Phala)

Quotes about Perceived Impact of Faith on Others

God gives wisdom for our family to develop.

God helped me progress and gave me wisdom to advise my family. I was afraid to share the gospel with them, but through my actions I can show to them little by little. God helps my family to develop more. Through my action, my family feels happy. (Linda)

Relationship with partner.

Before I got my partner, I also prayed to ask God for wisdom to know my partner's personality; was he good enough, would he love and care for me? I prayed that God would prepare a man for me. I prayed I would not have a problem with him. But since I prayed my partner is always doing good to me. So I am so happy about that. I believe that he truly loves me and we decided to love each other until now. (Chan)

Serving others.

I sometimes do something good for other people and I think God helps me. (Mony)

I want to serve Him. I want to share my experience. I want to meet young people and share my experience. I want to achieve my dream since I was small. When I was in the centre they asked me what I wanted to do when I am big. I said I didn't know. I only knew a little about cooking. If I learn more I think I love drawing and cooking. I have innovative ideas. I love singing and dancing. In the church we get love from them as they care about us. They try to encourage us. They support us with medical things when we have sickness. When I went to the church I helped them in some work and I visited the elderly as well. (Phala)

Now I help in teaching to help the rescued kids who are hated by society. I work with them to be better people. (Champey)

I helped a lot of people, which is why I am so poor today. Before I had a friend in the Centre who I was closest to. She faced a lot of problems but she never left me alone. It doesn't matter how angry she got, she always came back to me and do you know why? Because I gave a lot of support to her; I encouraged her and helped her but now she uses drugs. She worked in a nightclub close to my home and then lived with an older man who didn't like her going out but she escaped and came to live with me so now the old man hates me. (Sokchea)

I helped my sister's friend who was a garbage collector so she/he could finish early and come to the concert with us. She asked me, "Don't you feel ashamed [to help a beggar]." But I said I didn't feel shame. I helped to collect until the shack was full. I also brought bread and water for her so we could eat along the way. I also helped a man who was in a car accident. He broke his teeth and his legs were damaged as well. The other driver was really nasty. She said he was a gangster and wasn't careful driving when she was the one who crushed him. She gave him only 30 USD when even one tooth repair would cost 50 USD. I gave him water and tissue to help clean him up and later when we saw him we gave him 15 USD as a love gift. We gave them our number and now they invite us as their friends as a normal friendship. (Nary)

There was a man near my house who used to drink alcohol every day. He said to me, "Sister I could see that your life seems to be really fresh in your heart." I said, "How did you know about this, you are a teacher but how do you know about my heart?" He said he knew by the way I talk; he said he thought I was a Christian. Then I thanked him and it helped me to recognize that I am a Christian and people can see my identity through my speech. Normally when I talk to people around me they respect me. They said since I believe in Jesus I am so polite. Praise God. (Phana)

I told one man: "Don't use the drugs anymore because it will make you lose your beauty. Before you were so handsome but not now." I just told him this and I didn't care if he got angry with me but he said "When you tell me I will listen to you." I said "This way is not good for you to walk on because you already have a wife and children." He said, "Sister, I want to cut down on using and when you told me I want to follow you." Sometimes he wants to use it again but when he saw me sit nearby he is afraid to use it. He said he wants to minimize it because it is not giving benefit to him. So when I meet those who use drug I share with them and if they don't listen then I don't tell them anymore. I am worried nowadays that my child might follow them too. (Soda)

Be a light to others.

If we want others to believe I need to do good things. If we want them to see good things we need to have those things in our life and family first. There is no Christian in the village so I must shine so that is why I stay in the village. To shine the light on them. I think that this is the plan of God. (Nimul)

Speak kindly.

I tell people to observe those who believe in Jesus. "Have you observed them express their anger?" No they don't do that. Sometimes if you speak wrong to them they smile back. We all get angry but Christians know how to be more patient. For example, I will just walk away and not talk back to them; because I just leave it to God to solve it. When I talk with people they say I am so polite. I don't talk much and I am so kind. I said it is because I have God in my heart. (Soda)

Quotes about Anticipation of Faith in the Future

I have given my heart and life to the Lord. I can do it. I could not go anywhere else. (Vanna)

I don't think anything can change my love of God. I love God so much. (Nary)

There is no Christian in the village so I must shine so that is why I stay in the village. To shine the light on them. I think God wants me to shine the light in the village. When I am in trouble God helps. I am motivated and encouraged to do this. (Nimul)

I cannot go away from or forget God because He helps me so much. He has done great things in my life. Even if I am faced with problems. I was young and I didn't forget God before. I think my faith will become stronger. I want God to help me have a stronger faith. I want my family and sister's family to have children who believe in God too. I want God to do great things for me like that. (Ratanak)

I believe that in the future my faith will grow stronger because I have God to protect me and be near to me. When I have a problem, I call to God and he helps me. (Soriya)

My family are Buddhists. I can't cut the tie with Jesus either. I still think about God. I sometimes pray to Him when I face trouble in my life. I don't use the incense. I just close my eyes and talk to Him. God is always close to me. (Leng)

I do not think clearly yet about the way I should walk, I am now in the middle. My family is Buddhist. I am the Christian alone in the family and there are issues. It is difficult for me. I need to wait and see in the next two years. (Chivy)

In the future, I still feel that I will believe in God. If I get married I may change to their belief. Or when I visit my hometown when they celebrate ceremony, I may join them as I used to do. I am not sure about this yet. (Chea)

Discussion

Spiritual Practices

The responses from the researchers' questions appear to indicate that for the majority of participants faith was important in their lives. Spiritual practices, especially prayer, were an important part of their spirituality. This was also shown when they asked the pastors to pray for them/bless them.

Prayer was an important part of worship for many participants. For Christians, it is about a personal relationship with God of love and trust. When praying, some hoped that God would meet some or all of their needs. Sometimes this became unhelpful when they saw God as a "sugar daddy" of prosperity theology because, when God did not appear to provide what they wanted, they felt disappointed. But some Christians trusted that God would answer their prayers in the way that would be most helpful to them and in God's will.

Some Christian participants indicated that praying for physical and spiritual protection and safety for themselves and others was an important aspect of their faith. Some understood that bad spirits come under the power of Jesus.

Christian participants often talked about the Bible and referred to Scripture even if they didn't know the actual book or verse.

When Christian participants were unable to practice their faith practices due to lack of time or lack of accessibility to places of worship then they felt lacking. Those who identified more as Christians described being far away from God after re/integration. A number felt not as close to God as they had before in the aftercare programs (even though the Christian faith emphasizes that God is always close to people, e.g. Matthew 28:20 "I am with you to the ends of the earth"). They often looked back fondly on times when they did feel more connected to their source of spirituality.

For many, Christian faith involved being connected to others with the same faith, starting with their own family where possible and then with friends and members of the community. For those whose families, friends and community did not support them or who persecuted them for what they believed it was harder to maintain their faith, although not impossible.

For many, it was not helpful for them to have to say that they were one religion or another. Christianity had been helpful for some in the shelter but now they were home they didn't see the need to continue. For others, they felt loyal to their acquired religion for a while but then went back to the familiar, traditional beliefs. For some, they maintained their faith even when all the odds seemed against it. When other support was lacking, some felt that God's presence was with them.

Surprisingly, a significant number of participants maintained their acquired faith in Jesus/Christianity, even several years after being away from direct interaction with other Christians and churches.

Impact of Faith on Their Healing and Restoration

For those who identified more as Christians, their relationship with God was of particular importance. They described feeling loved, being able to talk to God, feeling understood by God. They felt they could hear God speaking to them through the Bible, they felt that the burdens they had were taken from them, that God helped them when they or their family were sick. They felt God's peace, safety and protection.

Some described specific ways in which their attitudes were changed, where they were less ashamed, less concerned about what others thought of them, where they were able to control their feelings more, where they could be more patient with others, less aggressive and violent. Some described how they didn't feel the need to lie, where they were willing to accept that they had made a mistake, where they were more confident of themselves and more trusting of others. Some described they were no longer afraid of death.

Christian participants described how their faith led to loving and respecting others and not discriminating against them. This included partners, parents and children but participants also helped friends and the vulnerable including elderly, street kids and alcoholics. Where they could not reach out directly, they described the importance of intercession. It seems likely that the example shown to them by the aftercare organizations contributed to their understanding of the importance of this.

This was not only true of the Christian participants, but also of the non-Christians. As researchers and up-close observers of participants in the study, we see that the program had played an important part in the life of survivors with regards to value formation. Those who reported non-Christian or mixed beliefs between Christianity and Buddhism were inspired/equipped with positive values during their stay in the program which we see was a valuable contribution to their rehabilitation. We would therefore encourage CFBOs and non-CFBOs to focus on value formation (instead of focusing on converting people which may lead to manipulation of rights).

For some, faith allowed them to overcome serious significant challenges in their personal lives, from relationship breakdowns to suicide. For others, they believed that an important part of their faith was reaching out compassionately to and praying for others in their community, especially the poor and needy.

Others realized that suffering was a part of life and that having a faith did not exclude those hard realities. Christ has personal experience of suffering, making a point of relieving the suffering of others and later experiencing suffering on the cross.

Figure 1 Shows how feeling connected to God, feeling connected in their beliefs to their natural family and feeling connected to their spiritual family/community can lead to experiencing positive emotions of self and towards others which can lead to empathy and reaching out to others. It can also lead to a sense of spiritual well-being and life satisfaction leading to resilience. It is possible to see the converse of this to be true when there is a perceived disconnect between the person and God, their own family and their spiritual family/community.

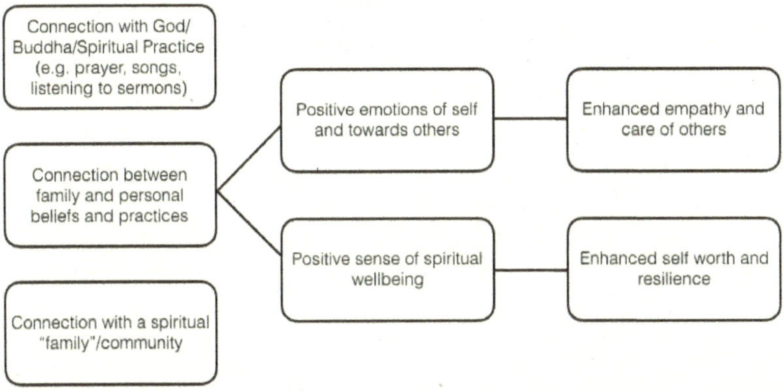

Figure 1: Spiritual wellbeing as a result of connections leading to resilience and empathy.

According to the American Psychological Association, resilience is the "process of adapting well in the face of adversity, trauma, tragedy, threats, or significant sources of stress – such as family and relationship problems, serious health problems, or workplace and financial stressors."[8]

The research also indicates that these factors are helped by a sense of spiritual wellbeing, a greater connection to understanding self, a connection with God, a connection with families' spiritual beliefs and a connection with a spiritual community/family. See Figure 2.

[8] American Psychological Association, "Building your Resilience" APA Website February 1, 2020, https://www.apa.org/topics/resilience/building-your-resilience.

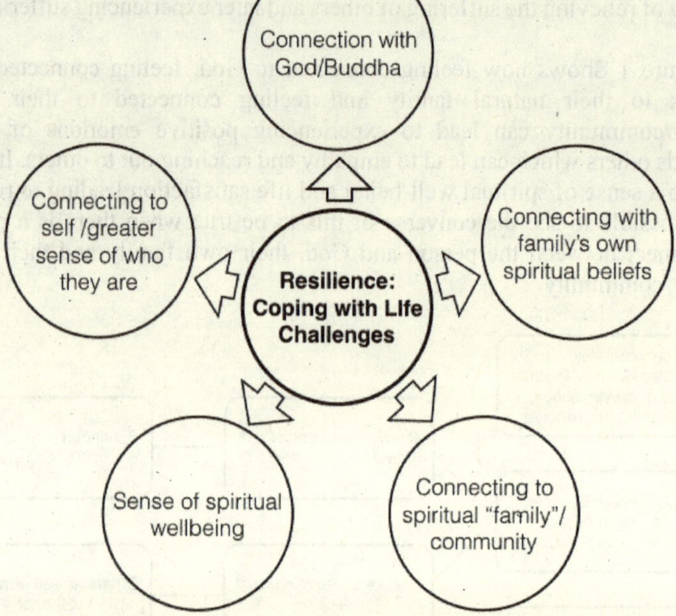

Figure 2: Resilience and its connection to spirituality

The research also indicates that it is much harder when they are unable to pray and worship and therefore communicate with God, when their family are opposed to their beliefs and when they are unable to be part of a faith community that they feel connected to. This is especially difficult in the context of pleasing elders and in a communal rather than individual society. In the absence of one or more of these connections, they can sometimes compensate but the more factors, the harder it may become.

It is of importance that very few participants indicated that they felt coerced to undertake faith activities in the aftercare programs, most had freedom to choose. However, some would say that the Christian culture of some organizations can be unhelpfully persuasive. Those who already had a faith usually continued in that faith. Some who had no serious faith beforehand were therefore able to weigh up whether the faith of the staff that was being offered to them could actually benefit them. Several tried it out and were not convinced. Others tried it out and took it on wholeheartedly.

Recommendations

Aftercare Centers and Community Programs

- Programs working with children and vulnerable adults should continue to provide them with holistic care that includes spiritual aspects of care. This means providing them a choice of faith options where they can go to church services or the Buddhist temple or none if they prefer. This research indicates that some who have experienced Christian spiritual input have experienced positive changes for themselves including feeling healed of traumatic events, forgiveness, reduction in anger and stress and also enabled them to pray and reach out to others. For some, the spiritual path from survive to thrive is a real one.

- Staff need to be screened and monitored to make sure that they are kind and patient towards survivors in their care, whether or not they have faith themselves. Survivors should have the opportunity to be able to complain about staff's behaviour so that it can be confronted. No-one is perfect but rudeness or unkindness is unacceptable and should be followed by apologies if and when it occurs. All staff should be signatories of the child and vulnerable adult safeguarding policies. All 14 NGO partners of Chab Dai Coalition involved in this project have their own policies which often include and address spiritual abuse. All Child Safeguarding policies should include the importance of prevention of spiritual as well as other kinds of abuse.
- "Spiritual abuse is the denial or use of spiritual or religious beliefs and practices to control and dominate a person. Spiritual abuse can have an impact on someone's self-esteem and confidence, make them feel guilty, damage their spiritual experiences and isolate them."[9] Spiritual abuse occurs when spirituality is used to manipulate or force someone into doing or thinking something rather than providing them with space to decide for themselves. Children and vulnerable people do not need further exploitation.
- Therefore, churches and faith-based organizations need to require accountability and transparency to ensure that leaders understand their role and how easily it can become negative.
- It is important that CFBO staff do not develop a culture of intolerance against other faiths. Survivors need to be able to freely choose whether or not they want to change religions or continue in the religion they are used to. Although most of the participants said that they were able to choose whether they were involved in Christian activities or not, some may have felt that they would be at a disadvantage if they stayed Buddhist. If there is one thing this research shows it is that staff with integrity, hope and love inspire others to their faith, far more than words.
- Christians should be confident enough in their own faith that they don't use fear or doubt to make others question their own faith. Going to the temple to please their parents, lighting the incense, eating food dedicated to the temple, wearing strings on the wrist, all of these are not inherently bad and they will still be able to maintain their Christian faith if they choose to. For some, prevention from doing these can cause anxiety, isolation from community, judgement from and against others. One positive example was

[9] (White Ribbon Australia).

a survivor with limited job opportunities, skills, and extremely poor living conditions who sold flowers at the temple as the only option to make living. The survivor hoped that God would understand what the survivor saw as a compromise. In this, they were able to maintain their faith in God, believing that God would understand that they needed to do this in order to survive.

- Some of the survivors had legitimate but very challenging questions about what happened to them and about other issues, for example, the genocide. Why did not God appear to intervene in their suffering? There must be discussions about these things rather than survivors feeling they cannot ask such questions or are embarrassing the staff. A theology of suffering must be explored with survivors where they understand that God may seem to be far away but that his grace and love is available for them always, even in their darkest moments.
- In assisting survivors to reintegrate with their families, reintegration and community programs should talk with the family about the importance of allowing them to practice their individual faith in their restoration and support them to pray, read and attend the place of worship if it is helpful to them and accessible. They should explain the importance of the right of freedom to believe, positive aspects of belief and dispel any misconceptions such as not being able to cry at funerals, lack of respect for parents, etc.
- Programs working with survivors should consider the long-term spiritual care of their recipients. With permission from the recipients, they should attempt to make contact with different options of churches and religious leaders so that, when they return to their communities, they are aware of where they can go to feel comfortable and welcome. These religious leaders may need help in understanding that the participants have been victims and did not choose to be exploited. With a deeper understanding of spirituality, they can heal and become active and strong members of the spiritual community. For those who want and request it, especially those far away from or too busy to attend churches/temples, information on radio shows, scripture to read or listen to and worship songs on CDs and radio could/should be made available to them, as well as other forms of media such as podcasts, streaming services, etc.
- It is gratifying to see that three of the participants said that their faith prevented them from suicide. One could find meaning and value to continue living in the hopeless situation through believing in God's presence and believing that their life has value. However, there is an understanding that suicide is not forgivable which can compound the grief of the families left behind. There appears to be nothing in the Bible that suggests that.
- Respectfully, all Christians who come in contact with vulnerable people in programs or in the community should be reminded of their responsibilities to be kind and not be abusive in any way.

Christian Leadership in Cambodia

- Christian pastors, priests and teachers should continue to welcome all types of people into the church. They should provide a place where people feel loved and cared for whatever has happened to them in the past or is happening to them now. They should have a strong emphasis on imago dei, i.e. that everyone is made in the image of God and avoid emphasizing teachings that focus on fear (e.g. "lake of fire"). They should encourage their entire congregation to seek the "fruits of the spirit" – that is love, joy, peace, patience, kindness, goodness, faith, long-suffering, gentleness, self-control (Gal. 5:23-25) – and reach out and pray for those who are in difficult situations. They should make the Bible and their sermons and worship songs available through radio, social media and television where possible.
- They should also encourage all their congregation to behave in a moral way, treating everyone with dignity and reaching out to those who are more vulnerable. Men should be encouraged to treat all women with dignity and respect.
- Many Christians who are fearful of the spirit world and ghosts need reassuring that they can pray and ask for protection at any time. Christian leadership needs to offer advice and ways to calm oneself/self-regulate fears and anxiety in healing through Christian prayers.
- Church leaders should understand that sometimes those who are recovering from abuse and exploitation will need help and support immediately after discharge from an aftercare program but later they can become the supporters of others.
- They should not discriminate against young people who have experienced abuse or treat them differently. Indeed, they should see the enormous leadership potential in survivors to care for other survivors in the future.
- Christian pastors and teachers who come in contact with vulnerable people should be reminded of their responsibilities to be kind and not be abusive in any way. Any people working directly in churches should be screened beforehand and sign a child and vulnerable persons protection policy. The policy/guidelincs should be developed for staff to align and adhere to while working with children and vulnerable adults. These policy/guidelines should encourage and foster an environment where each team staff can express their faith/core ethos into action (integrate their values into their work) with a Biblical foundation whilst still upholding child and human rights.

Researchers

- Researchers need to understand and explore the impact of spirituality and faith as a key part of holistic research.
- More research is needed in understanding how spirituality can help to heal trauma and help children become more resilient and how children and vulnerable people can move from survive to thrive.

- More research is needed on the connection between spirituality and resiliency.
- More research is needed on how spiritualty enables survivors to reach out to and empower their community.
- More research is needed on spiritual abuse, including its nature, types, causes, and ways to avoid inflicting it and recovering from it.

Reflection Questions

1. How can you understand and measure the impact of spirituality on survivors of sex trafficking? What challenges exist?
2. What can we learn from this chapter about how faith can be a positive or a negative part of aftercare programs? What more needs to be learned?
3. How can we challenge secular NGOs who say that it is unhelpful, indeed abusive, to include faith in programs working with survivors? How can we better ensure that spiritual and other abuse does not occur?

Resources

Chab Dai Butterfly Project Website. [Available at: https://chabdai.org/butterfly]. Especially, Chab Dai. *Butterfly Longitudinal Research Project Informational Overview Packet*. 2020.

Works Cited

Cormack, Don. *Killing Fields Living Fields: Faith in Cambodia.* Fearn, Scotland: Christian Focus, 2009.

Ennew, Judith. "What role does faith and spirituality have in caring for children at risk and other vulnerable people? How do we respond to those who say they were forcing children to believe things against their will?", In C. Crawford and G.M. Miles, Eds. *Finding Our Way through the Traffick: Navigating the Complexities of a Christian Response to Sexual Exploitation and Trafficking.* Oxford: Regnum, 2017.

Gray, Glori, Lilia Luna and Winston Seegobin. "Exploring resilience: strengths of trafficking survivors in Cambodia". *Int J Adolesc Med Health*. 24(4), (2012): 363-71. [Available at: https://www.ncbi.nlm.nih.gov/pubmed/23183739], [Last accessed: 24th October 2022].

Hay, David and Rebecca Nye. *The Spirit of the Child.* London: Jessica Kingsley Publications, 2006.

Hester, Tricia, Sopheak Kong, Srey Oun Seng, Chamreun Seng, Srey Mey Seng, Sam Ol Neang. "Experiences of Former Cambodian Entertainment and Sex Workers Integrating into Christian Churches". 2017. [Available at:

http://gmmiles.co.uk/wp-content/uploads/2017/08/Experiences-of-Former-Cambodian-Entertainment-and-Sex-Workers-Integrating-into-Christian-Churches-2.pdf], [Last accessed: 24th October 2022

International Justice Mission. "Children for Sale". *NBC News Website.* 24th January 2004.

[Available at: https://www.nbcnews.com/id/wbna4038249#.XSW2BpO6POR], [Last accessed: 24th October 2022].

Miles, Glenn, Vanntheary Lim, Nhanh Channtha. *Children of the Wood, Children of the Stone: The Journeys of Faith for Survivors of Trafficking.* Phnom Penh: Chab Dai, 2020. [Available at: https://chabdai.org/publications], [Last accessed: 24th October 2022].

Ponchaud, François, Yves Bishop Ramousse, Roger Etchegaray, Eds. *The Cathedral in the Rice Paddy: the 450 year long history of the church in Cambodia.* Trans. by Nancy Pignarre and Sharon Wilkinson. Second Edn. Phnom Penh, Cambodia Catholic Catechetical Centre Cambodia, 2012.

White Ribbon Australia. "What is Spiritual Abuse". Video, uploaded 21st May 2019. *White Ribbon Australia Facebook* [Available at: https://www.facebook.com/watch/?v=409156413038492], [Last accessed: 24th October 2022].

FORGIVENESS AND SEXUAL EXPLOITATION: A MULTI-DISCIPLINARY REFLECTION

Stephanie Goins

Introduction

The fascination with the transformative potential of forgiveness is more than academic for me; more than a working out of my own theological understanding. Forgiveness is a practice we may choose to utilize in everyday life and some circumstances offer seemingly endless opportunities to engage with it.

In my masters' thesis, I explored the comparative perspectives of forgiveness from Albert Ellis, a humanist and well-known psychologist who founded Rational Emotive Therapy, and Jay Adams, a well-known Christian psychologist at that time. Both practitioners talked about the benefits of forgiveness; Adams posited that a lack of forgiveness, particularly in relation to traumatic events, could be a contributing factor to some forms of mental illness. The research on the long-term effects of trauma was then in its infancy.

A more thorough understanding of the forgiveness process later found expression in my doctoral thesis. Forgiveness discourse offered varied descriptions of its meaning and practice, as understood through the disciplines of psychology, philosophy, and theology. And, as life requires of us, what we write about typically demands personal responses from us. Thus, I found myself applying those practices of forgiveness I had spent years exploring both in the literature and in the lives of others.

This chapter examines the relationship between forgiveness and sexual exploitation in light of what I've learned thus far through the discourse of various disciplines, and from survivors and practitioners. Different voices speak to one another to inform an understanding of forgiveness as it does, or does not, impact those who have been sexually exploited. In this process, I address specific questions about forgiveness and discuss common themes in forgiveness practices.

Learnings Thus Far

A 10-year civil war in Sierra Leone left the infrastructure of this beautiful country and the soul of its people all but destroyed.[1] The realities of this horrific war deeply challenged the Sierra Leonean people to learn to live alongside the very ones who had burned down their homes, mutilated their bodies, raped their wives and children, and required their abducted children to commit atrocities

---

[1] Sierra Leone's civil war began in 1991 and was officially declared over in January 2002.

meant to sever them from their communities. How would it be possible to reintegrate, to rehabilitate, to recover? This was the basic focus of my doctoral studies; and, as I considered what factors might contribute to recovery, I postulated that forgiveness might offer a positive impact.

Recovering from civil war was complicated by the fact that thousands of children had been abducted into armed groups (both rebel and civil or government backed). At the war's end, former child soldiers were, for the most part, seeking re-integration or integration within their own or others' communities. Re-integration was further complicated by the fact they were often at the same time both victims and perpetrators. Yet, without a move in the direction of forgiving, how could stability return and recovery have a chance?

After years of reading scholarly discourse, weeks of observation and reading children's narratives, and hours of listening to many stories, practices of forgiveness emerged as impacting the recovery process for Sierra Leone's people. Various factors that made a positive impact on forgiveness processes also surfaced. My research suggested that forgiveness would be supported by certain constructs, attitudes, and ways of being and living together.

I explored descriptions of forgiveness, how forgiveness could be enacted and realized, as well as with whom and between whom forgiveness processes could be seen. Sierra Leonean people saw forgiveness as a change in attitude and behavior by the victim, or both victim and perpetrator, encouraged by factors and attitudes of empathy, gratitude, hope, and acceptance. While forgiveness sometimes happened as a unilateral process, it was more often a bilateral process of forgiving others and being forgiven by others. It was most fully realized in the context of a community, and when repentance and/or some form of restitution was enacted by the perpetrator.

Forgiveness processes proved to be significant in the re-integration of former child soldiers, and in the transformation of relationships between people, in communities, between persons, and between civil society and government. Forgiveness functioned in different dimensions, such as between persons, between person(s) and a Supreme Deity, or between person(s) and ancestors. Forgiveness of self was critical for some, and yet some offences felt unpardonable and unforgivable by self, Deity and others. Trust, resilience, belonging, telling one's story, empathy – all functioning within a communal group culture – were the mitigating factors for this to happen. Conversely, other factors hindered practices of forgiveness, such as shame, a lack of supportive relationships, unrelenting anger, and a culture of revenge.

When we begin thinking about forgiveness from a philosophical perspective, things get complicated and messy. Foundational questions such as who deserves forgiveness, who does the forgiving, when is forgiveness called for, when should forgiving be withheld, are explored through the different disciplines and in religious practices. Answers are very often elusive on one extreme and conclusive on the other.

What initially drove me to explore forgiveness and its limits was imagining a child forced or coerced to commit atrocities that could destroy the child emotionally, psychologically, socially and physiologically. First a victim, the transition into perpetrator was nearly seamless. Defined by those deeds and particularly in the context of a communal culture, the future would look bleak indeed. However, if forgiveness practices came into the everyday way of living, then integration or re-integration into community and recovery of well-being were possible. Through the courageous efforts of the Sierra Leonean people, practicing forgiveness made re-integration possible and healing hopeful.[2]

Emotions that worked against forgiveness were anger and shame. Anger may have been mitigated by acts of restitution, depending on the offence and the form of restitution. In a culture of revenge, anger is acceptable and even desirable. Still, no matter one's culture, anger fuels action, which could work positively towards re-integration and restoration, or could work against it, such as when revenge was taken and forgiveness denied a place.

Shame, on the other hand, was significantly more difficult to address. This powerful emotion impels us to hide from others, even ourselves. During my fieldwork, I witnessed the power of shame over and above the reality of guilt. While guilt can be addressed through various practices of forgiveness such as offering restitution, paying a debt, or performing a ritual, shame does not so easily heal. What heals shame is to be welcomed back into relationship and community, whether this be relationship with others, with self or with Supreme Deity.[3]

What Others Say Through Research and Academic Writings

There has been significant research and writings about forgiveness and reconciliation as it relates to exploitation, specifically sexual abuse/exploitation. However, the relationship between forgiveness and sex trafficking is relatively unexplored in the different disciplines. I wondered if previous research and writings would apply to the current questions around forgiveness of sexual exploitation or trafficking, questions that I and others have posed. I also wondered how philosophical, theological, and psychological discourse would address these questions.

Before exploring this, there are two important points to note that are foundational to the discussion. First, forgiveness must begin with the recognition, by at least one of the parties, that a wrong has been identified and committed, a wrong for which the wrongdoer is responsible. Second, forgiveness generally begins as a motivation within an individual, whether it be the one wronged or the wrongdoer.

How Is Forgiveness Understood and Enacted?

One of the more common descriptions of forgiveness is a shift in attitude or feelings about the offender. Forgiveness begins with an internal process of overcoming or working towards relinquishing negative emotions and attitudes

---

[2] The question remained, and still does, as to the extent of the transformation resulting from practices of forgiveness within the individual and between individuals. However, there has been no resurgence of war since January 2002.

[3] See also: Shultz and Sandage, 2003.

towards the offender, such as anger or resentment, and working towards feelings of empathy and compassion for the offender. A change in attitude would be reflected in a change in behavior. Forgiveness might have begun as a unilateral process, but then leads to a bilateral or invitational process, as in an embrace.[4] Additionally, it is critical to distinguish between the offence and the offender. We do not forgive deeds; we forgive the people who committed deeds.

Forgiveness is often described as release from a debt or liberation from a burden, "carrying" or "taking away" the offence,[5] "setting free, dismissing or acquitting",[6] all which may benefit the offended and offender, and going so far as to release the offender from retributive justice. Being liberated from the past adds a dimension to forgiveness suggested in the most frequently used word for forgiveness in the New Testament: *aphiemi*, "to send or let off or away; to release or discharge." This can also be translated as liberation. The *aphiemi* kind of forgiveness is the kind that removes the marks left from sin, so that there is no trace of the offence for the parties concerned; thus, this becomes a liberation at the deepest personal level.[7]

Release from the burden of guilt and/or shame felt for the offences is complex but critical. These emotions refer to the humiliation felt at being the object of offences, the feelings of hatred towards the offender, and even the actuality or perception of moral shortcomings (e.g. the victim not defending themself, or the offender having committed the offense in the first place). Forgiveness that liberates overcomes this "burden of hatred",[8] and can be instrumental in enabling hope, resilience and the possibility of changed relationships – that is, a permission to live which is unencumbered by the past and hopeful for a better and different future.[9]

Rowden and Davis (2005) and Morris (1988) speak of forgiveness as having a transcendent or divine nature which, according to Muller-Fahrenholz (1998), brings freedom from shame, guilt and anger, and empowers a grace to forgive and be reconciled. This he calls a transcending element, "a spark of courage to open up, that moment of daring and trusting which causes the heart to jump over the fence. It is this surprising energy which lays down the dividing walls between us".[10] This grace seems to be a similar concept to *aphiemi* which implies a divinely empowered forgiving. Volf argues that the generous giving so

---

[4] This way of describing forgiveness is both literal and figurative. Literally, victim(s) and perpetrator(s) did embrace one another after there was repentance. In his book, *Exclusion and Embrace*, Volf (1996) explores the act of embrace as a symbolic and literal representation of forgiveness.

[5] From the word *nasa* in the Old Testament.

[6] From *apoluo* – a New Testament word.

[7] This understanding of "aphiemi" was given to me by a Greek pastor. Also, see: Watts 2004.

[8] (Murphy and Hampton, 1988: 106).

[9] See also: Chircop, 1998: 21; Murphy and Hampton, 1988; Soyinka, 1999; Willmer, 2001: 26.

[10] (Muller-Fahrenholz, 1998: 236; Rowden and Davis, 2005; Morris, 1998).

characteristic of God is what enables forgiveness, agreeing with Jones and Daly, who both say that the divine (in their perspectives, God) is indispensable.[11]

Others do not always agree. Arendt, while crediting Jesus with discovering "the role of forgiveness in the realm of human affairs", believes that forgiving is not necessarily dependent on the transcendent deity.[12] Other psychologists seem to agree, noting that the miraculous cannot be quantified or empirically measured,[13] thus attributing forgiveness to a decision and an act of the will.[14] However, Falconer responding specifically to Arendt's theory, argues that "Jesus stands alongside men and women empowering them to forgive", a position which suggests that Jesus is the divine transcendent source of forgiving. Falconer also notes the "nutrient power" of parents in enabling their children to do things beyond their present and immature state, and the "integrative power" of those who stand alongside and help others.[15]

This is clear: forgiveness is a process, not an event. Attitude and behavior changes take time. If forgiveness is viewed otherwise, it can easily become a source of confusion, accusation, and condemnation. We believe that we have forgiven someone, only to once again be confronted with those same negative attitudes and painful emotions associated with the offence and the offender. It may be better to think of forgiving, rather than having already forgiven.

For forgiveness to be fully realized, repentance – meaning a change of mind or attitude – is required.[16] The offender who repents confesses and commits to changed attitude and behavior. At its best, repentance signifies a turning back to the offended one with hope, enabling the offender to face the offended, and even (if appropriate) come into a renewed relationship with the offended.[17] Apart from this repentance, the wronged one is justified to remember the wrong "with resentment appropriate to a deliberate act of disrespect".[18]

While some psychologists make forgiveness contingent on repentance, others disagree. Here, the forgiveness process may be viewed as intrapersonal (unilateral), versus interpersonal (bilateral).[19] This is particularly true when reconciliation is not part of the process (which would be a unilateral practice). However, at the core of the spirit of forgiveness is "extending an attitude of real

---

[11] (Volf, 1995; Jones,2001; Daly, 1998).

[12] (Arendt, 1958: 238).

[13] (Flanigan, 1998: 97).

[14] See also: Denham *et al*, 2005; Enright *et al*, 1998; Konstam, 2002; Murphy and Hampton, 1988; Worthington Jr, 1998a, 2003.

[15] (Falconer, 1998a: 183-85).

[16] From the Greek word "*metanoia.*"

[17] (Shults and Sandage, 2003).

[18] (Biggar, 2001: 215).

[19] Forgiveness as an intrapersonal process means nothing is required of the offender. Worthington's (1998) intrapersonally based Pyramid Model to REACH Forgiveness requires only one actor – the forgiver – to do the work, with no interpersonal exchange between the two parties. In sharp contrast is Herman's (1992) perspective, which makes forgiveness contingent on the confession, repentance, and restitution of the perpetrator.

goodwill" towards the other, which is not realized with an intrapersonal approach.[20]

Forgiving and repenting do not imply that reconciliation follows, or even that it should. However, the wrongdoer's acknowledgement of the offence is essential to reconciliation.[21] Reconciliation which is based on acceptance, respect, and some degree of trust (or desire to rebuild trust) enables people to work towards better relationships.

What Constructs, Practices, and Attitudes Influence the Forgiveness Process, Both as Helps and/or Hindrances?

Forgiveness is influenced positively by particular constructs, practices, and attitudes; conversely, forgiveness is hindered by other constructs, practices, and attitudes.

Trust

Trust affects how we relate to one another, how we interpret events, and how we understand one another's actions.[22] Acknowledging the event is key to rebuilding trust. We jointly search for the truth by listening to one another and remembering.[23] Trust cannot be restored or rebuilt apart from this process of putting the pieces back together. Where trust is present, forgiveness is made possible.

Yet the act of remembering can be traumatizing in itself and grievous for victims of sexual exploitation/trafficking. "[T]he truth can as easily destroy as it can liberate".[24] Thus, coming to a place of forgiveness is extremely difficult.[25] As those who work with survivors know, disclosure of any form of abuse is contingent on an environment of trust, which is only possible when the survivor feels safe both physically and emotionally. Establishing the reality and perception of safety requires time and rebuilding trust on this foundation even more so.

It is not always appropriate, desirable or possible to rebuild trust between the one wronged and the wrongdoer. However, trust between the wronged one and a therapist, a spouse, a parent, a friend, or a group to which one belongs is a positive influencer for forgiveness processes. In these relationships, where the other is not the perpetrator, it remains true that building or rebuilding trust is crucial to forgiveness.

---

[20] See: Govier, 2002: 74; Holmgren, 2002; Volf, 1996.

[21] Many have written about this. See: Bash and Bash, 2004; Biggar, 2001; Jones, 1995; Shriver, 1995; van Deusen Hunsinger, 2001; Worthington Jr, 2003.

[22] (Govier, 2006).

[23] See also: Augsburger, 1996; Cose, 2004; Cyuma, 2005; Harris, 1998; Santer, 1998; Schreurs, 2001: Wright, 1998.

[24] (Biggar, 2003: 308).

[25] See also: Flanigan, 1998; Hamber, 2003; van Deusen Hunsinger, 2001.

Telling Their Stories in a Community of Belonging

It is critical in the healing process, as well as the forgiveness process, for survivors to give voice to their stories, if and when they feel ready to do so. Human trafficking victims "feel completely abandoned and alone, cast out by humanity and left without any sense of care or protection" – the result of which is a humiliating silence.[26] Yet, in voicing one's story, "painful emotionality in the narrative" is reduced. There is the opportunity for the victim to move beyond the old story "to a new and different story".[27] By listening to the voices of survivors, affirming and respecting their experiences, we support them in reclaiming their power.

Telling one's story in a place of safety provides the space for other helpful emotions to take their proper place, such as anger or humiliation. In the presence of other survivors, these types of emotions are shared and validated, and may even be utilized in productive ways.[28] Having supportive relationships, being accepted, and belonging are all critical to the recovery process for survivors of sexual exploitation.

> Trauma research overwhelmingly demonstrates that interpersonal support and love is absolutely essential for healing. The experiences of sexual abuse survivors – particularly those chronically abused as children – testify to the fact that persons are dependent upon the support and love of others to heal and realize their freedom to relate positively to themselves, others, and God […].[29]

However, confronting these emotions feels vulnerable, frightening, and even terrifying. Survivors may try to bypass the outrage of what has happened to them with a "fantasy of forgiveness", hoping that a "willful act of love" can erase the power of the trauma.[30] Additionally, survivors may feel pressured to enact this "willful act of love", which could do more to harm than help the recovery process.

Shame

"Shame is a master emotion", a critical component of the abuser's tactics: groom, arouse, shame and condemn.[31] "The shame of victims is generally hidden behind anger and indignation, but as soon as they express sorrow, anxiety or pain, feelings of shame come above the surface".[32] Shame silences a victim and, for survivors of sexual exploitation, this is most often an enforced silence. Unable to talk about their experiences, survivors will likely experience physical and

---

[26] (McCrory, 2015: 51).

[27] (Winter *et al.*, 2016: 293).

[28] A community of belonging was critical to recovery for victims of sexual exploitation and trafficking once Sierra Leone's civil war had ended. Because of the stigmatization they experienced, they often chose to remain in squalid conditions with others who had shared experiences, accepted them, and encouraged practices of forgiveness.
For further reading on this concept, see: Clawson, Salomon, and Goldblatt-Grace, 2008.

[29] (Beste, 2005: 94).

[30] (Herman, 1992: 189).

[31] (Allender, 2016: 71).

[32] (van Stokken, 2002: 344).

emotional health problems. Further, in many cases, there is a stigmatization that accompanies sex work, and possibly a sense of "social defilement" which lends to shame and a certain ambivalence about the self.[33]

Survivors of sexual assault most often assume responsibility for what has happened to them and feel a deep sense of personal remorse and shame, which reinforces silence. In this, we see a parallel to the experiences of others who are victims of domestic violence. "Slaves will also feel shame, even self-loathing, in a way that paralyzes them and prevents escape".[34] Conversely, freedom from shame contributes to well-being. This freedom impacts and is impacted by forgiveness processes.

Forgiving oneself is critical in addressing shame, the focus being on resolving feelings of guilt and shame. The conscience has been violated through transgression of cultural and/or religious standards, which determine how one understands and deals with shame and the self.[35] In communal cultures, self-forgiveness is strongly linked to restoration with the group, which, in a sense, may have held the victim responsible for violations committed against them. Yet, how one construes oneself in terms of bearing the responsibility for the violations committed against oneself will have direct implications on the shame they feel and further the ability to forgive oneself.

Forgiving self is more likely once the person has been restored communally. However, even with community restoration, the burden of shame may very well hinder forgiving. Past events can infiltrate and haunt the present.[36] As can a lack of restitution or a restitution that is so inappropriately small relative to the offence that it is insulting.

Resilience, Optimism, and Hope (or Future Mindedness)

Resilience, optimism, and hope are strongly linked to the forgiveness process, and at the same time mutually supportive of one another. These attitudes enable forgiving others, and support forgiving oneself, because forgiveness helps change one's relationship to the past. Having hope for a different future encourages survivors to take the painful journey of healing. This, in turn, supports the recovery of self-esteem and self-efficacy, characteristics of a resilient nature that are significant to the forgiveness process.[37]

---

[33] (Dodsworth, 2015: 63 citing McKeganey and Barnard, *Sex Work on the Streets: Prostitutes and Their Clients*, Buckingham: Open University Press, 1996: 83.

[34] (Bales and Soodalter, 2009: 23).

[35] See: Goins, 2015; Govier, 2002; Joseph, 2009; McCullough, Sandage and Worthington Jr, 1997.

[36] A case in point is a village chief held at gunpoint and, in that act, "destroyed for life." As he said, death would have been better, as the humiliation is forever with the one still alive.

[37] See: Anderson, 2001; Goins, 2015; Jones, 2014.

Empathy

Of all the attitudes that positively influence the forgiveness process, empathy is by far the most frequently discussed.[38] Carl Rogers describes empathy as entering the world of the other and responding accordingly.[39] Others describe empathy as a process of entering God's point of view, something that can happen through prayer and/or realistically assessing oneself and one's weaknesses.[40] Empathy for self and the other can make all the difference. Broome calls this "relational empathy", a construct of conflict resolution. It is co-directional and interactive, where both parties "bridge differences" and create common understandings and shared meaning through dialogue.[41] Armour and Umbreit say empathy for both parties reduces the injustice gap by helping victims to see themselves as less innocent and their offenders as less evil.[42]

Anger

There is no question that anger is a perfectly justified response in light of violations experienced by survivors of trafficking and sexual exploitation. Anger is also a phase in the grieving process and, as Worden notes, can encourage more productive reactions and even growth.[43] At the same time, anger and resentment are also the most commonly noted reasons for unforgiveness. Left on its own to fester, anger turned to resentment has incredible potential for destruction and is obviously a significant hindrance to forgiveness and re-integration.

Culture

Much of the forgiveness literature does not reflect the significance of societal, cultural, and religious impacts to its applications. For instance, forgiveness in an individualistic culture is seen as personal, whereas in a communal culture forgiveness is often a communal practice and even a prescribed duty.[44] Still, there is a growing body of discourse that emphasizes the importance of culture in understanding and enacting forgiveness, the appropriateness of forgiveness, and even the impossibility of it depending on the offences to be addressed via forgiveness processes. Two books, *Stolen Lives* and *Stigma: Survivor Experiences and Perceptions,* delve into the issue of cultural perceptions of trafficking survivors and how recovery is influenced.[45] Joseph said, "In the Eastern perspective, forgiveness is related to karma, so it is important that we consider the impact of this belief on the victim's ability to regain self-respect and deal with the complicated and difficult notion of forgiveness."[46] Karma undermines recovery because it shifts the blame to victims of trafficking

---

[38] (Shults and Sandage, 2003).
[39] (Rogers, 1980: 142).
[40] See: Adams, 1991; Biggar, 2001; Govier, 2002; Jones, 1995; Volf, 2005.
[41] (Broome, 1993: 100-109).
[42] (Armour and Umbreit, 2005).
[43] (Worden, 1991).
[44] (Sandage and Williamson, 2005: 45).
[45] (Joseph, 2009; Morrison, 2015).
[46] (Joseph, 2009: 57).

themselves, because of mistakes made in their past. Still, forgiveness is written about in sacred Indian writings. It "brings great power, and can result in healing, encouragement, hope, and determination".[47]

What Survivors and Practitioners Say

I will now shift focus to what I have learned through personal interviews with survivors and practitioners, through research focused on the voices of survivors, and through writings of practitioners who have worked with survivors.[48]

How Is Forgiveness Understood and Enacted?

Forgiveness begins with an acknowledgement that *a wrong had been committed.* "For me," one survivor said, "it is acknowledging what happened [...] acknowledging and facing it [...] You have to stop and acknowledge the horrible thing that has happened to you." "Face the fears," said another. Another survivor feels her healing was dependent on this. She felt God say to her, "I cannot heal what you won't acknowledge." All three survivors were motivated for various reasons to begin their forgiveness journey.

Forgiveness involves *a change in attitude, feelings, and even behavior.* "It's dealing with the negative feelings you have towards the perpetrator." "It is the way anger and pain are transformed." Forgiveness involves a process of transformation but also choice, what some call an act of self-determination.[49] "Forgiveness is not easy. Just like a drug addict has to choose not to pick up drugs, it's the same thing everyday [...] You have to make a choice every day. I choose to forgive. I choose to live a different life."

Forgiveness is *an offer of freedom, of liberation.* As one survivor said, "Step back, let it go. Give it to God [...] Keep doing it and doing it until it works." "I really feel like forgiveness is a choice and a state of mind so the factor (that helps forgiving) would also include a choice to not carry the burdens of unforgiveness and I think that by choosing to forgive you have also given yourself permission to heal and let go of those burdens." Thus, liberation is not just for the one being forgiven but also for the one doing the forgiving.

Forgiveness is *a transcendent and transformative process* attributed to the Supreme Deity.[50] "Forgiveness, self forgiveness especially, really requires something higher than yourself [...] that you can lean on in times of weakness.

---

[47] (Joseph, 2009: 61).

[48] My sample size was small. I interviewed three survivors and two practitioners, and corresponded via email with some who had worked with survivors. Also included in this section are several written works where the voices of survivors have been featured. I do not identify the survivors by name or number, in order to preserve identity although all survivors said I was free to share their identities. Where I am quoting survivors from a written work, I have referenced that work. Additionally, the survivors in this study are not clients being served by anyone in my organization.

[49] (Joseph, 2009).

[50] Not all discourse cited in this chapter comes from people of the Christian faith, and thus it is sometimes more appropriate to refer to the Supreme Deity rather than God.

Otherwise you're going to crumble." Another survivor said, "God gifted me with being able to see the whole picture, and that has helped me to forgive." "I've seen how God turns horrible things into beautiful things. God can transform everything."[51]

Various descriptions of forgiveness were offered: "Forgiveness – it is so uniquely individual, so very personal." "Forgiveness was a byproduct. For me, it was like 'look what happened as a result of loving people.'" "Forgiveness is different for everyone" a survivor said, and later, "It's not the same for me as it was before." This survivor's understanding has changed over time. "Forgiveness is something (a process) that happens over time" and conversely something that "can happen in a moment – an empathy moment."

How does repentance fit into the forgiveness process? For many survivors, repentance coming from their exploiters is unlikely; and, often there were too many of them. "I don't even remember their faces," one woman said. Another survivor said that without facing the person, you cannot see the repentance and behavior change; the process of forgiveness is short-circuited. However, for one survivor, the main perpetrator was her father. She tried talking with him but initially he denied everything. He later admitted that he was a horrible father. Her conclusion: "If you go looking for an apology, it makes it worse. You never know if you are going to get the response you actually feel you want or deserve." By their choice, engaging in the forgiveness process was not contingent on the repentance of the exploiter.

That said, one practitioner noted the importance of repentance and remorse for child survivors of exploitation. "Forgiveness could get them back on track developmentally, but that would only come if the perpetrator would express remorse, if the perpetrator was willing to take responsibility, or [...] was convicted. That can make all the difference. If there is no way a child can concretize the idea that someone could be remorseful, if they are left with their own experience of the incident(s) [...] they can't extrapolate forgiveness. They must have a concrete experience to balance what they've lived."

What Constructs, Practices, and Attitudes Influence the Forgiveness Process, Both As Helps and/or Hindrances?

Trust

One of the greatest challenges for trauma survivors is rebuilding trust; yet this is crucial to interpersonal relationships, overall recovery, and resettlement.[52] One survivor said she didn't trust anyone except her husband; she expects people to let her down and is always "taking a leap" when she relates with others. "Trust means doing what you say you are going to do." Two trafficked women in McCrory's study concurred: "[M]ost people can't or won't talk or open up unless they trust whoever they're talking to." Another echoed that trust is the most important aspect of aftercare. "Trust? I trusted nobody, no how, no way. I still

[51] Even believing this, one survivor said that "the hardest piece was God the father" because her father had been the exploiter.

[52] (van der Kolk, 2014).

have a hard time trusting anybody."[53] Particularly when working through trauma, there must be a safe place to share experiences, to develop trust with service providers or counsellors.[54]

Dodsworth said, "What is crucial in the development of a belief in one's acceptance and a consequent ability to move forward is the rebuilding of the ability to trust [...] that someone will be there for you and will listen in a non-judgmental, non-rejecting way. From this starting point, it appears that the women began to build a sense of self-esteem and self-worth and a belief in their own ability to say who they are [...]. 'Listening is the key [...] If I know that you're really listening then I'll tell you.'"[55]

Telling Their Stories in a Community of Belonging

All survivors stressed that telling their stories was inseparably linked to being in supportive relationships, feeling accepted and belonging. However, as one survivor said, "You never know what's going to happen." When she shared her story in her church, she expected her words would get twisted. "But it was one of those incidents where I felt the benefits could outweigh the risks." She found that to be the case.

A survivor in McCrory's research said,

> I feel like I improve my recovery and healing every time I stand up in front of a group or church to talk about trafficking and the sex trade. Every time I say the words I make a little more progress and when I talk to girls who have just escaped or been rescued or however they got out, I feel like I get a little piece of myself back.[56]

You don't tell your real story outside being accepted, having supportive relationships, and a community of belonging. For survivors, this is often with other survivors. "Meeting with survivors is the most healing thing on earth. We can say things to each other that we understand." Some survivors in India avoided re-integrating with family and community, but rather chose to remain in the group homes they became part of after their escape from the brothels. They found a "new family, forged out of a common identity [...] and find comfort in these groups".[57]

Two survivors from Joseph's study offer a contrasting illustration. For Nirma, dealing with feelings of anger and fear was helped through a religious support system. Another survivor, Madira, "feels alone, abandoned, and empty. Unlike Nirma, she seems to lack the support system or spiritual grounding to move beyond her anger".[58]

---

[53] (McCrory, 2015: 114).

[54] (Jones, 2014). One survivor told me that trust was the single most important quality or characteristic that someone should have, if that person were to be supportive of her in her journey.

[55] (Dodsworth, 2015: 191). This quote is from a woman in her study who was exiting sex work.

[56] (McCrory, 2015: 143).

[57] (Joseph, 2009: 41).

[58] (Joseph, 2009: 29).

That said, having supportive relationships and being loved and cared for can also be threatening to survivors. One remembered living with extended family members at one point: "It was difficult because they actually cared." She was not accustomed to that. However, the long-term viability of supportive relationships is not a guarantee. She and another survivor recounted that sharing their pasts with their husbands actually cost them their marriages.

While there are those who have been hurt and/or abused within the Christian community, we should not dismiss those whose involvement has been healing and transformative. The survivors I interviewed confirmed this, as did the observation of practitioners who work in a safe home for survivors of sexual exploitation. Additionally, one survivor spoke of a guided prayer session that directly addressed forgiveness, and was something she found helpful and healing.

Shame

"I tried everything I could to bury every secret I had hidden for years [...] Everything was led by shame for me [...] Everything was shame based [...] Shame around the industry, sexual labor shame, body shame, interpersonal shame, family shame, etc [...] but I realized if I say it, if I out myself, I'm in control [...] The moment I came clean about it, I spoke at our adult fellowship about my story [...] I felt like God honored it so much. My shame disappeared, almost like it happened in one day. I felt like I released it." She felt she could forgive herself.

How poignantly said! And yet, for other survivors, it has not been so easy to overcome the shame associated with their past. One woman said, "The shame piece – I'm still working through it. I know that none of what happened to me is my fault. It is a constant reminding myself, that's not my life anymore." Another woman explained how every day she looked at herself in the mirror and said, "I forgive you." After a few weeks of doing this thing that she thought was "really stupid", one day it seemed to land and she wept and wept. "The emotional release I had been waiting for my entire life came rushing forward." Later, she said, "True self-forgiveness is letting it go. Something you have to do every day. Accepting it for what it was."

A practitioner asserted that shame leads to people developing denial. "When you can't access the things you are ashamed about, you can't move towards forgiveness. It's really hard to get to a place where the shame can be experienced and resolved, but it is such a critical part."[59] She believes we have created a culture around shame. "People talk about it, but when you are one on one with it [...] to get it to a palpable place where it is shapeable is hard. In this culture, shame has been pushed away [...] We don't allow access to it." It's as if shame is "a dirty word, [...] like you are saying f*** in church. But shame is a human emotion that we can experience in order to understand what the opposite is. Without it we can't understand what it is to be proud."[60]

---

[59] This point is parallel to what one survivor said about being healed from what she was finally willing to acknowledge.

[60] This is also referenced in Van Stokken, 2002: 342.

If justice is considered in the process of dealing with shame and forgiveness, there must be justice and it must be appropriate to the offence. For survivors in Joseph's (2009) study, justice was critical to their ability to forgive and particularly to forgive themselves.[61] Otherwise, "the shame is worse [...] Because it feels like it's your fault." This, the survivor said, is what keeps many victims from speaking out. Certainly, we know this to be the case with victims of rape. However, if a perpetrator is willing to take responsibility, it can make all the difference.[62]

Empathy

For survivors to extend forgiveness to the exploiters, empathy proves to be an extremely helpful attitude. One survivor said that having understanding created a place of empathy and helped forgiveness. "I need to first fully accept that it is coming from a place of brokenness," she said, as she spoke about the traffickers. "With the purchasers, they would be different, they would find excuses. It would be harder to get to the core of what they are doing" and thus harder to develop empathy for them. Another said that empathy and compassion are the best interventions for healing, characteristics that have enabled her to forgive the exploiters in her life, and also what she encourages when working with other survivors. Although not explicitly stated, what was clear in these interviews was the empathy that survivors had extended to themselves as they had grown in understanding of their histories and vulnerabilities.

Anger

Anger, one of the stages of grieving noted by Kübler-Ross and Kessler, is also a necessary stage of the healing process for traumatized people.[63] Survivors must face and embrace their justified feelings of anger. However, anger is typically associated with an unforgiving attitude, where the exploiter is demonized. Certainly, there is considerable support for this way of framing the exploiter but it is not a helpful approach. Two survivors spoke of their willingness to forgive their exploiters, and how other survivors were in disbelief, angry and frustrated about this. "It can be a righteous anger [...] that [still] leaves us trapped and bitter and [...] fuels us but it also drains us." Another survivor was challenged by others with the question: Don't you hate your traffickers? She did not, although she knows other survivors who do.

Joseph tells the story of Husna, who is "held captive by her distress, anger, depression, and fear [...] Her dreams of freedom from poverty and a good married life were shattered by the deception and betrayal of a family friend and the resulting slavery [...] She seeks no healing or forgiveness at this point, but

---

[61] (Joseph, 2009).

[62] This was according to one practitioner who had worked with many victims of sexual abuse and exploitation.

[63] (Kübler-Ross and Kessler, 2005).

instead secretly desires revenge. She is filled with bitterness [...] She refuses to trust anyone and has no friends."[64]

Culture

The tendency to even pursue forgiveness processes is linked to the culture of the survivor. In Indian and Asian societies, to be able to forgive the perpetrator or oneself is linked to karma, fatalism, caste, gender, status, views on virginity, etc. Forgiveness and healing take a different path. One practitioner who worked at a safe home said, "Forgiveness has to be a part of the way we live. Everything is done in the context of community – so as a community we would call people to forgiveness. There was no event, no rituals, it was just in the context of learning and knowing Jesus. And then you ask the question, who are those people we need to forgive. I never had a girl say to me, 'I'm having a hard time forgiving my perpetrator.'"

In fact, the line is blurred as to who should be forgiven: the one who is perpetrating the exploitation or the one who is not fulfilling their family duty. Where this practitioner worked, there were many cases where the perpetrator felt like they were doing the survivors a favor by getting them jobs and enabling them to earn money to support their families. Additionally, when the culture is a highly sexualized one, "having sex in a brothel isn't a big deal." What is a big deal is not being able to do what is expected of you, "what you were born to do." The different attitudes about sex and familial obligation weigh in on whether forgiveness is necessary for well-being or a moot point.[65]

Gratefulness

While it was not specifically something postulated in the beginning of this chapter, gratefulness is regularly cited as a construct of forgiveness. Here, we are not talking about being grateful for sexual exploitation – this is an absurd thought to say the least – but rather the journey of recovery. Two survivors I spoke with talked about their perspective on this construct. "I'm grateful for the experiences I've had. Because so many good things have come out of it," said one survivor. In another interview, she said gratefulness is definitely related to forgiveness. "Being thankful for being able to forgive yourself, that you were forgiven, absolutely. Being able to be forgiving allows you to be thankful for all you have. Thankful that I'm still alive, thankful that I can forgive and move on and now I have hope." Another survivor, as she described her journey of healing, expressed her thankfulness to God. "For the first time, I felt like God was imparting wisdom."

---

64 (Joseph, 2009: 38).

65 This issue of familial obligation as it relates to sexually exploited/trafficking survivors in Cambodia is covered well in The Butterfly Research Project's second paper: *Economic Reintegration of Survivors of Sex Trafficking: Experiences and Expressions of Filial Piety and Financial Anxiety*, 2016.

What I Believe to This Point

As I have attempted to convey the thoughts of survivors, the word "forgiveness" was not always said. Yet as these women acknowledged, this construct has been foundational in the process of their healing. By their choice, engaging in the forgiveness process was also not contingent on the offender's repentance. And why should it be? Why should one's freedom of mind and heart be limited by someone else?

Processes of forgiveness seem to function similarly across issues, as do those elements that influence forgiveness. In Sierra Leone's communal culture context, forgiveness and reintegration worked in tandem as a two-wheeled bicycle, within a framework of a community being present and ready to take a chance and enact practices of forgiveness. Culture dictated how survivors of sex trafficking understood their lives and futures. In cultures where individualism prevails, supportive relationships and a community of belonging made all the difference. In communal group cultures, such as Indian and Asian, having adequate support systems helped survivors move through highly charged emotions, such as anger, for the good. Yet, having one's past known was risky; how much more so to reveal those things we find most humiliating. To risk rejection for the possibility of being more deeply known is a challenge most of us want to avoid.

One of the most challenging constructs of forgiveness is forgiving the self – the difficulty being underpinned by shame. Even when people are clearly the victims of others, there is the prodding of something like a poker iron, pointing to the possibility that "you could have done differently" and "it is your fault." Here, empathy for the self proves especially helpful. We all do the best we can at the time with the resources we have. In lacking agency, understanding, experience, protective support, and much more, why would we then hold ourselves in an unforgiven state? Nevertheless, despite these vulnerabilities, and compounded by the automatic responses of the amygdala (which is literally outside the victim's control), survivors struggle with self-blame.

One survivor said, "When I think negatively about myself, I stop and say 'If I was hearing this from someone else, what would the reaction be to that person?'" She doesn't expect to experience the forgiveness that she longs for until she sees Jesus. "That's how I'm going to face God, as his child. Maybe the consequence of that decision [made a while back] is feeling the pain for what I did."

Does forgiveness ever find its way to perfection? I think not. Forgive us our forgiving, even of ourselves.

Moving Forward

I find in the stories of these women a resilience and courage that is beyond admirable. I saw the same in the Sierra Leonean people. Resilience has been directly linked to the survivor finding her voice and using it in a way that is beneficial for her.[66] It is therefore not surprising that the stories of these women illustrate remarkable resilience and courage.

Still, what does this have to do with forgiveness? Is it even ethical to ask whether a survivor should consider forgiving? Should there be a cap on forgiveness, or a restriction on who should and should not be forgiven? In the words of a survivor:

> That's a choice […] but the bottom line for me is that I would always move in the direction of forgiveness being limitless. That is an ideal of mine. Whether or not I would be able to have empathy for some of these folks, to want the best for them – that's another practical question.

One survivor talked about enemy love; "the idea of loving the people who have wounded you the most. How can I honor your humanity? How can I recognize what you did and why you did it, how can I bring dignity and humanity to you, because it would be so easy to demonize." She said, "There's disbelief that I would actually forgive someone. There's frustration that I would offer someone the same kind of freedom we all want."

In fact, she did offer that. In speaking of the perpetrator, she said:

> I felt so much freedom. For him to understand that I forgave him, and then for him to have been able to move past it […] That's when I understood how significant it was for me to listen to him. God gave me a gift, and he got to die knowing that I was okay, that I was releasing him.

Herman believes that forgiving is "out of reach for most ordinary humans".[67] Arendt, on the other hand, refers to Jesus likening "the power to forgive to the more general power of performing miracles, putting both on the same level" and yet also within humanity's reach.[68] My personal experience of forgiving has not included being a victim of exploitation. Yet I have relied on God to move in a direction of forgiving that seemed utterly impossible otherwise. I regularly miss the mark, and must proactively call to mind the premise of practicing forgiveness I have come to rely on: Forgive us our forgiving. I can only imagine the challenge survivors of sexual exploitation must face.

Reflection Questions

1. In your work, have you seen practices of forgiveness impacting particular individuals? If so, what factors (constructs, practices, and attitudes) were involved in the process?
2. What are some ways that you can be proactive in incorporating constructs, practices, and attitudes of forgiveness that will facilitate and/or enable this process for people who have been sexually exploited? How can we incorporate this into our work with survivors?

---

[66] (Banyard and Williams, 2007).
[67] (Herman, 1992: 190).
[68] (Arendt, 1958: 247).

3. In your work, or your own life, how have you understood the role of shame and empathy, as it has to do with self-forgiving and recovery?

Works Cited

Adams, Marilyn M. "Forgiveness: A Christian model". *Faith and Philosophy* 8(3), (1991): 277-304.

Allender, Dan B. *Healing the Wounded Heart: The Heartache of Sexual Abuse and the Hope of Transformation.* Grand Rapids, MI: Baker Books, 2016.

Anderson, Pamela S. "A feminist ethics of forgiveness". In A. McFadyen and M. Sarot, Eds. *Forgiveness and Truth.* Edinburgh: T & T Clark, 2001: 145-55.

Arendt, Hannah. *The Human Condition.* Chicago, IL: University of Chicago Press, 1958.

Armour, Marilyn P. and Mark S. Umbreit. "The paradox of forgiveness in restorative justice". In E.L. Worthington Jr, Ed. *Handbook of Forgiveness.* New York: Routledge, 2005: 491-503.

Augsburger, David W. *Pastoral Counselling Across Cultures.* Philadelphia, PA: Westminster Press, 1986.

—–. *Helping People Forgive.* Louisville, KY: Westminster John Knox Press, 1996.

Bales, Kevin and Ron Soodalter. *The Slave Next Door.* Oakley, CA: University of California Press, 2009.

Banyard, Victoria and Linda Williams. "Women's voices on recovery: A multi-method study of the complexity of recovery from child sexual abuse". *Child Abuse & Neglect* 31(3), (2007): 275-290.

Bash, Anthony and Melanie Bash. "Early Christian thinking". In F. Watts and L. Gulliford, Eds. *Forgiveness in Context: Theology and Psychology in Creative Dialogue.* London: T & T International, 2004: 29-49.

Beste, Jennifer. "Recovery from sexual violence and socially mediated dimensions of God's grace: Implications for Christian communities". *Studies in Christian Ethics* 18(2), (August 2005): 89-112.

Biggar, Nigel. "Forgiveness in the Twentieth Century: A review of the literature, 1901-2001". In A. McFadyen and M. Sarot, Eds. *Forgiveness and Truth.* Edinburgh: T & T Clark, 2001: 181-217.

—–. *Burying the Past: Making Peace and Doing Justice after Civil Conflict.* Washington DC: Georgetown University Press, 2003.

Chircop, Lionel. "Re-membering the future". In A. Falconer and J. Liechty, Eds. *Reconciling Memories.* 2nd Edn. Dublin: The Columba Press, 1998: 20-29.

Clawson, Heather J., Salomon, Amy, and Goldblatt-Grace, Lisa. 2008. "Treating the Hidden Wounds: Trauma Treatment and Mental Health Recovery for Victims of Human Trafficking". *ASPE Website.* 14th March 2008. [Available at: https://aspe.hhs.gov/report/treating-hidden-wounds-trauma-treatment-and-mental-health-recovery-victims-human-trafficking - TOC], [Last accessed: 26th October 2022].

Cose, Ellis. *Bone to Pick: Of Forgiveness, Reconciliation, Reparation, and Revenge*. New York: Atria Books, 2004.

Cyuma, Samuel. "Conflict Reconciliation in South Africa (1990-1998) and its Significance for the Mediating Role of the Church in Rwanda (1990-2005)". PhD diss., University of Wales, 2005.

Daly, Gabriel. "Forgiveness and Community". In A. Falconer and J. Liechty, Eds. *Reconciling Memories.* 2nd Edn. Dublin: The Columba Press, 1998: 63-82.

Dodsworth, Jane. *Pathways into Sexual Exploitation and Sex Work: The Experience of Victimhood and Agency*. Palgrave Macmillan: Basingstoke, 2015.

Enright, Robert and Johanna North. *Exploring Forgiveness*. Madison, WI: The University of Wisconsin Press, 1998. See especially the following chapters:

Enright, Robert, Suzanne Freedman and Julio Rique. "The psychology of interpersonal forgiveness"; and

Flanigan, Beverly. "Forgivers and the unforgivable."

Harris, Jo. "Reconciliation as remembrance: It takes two to know one". In A. Falconer and J. Liechty, Eds. *Reconciling Memories.* 2nd Edn. Dublin: The Columba Press, 1998: 63-82.

Goins, Stephanie L. *Forgiveness and Reintegration: How the transformative process of forgiveness impacts child soldier reintegration.* Oxford: Regnum, 2015.

——. "The Concept of Forgiveness as Reflected in the Writings of Albert Ellis and Jay Adams." Masters Dissertation, University of West Florida, 1987.

Govier, Trudy. Forg*iveness and Revenge*. London: Routledge, 2002.

——. *Taking Wrongs Seriously: Acknowledgment, Reconciliation, and the Politics of Sustainable Peace*. Amherst, NY: Humanity Books, 2006.

Hamber, Brandon E. "Repairing the Irreparable: Dealing with doublebinds of making reparations for crimes of the past". Paper presented at the African Studies Association of the UK Biennial conference, Johannesburg, 1998.

——. "Does the truth heal? A psychological perspective on political strategies for dealing with the legacy of political violence". In N. Biggar, Ed. *Burying the Past: Making Peace and Doing Justice after Civil Conflict.* 2nd Edn. Washington DC: Georgetown University Press, 2003: 155-76.

Herman, Judith. *Trauma and Recovery*. New York: Basic Books, 1992.

Holmgren, Margaret. "Forgiveness and self-forgiveness in psychotherapy". In S. Lamb and J.G. Murphy, Eds. *Before Forgiving: Cautionary Views of Forgiveness in Psychotherapy.* Oxford: Oxford University Press, 2002: 112-35.

Jones, Gregory. *Embodying Forgiveness*. Grand Rapids, MI: Eerdmans, 1995.

Jones, Meghan. "Leaving the Life: The Recovery Journey of Sex Trafficking Survivors". Dissertation Presented to the Faculty of the School of Psychology and Counseling Regent University, March 2014.

Joseph, Victor. "Stolen Lives: Dignity, Forgiveness, hope, and Future-Mindedness for Victims of Sex Trafficking in India". *Agape Research*

Foundation Website. 2009. [Available at: http://www.agaperesearchfoundation.org/arf2013/wp-content/uploads/2013/03/Stolen-Lives.pdf], [Last accessed: 26th October 2022].

Kübler-Ross, E. and D. Kessler, Eds. *On Grief and Grieving: Finding the Meaning of Grief Through the Five Stages*. New York City, NY: Simon & Schuster, 2005.

Macaskill, A., J. Maltby and L. Day. "Forgiveness of self and others and emotional empathy". *Journal of Social Psychology* 142 (2002): 663-5.

McCrory, Michelle L. "Trafficking in Women: When Survivors Find Their Voice". Ph.D. diss., University of North Carolina at Greensboro, 2015.

McCullough, Michael E., Steven Sandage and Everett Worthington, Jr. *To Forgive is Human: How to Put Your Past in the Past*. Downers Grove, IL: Intervarsity Press, 1997.

McKeganey, Neil and Marina Barnard. *Sex Work on the Streets: Prostitutes and Their Clients*. Buckingham: Open University Press, 1996.

Morris, Herbert. "Murphy on forgiveness". *Criminal Justice Ethics* 7(2), (1988): 15-19.

Morrison, Todd, Siobhan Miles, Vanntheary Lim, Channtha Nhanh, Phaly Sreang and Davin Bun. *Survivor Experiences and Perceptions of Stigma: Reintegrating into Community*. 2015. [Available at: http://gmmiles.co.uk/wp-content/uploads/2016/02/Butterfly+2015+Stigma+Thematic.pdf], [Last accessed: 26th October 2022].

Murphy, Jeffrie G. and Jean Hampton. *Forgiveness and Mercy*. Cambridge: Cambridge University Press, 1988.

Rogers, Carl. *A Way of Being*. Boston, MA: Houghton Mifflin, 1980.

Rowden, Trampas J. and Sean D. Davis. "Forgiveness in Families". *Forever Families Website*. 22nd June 2005.

Sandage, Steven J. and Ian Williamson. "Forgiveness in cultural context". In E.L. Worthington Jr, Ed. *Handbook of Forgiveness*. New York: Routledge, 2005: 41-55.

Santer, Mark. "The reconciliation of memories". In A. Falconer and J. Liechty, Eds. *Reconciling Memories*. 2nd Edn. Dublin: The Columba Press, 1998: 30-36.

Schreurs, Nico. "Truth and reconciliation: Is radical openness a condition for reconciliation?" In A. McFadyen and M. Sarot, Eds. *Forgiveness and Truth*. Edinburgh: T & T Clark, 2001: 131-38.

Shriver, Donald. *An Ethic for Enemies: Forgiveness in Politics*. Oxford: Oxford University Press, 1995.

Shults, F. LeRon and Steven J. Sandage. *The Faces of Forgiveness: Searching for Wholeness and Salvation*. Grand Rapids, MI: Baker Academic, 2003.

Smith-Brake, Julia, Vanntheary Lim and Channtha Nhahn. "Economic Reintegration of Survivors of Sex Trafficking: Experiences and Expressions of Filial Piety and Financial Anxiety". The Butterfly Longitudinal Research Project: A Chab Dai study on (Re-) integration: Researching the lifecycle of sexual exploitation & trafficking in Cambodia. Phnom Penh: Chab Dai, 2015. [Available at: https://static1.squarespace.com/static/55a81f9be4b01a30079bb9d3/t/5705ec4b59827e22b3443991/1477607265832/BLR+2015+Thematic+Paper+Economic+Reintegration_Final.pdf], [Last accessed: 26th October 2022].

van Deusen Hunsinger, Deborah. "Forgiving abusive parents: Psychological and theological considerations". In A. McFadyen and M. Sarot, Eds. *Forgiveness and Truth.* Edinburgh: T & T Clark, 2001: 71-98.

van der Kolk, Bessel. *The Body Keeps the Score*. New York: Viking, 2014.

van Stokkom, Bas. "Moral emotions in restorative justice conferences: Managing shame, designing empathy". *Theoretical Criminology* 6(3), (August 2002): 339-360. [Available at: https://journals.sagepub.com/doi/pdf/10.1177/136248060200600306], [Last accessed: 26th October 2022].

Volf, Miroslav. *Exclusion and Embrace: A Theological Exploration of Identity, Otherness and Reconciliation.* Nashville, TN: Abingdon Press, 1996.

—. *Free of Charge: Giving and Forgiving in a Culture Stripped of Grace.* Grand Rapids, MI: Zondervan, 2005.

Watts, Fraser. "Christian theology". In F. Watts and L. Gulliford, Eds. *Forgiveness in Context: Theology and Psychology in Creative Dialogue.* London: T & T International, 2004: 50-68.

Willmer, Haddon. "Jesus Christ the forgiven: Christology, atonement and forgiveness". In A. McFadyen and M. Sarot, Eds. *Forgiveness and Truth.* Edinburgh: T & T Clark: 2001 15-29.

Worden, J. William. *Grief Counselling and Grief Therapy: A Handbook for the Mental Health Practitioner.* 2nd Edn. London: Routledge, 1991.

Worthington Jr, Everett L., Ed. *Dimensions of Forgiveness: Psychological Research and Religious Perspectives.* 1st Edn. Vol. 1. Philadelphia, PA: Templeton Foundation Press, 1998.

—. *Forgiving and Reconciling: Bridges to Wholeness and Hope*. Downers Grove, IL: InterVarsity Press, 2003.

Wright, Frank. "Northern Ireland and the British-Irish relationship". In A. Falconer and J. Liechty, Eds. *Reconciling Memories.* 2nd Edn. Dublin: The Columba Press, 1998: 248-60.

Wright, Norman T. *Jesus and the Victory of God*. London: Society for Promoting Christian Knowledge, 1996.

THE BIBLICAL STORY OF TAMAR AS A CHILD RAPE AWARENESS TOOL[1]

Genevieve James

Introduction

During 2020, as the world battles the ravages of the COVID-19 virus, many nations have restricted movement and implemented lockdowns to curtail the spread of the virus. And amidst the global pandemic a longstanding, unending war waged on the rights and wellbeing of children continues. Children's rights advocates are highlighting the painful impact of the lockdown on children (such as Human Rights Watch). As millions of children around the world are out of school, many children are bearing the brunt of increasing domestic violence. The COVID-19 death toll has left many children orphaned. Children's vulnerability has been exacerbated because of this global disaster.

In nations across the world, children experience gross human rights violations, trauma and suffering. Children are sexually abused by family members and care givers. Children are highly desired commodities that can be bought and sold for profit. Desperate communities fall prey to the sinister schemes of dubious criminals who offer "employment" to children who can supposedly send money back home. Used and abused, these children are often never seen again, as they disappear amongst the teeming multitudes in cities across the world. The bondage of enslaved child labor continues, despite certain governments' attempts to hide this from the world. Entire industries are being fueled by child labor.

The blood, sweat, and tears of children are not ignored by the God who has a special place for the broken, abused, and distressed. So critical questions that need consideration include: What is the role of the faith community in advocating for the well-being and safety of children? How can biblical texts be deployed in our child advocacy and awareness drives? This chapter explores one biblical story of exploitation found in the Old Testament book of 2 Samuel and makes a case for why this story should be included in children's Bibles. It then explains how this text became the basis of a child rape awareness tool and gives

[1] The article is a revised version based on two earlier publications: Genevieve James. "Tell It Like It Is! The Case to Include the Story of the Rape of Tamar in Children's Bibles as an Awareness Tool". *Journal for Semitics* 16(2), (2007): 312-332, and Genevieve James. "Resource for Children-at-Risk: The Story of Tamar as a Tool to Combat Child Rape", in John Baxter-Brown, Ed. *Mission To, For and With Children-at-Risk: A Kairos Moment for the Whole Church*, Papers from the Lausanne Movement's Consultation on Children-at-Risk, Quito, November 2014. Published 2017: 216-237.

an overview of the tool itself. Finally, it addresses issues and concerns that arise in using the tool and acting to combat child rape.

The South African Context

Before I explore the biblical story, in this section, I describe the South African context from which I write, and from which the motivation for the development of this tool originated.

According to 2016 Optimus Study:

- 35.4% of South Africa's children experience some form of sexual abuse,
- 34.8% of children experience physical violence,
- The South African child homicide rate is more than double the global average,
- Children younger than five years are at risk of fatal child abuse by someone close to them.[2]

The child rape situation in South Africa is nationwide, underreported, and devastating. We constantly read harrowing reports of child abuse and hear horror stories of the rape and murder of minors. Little children and even babies undergo colonoscopies and hysterectomies after being raped. The extent of the physical injury is distressing as some babies have had to undergo "extensive reconstructive surgery to rebuild urinary, genital, abdominal, or tracheal systems".[3] Despite several high-profile child and baby rapes that precipitated the anger and revulsion of the nation, tragically the incidence of child rape continues unabated, this despite stricter legislation. Sexual violence has perpetuated every place, even the sacred space of the home and the church. Children with chronic illness and or disabilities, and orphans, many of whom lost parent to AIDS, are often taken advantage of because of their vulnerability. Accompanying dangers, which include substance abuse, are at an all-time high and the average age of child addicts is decreasing.

Isaiah's vision of the New Jerusalem indicates the abnormality of infant death (Is. 65:17-25). Orphan is the word given to a child that has lost parents, yet in many languages there still is no word to describe parents who have lost their children since this goes against the natural order. It has become common for parents to bury their children. Children are dying of preventable causes due to improper health care in many regions. Other children are dying of opportunistic diseases brought about by HIV and AIDS. Sadly, children who are victims of sexual assault and abuse are even more vulnerable to HIV and AIDS. In South Africa, there is a decisive link between the high rate of sexual violence and HIV prevalence in young girls.

The situation is so toxic that there are now increased reports of violent crimes that are perpetuated by children themselves. A few years ago, a particular case reached the international media. A nine-year-old boy was "gang raped and

---

[2] (Jamieson, Berry and Lake, 2017).
[3] (Meier, 2002).

beaten with metal pipes and sticks by his friends,' two eight-year-olds, three eleven-year-olds and a thirteen-year old." According to CNN's Christiane Amanpour's blog titled, "The End of Innocence in South Africa: Children raping Children", his "friends" tied him to a tree and left him there over night.[4] In other cases, with accessibility to technology, children video record their violent sexual exploits and circulate it to their friends.

The failure to educate to children about the threat and dangers of rape has catastrophic results. Despite the crisis, there is still a marked deficiency of education and awareness on sexual violence. Children are hearing about rape and sexual violence from each other. They grow up amidst sexual assault, rape, and gender violence. They are exposed to sexual violence through every form of media. Sunday schools and children's churches rarely discuss the issue of rape and sexual assault, opting rather for Disney-styled entertainment. Sexual violence and rape certainly does not happen only in South Africa. Across the world, children experience unspeakable cruelty and reprehensible acts of sexual violence; there is therefore a critical need for vigilant and urgent action.

The Biblical Text

2 Samuel 13 (English Standard Version) reads:

> 1 Now Absalom, David's son, had a beautiful sister, whose name was Tamar. And after a time Amnon, David's son, loved her. 2 And Amnon was so tormented that he made himself ill because of his sister Tamar, for she was a virgin, and it seemed impossible to Amnon to do anything to her. 3 But Amnon had a friend, whose name was Jonadab, the son of Shimeah, David's brother. And Jonadab was a very crafty man. 4 And he said to him, "O son of the king, why are you so haggard morning after morning? Will you not tell me?" Amnon said to him, "I love Tamar, my brother Absalom's sister." 5 Jonadab said to him, "Lie down on your bed and pretend to be ill. And when your father comes to see you, say to him, 'Let my sister Tamar come and give me bread to eat, and prepare the food in my sight, that I may see it and eat it from her hand.'" 6 So Amnon lay down and pretended to be ill. And when the king came to see him, Amnon said to the king, "Please let my sister Tamar come and make a couple of cakes in my sight that I may eat from her hand."
>
> 7 Then David sent home to Tamar, saying, "Go to your brother Amnon's house and prepare food for him." 8 So Tamar went to her brother Amnon's house, where he was lying down. And she took dough and kneaded it and made cakes in his sight and baked the cakes. 9 And she took the pan and emptied it out before him, but he refused to eat. And Amnon said, "Send out everyone from me." So everyone went out from him. 10 Then Amnon said to Tamar, "Bring the food into the chamber that I may eat from your hand." And Tamar took the cakes she had made and brought them into the chamber to Amnon her brother. 11 But when she brought them near him to eat, he took hold of her and said to her, "Come, lay with me, my sister." 12 She answered him, "No, my brother, do not violate me, for such a thing is not done

[4] Christiane Amanpour, "The End of Innocence in South Africa: Children raping Children", *CNN*. 25th February 2014. [Available at: https://amanpour.blogs.cnn.com/2014/02/25/the-end-of-innocence-photos-of-child-sexual-abuse-in-south-africa/], [Last accessed: 26th February 2022].

in Israel; do not do this outrageous thing. 13 As for me, where could I carry my
shame? And as for you, you would be as one of the outrageous fools in Israel. Now
therefore, please speak to the king, for he will not withhold me from you." 14 But
he would not listen to her, and being stronger than she, he violated her and lay with
her.

15 Then Amnon hated her with very great hatred, so that the hatred with which he
hated her was greater than the love with which he had loved her. And Amnon said
to her, "Get up! Go!" 16 But she said to him, "No, my brother, for this wrong in
sending me away is greater than the other that you did to me." But he would not
listen to her. 17 He called the young man who served him and said, "Put this woman
out of my presence and bolt the door after her." 18 Now she was wearing a long
robe with sleeves, for thus were the virgin daughters of the king dressed. So his
servant put her out and bolted the door after her. 19 And Tamar put ashes on her
head and tore the long robe that she wore. And she laid her hand on her head and
went away, crying aloud as she went.

20 And her brother Absalom said to her, "Has Amnon your brother been with you?
Now hold your peace, my sister. He is your brother; do not take this to heart." So,
Tamar lived, a desolate woman, in her brother Absalom's house. 21 When King
David heard of all these things, he was very angry. 22 But Absalom spoke to
Amnon neither good nor bad, for Absalom hated Amnon, because he had violated
his sister Tamar.

The Tamar Campaign: A Biblical Resource to Raise Children's Awareness about Child Rape

The Tamar Campaign for Children originated out of the Tamar Campaign which began in South Africa. The basis of the campaign is the story of the rape of Tamar found in the Old Testament book of 2 Samuel 13 which has been used across the world to raise awareness about issues of gender violence and rape. This story has facilitated community discussions and action towards safer neighborhoods and public concern on the rights of women and children. The Tamar Campaign is being conducted around the world and was initially structured for adults.

The campaign has five major objectives:

- To create an awareness of gender issues to untrained readers of the Bible, both men and women with particular emphasis on women.
- To empower women to speak about their abuse and to deal with these issues.
- To target key leaders in church and community such as pastors, youth leaders, women's group leaders, and NGOs.
- To conduct Bible studies on texts relating to abuse in the Bible by using the Contextual Bible study method.[5]
- To develop community and church-based support groups for abused and/or HIV+ women.

[5] (see West, 2004).

The Tamar campaign for children arose out of the adult campaign. After attending a Bible study on the Tamar story conducted by Professor Gerald West of the University of Kwa-Zulu Natal, I was immediately convinced about the need for such a tool in churches and communities at large and about the effectiveness of the Tamar campaign. As I began conducting the Tamar Bible study with women and youth groups, I discovered that gender violence and rape defied age, race, socio-economic status, educational level, or religious affiliation. The churches I primarily worked in often believed that they had the monopoly on morality, yet I began to discover sordid acts of abuse behind the outward acts of holiness. Certain biblical texts, which contained references to power, triumph, prosperity, and blessing, seemed to be more favored. The story of a young girl by the name of Tamar, whose own brother violated her trust, was a lesser-known biblical text. After facilitating the Bible study amongst adults, I decided to share the story at a pre-school close to my home. The teacher, who attended the Bible study for adults, granted me the permission to prepare the Tamar story for pre-school children aged 3 to 5.

As I began my preparation, I explored the nature of children's Bibles. I discovered that many children's Bibles did not contain the story of the rape of Tamar found in 2 Samuel 13. The tragic story of the rape of the daughter of David is amongst the conveniently disregarded content for children's Bibles. Children's Bibles are, instead, filled with stories of the heroic actions of improbable candidates for success, the victories and triumphs of the weak and young, and escapes from cruel villains. Stories about the suspense of the natural order like the parting of the sea, the sun standing still, the talking donkey, and the burning-bush (that didn't burn) remain firm favorites for inclusion in children's Bibles because of their thrill factor.

According to Bottigheimer, early versions of children's Bibles did include the story of Tamar.[6] Children were not shielded from the stories of rape, murder, and adultery during the sixteenth and seventeenth centuries. These acts were included in order to serve as "cautionary tales depicting the punishment of vice".[7] Bottigheimer offers this description of the development children's Bibles:

> It generally contained stories from Old Testament histories, the Apocrypha, New Testament gospels and acts. As a group these books included a paradigmatic tales of the creation, Fall and deliverance, stories of patriarchal heroes, and New Testament fulfillments of Old Testament pre-figurations (also called "types" or "figures") and prophecies.[8]

In due course, children's Bibles sought to primarily provide children with good moral lessons and positive role models. In an *Introduction to the Child's Bible,* the author emphasizes his view that the use of the Bible for children is for the purpose of moral formation.[9] The true use of the Bible is to be found in the moral principles which it supplies. To gain these, the Bible needs to be read and

---

[6] (Bottigheimer, 1993: 74).
[7] (Bottigheimer, 1993: 74).
[8] (Bottigheimer, 1993: 68).
[9] (Carpenter, 1906: vii-x).

studied intelligently. The object of the issue of the *Child's Bible* is to give help in this direction. The simple and morally-suggestive stories of the Bible are set down in the words of the most recent translation. The child is introduced, as it were, into that great house of life's interpretations in which so many have found moral invigoration and inspiration.[10]

Bible story compilations have carefully passed over the "X-rated" content of the Bible with the intention to protect children from the horrors of rape, gender violence, and murder. The problem with the children's Bibles is that there is a failure to consider that children are becoming increasingly aware of violence, sexual abuse, and manipulation in the world that they live in due to their increasing victimization.

Children's Bibles today are big sellers in their own right. According to Garrett, booksellers know that it "makes sense to have a well-stocked Bible section."[11] There has been a boom in children's Bible sales and Bible stories, which occurred since 1996 and shows no sign of diminishing. Bookstores in South Africa stock a wide variety of children's Bibles and stories from the Bible. The Bible is still regarded as a source of moral and spiritual formation and it is clear that Christian parents want to pass on the stories of the Bible to their children for this purpose. The stories included in children's Bibles are very similar to present day Disney stories. There is a tendency to oversimplify and purposely hide the "X-rated" content of the Bible. Parents feel uncomfortable discussing stories that contain sexual content with their children. Hence, the story of the rape of Tamar is usually considered inappropriate for inclusion in children's Bibles.

In an article titled "Beyond Noah's Ark", Garrett argues that children's exposure to the Bible should not be restricted to stories of "Noah's ark, David and Goliath and Jesus blessing the children." She believes that children should not be shielded from the violent content in the Bible since "the world is a violent place – a place where the forces of death and destruction often have the upper hand." Children are being raped and sexually assaulted; as a result, this story has to be shared.[12]

The Development of the Tamar Story as an Awareness Tool

The story had to be child sensitive and presented in a child-suitable format considering the cognitive levels of children. It had to be streamlined and simplified in order to avoid confusion. The challenge I faced at this point was expressing the actual rape of Tamar to children. The question I struggled with was: how does one relate the story of rape to younger children? I then approached a counselor from the Office of the Family Advocate who had formerly worked with Child Line, a South African children's advocacy organization. She worked as a counselor for years and offered advice on how to discuss rape with children.

---

[10] (Carpenter, 1906: vii-viii).
[11] (Garrett, 1997: 29).
[12] (Garrett, 1997: 29).

The next step was to acquire information on writing stories specifically for children. According to Shephard, the theme of children's stories should emerge from the story as opposed to being blurted out.[13] It is advised that the theme should be expressed in dialogue instead of narration. Shephard warns that children's stories should be "explorations of life" and not sermons. With regards to the Tamar story, the children are not explicitly told that what was happening to her was wrong, instead, the powerful dialogue between Tamar and Amnon is where the theme of the story emerges. Shephard advises that the plot of the story should be built around a conflict involving the main character. In the case of the Tamar story, there is a steady build-up of the plot, which leads to a dramatic climax, namely, the actual rape of Tamar. The conflict in the moments before the rape establishes the riveting nature of the story and gives the main character, Tamar, the well-deserved title as "the most articulate character in the story" and "one of the most articulate women in the Bible".[14]

Finally, Shephard encourages a simple approach to the structuring of children's stories.[15] The Tamar story is loaded with specific details; it was important to choose which details the story needed to remain coherent yet simple and uncomplicated. There are numerous interpretations of the story which shed different light on the characters. I opted to keep the story as clear and uncomplicated as possible to place emphasis on the theme without getting bogged down in the details. The story is long and in depth; it has a slow deliberate sequence of events, this had to be abridged in order not to confuse the children.

I approached Durban-based artist Brad Nairn, who was later commissioned to develop graphics of the characters in order to make them more accessible to today's children. I discussed the story with Nairn and shared my vision of the story board. The pictures of the characters needed to be inclusive in terms of race in order to be relevant to all children. I rewrote the story in a child-sensitive manner closely following the chronological order of the chapter. I then allocated specific units of texts to each graphic frame. The content was checked by a child counselor expert. The graphic frames were shown to the children as the story was told; sometimes other props such as dolls or puppets were used instead.

What follows is the version of the Tamar story for children aged 5 to 10. I am of the opinion, that what I have actually done with the story of Tamar for children is write what biblical scholars call a *midrash. Midrash* comes from a Hebrew word meaning "to go in search of" or "to enquire." The midrash resulted when the rabbis went in search of the meaning of the text for their lives. A neo-midrash is a process where a new reading of the text is created for interested parties. In essence, I have re-read the story of Tamar, enquiring its relevance for children in our present context.[16]

---

[13] (Shephard, 2000).

[14] (West *et al*., 2004: 36; 24)

[15] (Shephard, 2000).

[16] See M. Williams, *The Storyteller's Companion to the Bible-Old Testament Women* (Nashville, TN: Abingdon Press, 1993): 129-134 for a readable discussion on the midrash.

The Tamar Story for Children Aged 5-10

Long ago in the land of Israel, lived a king whose name was David. Now King David had many children. This story is about three of his children: Amnon, Tamar, and Absalom.

(At this point, if using dolls repeat the names of the characters and get the children to say the names on their own as you point to the characters/dolls.)

2 Samuel 13:1-5

One day Amnon was behaving as though he was sick and sad because he thought he was in love with his sister Tamar. Amnon had a cousin named Jonadab who was a very cunning, sly person. Jonadab asked Amnon: "You are the king's son, Amnon, tell me why are you so sad and sick?"

Amnon answered, "I am in love with my sister Tamar!" So Jonadab said, "Lie down on your bed and pretend that you are sick. When your father comes to see you tell him to send Tamar to cook some food and feed it to you."

2 Samuel 13:6

So Amnon asked his father, King David, to send Tamar to cook for him while he was pretending that he was sick. (Children, how many of you have pretended to be sick when you did not want to go to school?)

2 Samuel 13:7

King David sent Tamar to the house of Amnon to cook for him so that he would feel better.

Samuel 13:8

Tamar obediently went to Amnon's house and baked cakes for him.

2 Samuel 13:9-11

When the cakes were ready, Tamar took the cakes to Amnon but he refused to eat them. He told her to tell everybody to leave his house. Everyone was sent out. Amnon said to Tamar "Sleep with me, my sister" (he wanted her to let him touch her private parts, he wanted to rape her.)

2 Samuel 13: 12-13

Tamar said "NO, my brother, do not make me do such a wrong thing; this is not done in our country. Do not do this shameful thing! I will be ashamed, and you will be a fool. Ask the king for permission."

2 Samuel 13:14-16

Amnon, who was stronger than Tamar, did not listen when she said NO. Instead, he forced himself on her. After he did this terrible thing, he hated her and sent her away. She begged him not to but he did not want to listen. She said to him, "No, my brother, for this wrong in sending me away is greater than the other that you did to me."

2 Samuel 13:17-19

Amnon told his servants to throw Tamar out of the house and lock the door. Tamar was wearing a beautiful long dress that day. The servants threw her out. Tamar was so sad and hurt about what Amnon did to her body that she cried aloud and tore her beautiful dress.

2 Samuel 13:20-22

When Absalom, Tamar's other brother, saw her he asked her not to cry aloud and kept her in his house. When the king heard what Amnon did to Tamar, he was very angry. Absalom did not speak to Amnon again. He hated him for what he did to Tamar.

Conclusion of the Story

So ends the story of Tamar, she lived sad and hurt in the house of her brother Absalom.

The Discussion Time

After the story is told, the children are invited to interact with the story through questions and discussion. These interactions are often lively and animated. A set of simply-worded questions are provided in order to engage the children in a reflection on the story.

The Discussion Questions

Below are the questions formulated for younger children, followed by the children's general responses. These questions are added to and deepened for older children.

1. What do you think this story is about?
   - *The story is about Tamar who was hurt and sad.*
   - *A brother who hurt his sister.*
   - *Rape.*
2. Who is the person that you like/is good/is right in the story? Why?
   - *Tamar is good/liked because she was kind and obedient. We feel sorry for her.*
   - *Absalom is good since he took his sister to his house.*
3. Who is the person that you dislike/is bad/is wrong in the story? Why?
   - *Amnon is bad/not liked.*
   - *He made Tamar cry when he touched Tamar where he was not supposed to touch her/ when he raped her.*
   - *He was cruel to his sister.*
4. What did you think about David, Absalom and Jonadab?
   - *David and Absalom are good.*
   - *Jonadab was naughty/bad because he told Amnon to lie, gave him a bad idea.*
5. What did Tamar say to Amnon when he was attacking her?
   - *Tamar said "No, do not do this." "You are my brother."*
6. How did Tamar feel in the story?
   - *Tamar was hurt, she felt sad and cried a lot.*
7. Do you know any children who was hurt/raped like Tamar?
   - *Yes.*
8. What can we learn from the story of Tamar?
   - *Be careful of people who want to be alone with you.*
   - *Family/people you know can also hurt you, not only strangers.*
   - *Scream and say NO when someone tries to touch you or grab you.*
   - *Do not be keep quiet, tell someone you trust if such a thing happens to you.*
   - *Do not listen to friends who tell you to lie.*

About the Discussion Time

The children are not explicitly told whose behavior in the story is right or wrong, or which characters they should sympathize with or reject. They make these choices on their own accord. The children are free to interpret the story as they choose to. The Tamar for Children program provides the space where children can express their evaluation of the characters in their own words and co-determine possible safety measures.

An interesting observation is that pre-school children were more likely to view the characters as either "bad" or "good." In the pilot programs, questions 2 and 3 asked "Who is the person that you like/is good and dislike/is bad in the story?" In later programs, the danger in this oversimplification of character was explained: People who can appear to be "good" and kind can be guilty of wrong behavior like rape and sexual abuse. After the time of questions and answers, a discussion takes place illustrating the difference between appropriate/right and inappropriate/wrong behavior. The children are cautioned that people who appear to be friendly and loving (hugging, kissing, and touching) are not necessarily to be trusted.

Another observation is that when the same story was discussed amongst adults, there was a tendency for some (particularly men) to question the moral standing of Tamar by suggesting that she had in some way brought the attack upon herself. Yet, in all the children's programs I have conducted, children have never seen Tamar as liable for her rape. Both boys and girls almost immediately sympathize with Tamar. This could indicate that younger boy children had not (yet) been socialized to consider girl rape victims as liable for their own rapes. Against this backdrop when discussing this story with adults, be sure to state that the intention is not to raise anti-men sentiment but to address a critical challenge in society facing all communities.

Practical Issues to Discuss with Children Arising from the Text

In addition to the questions about the story itself, the following practical issues should be discussed:

1. What kind of behavior/touching should be considered as inappropriate?
2. What areas of the body should be considered as personal and private?
3. What can children do if someone tries to harm them? Why is it important to scream, run, and tell?
4. Who are the people/child protection organizations that can be trusted and contacted in time of need? What and where are the contact details?
5. Are rapists always strangers? What is the process of grooming?
6. How can we respect our own bodies and others?
7. What is love, hate, and lust? (Generally, a discussion for older children around 10 years and older).
8. What is the value of children to God, family, and community?

As the children respond to the questions, it is important to reinforce important issues such as the importance of saying no to inappropriate touching. Clarify where the private places in the body are, by taking a picture of a woman and man in a swimwear and point to the areas that are private. Clearly explain to the children that despite these being private places their whole bodies are special and, as such, if they feel that they are being touched anywhere on their bodies that arouse strange or uncomfortable feelings, they must run away and inform someone they trust. Explain that not everyone who touches them means to hurt them, however they must be careful to detect risk. Discuss other issues such as the myth of stranger-danger, which falsely assumes that all abusers are strangers, as this is not the case. Make children aware that it is perfectly acceptable to fight off anyone who attempts to harm or abuse them. Sadly, it is also necessarily to explain that if a rape does occur, children are not to assume blame or remain silent.

Adaptations for Older Audiences

The story structure and method of operation presented in this article is specifically developed for younger children. The Tamar story has also been developed for teenagers and young adults. For each of these age groups, there are different methods of operation such as group readings and discussions, debates, and the use of art and music. The questions and issues for discussion are expanded on and conversation is deepened, particularly regarding the dysfunctional nature of the family (brother loves, then rapes, then hates, his sister; cousin gives bad advice; father does not know what's going on in the family; brother hates brother who raped sister; further back in the book, dad kills loyal soldier and impregnates soldier's wife, then marries her; further forward, brother kills brother who raped sister then wants to dethrone dad, then dies).

Training in the Tamar Story

Training has taken place across South Africa and with church workers across the world[17] to equip interested parties to facilitate this Bible story with children. The training is workshop-based and is designed to enable parents, community activists, teachers, church leaders, and NGO workers to sensitively facilitate community Bible studies for children that deal with rape, gender constructs, and gender violence. The facilitators are given the tools of creative engagement with children, storytelling, and information packages on rape and gender-violence issues.

Important Cultural and Ethical Considerations

Dealing with children requires special permission, skills, and abilities. The issues of gender violence and rape are particularly sensitive since they include issues of sex, power, and cultural taboos. It is imperative that facilitators tread carefully and sensibly. Before proceeding, a written ethical clearance and permission from the relevant gatekeepers must be sought. Explain clearly what the process would entail. Do not attempt to conduct the campaign without sufficiently exploring the specific cultural and ethical considerations of your context. Always request that a trained child abuse counselor and/or social worker is present when telling children the story.

What You Can Do to Strengthen Your Action to Combat Child Rape

Learn

It is necessary to carefully understand your specific context to act relevantly and effectively. It is also important to gather information about your context.

- Gather case studies and other information on child abuse from your local child safety offices.

[17] The program was launched by the Council for World Mission by Mission Executive Secretary Elizabeth Joy in March 2009 in New Delhi, India.

- Consult with police, child welfare and protection services, and children's advocacy groups.
- Collect newspaper articles, magazines, and blogs on the social concerns in your community. Search particularly for information which concerns children's health, safety, and well-being.
- Be part of community safety networks and children's advocacy groups.
- Check that police have victim-friendly facilities and sex offender registers.

Listen

Talk to your children, make time for conversation.

- Listen to the children; don't ignore their concerns and comments.
- Create spaces where children can be authentically heard.
- Facilitate the voice of children in church liturgy, sermons, and church bulletins.
- Read stories written by children and explore children's art.
- Listen to the music generated by your community and country; listen also to the popular music that children listen to, watch the popular shows children watch (TV or Internet).

Observe

Open your eyes and see your community in a way that you have never seen it before.

- Look at your surroundings and explore your own neighborhood as a social and physical space.
- As a social space, a neighborhood consists of families, friends, relationships, and all forms of social networks. Understand these social networks and explore what threats and challenges children could encounter.
- Understand also how virtual social networks are formed among children. Know the sites children visit on the Internet and the special media platforms they use. Become aware of cyber-bulling and report internet sites that lure and abuse children. Improve your cyber security.
- As a physical space, your neighborhood constitutes of buildings and infrastructure. Know the possible sites of danger and discover the thinking behind the planning of your community and neighborhood. Request that the city fix broken streetlights and clear bushes, as well as address other potential threats to safety.

Question

Ask questions. Become curious. Decide to ask deeper questions about news stories.

- Why are children becoming victims of rape in their own homes, schools, churches?
- What cultural or religious systems keep children vulnerable to secret abuse in the home?

- What are the economic systems that keep communities locked in chronic poverty and unemployment?
- What is the difference between safety and security?

Critique

Analyze the policies and laws affecting children, as well as their implementation.

- Consider the definition of child and child rape in your country.
    - Is there enough legislation on child safety and protection?
    - Are there aspects of child protection laws that need to be amended or revised? If so, how can you and your faith community advocate for this?
- Critically explore the acts, laws, public documents, etc. on Children's Rights (in general), children's access to safety and protection, children's access to education and health care.
    - Discuss the effectiveness and implementation gaps of the child rights and protection laws in your country.
    - What is the level of awareness and understanding of these laws in your community?

Final Thoughts

The story of the violation of Tamar in the land of Israel thousands of years ago still has a potent, compelling message for us today. The story provides children with a point of reference regarding what is acceptable and unacceptable physical behavior. The children realize that familiar faces do not automatically represent faces of trust and reliance. More importantly, they also become sensitized to discern other potential threats to their safety. Tragically, I am aware that this may not be enough to prevent the "stronger" from preying on the weak, however it certainly is proving to, at least, serve as a tool of awareness.

Much has been written about the need to treat children with dignity and care and how children are precious in God's sight. These warm theological sentiments must translate into a firm and unequivocal understanding that children are not sexual objects for the satisfaction of perverts. They are not beasts of burden. They are not unclean, unable, or incapable. They are not inferior.

Parents, teachers, and ministers must recognize and understand the signs of our times and include this text in their lesson plans and sermons. Sunday Schools or children's churches do not generally discuss the issues of rape and sexual assault. We need to provide adequate training to church workers serving children.

We must work to pursue national and international networks and alliances that resonate with the Church's social justice mission, so we are better able to address issues pertaining to child vulnerability and risk. We need to continue the tradition of collaborative practice so that we can contribute to the establishment of the just reign of God in the local and global communities we serve.

There is a need for vigilant, urgent action. According to De Beer, "children should be more central on the agenda of theological education and reflection." De Beer asks the following essential question:

> Why is it that so little is said or done about children by the most prominent theologians of our world? There is a theological silence that needs to be overcome. Pastors need to take the lead in placing children on congregational agendas and in integrating children meaningfully into worship services and other events of the church. They need to affirm childcare workers much more as key members of the ministry team. They need to invest in the development of effective and knowledgeable childcare workers.[18]

Reflection Questions

1. What is the significance of children in the theology of your church?
2. What is the meaning of the "Good News" to children in the context of a violent and abusive world?
3. How does your church use the Bible (including the "hard" passages) in teaching children about abuse and exploitation?
4. What is the role of the faith community in advocating for the well-being and safety of children within the church, community, and country?

Works Cited

Amanpour, C. "The End of Innocence in South Africa: Children raping Children". *CNN*. 25th February 2014. [Available at: https://amanpour.blogs.cnn.com/2014/02/25/the-end-of-innocence-photos-of-child-sexual-abuse-in-south-africa/], [Last accessed: 26th February 2022].

Bottigheimer, R.B. "Bible Reading, 'Bibles' and the Bible for Children in Early Modern Germany". *Past & Present* 139(1), (May 1993): 66-89.

Carpenter, W. *The Child's Bible*. London: Cassel & Co, 1906.

De Beer, S. *The Gospel, Children and the City*. Pretoria: Tshwane Leadership Foundation, 2006.

Garrett, L. "The Bible still matters". *Publishers Weekly* 244(42), (1997): 29.

Human Rights Watch. "COVID-19's Devastating Impact on Children". *Human Rights Watch Website.* 9th April 2020. [Available at: https://www.hrw.org/news/2020/04/09/covid-19s-devastating-impact-children], [Last accessed: 26th October 2022].

Jamieson, L., L. Berry and L. Lake. *Child Gauge*. Cape Town: Children's Institute, University of Cape Town, 2017.

Meier, E. "Child Rape in South Africa". *Medscape* 28(5), (2002). [Available at: http://www.medscape.com/viewarticle/444213], [Last accessed: 26th October 2022].

---

[18] (De Beer, 2006: 13).

Shephard, A. "Writing your story: tips on how to write children's stories". *Aaron Shephard Website.* 2000. [Available at: http://www.aaronshep.com/kidwriter/index.html], [Last accessed: 26th October 2022].

West, Gerald and Phumzile Zondi-Mubizela. *The Bible study that became a campaign in South Africa (and beyond).* Ministerial Formation, Geneva: WCC publication, 2004: 4-12.

West, Gerald, Phumzile Zondi-Mabizela, Martin Maluleke, Happiness Khumalo, Phidian Smadz Matsepe and Mirolyn Naidoo. "Rape in the house of David: The biblical story of Tamer as a resource for transformation". *Agenda* 61(2004): 36-41.

Williams, M. *The storyteller's companion to the Bible-Old Testament Women.* Nashville, TN: Abingdon Press, 1993: 129-134.

Additional Reading

Cooper-White, P. *The Cry of Tamar: Violence against women and the Church's response.* Minneapolis, MN: Fortress Press, 1995.

Gravett, S. "Reading Rape in the Hebrew Bible: A consideration of language". *JSOT* 28(3), (2004): 279-299.

Haddad, B. "Gender violence and HIV/AIDS: A deadly silence in the church". *JTSA* 114 (2002): 93-106.

Neff, L. "Bible Stories: Facing a flood tide". *Publishers Weekly* 248(42), (2001): 38-39.

Sloth-Nielson, J. and L. Ehlers. "Assessing the Impact: Mandatory and Minimum sentences in South Africa". *Political Science South African Crime Quarterly* 14 (Dec 2005).

Smith, A. "Born again, Free from sin? Sexual Violence in Evangelical communities", In C. Adams and M.M. Fortune, Eds. *Violence Against Women and Children: a Christian theological sourcebook.* London: A & C Black, 1995: 339-350.

PARENTS AS AGENTS IN COUNTERING CHILD SEXUAL EXPLOITATION

Haddon Willmer

Introducing Pace

Pace[1] is a voluntary charity (non-profit organization) in the UK that supports parents whose children are sexually exploited or at risk of being so. Pace sees parents as prime agents in countering child sexual exploitation (CSE) and has learnt much about how to work with *parents as partners* since it was founded by a parent in 1996.

Fiona was 17 when she was murdered in a Doncaster carpark in 1995. Her mother, Irene Ivison, strove intensively for several years to help her gifted and lively daughter find her way through some difficult relationships, but she could not prevent her from falling under the control of Zeb who put her on the streets. Three weeks later, she was dead. Irene channeled her overpowering grief and anger into rational campaigning action, bringing together supportive individuals from police, social services, the law, medicine, and from this CROP, the Coalition for the Removal of Pimping, began. Irene told her story at every opportunity, on television and elsewhere. Parents whose children were being sexually exploited, or had been killed, heard and made contact with her.[2] CROP grew as a coalition of affected parents in action with allies. It took some years before CROP became fully aware of the significance of this distinctive composition and dynamic. By 2003, Carol March, its first full-time support worker, was saying to parents, "You are the experts on CSE, you know it in the raw, as the pimp calls out your daughter in the middle of the night, and she feels compelled to go. You not only see what it does to her, you get close-up information about pimps, like their car numbers". CROP always had parents in its leadership, and that continued after Irene's premature death in 2000 and long before it had many paid staff. In 2013, CROP's name changed to Pace, Parents against Child Sexual Exploitation, and its affirmation of parents as prime agents was written into the constitution of Pace, requiring a majority of the board of directors to be "affected parents". Pace listens to parents, makes opportunities for them to meet and support each other, and gives them platforms to tell their stories in their own ways, thus disturbing professionals and politicians with their informed passion. Pace trains professionals so that they can make the most of

---

[1] Pace website: https://paceuk.info. Some CROP/Pace publications and papers are archived in https://library.leeds.ac.uk/info/1500/special_collections (search term: parents against child exploitation).

[2] Irene Ivison, *Fiona's Story: A tragedy of our times* (London: Virago, 1997).

parents; it does this by giving parents a significant role in the training, for they are not specimens but agents.[3]

But Irene's first explicit focus was not to build a co-operative agency of parents. She identified two main objectives for CROP. One was proclaimed in the title, the reduction of pimping (there was no shyness then about using this contested and yet still true word). Irene claimed that two men had killed her daughter: the man in the carpark, who was brought to trial and imprisoned, and the man who put her on the streets, yet was left free, untouched by the law, to carry on exploiting others. Now that the grooming of young people on a large scale in many places in the UK has been exposed in the media, law-courts and enquiries, it is hard to remember the complacency, even jocularity, with which pimping was widely regarded in the late 20th century. It was not a police priority; it was assumed that young people who were prostituted were making a free life-style choice, which should be respected; pimps were not seen because they were hidden behind the name of "boyfriend" and other disguises. Irene identified the strategic responsibility of the pimp in the sexual exploitation of young people: his was a power that could defeat all the agencies professedly arrayed in her defense as can be seen in the following diagram. All this was clearly argued by participants in the first large national conference held by CROP: "Who are the real criminals in prostitution?" Their answer: not the prostituted women and children (who were at that time not sharply distinguished) but the pimps.[4]

The second objective was closely related to the first: a reform of the laws touching on sexual exploitation, with more precise updated definitions of offences and heavier penalties. Better laws needed a step-change in enforcement, so that exploiters were sought out, brought to justice, disrupted, and deterred. This improvement required a change in attitude in law-makers and law-enforcers, including judges, magistrates, the police, and agencies such as social services. The greater challenge was to change the profit-driven media and the widely-held assumption that sexual appetites, especially male, were irresistible. This continuing battle has been half-won, and half-lost. It is now no longer respectable or legal to engage children in any sexual way, but the highly-sexualized liberalism of adult society is harder to criticize or to limit. It seems to be widely accepted that when "sexual services" are paid for, the sexual activity implies no further or deeper personal relationship and obligation. Humanity is lost when payment of money buys exemption from respecting the rights and dignity of another person.[5]

---

[3] This training by Pace is immensely valuable. Little attention seems to be given to parents in the normal training and formation of professionals. Remedying this omission at an early stage in their formation would make for significant improvement.

[4] The conference report, *Stopping the Pimp* (1998) is a significant historical marker, showing how much wisdom and vision was available then. It has an abiding challenge, not least in the testimonies of victims. Its neglect is to be regretted, although it is not surprising given the impatient forward-looking activism of many who are at the forefront of the struggle against sexual exploitation.

[5] Rachel Moran, *Paid For: My Journey through Prostitution: Surviving a Life of Prostitution and Drug Addiction on Dublin's Streets* (London: W.W. Norton, 2015).

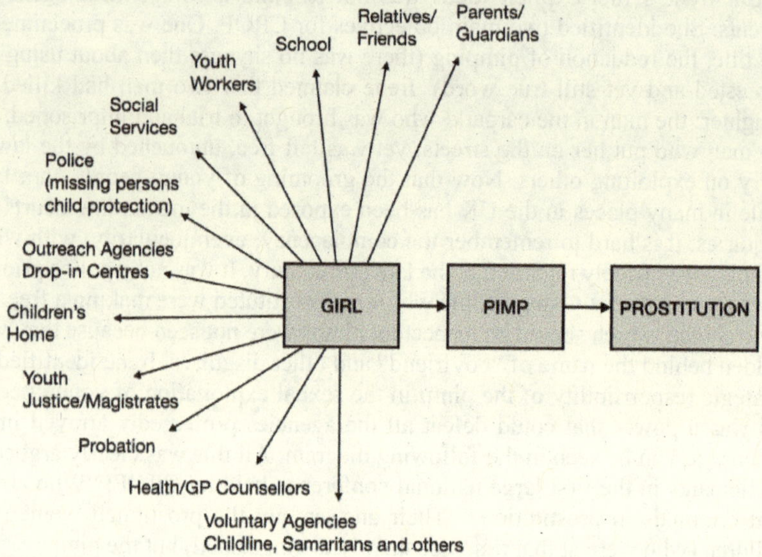

Figure 1

At the beginning, there was no mention of parents in the explicit objects of the coalition and the vision and program of work they pointed to. But as long as Irene was there, ardently drawing in and mobilizing other parents, it was impossible to deny the reality of parents and their striving for their children. They were the dynamic prophets of this distinctive new initiative; their witness had the authenticity of hard-won knowledge and costly engagement. CROP was on an inescapable journey to becoming aware of itself as *parents against child sexual exploitation*, and that involved the continuing struggle to ensure that parents were respected and included as agents and partners.

Parents – The Problem and the Promise

Can there be respect for parents as prime agents in responding to a major crisis in the child's life? Can they be taken as useful – even key – partners by professionals dealing with the issue? Parents are often marginalized, ignored, seen as incompetent, and thus part of the problem. Where professionals said "No" to parents as agents, Pace said "Yes" and it has contributed significantly to a shift in attitudes and practice over twenty years.

The problem has multiple causes.

Parents of teenage children are in a natural process of being left aside. The child makes her own way for better or worse.[6] Commonly, new adult-friendly relations are being forged within the family, if only painfully and erratically. Sometimes, there is a breakdown making repair unlikely.

The groomer exploits this natural process, offering a false prospectus to appeal to the young person's eagerness for life, presenting himself as the only one who really appreciates and understands, thus exacerbating his victim's impatience with the limitations of home and the irksome memory of being small. Alienating her from parents enhances the control of the clever exploiter.

Professional practice in its own way intensifies the marginalizing of parents. It meets some young people who have lost any practical connection with parents and so is bound to deal with them as detached individuals. This is obviously so with young people trafficked to a far country. But a majority of exploited teenagers in the UK live at home. Then the occurrence of exploitation is professionally interpreted as a sign of parental failure; the child comes from a "chaotic" family – an imprecise judgmental description that could cover many families where children do not fall to the exploiter. Often the family is suspected of neglect and sexual abuse, which is held to make the child vulnerable to extra-familial exploitation. So child sexual exploitation is treated as a sub-set of child sexual abuse. On the basis of evidence about affected families, derived from its work, Pace distinguishes sharply between intra-familial abuse and extra-familial exploitation.

Parents in the crisis present to professionals as naively innocent – they know little of CSE until it invades their lives, and at first they have no facility in the technical vocabulary. They are, however, forced quickly to become front-line experts. They are, not surprisingly, distraught, angry and impatient for action, sometimes out of tune with time-consuming professional procedures and detachment. They are inclined to disrupt orderly case reviews. Pace has worked hard to equip parents to engage with professional agencies, and to persuade the agencies that their effectiveness is enhanced by working with parents.[7] There has been significant improvement, but constant effort is needed to maintain it.

Against this triple tide of marginalization, a reminder of human basics is helpful. Parents are prime agents in the child's coming to be. The start of a new life often brings parents into a deeply felt lifelong commitment to a particular child or set of children. Even when parents make a sovereignly-free choice to adopt a child, or when they are fully armed against any accident of childbirth by contraception, the coming of a child speaks to their spirits at a deep visceral level; they find themselves profoundly committed, irked perhaps by the loss of freedom and the threat to their precious individuality, but also seduced into love by the little one, this epiphany of new life. The relation is in nature; it is prior to choice,

---

[6] Luke 15:11-24; Mark 10:7. In this paper, the feminine pronoun is used for convenience in referring to all victims of exploitation. Most victims are female, but not all. Pace has supported parents whose sons have been exploited.

[7] *Parents Speak Out: Crucial Partners in Tackling Child Sexual Exploitation* (Leeds, UK: Pace, 2016). [Available at: http://paceuk.info/wp-content/uploads/Parents-Speak-Out-final.pdf], [Last accessed: 26th October 2022].

sometimes against the will or the life-path parents choose for themselves. The origin lives powerfully in the memory: "my lovely baby" is a cry often heard when a mother mourns the devastation of her grown child at the hands of exploiters.

Parents are on call 24/7 over many years, and so, with whatever shortcomings, offer a practical reflection of the ideal of unconditional faithfulness. The relation of parent and child is resourced, as well as burdened, by the tangle of roots put down over the years. The long-developed habits of care and expectant dependency do not suddenly wither and die within parent or child. The father's house lurks within the memory of even the wanton prodigal, so that, when he "comes to himself", he decides to seek it again.[8] There is no need to idealize this relationship between parent and child: its having significance does not depend on any pretense of perfection. Parents and children mostly live together on a "good enough" basis. They learn resilience in the give and take of life. Parents who have not seen, or been unable to read the signs[9] of what is happening to their children often wake up and respond with energetic determination when serious trouble is obvious. They then show their responsibility and wisdom by seeking help and taking advice. Parents do not need to apologize or hide their failures when they come to Pace. They are accepted as they are, non-judgmentally, and then Pace highlights the strong positive significance of their coming: they are respected for their will to care for their child even in their impotence. A shared knowledge of the reality of CSE is presupposed in the community of Pace, so that no fuss is made of it. All energies are concentrated on appropriate support.

Against all marginalizations, the promise of the parent is to be welcomed in practical ways, for it is a rich resource.

Parenting in the Light of Theology

The lifelong commitment of parents to children, frail and faulty as it is, reflects the commitment of God to his children, to all his creatures. Parents are not God; but they are a little place where the potentiality of God in humanity is present and active. This presence may be partial, oblique and occasional. It is the kind of presence for which we wait, sometimes with thirsty impatience.[10] The presence of God is promise which calls for waiting with endurance; CSE gives parents testing practice in this style of life. Life is thus constituted as prayer, seeking for God and the fullness of life which God is; and as such, given this structure, parents in action for their children become living witnesses to forgiving redeeming grace, which abounds much more than sin.

[8] Luke 15:17.

[9] CROP's first publication, written by Irene Ivison, was *Advice to Parents who are concerned that their child is in an Exploitative Relationship,* and included a pioneering list of signs to alert parents to what might be happening.

[10] Psalm 42.

Pace and the Question of Secularity

This essay is intentionally a Christian theological reflection on CSE and Pace. Pace is a secular agency in a secular culture. Its secularity does not rest on a sharp division between religious and non-religious, but is an inclusive pluralism, open to people of any faith and none. Pace workers and parents are of all sorts, as varied in religious terms as in class and cultural terms. Secularity enables them to co-operate on what seem to be the practical issues of tackling CSE for the sake of the well-being of the young people, families and society affected by it. This non-militant secularity gently reduces any particular faith to silent privacy. Some religious people accept such an outcome with equanimity, but not all. Is an openly avowed and active religious faith bound to disturb the efficiency of the secularity? Does the wider community lose anything when the problem of plurality is solved by silence rather than by letting many flowers bloom? Is it possible to be profoundly Christian, as I want to be, and also constructively affirmative within the work of Pace, as I have been?[11]

There are two stages in my response. Firstly, to offer a Christian appreciation of the kind of secularity found in Pace, thus discovering Christian freedom to join in its action affirmatively. Second, from within that affirmation to point towards deeper dimensions of its service that might be enhanced by insights from Christian faith.

A Christian Appreciation of the Kind of Secularity Found in Pace

The Gospel calls for simultaneous openness to the reality of God and of humanity. It speaks to people who know well the tension between them, yet are hungry for life that does justice to both. God has made us for himself and our hearts are restless until they rest in Him. The Gospel does not call us to give up the world, and with it, our humanity, so as to be left with God alone. According to Christian faith, there is no "God alone", only God, Father, Son and Spirit, who is *for* his creation and is effecting his will to be *with* his creation.[12] This point is made simply in a formula found in the Gospels, and repeated every time we say the Lord's Prayer: "as in heaven, so on earth".

It is a dangerous temptation to pray as though that will lift us up intoxicatingly into the heavens; the quality of the prayer of trust in God is the humility that lives the earthiness of humus, the dust of which we are made. In prayer, we live humanly with God; we do not pretend to climb up to bring God down, but are open to finding God walking with us, as God does in Jesus. Prayer trusts and waits for God: it is a discipline of letting God be God; only thus does it enter into the practice of the Presence of God.

Prayer is *human* action which trusts God to be God and does not claim to take God's place. It takes responsibility to serve the "so on earth" side of the

---

[11] A lazy compromise between heaven and earth, where each loses its authenticity, is certainly useless and without taste (Revelation 3:15-22, Matthew 5:13-16).

[12] Karl Barth, *The Humanity of God* (Louisville, KY: Westminster/John Knox Press, 1961).

partnership. Prayer is a deliberate, fundamental sharing in the mediation the triune living God realizes between the divine and the human. Just as the divine Word emptied himself (kenosis) to be human in the specific way we have in Jesus Christ, so those who pray are called to make traffic between heaven and earth, from the earthly side, without holding on to any heavenly ambitions.[13]

Prayer thus means practicing translation between heaven and earth. All translation involves some loss of substance and nuance, and so the human interpreter can only convey what they see through a glass darkly. They pick up signs, gives hints and pointers, makes stabs at passing on what they have glimpsed. When Christians participate in secular pluralist operations, like Pace, they are not excused from mediation between God and world – God calls them to that service – but what they can share is fragmentary, occasional, even tentative. They present an invitation to share exploration rather than the exposition of an authoritative theory and business plan. If Christians were to try to impose a Christian plan or ideology on a secular operation, they would be abandoning the ministry of mediation to seek a dominance the Gospel forbids. In the name of Christ, they would lose Christ.

There are ways consistent with Christian truth whereby Christians may be free in spirit to work wisely and co-operatively within the secularity and even the godlessness of the world. A common obstacle in the way is that God is often imagined and spoken of as transcendent perfection, unchangeably complete and sure in itself. What presence, then, can God have in the world which is characterized by imperfect, incomplete uncertainty? Can there be any sharing or intimacy between them? Christian faith is rooted in the incarnation of God in Jesus, whereby God freely crosses the divide, becomes truly human without ceasing to be truly God, and so translates God for our hearing and understanding. As in any translation, there is some loss or clouding of meaning, besides real illumination. Any translation adds to and subtracts from the original, thus putting it in new light or creating a new darkness. God's free sovereign grace is evidenced in God's living patiently and hopefully with his being misapprehended to some degree, even by those who seek God sincerely. The Spirit of God is always pressing us beyond what we think we know, because we have not yet attained; we should not resist the Spirit by refusing to learn. The incarnation is in accord with the eternal way of God, witnessed to in Scripture and beyond it: God wills to converse with human being, to be known and heard, believed and obeyed, and God strives in the Spirit with the recalcitrance of matter and the resistance of humanity. Because God is love, God the Word becomes flesh and speaks in humanity, living and dying among us and for us.

Equipped with such theological insight and granted faith by the gracious Spirit of God, it becomes possible to affirm and learn to enjoy secular action, in the state, in voluntary action like Pace, in everyday life and in the family (which in Britain now is generally secular in spirit and culture). Put simply, the secular is to be affirmed theologically insofar as it is good, marked by faith, love and hope understood in ways that show human existence coming into line with God in Jesus Christ. Because of the forgiving grace of God, and God's good will for all

---

[13] Philippians 2:1-18.

creation, this affirmation is to be ventured and sustained against and through all contrary evil. If this is how the world and God are together, Christians are given the freedom and the call to affirm and engage in the secular with adventurous generosity and hope.[14] In response to the call, Christian conversion to hopeful secular engagement needs to be made again and again, in the manifold variations of the world, for it is never easy or unquestionable.

Into the Depths

Grooming disguises sexual exploitation so that it appears to the victim as an expansion of life into lavish entertainments, extravagant gifts, spurious attention, adventures into maturity. This excitement covers its own dark side, evident in the pimp's threatened and demonstrated sanction of cruel force against the victim's own body and spirit and against her family.

As the parents see through the disguise, which the child may collude in making, they are taken into the depths. They suffer with the child. Not being enamored by the exploiter, they have a clearer view of what this adventure might come to. The parent's experience of life and caring imagination leads them to fear dangers the young person dismisses. They see the child as she may be unwilling and slow to see herself: overborne, losing spontaneity, accommodating herself to disappointment by becoming emotionally erratic, depressed, even building a shell of cynical hardness. In a word, exploited. Loving parents see the child distracted and being destroyed.

Some people, including occasionally a parent, may be hard enough to write off the victims of sexual exploitation and other evils as hopeless losers. Realism, they think, requires some wastage, even of human beings, to be accepted. Is such helpless equanimity not, in truth, the way of the world?[15] But in relation to their own children, parents generally are like the Good Shepherd who will not accept even a 1% wastage rate, but searches until he finds.[16] Happily, the Good Shepherd is not alone in the world. Some parents venture into red light areas seeking their child, sometimes for months on end. That is just one of the costly ingenious ways of not giving up on the child. Such faithfulness, dogged by the realization of what the child is being put through, takes parents into the depths with the child.

Teenagehood is a time when young people experiment with life. They need space for protected learning through making mistakes that are grievous to them in the moment, but do no long-term damage. When a child is groomed that space is taken away: they are tightly controlled, by force and infatuation, by the exploiter. They do what he tells them, dissent and independence are ruled out. They lose the freedom essential to emotional and social maturing. They frequently become truant or lose interest in school. In some instances, the effects

---

[14] Jeremiah 29:4-7; Galatians 5:1-26.

[15] John 11:49; 50.

[16] John 10:11-15; Luke 15:1-7; Ezekiel 34. This exposure of false shepherds targets more than pimps. It reaches out to the pimping cultures in which we live.

of "the lost teenage" last for years, and people come into adult responsibilities deprived of competences they should have gained at the right time.[17] They are ill-equipped for adult independence and challenge, and their age makes it harder to access care from social services. No help is available to make up for lost time and opportunity and little research is devoted to their plight. Because the exploitation put them through years of malformation, they end up lonely, lacking the skills to make friends, to negotiate and to trust. Through all this abandonment and beyond, it is only the parents who stay the course with them in more or less close support. In time, parents may well become caring grandparents as the effects of CSE flow down to the next generation. The depths can be a long dark valley.

Parents are taken into deep darkness[18] by the child's being exploited. They are taken beyond the ordinary run of family troubles which come to most people and are topics of everyday conversation. CSE makes parents lonely, because conversation partners are often hard to find: who can be trusted to understand? Who will not give crass advice on the basis of their more secure family situation, implicitly criticizing while sympathizing? Friends are often embarrassed, not knowing how to respond. When "other helpers fail and comforts flee" people come close to the One who cried in the darkness, "My God, My God, why have you forsaken me?" CSE is one of those intolerable situations where we sense Death invading life. Fears and sorrows crowd upon us, so that loneliness is not enjoyable solitude, but exposure to enemies. It puts a great strain on parents.[19] Few succumb to pure despair, so that they can do nothing. Most carry on doing what they can, hiding the fear and grief within the run of little thoughtful acts that keep alive the tradition of love, which is the heart and substance of the parent-child relationship working well. But the darkness is a sapping sorrow, eroding the foundation rock. Good partnerships break up under the strain.

Parents know the evil of CSE by living through it with the child. They name it with no titillating fancy. They see it from within their resistance to it, holding on for the promise of the child's growing towards and along the way of freedom, in love, health and peace.

---

[17] "The Lost Teenage", in *Published Articles issued by CROP,* and in *CROP Annual Report, 2005.* Happily, not all lose their teenage, despite dreadful experiences of exploitation: see, for example, Emma Jackson, *Exploited* (London: Ebury, 2012).

[18] I draw on biblical symbolism here, finding its thesaurus indispensable. CSE is no place for healing the hurt of people lightly (Jer. 6:14;18:11). Here all God's waves and billows go over us (Ps. 42:7; Ps. 71:20). There is deep gloom over the land (Is. 8:20-9:2). It is "out of the depths" that we cry to the Lord (Ps. 130:1). It is also true that "if I make my bed in hell, Thou art there" (Ps. 139:8) but that does not cancel the reality of the depths, any more than resurrection takes the dark agony from the Cross, for Jesus or the world.

[19] Aravinda Kojaraju, "The True Cost to Families of Child Sexual Exploitation", CROP briefing paper, 2009.

What Does Supporting Anyone in the Depths Require?

CSE is usefully approached as a set of practical problems. Problems are defined according to the specific capability and duty of each agency in relation to the solutions they can affect. Police and social services, academics and politicians, media and parents make different contributions. It is good when they work closely together. The co-location of statutory and voluntary agencies in a town has made for great improvements in combatting CSE. Pace has helped significantly by bringing parents into closer engagement with the work at every stage.[20]

But CSE is more than a set of problems. It confronts us with our involvement in the mystery of being.[21] CSE, which embroils us in dark brokenness, cannot be adequately countered by functional solutions. Parents are undoubtedly encouraged and supported when they find that their troubles can be framed as problems to which there are viable solutions. They can then keep going in hope. But solutions are often mitigations rather than complete restoration.

Does solving problems dissolve the mystery so that it no longer bothers? Given that there is little or no discussion of the mysterious in responses to CSE, that would seem to be the working assumption in Pace and elsewhere.

Anyone who is in deep darkness because of CSE is involved in the mystery of the brokenness of the world, which cannot be turned entirely into soluble problems, leaving no remainder.

Support of parents must work by focusing problems and working on them as far as possible. There is no help in a magical or mystical leap into the mysterious, running away from the responsibilities and possibilities of earthly life. Parents are supported when they are respected by practical affirmations of their capacity and calling, so that they are enabled to do more for the child, as they want to do. They are not to be belittled by taking their work out of their hands, as though they are incompetent.[22] Nor is their humanity to be misunderstood as though there is nothing but mystery. Problems and intelligent, hard work and courage in trying to solve problems are all part of the grandeur of human being.

---

[20] Haddon Willmer, *CROP and Blackburn ENGAGE! Tackling Child Sexual Exploitation Together 2009-2011* (Leeds, UK: CROP, 2011); *A Professional's Guide to Supporting Families through the Court Process*, (Leeds, UK: Pace, 2018); Lucie Shuker, *Empowering Parents: Evaluation of Parents as Partners in Safeguarding Children and Young People in Lancashire Project, 2014-2017* (University of Bedfordshire, 2017).

[21] I am indebted, in a quite inexpert way, to Gabriel Marcel for this distinction. See "Gabriel (-Honoré) Marcel" *Standford Encyclopedia of Philosophy,* Available at: https://plato.stanford.edu/entries/marcel/ [Last accessed: 27th October 2022].

[22] Parents sometimes look to social services to provide a safe place for their child, when the home territory is infested by the exploiters: to ask for that help is an act of parental responsibility not to be interpreted, as it sometimes is, as a sign of parental unfitness. A child's being cared for in some way by social services does not afford an occasion to supplant the parent. When that is done, the parent is demeaned, not supported, because neither believed in nor hoped for.

All that must be done, but if it leads to ignoring the mystery in which we live, we get no farther than the man who kept all the law, as he should, yet lacked one thing necessary.[23]

Problem and Mystery, Proclamation and Prayer

I write religiously, theologically, because that seems to me to be what reality requires and enables.

For two decades, I have worked practically within the secularity of Pace. I have had a marginal share in its great story of innovation and effective service. And all along I have had a sense that something was missing in the enterprise. I cannot eliminate the depths, darkness and mystery from my understanding of CSE and how to respond to it – and yet I am uncertain what to say or do. Now before it is too late for me, I am trying to say something constructive about this question.

I am glad that many Christians around the world are active in combatting sexual exploitation. Sometimes the inspiration and values of Christian action are largely humanitarian and short on theological reflection and articulation. It shapes itself through engagement with problems and is in danger of reducing faith to a tool for solving problems. I have already argued for the validity of secular action in God's world. But the Christian contribution is stunted if it takes God for granted, or secludes God in the privacy of the religious circle. Can faith in God be *confessed* in the reality of hard secular practice? Can that practice be challenged and enriched by finding itself more intelligibly in *God's* world, which is wider than, but not exclusive of, *our human* world?

Christian speaking tends to come from those who are secure in faith, or at least in the conventions of religion. It may then come across to the struggling and breaking person as unreal and patronizing. The distance at which the confident Christian stands from those who are in the depths makes him vulnerable to pharisaism, pleased that he is not as other men. If the help offered includes the invitation to become religious in the form he represents, it may seem to be a leap of more than pure faith in God as God is in Jesus. The help offered in confident proclamation often rests upon material conditions inaccessible to the struggler; God's free grace is blocked off by the social and financial privilege of the messenger.

The problem here seems to me to lie partly in the possession of a defined faith which can then be proclaimed. Those who know tell those who don't know; but those who know are secluded by their knowledge from standing with[24] those who are in the depths and so don't know. Sympathetic and imaginative proclaimers may talk with care and insight about "the depths" and then point to the way out. But even such good talking can be false, because to be in the depths is to be *silenced.* The partial silence that secularity brings upon religious loquacity may

---

[23] Matthew 19:20.

[24] "Standing with" may suggest better things than the more obvious "understanding" does in this context.

thus be a merciful discipline and a sign for the confident believer who is open to learning.

What is left to us in the depths, where there is no proclamation, is the cry of prayer.[25] To pray to God, not to oneself, is to start from the depths of the reality of ourselves and the world; there is no boasting, no mastery in action, no confidence in the flesh, no insulating comparisons with others, but the simple plea: "God be merciful to me a sinner."[26]

How does this relate to a work like Pace? Pace is not to be faulted because religious proclamation is out of place in its pluralist inclusivism. It may already be a house of prayer, or at least not averse to becoming one. Prayer reaches places beyond proclamation, because it takes many different forms. God hears the cry of poor little Ishmael, too young to speak, and the wordless weeping of his mother Hagar and God notices the sparrow fall.[27] Following biblical hints of this sort, the unreligious everyday talk in caring families, between parents and with supporters, and in various therapies, may be seen as prayer. This talk is indeed often like weeping: hidden in the commonplace sharing of the latest trouble is the plea to be saved from seeing the dying of the child. Much that is done within secular limits by people who are pressed together in the depths can be understood as prayer, if we journey with God's servant who does not break the bruised reed or quench the dimly burning wick.[28] God is forever making something out of nothing, nurturing the little into life. All Christian practice should be developed in accord with this spirit and principle. Look for the heart and the substance of prayer, not for the outward form.

Putting Right and Staying With

In the depths, the assurance of Christian (and other faiths) is shaken. It is easy to sing in church of the omnipotence and constant presence of the victorious God, but what hold has it in the depths? Do we not come to see that "only the suffering God can help"?[29] Are we not cast on the paradox of the sufficient grace of God which appears as the weakness of God? If God is in Christ, who "took our infirmities and bore our diseases" and was squeezed out of the world on to the cross, God is in the depths. We do not then have to make a great leap to get started but find ourselves *accompanied* on the path we are already stumbling in.

---

[25] Dietrich Bonhoeffer, "Thoughts on the Day of the Baptism of Dietrich Wilhelm Rüdiger Bethge, May 1944" in *Letters and Papers from Prison:* "We are once again being driven right back to the beginnings of our understanding [...] Our earlier words [...] lose their force and cease, and our being Christian today will be limited to two things: prayer and righteous action amongst men. All Christian thinking, speaking, and organizing must be born anew out of this prayer and action."

[26] Luke 18:9-14; Revelation 3:17-20; Philippians 3:3-14.

[27] Genesis 2:15-19; Matthew 10:26-31. Remember the hymns "Prayer to a heart of lowly love/opens the door of heaven above" (Nirayah Vaman Tilak) and "Prayer is the soul's sincere desire/Uttered or unexpressed" (James Montgomery).

[28] Isaiah 42:3.

[29] Dietrich Bonhoeffer, *Letters and Papers from Prison,* 16th July 1944.

Like many others, I am indebted to Bonhoeffer. The encounter with circumstantial evil and his commitment to righteous action which took him into the depths with God was quite different from the evil and righteous action which takes a parent of an exploited child into the depths. But the essential human plight and divine grace are the same for both.

And from yet another circumstance, Frances Young has shone light on my path. Her son Arthur was profoundly disabled from birth. As a mother and as a theologian, this took her into "the wilderness", as she names what I have been calling the depths. There, the goodness and reality of God was hard to see. Conventional explanations and consolations did not bring release from the darkness. A hard way through the wilderness, eventually with surprising help, freed her from being caught in the puzzles of theodicy, trying to justify God who does not prevent or eliminate evil at a stroke. Rather, with Arthur, she gained access to "the deepest truths of Christianity".

> We don't begin by explaining evil away, justifying God, excusing God for the mess made of creation. We begin by contemplating the story which tells of God taking responsibility by entering the "gone-wrong" world, taking it upon the divine self, in all its horror, cruelty and pain.[30]

> Ultimately the sacrifice of Christ on the cross is [...] about the kind of love which exposes the truth about our moral ambiguities, about the way our very virtues may be the germ of our worst faults, the kind of love which stays with our pain, with the anguish of hearts before the inexplicable mysteries of life, with the suffering of innocents, with the absence of resolution in the face of tragedy. That "staying with" rather than "putting right" is a perception deepened by living with irremovable disability. The persistence of the marks of the nails on the resurrected body of Christ is a sign of God's commitment to be in it with us, and by solidarity with us God in Christ enables suffering borne in love or innocence to become itself redemptive through communion with Christ's redemptive suffering.[31]

"Staying with" rather than "putting right" reminds us of the distinction between problem and mystery. The way God takes with humanity, in creation and covenant, focused centrally in the life and death of Jesus is *accompaniment* on earth. Pace practices "staying with" parents even when matters are not being "put right", just as parents stay with their children. How is it done, how is it sustained, without a story, of an accompaniment and a solidarity of the sort that Frances Young reports? The dominant pressure in the work of agencies like Pace is to "put right". That is what Irene Ivison started CROP to achieve. But repeatedly in the struggle to "put right", it becomes clear that "staying with" is unavoidable. Experiments have been made by some agencies in which time-limited programmed assistance is offered to parents dealing with CSE, but experience shows that the comfortable efficiency of a timetable breaks down, because parents and children cannot be abandoned while there is still need. Care which stays within cost limits will fall short. Unresolved tragedy calls for "staying with".

---

[30] Frances Young, *Arthur's Call* (London: SPCK, 2014): 41.
[31] Young, *Arthur's Call*, 121.

Perhaps an organisation like Pace can do no more than be modest about, but not ashamed of, its secularity, by admitting that there are areas of reality it cannot enter – or cannot reside in, although it may mount forays into strange places. The religious, or if you prefer, the spiritual, may not be the only areas which are beyond ordinary reach. Just as the parent will go to the supermarket to buy food, not to Pace, so they will go elsewhere when they are searching for the sustaining meaning and hope of life.

If I have not love, wrote Paul, I am nothing. Love believes and hopes all things. Support of parents without such constructive affirming love is ineffective. Without love, support cannot get past the suspicion and distaste many parents have for officialdom and professionalism. Pace does not read the Bible or quote this text, but in its human warmth and caring, it knows this loving.

Support requires sensitivity, flexibility and freedom from prejudice – components of the capacity to work with the strangeness of real people. Support should not be ventured unless there is a readiness to go into the depths, even being led by the parent who is already there. It is widely accepted that support workers are vulnerable to stress; they too are at risk from the darkness they encounter in their work, and so they are directed to look after themselves. They have to navigate a path between being with the parent and caring for their own well-being. Unlike the parent, they work within protective structures: limited hours, holidays, sick leave, good management, and professional training. All this can inhibit the readiness and ability to venture into the depths. Support workers are not paid to give their lives, as does the Son of Man, who comes to serve and not to be served.[32] Because he was like that, his example is generally dismissed as dangerous and impractical. But parents are often reckless in their loving and sometimes pay for it. As are many who support them.

Guilt

Parents often have a sense of guilt when a child is sexually exploited. As their children grow up, most parents observe them, and see happy and less happy developments. Being responsible, and knowing how much influence they have over the young child, they question their own performance when the child is unhappy or wayward, just as they take pride in what is going well. This self-questioning and then trying to do better becomes a strong internal habit, part of the mind which belongs to the parental type of human being. It persists even when the child is an adult. Happy is the parent who is absolved from any sense of guilt and failure by being able to take unalloyed pleasure in the adult child: the knowledge that the fallibilities of earlier nurture have not had lasting effect is comforting. But this happiness is not available to many parents.

Parents of teenage children are not morally or practically free to break the habit of responsible care, although they have ever less influence over the child. Teenagers need parents and other caring adults around them, even while they are seeing through and breaking away from them. So when something goes badly

---

[32] Mark 10:45.

wrong in the life of the teenager the parent is bound to ask the question which awakens guilt: what have I done to let this happen? Where have I failed? These are responsible questions, quite different from the narcissistic self-pitying question: What have I done to deserve this?

Support of parents in this situation involves an analysis of guilt. A standard first move is to assure the parent, as Pace does, that the child's being exploited is not their fault, but the perpetrators'. Parents need to be clear about assigning responsibility precisely, however crushed and doubtful they may be. This is helpful to parents, liberating them to be pro-active for their child against the exploitation. But sometimes it can bring with it a too simple assertion of the innocence of parents: as though not being pimps, they must be good. As support for parents, this is superficial; it cannot reach to what they know and feel in the depths of their being, in their self-searching reflection on the whole of their life with the child. They are not the causes of the exploitation but they are part of the tangled history which it has invaded and is reshaping. Even when they are freed from the burden of causality, they are deeply touched by the regret and pain intrinsic to the situation.

I do not think parents should be encouraged to stop such reflection. That would be to ask them to achieve the impossible, and it would be profoundly disrespectful of them as responsible, sensitive and loving persons, committed to being true to the vocation they have accepted as parents. It would ask them to trash the person they have grown into through their parenting life experience. The parent wants to seek and find rescue and fulfilment in their parental mission.[33] That is what should be supported. It follows that the Christian gospel of forgiveness should not be shared in ways which simplistically promise freedom from the past or the achievement of a radical newness. Being forgiven is not a supernatural miracle but a reconciliation with God whereby we live the human life given to us by the accompanying grace and love of God. Living life starts afresh every moment with our here and now, which God makes his here and now.

Guilt in the experience of parents tends to be a nebulous dis-ease, not a precisely defined fault. That is why it is insidiously disabling, creeping into every nook and cranny of our being, lurking to jump out on us at any turning of the road. It may be helpful to distinguish between guilt as causality and guilt as responsibility. Commonly, guilt is ascribed to the cause of something wrong. The parent may rightly be relieved of this kind of guilt when the cause of the exploitation is identified as the exploiter. The parent's continuing sense of guilt is a reflex of responsibility. It is a refusal to excuse oneself from involvement in the rotten mess of human life. So, it does not content itself with searching for the cause and finding someone to blame. It asks, rather: What is to be done now, starting from where we are?

The concept of guilt is intricately, primordially, linked with debt. Paul sheds hopeful light on guilt, not as causality but as responsibility, when he writes:

---

[33] Young, *Arthur's Call,* 31-37, 17; Frances Young, *Face to Face,* (Edinburgh: T & T Clark, 1990): 142-143.

"Owe no one anything, except to love one another".[34] Indeed, do all you can to avoid the guilt that arises from causality. But even if you are quite free from that guilt, never deny the debt (that may be sensed as guilt) which calls us to love one another. Guilt from the cause has a limit when the cause is identified; guilt as the debt of love may be boundless.

One line of support for parents is to point up the significance of their being responsible and caring now, whatever has happened in the past. They are called to love by the present plight and possibilities of their child, and they are responding to the call. Support which enables them, by advice, resourcing and encouragement, to carry on in faithful struggle for their child, sets them free from guilt about the past by embracing them in constructive action. This is no cheap grace. And it is a way in which the non-magical forgiveness of God enters human life and sets it free where it is to live in present hope.

Paul's words open a wide vision. "Owe no one" implies that we are to love all within our reach, near and far. Anyone, including the parent who is affected by CSE, is in touch with the wider world from a particular angle. It is not only the child who the parent is called to love. Love as doing right and with good will (not love as soft feelings) is due to all. Love is not weak, it calls for speaking the truth, and being wise as serpents as well as harmless as doves.[35] Aiming at this kind of love is what is required in negotiating relations with support workers, social services, police, courts, media, politicians, neighbors, all of whom can make loving difficult, even when they aim to help. They do need criticism, the kind of pressure parents put on them but it needs to be in love which both understands their situation and won't let them off the hook.

And it goes even further. The exploiter is often, not surprisingly, a demonic hate-figure in the eye of the parent. One of the possible objections to the word "pimp" is that it is not cool or dispassionate, but loaded with fear and distaste. What if even the pimp is owed the debt of love? What form would it take? Certainly, it includes calling them to account and taking measures to disempower them. Does it also call for understanding: What made them pimps? No one is born a pimp. They need appropriate treatment and help to rescue them from their psychological and cultural mal-formation and bad practice. Such a constructive response does not come from a purely punitive hostility.

That this is a hard challenge became clear at a conference of the European Baptist Federation network on prostitution and trafficking, after the singing of a hymn. It began easily enough:

> God of the moon and stars, God of the near and far,
> God of the fragile hearts we are, I come to you
> God of the rich and poor, God of the princess and whore

But, a little later, dared to go on:

> God of the pimp and paedophile, I come to you

---

[34] Romans 13:8.

[35] Ephesians 4:15; Matthew 10:16.

That line provoked sharp discussion. What does it really mean? Should it be sung? If sung, how was it to be acted on? A crucial moral and Christian issue had burst upon them.[36] What is it to owe the pimp, love?

To Conclude Inconclusively

Christians may rightly desire to bring the "deepest truths of Christianity" to the notice of parents and others in Pace, believing that it speaks to a real need and is a real help which Pace can at most only skirt and lightly touch. Christian mission and proclamation should not invade the integrity of an organisation like Pace, disturbing its functional secularity. Pace can only point towards the spiritual and theological, for it is beyond its remit and secularity. The church can only make its offering, praying with the prayers that are there in the life of Pace. The church needs to be near and intelligible to a community like Pace, but on the other side of a *cordon sanitaire*. On both sides, we need to learn to communicate and share, without being intrusive, let alone aiming at domination.

Can anything be achieved on these terms? Many traditional forms of mission, such as campaigning, proclamation and chaplaincy are unserviceable. What then? I am inclined to think that the only way is for all who are in the depths or through the wilderness to speak the truth given them and to try to make it accessible to those for whom it is a foreign language. Christians and other religious believers speak in a tongue which is alien to many good secularized fellow-travellers.[37] The division of languages becomes the basis of exclusive sectarianisms and non-co-operation. Christians are vulnerable to the temptation to become an embattled sect against the secular, and then to split into embattled sects against each other. Much hard work and penitent living is required to swim against this tide. Secular society likes to think it is the escape from religious divisiveness but it manifestly has its own problems in this area.

Whatever faith Christians have to confess and share can only be communicated by speech which is integral to faithful practice, such as parents staying all the way with their child, and accompanying other parents and anyone else who is in the depths. It will be done through the manifestation of authentic rooted living, not by proclaiming an imported ideology. It will be inspired and enabled by sources from outside the territory and idiom of Pace, but translated into a language of life accessible in the secularity. It will take care not to be off-putting. The manifestation will fluctuate; sometimes a burst of light, an epiphany, sometimes a dim glow as dark clouds obscure the sun. Frances Young drew from Christian theology, but not so as to impose it on her experience, but to discover, in her sometimes-overwhelming experience, the reality theology does no more than point to. Along that path, she found what could be passed on in testimony. It is not given to all participants to testify as she does, but some testimony needs to be accessible in the particular depths to help many others.

---

[36] I owe this story to Hilary Willmer, Chair of Pace 1998-2013 and a member of the European Baptist Federation network. The issue deserves more attention than I can give it here.

[37] I Corinthians 14:1-25; verse 19 is the key principle.

Reflection Questions

1. What is Christian ministry *to* parents (and other close relations) of victims of sexual exploitation? And what is the ministry *of* parents and close relations in the context of sexual exploitation? Or are parents part of the problem or inoperative bystanders? Are they to be managed cautiously or valued for their distinctive insight and initiative?
2. What theology informs your action in secular contexts and with secular partners? Does our theological imagination and practice rest on faith in God's being in the secular as freely as in the church? Is God finding us in the secular?
3. What do we say are "the deepest truths of Christianity" and how, in our thinking and practice, do they interact with the deepest experiences of our living?
4. Everybody lives in the body, on earth, in human history. Christians and church cannot help being largely secular in practice. Does secularity trouble Christians because it dissolves or dispenses with God? Or is secularity surrounded, permeated and enjoyed by God?
5. "Christians stand by God in the hour of his grieving." (Dietrich Bonhoeffer) Where does this *take us,* spiritually, intellectually and emotionally, as well as practically and geographically, when God's hour of grieving comes again and again in sexual exploitation?

Works Cited

Barth, Karl. *The Humanity of God.* Louisville, KY: Westminster/John Knox Press, 1961.

Bonhoeffer, Dietrich. *Letters and Papers from Prison.* 16th July 1944. London: SCM, 2017 [1951].

Ivison, Irene. *Fiona's Story: A tragedy of our times.* London: Virago, 1997.

Kojaraju, Aravinda. "The True Cost to Families of Child Sexual Exploitation". CROP briefing paper. Leeds, UK: CROP, November 2009.

Moran, Rachel. *Paid For: My Journey through Prostitution: Surviving a Life of Prostitution and Drug Addiction on Dublin's Streets.* London: W.W. Norton, 2015.

Pace. *A Professional's Guide to Supporting Families through the Court Process.* Leeds, UK: Pace, 2018.

Pace. *Parents Speak Out: Crucial Partners in Tackling Child Sexual Exploitation.* Leeds, UK: Pace, 2016. [Available at: http://paceuk.info/wp-content/uploads/Parents-Speak-Out-final.pdf], [Last accessed: 26th October 2022].

Shuker, Lucie. *Empowering Parents: Evaluation of Parents as Partners in Safeguarding Children and Young People in Lancashire Project, 2014-2017.* University of Bedfordshire, 2017.

Willmer, Haddon. *CROP and Blackburn ENGAGE! Tackling Child Sexual Exploitation Together 2009-2011.* Leeds, UK: CROP, 2011.
Young, Frances. *Arthur's Call.* London: SPCK, 2014.
—. *Face to Face.* Edinburgh: T & T Clark, 1990.

MINISTERING TO HIJRA: THE CHALLENGE OF AMBIGUITY

Carl Jylland-Halverson and Timothy Gaikwad

Hijra refers to a unique community and cultural identity found in South Asia. Hijra communities may be found from Pakistan throughout India and Bangladesh and into Indonesia. They are often described as transgender people and/or eunuchs who fill a specific niche in their community.

There are multiple challenges of ministering to hijra. First, simply working with hijra requires being comfortable with the ambiguous. Identifying who is hijra can be a challenge. They may be eunuchs but not all of them are, they may be involved in religious work or prostitution, they may be of various or multiple religious backgrounds. Our own ambiguity may also be a source of discomfort. We may prefer to focus on values of family defined by a woman and a man, of purity versus promiscuity, of identity being clear. Further, we may feel called to do something, to act, to make a change when the reality is: whatever path a eunuch may take, the eunuch will remain a eunuch.

There is a complicated relationship between the Church and the Lesbian, Gay, Bisexual, Transgendered, Intersex and Questioning community (LGBTI-Q). Sometimes, the LGBTI-Q community is viewed as a targeted outreach community. At other times, the challenge is to meet the spiritual needs of congregants who identify as LGBTI-Q and are professed Christians. Both categories require those ministering to maintain the values and teachings of one's faith while being compassionate.

Issues of theology, identity, and causality require that those who are ministering to the LGBTI-Q community participate in value-clarification, engage in spiritual self-care, and ensure that one's behaviors are guided by faith, scripture, compassion, and love.

Issues of causality can be complicated. Assumptions of sexual orientation being the result of being "born that way" or of the individual making a choice have implications on whether homosexuality is an identity (this is who I am) or a behavior (this is what I do). In the case of intersex individuals, this argument is more complicated. Genetic factors, hormonal influences, abnormalities or incongruences between internal and external genitalia could hardly be considered a choice. Similarly, working with hijra requires moving away from looking at cause, which may be perceived as blame, and instead focusing on pastoral care.

Who Are the Hijra?

Hijra must be understood within a complicated cultural, behavioral, historical and religious context. However, first it is useful to have a clear understanding of identity in general.

Gender Context

Wishik and Pierce provide a simple definition: a person's sexual identity is their "acceptance of membership in a particular sex category".[1] Identity is more than a simple construct. "Transgender" is often used as an umbrella term to describe the expression of identity that challenges traditional conceptualizations of sexuality and/or gender.[2] "Cisgender" refers to individuals whose gender identity is congruent with their assigned sex at birth.[3] Transgender refers to individuals whose gender identity is incongruent with their assigned birth sex.

Plante provides other designations that may be useful in understanding hijra. According to Plante, "gender assignment" is a person's initial gender designation. In the case of the individual who will become hijra that designation is male. "Gender identity" refers to an individual's internal sense of self. For the developing hijra that may be initially female and then third gender (neither male nor female). "Gender role" refers to the social expression of that self. In the hijra community, consistency of feminine behavior is highly valued. Finally, "gender attribution" is the unconscious process of looking at someone and making a decision about what their gender is. A hijra who could not be readily recognized as hijra by others would be considered a very poor hijra.[4]

There are many terms used to identify transgender people in South Asia. Land van Wijngaarden *et al*. explains that the term *hijra* refers to the eunuch transgender people or "third gender" of northern India.[5] *Khushra* refers to transgendered men who dress mostly as women. *Khotki* refers to men who dress as men but have feminized traits. *Bantha* refers to men with a male gender identity. Not all hijra become emasculated. *Janana* refers to hijra who retain their penis while *chibry* refers to hijra who have been emasculated.[6] Hossain describes hijra as male-bodied individuals who desire "macho" men and who sacrifice their genitalia to a goddess and in return receive spiritual prowess. This sacrifice may include both castration (removal of testicles) and penectomy (removal of all or part of the penis).

Social Context

Men who become hijra often recall acting feminine as young boys and being ostracized by family and neighbors. Hijra have been identified as the most recognizably marginalized individuals in India.[7] The International Centre for

---

[1] (Wishik and Pierce, 1995: 187).
[2] (Ditmore, 2006: 499).
[3] (Ditmore, 2011: xix).
[4] (Plante, 2015: 70).
[5] (Wijngaarden *et al.*, 2013: 73).
[6] (Hossain, 2012: 497).
[7] (Reddy, 2005: 257).

Diarrhoeal Disease Research, Bangladesh (ICDDR,B) initiated an ethnographic study using the Social Exclusive Knowledge Network Model. They reported that while all sex workers were concerned about violence, hijra reported more violence toward them than other male sex workers.[8] These findings are consistent with Land van Wijngaarden *et al.*'s research, which found that about a third of transgender men (khusras) had experienced violence from the police, from clients, and, to a lesser degree, from neighbors.[9] Khan *et al.*'s research at the ICDDR, B found evidence that exclusion of hijra was the result, in part, of early childhood feminine development, rejection by peers, feminine behavior and mannerisms not being tolerated in schools, and identity confusion by the boys who became hijra.[10]

Many who become hijra leave their homes as boys or teens and join hijra households. These households (*hijra dera*) function as surrogate families. They are led by an older hijra who is referred to as the *guru*. The relationship between the guru and the student (*chela*) is life long and reciprocal. The guru provides guidance, a family, and entry into hijra life. The student provides loyalty and financial support to the guru and the household.

Hijra identity develops over time. How good a hijra the individual becomes is measured by the reactions of the hijra community and the larger community. Two constructs are used to measure status. One is *Izzat* or moral currency. This is bestowed upon a hijra for the consistency of feminine behavior in all situations. A hijra who only acted feminine when working would accrue less *izzat* than the hijra who behaves in a feminine manner even when there is no audience.[11] The other construct that indicates that others view the hijra as a true hijra is *sharam* or shame. When emasculated hijra are ignored, one response is for them to publicly raise their sari and expose their excised genitalia to shock those who would otherwise ignore them. During such behavior, the hijra are described as having no *sharam* or shame. It is these two constructs – the *izzat* bestowed by members of their own group and *sharam* or judgment of them by outsiders – that measures how successful one is at becoming the third gender.

Hijra have limited vocational options. *Bazaar tola* refers to the practice of hijra collecting money from the market, that is, those arenas open to hijra interaction. That may include begging in the street market, providing blessings for weddings, baby dedications, rites of passage, dancing at social events, and engaging in prostitution. *Bedhas* or blessing of newborns is an example of practicing one's vocation as a person with spiritual powers. If a hijra is not paid for a dance, blessing, or other service they may respond with *tin tali* – the traditional open palm hand clap followed by raising their sari and exposing their castrated genitalia.[12] It is through hijra occupations that the individual develops their hijra skills, accumulates *izzat*, and is recognized by others as hijra.[13]

---

[8] (Azim *et al.*, 2008: 320).
[9] (Wijngaarden *et al.*, 2013: 74).
[10] (Khan *et al.*, 2009: 442).
[11] (Reddy, 2005: 261).
[12] (Khan *et al.*, 2009: 446).
[13] (Reddy, 2005: 261).

There are often vocational implications to being transgender. According to Ditmore, transgender individuals are disproportionately represented in the sex industry. This is believed to be, in part, the consequence of disrupted education, family rejection, and, in the case of runaways, precarious legal status. Homeless individuals often participate in "survival sex" (the exchange of sex for food, shelter, and necessities). Less desperate individuals may participate in "transactional sex", defined by the *Encyclopedia of Prostitution* as neither the exchange of a professional service with a client nor survival sex but rather "something is given in exchange for sexual services".[14]

Sex workers, no matter how they are defined, are viewed as having multiple vulnerabilities for violence. For males involved in prostitution, the violence toward them may be a product of homophobia and transphobia. In fact, some of the planners of the 2009 Transgender Day of Remembrance (commemorating transgender people killed in the previous year) assumed that all the transgender people who had been killed in the United States were involved in prostitution.[15]

Brothels specifically for hijra may be found throughout South Asia.[16] In Kolkata, sex workers have been organizing to protect themselves since 1992. Ditmore explains that this was a response, in part, to the state-sponsored STD and HIV Intervention Program (SHIP).[17] In Dhaka, hijra have the highest rate of syphilis in the city.[18] In some communities, the HIV-sero prevalence rates are above 72%.[19] One possible explanation for such a high rate of infection may be the low rate of condom use and other protection. In Bangladesh, responses to the Behavioral Surveillance Survey indicate that hijra used protection consistently only 25% of the time during the week prior to the survey.[20]

Historical and Religious Context

Hijra and other transgender groups have a long history in South Asia. Dutta states hijra were recognized as a distinct caste in India in 1885.[21] Section 377 of the British Law of 1860 was the first law banning "carnal intercourse against the order of nature." The British Criminal Tribe Act of 1871 criminalized sexual relations between hijra and other men.[22] Nanda postulated that acceptance or at least tolerance of a third gender group was possible because of the earlier Hindu veneration of androgyny.[23] It is perhaps because of this long history of a distinct caste and clear niche that, in March 2004, the Madras High Court struck down the laws against hijra and granted the hijra voting rights, along with the right to education, marriage, adoption, and formal recognition of the third gender.[24]

---

14 (Ditmore, 2006: 449).
15 (Ditmore, 2011: xxviii).
16 (Shah, 2014: 16).
17 (Ditmore, 2011: xix).
18 (Shah *et al.*, 2009: 441).
19 (Reddy, 2005: 257).
20 (Azim *et al.*, 2008: 316).
21 (Dutta, 2012: 829).
22 (Dutta, 2012: 829).
23 (Hossain, 2012: 497).
24 (Reddy, 2005: 263).

The hijra identity is old and predates the introduction of Islam to the subcontinent. The rituals and spiritual power associated with hijra is connected to the Hindu cosmology. According to Hossain, even hijra who were born and remain Muslim may trace their genealogy to two hijra goddesses, Maya and Tara.[25] The goddesses or avatars may change from region to region. In India, they may be Maya Ji and Bachucara Mi. This connection to the goddesses is powerful. The *Baraiya* is the ceremony that marks transition from male to third gender and hijrahood. The length of days varies from 12 or more after the emasculation. The individual is seen as leaving the world he was born into and reincorporating herself, without a penis, into the community of hijra.[26] It is like they are reborn into their new community.

For hijra who are Hindu, there are also specific festivals and holidays to reinforce their relationship with the Hindu cosmology. The Koovagam Festival in southern India is a major gathering of hijra in which they participate in the ritualistic marriage to the Hindu god Aravan. Again, Nanda postulates that South Asian nations accommodate and create a niche for third gender communities because of the Hindu veneration of androgyny.[27]

In some parts of South Asia, hijra may identify as both Hindu and Buddhist because people in South Asia may have multiple religious identities. The British legal code that defined homosexual behavior as criminal was not consistent with the theology of Buddhism. For Buddhists, sexual behavior was not divided into "good heterosexual behavior" and "bad homosexual behavior." Instead, the dichotomy was between celibacy (which was the ideal) and sexuality.[28]

Islam has a complicated relationship with the concepts of transgender and third gender people. This is illustrated in South East Asia, especially in Indonesia, the nation with the largest Muslim population in the world. Indonesia is known as a tolerant nation and yet the Indonesian Ulema Council (MUI) has issued a fatwa reminding citizens that gay sex is a sin and called for the death penalty for those found participating in gay sex.[29] However religious responses to gender are rarely one dimensional. Syahirah reports that Indonesia is also home to *Pesantren Waria*, an Islamic boarding school for transgender men or "*waria*." At the school, the *waria* are able to learn new professions, receive lectures from Islamic scholars, and worship as a community.[30]

Muslim hijra or eunuchs have a place in the history of Islam. They were viewed as loyal protectors of Sultans and harems. Hajji hijra are the custodians of the prophet's grave and as such hold a special place in the faith.[31] Hijra make the pilgrimage or haj to Mecca. At such times, they dress as men and participate with men in worship.

---

[25] (Hossain, 2012: 507).
[26] (Hossain, 2012: 506).
[27] (Hossain, 2012: 497-8).
[28] (Bronski *et al.*, 2012, Part Three, Myth 10, 5).
[29] (Green, 2015).
[30] (Syahirah, 2014).
[31] (Hossain, 2012: 502).

Ministry to Hijra and Transgender People

Against this backdrop, this chapter will now look at the question of what is being done to minister to hijra in a particular context in India, and what are some principles that can be useful in ministering to transgender people in any context.

Case Study: Imcares

IMCARES (Inter-Mission Care and Rehabilitation Society) is a registered charitable organization whose objective is to reach out to the poorest of the marginalized poor in Mumbai, India. It consists of a group of people who love the Lord Jesus and who reach out to those who are left out. The personal spiritual focus of our workers takes us beyond issues of social justice. IMCARES is not a Christian organization but it works with community organizations, including the church and faith-based organizations that serve people in need.

The following is an interview with Timothy Gaikwad, the CEO of IMCARES

How did IMCARES get involved in working with the hijra community?

Our encounter with the hijra community began over 30 years ago. We were starting a safe home for children raised in brothels. Some of the brothels were run by the hijra community. Some of the hijras intimidated our staff. We talked to the hijra about the value of life and of the children we wanted to help. They believed we cared and they stopped harassing us. One of the children we rescued was a four-year-old boy. The boy had had a very traumatic early childhood and for a couple of years would not speak. But, with tender loving care, he began to open up and recover. At first, the hijras would come back wanting to take back the boy. But when they saw that we genuinely cared for the boy and his welfare, they allowed us to keep him and never again came back. Today, that boy is a man. He is married and the father of a baby girl.

Twenty years ago, we were working with the very, very poor. We consider hijra part of this marginalized community. This includes MSM (men who have sex with men), HIV+ clients, and those involved in prostitution. Initially, we came in contact with one hijra. He was very scared. He reported that bringing in money to the hijra household was very important. He was HIV+ but was afraid to tell anyone. He was afraid that he would be beaten, kicked out, and possibly killed. He had already been ostracized. He lived in isolation in a slum house. Our people cared for him. As there was no antiretroviral treatment then, recovery was very difficult; all we could provide was end-of-life care. This hijra gave his life to the Lord. He died one year later but he died being loved. The church (embodied by our members) went to him. This is when we learned just how damaging HIV is in the hijra community. "We hijra may live lives as queens but we die as dogs", said one of the hijras. This is because their HIV status scares away customers and the hijra lose their livelihood.

Help us get a picture of the community. Approximately how many hijra are in India?

In 2014, the first official census of hijra by the Indian government identified 450,000 hijra in all of India. Half of this population is in Mumbai. Activists believe this is a low count and the actual number is somewhere between 6 to 7 times higher.

How do issues of religion and gender intersect? Are there any special challenges ministering to hijra?

Hijra are part of the transgender and LGBT communities in India. Hijra are deeply rooted in religious practices. To be a Christian requires that Jesus is your only God. That is a problem for hijra.

Attaining a "nirvana" or a complete change of life from male to female is the highest respect a hijra can acquire. The conventional way of attaining "nirvana" is deeply rooted in religious beliefs. Because of conventional and unsafe methods of castration, the mortality rate is very high. Today, many hijras are going through sex change operations conducted illegally by some surgeons in India. When hijra become the third gender, they do not go to a hospital; there is no proper surgery or medications. The surgery and rituals are performed in compliance to religious beliefs. Being conscious during bleeding is important to appreciate the sacrifice and the transformation from impotent male to the third gender and the embodiment of the Goddess. Should they become Christian, they will remain eunuchs and probably view themselves as members of the larger LGBT-Q community. Our challenge is to love them and offer them a safe community in which to grow in their new faith.

According to reports from pastors, over the years, many hijra have given their lives over to Jesus. But local churches are often reluctant to welcome them into their community so these hijras created a small church group. Some of these members reported to IMCARE that in the church they experienced God's love in words and deeds. They have told us that they experienced this love because "they touch us, they walk with us, they visit us."

Seema[32] is 25 years old and was born with an effeminate personality. Seema had been sexually abused from the time of early childhood until a few years ago. Seema, whose masculine name is Sandeep,[33] was living with a group of hijras in the slums of Dharavi when our staff met them during a regular HIV/AIDS awareness drive. We came to know Seema's story and learned that he had already committed his life to Jesus and no longer engaged in promiscuous sexual activity. Seema wanted to come out of the hijra community but insecurity due to lack of a proper rehabilitation program deterred him from daring to step out. In addition, his guru would not let him go unless he paid back a huge amount of money. IMCARES counseled him, helped him with some financial aid to pay back the guru, and offered him a job. Seema also gave the guru a few belongings that had been purchased through asking for alms. The guru told him that he could go out but must dress as a female in public so that other "chelas" (disciples) would not quit the hijra seeing his example. Seema would leave dressed as a

[32] A pseudonym.

[33] This is not deadnaming but relevant to Seema/Sandeep's story.

female, change into male clothing in a public toilet at the train station before coming to work, and change back into female attire on the way home. We at IMCARES told him to wear whatever he felt most comfortable wearing but Seema wanted to change back to Sandeep. Seema's peers were not very comfortable with his decision so he eventually quit the job and went back to asking alms dressed as a hijra. But Seema's love for Jesus was only getting stronger. Two years ago, he met another hijra who had also given his life to Jesus and was in a pastoral ministry reaching out to other hijras. Soon, Seema joined his friend and is now an assistant pastor and reaches out to hijras in need of love.

What are IMCARES goals for ministering to the hijra community?

- Treat them with the respect you would give to any other person. Have them be part of peer groups.
- For those who voluntarily request us to connect them to a local church, do make that connection for them.

Are there any special considerations when working with the hijra community?

We believe we should respond as follows:

- Hijra live in community and must be treated in a community.
- A good working relationship with the guru is needed.
- If they are Christians, the church expects them to stop prostitution because the body is the temple of the Living God.
- We must remember that they will still be LGBT or trans or eunuchs.
- The Apostle Phillip's encounter with the Ethiopian eunuch provides us a model of interaction. We are to serve, love, and not sit in judgment. After the eunuch was baptized, he remained a eunuch. Should a hijra become a follower of Christ, the hijra will also remain a hijra.

What Bible verses or teachings guide your work?

The Holy Bible says that we are not meant to judge anyone. Also, God looks at the heart and not on the outward appearance of man. God also promised for the eunuchs a special place in His temple, much better than even sons and daughters, with a condition that they keep His commandments and follow the Sabbath. The Bible also says that we have all sinned and fallen short of the Glory of God. The most commonly-used passage to preach salvation through Jesus – John 3:16 – says that "whosoever" believes in Him shall not perish but have everlasting life. So who are we to judge? It is good that we get on with the work of sharing God's love in action to those in need.

Does IMCARES provide any special guidelines for those providing the ministry to hijra?

IMCARES workers are passionate about and committed to serving the ones most in need of love and care. IMCARES has served the poor of Mumbai for the past 30 years. IMCARES serves the homeless, the sick, undernourished children, children in need of an education, victims of domestic abuse, people who are HIV+, abused children, and hijra. IMCARES consists of paid staff in ministry, counseling, public relations, and health services, but it also maintains an active corps of volunteers from many professional fields.

We believe that every human being is created in the image of God and that it is our call and duty to wait upon them in the time and point of their need. Our primary focus group are the marginalized poor. Hijras are a marginalized group and a majority of its members are socio-economically and emotionally poor. However, working among this group of people requires a lot of courage and commitment. IMCARES's policy is that staff will always go in pairs or a team. No staff member will ever be alone. We also provide periodic training and updates to our staff to make their work more relevant and safer. Because of the religious dynamics involved in working with the hijra, the staff themselves need to be spiritually motivated and strong. IMCARES provides its workers and volunteers with training to ensure healthy boundaries and effective working conditions while maintaining morale. The UNAIDS document, "Preventing Carer Burnout Inter-Mission Care and Rehabilitation Society (IMCARES)" explains the guidelines IMCARES uses to supports its staff and volunteers. The staff are covered with prayer and spiritual motivation. Moreover, IMCARES does not proselytize. For those hijra who show a desire to follow Jesus, they are connected to a local church.

During the course of training, faith-based organizations to care for the poor and marginalized in their communities, many pastors came to me and shared in confidence about coming across hijras who were asking for a baptism, or a funeral, or even acceptance in the church. Some of those pastors told me that they would often offer spiritual services to the hijra discreetly because they feared a backlash from their congregation. In order to sensitize faith-based communities and the larger community about the need to accept hijras, IMCARES (with gracious funding from Love146) produced a Bollywood-style short film called *Ashu: Break the Silence*. This was history in the making. Never before had the church in Mumbai addressed this issue so openly. This film has been screened in many churches, NGOs, and groups in Mumbai and across India, thus breaking the silence regarding male-child sexual abuse and the hijra fold.

I feel strongly that the church should never compromise on Biblical principles on sexual practices. These practices include valuing sexual purity, believing that sex is reserved for the relationship between husband and wife, and accepting that our body belongs to God and we must therefore respect it. At the same time, the church must not allow these issues to deter them from reaching out to those in need, regardless of their socio-economic, mental, physical or sexual status. We are no better than them, they are no worse than us. We all fail and need God's abundant grace and the keys to the Kingdom are given to the followers of Jesus. The church should be an open door and should open doors to the Kingdom of God to all who seek Him earnestly. The Holy Bible says that the poor will always be in the land and we are supposed to be openhanded towards them.

So here is another area of ambiguity. We are called upon to be faithful to our religious laws and values and at the same time be available to serve "the other", our neighbor, even if they act in a way contrary to our values. The "dance" for us is to be faithful, to love others, and to let God judge – to let God be God.

Principles for Ministry with Hijra

Clearly, the hijra make up a unique community and the ministries that provide pastoral care and vocational training are also unique. To meet the needs of this community and to aid in caring for the ministers, it is critical to meet the pastoral needs of both groups.

Guidance from the Hijra Theological Context

This requires an understanding of theological foundations of the hijra community (discussed at the beginning of this chapter) and how some of their needs may be met.

All of this has implications for the person attempting to minister to the needs of the hijra. Assumptions that the hijra are Hindu could be incorrect. As may assuming they may be attracted to Christianity because they want to escape the caste system. Assuming that a Buddhist or Muslim hijra or Christian convert has not incorporated the cultural aspects of the caste system into their worldview could also be wrong.

Guidance from Catholic Social Teaching

It is also important for the Christian ministering to hijra to be clear about the theology that guides them in their ministry. One guide may be the seven themes of Catholic Social Teaching.[34]

The first theme is to respect the *Life and Dignity of the Human Person.* This may best be understood in this context as caring for the hijra in a respectful manner as opposed to judging her.

The second theme calls for *Family, Community, and Participation.* The challenge here is to find ways to provide a sense of belonging for the hijra, especially if they are experiencing rejection from their hijra community and their larger local community. An additional challenge is for the ministers to work with local parish communities to be accepting of hijra who wish to join them. Glenn Miles, in his documentary film *Accepted or Rejected: The Life of a Hijra*, points out that the life of hijra is often marked by rejection. This includes rejection by their family of origin and the community they grew up in. Even though they are accepted into the *hijra dera*, if they become HIV-positive they may be rejected again. If members of the Church are indeed being the hands and feet of Christ, then it is important for the hijra not to be further rejected should they seek membership to a congregation. This may take the form of active acceptance into the local church, invitations to church and community participation, and opportunities to learn about their growing faith and to serve their new community.

The third theme is *Rights and Responsibilities.* This is a theme that Christians should feel comfortable addressing. It calls for us to be advocates for social justice. Christians are called to help the poor (Lev. 25:35), to open your mouth for the destitute (Prov. 31:8), and to learn to do good, make justice your aim, and redress the wrong (Is. 1:16-17).

---

[34] (United States Conference of Catholic Bishops, 2005).

The fourth theme is the *Option for the Poor and Vulnerable.* This is consistent with the third theme. In a prioritized list of what we should care about, caring for our poor and vulnerable siblings should be on the top of the list.

The fifth theme, the *Dignity of Work and the Rights of Workers*, is the result of combining the previous two themes. The result is reflected in ministries advocating for fair work conditions, vocational training, and communities free of harassment. When we provide vocational training to hijra, we are addressing this cluster of themes.

The sixth theme is *Solidarity.* As children of God, we are to recognize our connectedness to one another. It is sometimes easy to behave in an Us-Them manner when ministering to others. We are the Christians; they are not. We have resources; they are the exploited. We have salvation; they are broken. This type of thinking ignores that we are called upon to see Christ in the stranger and to know we are brothers and sisters in Christ. Jonathan Hancock, former executive director of Emmaus Ministries, an urban ecumenical ministry that serves homeless males who participate in prostitution, has some practical advice on how to see the people we serve as our siblings.[35] He suggests that we imagine the folks we serve as our own children. Further, he recommends that we imagine we are helping Jesus when we care for others. He recommends that we should pray for wisdom about how to respond to the people we serve and that we also pray for our heart to reflect God's heart.[36] Hancock's advice suggests that our service is not about us, it is about God and the people we serve as fellow children of God.

The last theme is *Respect for Creation.* This theme is most closely connected to issues related to pollution, climate change, and degradation of ecological habitats. The reality is that hijra, along with much of the greater communities in which they are found, are often living in conditions of pollution, tainted water, and poverty. Caring for Creation in such setting would include advocacy, caring for the poor, and reflecting solidarity.

Guidance from Work with Transgender Communities in Other Contexts

Glenn Miles researched the relationship between the church and the hijra community in Mumbai. The result of that research was the documentary film *Accepted or Rejected: The Life of a Hijra* (2010). The film provides a number of observations that are useful for the Christian ministering to hijra, including the following. Lalita Edwards, M.D., the founder of a transgender project reflected on the connection between a desire to become hijra and a history of experiencing domestic violence. She stated that most did not become hijra simply from a desire to join the community but that they often fled their homes because of domestic violence or sexual abuse in the home or community. Blessi Kumarvia, a public health consultant, pointed out that children are exposed to sexual abuse and pornography via print, internet and CDs. This easy access to pornography makes early intervention critical. Jasmir Thakur, CEO of Sambhavana Society,

[35] (Miles and Crawford, 2014: 193).
[36] (Miles and Crawford, 2014: 193).

agreed with this assessment and recommended educating young children about sexual abuse and about sexual minorities. Timothy Gaikwad, CEO of IMCARES, reported there were an estimated 250,000 hijra in Mumbai. His concern was that this was a community that had experienced rejection and yet "the church response has been passive and guarded".[37]

Gaikwad's observation that the church is limited in its response to the hijra community is not unique. In Thailand, Celeste McGee provides a ministry for transgender people (ladyboys). The ministry, Dton Naam, provides acceptance, love, and an introduction to Jesus. It also provides vocational training. The ministry is visited often by ministers passing though Bangkok. However, McGee notes that there is very little evidence that the Christian community is ministering to the transgender community in Thailand.[38] This is in contrast to the multiple ministries for women and children who are involved in prostitution or trafficking. She suspects this is due in part to the stigma of males involved in prostitution. Her recommendation is that ministers drop "Us and Them" dichotomies that get in the way of helping and caring for others. Instead, McGee states, "the church needs to remember that believers are also all a bunch of misfits".[39] Her approach keeps the ministers humble and connected to the people they are working with.

In the United States, Nicole Foster reminds us to preach not only from our lips but also from our actions.[40] The people we serve will know if we care about them by how we live among them. Doug Van Ramshorst calls on us to build a presence in the communities in which we work. In the process, we build trust through our visible commitment and consistency.[41] The work we do is difficult and Van Ramshorst calls us to cover ourselves in prayer but to not shy away from discomfort.

Finally, the wisdom and experience of IMCARES ministry is valuable to Christians serving this unique community. Hijra live in community and must be ministered to in community. If hijra are not welcomed into a local church then we must be prepared to bring the church to them. Be humble, not judgmental, and be true to the teachings of our faith. Build up and support one another so that we may be effective hands, feet, and instruments of the Body of Christ: the Church. When that occurs, we, the Christians ministering to the hijra community, may experience what John Green refers to as "breaking out of our own conditioning".[42] Green says we will be living justly and able to step into the lives of our siblings showing mercy and serving humbly.

---

[37] (Miles, 2010).
[38] (Miles and Crawford, 2014, 231).
[39] (Miles and Crawford, 2014, 233).
[40] (Foster, 2010: 10).
[41] (Miles and Crawford, 2014, 197).
[42] (Green and Jewell, 2010: 10).

Reflection Questions

1. The difference between you and a hijra/transgender person can be very distracting. How do you stay focused not on your differences but on your goal of being a servant to the hijra/transgender person?
2. How can you serve your local church, which may be very uncomfortable having hijra among them, and faithfully serve the hijra/transgender person seeking to become a part of the church?
3. How can the example of Philip the Evangelist in the book of Acts serve as a guide in our work with hijra/transgender people?
4. Reflect upon the ways in which engaging The Triangle in the hijira/transgender context might impact your understandings around theology, sexual exploitation and response.

Works Cited

Azim, Tasnim, Sharful Islam Khan, Fariha Haseen, Nafisa Lira Huq, Lars Henning M.D., Moshataq Pervez, Mahbub Elahi Chowdhury, and Isabelle Sarafian. "HIV and AIDS in Bangladesh". *Journal of Health, Population and Nutrition.* 26(3), (September 2008): 311-324. [Available at: https://doi.org/10.3329/jhpn.v26i3.1898], [Last accessed: 28th October 2022].

Bronski, Michael, Ann Pellegrini and Michael Amico. *You Can Tell By Looking*. Boston, MA: Beacon Press. 2013

Ditmore, Melissa Hope. *Prostitution and Sex Work. Historical Guides to Controversial issues in America.* Westport, CT: Greenwood, 2011.

——. *Encyclopedia of Prostitution and Sex Work.* Westport, CT: Greenwood, 2006.

Dutta, Aniruddha. "An Epistemology of Collusion; Hijras, Kothis and the Historical (Dis)continuity of Gender/Sexual identities in Eastern India". *Gender & History*. 24(3), (2012): 825-849.

Foster, Nicole. *Light in a Dark Place: My Experience Working with Men in Prostitution.* Grand Rapids, MI: Zondervan, 2010.

Gaikwad, Timothy. *ASHU: Break the Silence,* Producer IMCARES and Love146. Mumbai. 2010.

Green, John and Dawn Herzog Jewell. *Streetwalking with Jesus: Reaching out in Justice and Mercy.* Huntington, IN: Our Sunday Visitor, 2010.

Green, Jon. "Indonesia's top clerics issue fatwa against gays". *America Blog*, 17th March 2015. http://americablog.com/2015/03/indonesian-clerics-fatwa-gays.html. [Last accessed: 11th April 2020].

Hancock, Jonathan. "Advice from Practitioners", in Glenn Miles and Christa Foster Crawford Eds. *Stopping the Traffick: A Christian Response to Sexual Exploitation and Trafficking*. Oxford: Regnum, 2014.

Adnan, Hossain. "Beyond Emasculation: Being Muslim and Becoming Hijra in South Asia". *Asian Studies Review* 36(4) (December 2012): 495-513.

Inter-Mission Care and Rehabilitation Society (IMCARES). *Preventing Career Burnout*. UNAIDS Best Practice Collection. Geneva: UNAID, December 2007. [Available at: http://www.unaids.org/sites/default/files/media_asset/jc1538_imcares_full_en_0.pdf], [Last accessed: 28th October 2022].

Khan, Sharful Islam, Mohammed Iftekher Hussain, Shaila Parween, Mahhbubul Islam Bhuiyan, Gorkey Gourab, Golam Faruk Sarker, Shohael Mahmud Arafat, Joya Sikder. "Living on the Extreme Margin; Social Exclusion of the Transgender Population (Hijra) in Bangladesh". *Journal of Health, Population and Nutrition* 27(4), (August 2009): 441-451.

McGee, Celeste. "How Can the Church Effectively Minister to Transgender People Who Are Sexually Exploited?" In Glenn Miles and Christa Foster Crawford, Eds. *Stopping the Traffick: A Christian Response to Sexual Exploitation and Trafficking*. Oxford: Regnum, 2014.

Glenn Miles, *Rejected or Accepted. The Life of a Hijra*. Producer Love146, Mumbai. 2010. Available on YouTube, Channel: Glenn Miles, Uploaded: 24th June 2021. https://www.youtube.com/watch?v=_m9aZ1nJvUA, [Last accessed: 28th October 2022].

Plante, Rebecca F. *Sexualities in Context: A Social Perspective.* Ithaca, NY: Routledge, 2015.

Reddy, Gayatri. "Geographies of Contagion: Hijras, Kothis, and the Politics of Sexual Marginality in Hyderabad". *Anthropology and Medicine*. 12(3), (December 2005): 255-270.

Van Ramhorst, Doug. "How Should Christians and the Church Engage with Boys and Men?" In Glenn Miles and Christa Foster Crawford, Eds. *Stopping the Traffick: A Christian Response to Sexual Exploitation and Trafficking.* Oxford: Regnum, 2014.

Shah, Svati P. *Street Corner Secrets: Sex, Work and Migration in the City of Mumbai.* Durham, NC; London: Duke University Press, 2014.

Syahirah, Nurul. "Indonesia's Trans Muslim Maryana: Seeking Paradise is Not Limited to our Sex or Clothing". *Patheos*, 28th April 2014. [Available at: http://www.patheos.com/blogs/mmw/2014/04/indonesias-trans-muslim-maryani-seeking-paradise-is-not-limited-to-our-sex-or-clothing/], [Last accessed: 28th October 2022].

United States Conference of Catholic Bishops. "Seven Themes of Catholic Social Teaching". *USCCB Website.* 2005. [Available at: http://www.usccb.org/beliefs-and-teachings/what-we-believe/catholic-social-teaching/seven-themes-of-catholic-social-teaching.cfm], [Last accessed: 28th October 2022].

van Wijngaarden, Jan Willem de Lind, Bettina T. Schunter and Qasim Iqbal. "Sexual abuse, social stigma and HIV vulnerability among young feminized men in Lahore and Karachi, Pakistan". *Culture, Health & Sexuality.* 15(1), (January 2013): 73-84.

Wishik, Heather and Carol Pierce. *Sexual Orientation and Identity: Heterosexual, Lesbian, Gay, and Bisexual Journeys.* Laconia, NH: New Dynamics Publications, 1995.

"Reserved for a Special Place in Hell" Perpetrators Who Abuse: What Is the Place of Forgiveness, Healing, Hope?

Samantha Miller and Glenn Miles

Is there a place for understanding the exploiter better? Not the vile monster and pervert popularly demonized in current media but the ordinary man, including the Christian man, who is vulnerable (a seemingly out of place word in the context) to engaging a person in prostitution or who is a sexual exploiter who has already "crossed the line"? How can men be challenged to make better choices, to treat people with dignity both practically and theologically? When they are apparently "addicted" to sex, where is the path to redemption? Why do they so often feel unwelcomed by the church who claims to be open to "whosoever" are repentant?

Introduction

When speaking at churches and with people working with survivors (practitioners), we encourage them to get involved in the demand side of human trafficking, perhaps with a ministry reaching out to men in red-light districts. In response, we have received a number of reactions, most frequently exasperation. A common question is: "Why spend time and resources with those 'pervs'?" One person flatly stated: "There is a special place in hell for those kinds of men." We have heard responses such as: "I'd like to have a few minutes in a room with one of those guys and give them some of the pain they've inflicted on others" and "A bullet is too good for them." Others have told us that we must have developed a kind of liberal pastoral theology, a long way from proper systematic conservative theology, to want to be involved in reaching out to the exploiters. Even the men we have met in the red-light areas tell us to focus our attention on the "victims."

In a discussion about sexual exploitation and theology, is there a place for understanding the exploiter better? There are many objections to committing time and other resources to understanding the exploiter. First of all, sexual exploitation is vastly underreported and largely unpunished. In a modern-world context where victim advocates must cite a "rape culture" in order to raise awareness to the injustice present in even the most obvious forms of sexual exploitation, should there be space to challenge common assumptions about offenders? Many organizations fighting sexual exploitation face serious difficulties in raising the necessary resources to offer services to the victims of sexual exploitation. Why should organizations expand their theology and their practice to include restoration of exploiters as a vital component of demand reduction?

This chapter will include an honest look at offenders as part of the complexity of the problem of sexual exploitation. We will consider the Hebrew word *shalom* in the Bible and examine Jesus' example as a way of understanding biblical justice. *Shalom* is commonly translated as peace and refers to completeness, a state where nothing is missing and nothing is broken. Jesus' ministry prioritized the broken and included the ignored. The gap in current response efforts of Christian ministries hints at an incomplete theology underpinning the understanding of biblical justice and reconciliation. We want to challenge the theological presuppositions of Christian practitioners and call ministries to reconsider their response to Jesus' call to join him in his work of reconciliation.

Theological Presuppositions

Where are we, as the authors of this chapter, coming from? What theology drives us to write this chapter and challenge the assumptions of others? Put most basically, we believe Jesus came for sinners. Many see sexual exploiters and put them beyond redemption; who could not be shocked by their immoral behavior? God looks at the sexual exploiter and sees yet another sinner in need of a savior. Jesus confronts sinners and is not shocked by their immoral behavior.

We think about the act of sexually exploiting another person and consider it one of the worst evils imaginable.

> Jesus points out that we too are sinners (John 8:7) and all sins are morally equal in his eyes. Jesus challenges our assumptions with his parables and says that those forgiven of much will love him more. God asks his followers to love mercy and walk humbly with him. Jesus asks his followers to join him in his mission of reconciliation. God alone is the judge and vengeance is his alone.

We, with our human limitations, do not know the extent of pain and brokenness. Research indicates that most exploiters have been exploited themselves and are in deep pain; they have numbed their pain and exploiting others is their form of coping. Research done on the victim-to-victimizer cycle shows that having been a victim of child sexual abuse was a strong predictor of becoming a perpetrator.

> God sees all of the brokenness and has compassion for offenders. His grace changes hearts. A changed life has the power to connect with God and reach others for God. Think about how Paul's salvation and restoration changed the Church.

We see sexual exploitation and get angry.

> God sees this brokenness and missing pieces and longs for restoration and shalom.

Complexity Surrounding Exploiters

The first step in expanding the discussion of sexual exploitation and theology to better understand the exploiter requires acknowledging the complexity of sexual exploitation. Exploiters include everyone from the "john" to the trafficker, and all the pimps, madams, and recruiters in between. But what about the casual pornography viewer or the patron of an erotic massage? With the inclusion of these categories, it may be easier to agree that exploiters could include the Christian man who is vulnerable to sexual addiction and becoming a client of prostitutes. Even Christian expatriates, those working for development organizations doing significant work in poverty eradication programs and even developing policy, are vulnerable to erotic massage and other types of prostitution, particularly in areas of the world where it is relatively cheap and accessible.[1]

Purchasers of sexual services vary widely, so it is difficult to identify specific demographic similarities between these individuals. However, current studies suggest that men are much more likely to purchase sexual services than women. Additionally, studies suggest that men who work in occupations that require them to travel often or be separated from their families for long periods of time are often inclined to purchase sexual services. These occupations may include the armed forces, traveling businessmen, truckers, seafarers, and migrant workers. Men working in occupations that are associated with hyper-masculinity or that are sex-segregated may also be more likely to purchase sexual services. In a London study, 20 percent of participants had purchased sex while they were serving in the military. Lack of a relationship or sexual partner does not seem to be a determining factor in men's decision to purchase sexual services. In the study "Men Who Buy Sex", over half of the participants were in a relationship and still purchased sex. Local men provide an even larger customer base for sexual services.[2]

Without in any way minimizing the fact that the majority of abusers may be men, we need to be more open to the possibility that women can also be abusers. If we deny it, then abuse of boys by women will continue to be trivialized and under-reported. Those who minimize what has happened accentuate a survivor's suffering and make reporting harder. The problem is more complex than we often anticipate. A biblical example is the case of Joseph in Genesis 39. After being sold as a slave by the Ishmaelites to Potiphar, the captain of Pharaoh's guards, 17-year-old Joseph found favor with his master as well as with God. He lived in the house of his Egyptian master and became his attendant. Joseph was handsome and well-built and Potiphar's wife wanted Joseph to come to bed with her. Day after day, she sexually harassed him, even though he refused and pushed her away. Being the one with the power and not getting what she wanted, Potiphar's wife accused him of raping her. As a result, he was put into prison and was left there for several years (before he was released to interpret Pharaoh's dreams). This story portrays what might be considered an unusual case where the wealthy, powerful woman is the exploiter and the vulnerable slave is a young

---

[1] (Ainsworth, Miles and Taylor, 2016: 153).
[2] (Farley, Bindel and Golding, 2009).

man, but there are increasing reports that sexual abuse and exploitation of boys and young men by female teachers, youth leaders, counselors, and tourists may not be as uncommon as we would like to think.

The complexity of the problem of sexual exploitation also needs to include a discussion of those who pay to use children sexually. There are various reasons for sexual exploitation of children. In some settings, the person being sold for sex is under the age of 18 and the purchaser does not realize that that person is a minor. In other cases, the purchaser practices pedophilia and prefers to sexually abuse children. Pedophiles are often characterized by a consistent behavioral pattern: a preference for sex with children, a refined method of securing victims, and sexual fantasies about children. Although generalizations about pedophiles may not be helpful, common behaviors may include an inability to socialize within their own society's standards, a self-identification as child-lovers, difficulty in identifying the gaps between their behavior and normal behavior, and a strong need for visual stimulation.

Perspectives on Prostitution

While the profile of an exploiter varies widely, attitudes towards prostitution appear to have some similarities throughout the world. Societal assumptions often suggest that men are naturally inclined to stronger sexual urges that must be satisfied, while women (apart from those in prostitution) are viewed as more passive and controlled in their sexual behaviors. In our discussions with men in red-light areas, sexual behavior can be segregated into two categories: sex in marriage for comfort and procreation, and sex buying for fun and recreation with friends. Most societies view prostitution negatively as it compromises the treasured virginity and purity of women. Nonetheless, prostitution has often been seen as a "necessary evil", including by those in the church, as it serves to satiate men's excess sexual urges, which, if not satisfied, may cause additional societal or familial problems. These views often result in men who purchase sex being dismissed or let off lightly from punishment on the basis of their need for sexual release, while women who work as prostitutes are viewed as culturally and naturally deviant.

In the West, prostitution appears to be increasingly acceptable. In a London, UK, study by Farley (2009), men shared that after visiting a place where prostitution was actively promoted, such as a red-light area, they were more inclined to seek out prostitution, even if it was illegal. Sixty-five percent of men in this study also believed that the majority of men buy sex, even though the actual number of men who purchase sex may be less. Perhaps this belief that prostitution is common normalizes it and further encourages its use. Views on prostitution are typically understood to be socially constructed and are affected by beliefs about gender relations, familial relations, and attitudes toward minority groups. In another London study, respondents acknowledged that they do think prostitution and paying for sex is wrong but believe it is inevitable.[3] The

---

[3] (Coy, Hovarth and Kelly, 2002).

majority of men interviewed expressed feelings of guilt or shame over purchasing sex. Others claim that their use of prostitutes is the result of a sexual addiction. Legalization and increasing tolerance of prostitution seems to be one of the factors that enables men to purchase sex.

Role of Pornography

Pornography does appear to be linked to prostitution.[4] Research among Cambodian men revealed several connections.[5] Some men used pornography as a stimulus before seeking a prostitute. Some men used pornography as a way of educating themselves about how to do sex, but because they believed that their wives and partners would not want to do certain sexual techniques, they sought out a prostitute to relieve sexual tension. The Gottman Effect states that the more someone views images, the more disinteresting those images become, which leads to more violent and alternative types of sexual behavior, and might lead someone to seek after other forms of sexual stimulation, such as prostitution.[6]

A number of programs in the United States have focused on enabling men to stop using pornography. Many of these have a Christian focus (e.g. Covenant Eyes). Research conducted with and by these organizations suggests that there is very little difference between those who say they are Christians, and those who do not. Those in Christian leadership are also prone to use pornography.[7]

Having been involved in the MST Project and then GLUE Ministries in Cambodia, we noticed the challenges we had in keeping expatriate male volunteers. Although we have not been able to do systematic research on the issue, discussion with some church leaders have led us to think that for some men their struggle with lust, pornography, and shame makes it difficult for them to continue or even start volunteering with us (even though confessing to each other and praying before outreach is part of the ministry). Today's Internet provides an unprecedented opportunity to access pornography. Internet pornography goes beyond the still photographs in magazines of the past. Viewing pornography can alter the brain to produce an addiction; teenager's brains are especially vulnerable. This type of addiction, perhaps especially in the church context, often develops in secret.

Disciplines and Services

The exploiter is the ordinary man or woman, not the vile monster and pervert popularly demonized in current media. The exploiter can be a Christian who is vulnerable to buying sex. If any ordinary person is capable of being an exploiter, then why is there such a gap in current response efforts? Organizations working

---

[4] Editor's note: Also see Part 3 of the first volume in this series regarding the connections between pornography and prostitution. Miles and Crawford, *Stopping the Traffick* (Regnum 2014).

[5] (Davis, Miles and Miller, 2016).

[6] (Gottman, 2016).

[7] (Barna, 2016).

to address the injustice of sexual exploitation disproportionately focus on women and children being exploited. Reaching out to exploiters is rarely a part of the mission of organizations and it appears that the perspective of the exploiter is preferably unheard.

In Cambodia, there are around 50 organizations working under the umbrella of the *Chab Dai* coalition to address sexual exploitation. Only three of these are working to address the "demand" side; one with the police and the law, and the other two with pimps and sex tourists/expatriates in their context. There is a need for further research on the demand for the sex industry, specifically the psychology behind why men pay for sex.

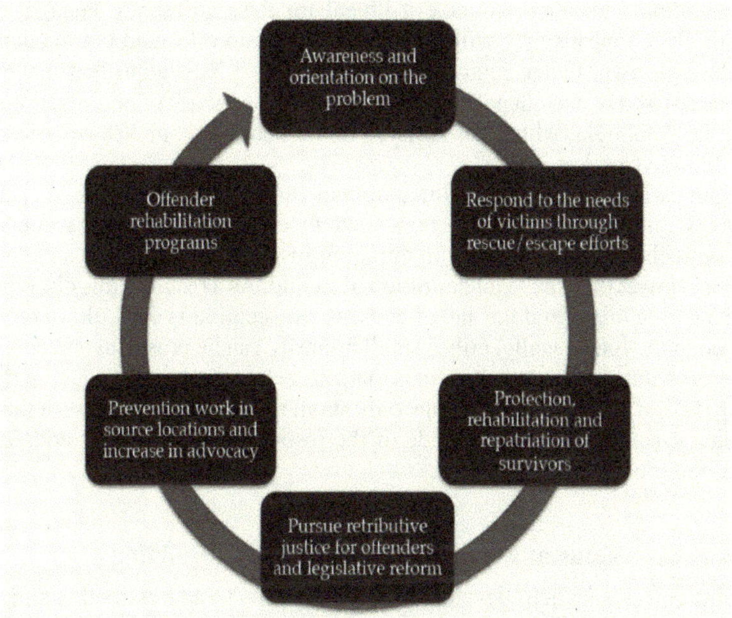

Figure 1: Cycle of response to trafficking[8]

To further explain the gap in response efforts, Figure 1 shows the cycle of response to one example of sexual exploitation, sex trafficking. At the beginning of the cycle, there is an acknowledgement that the awareness of the problem of sex trafficking leads to some type of response. Individuals and organizations combating sexual exploitation respond to the problem by meeting the needs of victims through rescue efforts. Rescued victims and other survivors are offered protection, rehabilitation, and repatriation to their countries of origin. As rehabilitation progresses and the stories of survivors are told, the desire to pursue retributive justice for exploiters increases. Legislative reform is often needed to properly address the injustice. At this point in the cycle, the responders take a step back and there is a renewed focus on preventing the problem. Advocacy

[8] Adapted from Miller, 2013: 73.

groups begin education programs in source communities and initiate demand reduction techniques. While each of these steps follows an understandable cycle of response, there is a gap in response efforts because those offering services rarely offer rehabilitation or a path to redemption to exploiters. The focus tends to be on retribution and only on child sex offenders, because having sex with children under 12 years in particular is seen as much more serious than buying sex from adults.

Why is there a gap in programs addressing the demand? Many factors are necessary to consider in an effort to address the demand for prostitution, sex trafficking, and sex tourism. An increase in legislation regarding ethical tourism could be helpful in curbing the demand for sex tourism. Some governments are implementing legislation to make it illegal for their citizens to engage in sex tourism, which means they will experience extradition if found out in countries outside their own. Other countries have established legislation that makes the purchase of sexual acts illegal. These laws support the work of organizations like APLE in Cambodia, which has assisted in the conviction of 128 sex offenders from 2003 to October 2011.

Organizations such as the International Justice Mission, due to limited resources, public concern, and donors, have focused their energy on prosecuting those who choose to have sex with children. In some countries, the legal age of consent is lower than the legal definition of a child. As a result of this discrepancy in the age of a minor and the age of consent, prosecution is difficult. In terms of addressing the issue legally, only a small minority can be prosecuted in countries where prostitution is legal. It is important to acknowledge that legal action is expensive and time consuming; thus only small number of cases make it through the legal system. This punitive side of the justice system does not address the root of the problem.

Value of Education and Awareness Building

In addition to legislation, development of programs to address both supply and demand sides of trafficking is necessary. Before comprehensive programs can be developed, the anti-trafficking community needs to seriously consider including outreach to the exploiter in demand reduction. The International Christian Alliance on Prostitution (ICAP) "exists to care for and connect practitioners who serve survivors of commercial sexual exploitation around the world, promoting collaboration, providing encouragement, offering resources and creating environments for worship" and yet ICAP recognizes the need to include those working with the exploiter as speakers during their global conference. How much more comprehensive could response efforts be if other anti-trafficking conferences were intentionally including speakers who work in restorative ways to reduce the demand side of sexual exploitation?

Discussion addressing the demand side of sexual exploitation can lead to useful programming. While more research is needed to determine the effectiveness and appropriateness of various types of interventions to address demand, the following are a few examples. One intervention that may be effective involves providing educational programs that deter men from buying sex, especially with men who have mixed feelings about prostitution, e.g. posters used in Cambodia to discuss the positive and negative aspects of using prostituted people.[9]

If these men were provided with reasons to avoid purchasing sexual services, they may be less inclined to support prostitution. Community programs have developed through neighborhood safety organizations and publication of the names of sex offenders. Other programs to address demand have included faith-based healing and treatment programs, which work with men to address behaviors regarding sexual sin or addiction. Additionally, campaigns have been developed in many countries to promote awareness and prevention of child sex tourism in an effort to prevent sex offenses rather than merely respond to men who have already been arrested for an offense. The solution to demand is not a simple one and requires much more attention and research.

Another approach is to use John Schools, educational interventions, and diversion programs for men arrested for soliciting the services of a prostitute. These schools are several days where "Johns" are exposed to the dangers to themselves and to the prostitutes. It attempts to elicit a compassionate response from sex buyers of the real risks and life cycle of prostitutes so that they do not choose to do it in the future. Limited resources are available to those who are addicted to sex and looking for counseling.

Effectiveness of Circles of Support and Accountability

There is also a model for working with sex offenders after they are released from prison. Circles of Support and Accountability (COSA) is a collaborative model of risk management and restoration. A Mennonite community in Canada conceived the project and it is now used in many communities and in many countries around the world. In this restorative justice approach, "professionally-supported community members volunteer time to assist high-risk, high-need sex offenders as they attempt to integrate to society after release from prison".[10] The COSA model is based on the idea that ex-offenders need housing, employment, and pro-social support in order to successfully re-enter a community. Studies comparing the relative rates of reoffending between COSA Core Members and matched-comparison subjects showed that COSA Core Members had significantly lower rates of any type of reoffending than did the comparison subjects, specifically a 70% reduction in sexual recidivism. A recent study on the Minnesota Department of Corrections COSA showed participation in a COSA significantly reduced sex offense recidivism, lowering the rate of being rearrested by 88%. COSA has given community members a tangible and positive

---

[9] "What Men Should Consider", posters. Available at: [http://gmmiles.co.uk/wp-content/uploads/2013/05/Man-Eg.pdf and http://gmmiles.co.uk/wp-content/uploads/2013/05/Soldier-Eg.pdf], [Last accessed: 28th October 2022]. In addition, a Volume II in this series includes as section on demand (*Stopping the Traffick*, 2014).

[10] R.J. Wilson, "Circles of Support & Accountability" Website: http://www.robinjwilson.com/circles.shtml.

way to engage with ex-offenders and provides a balance between accountability and support that results in increased community safety.

Despite the proven success, most practitioners believe that it would not work. In a recent informal survey, contacts of the authors were asked whether or not the COSA program would be successful, and the majority indicated their belief that the recidivism rate would be very high. The view of many is that if one is a pedophile, change is unlikely. But the above research indicates differently. We are not suggesting that people should be put in situations where they could be tempted, but we must question why it is so hard for us to think that change might be possible for this group of people. Is it because we find it easier to separate ourselves from them if they continue to be evil, are othered and demonized?

There is an assumption (that is most certainly not challenged in public discourse, especially highlighted in the threads of social media posts on the topic) that pedophiles can never change. This assumption, taken to its natural conclusion, normalizes extraordinary punishments for child sex offenders. For example, in June 2019, Governor Kay Ivey of the US state of Alabama signed a chemical castration measure into law. The law requires those who were convicted of certain types of sexual offenses, including child sex offenders, to be chemically castrated as a term of their parole. Chemical castration uses a drug to reduce testosterone to affect the sex drive. In 2016, Indonesian President Joao Widodo signed an executive decree allowing judges to hand down a sentence of chemical castration at their discretion to convicted child sex offenders. Russia, Poland, Australia, South Korea, Israel, the UK and other states in the United States have used chemical castration on sex offenders. There is a belief that severe punishments like chemical castration will deter perpetrators from committing crimes against children and that therefore, in some way, society will be a safer place. Once again, this is an example of a justice measure that does not deal with the root cause of the problem of sexual offending. Does a chemical castration law satiate society's desire for vengeance? AP News published an interview with Steve Hurst, the Alabama representative who introduced the chemical castration bill, who said, "If they're going to mark these children for life, they need to be marked for life."[11] Does public outrage justify a total lack of interest in preventative work? In this article, we want to challenge this lack of interest and call on the Christian community to be counter-cultural in its thinking about sex offenders.

Organizational Approaches

Even though there is an increasing amount of research that Christians are vulnerable to losing their sexual integrity, there is limited evidence that understanding and maintaining sexual integrity is being included in training and being screened for during the application process. Christian organizations need to think creatively about child protection and sexuality well before an individual is accepted into ministry. The Child Safety and Protection Network is an example of an inter-agency response to issues of child abuse and safety in Christian

---

[11] https://apnews.com/article/77cd155339744a9396399ae641096230.

missions. Christian missionary agencies and mission-related schools are encouraged to collaborate in developing child safety curriculum, sharing quality resources, and developing effective response and care protocols.

Ultimately, there are limits to screening and training. All you have to do is simply speak with the children's ministry director at a church about their child safety policy and you will be told matter of factly that they conduct background checks on all volunteers. Should that make you feel safe as a parent leaving your child with strangers at church? Conducting background checks for previous sexual convictions would rule out only a very small number of individuals who could pose a risk to children. Many with addictions to child pornography for instance may have never been caught. Those with child pornography addictions do not have a safe place to turn for counseling due to mandatory reporting laws (which is an entirely larger conversation in the discussion of the "demand" side of sexual exploitation).

Often, protecting an organization from sexual exploiters comes after a devastating incident has been uncovered. For example, the Christian organization Kanakuk Kamps responded to sexual misconduct within its organization by developing a comprehensive child safety system to prevent, detect or respond to child abuse in a camp setting. They now empower and equip camping organizations throughout the United States with a training program that includes a demand-focused prevention strategy. Specifically, the Kanakuk Child Protection Plan provides an "Opt Out" opportunity for those struggling with pedophilic tendencies or desire to harm children to opt out of employment or service before harm occurs.[12] This type of innovative approach is needed in other ministry settings. Missionaries and development workers working in high-risk environments where prostitution and erotic massages are cheap and very accessible should take organizational approaches that recognize the vulnerability.

The biblical example of Amnon and Tamar contributes to a holistic theological understanding of reaching out to the exploiter (2 Sam. 13). Amnon "became so obsessed with his sister Tamar that he made himself ill" and his advisor Jonadab asked him why he looked so terrible day after day. Amnon admitted being "in love with Tamar" and, together, Amnon and Jonadab came up with a scenario that gave Amnon access to his virgin half-sister. Amnon pretended to be ill and asked his father, David, to send his sister Tamar to give him something to eat. David sent Tamar to Amnon's house and Amnon went on to rape his sister. This example shows multiple points where intervention could have prevented the sexual exploitation of Tamar. After Amnon raped Tamar, Tamar's brother Absalom told her to stay quiet. Absalom hated Amnon because he had disgraced his sister and went on to order his men to murder Amnon. The lack of properly addressing Amnon's wrongdoing led to intense hatred and death, no *shalom*. Absalom fled and King David longed for both Amnon and Absalom. In this situation, the result was further brokenness and damage to all of those surrounding the exploitation. How do we contribute to the culture of

[12] https://kanakukchildprotection.org/the-plan/.

exploitation? How can addressing the demand side of sexual exploitation include a conversation with the community about ways everyone plays a part in the problem, if only indirectly.

In Christian ministries, where there is a lack of any form of discussion or training about sexual exploitation and transparency, it is unlikely that someone who has a developing problem with sexual temptation will receive the assistance needed to prevent sexual exploitation. In conducting training in Cambodia, one participant described to one of the authors about how difficult it had been for him to come to the training, even though it was a general discussion about the issue rather than being described as a session for those with a problem.

Christian programs about sexual integrity tend to be aimed at youth and focus on abstinence and preventing access to pornography. The majority focus on heterosexual youth; talking with adults is usually done in the confines of "marriage preparation" courses, where sexual activity outside of marriage seems improbable.

Clergy abuse has taken center stage in the media, especially with the Catholic Church and more recently with the Southern Baptist Convention in the United States. This may largely be because money is involved; research into clergy abuse has been conducted to try to reduce the number of insurance payouts. Imagine how implementing and researching restorative justice programs with clergy who have been removed from their positions and been punished punitively could benefit practitioners addressing sexual exploitation.

There is room for improvement in the services offered to prevent sexual exploitation and properly address its impact. However, improving current response efforts begins with challenging theological assumptions and beliefs about exploiters.

Christian Theology

The lack of disciplines and services related to the restoration of exploiters hints at the Church's limited theological perspective on this matter. People and organizations working in this field should ask: "What is justice and whose justice should be pursued?" Is it possible practitioners are missing part of God's call and heart for restoration and reconciliation? Jesus came to earth as the example of the perfect human, offering reconciliation to all people. In Jesus' teachings, actions, and death, his followers learned about God's character and how to join him in his work of reconciliation.

Thinking deeply about Jesus' approach to restoration and reconciliation includes his response to both the sexually exploited and the exploiter. He makes the comment regarding the woman caught in adultery in John 8:7: "Let any one of you who is without sin be the first to throw a stone at her." Although we are unclear about the context of this story and why the man is not being addressed, Jesus' comment to the teachers of the law to throw the first stone is a reminder that we have all sinned and have no right to judge others. This is left to God and, in this story, Jesus says he too will not throw a stone.

The parables included in Luke 15 offer a picture of Jesus seeking and saving the lost as a crucial aspect of his approach to restoration and reconciliation. The model of forgiveness includes the prodigal son who went off to a far country and spent the inheritance money on women and wine. The prodigal son could be described as a sex tourist in modern language. Jesus seems to warn his audience that his followers should expect the "older brother" type of response when there is celebration to mark the restoration of the lost in the prodigal son parable. We were challenged to think even deeper about this story of the prodigal son by one reviewer of this chapter. Not only should we expect to receive the "older brother" response to the work of restoring offenders but, unless we are welcoming the returning "prodigal son" and rejoicing with the father, we are excluding ourselves from the party – and thus will be like the son who went into a far country.

The Old Testament example of Tamar and Judah is another example of a sex tourist (Gen. 38). After the death of her husband, and her brother-in-law's refusal to father children for his brother, Tamar was left childless. Her father-in-law, Judah, refused to give her his other son and told her to return to her father's house. After Judah's wife died, he went to another town to shear his sheep. Tamar concealed her identity and dressed as a prostitute, waiting for Judah. Judah did not recognize her and propositioned her for sex. Tamar became pregnant from Judah; and, being a widowed woman, was therefore considered guilty of prostitution. Judah wanted Tamar burned to death, until she sent a message to him notifying him that he was the one who had impregnated her. Judah was confronted with his wrongdoing, recognized his guilt in the situation, and did not sleep with her again. Judah considered Tamar more righteous than himself, and God blessed Tamar with twin sons.

Jesus is often criticized for dining with prostitutes and tax collectors (Mt. 9:10-17, Lk. 19:10, Mt. 21:32). Tax collectors were often linked to prostitution: "tax collectors are connected in Greco-Roman literature to those who trafficked in prostitution and slavery, particularly to brothel keepers and pimps, those most responsible for supplying women and slaves for banquets".[13] In Luke 19, the fact that Jesus not only noticed Zacchaeus, but also chose to enter his home and share a meal with him suggests another often overlooked group who need to be considered. Jesus went to where Zacchaeus, the chief tax collector, lived and all the people begin to mutter because he went to be the guest of a sinner. Those working with exploiters often experience Christians objecting to their work. Jesus came to help souls find their worth, even exploiters. In Jesus Christ's incarnation, crucifixion, and resurrection, he fully identifies with victim and offender. He takes the place of an offender on the cross, including his direct comment to the perpetrator on one side of him, although Jesus is an innocent victim. The Church has a lot to learn from Christ's example of love and his willingness to search for those who are lost.

Those responding to sexual exploitation should question whether their view of justice is as just as they think. Only God is all knowing; humans often have a distorted and limited view of the world. Oftentimes, this leads to perpetuating injustice in the name of justice. One way that this is done is by dehumanizing the

---

[13] (Corley, 2002).

exploiters and putting them beyond redemption. Justice includes naming the deed as evil and protecting the innocent but also seeking to forgive and reconcile with the exploiter. Restoration means re-establishing right relationships with God and others. How often do practitioners hold a view of justice that includes the exploiter in a restorative way?

Christian organizations combating sexual exploitation will often use Micah 6:8 as a guiding verse for their work. They tell supporters that the requirement is to do justice, to love mercy, and to walk humbly with God. In doing so, they overlook the implication of the very meaning of mercy – God not punishing sinners as they deserve. If Christians are supposed to love mercy, what does that mean for offering restoration to exploiters? Revenge is God's (Rom. 12:19), and his followers are given the ministry of reconciliation (2 Cor. 5:18-21). Christians are called to seek and struggle for God's justice, not their own. The sinner – yes, even the sexual exploiter – is justified by the blood of Jesus; this is God's idea of justice.

What about another often-quoted Bible verse by anti-trafficking practitioners? This verse says if anyone causes a little one to stumble it would be better for them to have a millstone hung around their neck and to be drowned in the depths of the sea (Mt. 18:6). The context of this conversation is Jesus speaking to his disciples (after they ask him which one of them is the greatest) about having the humility of a child to enter the kingdom of heaven. He uses the example of the innocence of childhood as a representation of how those converted must be made like little children to enter heaven. Jesus says he desires his followers to be simple and humble as children. As *John Gill's Exposition of the Entire Bible* points out, "little ones" is not only an indication of age but also of the esteem of the world.[14] Jesus does not want the laying of a stumbling block before anyone, and elsewhere he shows his deep love for children. But this verse (Mt. 18:6) may not be the damning evidence justifying the harsh type of justice that forgets the sex offender in the work of reconciliation. The story of Jesus talking to the other man being crucified alongside him is one of reconciliation and forgiveness that was completely undeserved.

The seemingly impossible task of loving the exploiter (Mt. 5:43-48) is only possible with God. Jesus was the perfect example of what it looks like to sacrifice for sinners (Rom. 5:6-11). Croatian theologian Miroslav Volf put it this way: "If we believe rightly in Jesus Christ who unconditionally embraced us, the godless perpetrators, our hearts will be open to receive others, even enemies, and our eyes will be open to see from their perspective."[15] Jesus came to seek and save the lost, even the exploiter. Can we ever offer forgiveness, healing, and hope to these exploiters theologically, if not legally? Are we willing to step back from the seemingly-righteous anger we feel toward those who offend sexually and ask God what he sees in someone so "offensive?" Can we see their humanity and brokenness and work with them for restoration?

---

[14] (Gill, 2016).

[15] (Volf, 1996).

Conclusion: How Do We Face the Challenges Going Forward?

Have you noticed that we like to put sin into a hierarchy telling ourselves that we are not so bad? When we talk to men in the red-light area in Cambodia, some tell us that they would never hurt children, not seeing that the person they are having sex with tonight likely started their career in prostitution as a child. Even Christian leaders, in the safety of our home offices, change the website to something sexy. We may forget that those images were created using real people and are not as untainted as they might seem; they are likely to have involved coercion and pain.

There seems to be a view in the anti-trafficking community that if a ministry only reaches or rescues one girl, woman, or victim, that is enough. Why is this same logic not applied to the exploiters? If only one man was stopped, how many children (or victims in general) could be spared? For example, the documentary film "Nefarious: Merchant of Souls" addresses the sex industry and includes an interview with Ohad Shaul, a man who was involved in trafficking for 11 years. He is now a Christian, is married and, together with his wife, works with vulnerable youth in Sea of Galilee, Israel to prevent them from entering the sex industry. In addition, the community underestimates the value a reformed offender could have, the ways in which this person's insights could improve response and rescue efforts. The inside knowledge of a trafficker, for instance, could lead to better prevention education among those at risk as well as more effective identification of other exploiters.

Another example is former porn producer Donny Pauling. He advertised his pornographic content on Christian web pages and forums and said he had success recruiting some of his greatest number of clients on these sites. His time working in the porn industry led him to his view that it is degrading and damaging to all parties involved. He was drawn to the tolerance message being preached to a church called *XXXChurch.* Author Tim Smith quoted Pauling as saying, "The Christians I grew up around would never talk to a porn producer, much less broadcast it to their listeners [...] but they were doing things in such a different way. They were actually loving people [...] I couldn't help but say, if I was going to be a Christian, this is the kind of Christian I would want to be."[16] Pauling went on to convert to Christianity and left the porn industry. He became a pastor and anti-porn activist.

Sadly, in December 2014, Pauling was arrested on three felony sex charges including statutory rape. In 2015, he pleaded no contest and agreed to a prison sentence; he said he was "motivated by an unnatural or abnormal interest in children" according to his plea. We wonder if there was anyone in his Christian ministry circle who he felt he could approach about his sexual interest in children. This was a man who toured the world using words like sex and porn and addiction, yet it seems he did not have a mechanism for naming or addressing his root sin and brokenness. After his conviction, Christian ministries understandably distanced themselves from him. Our culture likes to assign guilt and shift blame and this impacts Christians living in this culture. His affiliate

---

[16] (Smith, 2014).

ministries prepared public statements, should they be asked to comment. Did Donny Pauling deserve to serve time for his crimes and to be removed from ministry positions? These questions seem easy to answer; almost a gut reaction will give you the answer. But we are compelled by a deeper question that needs to be asked, beyond the easy assigning of guilt and blame: does Pauling deserve someone to come alongside him to help him find another experience of the healing grace and love of God?

What does the limited response to sexual offenders from Christian groups say about our theological presuppositions? There seems to be an assumption that the exploiter deserves to die or spend their afterlife in hell because a sexual sin ruins a life (a sexual sin is worse on the hierarchy than other offenses). Is being exploited the end of a life? Where is the hope for restoration? This view of the irreversible impact of sexual exploitation seems to be limiting the restoration efforts for victims as well as offenders/exploiters.

In order to thoroughly address issues of prostitution and sex trafficking, the demand for sexual services must also be addressed. There is not a simple fix to such a complex problem with so many individuals involved. Programs to support those working in prostitution or those who have been trafficked have been established, and while these programs may not yet be sufficient for the need, they are more prevalent than programs available to support men and women who exploit others sexually. Through outreach in red-light districts in Thailand and Cambodia, the MST Project and GLUE Ministries seek to understand and to support men who frequent these areas. As information about these men has been gathered, there has been more opportunity to discover their needs, to educate them about alternatives, and to provide them support.

As existing literature suggests, it is difficult to label a specific type of person as a sexual exploiter. However, recent research in Thailand and Cambodia reveals some possible trends about men who frequent red-light districts. There are a significant number of men who view prostitution negatively, which means they acknowledge there are concerns. Providing them with information has the potential to be very helpful, and it may leave room for further opportunities to provide additional educational and support programs. While this data provides a foundation, there is still much room for further research and understanding about the best ways to address demand and to provide effective programs for men who purchase sex.

God's justice is holistic and transformational, and his followers are called to join him in his work of reconciliation. People who exploit are created in the image of God, broken and in need of a savior. The solution starts with a Christian's desire to include the exploiter in the response to the problem. Should justice hurt or heal? Is it about retribution or rehabilitation? Where is the place for forgiveness? How can exploiters be challenged to make better choices, and treat people with dignity both practically and theologically? It may be more easily understood theologically than practically, especially in the case of the abuse of children, but seriously considering the restoration of offenders will expose Christians to their own views of the hierarchy of sin and approach to hidden sin. Serious reflection could result in a very transformative view of human nature without God, not to mention the great task God has invited his followers to join. Understanding God's compassion for the exploiter will open a world of possibilities for a holistic, wise, and constructive response to sexual exploitation.

Reflection Questions

1. How do you define justice? What is the purpose of justice? Should it be punitive or restorative? In what ways should justice hurt and in what ways should it heal? Describe your understanding of biblical justice and reconciliation.
2. Do you feel that the Church welcomes the sexual offender who is repentant? What does repentance mean? What does it require?
3. Do you think Christian ministries are interested in creating programs to help offenders experience the healing of God's restoration and justice? If not, why? What is needed to do so?
4. After reading the chapter, did you feel any new stirring of the Holy Spirit regarding how you can join in his work of reconciliation? How can you respond in practical ways?

Works Cited

Action Pour Les Enfants. "Casework Statistics". *APLE Website*. 2011. [Available at: http://www.aplecambodia.org], [Last accessed: 28th October 2022].

Anderson, B. and J.O. Davidson. *Trafficking: A demand led problem?* Stockholm, Sweden: Save the Children Sweden, 2004.

Barna Group with Josh McDowell. *The Porn Phenomenon: The Impact of Pornography in the Digital Age.* Ventura, CA: Barna Group, 2016.

Bible Hub. "Matthew 18:6", *Bible Hub Website.* [Available at: https://biblehub.com/commentaries/matthew/18-6.htm], [Last accessed: 28th October 2022].

Corley, Kathleen E. *Women and the Historical Jesus: Feminist Myths of Christian Origins*. Santa Rosa, CA: Polebridge, 2002.

Coy, M., M. Horvath and L. Kelly. *"It's just like going to the supermarket": Men buying sex in East London report for safe exit at Tonybee Hall.* London: Child and Woman Abuse Studies Unit London Metropolitan University, 2007.

Davidson, J.O. *The Sex Exploiter*. Nottingham: University of Nottingham, 2001.

Duwe, Grant. "The Promise and Potential of Circles of Support and Accountability: A Sex Offender Reentry Program". *American Enterprise Institute Website.* 21st February 2018. [Available at: https://www.aei.org/research-products/report/the-promise-and-potential-of-circles-of-support-and-accountability-a-sex-offender-reentry-program/], [Last accessed: 28th October 2022].

Ericson, E. and A. Rönning. *Sustainable Tourism Development in Cambodia.* Karlstad: Karlstad University, 2008.

Farley, M., J. Bindel and J.M. Golding. *Men Who Buy Sex: Who they buy and what they know.* London: Eaves, 2009.

Gill, John. *John Gill's Exposition of the Bible* [online] Bible Study Tools. 2016. [Available at: http://www.Biblestudytools.com/commentaries/gills-exposition-of-the-bible/], [Last accessed: 28th October 2022].

Glasser M., I. Kolvin, D. Campbell, A. Glasser, I. Leitch, S. Farrelly. "Cycle of child sexual abuse: links between being a victim and becoming a perpetrator". *Br J Psychiatry*. 179 (December 2001): 482-94.

GLUE Ministries Website. [Available at: www.glueministries.com], [Last accessed: 28th October 2022].

Gottman, John and Julie Gottman. "An Open Letter on Porn". *The Gottman Institute Blog*. 5th April 2016, https://www.gottman.com/blog/an-open-letter-on-porn/

Grillot, C. *"Street Pedophilia" in Cambodia: A survey on Phnom Penh's suspects and victims.* Phnom Penh: Action Pour Les Enfants and British Embassy in Cambodia, 2005.

Havey, J., J. Halsey, C. Scales and M. Stumpf. *"Listening to the Demand" Men who buy sex from men in Cambodia.* Love 146, 2014. [Available at: http://gmmiles.co.uk/wp-content/uploads/2014/05/MSF-Demand-Final-Report.pdf], [Last accessed: 28th October 2022].

Hughes, D.M. *Best practices to address the demand side of sex trafficking.* Kingston, RI: University of Rhode Island, 2004.

International Christian Alliance on Prostitution Website. [Available at: https://www.icapglobal.org], [Last accessed: 28th October 2022].

Lenty, C. and G. Miles "Surveys of Men in Red Light Areas in Bangkok". Unpublished research by MST Bangkok. 2011. For more info contact: drglennmiles@gmail.com.

Lim, L.L. *Trafficking, demand and the sex market*. International symposium on gender at the heart of globalization. Geneva: International Labour Organization, 2007.

Miles, Glenn and Christa Foster Crawford. *Stopping the Traffick: A Christian Response to Sexual Exploitation and Trafficking*. Oxford: Regnum, 2014.

Miles, G. and J. Yoder. "Surveys of Men in Red Light Areas in Phnom Penh, Cambodia". Unpublished research by GLUE Ministries. For more info contact: drglennmiles@gmail.com.

Miller, Samantha, Glenn Miles and James Havey. "Listening to Local and Foreign Sex Buyers of Men and Women in Cambodia." *Slavery Today Journal* 3(1), (August 2016): 1-24.

Miller, Samantha S. "Beyond Prison Bars: The Intersection of the Perspectives of Christians Working in the Anti-sex Trafficking Field in Kolkata, West Bengal, India and the Theory of Restorative Justice". Master's thesis. Wheaton, IL: Wheaton College, 2013.

MST Project Website. [Available at: www.mstproject.com], [Last accessed: 28th October 2022].

Nolot, Benjamin (director). "Nefarious: Merchant of Souls". Exodus Cry, 2011.

Raymond, Janice. "Ten Reasons for Not Legalizing Prostitution a Legal Response to the Demand for Prostitution". *Journal of Trauma Practice* 2 (2003): 315-332.

Smith, Tim. "Donny's Escape from Pornography". *CBN.* Archived from the original on 25th July 2014.

The Independent. "Sex offenders to be castrated under new law approved by US state". *The Independent Website.* 11th June 2019. [Available at: https://www.independent.co.uk/news/castrate-sex-offenders-alabama-us-chemical-pedophile-a8953971.html], [Last accessed: 28th October 2022].

Volf, Miroslav. *Exclusion and Embrace: A Theological Exploration of Identity, Otherness, and Reconciliation.* Nashville, TN: Abington Press, 1996.

Williams, Antwan. "Episode 13: Dirty Water". Audio blog post. *Ear Hustle.* Radiotopia, 28th March 2018. [Available at: www.earhustlesq.com], [Last accessed: 28th October 2022].

Wilson, R.J., J.E. Picheca and M. Prinzo. "Evaluating the effectiveness of professionally-facilitated volunteerism in the community-based management of high-risk sexual offenders: PART ONE – Effects on participants and stakeholders". *Howard Journal of Criminal Justice* 46 (2007): 289-302.

Wilson, R.J., J.E. Picheca and M. Prinzo. "Evaluating the effectiveness of professionally-facilitated volunteerism in the community-based management of high-risk sexual offenders: PART TWO – A comparison of recidivism rates". *Howard Journal of Criminal Justice* 46 (2007): 327-337.

Wilson, R.J., F. Cortoni, and A.J. McWhinnie. "Circles of Support & Accountability: A Canadian national replication of outcome findings". *Sexual Abuse: A Journal of Research & Treatment* 21 (2009): 412-430.

Wilson, R.J. "Circles of Support & Accountability" Website. [Available at: http://www.robinjwilson.com/circles.shtml], [Last accessed: 28th October 2022].

XXX Church Website. [Available at: www.xxxchurch.com], [Last accessed: 28th October 2022].

Contributors

Editors

Christa Foster Crawford, JD, is an international expert in human trafficking and sexual exploitation with more than 25 years of grassroots and policy experience in Thailand and around the globe. As founder of *Freedom Resource International,* she spends her time teaching, training, writing and speaking about how to help the anti-trafficking movement have more strategic and effective impact. She also co-chairs the *Joint Learning Initiative's Modern Slavery & Human Trafficking Hub* and is Specialist with the *Payap University Center on Human Rights Law.* Her previous experience includes heading anti-trafficking organizations including *Chab Dai* and *International Justice Mission's Thailand Justice Center*, co-founding *Just Food Inc.*, an early pioneer in Freedom Business, and writing a book on how to use the law to combat human trafficking for the *United Nations*. Christa teaches graduate courses for *Fuller Seminary* and *Multnomah University*, and has authored and edited numerous books, chapters, and articles. Christa holds a Juris Doctorate from Harvard Law School and a BA in Philosophy & Public Affairs from Claremont McKenna College. www.freedomresource.org

Glenn Miles, PhD, is an international expert on human trafficking, sexual exploitation and child welfare, with more than 30-years experience in Southeast Asia. He pioneered several international NGOs in Cambodia and helped to develop a series of toolkits for children to reduce sexual exploitation (e.g. www.goodtouchbadtouchflipchart.org). A senior researcher with the *Global Association of Human Trafficking Scholars*, Glenn has conducted research into demand, including porn use, and has led multiple studies on the vulnerabilities of sexually exploited children/young people (including boys, young men and transgender people) in partnership with *up! Collective International* and other organizations. In addition to his academic research, Glenn has published numerous books, workbooks and other resources to improve the practice of grassroots workers. He is academic advisor for the *Chab Dai Longitudinal Butterfly Research Project* and teaches courses for graduate programs in Asia. In addition to his PhD in Childhood Studies, he is a graduate of All Nations Christian College where he received a Diploma in Biblical, Cross Cultural and Pastoral Studies. www.gmmiles.co.uk

Bill Prevette, PhD, is a mission scholar and practitioner. His research focuses on youth and children at risk in the developing world. He also conducts studies on human trafficking and interventions, urban research, community development, and Pentecostalism in global mission. Bill is currently serving as the Mission Scholar in Residence at *Vanguard University*. He and his wife, Ky, are appointed missionaries to Europe with the *Assemblies of God World Mission.*

He is a member of several international not-for-profit boards and a technical advisor to faith-based organisations in the United States, Romania, Moldova, Cambodia, and Africa. He regularly teaches academic seminars and lectureships. Bill has a PhD from with Oxford Centre for Mission Studies and a MA from the Fuller School of World Mission.

Contributors

Jarrett Davis, MA, is an independent social researcher with more than 10 years' experience specialising in gender, exploitation, and violence. His work has focused on developing a better understanding of the vulnerabilities of people groups that are often overlooked in research, policy, and social development initiatives. He has led a variety of research projects with international organizations in Southeast Asia focusing on sexual violence against males and LGBTQ persons. More recently, he conducted research on Online Sexual Exploitation in Cambodia and the Philippines. He is currently based in New York and is a member of *up! Collective.*

Tim Davy, PhD, is Lecturer and Head of Research and Consultancy at *All Nations Christian College* in the UK. His two research focuses are the missional interpretation of the Bible, and vulnerable children. He is currently working on a book on vulnerable children in the Old Testament. Tim is Theologian in Residence at *Home for Good*, a charity working to mobilise the UK Church to respond to the needs of vulnerable children. He also led a research project funded by the Gloucester Diocesan LIFE Development Fund on Unaccompanied Asylum-Seeking Children, which included helping set up an educational mentoring scheme.

Leah Edwards, PhD, is a freelance research consultant based in The Netherlands. She is the founder of *Kaart Consulting* and is currently focused on researching and publishing on the experiences of vulnerable migrants within the Middle East and Islamic world. She works with anti-trafficking NGOs to strengthen programming and develop innovative tools for conducting research, assessments, and evaluations. Dr. Edwards is a member of the operational team for the *European Freedom Network* where she steers the Research Action Group and consults on European Union advocacy projects. Prior to her PhD study, Dr. Edwards worked in the humanitarian sector with faith-based organisations.

Timothy Gaikwad is the CEO of *IMCARES*, an NGO based in Mumbai, India. He is also an award-winning independent documentary and feature filmmaker, a composer/songwriter ad music director, and has made landmark productions to sensitise people about those who are lost, poor, abused, and vulnerable. His films on HIV & AIDS, child trafficking, boy-child sexual abuse, and domestic violence against women are widely used as resource materials in different parts of India and worldwide. Timothy is passionate about expressing the agape love and the justice heart of God through all his endeavours.

Stephanie Goins, PhD, has worked in program development, management, and research for over 25 years, focusing on issues concerning vulnerable children, well-being, and culture. Having begun her career in psychology, Dr. Goins is currently serving as faculty with *NAIITS*, an indigenous learning community. Prior to this, Dr. Goins was the program director for an international human rights organisation focusing on prevention and aftercare for trafficked and exploited children. Dr. Goins has lived and worked in Africa, Europe and the United States alongside her husband. Her doctoral work focused on processes of forgiveness as they related to reintegration for former child soldiers in Sierra Leone.

Glenn M. Harden, PhD, is Assistant Professor, Social Science & History at *Asbury University* in Kentucky, US, where he lives with his wife and dogs. From 2003 to 2015, Glenn lived in the Dominican Republic where he started a ministry to victims and survivors of the sex trade and their families. He has a PhD in Political Science from the University of Kentucky, a MA in History from George Mason University, and a MA in Theological Studies from Asbury Theological Seminary. He is the author of *The Sex Trade, Evil, and Christian Theology* (Wipf & Stock).

Leslie Harley is a survivor of commercial sexual exploitation. She participated in *Rahab Foundation*'s recovery program for victims of human trafficking and sexual exploitation. After finishing the program, she volunteered helping other victims, both at *Rahab Foundation* and at her local church. She has a BA in Philosophy from the Universidad de Costa Rica and a BA in Theology from Universidad Evangélica de las Américas. She lives in Alajuela, Costa Rica.

Genevieve James, PhD, heads the Community Engagement and Outreach division at the *University of South Africa*, which provides oversight to more than 100 development projects. She also created the *Chance 2 Advance* programme, an education for justice initiative and best practice in knowledge mobilisation. Chance 2 Advance is designed to create wider access to knowledge produced in the higher-education sector and encourage mutual knowledge mobilisation between universities and external communities. It has reached more than 100,000 participants. Prior to this, Genevieve served as senior lecturer in Missiology. Her PhD is in the field of Urban Missiology.

Carl Jylland-Halverson, PhD, is a Professor in the Department of Psychology and Counselling at the *University of Saint Francis* (Indiana, US), where he also directs the clinical mental health counselling program. He has presented on human trafficking at international and national conferences and provided training for counselors of survivors of human trafficking in Nepal, Thailand, and India. Carl served his sabbatical at *Emmaus Ministries* which works alongside homeless men who participate in prostitution. He holds a PhD in clinical psychology, an MA in Theology, an MA in Counselling Psychology, and an Advanced Certificate in Pastoral Counselling.

Amanda Avila Kaminski, PhD, is Assistant Professor of Theology at *Texas Lutheran University* where she also serves as director of the Social Innovation and Social Entrepreneurship program. She also belongs to the *International Fellowship of Mission for Transformation*, a global network that seeks to reimagine and mobilize theological education and to diversify seminary curricula for preparing mission laborers in contexts of suffering and extremity. She completed her undergraduate degree at Wheaton College and a dual Master's in Divinity and International Development at Eastern University before completing her PhD at the Graduate Theological Union.

Vanntheary Lim, MA, began work on the *Chab Dai Butterfly Longitudinal Research Project* in 2011 as part of Butterfly's original research team, and has spent over nine years conducting interviews, analysing data, producing reports, and giving presentations. From 2015-2019, Vanntheary was leading the Research Project as Project Manager and Researcher. Now, she is a Project Assistant at the *International Organization for Migration* (IOM) in Phnom Penh, Cambodia. Vanntheary holds a double bachelor's degree in Sociology and English Education in addition to a Master of Development Studies, all from the Royal University of Phnom Penh.

Bryon Lippincott, MA, is Communications Manager for *Free the Slaves*. He is passionate about helping people who are marginalized or vulnerable experience safe and abundant lives within healthy communities, as well as helping organizations represent these beneficiaries in ways that honor their dignity and respect their value as human beings. Prior to working for Free the Slaves, Bryon ran *Sharing Dots*, a creative agency specializing in strategic communications and media production for NGOs in Asia. He has partnered with more than 100 organizations and individuals in 13 countries, including organizations working with child vulnerability, anti-trafficking, HIV/AIDS, refugees, agriculture, poverty alleviation / community development, and education. Though born and raised on a family farm in Nebraska, US, his love for culture and humanitarian causes brought him to Asia where he has lived and worked for more than 10 years in China, Cambodia and Thailand, along with his wife, two teenage children, and two cats. Bryon holds an MA in Strategic Communication from California Baptist University, and is pursuing a PhD in Peace Studies from Payap University.

Heike Lippmann, MA, was an independent consultant known for her heart for justice and passion to see enslaved women set free. She was a post graduate at All Nations Christian College and co-author of "More Than Gender: A Baseline Study of Transgender Persons in the Phnom Penh Sex Industry." Her work involved setting solid theological foundations for work among people who are exploited, and helping people journey well on the long road to justice. Originally from Germany, she served with *Tamar*, a ministry of *All Souls Langham Place* in London, and also served in Kyrgyzstan, a country she loved, until shortly before her death in 2022.

Joni L. Middleton, MA, has served as a training and network consultant with *Project Rescue* since 1998. After spending 16 years in South Asia learning from human trafficking survivors, their children, and staff, and facilitating the formation of two networks, she moved to Paris in 2016. She now co-leads a ministry for Spanish-speaking transgenders and women in prostitution. She has been a contributing writer and trainer for the *Hands That Heal* curriculum (FAAST 2007). Currently, she is completing a PhD in Intercultural Studies (Relief and Development). Her professional aim is to facilitate learning experiences which enhance best practices in human trafficking responses, mentor new workers, and encourage survivors along their healing journey.

Siobhan Miles, MN, was a nurse practitioner/physician assistant who worked in clinical roles in California as well as the UK, Costa Rica, Thailand and Cambodia where she lived for more than two decades. Her work always focused on the most marginalised. She specialised in HIV/AIDS and then later managed the *Chab Dai Butterfly Longitudinal Research Project*. Siobhan held an MN (Masters in Nursing) and PAC (Physician Assistant Certified) from the University of Davis and the University of San Francisco and a Diploma in Theology from All Nations Christian College. She was working on her PhD at Oxford Centre for Mission Studies when she died suddenly and unexpectedly in 2016. The chapter in this volume was put together from additional research conducted before she died.

Samantha Miller, MA, MPA, is the founder of *Voices Heard LLC*, and serves as an independent investigative consultant. She conducts training of child safety teams worldwide and acts as an external consultant, leading inquiries into allegations of current and historic child abuse, primarily within the Christian missionary context. Ms. Miller is a certified child forensic interviewer and spent years interviewing and leading investigations as an active-duty military officer and Special Agent in the *United States Air Force Office of Special Investigations*. She has a MA in Intercultural Studies from Wheaton College as well as a second master's degree in Public Administration. Ms. Miller volunteers with restorative justice initiatives, including *Circles of Support and Accountability*, in her home state of Colorado.

Channtha Nhanh, MA, is the assistant project manager for the *Chab Dai Butterfly Longitudinal Research Project*, where she has conducted interviews, collaborated on data analysis, and disseminated study findings. She has also co-authored numerous publications addressing survivor resilience, perceptions of stigma, economic reintegration, experiences of male survivors, and experiences in shelter care. She holds a BA in sociology from the Royal University of Phnom Penh and a master's degree in Holistic Child Development from Malaysia Baptist Theological Seminary.

Rev. Dan Pratt, PhD, is Founder and Antislavery Co-ordinator for *The Together Free Foundation* and the *Southend Against Modern Slavery Partnership.* Both seek to partner with and resource communities and churches to combat modern slavery and human trafficking. He is an Associate Researcher with the Baptist Centre for History and Heritage at *Regent's Park College, Oxford.* Previously, Dan founded and pioneered *57 West*, a Baptist church rooted among rough sleepers in Essex. Dan's doctoral research was in Christian Education and Contextual Theology within South African townships. He is author of *Covenant and Church for Rough Sleepers* (Whitley Publications).

Jill Reimer, PhD, is passionate about social justice. She has been engaged in various capacities in the field of international development and education for 30 years, and lived in Cambodia for 15 years. She is co-author of several key pieces of research relating to human trafficking in Cambodia. Her doctoral dissertation through the University of British Columbia explored the intersection of culture and formal education in the context of Southeast Asia. She also holds a MSc from University of Guelph.

Andrew J. Schmutzer, PhD, is Professor of Bible at *Moody Bible Institute.* Among other biblical interests, he has written extensively on issues of sexual abuse and its practical and theological implications. His work has been published in *Journal of the Evangelical Theological Society*, *Journal of Spiritual Formation*, and others. His books on sexual abuse include *The Long Journey Home* (Wipf & Stock) and *Naming Our Abuse* (Kregel). He regularly works with church leaders about ministering to abuse victims and leads seminars around the US. He also serves on the Board of Directors for *Male Survivor*, an organization dedicated to help male survivors of sexual abuse. He holds a PhD from Trinity Evangelical Divinity School.

Jennifer Singh, PhD, is Associate Professor of Intercultural Studies at *Ambrose University* in Alberta, Canada. She also currently serves as a lay minister with a First Nation community in Southern Alberta. Prior to this, Dr. Singh was engaged in international development work for 15 years among vulnerable women in Southeast Asia, Africa, Latin America, Central Asia, and the Caribbean. Dr. Singh is committed to listening to and learning from those on the margins wherever her work takes her. She holds a PhD from Oxford Centre for Mission Studies and an MDiv from Regent College.

Hannah Sworn, MSc, is a researcher with extensive experience in Southeast Asia. She worked at the *USAID Cambodia Countering Trafficking-in-Persons* project before moving into monitoring and evaluation consulting for non-governmental organisations in Cambodia, Thailand, and Uganda. Her research interests lie in development, governance, and transnational crime and she is currently pursuing a PhD in Political Science. Hannah grew up in Cambodia from the age of four before undertaking a BA in Social Sciences at Monash University, Malaysia, and a MSc in International Relations from the S.

Rajaratnam School of International Studies at Nanyang Technological University, Singapore.

Myrto Theocharous, PhD, is a lecturer of Hebrew and Old Testament at the *Greek Bible College* in Athens, Greece. She is author of *Lexical Dependence and Intertextual Allusion in the Septuagint of the Twelve Prophets: Studies in Hosea, Amos and Micah* (LHBOTS 570; T & T Clark). Myrto has been active in anti-trafficking street work for many years and her current research interests include the book of Deuteronomy and the relationship between the Old Testament and Christian ethics. Born in Nicosia, Cyprus, she studied theology and biblical studies at the Greek Bible College. She holds a MA in Biblical Exegesis from Wheaton College and a PhD in the area of Septuagint studies from University of Cambridge, UK.

David Tombs, PhD, is the Howard Paterson Chair of Theology and Public Issues at the *University of Otago,* Aotearoa New Zealand. Originally from the United Kingdom, he previously worked at the *University of Roehampton* in London, and at the *Irish School of Ecumenics, Trinity College.* He has a longstanding interest in contextual and liberation theologies, and his current writing focuses on the crucifixion. He holds a PhD (London), an MA (Oxford), and STM (Union Theological Seminary).

Haddon Willmer, PhD, is emeritus Professor of Theology at the *University of Leeds,* where he taught for 32 years. He was a trustee of *Pace (Parents against Child Sexual Exploitation)* from 1997-2014 and a trustee of the *Child Theology Movement* from 2002-2016, writing *Entry Point* with Keith White. He has special interests in Barth and Bonhoeffer; political theology (especially exploring the relation of politics and forgiveness); and the future of Christian faith in a threatened humanity. He is glad to have lived with Hilary for over fifty years, and together they have three children and eight grandchildren.